Cambridge Studies in the History and Theory of Politics

EDITORS
MAURICE COWLING
G. R. ELTON
E. KEDOURIE
J. G. A. POCOCK
J. R. POLE
WALTER ULLMANN

FRANCOGALLIA

BY FRANÇOIS HOTMAN

FRANC.
HOTOMANI
IVRISCON-
SVLTI,
Francogallia.

Ex officina Iacobi Stœrij.
1573.

FRANCOGALLIA

BY FRANÇOIS HOTMAN

Latin text by Ralph E. Giesey
Translated by J. H. M. Salmon

CAMBRIDGE

At the University Press

1972

Published by the Syndics of the Cambridge University Press
Bentley House, 200 Euston Road, London NW1 2DB
American Branch: 32 East 57th Street, New York, N.Y.10022

Library of Congress Catalogue Card Number: 73-172835

ISBN: 0 521 08379 6

Printed in Great Britain
at the University Printing House, Cambridge
(Brooke Crutchley, University Printer)

CONTENTS

v

034263

vi

vii

viii

ix

APPENDICES

BIBLIOGRAPHIES

EDITORS' PREFACE

The two editors began their collaboration when they discovered in 1965 that they were both at work on Hotman's *Francogallia* in differing but complementary ways. Giesey had already prepared a variorum edition of the Latin text with an apparatus of Hotman's sources, while Salmon had accepted an offer from the Cambridge University Press to prepare a new English translation. The Press was pleased to have the two projects fused to produce a critical variorum Latin edition with a parallel English translation and a joint introduction by the two editors.

Hotman greatly altered and expanded the original edition (1573) on each of two occasions when he issued new editions (1576, 1586), and no serious discussion of the work's contents can be undertaken without close consideration of the major textual variants. For instance, the 1586 edition contains long sections upholding the right of legitimate succession to the crown of France, whereas the *Francogallia* as a whole has always been regarded as an attack upon the dynastic, as well as the constitutional, practices of the French monarchy under the last Valois kings. This and other anomalies are explained through a patient collation of the three major editions and the provision of a critical apparatus.

The preparatory study for this edition has afforded new insight into the provenance of the *Francogallia* and has clarified the complex motives that led to its composition. It has enabled the work to be related to both Hotman's juristic studies and his political activities. Furthermore, informed comment is now possible on the relationship between the *Francogallia* and contemporary works by critics and sympathizers in the fields of history and constitutional theory. This, in turn, provides a new basis for the study of the influence exerted by the *Francogallia* on subsequent European political thought.

Although the present editors made suggestions regarding each other's work on the text, Giesey is responsible for the Latin text and its apparatus on the left-hand pages, and Salmon for the facing translation. They share responsibility for the introduction, however, and they divided up the compiling of the bibliographies, appendices and index. Attention is drawn to the fact that there are two bibliographies: the first lists sources quoted by Hotman in the *Francogallia* and items shown in abbreviated form in source footnotes to the text will be found fully identified here; the second refers to secondary works on Hotman. The first appendix contains three substantial passages suppressed in later editions: the second collates the pagination of all previous editions, in all languages, with the present text.

The editors wish to thank Professors Donald R. Kelley, J. G. A. Pocock and Caroline Robbins, who made many helpful suggestions concerning the introduction. They also thank Professor G. R. Elton for the interest and encouragement which has led to the inclusion of the work in the series 'Cambridge Studies in the History and Theory of Politics'. The staff of Cambridge University Press gave expert advice in preparing this edition for publication. Giesey would like to make these separate acknowledgements: to Mrs Judith George and Dr Ronald Althouse, former students with whom he first began the task of identifying the precise bibliographical citations for Hotman's sources; to the Rockefeller Foundation for a grant to work in Europe in the summer of 1962; and to the Institute for Advanced Study for having welcomed him to work in its congenial setting many times.

February 1971   R.E.G. AND J.H.M.S.

EDITORS' INTRODUCTION

SECTION I – GENERAL

1. Problems of context

François Hotman was both a professional revolutionary and an eminent professor of law respected for his learning throughout the European world. He venerated classical antiquity in the best humanist manner, and at the same time he magnified the warlike valour and political prudence of the German barbarians who destroyed imperial Rome. Despite his Germanism and the Silesian origin of his family, he was a fervent French patriot. While he preached the virtues of the French language in legal practice, he wrote most of his legal treatises in a precise and sometimes elegant Latin. Although he was associated with a political faction that demanded the dispersion of authority in quasi-feudal terms, he was also linked for a time with the centralizing, reformist movement led by the chancellor, Michel de l'Hôpital. As a jurist he followed the legal humanist school that applied history to the interpretation of law: yet he also sympathized with its critics, the neo-Bartolists, who sought to educe a perfect system from the comparative study of jurisprudence. He was both an innovator disguised as a reactionary and a renovator masquerading as a radical. He was a man of narrow convictions and doctrinaire outlook who, nevertheless, allowed his conscience to adapt itself to changing political circumstances. Although he took pride in his rôle as an objective historian, he regarded any departure from pristine models as a process of corruption. While he respected the past, he bent it to serve the needs of the present. He looked to custom as the touchstone of constitutionalism, and invented an ancient assembly endowed with enough authority to make a mockery of consuetudinary mystique. All these paradoxical elements were contained in the *Francogallia*. Their reconciliation involves the reconstruction of a complex of ideas which profoundly affected the development of European thought. A genera-

3

tion after Hotman, Francis Bacon expressed the intellectual dilemma of an age when he remarked that 'a retention of custom is as turbulent a thing as an innovation, and they that reverence too much old times are but a scorn to the new'.[1]

In the decade of the 1560's revolts of aristocratic parties associated with Calvinism occurred in Scotland, France and the Netherlands. It is tempting to see these movements as an international revolutionary force whose military leaders were linked in a common cause and whose apologists formed a close-knit intellectual élite.[2] Yet, equally, it is possible to distinguish differences in direction derived from national experience, and it is dubious whether revolt proclaimed in the cause of the past rather than the future can be termed revolutionary in the modern sense.[3] In the ensuing decade, when the *Francogallia* was published in company with a spate of Huguenot treatises in which a more radical note was sounded, there emerged a more generalized 'Calvinist' ideology. Beza issued the *De jure magistratuum*, Mornay the *Vindiciae contra tyrannos*, Buchanan the *De jure regni apud Scotos*, and Languet, if he did not contribute to the *Vindiciae*,[4] most likely had a hand in the *Apology of the Prince of Orange*, published in 1581. The leading Calvinist polemicists, Hotman among them, certainly knew one another's works, and were members of the same personal circle. They drew upon the same general sources. They cited the same passages from classical authors and the same texts from the Bible. Their legal training often enabled them to discourse upon the transfer of power under

[1] *The Essays* (London, 1883), XXIV, 146.
[2] Cf. H. G. Koenigsberger, 'The Organization of Revolutionary Parties in France and the Netherlands during the Sixteenth Century', *The Journal of Modern History*, XXVII (1955), 335–51; and R. M. Kingdon, 'The Political Resistance of the Calvinists in France and the Low Countries', *Church History*, XXVII (1958), 3–16.
[3] J. H. Elliott, 'Revolution and Continuity in Early Modern Europe', *Past and Present*, XLII (1969), 44.
[4] A third candidate, in addition to Mornay and Languet, has been suggested for the authorship of the *Vindiciae*. He is Johan Junius de Jonge, councillor to both the elector Frederick III and William of Orange, and an acquaintance of Beza, Hotman, Languet and Mornay. Cf. Derek Visser, 'Junius: the Author of the *Vindiciae contra Tyrannos?*', *Tijdschrift voor Geschiedenis*, LXXXIV (1971), 510–25.

4

the *lex regia* and to make use of Roman Law corporation theory. They could adapt the concept of popular sovereignty expounded in scholastic fashion by Jacques Almain and John Mair early in the century. They were aware of German Lutheran experience in the Schmalkaldic wars, and some, such as Beza, were familiar with the teaching of the Magdeburg *Bekenntnis*, from which they may have developed the concept of the duty of inferior magistrates to lead resistance. They were probably familiar with the ideas of the exiles from Marian England, especially with the *Shorte Treatise of Politicke Power* by John Ponet, who published his book in Strasbourg in 1556, the year when Hotman arrived there. Above all, they were familiar with the passage in the penultimate paragraph of the fourth book of the *Institution of the Christian Religion*, where Calvin so far departed from the doctrine of non-resistance as to suggest that certain magistrates, notably the assembled deputies of the estates, had a legitimate ephoral authority to resist a tyrannical prince.

For all this, Hotman's *Francogallia* differs markedly in emphasis from the generalized doctrines of political obligation presented by the classical works of Calvinist resistance theory in the 1570's. It reflects a reliance upon constitutional custom rather than upon rational abstractions, an attitude which characterized an earlier phase of the conflicts. However, while certain aspects of the work are the particular product of the author's own intellectual development, others are part of a more general phenomenon. Dependence upon a *national* past and a *Francogallican* ancient constitution seems to imply a stress upon the empirical rather than the normative, upon history rather than philosophy, upon the particular rather than the universal. At the same time there are evident principles of organization employed by the historian to re-arrange the past in the light of present preoccupations. Equally, the more generalized polemics of Hotman's associates reflect a conviction that historical precedents will demonstrate the truth of abstract propositions. The period exhibits, in short, a continuing tension between philosophical and historical priorities. Apart from the mystique of French constitutionalism, ancient

5

constitutions were also discovered for Scotland and the Netherlands. Just as we may compare Hotman's *Francogallia* with Beza's *De jure magistratuum*, so also we may place Buchanan's *Rerum scoticarum historia* beside his own *De jure regni*, or Grotius' *De antiquitate reipublicae Batavicae* beside Althusius' *Politica methodice digesta*.[1] It is clear that in the climate of opinion prevailing in Scotland, France and the Netherlands during certain phases of Calvinist revolt neither mode of thought was adequate without the other.

The problem of reconciling historical and philosophical priorities, and of setting such a reconciliation within the framework of political action, is illustrated by a curious parallel between the *Francogallia* and the works of Buchanan. Although Hotman and Buchanan had many common friends and correspondents,[2] there is no record of any personal contact between them. Since there would appear to be no direct reciprocal influence, the similarity of ideas and coincidence of situation may be seen as a patterned response within the general European context of Calvinist revolt – unless it be merely the product of an ironic play of contingency. Early in 1567 each was assembling material for the history of their respective countries, albeit from different viewpoints and for different purposes. By the end of that year each had become involved in a new political crisis and had simultaneously changed his focus on the past. For Hotman the crisis was the resumption of the civil wars: for Buchanan it was the deposition of Mary Queen of Scots. Buchanan was responsible for both the historical and the general arguments with which the confederate Scottish lords justified their act to the English ambassador. He propounded these

---

[1] On the relationship of the *Politica methodice digesta* (1603) and the *De antiquitate reipublicae Batavicae* (1610 – best known in *Chronicon Hollandiae de Hollandorum republica et rebus gestis* [Leyden, 1617], pp. i–lx) to the revolt of the Netherlands see E. H. Kossmann, 'The Development of Dutch Political Theory in the Seventeenth Century', in *Britain and the Netherlands*, edited by J. S. Bromley and Kossmann (London, 1960), 92–4. Although Kossmann remarks that Grotius owed much in *De antiquitate* to 'French Calvinistic writers like Hotman', Grotius did not actually cite the *Francogallia*.

[2] Including Johann Sturm, Rodolph Walter, Languet, Beza, Mornay and Pierre de Montdoré.

arguments as the moderator of the Presbyterian assembly in June 1567, in the first draft of *De jure regni* composed soon afterwards, in the regent Moray's embassy to York in October 1568, in a statement submitted to Queen Elizabeth's commissioners in London early in 1571, and in the history of Scotland he was writing throughout these years.[1] However, *De jure regni* did not appear in print until 1579, while *Rerum scoticarum historia* was not published until 1582.

Hotman probably began the first version of the *Francogallia* late in 1567 and may still have been engaged upon it early in 1568, when his rôle in the entourage of the Huguenot leader, Louis de Condé, was not unlike that of Buchanan beside the Earl of Moray. During these years Huguenot polemicists were demanding the convocation of the estates general, appealing to immemorial custom and, in at least one pamphlet, recalling liberties once supposedly enjoyed by the conquering Franks before the establishment of the monarchy.[2] The *Francogallia* was a part of this background. Where Buchanan had depicted the mingling of Picts and Scots, Hotman saw the assimilation of Franks and Gauls. Where Buchanan endowed his 2,000-year-old constitution with a supreme council of nobility, Hotman more modestly fixed the origin of his ancient constitution in the fifth century A.D., and observed that 'the highest administrative authority in the kingdom of Francogallia lay in the formal public council of the nation, which in later times was called the assembly of the three estates'.[3] Where Buchanan, following the fables of Hector Boece, held the Scottish monarchy to be elective in one family, and recited a litany of the kings of the house of Fergus whose fearful crimes had led to their deposition and, sometimes, to their death, Hotman chronicled the election and deprivation of Merovingians and Carolingians by his public council. And, as Buchanan departed from national history to reveal the principles of the ancient Scottish constitution as but a particular representation

---

[1] This follows H. R. Trevor-Roper's ingenious reconstruction of Buchanan's historical and political ideas in *George Buchanan and the Ancient Scottish Constitution* (Supplement 3 to *The English Historical Review*; London 1966). See also W. A. Gatherer, *The Tyrannous Reign of Mary Stewart* (Edinburgh, 1958), 3–5, 11–19.
[2] See below, p. 39.   [3] See below, p. 291.

of an ideal form designed by God and nature, so Hotman (although he never wrote an equivalent of *De jure regni*) cited Plato, Aristotle, Polybius and Cicero on the model of the mixed and tempered form of government, to which he held the Francogallican constitution to conform.

To complete the parallel, the *Francogallia*, like the *De jure regni* and the *Historia*, was not to be published for several years. When it did appear, a year after the massacre of Saint Bartholomew, its purpose was understood in terms as different from the spirit in which it had been drafted as that spirit was different from Hotman's original interest in constitutional history. As Buchanan has been imperfectly understood through the misdating of his work, through the confusion of motive and event, and through the failure to identify the successive phases of his thinking, so, too, has Hotman. With Hotman the fault may be venial, since the author conveyed the impression in the 1573 dedication of the *Francogallia* that he had written it under pressure of events in the preceding year, and yet the consequent distortion has been far greater than ever it was with Buchanan. Thus the problem of the *Francogallia* is not unique. However, the reconstruction of the mental processes that went to its making, and to its remaking in subsequent editions, involves the study of certain aspects of Hotman's life and writings in their own right. It is to this task that we must now turn.

2. *Legal influences*

An important theme in the *Francogallia* was Hotman's contempt for the class of legal officialdom to which his own family belonged. His grandfather had settled in Paris in the reign of Louis XI. His father, Pierre Hotman, sieur de Villiers-Saint-Paul, was the youngest of several sons who found successful careers in finance, church or state.[1] In June 1524, two months before the birth of François, his

---

[1] Biographical and family details are provided in many of the works listed in the bibliography. Among the most thorough biographies are Rodolphe Dareste, 'François Hotman, sa vie et sa correspondance', *Revue historique*, II (1876), 1–59, 367–435; David Baird Smith, 'François Hotman', *Scottish Historical Review*, XIII (1915/16), 328–65; and Ludwig Ehinger, *Franz Hotmann, ein französischer Gelehrter*,

eldest son, Pierre Hotman left his practice at the bar of the parlement to assume administrative responsibilities in the department of *eaux et forêts*. He had married into a family of the *noblesse de robe* and in 1544 became a *conseiller* in the parlement itself. When a special tribunal, the so-called '*chambre ardente*', was established to try cases of heresy, Pierre Hotman became one of its judges. A stern father, a conservative and conformist, he expected his six sons to follow in his footsteps. Most of them did so. Antoine Hotman was to become *avocat-général* in the parlement in the time of the Catholic League. Jean Hotman was chancellor to the cardinal of Lorraine, the most influential figure in the ultra-Catholic cause during the early phases of the wars of religion and the target of one of François' polemics. There was also a Charles Hotman who was to be one of the organizers of the conspiratorial wing of the League in Paris in the 1580's. François Hotman reacted against both his father's profession and the extreme Catholic orthodoxy to which his brothers adhered.

At the age of fifteen François began his legal education at the University of Orléans. A decade earlier Calvin had deserted the Orléans law school for its rival at Bourges, where Andrea Alciato had just begun to teach. Pierre de l'Etoile, the professor at Orléans who guided Calvin's studies, had died shortly before Hotman's arrival, but his influence still dominated the school. L'Etoile, besides being a capable, if conservative, teacher of Roman Law, was also a biblical humanist, and Calvin had so admired him that he had contributed to a published defence of his first master against the criticism of Alciato.[1] L'Etoile employed the traditional Italian method of legal exegesis, with its laborious study of Justinian's codification and its labyrinthine comparison of the glosses of the great medieval civilians, from Accursius to Bartolus and his

Staatsmann und Publizist des XVI. Jahrhunderts (Basel, 1896). The first biography was that of Pierre Nevelet (Doschius) composed soon after Hotman's death in 1590 and published in 1592 and again with the *Opera* of 1600. The editors are indebted to D. R. Kelley, who is engaged upon a full-length biography of Hotman, for his advice on biographical matters throughout this introduction.

[1] John T. McNeill, *The History and Character of Calvinism* (New York, 1967), 103.

successors. In his own generation Alciato was the leading representative of legal humanism and the French method of teaching law, as Guillaume Budé had been before him and Jacques Cujas was to be after him. The realization that Justinian's codifiers had heaped together aspects of Roman Law from many ages, and that the glossators and commentators had magnified confusion and contradiction by their endeavour to adapt Roman and Byzantine texts to the society of their own day, discredited the Italian method in the eyes of those who employed history to disentangle the various elements of jurisprudence. As a celebrated exponent of Roman Law, Hotman was to condemn the style he first encountered at Orléans, but he was also to criticize the pedantry of the 'grammarians' of Bourges. Orléans also provided his introduction to heterodox religious opinion.

When Hotman returned to Paris in 1540 to begin his practical apprenticeship to the law, he found himself in contact with three minds whose special interests came to represent three distinct strands in his own intellectual development. They were Charles du Moulin, François Baudouin and François Connan, and their influence upon Hotman was felt respectively in the fields of customary law, the techniques of historical exegesis, and the synthetic reconstruction of jurisprudence. He was personally acquainted with Du Moulin and the latter's secretary, Baudouin, but he seems to have had no direct association with Connan, whose works he helped to edit. His relationship with Du Moulin and Baudouin was complicated by the fact that they anticipated Hotman's conversion to the reformed faith, and then betrayed the cause which he defended so staunchly. Hotman retained his respect for Du Moulin's juristic writings, but Baudouin became his bitter personal enemy. His admiration for Connan was tempered by the latter's insistence upon finding a Celtic origin for the Franks and a Gallic source for feudal institutions – themes which belonged to the 'Gaulois' school of French savants in the 1550's. Hotman was to accept the Germanic solution expressed by Du Moulin. He borrowed from all three, but their ideas assumed subtle modifications when assimilated within the corpus of Hotman's work.

Du Moulin deservedly enjoyed a high reputation in many fields of law, but he was best known as the spokesman for a unified national system of private law, based upon what he held to be best in existing custom. In 1539 Du Moulin suggested that the custom of Paris might serve as a national model, and that the multiple systems of private law in the northern provinces of France should be brought into consonance with it.[1] It was implicit in customary law that, in origin at least, it should be unwritten, that its validity was established by consent, and that it applied outside the sphere of public law, where the ordinances of the king held sway. Its efficacy in the courts, however, depended upon the clear demonstration of its content. Since the edict of Montils-lès-Tours of 1454 commissions had been sporadically recording the evidence of local representative estates as to what constituted regional custom. But as the commissioners who wrote down and proclaimed custom were royal judges from the parlements, the process appeared to contradict the very basis of customary law. Moreover, the lacunae and internal contradictions incorporated in many early *rédactions* suggested the need for a systematic reformation, which would imperil its regional nature and render consent a hollow formality. There were some who, because of their training in the law schools or because of their association with the *droit écrit* that prevailed in the south, wished either to see Roman Law as French common law or to use Roman Law principles to codify French custom.[2] At the other extreme were those who wished merely to record local custom

[1] *Prima pars commentariorum in consuetudines parisienses* (Paris, 1539).

[2] In the 1530's, président Lizet, who later sat on the bench of the *chambre ardente* with Pierre Hotman, was a zealous reformer of French custom by means of Roman Law. In 1567 Pierre Versoris pleaded on behalf of the courts of Lyon that the southern provinces had received their *droit écrit* from the Romans in ancient times and therefore observed a law superior to the customs of the north. The *avocat du roi*, Guy du Faur-Pibrac, replied that the existence of *droit écrit* in the south exhibited a deficiency of original custom, for the Romans had permitted the Gauls to apply their own custom in regions where they had possessed it. In the north, Pibrac argued, Roman Law could only be cited where it did not conflict with custom. It is significant that this celebrated case should have been heard in the year when Hotman, having finished his *Antitribonian*, commenced the *Francogallia*. See René Filhol, *Le premier président Christofle de Thou et la réformation des coutumes* (Paris, 1937), 125–8.

without reforming or unifying it. Du Moulin, who opposed both attitudes, was not averse to the use of Roman Law principles to subvert the latter school, but he was too much a part of what Vittorio de Caprariis has called 'questo nuovo nazionalismo giuridico' to countenance the substitution of Roman Law for national custom.[1] In 1543 Du Moulin set out his general proposals for the national codification of custom,[2] and twenty years later he suggested the annotating of all local customs to produce a systematic body of national customary law, which could then be examined by an assembly of jurists.[3] Hotman's proposals for a national body of private law in his *Antitribonian* of 1567 were more radical than this, but they revealed a debt to his predecessor.

Hotman apparently did not devote much attention to the details of the problem of the *coutumiers*, but he shared Du Moulin's reverence for custom, and in the nationalistic climate of the age it is not surprising that he improved upon Du Moulin's anti-Romanism. Du Moulin was an advocate of the secular state, holding that the church had been ruled by the king in early times, and that the royal authority had been usurped, and ancient law corrupted, by the papacy and its Canon Law. In the circumstances of the early religious wars Hotman could not follow the defence of stong monarchy consistently asserted by Du Moulin,[4] but in later years his anti-papalism allowed him to defend Henry of Navarre against his excommunication by Sixtus V in pseudo-Gallican terms reminiscent of Du Moulin. Moreover, Hotman seems to have taken from Du Moulin the concept, expressed in both the *Antitribonian* and the *Francogallia*, that Canon Law was the principal instrument

[1] *Propaganda e pensiero politico*, 237.

[2] *Oratio de concordia et unione consuetudinum Franciae* [1543], in *Tractatus commerciorum et usuarum, redituumque pecunia constitutorum et monetarum* (Paris, 1555).

[3] *Notae solemnes* (Lyon, 1563). The work by Filhol (above, p. 11, n. 2) shows how Du Moulin's writings influenced the commissions to record custom over which Christofle de Thou presided, beginning with the commission for Sens in 1555 and ending with that for Orléans which De Thou was about to undertake when he died in 1582.

[4] In his *Apologie* (Lyon, 1563) Du Moulin denied that any of his books had impugned the honour of the French crown, and declared that doctrines of sedition had been repugnant to him throughout his life (Caprariis, *Propaganda*, 113).

by which the national juristic tradition was corrupted. In his treatise on the custom of Paris, Du Moulin had proclaimed the relevancy of the institutions of the Germanic Franks to the study of feudalism. Hotman was also indebted to him in this respect, for he came close to his view of the Germanic origin of the fief. What is more, some of Hotman's remarks about the Franks may have been drawn from the polemical work in which Du Moulin most cogently expressed his opposition to Rome.[1]

Baudouin's legal interests were as many-sided as Du Moulin's, but his major contribution lay in the historical study of Roman Law. He approached his subject with a deep admiration for Alciato and a mastery of the techniques of humanist philology. His first work, a study of Justinian's agricultural laws, was followed by an introduction to the study of the *Institutes*, which revealed his understanding of the historical development of Roman Law.[2] His association with Hotman was sufficiently close for the latter to accuse him of plagiarizing his notes. In 1546 both were providing supplementary courses for the faculty of Canon Law at Paris. Another celebrated jurist, Etienne Pasquier, was later to recall his youthful impressions of their lectures.[3] Baudouin anticipated Hotman in making his way to Geneva and becoming a secretary to Calvin. In 1548 he deserted Geneva to assume a chair of law at

[1] Cf. Kelley, *Foundations of Scholarship*, 191–4. Du Moulin's first Gallican polemic took the form of a defence of Henry II's edict against papal abuses in the disposal of benefices (cf. *ibid.*, 166). This was the basis of much in his later work, *Premiere partie du traicté de l'origine, progres et excellence du royaume et monarchie des Francoys et couronne de France* (Lyon, 1561). This book discussed Frankish history in some detail, but included fables about Pharamond and his successors which Hotman rejected. It held that the Carolingian and Capetian lines had been appointed to the crown 'par le consentement des estats' (pp. 28–9), a statement which might have seemed suggestive to Hotman had Du Moulin not qualified it by trying to show that Pepin, the first Carolingian king, also had an hereditary claim, and that the laws of succession for the Frankish monarchy antedated the arrival of the Franks in Gaul. He did not, however, suggest any hereditary right for Hugues Capet. Du Moulin's remarks on the subversive influence of Canon Law occur on p. 93, and the preceding fifty pages constitute a general diatribe against Rome. All Du Moulin's historical sources are to be found in *Francogallia*.

[2] *Justiniani...de re rustica* (Louvain, 1542); *Prolegomena sive praefata de jure civili in annotationes in libros IV institutionum Justiniani* (Paris, 1545).

[3] *Lettres* (Paris, 1619), II, 501.

Bourges, where he continued to apply his humanist methods to the law of the early Roman republic. A violent quarrel with another Bourges professor, François le Douaren, obliged Baudouin to quit the university in favour of a new chair at Strasbourg, whence Hotman displaced him in 1556. The feud between Hotman and Baudouin reached a crescendo of invective in the years that followed. This would not, however, have prevented Hotman from reading Baudouin's best known treatise, *De institutione historiae universae et ejus cum jurisprudentia conjunctione prolegomenon* (1561). This work proclaimed the error of regarding Roman Law as a logical system, and demanded a comparative study of the early history and customs of the barbarian peoples who had conquered Rome.[1]

Like Calvin, François Connan had been attracted to Bourges in his student days by Alciato. He subsequently became one of the *maîtres des requêtes* who arranged the business of the royal council and provided a liaison between it and the parlement. When the earlier systems of the civilians were shown to have been defective, some jurists sought a new system of universal jurisprudence by such comparative methods as Baudouin suggested in *De institutione historiae universae* or Jean Bodin proposed in his *Methodus ad facilem historiarum cognitionem*. An alternative was the reorganization of the existing material in Roman Law. It occurred to Connan that it was the very categories employed by the sixth-century codifiers of the *Corpus juris civilis* which had resulted in confusion and error. He therefore selected new categories with which he hoped to produce a systematic jurisprudence from the established texts. He did not live to complete the task, but in 1553 his preliminary commentaries were edited by Barthélemy Faye, one of De Thou's most able lieutenants in the *rédaction* of custom.[2] Faye's preface attacked not only Justinian's compilers but also the glossators seven centuries after them. Hotman helped to arrange the material and himself

---

[1] Franklin, *Bodin*, 45. See also Kelley, *Foundations of Scholarship*, 115–48.

[2] *Francisci Connani...Commentariorum iuris civilis libri X* (Basel, Episcopius; 1557). Faye's prefatory letters to Oliver and L'Hôpital are dated 1553; Hotman's epistle, 1557. This first printing carries an Imperial letter of privilege dated 1557, but the second printing (Paris, Vascon; 1558) has a letter of privilege from Henry II dated 1551. The work was republished in 1566 and 1609.

contributed a prefatory note which served to shape the ideas that achieved their final form in his *Antitribonian*. A few years later he also attempted his own rearrangement of the basic elements of the civil law in Connan's tradition.[1] Furthermore, Hotman was closely associated with two other systematizers, Le Douaren, the opponent of Baudouin, and Hugues Doneau, who was also for a time a professor of law at Bourges, and became the close friend and colleague of Hotman in Geneva after the massacre of Saint Bartholomew.

Rebelling against his father and the persecutions with which Pierre Hotman was associated, Hotman fled first to Lyon and then to Geneva, where he arrived in October 1548. Beza, who had been his contemporary at the Orléans law school, went to Geneva at about the same time, and the partnership which was to direct Huguenot political propaganda in subsequent decades was established. Hotman venerated Calvin as his spiritual father, and the intensity of his own conviction was such as to impress Calvin's fiery predecessor and associate, Guillaume Farel. He married and moved to the school at Lausanne founded by another celebrated reformer, Pierre Viret. There he cooperated with Beza, who was professor of Greek at Lausanne, in teaching classical literature. He had published several minor treatises before arriving in Geneva, and a number of other legal works, together with a French version of Plato's *Apology* and an edition of a commentary upon Cicero's speeches, appeared in rapid succession under his name.

In 1553 Hotman came to the defence of Du Moulin, who had been cited by the parlement for his anti-papalist writings and had found a temporary haven in Tübingen. A Sorbonne theologian had printed a tract questioning Du Moulin's observations on the early church and the priesthood, and Hotman's defence closely followed Calvin's view of primitive Christianity. He embroidered Du Moulin's earlier criticism of Canon Law and repeated the latter's belief that each branch of the Christian church was a national organization.[2] Beza also contributed to the controversy

---

[1] *Partitiones iuris civilis elementariae* (Basel, 1560); cf. Franklin, *Bodin*, 36.

[2] *De statu primitivae ecclesiae...ad Remundum Rufum defensorem pontificiis Romanis adversus Carolum Molinaeum jurisconsultum* (Geneva, 1553).

by publishing an attack upon Du Moulin's persecutor and rival as a reformer of customary law, président Lizet. Hotman revealed in this affair that *renovatio* was as much an item of his religious faith as it was later to become an aspect of his constitutionalism. Moreover, the assault that he and Beza delivered against the Canon Law in defence of Du Moulin was another element which would receive a prominent place in his later writing.

Hotman became increasingly impatient at the conditions of his life at Lausanne. In 1555, the year in which his father died, he obtained letters of recommendation from Calvin to Peter Martyr at Strasbourg and to Johann Sturm, the rector of the gymnasium there. At Strasbourg he found his enemy, Baudouin, holding the chair of law. Within a few months of bitter exchanges which brought credit to neither contender, Baudouin retired from the field, and in June 1556 Hotman was installed in his place. The next few years were among the most active and productive in Hotman's life. His teaching, his juristic publications and his political activism in this period were to bring the earlier influences in his life to sharper focus, and to prepare the way for his more significant political writings.

3. *Political commitment*

At least twelve works on Roman Law and Roman history appeared under Hotman's name in the years 1556–60, including a short life of Justinian, commentaries on the *Institutes* and the *Digest*, studies in ancient Roman political and legal usage, and the systematic reclassification of Roman Law principles already mentioned. In his sketch of Justinian Hotman was severely critical of the methods used to produce the *Corpus juris civilis*. This work was reprinted with Hotman's commentaries on the *Institutes*, which contained a prefatory letter also condemning Tribonian's labours.[1] Even at this stage in the development of Hotman's ideas, there appeared the contrapuntal suggestion that the primitive customs of the Germanic peoples could be favourably compared with more sophisticated

---

[1] *Justiniani imperatoris vita* (Strasbourg, 1556); *Commentarius in quatuor libros institutionum juris civilis* (Basel, 1560).

legislation. The quotation from Tacitus with which he supported this viewpoint was to be repeated in similar context in a later work, closely associated with the *Antitribonian* and the *Francogallia*, the *De feudis*.[1] Hotman's scholarly works were well received, and with the aid of his friend Amerbach he obtained a doctorate from Basel. His students came to him from Germany, France, Poland, Scotland and England, and his career as an eminent jurist seemed assured.

Yet this was also a period of frenetic political activity. It seemed to Hotman that Protestantism throughout Europe was threatened by sinister Catholic forces. He was closely in touch with the circle of the Marian exiles, whose revolutionary doctrines of resistance suddenly lost their immediate focus when Elizabeth succeeded her sister on the English throne in November 1558. The oppression in France moved him deeply, and he wrote constantly to Calvin in Geneva and Bullinger in Zurich upon this theme. He saw that the Protestant churches were vulnerable because of their disunity. Strasbourg itself was a battlefield in the conflict between Calvinists and Lutherans. Hotman accompanied Calvin to a colloquy at Frankfort, and attended another at Worms. His own inflexible faith reflected the inability of the churches to settle their doctrinal differences, and he became more interested in a common diplomatic front against Catholicism than he was in a confessional reconciliation that would attenuate Genevan theology. In 1558, and again in 1559, he took part in missions to the elector palatine, the duke of Würtemberg and other Protestant German princes, to plead for their intercession with Henry II in favour of the French Calvinist churches, and especially the congregation threatened with expulsion from Metz. These activities led to his personal involvement in the French crises which followed the death of Henry II in July 1559.

The rivalry of the great aristocratic houses of Guise, Montmorency and Bourbon served as the *primum mobile* for the anarchy that convulsed France in the ensuing decades. Since 1555, when

---

[1] 'Etsi autem verissima dictum est ab antiquis, plus valere apud Germanos bonos mores, quam apud alios, bonas leges.' Cf. Caprariis, *Propaganda*, 226, and Smith, 'Hotman', 350.

Beza's company of Genevan pastors commenced their mission to evangelize France, Calvinism had attracted many proselytes, and had even gained a foothold at the court and in the parlement. In the late 1550's it began to find an increasing number of converts among the rural nobility, the class who formed the clientele of the aristocratic factions. During the short reign of the boy king, Francis II, his wife's uncles, the duke of Guise and the cardinal of Lorraine, were the effective rulers of France. Their policy intensified the persecutions already forecast by the Spanish peace of Cateau-Cambrésis, which had been signed a few months before the death of Henry II had left a vacuum at the centre of power. The parlemen purged itself of fellow-travellers, and the burning of a leading magistrate, Anne du Bourg, was the signal for fresh fires of martyrdom elsewhere. The Guisard régime inherited a bankrupt government and a legion of social discontents among the country *hobereaux*, deprived of their employment in foreign war and suffering from inflationary processes. At this point opposition to the Guises was centred less in their traditional rivals, the house of Montmorency, who, except for the three Châtillon brothers, adhered to the orthodox faith, than in the Bourbon princes, Antoine de Navarre and Louis de Condé. The Calvinist wing of the rural *noblesse* looked to the leadership of these descendants of St Louis, whose royal blood gave them an advantage scarcely offset by the association of the Guises with the house of Lorraine and hence with Carolingian tradition. As the combination of religious and political motives turned this opposition towards armed conflict, the political justification of the movement assumed a conservative hue. Neither Huguenot theory in general, nor Hotman's contribution to it in particular, was a programmatic ideology of social change. It did not represent a revolution of the saints,[1] but espoused arguments of custom and tradition against a régime whose activities seemed to threaten local privileges and immunities as well

---

[1] Michael Walzer, *The Revolution of the Saints* (Harvard, 1965), 68–92. Walzer's application of a political variant of the thought of Max Weber to the Huguenot movement may have some relevance to the intellectual wing of the party, but it is quite inappropriate to the dominant element, the rural *noblesse*, as the author seems, indeed, to acknowledge (p. 90).

as religious freedom. Nevertheless, Huguenot political thought was a coherent amalgam of theories of law, history and government, which derived its strength from the firm political and religious convictions of its principal progenitors, Hotman and Beza.

Hotman first exercised his pen as the propagandist of Huguenot resistance theory in connexion with the Tumult of Amboise of March 1560 – a conspiracy to remove the king from the tutelage of the Guises. The plot failed and many of the conspirators lost their lives. Their leader was a nobleman named La Renaudie, and their secret figurehead was Louis de Condé. Calvin, while he wished Antoine de Navarre to oppose the Guises in virtue of his constitutional status as first prince of the blood, refused to support the Amboise affair. However, Beza and a number of other pastors were implicated in greater or less degree, and Hotman was the most actively involved of all Calvin's immediate circle.[1] The protection of Protestant interests in Metz, the diplomatic front in Germany, and the endeavour to strengthen the resolution of Antoine de Navarre, were all activities which led Hotman into the plot. He kept in close touch with Beza, who visited Strasbourg in October 1559 and Heidelberg in November, and worked with Sturm to construct an alliance with the elector palatine. After the conspiracy was frustrated by the betrayal of its plans, he and Beza visited the Bourbon court at Nérac. On his return to Strasbourg he quarrelled bittery with Sturm, whom he rashly accused of responsibility for the betrayal. Sturm defended himself in letters which eventually became known and reflected little credit on Hotman.[2]

It is uncertain which of the many tracts justifying the Amboise plot were personally composed by the author of the *Francogallia*, but his influence in the literature concerned with the affair has been established beyond reasonable doubt. In two polemics published in 1562 Baudouin proclaimed him as the instigator of the whole conspiracy, together with Calvin and Beza. Referring to an

---

[1] Such is the conclusion of Naef, *Conjuration d'Amboise*, 70–2, 81, 151–2, and Kingdon, *Geneva and the Wars of Religion*, 69–74. For Calvin's attitude see N. M. Sutherland, 'Calvinism and the Conspiracy of Amboise', *History*, XLVII (1962), 111–38.

[2] Dareste, 'Hotman et la conjuration d'Amboise', 360–75.

honorific title Hotman had been awarded by the Bourbons, Baudouin remarked that rather than being known as master of requests he was more properly master of libels. He named the *Epistre envoyée au tigre de la France* and the *Histoire du tumulte d'Amboyse* as two specific examples of Hotman's style.[1] Hotman's *Tigre* was less a reasoned statement of constitutional opinion than a vituperative and rhetorical attack upon the cardinal of Lorraine, modelled upon Cicero's denunciation of Catiline. The author maintained, however, that when the king was an adolescent the government rightfully belonged to the princes of the blood, and that the cardinal had usurped it in order to transfer the crown to the house of Lorraine.[2] Hotman also touched upon one of his favourite themes when he held the cardinal responsible for deliberately corrupting justice by widening venality of office in the parlement.[3] The *Histoire du tumulte* was published at Strasbourg in French, Latin and German soon after the failure of the conspiracy. Two other pieces in which Hotman's influence is discernible were the leaflet known as the *Livret de Strasbourg* and the tract entitled *Supplication et remonstrance addressée au Roy de Navarre*. Beza admitted sending the first of these to France,[4] while Hotman and Beza presented the second to the Bourbon princes at Nérac.[5] These writings, and others connected with Amboise, show signs of collaboration and are often derivative one from another. All reveal a desire to establish the legitimacy of the plot in terms of ancient constitutional practice infringed by Guisard rule.

It is possible to reconstruct the reasoning that may have led to some of the arguments later expressed in the *Francogallia* from inferences drawn from the propaganda connected with Amboise. Although the house of Lorraine did not at this time vaunt its descent from the Carolingians (albeit on the distaff side), Huguenot writers

---

[1] Naef, *Conjuration d'Amboise*, 61–3, 356–7, 362. The works attributed to Baudouin are: *Religionis et regis adversus exitiosas Calvini Bezae et Ottomani conjuratorum factiones defensio prima*, and Fr. *Balduini responsio altera ad Ioan. Calvinum.*
[2] *Le Tigre de 1560*, ed. Charles Read (Paris, 1875), 43.
[3] '...pour rompre la force de la justice de France et pour avoir les juges corrompus et semblables à toy, tu as introduit un semestre à la cour de Parlement'. *Ibid.*, 42.   [4] Kingdon, *Geneva and the Wars of Religion*, 70.
[5] Naef, *Conjuration d'Amboise*, 362.

were quick to assert a Guisard plan to usurp the crown. Huguenot literature also stressed the inviolate Salic Law of succession, declaring it to have been established in remote antiquity, not only to exclude descent from the female line but also to prevent those connected to the ruling dynasty through women from acting as tutors to the royal house. But stress upon the sanctity of the laws of succession raised the spectre of the legality of the whole Capetian line. Hotman was later to maintain that the Salic Law was the general custom of the Salian Franks and had nothing whatever to do with succession to the crown, which had been elective through the public council of the realm, and had become successive under the Capetians. Such arguments overcame the contradictions implicit in the Amboise literature, and rejected the subsequent claims of Lorraine and Guise.

The public council or estates general, which was later to prove the *deus ex machina* in Hotman's constitutional thought, also played a part in the polemics associated with Amboise. It was represented as an ancient constitutional practice that no government was legitimate during a royal minority unless it was appointed by the estates and the princes of the blood. The *Supplication et remonstrance* illustrated this principle from periods of royal incapacity in the reigns of Charles the Simple, Philip I, Louis IX, Charles VI and Charles VIII. Whenever the estates general had not been consulted, this tract maintained, civil war had been the consequence. The most recent and telling precedent, the discussion of the composition of the regency council at the 1484 estates of Tours in the minority of Charles VIII, had a special place among these examples. This meeting of the estates had been eulogized in the memoirs of Philippe de Commines, following the celebrated passage where Commines described any king who taxed his subjects without their consent as a tyrant. The passage was to be used to good effect in the *Francogallia*. In the aftermath of the Amboise plot the *Histoire du tumulte* contained an extract from the relevant section of Commines' memoirs,[1] while another anonymous tract, the *Response*

[1] Philippe de Commines, *Mémoires* (ed. Société de l'Histoire de France; Paris, 1840–7), II, 141–4.

au livre inscrit: pour la majorité du Roy François second, provided a more complete version of the same passage.[1]

The work to which the last-named libel constituted a reply gave a new direction to the controversy, and anticipated the theme of the *Francogallia*. The author of *Pour la majorité du Roy Treschrestien, contre les escrits des rebelles* was Jean du Tillet, registrar to the parlement and historian of the constitution. Du Tillet did not deny that the estates had played an important rôle in past royal minorities, but he argued that Francis II had passed the customary age of majority. Moreover, he claimed to discern in the writings of his opponents the implication that the estates were in some sense superior to the crown, and this, he held, was to advance the absurd tenet that the king was placed under the authority of his subjects. Not content with rebutting in advance what was popularly assumed to be the thesis of the *Francogallia*, Du Tillet, who, in the previous decade, had accepted a Germanic origin for the Franks, attacked the polemicists of Amboise on their own ground. Pursuing the constitutional issue into the mists of antiquity, Du Tillet could not resist citing a passage from Tacitus, which appeared to support his argument for the capacity of the young king, but which in fact opened the way for a powerful riposte. According to Tacitus' *Customs of the Germans*, Du Tillet remarked, it was the practice of the Germanic peoples, from whom the Franks were derived, to appoint the adolescent sons of the great to high office as a reward for the achievements of their fathers.[2]

Du Tillet's Germanism may well have inspired that of his friend Etienne Pasquier, who published the first book of his *Recherches de la France* in the year of the Tumult of Amboise. Although Pasquier was by no means the first to dispel the myth of the Trojan descent of the Franks and their eponymous King Francion, he displayed an unrivalled sophistication in his treatment of chronicle sources, and described the gradual incursions of Germanic war bands into Gaul and its final conquest in the fifth century. Like Hotman in the *Francogallia*, he repeated the opinion of medieval chroniclers that

---

[1] Naef, *Conjuration d'Amboise*, 357.
[2] Caprariis, *Propaganda*, 50-1

the word 'Frank' bore the Teutonic connotation of liberty,[1] and refuted Connan's belief that the Franks had originally been Gallic colonies established east of the Rhine.[2] Through the influence of the German historian, Beatus Rhenanus, Germanic themes were gaining popularity in this period. But Germanism had no necessary connexion with resistance theory. Like Du Tillet, Pasquier defended the government against its critics and entered the controversy provoked by the Amboise plot with his *Pourparler du Prince*, which also discovered subversive implications in Huguenot themes of the estates general. Five years later, in the second book of the *Recherches*, Pasquier allowed his historical judgment to lapse by tracing the descent of the parlement from early assemblies of Frankish warriors.[3]

In 1560 two replies to Du Tillet, the *Response au livre inscrit* and the *Légitime conseil des Rois de France pendant leur jeune age*, advanced the debate a step further. The former argued that, while kings might attain a formal majority in their fourteenth year, they were not accorded full authority until their twenty-fifth. This, too, was to be mentioned in the *Francogallia*.[4] The *Légitime conseil* held Du Tillet's doctrine to be contrary to both custom and good sense, and branded his history as false. This tract came even closer to the kind of argument later proposed in the *Francogallia* when it suggested that the king must accept counsel at all times, and at none more urgently than during adolescence.[5] In his *Pour l'entiere maiorité du Roy Treschrestien, contre le légitime conseil malicieusement inventé par*

[1] *Les recherches de la France*, lib. I, cap. vi (ed. Paris, 1633, 17).
[2] *Ibid.*, lib. I, cap. vii (*ed. cit.*, 21).
[3] The second book of the *Recherches* was expanded and rearranged by Pasquier in later editions. The 1581 edition introduces a new chapter on the estates, which Pasquier had previously neglected. He claimed that that institution, like the *grand conseil*, was unknown until after the parlement had been established as a sedentary court at Paris. He went on to make a derogatory comment about the kind of historical argument for the estates used in the *Francogallia*: 'Ie di l'assemblée des trois Estats: car encores que quelques uns qui pensent avoir meilleure part aux Histoires de la France, la tirent d'une bien longue ancienneté, voire sur elle establissent toute la liberté du peuple, toutefois ny l'un ny l'autre n'est veritable.' *Les recherches de la France livre premier et second*, lib. II, cap. vi (ed. Paris, 1581, 128ᵛ; cf. ed. Paris, 1633, 81).   [4] See below, p. 260.
[5] Caprariis, *Propaganda*, 52–3.

23

les rebelles Du Tillet reiterated his attack upon the alleged concept of the supremacy of the estates.

Thus the debate that followed the Tumult of Amboise set the scene for the constitutional theories advanced later in the decade. It caused a searching of the past under urgent need to justify political action in the present. It raised issues about the laws of succession and the rôle of the estates general, and associated these issues with early Frankish history. The precise extent of Hotman's participation in the controversy cannot be determined, but it is certain that he was a major influence in some of the first Huguenot libels after the plot, and probable that he was fully aware of the later stages of the debate. It was ironical that two of the foremost historians of the day should have entered the lists against the conspirators, for the inferences they drew from some of their opponents' arguments were often closer anticipations of the *Francogallia* than the explicit theories of Hotman and his fellow polemicists in 1560. If Pasquier had associated the Franks with a pristine liberty and had later chosen to suggest that it was the parlement, and not the estates general, that was the legitimate heir to the early Frankish assemblies, then Hotman, brooding on his anti-Romanism and his hatred for the magistracy to which Pasquier and Du Tillet belonged, might simply reverse the priorities. But the situation was not yet ripe for him to become fully conscious of these implications, and for several years other preoccupations absorbed his attention.

It is true that for more than a year after Amboise constitutional problems kept the rôle of the estates during a minority a live political issue. Francis II died in December 1560, immediately before the assembly of the estates at Orléans, and, although Antoine de Navarre disappointed the Huguenots by declining to insist upon his claim to govern in the minority of Charles IX, the proper composition of the regency was raised again when the estates reassembled at Pontoise in August 1561. The spokesman for the nobility at Orléans agreed with L'Hôpital, the chancellor, that the estates should not give law to the crown, but warned that the ancient customs of the realm should bind the government.[1] The *cahiers* of

[1] *Ibid.*, 63, 66, 77.

the nobility at Pontoise stated explicitly that the estates must be consulted on the persons to be appointed to the regency council, while the third estate again affirmed the need to preserve ancient law and custom. The idea of the ancient constitution was clearly not confined to the pamphlets of the previous year. Hotman, however, said nothing about such general issues in the letters he wrote early in 1561 to Bullinger and Peter Martyr. He was concerned solely with the tactics within the assembly most favourable to the reformed religion, and attacked what he regarded as the tyrannical ambitions of the new Semiramis, the queen mother, Catherine de Medici. A new theme, his suspicions of the Machiavellian subtlety of 'l'Italienne Médicis' and her entourage, now occupied his thoughts.[1]

Nevertheless, Hotman still dwelt upon constitutional formalities. After his return to Strasbourg he continued to serve as an intermediary between the Bourbons and the Protestant German princes. On 19 March 1561 he wrote to Philip of Hesse declining a chair which the landgraf had offered him at the university of Marburg. In the same letter he reported how Condé had finally been absolved of complicity in the Amboise affair, remarking that the decree of absolution had been pronounced by the parlement, the princes of the blood and the peers, 'en sorte qu'il soit absous avec toutes les formalités usitées de toute ancienneté'.[2] In the year that followed he busied himself with further missions in Germany and the composition of a stream of reports on French affairs for his German patrons. He was no longer fulfilling his obligations to the university of Strasbourg, and his quarrel with Sturm, combined with the triumph of Lutheranism in the city, made his post seem a less congenial base for his political activities.

In February 1562 the increasingly liberal attitude of the regency towards the Huguenots resulted in Hotman's being associated with a French embassy to Brandenburg. But in France the forces of Catholic reaction were determined to check L'Hôpital's policy of

---

[1] Dareste, 'Hotman, sa vie et sa correspondance', 28–30.
[2] Dareste, 'Hotman, 1561–1563', 298. The wording is that of Dareste's translation from the Latin.

provisional toleration and Catherine de Medici's rapprochement with Condé. The court was obliged to accept the protective custody of Guise and Montmorency, and in April Condé occupied Orléans and prepared for war. Hotman hastened to join him and remained in Orléans for a month. He evidently resumed his rôle as apologist for the faction, for he sent Beza a Latin account he had prepared of the massacre of a Protestant congregation at Vassy by the duke of Guise. He also wrote letters to foreign courts on Condé's behalf, justifying the revolt as an attempt to rescue the king from those who had usurped his authority.[1] No new themes were put forward in Huguenot propaganda, and its tone was generally less original and less radical than the pamphlets of 1560. Hotman spent the remainder of the war in Strasbourg, where, once again, he acted as an agent to win the support of the German princes for the Huguenot cause. In March 1563 the death or capture of the leaders of the factions enabled the government to negotiate a peace. There may have been a note of disillusionment in Hotman's attitude to the military leadership of his party. In any event he decided to return to his former mode of life, and accepted a professorship at Valence.

4. The complex of Tribonian

Hotman owed his new position, which had formerly been held by Cujas, to the patronage of the latitudinarian bishop of Valence, Jean de Monluc. The peace allowed the re-emergence of liberal elements, and the tolerant and reformist influence of L'Hôpital dominated the policy of the government of Catherine de Medici. Hotman visited the court at Fontainebleau and found that his own attitudes often coincided with those of the chancellor. L'Hôpital sought to strengthen and rationalize government through the reform of justice. He was prepared to discipline the parlement, and, as he showed in the celebrated ordinance of Moulins in 1566, he intended to limit the courts to their judicial rôle and even to attack venality of office.[2] Indeed, in his address to the *présidents* of the

---

[1] Dareste, 'Hotman, sa vie et sa correspondance', 35–6.
[2] Roger Doucet, *Les institutions de la France au XVIᵉ siècle* (Paris, 1948), I, 185, 413.

sovereign courts assembled at Moulins in January of that year, he extolled the simple and direct justice of earlier times and denounced the judicial system of his own day as a corrupt departure from a better ordered régime.[1] His *Traité de la réformation de la justice* also revealed a distinct anti-Romanism, for it declared that Roman Law had never been received in France and that it was associated with alien and tyrannical practices.[2] Elsewhere, it is true, he acknowledged the worth of the equity contained within it,[3] but this, after all, was also Hotman's position in the *Antitribonian*.

There was, however, another aspect of L'Hôpital's thought which Hotman found more difficult to accept. The reforms which he proposed bore a somewhat autocratic air, and the preservation of ancient custom was not always compatible with the legislative authority that this new Solon, as Hotman called him, wished to repose in the crown. He argued that, while certain fundamental laws were immutable, there was a wide area where the king alone could make and unmake law for the changing needs of his people. Although L'Hôpital had advocated the calling of the estates at Orléans, he had made it clear in his speech to that assembly that its function was merely to petition and advise. The king, he had declared, did not hold his authority from the nation, but from God and the ancient laws of the realm.[4] Yet, if Hotman found such ideas opposed to the doctrines he had espoused at Strasbourg, he also found it hard to deny that the reform of French justice and the codification of French law – a programme equivalent to that assigned Tribonian by Justinian – required authority for its success. Hotman effected his own kind of compromise, but the problem created for him what has been called the complex of Tribonian.[5]

[1] *Remonstrance de Monsieur le Chancelier faite en l'assemblée tenue à Moulins au mois de Ianvier, 1566* (n.p., n.d.).
[2] *Oeuvres inédites*, ed. R.-J.-S. Dufey (Paris, 1825), I, 3–406 and II, 1–316. This edition contains a number of later interpolations.
[3] Caprariis, *Propaganda*, 206–10.
[4] *La Harangue faicte par Monsieur le Chancelier de France le treiziesme iour de Ianvier mil cinq cents soixante – estans les estats convoqués en la ville de Orleans* (n.p., n.d.).
[5] Pierre Mesnard, 'François Hotman (1524–1590) et le complexe de Tribonien', *Bulletin de la Société de l'Histoire du Protestantisme français*, CI (1955), 117–37.

L'Hôpital's proposals were not, after all, very different from those of Du Moulin. The suggestion made in the *Antitribonian* that a judicial assembly should codify both public and private law, and that in private law it should proceed from first principles, rather than by the *rédaction* and comparison of the *coutumiers*, was certainly more radical. It reveals that Hotman's admiration for the policy of L'Hôpital had led him far from the constitutional convictions he had made manifest in the preceding three years.

Although he was far away in Valence, Hotman kept in touch with the reformist circle through his friend Henri de Mesmes, a *maître des requêtes*. Soon after his installation in his new chair he dedicated to the chancellor a new study of the Twelve Tables, the ancient basis of the law of republican Rome.[1] It resumed the old theme, already manifest in his life of Justinian and his commentaries on the *Institutes*, that Tribonian had entirely misunderstood the spirit of early Roman institutions. Hotman's own exegesis of the origin of the Twelve Tables in the fifth century B.C. revealed his awareness of the fact that Roman public law had been adapted to the new circumstances accompanying the establishment of the republic. In his teaching at Valence it seems that at first Hotman had to modify his historical method to suit the expectation of the students, who, as he told Henri de Mesmes in a letter in January 1564, were accustomed to the disputations of the Bartolists.[2] Two years later the situation had changed. Writing to request De Mesmes to use his influence to help him recover his sequestered patrimony, Hotman displayed another focus of interest: 'Nous nous occupons moins (he wrote) d'interpréter le droit civil, que de renverser les inventions sophistiques des praticiens, et de nettoyer pour ainsi dire les écuries d'Augias.'[3] In Dauphiné, he complained, the lawyers used Roman Law as a cover to import rules of duplicity borrowed from the Italianate dregs of the profession. The kind of issues which concerned the courts of Dauphiné were those listed in Guy Pape's compilation of the judgments of the parlement of

[1] *De legibus XII tabularum tripartita.. commentatio* (Lyon, 1564).
[2] Dareste, 'Hotman, sa vie et sa correspondance', 46.
[3] *Ibid.*, 47. The French translation of the Latin is Dareste's.

Grenoble, a source book which Hotman used in the *Antitribonian* and the *Francogallia*.

In fact, Hotman spent his years at Valence in refining his humanist practice of interpreting law in the light of its historical provenance and in using his conclusions to discredit the civilians. It is likely that, following suggestions made earlier in his career, he was also contrasting Roman Law unfavourably with Germanic custom, and accumulating a scholarly apparatus on early Frankish history. The *Antitribonian* itself was probably composed at Valence.[1] It was not to be published until 1603, when the title page bore the statement: 'Fait par l'advis de feu Monsieur de l'Hospital chancelier en France en l'an 1567.' As he was to remind his former student, Caspar Seydlitz, in a preface to his study of feudal law, *De feudis*, dated June 1572, Hotman and Seydlitz had been graciously received by L'Hôpital in Paris in the late summer of 1567. There is no reason to suppose, however, that it was at this meeting that the chancellor suggested Hotman should write the *Antitribonian*. The suggestion probably antedated the 1566 assembly of Moulins, and may well have been made when he visited the court at Fontainebleau in 1563.

Hotman had quarrelled with his employers over his salary in Valence late in 1566. With the support of L'Hôpital, and, through his influence, with that of the king's aunt, Marguerite de Savoie, he had obtained a chair of law at Bourges, and moved there in April 1567. He stayed for four or five months only. Immediately before his visit to Paris, he fled from Bourges as the result of a student riot, similar to the violence which had caused Baudouin's flight in 1554, and doubtless exacerbated by Hotman's aggressive Protestantism. After remaining at court for a short period and studying again in the library of Fontainebleau, Hotman escaped to Orléans when the second civil war began in September 1567. For the six months' duration of the war he was again in Condé's service, acting as the prince's commissioner in Blois from January 1568. After the peace of Longjumeau in March he remained in Orléans until the outbreak of the third war in August of the same year. He then took refuge in Sancerre, where he and his family endured the hardships

---

[1] Such is the opinion of Smith, 'Hotman', 339.

of a long siege. The only literary product of this period was his posthumously published *Consolatio e sacris scripturis*, in which he explained that his only books at Sancerre were the Bible and Saint Augustine's *City of God*. His library had been lost either during the Bourges riot or at the beginning of the third war. He remained in Sancerre for three months after the peace of Saint-Germain in August 1570, and in November of that year moved to another Huguenot fortress town, La Charité. He returned to Bourges in June 1571, where he recovered or reconstituted his library. In August 1572 he fled to Geneva during the slaughter of Saint Bartholomew's day, once again losing his books and manuscripts.[1]

The *Antitribonian* is closely related to a number of works, including the *Francogallia*, composed during this disturbed period of Hotman's life, although not, of course, during the time he spent at Sancerre. In the first eighteen months after his return to Geneva he published six such manuscripts, of which the first three are interconnected. They were the *De feudis commentatio tripertita* (March 1573),[2] the *Quaestionum illustrium liber* (June 1573), the *Francogallia* (August 1573), the *Dialecticae institutionum libri III* (August 1573), the *Observationum liber III* (January 1574), and his commentary on Caesar's *Gallic War* (*De bello gallico commentarii VII*, 1574). In the year following his arrival in Geneva he composed his account of the massacre of Saint Bartholomew (*De furoribus gallicis*, 1573) and his tribute to its principal victim, Admiral Coligny (*Gasparis Colini Castelloni vita*, 1575). The manuscripts he had lost in his flight were returned to him at intervals. The date of the dedicatory letter to Caspar Seydlitz in *De feudis* (June 1572) indicates that the work had been sent to the printer before the catastrophe. A second prefatory letter was added to *De feudis* in March 1573 and addressed to another former student, Reuber, who was later a member of the council of the elector palatine. This second letter discussed the recovery of the various missing manuscripts. It mentioned that the *Dialecticae* had also gone to the printer before the massacre, that the *Consolatio* composed at

---

[1] Giesey, 'When and Why', 591. Cf. Dareste, 'Hotman, 1563–1573', 529–44.
[2] Dates are those of prefatory letters in the works concerned.

Sancerre was safe, and that the notes for the commentaries on Caesar had recently been received. Some exercises he had written to controvert the opinions of Guy Pape, Jean Papon, and other compilers of the decrees of the parlements, whom Hotman disparagingly called *pragmatici*, had been borrowed by Christofle de Thou, but, he said, he had written others in their place.[1]

The dedication of the *Dialecticae* also referred to lost manuscripts, although it did not mention titles or content. The text of the *De feudis* cited the titles of the *Francogallia*, the *Quaestionum illustrium liber* and the *Observationum liber III*, indicating that it was drafted after these three works. Finally, the preface of the *Observationum liber III* remarked how the author had twice lost his library, and how his papers had gradually come back to him through the influence of his patrons.[2] These cross-references help to determine the order of composition of the works concerned, and the sequence so established enables the reconstruction of Hotman's thought in the years preceding the massacre of Saint Bartholomew. Both the *Francogallia* and the *Quaestionum* were composed before the *De feudis* and bear a special relationship to it. All three of these books reflect the influence of a general design forecast in the *Antitribonian*. It is now appropriate to return to the latter work, which provides the key to many of the problems of the provenance of the *Francogallia*.

Hotman's sympathy for L'Hôpital's projected reform of justice relegated the ideas expressed in the context of the Amboise conspiracy to secondary importance. The new political situation made the life of the jurist of Valence very different from that of the propagandist and political agent of Strasbourg. Nevertheless, the

---

[1] Giesey, 'When and Why', 592–3. The exercises last mentioned are termed 'Disputationes contra Guidonem Papium & Paponium Arrestographum, & aliquot eiusmodi Pragmaticos'. No work by this title was ever published, but Hotman's fulminations against Guy Pape abound in his *Observationes*, viz.: *Observationum liber quartus* (Basel, 1575), cc. xi, xvii, xxiv, xxix; *Observationum liber quintus* (Basel, 1577), cc. xi, xiv, xv, xvii, xx, xxi. Then, too, he railed against Guy Pape and Jean Papon in the *Francogallia* – see the index to the present volume. Hotman refers to Christofle de Thou as 'is quem tu ioculariter Christopherus Porcus appellabas'.

[2] Giesey, 'When and Why', 594.

complex of Tribonian was not without its paradoxes, and not all of them operated at the political level of a conflict between constitutional respect for custom and the chancellor's centralizing, reformist spirit. Within the context of his intellectual development the tension remained between those two coexisting attitudes to law which saw understanding in terms of history and yet demanded the demonstration of absolute values. The *Antitribonian* revealed Hotman's habitual respect for custom, and even contained a flavour of the Germanist historicism that was becoming increasingly important to him.[1] Yet the purpose of the book required a positive reshaping of law rather than a simple return to the past. It was in these terms that he outlined his proposal for the assembly of jurists:

[Il] seroit fort aisé (ce me semble) & principalement en ce temps qu'il a pleu à Dieu nous prester un Solon en nostre France, qui est ce grand Michel de l'Hospital, d'assembler un nombre de Jurisconsultes, ensemble quelques hommes d'Estat, & autant des plus notables Advocats & Practiciens de ce Royaume, & à iceux donner charge de rapporter ensemblement ce qu'ils auroient advisé & extrait tant des livres de Justinien (dont ils pourroient choisir le plus beau & le meilleur; qui seroit à vray dire un thresor inestimable) que des livres de la Philosophie; & finalement de l'experience qu'ils auroient acquise au maniement des affaires... Doncques apres une telle conference & rapport, il s'ensuivroit que les Deputez dresseroient un ou deux beaux volumes en langage vulgaire & intelligible, tant du droit public, qui concerne les affaires d'Estat & de la Couronne, que de toutes les parties du droit des particuliers, suivant en ce que bon leur sembleroit, l'ordre & continuation desdits livres de Justinien, & accommodant le tout ainsi que du commencement a esté dit estre necessaire à l'estat & forme de la Republique Françoise.[2]

The commissioners were also expected to derive principles of equity from Mosaic law, since Christian legislators should prefer God's chosen commonwealth before the natural law theories of pagan Rome, whence had issued 'les plus infames & detestables Tyrans'. Moreover, lest the reader should think his plan too

---

[1] Cf. Caprariis, *Propaganda*, 234.
[2] *Antitribonien*, c. 18 (ed. Cologne, 1681, 139–40).

audacious, Hotman recalled a passage in the memoirs of Philippe de Commines where the author described the intention of Louis XI to 'mettre une grande police au royaume', to simplify justice and limit the parlement, to adopt a single body of private law and a single system of weights and measures, and to record all custom in one volume written in French 'pour eviter la cautelle & pillerie des chicaneurs'.[1]

The *Antitribonian* appears to be an attack upon Roman Law which concludes with the proposal that Justinian's codification should play a prominent part in the reform of French law. This seeming contradiction is resolved by two statements early in the work: the distinction between public and private law, and the citing of Aristotle's opinion that the laws of a commonwealth should be accommodated to its political form and not the form to the laws.[2] The proposed commission had less freedom to remould the public law and constitution because these were the product of history; but in the sphere of private law Hotman was not so much concerned with history as he was with order and simplicity. It was principally in this area that he called for a neo-Bartolist pursuit of relevant principles, and cited the design of Louis XI. Nevertheless, the separation was not complete,[3] and the ideal of Saint Louis administering justice in terms of equity beneath the oak of Vincennes (in contrast to the author's contempt for the *practiciens*) underlies the whole work.[4] The Hotman of the *Antitribonian* generally resembled the L'Hôpital of the Moulins address and the *Traité de la réformation de la justice*, but he was closer to him on private law and the administration of justice than he was on constitutional issues. As has been shown, there were many opinions on the proper method to be adopted in codifying customary private law. Hotman rejected the practice of président Christofle de Thou, who was proceeding slowly to record and edit it piecemeal in the

[1] *Ibid.* (*ed. cit.*, 140–1). Cf. Commines, *Mémoires*, II, 209.
[2] *Antitribonien*, c. 2 (*ed. cit.*, 11, 8).
[3] This problem is discussed, although not fully resolved, by Franklin, *Bodin*, 46–58; by Pocock, *Ancient Constitution*, 22–5, 28; and by Fournol, 'Quelques traités de droit', 298–325. Cf. Giesey, 'When and Why', 596–604.
[4] *Antitribonian*, c. 17 (*ed. cit.*, 115–17).

direction of greater equity and uniformity. Nor could he wholly accept the method of Du Moulin, who wished to unify through the use of the model of Paris and a French comparative method. Instead, Hotman sought to impose an equitable custom devised on neo-Bartolist lines. It is understandable that his impatience with the century-old process of *rédaction*, and his enmity for the *parlementaires* who conducted it, should have led him to prefer a method aligned with the autocratic centralization of L'Hôpital. But the contrast between this approach of the *Antitribonian* to private law and the attitude to public law revealed in the *Francogallia* could scarcely be more marked. In the latter, Louis XI, who in the *Antitribonian* is represented as the progenitor of a scheme parallel to L'Hôpital's, becomes the tyrannical subverter of the ancient constitution.

In terms of public law Hotman insisted upon the irrelevance of the legal codes and constitution of the Roman republic and empire to France. Not merely the form of state but also the structure of society and its different historical background rendered the study of the Roman magistracy in a French context an absurdity. In any event, Tribonian had jumbled together sections of Roman Law with regard neither for their historical provenance nor for the various forms of state to which they were appropriate. The legal humanists had revealed the errors of their predecessors both in failing to see the distortions introduced by Justinian's codification and in attempting to apply the *Corpus juris civilis* to their own society. However, these grammarians had also erred, for in their insistence upon restoring original meaning and context they had lost sight of the relevance of certain enduring principles of equity. Hotman clearly did not mean by this that sections of Roman private law could be applicable to France, for he remarked that a French lawyer entering a French court after learning Roman rules of property and inheritance would be as well equipped as if he had arrived among American savages.[1] Moreover, French legal procedure had nothing in common with its Roman equivalent. French advocates had their own jargon and employed it as if it were a set

[1] *Ibid.*, c. 5 (*ed. cit.*, 32).

of magic incantations, but this language and method of pleading was as remote from the practice of the ancient Romans as French methods from those of Tartars or Troglodytes.[1]

While Hotman proclaimed the irrelevance of Roman Law to practical French legal needs, he also suggested methods for the reform of legal education. Some of his suggestions for the material he wished to substitute for the study of Roman Law texts explain the original purpose of the *Francogallia* and the *De feudis*. Instead of preparing a young man for the administration of French justice by teaching him the functions of magistrates in Rome and Constantinople, he should be instructed to learn:

le droit de la souveraineté de nos Rois, de la puissance & authorité des trois estats, des droits de la Reine, du Dauphin, des freres du Roy & de leurs appennages, des Princes, des bastards du Roy & de ses freres, du Conestable, des Pairs, des Mareschaux de France, du grand Maistre: du grand Chambellan, de l'Admiral, des Ducs, Comtes, Vicomtes, Vidasmes, & Barons: Item des Thresoriers de France, des Generaux des finances de la chambre des Comptes: quant à la Justice, des droits du chancelier, des gens du privé Conseil; des Maistres des Requestes, des Parlemens, Baillifs & Seneschaux des Provinces.[2]

What Hotman here proposed was a study of the constitution and the principal military, administrative and judicial officials, local and national, household and conciliar. The titles of the nobility were included because of their historical origin as public offices, for it was part of Hotman's habitual method that public functions should be explained in terms of history. Another clue is provided by the host of technical terms which, Hotman suggested, must be known by anyone wishing to practise law in the courts. They included such matters as the law of:

d'heritages cottiers ou surcottiers, des droits seigneuriaux, de justice directe, censive, recognoissance, de retraits lignages ou feodaux, de rente fonciere ou volage, vest, desaisine, dessaisine [*sic*] droit de quart ou requart, quint ou requint, droit d'afeurage ou chambellage, droit de champart, de frarenseté ou escleiches, de doüaire coustumier ou prefix, de communauté de biens, et autres semblables propos...[3]

[1] *Ibid.*, c. 9 (*ed. cit.*, 56–7).　　[2] *Ibid.*, c. 3 (*ed. cit.*, 18).　　[3] *Ibid.*, c. 5 (*ed. cit.*, 32).

These were issues of seigneurial and private law, the subject matter of the *coutumiers*. Yet Hotman did not essay the impossible task of tracing in detail the evolution of private law. He treated the *feudum* as a public office, but he was aware of the ambivalence of feudal law, which did not fit the clear-cut Roman distinction between public and private law. Hence in the *Francogallia* he set out to discover the historical roots of constitutional law, excluding the public aspects of the feud, while later in the *De feudis* he pursued many of those aspects of public law omitted from consideration in the *Francogallia*.

Certain sections of the *Antitribonian* reveal that Hotman had made considerable progress with his historical investigation of early French institutions before he came to describe in formal terms how knowledge of the constitution should form part of his suggested programme for legal education. In the seventeenth chapter he reviewed the course of early and medieval French history in order to determine whether Roman Law influence had been a blessing or a disaster.[1] Long after the foundation of the Merovingian kingdom in France, he argued, the country had generally remained ignorant of Roman codes. He admitted that traces of Roman Law had lingered for a time in Gaul after the Frankish occupation, but its memory was buried beneath the *seigneurie* of the Franks. Like other *nations septentrionales*, the Franks had brought with them their own law out of Germany, and its relics were to be found translated into Latin in the Salic Law. Hotman quoted its preface to show that Frankish 'princes, barons et notables' had composed the Salic Law long before the baptism of Clovis, and that subsequent kings had corrected and revised it. For 300 years the Merovingians had ruled by the Frankish code. Under Charlemagne a further reformation of this law had taken place. Hotman cited Einhard's remarks about this revision, which displayed entire ignorance of the existence of Justinian's codification. Moreover, for another five centuries France had continued to be governed without reference to the *Corpus juris civilis*. The constitutional emphasis in all this is in marked contrast with his views in the subsequent

---

[1] *Ibid.*, c. 17 (*ed. cit.*, 111–37).

Francogallia. His readiness to grant authority to the kings in the reform of Frankish law shows that he had not yet defined the theme of the ancient and invariable authority of the public council in such matters. The estates general were never mentioned in this context throughout the *Antitribonian*. Neither did he use the expression 'Francogallia' or 'France-Gaule', nor did he depict the Franks as the standard-bearers of liberty.

At the same time, there are obvious similarities between the *Antitribonian* and the *Francogallia*. The citations from historical sources are much less in evidence in the earlier work, but many of the same authorities, Gregory of Tours, Einhard, Aimon of Fleury, and certain Roman and Byzantine historians, are quoted in both. The passage from Joinville describing the administration of a direct and simple justice by Saint Louis at Vincennes occurs in both works.[1] The account of the establishment of the parlement of Paris (in itself an oblique response to Pasquier), together with the criticism of the expansion of the magistracy and the needless complication of legal procedure, are stated in the two books in similar terms.[2] So, too, is the discussion of the introduction of Canon Law into France, which is held responsible for the corruption of justice and for the 'sotte et barbare coustume' of expressing legal documents in Latin, a practice only abolished in respect of private law, by the edict of Villers-Coterets in 1539.[3] The proverb 'magnus canonista, magnus asinista' epitomizes Hotman's unvarying disdain for Canon Law, an area where he inherited all the bias of Du Moulin. Apart from the repetition of particular themes, there is, of course, the general characteristic common to the *Antitribonian* and the *Francogallia* of a reliance upon the national past and the rôle within it of the Germanic influence of the Franks. For all this, however, the political theme of the *Francogallia* is absent from the *Antitribonian*. The implications of the Amboise propaganda had not yet been recalled, and the authoritarian element in the complex of Tribonian still influenced

---

[1] *Ibid.*, c. 17 (*ed. cit.*, 116–18). See below, p. 508.
[2] *Ibid.*, c. 17 (*ed. cit.*, 120–2, 131–7). See below, pp. 510–16.
[3] *Ibid.*, c. 13 (*ed. cit.*, 88–9). In a later passage (c. 15; *ed. cit.*, 105), Hotman refers to the corrupting influence of Canon Law in the education of youth. See below, p. 522.

his thinking. The shift in emphasis occurred after the composition of the *Antitribonian*, and it seems to have been associated with the resumption of the civil wars.

5. *The genesis of the 'Francogallia'*

A substantial part of the text of the *Francogallia* seems to have been written before Hotman fled to Sancerre in August 1568. This may be established from evidence within the text itself. At the conclusion of his fifth chapter Hotman declared that the Capetians were in the five hundred and eightieth year of their régime at the time of writing.[1] In the revised edition of 1576 he altered the phrase to read that the Capetians had been ruling for five hundred and eighty years.[2] The change was probably made for reasons of style, yet Hotman did not alter the numeral, which suggests that this part of the original draft was written in 1567.[3] There is support for this calculation in two passages in which Hotman refers to an occasion, 'since when the hundredth year has not gone by', on which the estates general of Tours supposedly deputed thirty-six guardians of the commonwealth (*XXXVI Reipublicae curatores*) to supervise the government of Louis XI.[4] However, Hotman's remarks about the restraint of the monarch who, in contrast to his rôle in the *Antitribonian*, had now become the enemy of the ancient constitution, were singularly inaccurate. The estates met at Tours in April 1468, but it was not this subservient assembly that appointed the guardians.

[1] 'Qui ab Hugone Capetto prognati quingentesimo iam et octogesimo anno Regnum obtinent.' See below, p. 218.

[2] 'Qui ab Hugone Capeto prognati per quingentos iam et octoginta annos Regnum obtinent.' See below, p. 218.

[3] Early in the sixteenth chapter of the 1573 edition (below, p. 406) Hotman accepts the year 987 for the advent of Hugh Capet. Since he moved from an ordinal to a cardinal number, and may not have been counting inclusively, the date 1566 would appear possible, but this can be discounted because of the priority of the *Antitribonian* and the likelihood that the *Francogallia* was composed in the political climate of the civil war of 1567–8. Cf. Salmon, '*Francogallia*', *Times Literary Supplement* (11 December 1969), 1,426.

[4] See below, pp. 446, 480. The two phrases used in the Latin are: 'nondum centesimum annum abiisse' and 'neque centesimum adhuc exisse annum'.

These were created by the treaty of Saint-Maur of October 1465, when Louis XI, after his war with the princes of the League of the Common Weal, agreed to accept the presence of twelve deputies from each of the three estates at the royal council. Moreover, the arrangement had such little effect that it was terminated before the end of the year. Yet inaccurate as was Hotman's account, the passages do confirm the belief that he was engaged upon the composition of the *Francogallia* in 1567 and 1568.

It so happened that the year 1567 marked the revival of Huguenot constitutional thought, and that among the arguments used to justify armed resistance was an explicit parallel between the action of Condé's party and that of the League of the Common Weal against Louis XI over a century earlier. The *Memoires des occasions de la guerre appellée le Bien-Public, rapportez à l'estat de la guerre presente* suggested that Louis XI had broken constitutional conventions, which, from the very origin of the French monarchy, had limited the king through the authority of the nobility and the *communautés* of towns and provinces. The princes of the Common Weal had taken up arms in the public interest to require the convocation of the estates. It was the aim of Condé and his associates, argued the author of this pamphlet, to put into effect the decisions of the Orléans estates of 1560, which, despite the royal promise, had not been respected.[1]

Other Huguenot pamphlets of 1567 advanced arguments related to those of the *Francogallia*. The *Protestation de Monseigneur le Prince de Condé* demanded the assembling of the estates to review the unjust exactions of the 'Italians'. The *Nécessité d'assembler les états* reproduced extracts from the memoirs of Commines about the constitutional rôle of the estates, and quoted the advocacy of the estates presented by Charles de Marillac, archbishop of Vienne, at Fontainebleau in August 1560, together with L'Hôpital's speech at the opening of the Orléans estates. The *Protestation de plusieurs gentils-hommes* recalled the ancient liberties of the Franks, existing before and after the foundation of a monarchy that would now

---

[1] This and the pamphlets mentioned in the next paragraph are summarized by Caprariis, *Propaganda*, 387–99.

replace liberty with slavery. Yet another 1567 tract was reminiscent of the arguments of Amboise. This work, the *Requeste et remonstrance du peuple*, held the crown to be restrained by inviolable laws that prevented the alienation of the royal domain and required the king to rule with legitimate counsel, whether or not he had attained majority.

Themes close to those of the *Francogallia* were also contained in the literature with which the Huguenots justified their opposition during the third war. The *Discours par dialogue sur l'edict de la revocation de la paix* (1569) declared a king who did not fulfill his obligations to his subjects a tyrant, and argued that the process by which consent was obtained for taxation showed that the constitution was a mixture of monarchic, aristocratic and popular elements. If kings exceeded their constitutional authority, it was legitimate to submit private or public remonstrances. The latter were advanced:

en assemblee d'estats, comme il s'est tousiours pratiqué en la France dès la premiere institution de tel regne, en quoy l'on congnoit que l'intention du peuple François et Gallicque n'a pas esté par la loy Royalle du pays, de souffrir un Roy tyran ny qui usast d'absolue puissance contre toutes loix...[1]

A tract of the third war entitled *Question politique, s'il est licite aux subiects de capituler avec leur Prince* advanced contractual theories, and suggested that legitimate monarchy arose originally from elections in which kings were bound by specific capitulations. The first kings, who had delivered Gaul from Roman tyranny, had done so with the aid of their subjects, and had governed in partnership with them through assemblies which were part noble and part *roturier*. The estates, which had once met annually, were now summoned once or twice in a century. The name of 'parliament', which had formerly designated these assemblies, was now restricted to a purely judicial court, whose judges dealt only with particular cases. The authority of the peers had been destroyed. The ancient constitution had been subverted, and ought to be restored.[2]

[1] *Ibid.*, 427. See also Allen, *Political Thought in the 16th Century*, 305–6.
[2] Caprariis, *Propaganda*, 428–34, 438.

It is conceivable that François Hotman played some part in the direction of Huguenot propaganda during the second war of 1567–8, but his exact contribution is even more problematical than it is to the literature of Amboise. What matters for our purpose is that many of the arguments of the *Francogallia* were being delineated in contemporary polemics when he was composing his first draft. In this context it is not difficult to see how what was outlined as a study of the constitution in the *Antitribonian* (where it fitted the context of the reform of justice and legal education) suddenly assumed a sharp political focus. This is not to suggest that Hotman consciously subordinated his standards of historical judgment to the political needs of the moment, nor even that he borrowed themes from the Huguenot tracts of the time. It has been seen that his ideas on the nature of the French constitution were prepared over many years in the course of both his juristic writings and his political activities in the Huguenot cause. He had begun to collect his apparatus of historical references bearing on these issues well before he wrote the *Antitribonian*. Now the various elements in his thought coalesced with all the force of a revelation. His desire for certitude overcame the critical bent of his juridical training. Fundamentalism in religion and politics was transmuted to the kind of history that saw essential values implanted in positive origins, and subsequently corrupted in the passage of time. The mood of the moment was propitious to an historical justification of constitutionalism. The conviction of the historical rôle of the public council in the constitution, and of its derivation from Frankish tradition, came to him with greater force because the elements of these ideas had for long been hidden in his mind. Other Huguenot writers of the time expressed similar viewpoints, but none of them set out with such unremitting energy to ransack the chronicles of the past in order to demonstrate what Hotman fervently believed to be an historical fact. The mingling of this attitude with the antiquarian research he had already conducted produced the strange amalgam that became the first draft of the *Francogallia*.

It has already been suggested that the *Francogallia* has a special relationship to other works besides the *Antitribonian*, notably the

Quaestionum illustrium liber and the *De feudis*. The *De feudis*, as we have seen, cited the *Quaestiones* as well as the *Francogallia*, and seems to be the last to be written of this group of works which Hotman published only after his return to Geneva.[1] The *Quaestiones* contained several themes also to be found in the *Francogallia*, indicating that parts of it were probably composed before Hotman's flight to Sancerre or during his second sojourn at Bourges. However, other sections were clearly inconsistent with the *Francogallia* and may have been drafted much earlier. The third question, for example, discussed the respective claims of a younger brother of a king and of a king's son to succeed to a crown.[2] Arguments from Roman Law were presented on both sides, and the conclusion favoured the uncle before the nephew (provided that the uncle was the elder of the two). Among the many examples proffered was the succession of Guntram before his nephew Childebert after the death of Lothar I.[3] There was a double contradiction with the *Francogallia* here. In the first place Hotman was using Frankish history to illustrate a supposedly universal principle, whereas the *Antitribonian* and the *Francogallia* stressed that each nation had its own constitution and custom, and that the Franks owed nothing to Roman Law. Secondly, the *Francogallia* argued that under the ancient constitution the succession to the crown was at the disposal of the public council. In later editions Hotman changed his ground by distinguishing between the opinions of the civilians and the national practice of the French. He only did so, however, under pressure of a new shift in political circumstances that occurred in

---

[1] The problem of order of composition is complicated by a reciprocal citation of the *De feudis* in the *Quaestiones* (p. 17). The reference, however, is to the third section of the *De feudis* (*Dictionarium verborum feudalium*), which was composed before the other two. The edition of the *Quaestiones* used here is the second (Paris, 1576). There are few changes from the first (1573) edition, except that a new question (xxxv) is added, and *Quaestio* xxxv of the 1573 edition of the *Quaestiones* becomes *Quaestio* xxxvi in the 1576 version. The 1573 edition of the *Quaestiones* was issued with a tract first published at Bourges in 1567 attacking Canon Law views on wills (*Disputatio in c. Raynutius ext. de testam.*). This work is cited in the *Francogallia* (below, p. 416).

[2] *Quaestionum illustrium liber*, qu. III (ed. Paris, 1576, 27–34).

[3] *Ibid.* (*ed. cit.*, 29).

42

1584, the need to support the claim of the Protestant Henry of Navarre to succeed to the throne in preference to his uncle the cardinal of Bourbon.[1] This in itself obliged him to admit that the elective practices of the ancient constitution had long been replaced by hereditary succession. The admission was less of a *volte-face* than it appeared, for in the early debates occasioned by the publication of the *Francogallia* he denied that he had advocated a return to elective kingship.[2]

That section of the *Quaestiones* which more closely resembled the *Francogallia* was the first, which discussed whether or not kings had a right to alienate part of their kingdom by their own decision.[3] This *Quaestio* was framed in universal terms and, in fact, offered more examples from German history than it did from French. It contained the same passage from Seneca as did the *Francogallia* about the respective rights of kings and subjects in property.[4] More importantly, it contained an identical account of the four kinds of property which might in some sense be said to be within the authority of Caesar.[5] The corresponding section of the *Francogallia* was not, however, inserted until the 1586 edition, where it replaced a shorter and less consistent passage. Other passages common to both *Quaestio* 1 and the *Francogallia* included the general arguments that subjects did not exist for the sake of kings, but rather kings for the sake of subjects, and that, while there could be subjects without a king, no king could exist without subjects; that, as Cicero had said, magistrates were like tutors, and were appointed for the utility of their wards, not *vice versa*; and that a king who conquered a territory with the aid of his subjects could not alienate any part of it without their consent.[6]

Hotman suggested in *Quaestio* 1 that there were four ways in

[1] Cf. Smith, 'Hotman', 353.

[2] See below, pp. 78, 80.

[3] Cf. Beatrice Reynolds, *Proponents of Limited Monarchy in Sixteenth-Century France: Francis Hotman and Jean Bodin* (New York, 1931), 66–8.

[4] 'Ad reges potestas omnium pertinet; ad singulos proprietas.' *Quaestionum illustrium liber*, qu. 1 (*ed. cit.*, 14). See below, p. 252.

[5] *Ibid.* (*ed. cit.*, 5–7). See below, pp. 246–52.

[6] *Ibid.* (*ed. cit.*, 10, 12, 14).

which authority might be conferred: by election as in contemporary Poland, by laws of succession established by the founders of a commonwealth, by testament and by conquest. When a kingdom was conveyed by election, it was usual for capitulations to be imposed to prevent the ruler from alienating any part of the realm, as with the oath of the kings of Hungary. This was not an example offered in the *Francogallia*, but the principle was there reiterated. Even where there was no specific covenant, the king should act as the moderator, not as the destroyer, of the commonwealth because of the purpose for which he was elected. It was particularly important that the fundamental laws of a constitution be kept inviolate, and not altered by new conventions.[1]

In another passage in *Quaestio* I Hotman used an expression frequently employed in the *Francogallia* when he remarked that it was inconceivable that any people, unless they were like the Turks and were so stupid and barbarous that they were more like cattle than men, could appoint a king to protect a commonwealth and fail to exact from him an oath to bind him to his duty. He elaborated the point in terms of reciprocal obligations reflected in feudal oaths of vassalage and in the Roman Law relationship between patron and client. Then he observed that in France the king cannot alienate anything without the consent of a public council of the nation, commonly called the assembly of the three estates.[2] History provided examples, such as Charles VI's treaty with Henry V of England, that contravened such rules; and yet, wrote Hotman, the question should not be decided by precedent but by the law, according to the usage of the civilians.[3] This is a startling doctrine from one to whom history is the key to law, and reliance upon custom the essence of constitutionalism. The *Quaestiones* were, of course, a series of general legal problems, debated and resolved for the benefit of law students. Nevertheless, the paradox of the relationship between the universal and the particular remains. The discussion presented by Hotman in *Quaestio* I, and the close parallel between it and certain parts of the *Francogallia*, illuminate the problem of the association in Hotman's mind

[1] *Ibid. (ed. cit.,* 11–12).   [2] *Ibid. (ed. cit.,* 15–16).   [3] *Ibid. (ed. cit.,* 16).

between the force of constitutional precedent and the definition of eternal truths about the nature of politics.

The *De feudis*, like the *Francogallia*, was partly the result of the programme outlined in the *Antitribonian* and partly the product of other phases in Hotman's life. While the book owed much to the opinions of Du Moulin and Le Douaren on the origin of the fief, it was very much a part of his own experience. As he remarked in the preface, he had lectured on the subject at Strasbourg twelve years earlier. There was also a section on the problems of the feudists in his *Observationum liber secundus* (Basel, 1561). He returned to the topic in his teaching when he resumed his chair at Bourges in June 1571, and it is likely that the first two sections[1] of the work were composed in the ensuing year. The third section, his dictionary of feudal terms, was evidently collected some years earlier, perhaps when he was at Strasbourg. The political situation in the summer of 1571 was very different from that in which Hotman had drafted the *Antitribonian* and, equally, from the climate prevailing when he had begun to write the *Francogallia*. After some early uncertainties the peace of Saint-Germain appeared relatively stable. The reformist zeal of L'Hôpital no longer influenced the government, and constitutional polemics that revealed the trend of Huguenot thought in the war years no longer appeared from the presses of La Rochelle. Hotman still had the *Francogallia* in mind, for he used the word to describe France twelve times in the text of *De feudis*, and once, when explaining how the German peoples had commonly been called Franks in earlier times, he added the phrase, 'just as we have taught in our *Francogallia*'.[2]

Hotman's prefatory letter to Seydlitz dated June 1572 recalled that he had noted at Strasbourg that feudal law was distinguished by the three vices of ambiguity, contradiction and absurdity. He had, he declared, already stated in a book of *Observationes* that its barbaric Latin submitted the mind to a veritable torture-rack, and that it provided an Augean stables for any Hercules who tried to set it in order. The further study and explication of the *Libri*

---

[1] *Disputatio de iure feudali* and *Commentarius in usus feudorum*.
[2] Giesey, 'When and Why', 589.

feudorum he had attempted at Bourges confirmed and strengthened his earlier opinion. Nevertheless, it was necessary to expound the feudal law for the instruction of youth, and his own judgments might encourage others to undertake its reform. The texts he had chosen were not confined to one particular state, but were drawn from a medley of sources and opinions in which so-called law was often contrary to equity and reason. Since feudal institutions had originated among the peoples of Germany, he intended to elucidate them mainly in terms of German history. The issues were those of public law, for the exercise of feudal rights was the function of a public office.[1] This statement of purpose linked the *De feudis* with the design of the *Antitribonian*.

Although the *De feudis* was based upon an apparatus of historical and legal sources similar to that used in the *Francogallia*, it betrayed little of the veneration for Germanic institutions manifest in the latter work. It is true that Budé and Zasius were criticized for finding a flavour of vassalage in the relationship between patron and client in ancient Rome.[2] Equally, Connan was found to be at fault for suggesting that feudal customs originated with the Gauls, and the words 'feud', 'vassal' and 'seigneur' were all alleged to be Teutonic in derivation.[3] However, Hotman could not identify feudal practice with the primitive military customs of the German peoples because those customs were not associated with land-holding. The humanists, on the other hand, were mistaken because they failed to appreciate the essentially military nature of the feud. Hotman's own conclusions on the origin of the feud were mainly negative.[4] It seems that he thought feudal relationships first developed when the Franks, the Goths, the Lombards and the Saxons moved from their homelands into imperial territory, but he refused to be explicit. He was much more precise when he came to describe types of vassalage, the kind of person who might constitute feuds, and whether an entire kingdom could be held as a fief.[5]

It was in regard to this latter question that Hotman touched in

---

[1] *De feudis commentatio tripertita* (Lyon, 1573), 1–6.   [2] *Ibid.*, 8.
[3] *Ibid.*, 7, 9, 12, 14.   [4] Cf. Pocock, *Ancient Constitution*, 77–9.
[5] *De feudis* (above, n. 1), 31.

De feudis upon a sensitive issue in the *Francogallia*. The deposition of Childeric and the substitution of Pepin with the approval of Pope Zachary was discussed at length in the *Francogallia*, which concluded that it was the national assembly that replaced the Merovingians with the Carolingians, having first sought and obtained the advice of the pope. But in the *De feudis* Hotman suggested that Pepin himself took the initiative, and arranged for Zachary to depose his rival. The rôle of the public council was nowhere mentioned. Gelasius and the nine chroniclers whom Hotman cited in the *De feudis* all seemed to say that Zachary deposed Childeric, and the only way in which he could avoid agreement with this papalist conclusion was to assert that it was Pepin who forced Zachary to act. His opinion in the published version of the *Francogallia* was the result of subsequent consideration. The chapter in the *Francogallia* concerning this incident[1] may well have been one of those passages which he added or revised immediately before publication. In the 1573 version he cited eight of the ten original sources to suggest that some authorities appeared to credit Zachary with the deposition, and then added a new source, Walramus, to show this opinion to be mistaken. Re-reading three of the earlier references, and adding three more who could be construed to support Walramus, he concluded that the decisive element was the supreme authority of the public council. He then added the account of the deposition by Marsilius of Padua for good measure. The 1576 edition enlisted the support of Johannes Trithemius, and the 1586 version included yet another authority, a manuscript purporting to give the substance of an address to Pepin by the archbishop of Mainz.

The variant accounts of the deposition of Childeric in the *De feudis* and the *Francogallia* reveal Hotman's methods and the complex problems of provenance those methods entail. Two other passages in the *De feudis* concerning the respective powers of pope and king are related to the *Francogallia* in a much simpler manner. They deal with the conflict between Boniface VIII and Philip IV and with that between Benedict XIII and Charles VI. The same

---

[1] See below, pp. 360–70.

analysis is provided in both works and the same documents reproduced.[1] However, in these instances Hotman was more concerned in the *Francogallia* to attack the papacy than he was to demonstrate the rôle of the public assembly. The estates general did not appear as an important institution in the *De feudis* because, after all, it was the king, not the estates, who could create a feud.[2] It is surprising, nonetheless, to compare the two accounts of the arrangements for the partition of the Carolingian empire on Charlemagne's death. In the *De feudis*, where Hotman's purpose was to show that the kings of France were in no way inferior to the German emperors, the public assembly again plays no part. In the *Francogallia*, on the other hand, it is the assembly and not the will of Charlemagne that authorizes the partition.[3] The discrepancy results from the differing emphases of the two works. Although there was no demand for the convocation of the estates in 1571 and early 1572, Hotman had not abandoned his historical vision of the rôle of the estates. Even in the *De feudis* his general attitude was revealed by his account of the election of Flavius as king of the Lombards by their common council, and by his observation that this council had refused to allow the king to designate his successor. Technically, he argued, a king who is elected either by the people or by the *duces* becomes and remains their client.[4]

Now that the order and relationship of the works composed over the five years preceding the massacre of Saint Bartholomew have been established, it is possible to reconstruct Hotman's attitude to the *Francogallia* once its lost manuscript had been returned to him in Geneva. While he was preparing the book for the printer, his friend and associate, Théodore de Bèze, was composing *De jure magistratuum*. The latter set forth general grounds for public resistance to a tyrant, led by inferior magistrates when the estates could not be convened. Beza's doctrines were illustrated from the Old Testament, from the *Libri feudorum*, from conciliarist arguments subordinating the pope to the council of the church, from Roman

---

[1] *De feudis*, 31–2. See below, pp. 428–38, 452–6.   [2] *Ibid.*, 37.
[3] *Ibid.*, 32. See below, p. 264. Charlemagne's will was published as an appendix to the 1573 Lyon edition of the *De feudis*.   [4] *Ibid.*, 36.

history, from Athens, Sparta, Denmark, Sweden, Scotland, Spain and England. Like Hotman, Beza reproduced the supposed 'Oath of the Aragonese' in the quaintly nonsensical form which they were the first to adumbrate, and which afterwards became traditional in resistance theory. A special section on the French constitution used the word 'Francogallican' and summarized the precedents for the supremacy of the estates listed in the *Francogallia*, including the thirty-six guardians supposedly appointed to discipline Louis XI at the estates of Tours in 1468.[1] The many close similarities between the *De jure magistratuum* and the *Francogallia* suggest that Beza had read Hotman's manuscript. For his part, Hotman must have been tempted to extend his own general arguments from the more coherent reasoning of his colleague's work. That he did not do so to any great extent may indicate that he still saw the work primarily as a carefully documented history of the ancient constitution of France. It is obvious, however, that he saw its relevance to the contemporary crisis, and he said as much in his dedication to Frederick III, the elector palatine. Later in the decade Simon Goulart was thrice to publish together the *Francogallia* and the *De jure magistratuum*, both in French versions. Were it not for the evidence to the contrary, it would be easy to believe, as so many have believed, that Beza and Hotman together planned their ideo-logical response to the massacre, and that Beza agreed to provide a generalized argument while Hotman composed an historical justification, subtly disguised as antiquarianism.

When Hotman submitted the manuscript of the *Francogallia* to the Genevan council to obtain permission for its publication, the book was described in the register as '*ung livre de l'estat des afaires de France avant qu'elle fust reduite en province par les Romains*'.[2] It is likely that Hotman suggested this title, which was in fact that of

---

[1] *De jure magistratuum in subditos, et officio subditorum erga magistratus*, (n.p., 1580), 277–86. On the joint use of the Aragonese oath by Hotman and Beza see Giesey, *If Not, Not*, 20–3.

[2] Archives d'Etat (Geneva), régistres du conseil pour les particuliers, VIII (1573) 145. Full documentation of the incident is provided from the archives by H. Fazy, 'La Saint-Barthélemy et Genève', *Mémoires de l'Institut national Genévois*, XIV (1878–9), 76–8.

the first chapter, to appease the censors. The French government was at this time exerting pressure on Geneva through the city of Berne in an endeavour to prevent the publication or distribution of hostile literature. Beza had come before the Genevan council in June to argue that freedom of conscience mattered more than diplomatic expediency, but the council rejected his opinion. On 6 July the French ambassador's thanks for the ban were received in Geneva: on 7 July Hotman's work was approved for publication. Clearly the council failed to see in the *Francogallia* the incendiary tract that subsequent readers assumed it to be. The council regarded it, as Hotman hoped they would, as antiquarianism. Beza submitted the *De jure magistratuum* on 30 July. Two weeks later the examiners recommended that a licence be withheld, and added a report of a disturbing rumour that the work was already being printed. On 20 August Beza appeared before the council to deny this, saying that the manuscript had left his hands only to go to a copyist and to 'M. Hotman', who had perused it.[1] Denied approval in Geneva, Beza's tract was not printed until the following year, when it appeared anonymously in a French translation. The *Francogallia*, however, appeared without hindrance under Hotman's own name. That Hotman was prepared to see the book published in this way, when he had issued his account of the massacre under the pseudonym of Ernestus Varamundus, indicates his conviction that the *Francogallia*, relevant as it might be to the times, was less a polemic than a sound and erudite exposition of historical truth.

When Hotman was composing the dedication of the *Francogallia* in the weeks when the *De jure magistratuum* was under review, he said specifically that it was in the course of brooding on recent calamities some months earlier that he had turned to examine the

---

[1] Cf. Alfred Cartier, 'Les idées politiques de Théodore de Bèze d'après le traité: "Du Droit des magistrats sur leurs sujets"', *Bulletin de la Société d'Histoire et d'Archéologie de Genève*, II (1900), 187–206. See also the introductions in recent editions of the Latin, French and modern English versions of Beza's work: *De jure magistratuum*, ed. Klaus Sturm (Neukirchen, 1965); *Du droit des magistrats*, ed. Robert M. Kingdon (Geneva, 1970); *Concerning the Rights of Rulers over their Subjects and the Duty of Subjects towards their Rulers*, ed. A. H. Murray, tr. H.-L. Gonin, intr. A. A. Van Schelven (Capetown, 1956).

historical roots of the ancient constitution. In the edition of 1586 this remark was made yet more precise by the addition of the marginal note 'anno 1572 & 1573'. In 1573 his horror and anger at the atrocities of 24 August may have induced him to represent the work as the product of very recent research, without in any way modifying his conviction that it represented objective historical fact. By 1586 he had cause to recognize and regret some of the more radical and generalized passages, and the marginal note may, perhaps, have been meant apologetically to convey to the reader that his less temperate opinions had been provoked by the massacre of 1572. If it seems that Hotman misled the reader on this point, then it should also be said that he never wavered in his belief in the ancient assembly of the Franks. In any event, some revision of the manuscript took place immediately before the initial publication, so that the statement in the dedication was not entirely untrue.

There were, then, three stages in the composition of the *Francogallia* that appeared in 1573. The first took the form of a wide-ranging historical investigation in which the references Hotman had been accumulating were shaped towards the educational purpose defined in the *Antitribonian*. Here his dislike of the judicial system, his nationalism and his anti-Romanism sharpened his pen and cast objectivity in doubt. The second stage was the imposition of the historical myth of the warlike liberty-loving Franks with their public assembly and elective monarchy. Here, as he turned away from the now irrelevant policies of L'Hôpital, his thesis drew strength from the new tones and stresses of the Huguenot literature of the second war of religion. The third stage was the preparation of the manuscript for the printer, when one might expect some heightening of tone, expansion of general argument, and elimination or correction of weak or contradictory evidence. Yet, despite the association with Beza and the remarks made in the dedication, the impression remains that revision of the *Francogallia* at this point was slight, and probably much less than the alterations of 1576 and 1586. Indeed, it may be true to say that before the publication of the first edition no one of the three phases of composition succeeded fully in imposing itself upon the design associated with the others.

EDITORS' INTRODUCTION: GENERAL

It is for this reason that the *Francogallia* has been variously interpreted as an antiquarian exercise, as the genesis of a constitutional myth based upon the mystique of custom, and as an oblique attack upon the Valois monarchy resting upon the tacit assumptions of popular sovereignty. In a sense the *Francogallia* of 1573 is all these things.

6. *The sources*

Just as the *Francogallia* should be understood against the background of the author's preoccupations for many years preceding its first publication, so, too, should its subsequent revisions be read within the context of later phases of Hotman's life. The first edition comprises only 56 per cent of the final text. Additions to the second Latin edition of 1576 make up 24 per cent, and further insertions in the third Latin edition of 1586 20 per cent.[1] Yet, although these changes involve some modification of ideas and adjustment of emphasis upon particular issues, four-fifths of the new material consists of further historical examples supporting the original argument. Thus the book retained its most striking characteristic – the massive concatenation of historical references designed to demonstrate the themes that Hotman believed important. A total of some 800 references spread among 158 separate authorities occur in the final edition. Nearly 200 of these citations refer to classical writers; almost 300 to medieval authors in the period 500–1400; while the remainder are divided in roughly equal proportion between fifteenth- and early sixteenth-century historians, legists, and legal codes and documents. Within the two latter categories most of the references to Roman, Canon and Feudal Law are inserted in the later editions, especially that of 1586.

Among classical writers Caesar (39 references) and Tacitus (21) are the preferred authorities, but there are also frequent allusions to Cicero (10), Ammianus Marcellinus (10), Pliny (8), Suetonius (7) and Livy (6). Hotman also makes good use of the letters of Sidonius

---

[1] The 1574 Latin version was described on the title-page as the second edition but it was in fact a reprinting. Similarly, the 1576 and 1586 editions describe themselves as the third and fourth.

Apollinaris, the fifth-century poet and bishop of Auvergne. References to other Roman men of letters and historians are scattered throughout the early chapters of the *Francogallia*. Among the Greeks Xenophon, Plato, Aristotle, Polybius, Strabo and Plutarch are all mentioned; Agathias, Procopius and Zosimus are cited from the fifth and sixth centuries: and Cedrenus, Suidas and Zonaras from the later annalists of Byzantium.[1]

The medieval chronicles most often quoted are those of Aimon or Fleury (79 references), Gregory of Tours (40), Sigebert of Gembloux (26), Regino of Prüm (25), Otto of Freising (22), Godfrey of Viterbo (17), Einhard (13) and Ado of Vienne (11). Hotman cited the chronicles of Frodoard of Reims and the abbot of Ursperg (Aura) 9 times each, and that of Walramus of Naumburg (Venericus Vercellensis) 8 times. He added 11 references in the 1576 edition to Hunibaldus, the supposed fifth-century contemporary of Clovis, who had been discovered, or, more probably, invented, by Johannes Trithemius at the beginning of the sixteenth century. The 1586 edition of the *Francogallia* contains 10 citations of the Burgundian chronicles of Besuensis which Hotman had consulted in manuscript.[2] Although his use of such chronicles was often capricious and his attitude to their provenance naïve, Hotman revealed a grasp of these sources remarkable for his time. Many of his contemporaries used as wide a diversity of sources, but no one marshalled battalions of medieval annalists on particular points with such effect. His closest rival in this respect was Matteo Zampini, who included 250

<hr />

[1] Hotman's sources are identified below in Bibliography A.

[2] This is attributed to the monk Jean de Bèze of the late eleventh and early twelfth centuries. The chronicle was continued anonymously to 1255. Part of it was drawn from the work of a monk in the monastery of Saint Bénigne in Dijon, with which it was later conflated (cf. Auguste Molinier, *Les sources de l'histoire de France* [Paris, 1901], II, 89; and Migne, *Patrologia Latina*, CLXII: *Anonymi chronicon S. Benigni Divionensis*). It is to be expected that Hotman should lack the sophistication of modern scholarship in distinguishing problems of borrowing, continuation and authorship for medieval chronicles. He was apparently unfamiliar with, or else did not choose to cite, the compilation of Fredegar and his continuators, which did not appear in print until it was published at Basel by Flacius Illyricus in 1568 (cf. J. M. Wallace-Hadrill, *The Long-Haired Kings and other Essays in Frankish History* [London, 1962], 151). Nor did he know of Hincmar of Reims, although he used part of his work unwittingly when he consulted the chronicle of Frodoard.

such citations, out of a total of 319, in *Degli stati di Francia et della lor possanza* (1578), a treatise comparable in size and theme with the *Francogallia*.[1]

Many of the fifteenth- and early sixteenth-century historians of France are quoted in the *Francogallia*, including the Veronese Paulus Aemilius, Commines, Gaguin, Gilles, La Marche, Monstrelet, Jean de Roye, Seyssel and the fourth volume of the *Grandes Chroniques*. Among recent provincial annalists Hotman cited his contemporary Guillaume Paradin on Burgundy and the compilers Alain Bouchart (on Brittany) and Jean Bouchet (on Aquitaine), who belonged to the elder generation. The names of several German historians of the same, or a slightly earlier, period, also appear with frequency. They include Beatus Rhenanus, Albert Krantz, Henricus Mutius, Johannes Nauclerus, Dietrich von Nieheim and Johannes Trithemius. Of these Beatus Rhenanus may have been more important in the genesis of the *Francogallia* than Hotman acknowledged, for it was his *Rerum germanicarum libri tres* (Basel, 1531) that first offered any convincing historical evidence of the Germanic origin of the Franks. Moreover, Rhenanus had published a collection of panegyrics from the third century which seemed to support his thesis (*Panegyrici veteres*, Basel, 1520).[2] Hotman used the panegyrics for the same purpose, but he differed from Rhenanus on several issues, and ignored the latter's accusation that the chronicles of Hunibaldus had been forged by Trithemius. Polydore Virgil and Thomas of Walsingham are among the sources used for English history, while Joannis Vasaeus and Géronimo Zurita are cited on Spain. Despite the comparative discussion of the constitutional history of other states, it is France that dominates the text, in terms of the preponderance of sources as well as of the shape of the argument.

---

[1] Zampini's references to medieval chroniclers before 1400 included Aimon of Fleury and his continuator (123), the abbot of Ursperg (34), Regino of Prüm (29), Sigebert of Gembloux (15), Gregory of Tours (15), Ado of Vienne (12), Otto of Freising (9), Einhard (5), Godfrey of Viterbo (3), Froissart (3), and Turpin of Reims (2) (cf. L.-P. Raybaud, 'La royauté d'après les oeuvres de Matteo Zampini' in *Le Prince dans la France des XVIe et XVIIe siècles* [Paris, 1965], 151). See below, p. 94.

[2] Cf. Huppert, *Perfect History*, 77–81.

Although the Roman Law sources introduced into later editions of the *Francogallia* tend to give universal significance to what had been primarily French, enough references remain to the legal traditions of France to redress the balance. The jurist most often quoted, though not always with entire approbation, is Guillaume Budé. Among the collectors of the judgments of the parlements Nicolas Bohier, together with the two 'arrestographi' already mentioned, Jean Papon and Guy Pape, are the authorities cited by Hotman. On judicial procedure he refers on several occasions to the fourteenth-century textbook by Guillaume du Breuil, as revised by Etienne Aufrier and annotated by Du Moulin. He uses the commentaries on Burgundian and French custom by Barthélemy Chasseneux and makes several important quotations, in anonymous form, from the treatise on the royal domain by his bitter personal enemy, René Choppin. He is also familiar with Jean Montaigne's work on the prerogatives of the parlements and with Cosmas Guimier's commentary on the pragmatic sanction. The treatise of the French jurist, Guillaume Benedicti, on testamentary problems in Canon Law, which had already been the subject of a separate disquisition by Hotman, is cited several times in the *Francogallia*. On occasion, too, he seems to prefer medieval French civilians to their Italian counterparts, for he quotes Guillaume Durand (Speculator) and Jean de Faure in the context of Roman Law. The *Francogallia* includes references to early Germanic codes, especially those of the Salians, Ripuarians, Angles and Saxons as published in the collection of Johannes Herold in 1557. Carolingian capitularies are quoted from the ninth-century compilation of Ansegius of Fontenelle, and there also are occasional references to much more recent collections of royal ordinances. Beside all these French jurists and sources, the later editions of the *Francogallia* contain the names of a dozen celebrated Italian canonists and civilians and a total of thirty-four direct references to the *Corpus juris civilis* and the *Corpus juris canonici*.

Hotman was accused by his critics of falsifying his sources and deliberately deceiving his readers. For the most part these criticisms are merely matters of opinion, since the sources themselves were often corrupt and ambiguous. Hotman's standards of historical scholarship were as good as those of the majority of contemporary writers. Some instances of distortion do appear, however, when his quotations are checked against the texts he used. For example, he quotes Aimon in the first edition to the effect that the Franks 'raised up' Theuderic as king ('Franci Theodoricum...erigunt'), but in 1576 'erigunt' becomes 'eligunt' ('elected'), a change which suggests that this is no innocent error.[1] There are many cases of abbreviating quotations to suit the argument. These range from a trivial instance of the omission of a reference to Roman virtue to a crude misinterpretation of Gaguin's account of the succession crisis of 1328, when Hotman conveniently omits a reference to the Salic Law.[2] Moreover, on two occasions he quotes the same passage from Sigebert on events in 622 to different effect. In the first, where he desires to establish that the public council of Francogallia met regularly at that time, he fails to quote Sigebert's words explaining the inadequacy of the ruler ('regibus solo nomine regnantibus'): in the second, where he is describing the rise of the mayors of the palace, he retains the phrase because it fits the argument at this point.[3]

Hotman also manipulates French sources at times when rendering them in Latin. When he remarks that his quotations are verbatim, this does not always mean that they are complete. He claims to quote the *Grandes Chroniques* to the letter as to the convocation of the estates at Tours in 1468, but fails to mention that Louis XI took the initiative in calling them and that his source does not support his view that the king was forced to do so. Further, he gratuitously inserts the word 'republic' not found in the source.[4] Perhaps the most telling example of deception is his citation from Joinville concerning the regency of Blanche of Castile. It is his purpose to reveal the unconstitutionality and the evil consequences of rule by

---

[1] See below, p. 230. Hotman's critic, Matharel, pointed out this error (*Ad Franc. Hotomani Francogalliam...responsio* [Lyon, 1575], 80), and Hotman replied with the assertion that the word 'elegerunt' occurred frequently in Gregory of Tours (*Monitoriale adversus Italogalliam* [n.p., 1575], 32).

[2] See below, p. 268.   [3] See below, p. 326 and p. 354.

[4] See below, p. 444; also p. 448, where Commines is not quoted *ad verbum* as Hotman promises.

women, and he deliberately omits Joinville's praise of Blanche for inculcating a sense of religion and morality in her son, Louis IX. He twists Joinville's account of the baronial revolt in the minority of Saint Louis, and makes it a justifiable resistance to the queen mother's misgovernment instead of a factious piece of opportunism.[1] He also corrupts the spirit of the text in other ways, and then, in the 1576 edition, adds a passage in the same chapter from a collection of royal ordinances which shows how Blanche was legally authorized again to exercise the regency when Saint Louis was on crusade in North Africa.[2] Although this later addition is textually accurate, it is curiously out of harmony with the argument, and illustrates the contrary tendency where the antiquarian could sometimes dominate the polemicist. Indeed, it may be said in general that, despite the examples mentioned, Hotman respected his sources as a jurist and an historian, and that his integrity in this regard was probably higher than that of his critics. Believing, as he did, that he had discerned an essential truth about the nature of the French constitution to which others were blind, he may often have bent his sources unconsciously.

A large number of Hotman's sources were available in published form before he began to draft the *Francogallia*, many of them appearing shortly before he took up his pen. As he revised the draft, and in later years altered the printed version in its subsequent editions, he alluded to publications after 1567.[3] It is significant,

[1] See below, pp. 490–2.
[2] See below, pp. 478–80.
[3] Among sources of the *Francogallia* published in the decade before Hotman began his draft are: Ado of Vienne, *Breviarium* (Paris, 1561); Aemilius, *De rebus gestis Francorum* (Paris, 1565); Aimon, *Historiae Francorum libri V* (Paris, 1567); Bohier, *Decisiones Burdegalenses* (Lyon, 1567); Budé, *Annotationes in Pandectarum libros* (Basel, 1557); Connan, *Commentariorum iuris civilis* (Basel, 1557); Einhard, *Annales* (Cologne, 1561); Fortescue, *A Learned Commendation of the Politique Lawes of England* (London, 1567); Froissart, *Chronicon* (Basel, 1563); Godfrey of Viterbo, *Panthéon* (Basel, 1559); Gregory of Tours, *Historiae Francorum* (Lyon, 1561; an edition at Basel in 1568 contains the appendix, liber xi, to which Hotman frequently refers); Krantz, *Ecclesiastica historia* (Basel, 1568); Lambert of Hersfeld, *Historiae Germanorum* in *Germanicarum rerum quattuor celebriores vetustioresque chronographi* (Frankfort, 1566; this contains the chronicles of Regino, Sigebert, Turpin and Urspergensis); Nieheim, *De schismate* (Basel, 1566).

however, that he referred to no contemporary historical work in the *Francogallia*, although the years 1560–80 were marked by an unprecedented number of histories of France which used the same sources and touched upon the same themes, and which Hotman had indubitably consulted.[1] Hotman cited neither Ramus' treatise of 1559 on the customs of the ancient Gauls, which could have suggested his views on Gallic political institutions,[2] nor Du Moulin's *Traicté de l'origine* (1560) already referred to. The political bias of the historical works of his two polemical opponents of 1560, Pasquier and Du Tillet, was hardly to his taste. As we have seen, both these writers accepted the Franks as Germans. However, the exaltation of the parlement in Pasquier's *Recherches* was anathema to Hotman, and, while Du Tillet's *Recueil des Roys de France*, largely composed in the 1550's, also echoed the chroniclers on 'Frank' as the German word for liberty, and admitted the ancient Germanic practice of electing and deposing kings,[3] it, too, was the work of a *parlementaire* and a critic of Hotman's politics. The references to French history in Bodin's *Methodus ad facilem historiarum cognitionem* of 1566 were distasteful to Hotman because of their Celticism. Nor is it likely that he could stomach the adulation of the crown in Louis Le Roy's *Consideration sur l'histoire françoise et universelle de ce temps* (1567).

Two other contemporary historians who acknowledged a debt to Pasquier and Du Tillet were François de Belleforest and Bernard de Girard, seigneur du Haillan. Belleforest's *Chroniques et Annales de France* (1573) was in many respects an antidote to the *Francogallia*, although it took the form of a revision and continuation of the

---

[1] Hotman does cite Du Tillet's *Recueil* in the 1586 edition of the *Francogallia* to provide factual details of the dispute between Boniface VIII and Philip IV (below, p. 430). His close reading of the works of two other members of the group of Catholic historians to which Du Tillet belonged – Pasquier and Du Haillan – is revealed by his reference to them in his reply to Matharel, one of the *Francogallia*'s critics. Cf. *Monitoriale* (above, p. 56, n. 1), 55.

[2] Cf. Cougny, 'François Hotman, la "France-Gaule"', 300–1.

[3] *Recueil des Roys de France, leur couronne et maison* (ed. Paris, 1580), 1, 3, 15. The work was still being written in 1565, as can be seen from the remark on p. 169 that Charles IX was fifteen years of age. The text in this edition accompanies a chronicle of French kings composed by Du Tillet's brother, the bishop of Meaux.

fifteenth-century history of Nicole Gilles. Belleforest, too, sought to trace the origin of institutions revered by 'le peuple Gallo-François', and he proclaimed his history a purely factual exposition, avoiding the deductive methods he professed to find in Machiavelli's discourses on Livy.[1] The author extolled the antiquity of the Salic Law as applying to the succession, and denied the argument that it was invented in 1328. However, he defended the rights of French queens to participate in government. The League of the Common Weal was described as a rebellion of a factious group of nobles under pretence of the public welfare, and the estates of Tours in 1468 were regarded as merely an occasion for Louis XI to inform his people that Guyenne would constitute a more appropriate appanage for his brother than Normandy.[2] Writing in the immediate aftermath of the massacre of Saint Bartholomew, Belleforest justified the slaughter as a legitimate response to a Huguenot plot against the crown.[3] The king, he argued, had the sovereign right to alter law and custom, but in normal times he should rule with gentleness and allow his subjects to dispute his decisions in the courts.[4] Like Hotman, he described kingship as a public office, not a patrimony. He provided a critical account of the arrival of the Germanic Franks in Gaul, and admitted the early practice of election and deposition of kings. He used the same sources as Hotman, but with greater critical acumen. He mounted a more extensive attack upon the myths attached to the early history of the Franks than did the author of the *Francogallia*, and, like Beatus Rhenanus, exposed the errors of Trithemius and the putative Hunibaldus.[5]

Du Haillan's *De l'estat et succez des affaires de France* went through

---

[1] *Les Chroniques et Annales de France dez l'origine des Francoys et leur venues es Gaules* (Paris, 1573) (privilege dated 2 October 1572), p. a iii. Belleforest's historical attitude and his indignant contempt for the history of the Huguenot writers of the late 1560's are revealed in the following rhetorical question in the book's dedication: 'D'ou est-ce qu'on a tiré en consequence le droict des estatz, l'authorité du conseil, la puissance des Pairs, et les libertéz de l'Eglise Gallicane, si ce n'est de ceste histoire Galle-Francoise, que plusieurs mesprisent tant apres avoir ravy d'elle ce qu'ils scavent de bon?'   [2] *Ibid.*, pp. a iii, 5ʳ⁻ᵛ, 397ᵛ, 399ʳ.
[3] *Ibid.*, 529ᵛ–530ʳ.   [4] *Ibid.*, 4ᵛ.
[5] *Ibid.*, 13ʳ, 15ᵛ–16ʳ, 1ʳ–3ᵛ.

many editions after its first publication in 1570, in the course of which the third book (on the development of the French constitution) was entirely rewritten. Du Haillan maintained, as did Hotman, that contemporary forms of government had been corrupted, and that France retained only the shadow of 'ces belles premières constitutions'.[1] He closely followed the opinion of Claude de Seyssel, author of La Monarchie de France (1519, second edition 1557) and counsellor of Louis XII, that the form of government was a mixture of monarchy, aristocracy and democracy, and that the crown, although absolute in theory, voluntarily accepted the limitations of customary laws and long-established institutions. Under the influence of Bodin's theory of sovereignty, he modified his view of mixed monarchy without entirely abandoning it, but Bodin publicly answered his opinion in his Six Livres de la République.[2] Du Haillan praised the Carolingians and Capetians at the expense of the Merovingians. The existing constitution was the work of the Capetian kings, who had preserved what was best from earlier ages. The estates had been first summoned by the Carolingians and consisted of the four orders of the church, the nobility, the officers of justice, and the common people. Their ancient rôle in preserving the constitution and the fundamental laws had been distorted by their recent opposition to the crown and their tendency to foment rebellion. Equally, the rôle of the parlement had been corrupted by venality of office and the chicanery of the professional lawyers.[3] In the tradition of Seyssel, Du Haillan bitterly condemned the character and policies of Louis XI, with language

[1] De l'estat et succez des affaires de France (Paris, 1613), 195ᵛ.

[2] Ibid., 190ᵛ–191ᵛ. Cf. Claude de Seyssel, La Monarchie de France, ed. Jacques Poujol (Paris, 1961), 115–21. Seyssel's orders were noblesse, peuple gras and peuple menu. Bodin accused the advocates of mixed monarchy of treason (Six livres de la République [Paris, 1580], 262–3). In the first Latin edition of 1586 he added a specific marginal reference to Du Haillan's De l'estat (The Six Bookes of a Commonweale, ed., K. D. McRae [Harvard, 1962], p. A 117). Du Haillan indignantly repudiated the accusation in the 1594 edition of De l'estat, and hinted that Bodin had himself committed treason by joining the Catholic League (see J. H. M. Salmon, 'Bodin and the Monarchomachs', in Jean Bodin: Verhandlungen der internationalen Bodin Tagung in München, ed. Horst Denzer [München, 1972]).

[3] De l'estat, 196ᵛ, 190ʳ, 200ʳ, 195ᵛ, 189ᵛ, 194ᵛ.

even more explicit than that used by Hotman.[1] His *Histoire de France* (1577) discussed early Frankish history more extensively than did *De l'estat*, and included in the preface a long critical review of sources and recent historians. He seemed to have the *Francogallia* and its imitations in mind when he concluded this review with the observation that some had written history to encourage sedition, and went on:

Leur imposture a esté descouverte au bastiment de leurs oeuvres: car outre leur crime de blasmer nos Rois, ils ont esté si impudens que d'emprunter, en ce qui est bon en leurs edifices, la main & l'oeuvre des meilleurs massons qu'eux pour les faire.[2]

Like Hotman, Du Haillan was bold enough to declare that the Salic Law originally had nothing to do with the succession.[3] He discussed at length the election and deposition of Frankish kings, and, despite his critical tone, included many fabulous stories and anecdotes.[4]

The circle of antiquaries including Du Tillet, Pasquier, Belleforest and Du Haillan generally excluded and ignored Hotman. Claude Fauchet, who seems to have influenced the most erudite historical scholar of them all, Jean Bodin, was also on the fringe of the group. His *Recueil des antiquitez Gauloises et Françoises* appeared in 1579 and set new standards in the objective appraisal of the sources used by Hotman and the group of antiquaries. Fauchet used the chronicle of Fredegar and suspected the reliability of Trithemius and the existence of Hunibaldus. He held all the stories of the Franks before their arrival in Gaul to be unproven. Many of his quotations in this respect were closer to the *Francogallia* than were those of his predecessors.[5] Questions of mutual influence must, however,

---

[1] *Ibid.*, 164ᵛ–187ᵛ. Seyssel's criticism of Louis XI was set out in his *Histoire de Louys XII* (Paris, 1515), 79–117. Hotman quoted this in *Monitoriale* (above, p. 56, n. 1), 61.

[2] *L'Histoire de France* (Paris, 1577), I, préface au lecteur.

[3] *Ibid.*, 20.

[4] E.g., the supposed debate between Charamond [sic] and Quadrek before the election of Pharamond and the establishment of the form of government; *ibid.*, 3–18.

[5] *Recueil des antiquitez Gauloises et Françoises* (Paris, 1579), 58ʳ–59ʳ.

remain problematical. Hotman certainly did not wish to cite Fauchet in the 1586 edition of the *Francogallia*, and none of the changes that he made in this or in the 1576 edition appear to have been the direct result of his reading the works of major contemporary historians. For the most part their work was far more discursive and less thematic than the *Francogallia*. Hotman chose to ignore them, as they ignored him, and he could claim with some justification that his history was written *de novo*. He singled out the older work of Du Bellay, *Epitome de l'Antiquité des Gaules en France*, as the object of his scorn for all the retailers of old fables.[1] The Catholic antiquaries, of course, were by no means uncritical fabulists. Their work, and the sources they used, provide a broader context for evaluating the historical argument of the *Francogallia*.

7. *The argument*

Just as Hotman refuses to name contemporary historians in the *Francogallia*, so too he resolutely avoids mention of the political events of his own day. Nowhere in the actual text of the work does he refer to the Huguenot wars and the massacre of Saint Bartholomew. The Genevan council approved its publication under the impression that it was a purely historical study unlikely to offend the French crown. This, after all, was what Hotman originally had in mind at the time he was writing the *Antitribonian*. The reader who was not alerted to the new purpose conceived in the autumn of 1567 might not at first discern the book's political relevance, especially when he read the early chapters on the Gauls and the coming of the Franks. But in the dedication, which was not submitted to the Genevan council, Hotman makes the relevance of the *Francogallia* explicit. There he asserts that the problems of contemporary France were the result of an attack by Louis XI, about a century earlier, upon the constitution which the public council of the realm had preserved, albeit in an attenuated form, from the very foundation of *Francogallia* in remote antiquity. The remedy for present discontents is the revival of the ancient form of the constitution.

[1] See below, p. 198.

With these remarks from the dedicatory letter in his mind, the reader would find political significance in every aspect of Hotman's account of early history and ancient customs, and the immediate notoriety of the *Francogallia* becomes comprehensible.

What had appeared necessary in 1567 was at least as important in 1573. As we have seen, the general theme of *renovatio* was present in Huguenot thought almost from its inception. The various strands of constitutional historicism that gave it expression were woven into Huguenot polemics at the time of the Amboise plot and emerged in stronger colours in the political literature of the years 1567–9. Hotman designed the final pattern, and it remained foremost in his thought after the atrocities of 24 August. He could not refrain from incorporating some of these ideas in the two anonymous works composed in 1572 and 1573, *De furoribus gallicis* and *Colini Castelloni vita*, although these were intended simply to describe the horrors of the massacre and the virtue of the principal martyr.[1]

The *Francogallia* begins, however, as perhaps it has originally been meant to begin, with an account of Gaul before its subjugation by the Romans. It discusses the valour of the Gauls and their dislike of tyranny, suggesting that, despite the division of the Gallic tribes and the fact that some were ruled by kings and others by councils of leading men, there was also a general public assembly for all the Gallic regions. Hotman cannot refrain from observing, even at this point, that Plato, Aristotle, Polybius and Cicero all advocated placing restraints upon kingship. The second chapter essays an antiquarian digression designed to show that the ancient Gauls did not speak Greek except in so far as they learnt it in the schools of the south, and that the ultimate language of the French is derived half from Latin, and the rest in equal proportions from Gallic, Greek and the Germanic tongue of the Franks. The third chapter describes the oppression and exploitation of the country by the Romans, when the Gauls lost their valour with their liberty. Hotman here introduces the first incursions of the Franks into Gaul in the second half of the third century, although he treats these

---

[1] Cf. Dareste, *Essai sur Hotman*, 65–6.

forays not as raids against Gaul and Roman alike but rather as actively encouraged by the Gallic victims of Roman tyranny.[1]

The discussion of the Franks is continued in the next chapter, where Hotman wrestles with the problem, beloved of the antiquaries, of the origin of the Frankish people. Like the antiquaries, Hotman rejects the legends that their original home was either Troy or Scandinavia. Unlike Du Haillan and Fauchet, he makes no mention of the letter which Cicero wrote to his friend Titus Pomponius Atticus referring to the German tribe of the Francones.[2] The first tangible identification of the Franks under their own name is held to be in the reign of the Emperor Gallienus, that is A.D. 260–8. Hotman declares them to be a Germanic people living near the coast between the mouths of the Rhine and the Elbe. Gregory of Tours had associated the Franks with the Sicambri living among the swamps of the Rhine delta, and had suggested they had come from Pannonia. The latter statement was regarded with suspicion by the antiquaries, although they did not hesitate to accept the story that a group of Franks had been removed to the Black Sea by Probus, whence they escaped to ravage Syracuse and other Mediterranean towns before sailing home through the pillars of Hercules. Hotman also recounts this episode.[3] The association of the Franks with the Sicambri offered certain difficulties for Hotman. Pasquier doubted the identification and pointed out that the Sicambri had been mentioned in the first century B.C. by Strabo as living at the mouth of the Rhine, while Fauchet remarked that Tacitus believed the Sicambri and the Batavi to be more Gallic than German.[4] In the fourth chapter of the *Francogallia* the Sicambri and the Franks are associated, but in the fifth they are distinguished as two different peoples. In consequence Hotman is obliged to disparage the story of the chroniclers that Saint Rémi

[1] Cf. Ferdinand Lot, *Les invasions germaniques* (Paris, 1945), 33–4.

[2] Du Haillan, *Histoire* (above, p. 61, n. 2), I, préface; Fauchet, *Antiquitez* (above, p. 61, n. 5), 58ᵛ.

[3] It is accepted by modern historians. Cf. Wallace-Hadrill, *Long-Haired Kings* (p. 53 above, n. 2), 81.

[4] Pasquier, *Recherches* (p. 23 above, n. 1), lib. I, cap. vi (*ed. cit.*, 17–18); Fauchet, *Antiquitez*, 58ʳ.

addressed Clovis as a Sicambrian on the occasion of the baptism of the first Catholic king. Fauchet, who accepted the words of Saint Rémi without hesitation, had no such difficulty, for he held that the two peoples had become assimilated.[1] Hotman, however, links the Franks with the thoroughly Teutonic tribe of the Caninefates, whom Tacitus had mentioned early in the second century as living near Batavia and Frisia. Tacitus had described their custom of electing their kings and elevating them upon a shield. He had also spoken of their claim to be the authors of liberty after their victories over the Romans. Clearly, they were suitable candidates in Hotman's eyes to be regarded as the ancestors of the Franks. He goes on to introduce the theme of the election of early Frankish kings and their appointment as protectors of liberty and guardians of the commonwealth.

The fifth chapter discusses the etymology of the word 'Frank' in terms of the Teutonic roots of the words 'free' and 'fierce', which were associated in punning fashion in the chronicles. Here, as we have seen, Hotman is by no means original. He also associates the name of Frank with the refusal of his heroes to pay tribute to Valentinian I, and on this issue, as in some other aspects of his etymology, he was contradicted by Du Haillan.[2] This chapter deals generally with the expansion of the Franks in the second half of the fourth century, and relies upon the surviving fragments of the history of Ammianus Marcellinus. Leaving the deeds of the

[1] *Ibid.*, 59^r. The meaning of St Rémi's exhortation to Clovis, 'Mitis depone colla Sicamber', is the subject of modern controversy (cf. Wallace-Hadrill, *Long-Haired Kings* [above, p. 53, n. 2], 172). The translation given below (p. 206) does not follow the suggestion that the words invited Clovis to divest himself of a magic necklace, but rather the sense proposed originally by Fauchet: 'Laisse ton orgueil, Sicambre, et devient doux et courtois.' Fauchet, it may be noted, also followed Hotman in quoting both the lines in which Sidonius Apollinaris wrote of the Sicambri and the Franks living among the marshes, and those in which Claudian had spoken of the Franks and Sicambri (below, pp. 190, 192).

[2] Du Haillan asserted that the word 'Frank' was derived neither from the ferocity of Frankish warriors nor from their claim to immunity from imperial tribute. He also remarked on the absurdity of associating the word 'franchise' with the Franks, pointing out that 'franchise' came into use a thousand years after the first known appearance of the word 'Frank'. Hotman was clearly the object of this piece of asperity. Cf. Du Haillan, *Histoire* (above, p. 61, n. 2), I, préface.

Franks in the early fifth century in the obscurity which the vagueness of acceptable sources suggests, Hotman moves on to the defeat
of the Huns by Aetius and the conquest of northern Gaul by his
ally, the Frankish king Merovech. It is Childeric, Merovech's son,
who for Hotman becomes the first king of Francogallia, being
elected jointly by Franks and Gauls, raised upon a shield according
to custom and carried thrice round the assembly. Thus the kingdom
was inaugurated by the primal elective act, for which it is necessary
to assume the rapid intermingling of the two peoples. Hotman is
not alone in this, however. Du Haillan provided a similar description, and went so far as to call the first Francogallican assembly
'une forme d'estats generaux'.[1]

At this point the argument of the *Francogallia* abandons its
loosely chronological construction, and for the next six chapters of
the 1573 edition surveys the main elements of the Francogallican
constitution analytically. One exception to this, the ninth chapter,
is concerned with the right of the Frankish kings to wear long hair
and would appear to be an antiquarian digression from Hotman's
political themes. It has been ingeniously suggested that this is less
irrelevant than it seems, since Hotman declares that originally all
Gauls and Franks wore their hair long and so disproves the opinion
that the Franks acknowledged an hereditary line of *reges criniti* who
from the first were distinguished from their subjects by their
hirsute characteristics.[2] This is unlikely, however, for Hotman
admits an hereditary element in Frankish kingship. The chapter is
unusually anecdotal, and includes the story of the queen mother
Clothild who, when presented by her younger sons with the
choice of tonsuring the sons of their deceased elder brother or of
killing them, preferred to cut off their heads rather than their hair.
The issue of the long-haired kings was, in any event, a stock subject
with the antiquaries and was discussed by Pasquier and Belleforest.[3] In so far as it suggests sacral kingship among the Franks,

[1] *Ibid.*, 40.

[2] Georges Weill, *Les théories sur le pouvoir royal en France pendant les guerres de
religion* (Paris, 1891), 101.

[3] Pasquier, *Recherches*, lib. I, cap. vi (ed. Paris, 1633, 18). Belleforest,
Chroniques (above, p. 59, n. 1), 3ʳ.

the practice is, of course, relevant to the general problem of royal authority with which the *Francogallia* is concerned. But Hotman heard no whisper of the Golden Bough.

The chapter on whether the kings of Francogallia were hereditary or elected begins with the celebrated lines of Tacitus to the effect that the Germans chose their kings *ex nobilitate*, and their military leaders *ex virtute*.[1] Hotman does not pause to comment on the possibilities in this passage of the distinctions between the two offices or between *nobilitas* and *virtus*. He uses it simply to show that kings among the Germanic peoples were elected without possessing any overriding hereditary right, and points out that this is still the practice in Germany, Scandinavia and Poland. His method is to mass citations from the chroniclers referring to the election and deposition of particular Frankish kings and to the ritual of shield-elevation. On these issues the antiquaries, who cited the same sources, did not disagree with him. He sees no essential difference between the practices of the Merovingian monarchy and the small tribal war-bands of an earlier age. He acknowledges that it was the practice of the Francogauls to choose their kings from a particular family, though they did not invariably do so. Thus a king's brother might be elected before a king's son if the latter were a minor or otherwise unsuitable. The 'throne-worthiness' of a candidate depended partly upon his membership of the royal dynasty (and hence his right to long hair) and partly upon his personal capacity. Hotman mentions disputed successions and the many murders of nephews by uncles, but he makes no general condemnation of the ferocious blood lust of some of his Merovingians. He seems to regard the retention of the crown within the Merovingian line as providing a measure of stability, but he undercuts this argument by quoting Plutarch's judgment that one chooses a horse or a dog for its own qualities and not for its pedigree.

The important element for Hotman's argument is, of course, that it was the public assembly that elected and deposed kings.

[1] The translation of this passage (below, p. 221) rejects the view that *ex nobilitate* meant 'from the ranks of nobility'. Cf. P. Grierson, 'Election and Inheritance in Early Germanic Kingship', *Cambridge Historical Journal*, VII (1941), 1.

3-2

Neither he nor his contemporaries accepted the modern view that the Merovingian Franks differed from other Germanic peoples by following the practice of dividing the kingdom equally among the male heirs.[1] This practice presents him with a considerable problem, and he overcomes it by claiming that the assembly decided not only who would be king, but also whether the succession should be shared among several. At the same time he writes at length upon the importance of preserving the royal domain, which belonged to the kingdom rather than the king, although the latter had the usufruct of it by virtue of his public office. He also describes how the assembly could create appanages for the king's brothers, which thereupon ceased to be part of the public property of the kingdom. Finally with regard to the succession, Hotman launches a powerful assault on the contemporary concept of the Salic Law. He claims in the first place that it belonged more to the Salian Franks than to the conquerors of Gaul, and, secondly, that it concerned private law and not the public law of the succession. That it had been applied in the succession struggle between Edward III of England and Philip VI of France in 1328 was accepted as fact by Hotman, as by all others in his time; Hotman argued that this had been improper, and modern scholarship has more than vindicated his scepticism by showing that the supposed evocation of Salic Law in 1328 is an historical myth propagated in the next century.[2] It was necessary for Hotman to refute the antiquity of the Salic Law of the succession if he were to maintain the ancient rôle of his public council. That he was right in respect of the Salic Law does not mean, of course, that he was also correct about the nature of succession to the Merovingian crown.

The tenth and eleventh chapters of the 1573 *Francogallia* constitute the core of the argument and, more than any other sections of the book, reveal the tension between the universal and the parti-

[1] Cf. Wallace-Hadrill, *Long-Haired Kings* (above, p. 53, n. 2), 3: 'The Frankish crown was hereditary within the Merovingian dynasty on the basis of equal partition between male heirs, and there is no trace of an elective element in it at all.' Grierson points out, however, that there are some who dissent from this view.

[2] Cf. Giesey, *Juristic Basis of Dynastic Right*, 18.

cular, the philosophical and the historical. They concern the nature of the Francogallican constitution and the dominant rôle of the public council within it. The government of the Gauls before the advent of the Romans is said to have been essentially the same, and a general model of perfection is presented in terms defined by Plato, Aristotle, Polybius and Cicero. It is the mixed or tempered form, combining monarchy, aristocracy and democracy, in which ultimate decisions are made by a common council. Such, says Hotman, was the ancient Greek Amphictyonic council, and such is the form of government in England and the German empire. The practice of restraining the authority of kings is a universal one, reflected in the ephors of Sparta, the rectors of Ceylon and the justicia of Aragon. At the same time, Hotman does not forget that he is providing an historical explanation of the French constitution. The three signs of tyranny – the absence of consent, the use of foreign bodyguards, and government in the interest of the ruler rather than the ruled – are exemplified in terms of French history, and the public council is explicitly associated with the estates general as the supreme authority in the kingdom. In earlier times this body is curiously identified with such terms as *curia, parlamentum, placitum* and *conventus generalis*. The opinions of the chroniclers are paraded as to the procedure of the annual meetings on the kalends of May, the arrival of the Frankish kings upon an ox-cart, and their presiding from a golden throne. The authority of the assembly is defined in terms of the election and deposing of kings, public laws, appointing public officers, assigning appanages and royal dowries, and the control of all important affairs of state. Not only is there a refusal to accept change and development in representative institutions in these passages, but there is also a clear implication of popular sovereignty that contradicts reliance upon custom. These revolutionary aspects may not be explicit, but if Hotman intended to revive the authority of the estates in these terms, he would indeed have accomplished fundamental changes in the structure of French government.

The next four chapters of the 1573 edition discuss the continuance of the Francogallican constitution under the Carolingians. The mayors of the palace, who assumed the royal power in the name of the last Merovingians, are described as the creation of the public council. Hotman admits the decadence of the later generations of the Merovingian line, but refuses to condemn the dynasty. He remarks that Einhard is a suspect source in this respect, since he was anxious to extol the Carolingians at the expense of their predecessors, and Hotman recalls the great victories of Clovis against the Romans, the Alemanni and the Visigoths. The advent of the new dynasty is treated as the work of the common assembly, as already described, and not of the papacy nor of Pepin himself. In discussing the origin of the offices of the constable and the peers Hotman associates the latter with the legendary King Arthur, an error which he subsequently corrected. The annual council is said to have continued with undiminished vigour throughout the Carolingian régime, even at the height of Charlemagne's power. This section of the *Francogallia* closes with the universal theme of the superiority of the kingdom to the king, a doctrine developed in Huguenot theory after 1572 from medieval ideas of popular sovereignty, and commonly expressed through the maxim 'rex singulis major, universis minor'. Unlike his fellow polemicists, however, Hotman refrains from expanding the concept in terms of the Roman Law corporation theory of the *universitas*.

When he comes to the transfer of the kingdom to the Capetian dynasty, Hotman surprisingly does not depict the advent of Hugh Capet as the result of the election of the public council. Indeed, to Capet is attributed a significant change in the Francogallican constitution. He is said to have astutely placated the nobility and confirmed his own authority by making the great feudal offices hereditary, instead of their being conferred by the assembly of the realm. This censure of Capetian feudalism suggests an appeal to the lesser *noblesse*. To modern eyes it is a commentary on feudal institutions as curious as Hotman's view of the superiority of Frankish government to Roman, when in fact the early kings imitated the trappings of imperial Rome. In the next chapter Hotman hurries on to some of the great assemblies of the estates general in the fourteenth and fifteenth centuries in an endeavour to show that his council retained its authority undiminished under the new line of kings. The 1573 edition then passes to the period of the great betrayal of the ancient constitution by Louis XI, a point where one might expect the argument to conclude. Although he discusses the failure of the king to keep his promises to accept the thirty-six guardians in this chapter, the high point of his general argument is that the very appointment of the guardians demonstrated the vitality of the pristine constitution. It is also in this chapter that Hotman mentions that the ancient assembly had changed in form since the days of the long-haired kings, and that the clergy had become one of the three estates.

The two concluding chapters of the 1573 *Francogallia* appear almost as if they were afterthoughts. In the first Hotman resumes a theme he had first taken up in the early 1560's and sets out to show that under the constitution of Francogallia women were as much excluded from administering the government as they were from inheriting it. At least he returns to one paramount principle which he frequently forgets in other parts of the book: he is concerned, he says, not with the practices of other peoples but only with those of Francogallia. From the long list of queens whose misgovernment brought bloodshed and tyranny one might easily assume that ancient practice had not excluded women, and that Hotman is really demonstrating feminine incapacity to govern. The crimes of Clothild, Fredegund and Brunhild are paraded through copious citations from the chroniclers, together with those of Plectrudis, the widow of Pepin of Herstal, and of Judith, the queen of Louis the Pious. The most recent examples are those of Queen Blanche, the mother of Louis IX, and Isabella, the queen of Charles VI. There is reference neither to the regency of Anne de Beaujeu in the minority of Charles VIII nor to that of Louise de Savoie during the captivity of Francis I. The reader is left to draw his own conclusions about the government of Catherine de Medici.

The final chapter consists of a long and vituperative attack upon the parlements, whose practices, as we have seen, formed one of the deepest of Hotman's prejudices. The discussion is loosely linked with the general argument, for the author criticizes the Capetians for the establishment of the sovereign courts at the end of the thirteenth century and for allowing them to usurp certain functions which, he believes, are the prerogative of the estates general. These judgments involve a contradiction already implied in the censures expressed against Hugh Capet and the alleged creation of an hereditary feudal nobility. If the decay of the constitution had begun so early, then the blow dealt it by Louis XI appears less significant. Hotman will not allow the antiquity of the parlement asserted by those writers who traced it back to the time of Charlemagne, and his diatribe reflects his scorn for the history of Pasquier and the *parlementaire* antiquaries. He is unable to see that the estates general had no better claim to be the successor of the *Champs de Mai* than the parlement, and that both institutions developed constitutional significance in the course of the fourteenth century. His plea for the simple, direct justice of Saint Louis, and his assaults upon the chicanery, venality and unjustified expansion of the *pragmatici*, follow the same line as his attack in the *Antitribonian*. In the 1576 edition he associates the decay of justice with another of his prejudices – the introduction of Canon Law through the influence of Rome. This is only one of a number of changes in the second edition that gave the argument greater vehemence.

8. *Early responses*

As soon as it was published, the *Francogallia* was universally accepted, not as antiquarian history, but as a tract for the times. In September 1573 the French ambassador at Soleure wrote to the Genevan council to denounce the book and to demand its suppression. In some embarrassment, the Genevan council debated the issue and took no action.[1] Hotman ensured that his work was widely distributed. In December he wrote to Rodolph Walter remarking that he had sent a copy to Bullinger, and that it was necessary, in the context of the peace negotiations then taking place in the south of France, not only to restore repose but also to recon-

---

[1] Council Registers (above, p. 49, n. 2), 185, 208ᵛ; also Fazy (*ibid.*), 78.

stitute the French government upon its ancient basis. In March of the following year he wrote to Daniel Toussaint, a Huguenot pastor at the court of the elector palatine, calling down the wrath of God upon the cruel and intolerable French tyranny. He added in a post-script that the *Francogallia* had been translated into French and widely disseminated, despite the success of the envoy at Soleure in persuading the council of Berne to interfere. In late April he sent another letter to Walter commenting on a recent conspiracy among the politiques at the French court. He observed that the *Francogallia* was having its effect upon fair-minded papists, and noted that the plotters were reported to have demanded the revival of the ancient constitution through the convocation of the estates general. This, he said, was the only remedy for the many evils that beset the state, and at the same time it was the surest possible blow against tyranny.[1]

Catholic condemnation of the *Francogallia* increased its notoriety, and hence its appeal. In June 1574 a letter from the papal curia to the inquisitor in Bologna spoke of the censuring of Hotman's work because of his being a heretic, and clearly alluded to the *Francogallia*.[2] On 1 January 1575 an edict was issued by the government of Savoy banning the *Francogallia* together with a tract described as 'the other new book about magistrates', presumably the *De jure magistratuum* in its French version. Hotman remarked in a letter to Jacob Cappel, the Protestant *conseiller* in the parlement of Rennes who, from his place of exile in Sedan, had been one of the first to congratulate Hotman on the appearance of the *Francogallia*, that the news of the Savoyard interdiction had caused the printers to press for a new edition.[3]

[1] This letter, and the other correspondence in this paragraph, is summarized by Dareste, 'Hotman, sa vie et sa correspondance', 372–5. See also below, p. 82, n. 2.

[2] 'V. R. ha fatto bene a retenere quel libro di Francesco Ottomani perche que medes imamente si retiene et tutte le altre opere sue, intendendosi che gli e diventato heretico.' Cited by Domenico Maffei, *Gli inizi dell'Umanesimo giuridico* (Milan, 1956), 189, n. 38, out of E. Costa, *Ulisse Aldrovandi* (Bologna, 1907), 77, n. 43.

[3] 'De qua [i.e. *Francogallia*] in memoriam redeo, quod heri mihi nuntiatum est. Nudius octavus a Chamberi tres buccinatores in foro Ducis Sabaudiae et Senatus interdixerunt, ne quis eum Libellum, et novum alterum de Magistratibus et

By this time other Huguenot tracts had taken up the themes of the *Francogallia* without any attempt to conceal their political import. One such, of course, was Beza's *De jure magistratuum*, but a work which attained even greater notoriety was *Le Reveille-Matin des François*. This pseudonymous work, perhaps the most radical of Huguenot responses to the massacre of 1572, appears to have been composed by several hands.[1] The preface used the term 'Francogallia' seventeen times, but the first dialogue has little in common with Hotman's themes. It surveys recent French history from the Huguenot viewpoint, discusses Frankish history in terms of Ronsard's *Franciade*, attacks the 'Machiavellian' influence in the circle of Catherine de Medici, and provides a sketch of a new constitution in the form of forty fundamental laws. Much in the second dialogue, however, is a direct commentary on the *Francogallia*, and makes explicit many general arguments at which Hotman had merely hinted in his own work. The discussion is monopolized by 'Politicus' and 'Historiographus', an unconscious reflection of the tension between the two aspects of Huguenot resistance theory. All government, the argument runs, rests upon the consent of the governed and is in effect their creation, although it may have different forms. The people elect their magistrates and enter into a contract with them which is expressed in the form of a royal oath setting forth the conditions under which a king exercises authority and a people grants obedience. Sometimes, as in the Old Testament, it is God who is the author of the form of contract. Elsewhere the formulae may be found in histories, as in the oaths of the rulers of the German empire and Hungary or that

veritate, vendere aut domi habere, legere, contrectare auderet. Hoc nuntio accepto typographi certatim occurrunt ut alteram editionem adoriantur.' Hotman to Cappel, 7 January 1575; *Hotomanorum epistolae*, 46.

1 The tract is variously attributed to Nicolas Barnaud, Hugues Doneau, Beza and Hotman, but it is unlikely that either Beza or Hotman contributed to it. The full French title under which the two parts were first published together, in 1574, is *Le Reveille-Matin des François et de leurs voisins composé par Eusebe Philadelphe Cosmopolite en forme de dialogues*. The version cited here is the Latin one containing both parts, *Dialogi ab Eusebio Philadelpho Cosmopolita in Gallorum et caeterarum nationum gratiam compositi, quorum primus ab ipso auctore recognitus et auctus: alter vero in lucem nunc primum editus fuit* ('Edimburgi', 1574).

of the king of France as described in the chronicle of Aimon of Fleury. When a king such as Charles IX attacks his people and breaks his oath, he is a tyrant and need not be obeyed. Kings who have usurped their power, as the Capetians originally did, have broken the laws of the constitution. Since purely hereditary succession may lead to minorities and the rule of evil queen mothers, and since a system of simple election may result in civil war, the best method of choosing kings is a mixture of election and heredity. The original form of the French constitution was one where supreme authority lay not with the king but with the public council of the realm, that is with the three estates, consisting of the officers of justice, the nobility and the people.[1] The estates were empowered to depose kings, and from the fifth to the tenth centuries eight kings were deposed in this fashion. Charles IX would also have been deposed were it not for the fact that his mother has been held responsible for his misdeeds. The estates, then, are the supreme magistrates, superior to the king, according to the old constitution of the Gallic and Frankish peoples. Yet in recent memory the estates lost their liberty, and their powers have been undermined by ambitious ministers and by the parlements. The prescription of time, however, cannot infringe the rights of the nation. If the whole estates general cannot be convoked, then the inferior magistrates who represent some part of that institution may lead resistance against the tyrant.[2]

Such are the main tenets of the second dialogue, and the reader is exhorted to read Hotman's *Francogallia* to see them exemplified in French history with a full and accurate documentation. The unique remedy for the dangers that threaten France is to adopt Hotman's advice and return to the old customs and the ancient

---

[1] *Dialogi*, II (*ed. cit.*, 65): 'Eadem Reipublicae forma constituta est olim in Gallia, adeo ut summa rerum non esset penes reges, sed penes tres Status, id est penes publicum Regni concilium sive Parlamentum, ut vocant in Anglia: ita ut non liceret regibus bellum facere, aut imponere nova vectigalia, quin consentirent tres illi Status; in quibus non numerabatur Ecclesia, ut nunc; sed Iustitia, Nobilitas et Populus.'

[2] For the arguments from the second dialogue summarized in this paragraph, see *ibid.*, 61–70.

constitution (*antiquus status*).[1] 'Politicus', agreeing with this advice, remarks that this is really what Machiavelli had intended in the third book of his *Discourses* when he wrote that a commonwealth can only be preserved by a continual return to the principles underlying its foundation. In the concluding section of the tract the author attacks the parlement and the Italianate retinue of Catherine de Medici, and continues to demand the restoration of the pristine form of government (*pristinus status Galliae*) and the authority of the estates general, 'as so elegantly summarized in Hotman's Francogallia'.[2]

Popularization of this kind by his friends must have worried Hotman more than the official denunciations of the *Francogallia* by his enemies. Jacob Cappel wrote to him expressing fears about the misrepresentations of his imitators and the danger of publishing a work under his own name when it criticized the magistrates of the parlement, who had the power to proscribe his book.[3] Hotman replied with indignation against those whom he described, with the word he had used in the final chapter of the *Francogallia*, as *rabularii*:

First, if the pettifoggers are anxious to do business with me, I have it in mind to deal with their Papponian judgments as they deserve, and to declare their eternal dishonour. It is an historical book, the history of a fact. What impudence have we here, since hardly three propositions are set forth without the clearest evidence and documents? If they complain that I have set anything forth improperly, or invented anything, or advanced as true some forgery, let them bring it forth in a public writing. I will submit to a debate even at the risk of my head.[4]

Two months after composing this letter Hotman read just such an attack upon the *Francogallia* by one of these very *rabularii*. It was the *Responsio*[5] of Antoine Matharel, procurator-general for

---

[1] *Ibid.*, 88. The author also suggests reference to Pasquier.

[2] *Ibid.*, 94, 134.

[3] Cappel to Hotman, 13 February 1575; *Hotomanorum epistolae*, 48. Cappel's remark on the power of proscription was a quotation from Macrobius, *Saturnalia*, II, 4.   [4] Hotman to Cappel, 2 March 1575; *Hotomanorum epistolae*, 49.

[5] *Ad Franc. Hotomani Franco-galliam Antonii Matharelli, reginae matris a rebus procurandis, responsio* (Paris, 1575).

Catherine de Medici, and Hotman wrote to Cappel that it was such a clumsy, barbarous and stupid work that he did not know how to reply and hoped to find someone to enter the lists on his behalf.[1] But in fact he was still in the combative mood his earlier letter suggested, and he wrote the refutation himself, disguising his identity with a pseudonym.

Matharel's *Responsio* undertakes a chapter-by-chapter refutation of the *Francogallia* that is longer than the original work. The author mentions that his tract is largely collaborative, and it is likely that much of it was written by a young humanist at the royal court, Papire Masson. Masson was himself engaged on a lengthy historical work at this time, but, as his name was as yet unknown, it is quite possible that he was willing to allow Matharel the credit. He openly acknowledged his authorship of a short commentary that served as the preamble to the *Responsio*, and a few months later he alone assumed the task of rebutting Hotman's answer to Matharel.[2] In his commentary (*Iudicium Papirii Massoni de libello Hotomani*) Masson declares the *Francogallia* a work of subversion, based on the distortion of the annals and designed to show that kings should be elected. He admits certain instances of deposition in early French history, but asserts, as Hotman had once himself asserted in another context, that it is the law, and not the precedent, that matters.[3] In that part of the book ostensibly written by Matharel, Hotman's Germanism is assailed, and his history declared as fabulous as the stories of the Trojan ancestry of the Franks. The author quotes Du Tillet on several occasions, and holds that election is a seditious, bloody and bestial process, and that Hotman frequently misinterprets examples of inaugural ceremonies, acclamation and consent as if they were the popular creation of kings.

---

[1] Hotman to Cappel, 20 April 1575; *Epistolae*, 51. 'Henrici [sic] Matharelli nescio cujus scriptum vidi contra Franco-Galliam nostram, adeo stultum, barbarum, stolidum, ut satis constituere non possim quemadmodum illi respondeam.'

[2] The arguments supporting Masson's authorship of the *Responsio* are provided by Pierre Ronzy, *Un humaniste italianisant, Papire Masson (1544–1611)* (Paris, 1924), 171–5.

[3] *Responsio*, 8. The same point is made in a later passage (*ibid.*, 34); cf. above, p. 44.

He agrees with Hotman that Pepin, the first Carolingian king, was not appointed by Pope Zachary, and states that Pepin made use of force and a measure of consent to seize the throne.[1] He rejects Hotman's view of the Salic Law and mocks his error about the institution of the peers, citing the authority of René Choppin.[2] The chapter of the *Francogallia* which provokes Matharel's longest rebuttal is that concerning government by women. Here he defends the honour of Catherine de Medici, his patroness, together with that of Clothild, Brunhild and Blanche of Castile.[3] Another long refutation assails Hotman's treatment of the parlement. Hotman is accused of damning the profession that created him, and of bitter prejudice against Roman Law.[4]

In his *Monitoriale adversus Italogalliam sive Antifrancogalliam Antonii Matharelli*, completed early in May 1575,[5] Hotman adopts a facetious and mercilessly sarcastic tone under the pseudonym of 'Matago de Matagonibus', a supposed student of Canon Law. He includes Masson's *Judicium* as one of his targets, and observes that the *Francogallia* is not concerned with the method of succession under the Capetians, which he is quite prepared to admit as hereditary, but only with the question of whether kings were elected in early times.[6] Returning to the same point in a later passage, he remarks that Matharel is mistaken in thinking the *Francogallia* advocates a return to elective monarchy, and that his opponent, who ought, perhaps, to suggest a new method for electing the king's archfool, will not find the slightest mention of such a suggestion in any place in Hotman's work.[7] The supposed 'Matago' virtually admits his real identity when he speaks of new evidence, particularly that of Hunibaldus, which will appear in the next edition of the *Francogallia*.[8] The *Monitoriale* serves, indeed, as

[1] *Responsio*, 37, 38, 91, 92.　　[2] *Ibid.*, 51, 99, 102.　　[3] *Ibid.*, 132–48.

[4] *Ibid.*, 148–64, 133 ('Hotomanus ius Romanorum respuit').

[5] The Geneva Council Registers (above, p. 49, n. 2), vol. 70, fol. 79ᵛ, record Hotman's submitting the manuscript for approval on 2 May. They also show the council's provisional approval, pending reports from Beza and Lambert Daneau.

[6] *Matagonis de Matagonibus decretorum baccalaurei, Monitoriale adversus Italo-galliam Antonii Matharelli, Alvernogeni* (n.p., 1575), 13.

[7] *Ibid.*, 22. 'Ubi vero ulla istius reductionis vel tenuissima mentio fit in toto libro Francogalliae.'　　[8] *Ibid.*, 16.

advance notice of the revisions that Hotman was to make in the text of 1576. 'Matago' has none of Hotman's hesitations in quoting the work of contemporary historians such as Pasquier, Du Haillan and Le Roy,[1] but he defies Matharel to show him where the *Francogallia* has any reference to contemporary events, or, indeed, to any ruler in the last hundred years.[2] Hotman counter-attacks by describing Matharel as an 'Italogaul' and inveighing against Italian favourites and financiers. The *Monitoriale* concludes with some passages of violent anti-feminism, and an attack upon the corruption and venality of the parlement more detailed and up-to-date than any in the *Francogallia*. Hotman's letters to his friends at this time reveal his pride in the way the *Francogallia* had brought his opponents into the open, and he clearly delights in his notoriety.[3]

Masson answered the *Monitoriale* in June, declaring in the title of his tract that 'Matago' was an inadequate disguise for his enemy.[4] He tried to adopt the same ironical style, but his writing lacked the verve and bite of Hotman's polemic. A month later Hotman responded with his *Strigilis Papirii Massoni*,[5] a *strigilis* being a surgical instrument which, Hotman suggested, might be used to cure Masson's madness. He varied his pseudonym, calling himself 'Matagonides de Matagonibus' and claiming to be *baccalaureus formulatus* in medicine as well as Canon Law. Hotman had been abusive enough in his *Monitoriale*, but in the *Strigilis* his vituperation knew no bounds. He accuses Masson of being an inmate of the lunatic asylum of the Mathurins in Paris, a libel he repeats in the 1576 edition of the *Francogallia*. He calls him a 'scrofulous dung beetle', 'a stupid monkey with a tail', and the 'filth of a Jesuit latrine'. The

[1] See above, p. 58.

[2] *Monitoriale*, 61: 'Suus [i.e. Hotomani] liber de nullo principe vel principissa, qui vel quae fuerit de post centum annos non fecit ullam mentionem.'

[3] Cf. Dareste, 'Hotman, sa vie et sa correspondance', 380–1.

[4] *Papirii Massoni responsio ad maledicta Hotomani cognomento Matagonis* (Paris, 1575). The treatise is discussed by Ronzy (above, p. 77, n. 2), 197–201.

[5] *Strigilis Papirii Massoni sive remediale charitatiuum contra rabiosam frenesim Papirii Massoni Iesuitae excucullati: per Matagonidem de Matagonibus, baccalaureum formatum in iure canonico et in medicina, si voluisset* (n.p., 1575). Subsequent references are to the 1578 edition. Cf. Ronzy (above, p. 77, n. 2), 201–8.

Genevan censors required certain corrections to be made before publication, but, if they suggested a more temperate term of phrase, their recommendations were ignored.[1] The added virulence in Hotman's epithets may have been caused by his discovery that Masson, besides having connexions with the Jesuit order, had been the pupil of his enemy, Baudouin. Nor could he have been immune to some of Masson's insults, such as the proposal that he should be torn apart by mad dogs and his remains cast into Lake Geneva. The *Strigilis*, however, contains more than a storm of picturesque abuse. Once more the author declares that the *Francogallia* does not deny that hereditary succession became customary with the Capetians.[2] He defends the authenticity of Hunibaldus, and adduces new examples of the election of kings which he subsequently inserted in the 1576 *Francogallia*.[3] Hotman concludes by attacking the anti-Germanist prejudice of his 'Italogallican' critics, whom he accuses, with a fine disregard for national images, of building castles in Spain.[4]

His pose remains that of one who is dealing with concrete historical realities, as opposed to the propaganda of court sycophants and royalist 'mythistorici'. As he said in a letter to Amerbach, it should be enough to beat the dogs to which Semiramis had thrown a crust to make them bark, without wasting words upon them.[5] One such piece that he did not bother to answer was the *Contra Francogalliam* of Pierre Tureau, an *avocat* at the parlement, whose humanist refutation contained far more allusions to classical history than it did to the ancient Franks and their constitution.[6] He also ignored an attack upon the themes of the *Francogallia* contained in Louis Le Roy's *De l'excellence du gouvernement royal*, which denied the proposition 'que le Royaume de France estoit anciennement electif, & gouverné plus par l'advis du peuple que par l'authorité du

---

[1] Council Registers (above, p. 49, n. 2), fols. 119–20 (5 and 7 July).
[2] *Strigilis*, 19.   [3] *Ibid.*, 18–23.
[4] *Ibid.*, 31. 'Edificant castra in Hispania.'
[5] Dareste, 'Hotman, sa vie et sa correspondance', 380–1.
[6] *Petri Turelli Campani et in supremo Galliarum senatu advocati contra Othomani Francogalliam libellus* (Paris, n.d. – dedication to Christofle de Thou dated August 1575).

Roy et de son conseil'. Le Roy stressed the inevitability of historical change and scorned the concept of *renovatio*. He described
the early Franks as a rude and barbarous people emerging from
their swamps and forests under the rule of long-haired kings, who
were elevated upon the shields of their warriors at their institution
and transported to their palaces on ox-carts. To advocate return to
such uncivilized ways seemed to Le Roy to be absurdity. Those
who rummaged in the old chronicles to produce ancient customs as
models for reform engendered discontent and sedition. Nor could
their thesis on the authority of the estates general be sustained. The
institution was useful as an agency for the voicing of complaints,
but kings had always found it necessary to conceal high affairs of
state from the vulgar multitude, lacking knowledge and experience
of government.[1] Tureau and Le Roy were critics Hotman chose to
ignore, but, although he did not admit it to Amerbach, his own
pen had been very active in the controversy with Matharel and
Masson. The exchanges reveal the double standard Hotman
observed. Behind the dry-as-dust postures of the author of the
Francogallia was the passionate polemicist, who was prepared to
show this *alter ego* only in the disguise of pseudonymity. However,
hints of the latter rôle make their appearance in the 1576 edition of
the *Francogallia*, and his motive for revising the text must now be
seen as far less scholarly than he pretended.

9. *The edition of 1576*

The new edition was nearly half as large again as the original. Some
of the new material was mentioned in the *Monitoriale* and the
Strigilis, and some may have been contributed by Hotman's friends,
whom he frequently urged in the summer and autumn of 1575 to
send him any notes they might have made on the first edition. He
also tried to have friends see the revised text through the press at
Basel, and then began negotiations with a Genevan printer. He was
uncertain, however, whether the Genevan magistrates would

---

[1] *De l'excellence du gouvernement royal avec exhortation aux François de perseverer
en iceluy, sans chercher mutations pernicieuses* (Paris, 1575), 25ᵛ–27ᵛ.

again approve the book, and he finally had it published by Bertulphe in Cologne.[1]

With one important exception, it does not seem that Hotman based any of the textual changes upon alterations in the first French edition of 1574, which was also published by Bertulphe. The identity of the translator is unknown, and although Simon Goulart, who was responsible for the three editions of the *Mémoires de l'estat de France sous Charles Neufiesme* (1576-9), has been suggested,[2] there is no certain proof in the matter. The *Mémoires* included the *Francogallia* beside the *De jure magistratuum*, both in French. This French version consisted of the 1574 French text with the addition of the new material translated from the Latin edition of 1576, as Goulart mentioned in a prefatory note.[3] Goulart also

---

[1] Dareste, 'Hotman, sa vie et sa correspondance', 381. See also two Basel MSS: G. 11. 19. fol. 164 (Hotman to Amerbach, 15 June 1575) and K. Ar. 18a, fol. 242 (*ibid.*, 13 August 1575).

[2] Cf. Leonard C. Jones, *Simon Goulart, 1543-1648* (Geneva, 1917), 12. This assertion seems no more than speculation. The tradition of attributing the translation to Goulart goes back no further than the *Opuscules françoises des Hotman* (Paris, 1616), and if the editor of the work knew only Goulart's publications of the French translation in his *Mémoires de l'estat de France* and not the earlier publication of it separately in 1574, then it would have been natural for him to assume that Goulart was the translator. Part of the postscript in Hotman's letter to Daniel Toussaint (see above, p. 73, n. 1) makes it unlikely that Goulart was the translator. The printed version (*Epistolae*, 44) reads: 'Oblitus eram de Franco-Gallia nostra, furtim a malevolis quibusdam...translata et impressa. Nam Bernenses a Legato Solodurensi rogati impetrarent a nostris, ut haed...trahatur. Interim istorum clientes furtum...ferunt. Spero eos poenas daturos. Habemus hic translationem, quam Velsero imprimendam vel ad vos mittemus.' The lacunae in the text doubtless account for Dareste's omission of the first sentence from his summary ('Hotman, sa vie et sa correspondance', 373-4). The sense appears to be that the authorities at Berne procured a copy of the Latin text of the *Francogallia* at the request of the French envoy at Soleure, and that the text was translated and printed by men who, Hotman felt, had deceived him. However, he refers at the end of the postscript to a translation which is being printed by Welser, a project of which he evidently approved and therefore is more likely to have been done by Goulart, his co-religionist and fellow exile in Geneva, than the Berne-Soleure project. But the only known edition of 1574 in French is by Jerome Bertulphe in Cologne, who also reprinted the first Latin edition in that year.

[3] Goulart, *Mémoires de l'estat de France* (Meidelbourg, 1577), III, 576. , In 1578 this text was reprinted twice in typographically different editions of the *Mémoires de l'estat*; see below, Appendix B.

added further comment at the end of the text he published in the *Mémoires*, summarizing the controversy with Matharel and Masson in terms favourable to Hotman.[1] In general Hotman seems to have ignored the French version. The translation was a free one, and the translator added many explanatory comments not to be found in the Latin. For instance, he carefully identified the regions of France inhabited by the Gallic tribes mentioned by Caesar in Hotman's citations.[2] When Hotman referred to the Great Beast of 'holy scripture', the translator substituted: 'ainsi qu'elle est appellee par Daniel le prophete'.[3] When Hotman mentioned the victory of Posthumus and his Frankish allies over Victorinus, the translator explained that Victorinus was the general of Gallienus, an addition which makes the passage much more intelligible to a reader unfamiliar with the events described.[4] Similarly the translator added to Hotman's remark that the public council had the authority to depose kings the observation that this power was only exercised when kings merited deposition.[5] He also expanded the account of Ebroinus, the first mayor of the palace,[6] and he explained Hotman's cryptic quotation of Cato's condemnation of women by saying that Cato was referring to the need to keep Roman wives at home.[7]

Sometimes the translator left out passages,[8] and at other times his changes tended to intensify the argument. For instance, where Hotman had said that before the Romans certain Gallic tribes had possessed kings ('ceterae Reges haberent'), the French read: 'Les autres elisoyent des Roys.'[9] Similarly, where Hotman had written of the attendance at his public council of the nobility and others described as 'delecti', the translator had insisted that these were

---

[1] *Ibid.*, 733–4.

[2] *La Gaule Françoise de François Hotman Iurisconsulte* (Cologne, 1574), 3 (Reims), 6 (Berry), 8 (Beauvais). Cf. below, pp. 148, 150, 152.

[3] *Ibid.*, 24; cf. below, p. 172.   [4] *Ibid.*, 51; cf. below, p. 208.

[5] *Ibid.*, 66; cf. below, p. 234.   [6] *Ibid.*, 69; cf. below, p. 236.

[7] *Ibid.*, 184–5; cf. below, p. 482.

[8] E.g. the omission from the preface of a reference to Seneca. Cf. below, p. 140. The omission of a 1576 Latin insertion, referring to the *parlementaires* as 'pettifoggers and robed vultures', from the text of the 1577 French version appears to have been deliberate. Cf. *Mémoires de l'estat*, III, 727, and below, p. 512.

[9] *La Gaule Françoise*, 2; cf. below, p. 147.

delegates and representatives of the people.[1] Wherever he found the words 'concilium publicum' he translated the term as 'le conseil general des estats de la France', 'l'assemblee des estats', 'le parlement general de nos estats de France', or, simply, 'les estats'.[2] In the same spirit he translated the phrase 'iudicio et suffragiis Populi' as 'par l'advis des estats et par les voix du peuple'.[3] *Populus* and *peuple*, of course, might mean the nation, and had no necessarily democratic connotation in the usage of the Huguenot theorists. That the translator was prepared to expand Hotman's view of the estates on his own initiative is clear, however, from his insertion of four additional lines in his text which claimed that the authority of the estates was so venerable that kings accepted their advice.[4]

The French translator's tendency to render the term 'concilium publicum' as 'états' has many echoes in Hotman's 1576 version of the Latin text. Whether influenced by the translator or not, Hotman himself inserted the term 'orders' (*ordines*) in at least nine places to amplify what in 1573 had been simply 'people', or 'council' or 'public council'. The resulting phrase was '(public) council of the orders', or the like.[5] The word 'estates' (*status*) is used much more sparingly. It appears in 1573 related to *parlamentum* in the phrase 'parliament of the (three) estates', and in 1576 that same phrase is made synonymous with the 'curia regis' or the 'curia Franciae'.[6] In 1576 Hotman also added a passage from Seyssel which appears at first glance to explain what 'orders' meant.[7] Seyssel had defined the 'three estates or orders' as the nobles, the middle estate (the wealthy) and the lowly commoners, specifically

[1] *Ibid.*, 103; cf. below, p. 302. The words in which *delectorum* are rendered in French in this passage are: 'des plus notables choisis et deputez par le peuple'. Cf. another passage (*La Gaule Françoise*, 12, and below, p. 154) where *delectorum* is rendered: 'des gens de bien et d'honneur'.

[2] *Ibid.*, pp. 72, 73, 124, 132, 151 (twice); cf. below, pp. 246, 322, 350, 390, 528.

[3] *Ibid.*, 72; cf. below, p. 246.

[4] *Ibid.*, 172; cf. below, p. 440 (after the words 'ex superioribus testimoniis' in the Latin—this is the passage introducing the chapter on the memorable authority of the council against Louis XI).

[5] See below, pp. 234, 246, 262, 264, 266 (thrice), 286, 342.

[6] See below, p. 322 for 1573, pp. 330, 500 for 1576.

[7] See below, p. 292. Cf. Claude de Seyssel, *La Monarchie de France* (above, p. 60, n. 2).

excluding the clergy. The reader might expect to find some comment upon the composition of that institution about which the central argument of the *Francogallia* revolves. Yet Hotman merely explains that Seyssel was referring to the public council rather than to the structure of society, and, while he accepts Seyssel's description, he goes on to remark that the three orders or estates are more conveniently understood as corresponding to 'the three kinds of government embodied in the council'. There follows the account of the mixed form of monarchy, aristocracy and democracy advocated by the classical philosophers which was already provided in the 1573 version, and clearly associated with the ancient Francogallican constitution.

Despite their vagueness, the 1576 insertions amplifying the description of the public council would seem to intensify the general argument. This is also the effect, and less equivocally so, of the numerous additional passages placed in the final chapter, the diatribe against the parlement. In 1573 Hotman provided evidence to show that the increasing specialization which separated the modern parlement from the ancient *parlamentum* could be dated from the reign of Philip the Fair, specifically from the edicts of 1293 and 1302: in 1576 he adduced evidence to prove that the public council or *parlamentum* had been able in the 1270's to meet all judicial needs by meeting regularly.[1] He also added citations from Aufrier, Bartolus and Johannes de Platea to show that the intrinsic meaning of *parlamentum* was not what the modern parlement had come to represent.[2] He noted the true usage of the word in the passage where Commines had described the powers of the English parliament, which that author held to be the equivalent of the French estates.[3] He cited Seyssel's condemnation of the multiplication of lawyers and litigation, and inserted a passage from Einhard on the simplicity of direct justice under Charlemagne to parallel the 1573 citation from Joinville on Saint Louis and the oak of Vincennes.[4] The quotation from Commines already used in the

[1] See below, p. 510.
[2] See below, pp. 500–2. See also his gloss on *placitum*, below, p. 344.
[3] See below, p. 500.   [4] See below, pp. 498, 506–8.

Antitribonian about Louis XI's proposed reform of the judicial system was also added.[1] Moreover, the account of the establishment of the parlement of Paris and its provincial counterparts was made more persuasive by the insertion of passages connecting the latter with prior provincial assemblies, and explaining how the various chambers in the Paris parlement had been expanded on the basis of venality.[2] The new section on venality of judicial office made use of material contained in the *Monitoriale*, and discussed the sale of office under Francis I. This more searching attack upon the practice was supported by reference to its condemnation by the Emperor Alexander Severus, whose opinion was also reproduced at this time in the *Anti-Machiavel* of Innocent Gentillet, a protestant magistrate from Dauphiné.[3] Hotman heightened the acrimony of his criticism by increased use of the term *rabularii* (pettifoggers) for the professional lawyers, and by personal abuse of Matharel and Masson. Finally, the revised chapter on the parlement received a new cogency by assigning responsibility for the whole process of judicial corruption to Avignon and the Canon Law – another theme resurrected from the *Antitribonian*.[4]

These new observations on the public council and the parlement accentuate the paradox which, as we have earlier observed, was contained in the argument of the 1573 edition. There Hotman had admitted that the clergy had usurped a place in the estates general,[5] and in his 1576 citation of Seyssel on the composition of the estates he quoted Seyssel's exclusion of the ecclesiastical order from that body.[6] Yet the issue was not pursued. With the parlements, on the other hand, Hotman made his 1573 views even more explicit in 1576 by explaining precisely how the professional lawyers had invaded a domain which had been that of national assemblies since

---

[1] See below, p. 498.   [2] See below, pp. 510–18.

[3] See below, p. 518. Cf. Innocent Gentillet, *Anti-Machiavel* [1576], ed. C. Edward Rathé (Geneva, 1968), 51–3.

[4] See below, p. 522, and above, pp. 37, 72. A second passage is inserted in an early chapter of the 1576 version to the same effect (below, p. 168).

[5] See below, p. 444.

[6] It may also be noted that a long passage of the 1573 edition which was suppressed in 1576 contains two thirteenth-century chroniclers' references to the clergy's participation in assemblies (below, p. 532, appendix A).

the founding of the nation. The juridical parlements were seen as corruptions of the old constitution, and not (as we should view them today) a natural step in the emergence of a centralized judiciary to serve the new national state. The clerical invasion of the *parlamentum* could have been matched by the legal appropriation of a part of its authority by the parlements, which were themselves tainted by the *odium theologicum* of Canon Law. But Hotman did not choose to develop the former argument, and this was doubtless because the parlement existed as an institution quite distinct from the estates, and he could not accept major historical changes of this kind.

The reader is led to assume a parentage, if not an identity, between the Francogallican assembly and the modern representative body. The chapters devoted to the unabated authority of the council under the Carolingians and the Capetians (including the Valois) suggest unbroken continuity. From what he declares to be a multitude of examples available in the fourteenth and fifteenth centuries, Hotman chose six in 1573 and added a seventh in 1576.[1] These range from the year 1328, when the succession was decided in favour of Philip VI, to 1484, when the regency in the minority of Charles VIII was decided at the estates of Tours.[2] Moreover, the chapter on the public council under Louis XI does not suggest, as does the preface, that Louis XI had fatally weakened the constitution, but that the estates were still strong enough to restrain the king. Significantly, Hotman has nothing whatever to say in the *Francogallia* about the estates general of 1560–1 at Orléans and

[1] See below, pp. 418–24. See next note.

[2] The other examples concern three instances of royal incapacity and the appointment of a regency (1356, 1375 and 1392), the dispute between Humphrey of Gloucester and Philip of Burgundy (where the arbitration actually took place in 1425 in the *conseil du roi*), and the dispute between Louis XI and his brother Charles de France over the latter's possession of the appanage of Normandy (estates of Tours, 1468 – this is the example added in 1576). An eighth instance cited by Hotman in this chapter (although it is actually the fifth in order of presentation) does not concern a meeting of the estates, but refers to the opinion pronounced in the parlement in 1525 that the captured Francis I could not cede the province of Burgundy to his conqueror, the Emperor Charles V, without the consent of the estates.

Pontoise, and, although, as we have seen, he might write with approval of the report in 1574 that the politiques were demanding an assembly of the estates general in terms of his book,[1] he did not in 1576 improve upon his signpost in the 1573 preface that the remedy for present ills was to return to the principles of ancient times.

Hotman was correct in deriving the parlement in the early fourteenth century from the *parlamentum* of immediately preceding times, which was a synonym for the feudal *curia regis*. He was not prepared to discuss the parallel and simultaneous development of the national estates. Perhaps he was aware that 1302 was also the date of the first national assembly where the third estate was separately represented – an event which for Pasquier meant the beginning of the estates general as he knew that institution – but Hotman is no more prepared to discuss so fundamental a change than he is to accept the admission of the clergy as the first estate. Nor has the *Francogallia* anything to say about the separation and reunion of the estates of Languedoil and Languedoc or the variegated history of provincial estates. Certainly Hotman had no wish to make evolutionary distinctions under the stress of his polemical mood in 1575. The institution which represented society as a whole, and hence possessed the authority to discipline a king, was seen as unchanging in essence throughout all ages, the epitome of the ancient Francogallican constitution. Hence some of those additions in the 1576 *Francogallia* which concerned the public council allowed the reader more readily to draw the inference that this was the body that could solve the problems of the age. Yet Hotman had sufficient respect for his earlier conception of the *Francogallia* not to say explicitly, as did Beza and the author of the *Vindiciae contra tyrannos*,[2] that the estates general were still a regular part of the existing constitution and could serve at any time (if they could be convoked) as a check upon arbitrary royal rule. In any case Hotman could hardly reconcile such an assertion with his account of the processes of corruption that had eroded the ancient constitution, beginning

[1] See above, p. 73.
[2] Cf. Giesey, 'Monarchomach Triumvirs', 43–4.

from the installation of an hereditary feudal nobility under the early Capetians, proceeding through the infiltration of the clergy into the estates and the arrogation of authority by the parlement, and receiving a final and fatal canker from Louis XI. The work remains one of history by exegesis and politics by implication. The *Monitoriale* and the *Strigilis* might defy the reader to show where the 1573 *Francogallia* advocated a return to the election of kings.[1] The 1576 *Francogallia* neither admits the ancient practice has been replaced by new customary laws of the succession nor denies that the old methods are still viable. When Hotman composed a new conclusion for the 1576 version he did not repeat the theme of constitutional *renovatio* proclaimed in the preface, but preferred a more fundamental kind of renewal – a return to the scriptural principles which would dispel the clouds of superstition that enveloped his fatherland.[2]

The impression of greater vehemence, and consequently of greater tension between the political concept of the *a priori* rights of the national assembly and the historical account of its corruption, is strengthened by a number of other additions to the 1576 version. A striking change is the insertion in capitalized print of the Ciceronian maxim SALUS POPULI SUPREMA LEX ESTO. This occurs on six occasions, usually in contrapuntal relationship with additions describing the tyranny of the Turks, whose subjects are said to live like cattle.[3] The insertions are placed strategically in such key chapters as those describing the form of the ancient constitution, the authority of the council, and its challenge to Louis XI. The authority of Budé and Du Moulin is invoked in a new passage giving the public council control of monetary affairs, while the distinction between the king and the kingdom is given fresh emphasis by reference to the practice of naming the great officers of state as officers OF FRANCE, in contrast with officials of the royal household.[4]

---

[1] See above, pp. 79, 80.   [2] See below, pp. 522–4.

[3] See below, pp. 296, 300 (twice), 342, 414, 450. The Ciceronian maxim (from *De legibus*, III, iii, 8) had been used in the fifteenth century to support the right of resistance. Cf. Sofia Rueger, 'Gerson, the Conciliar Movement and the Right of Resistance', *Journal of the History of Ideas*, xxv (1964), 467–86.

[4] See below, p. 404.

Moreover, approval for armed resistance to the king in the name of the estates is underlined by the insertion of the words 'by force' in the quotation from Commines describing the defiance offered Louis XI by the League of the Common Weal.[1]

Hotman also includes new examples of early elections and depositions, together with the testimony of sources he had previously overlooked, notably Hunibaldus and Paul the Deacon.[2] He suppresses the passage where he had attributed the origin of the peers to the legendary Arthur, and inserts a new account of their rôle and institution. This is the occasion when he cites, in anonymous form, the authority of René Choppin, whom he detested and whom Matharel had used in his refutation.[3] A few fresh elements are introduced which contribute little to the polemical aspect of the book. These include an anecdote from William of Newburgh concerning the use of French bodyguards against the supposed treachery of Richard of England in the third crusade; a letter from the Emperor Constantine to Agricola, then viceroy of Gaul; a discussion of the office of seneschal; and the ordinance empowering the later regency of Blanche of Castile which has already been mentioned.[4] Then, too, there are numerous stylistic improvements. Finally, the only change in the chapter arrangement of the *Francogallia* in the 1576 edition is the addition of a chapter concerning the authority of the council in religious matters, which describes the conflict between Boniface VIII and Philip the Fair. Thus the *Francogallia* appeared in its revised version with a more vigorous but even less coherent argument, where the augmented historical material strengthened the general flavour of the first edition.

10. *Change of front*

In the late spring of 1576, soon after the publication of the second edition of the *Francogallia*, the war which Henry III had been conducting against the alliance of Huguenots and *politiques* came to an end. Alençon, the king's younger brother and leader of the

---

[1] See below, p. 440. [2] See below, pp. 352, 356, 366.
[3] See below, p. 380. [4] See below, pp. 288–90, 316–20, 358, 480.

parties of opposition, offered Hotman patronage, but he accepted
the advice of a more trustworthy patron, the landgraf of Hesse, and
decided not to leave Geneva for France.[1] The decision was prudent,
for Alençon, who became duc d'Anjou at the peace, soon deserted
his Huguenot allies. Meanwhile, the Catholic League, formed under
the leadership of the Guise family to oppose the tolerant terms of
the peace, arose as a threat to the crown from a new quarter.
Strangely enough, it was the League that now began to advance the
teaching of the *Francogallia*, and even to improve upon it. The third
of the twelve articles adopted by the Catholic faction promised to
restore 'les droits, preeminences, franchises et libertés anciennes
telles qu'elles estoient du temps du roy Clovis, premier roy
chrestien, et encore meilleures plus profitables si elles se peuvent
enventer, sous la protection susdite [de la ligue]'.[2] Frankish
history had become very relevant to contemporary politics. When
a Guisard envoy to Rome, the *avocat* David, was slain by the
Huguenots on his return, his papers, which the Protestant faction
was quick to publish (if indeed they did not forge), contained a
history of the elevation of Pepin to the throne and the seclusion of
the last Merovingian in a monastery. An explicit parallel was
drawn between this event and the present *roi fainéant*, whom, the
author suggested, might be similarly displaced by the Guisard
house of Lorraine, the descendants of the Carolingians. It is
interesting to find that Hotman sent a manuscript copy of the
articles of the League, and a printed Latin version of David's
argument, to his friends in Hesse.[3]

A second irony for the author of the *Francogallia* was the convocation of the estates general at Blois late in the same year, and the
subsequent attempt to appoint thirty-six of the deputies to sit with
the royal council and draw up an ordinance granting redress to the
cahiers. This faint echo of Hotman's guardians of the constitution

[1] Dareste, 'Hotman, sa vie et sa correspondance', 382–4.
[2] Palma Cayet, *Chronologie novenaire* in *Mémoires relatifs à l'histoire de France*,
ed. Petitot, 1st series, XXXVIII (1823), 255.
[3] Darmstadt, Hessisches Staatsarchiv, A. IV, Konv. 50, Fast. 3. Hotman sent
the documents to Georg von Hesse. Cf. Anquetil, *L'Esprit de la Ligue* (Paris, 1770),
II, 165–9; and Cayet, 254–7.

against Louis XI was entirely the work of the Catholic party, for the League dominated the estates, and the Huguenots, in whose cause the *Francogallia* had been written, chose to boycott the assembly. The French Calvinist cause no longer associated its hopes with the estates general, and when, three years later, Mornay's *Vindiciae contra tyrannos* took its place as the third item in the trilogy of which the *Francogallia* and the *De jure magistratuum* formed the first two parts, little reliance was placed upon the possibilities of that institution.[1]

Two other theorists and historians, whose works were to exert an influence rivalling, if not surpassing, that of the *Francogallia*, were connected with the Blois estates of 1576 and 1577. These were Jean Bodin and Matteo Zampini.[2] Bodin, who played the rôle of a constitutionalist in the debates of Blois, ultimately succeeded in defeating the proposals for the thirty-six deputies to sit with the council on the ground that it would imperil the right of the third estate to differ from the clergy and the nobility. His *Six Livres de la République*, published shortly before the assembly, may be construed as in several respects a direct reply to the Huguenot pamphlets of 1573–5, including the first edition of the *Francogallia*. Indeed, Bodin stated in his first preface to the *République* that his book was intended to refute the errors, first, of those who followed Machiavelli and, second, of those 'qui, soubs voile d'une exemption de charges et liberté populaire, font rebeller les sujets contre leurs princes naturels, ouvrant la porte à une licentieuse anarchie, qui est pire que la plus forte tyrannie du monde'. That he had the Huguenot writers in mind is certain from the fact that he admitted that the second variety of seditious men criticized the immorality of the first. The anti-Machiavellian theme in Huguenot literature was a

[1] Cf. Giesey, 'Monarchomach Triumvirs', 43–5.

[2] The European influence of Bodin's *République* requires no demonstration; that of Zampini's *Degli stati di Francia* may be judged from the fact that editions in Italian appeared in 1578, 1625, 1628, 1637, and 1679, in French in 1588, in an abbreviated Latin version (*De statibus Franciae*) in 1578, and in English in 1680 (*Of the French Monarchy and Absolute Power and also a Treatise of the Three States and their Power*, London). Cf. Raybaud (above, p. 54, n. 1), 149–50, who fails, however, to mention the English version.

strong current in the years immediately after the massacre of Saint Bartholomew. However, Bodin never referred to the Huguenot authors by name in the *République*, although he did once refer to Hotman's opinion as a civilian.[1] He specifically attacked the doctrines that the estates were in some sense superior to the king, that the supposed Aragonese oath implied original election or had any modern application, and that there could be a mixture of forms of government, of which France was an example.[2] Bodin maintained the sanctity of fundamental laws such as the inalienability of the royal domain and the law of succession. Yet he defined sovereignty as the power to make and unmake law, and held all the other attributes of authority to be included within the legislative power.[3] It may well be that he discerned within the works of Beza, Hotman and their imitators an implicit theory of the legislative supremacy of the estates, and that his own doctrine of the indivisible legislative power of the French crown was defined in contradistinction to this implication in monarchomach thought. Moreover, his chapter attacking election contained passages which seem a direct critique of the *Francogallia*, or, possibly, of its vulgarization in the second dialogue of the *Reveille-Matin*,[4] and he even pursued his opponents into the detailed examples they provided from early French history in order to deny the claim that 'les Rois de France estoyent electifs, et que le royaume tomboit en choix ancienne-

---

[1] *République*, III, iii (ed. Paris, 1580, 402).

[2] *Ibid.*, I, viii (*ed. cit.*, 137–8), on the estates' not being superior to the king; I, viii (*ed. cit.*, 129–30), on the Aragonese oath; II, i (*ed. cit.*, 262–3), on the denial of the mixed form. On the last issue, as we have seen (above, p. 60, n. 2), Bodin made specific reference to Du Haillan. The form of the Aragonese oath used by Bodin was evidently copied from Hotman or Beza (cf. Giesey, *If Not, Not*, 23, 221). For the general relationship between Bodin and the Huguenot theorists of resistance see Salmon, 'Bodin and the Monarchomachs', *passim*.

[3] *République*, I, x (ed. 1580, 223).

[4] E.g., 'Ce qu'il est besoin d'esclaircir par raisons necessaires, et par exemples, pour lever l'opinion que plusieurs impriment aux subiects d'autruy, et par ce moyen entretiennent les rebellions pour changer les monarchies bien ordonees, et remuer ciel et terre. Et tout cela se fait sous le voile de vertu, de pieté et de iustice. Et mesmes il s'en trouve qui osent publier livres et soustenir contre leur Prince naturel venu à la couronne par legitime succession, que le droit de choix est meilleur en la Monarchie.' *Ibid.*, VI, v (*ed. cit.*, 973).

ment'.[1] As it will be shown, Hotman seems to be replying to some of Bodin's points in the changes he made in the third edition of the *Francogallia*.

The connexion of Zampini with the Blois estates is merely that his treatise on the estates general was composed with this occasion in mind, although it was not published until a year after the dissolution of that assembly. As a protégé of Catherine de Medici and the perfect model of an 'Italogaul', Zampini appeared a likely target for Hotman, and the latter was to engage him in a bitter controversy over the succession during the ascendancy of the League in the late 1580's. Hotman did not, however, attack Zampini's book on the estates, perhaps because in some respects it confirmed his own findings in the *Francogallia*, and in others it would not have been easy for Hotman to answer without a complete adjustment of focus. Zampini admitted the authority of the estates to elect kings, but he argued that this applied only where the succession was uncertain and that the estates only held the supreme authority until the election had taken place.[2] Many instances of supposed elections were merely declarations of blood right.[3] If the king was incapable, then his successor should act as regent, and it was only when the successor was in doubt that the estates exercised the right to name a regent during a royal minority.[4] Many early writers seemed to indicate that the estates had been called regularly, but there were even more authorities to show that they were summoned when kings thought them necessary.[5] At the same time, Zampini's list of the reasons for which the estates had been summoned in the past included the appointment of the great officers of the kingdom, the making of law, the extirpation of heresy, the despatch of great affairs, and the right to consent or dissent to the alienation of part of the kingdom, to the making of offensive war, and to taxation.[6] As we have seen,[7] Zampini used the same methods as did Hotman in massing citations from

---

[1] *Ibid.*, VI, v (*ed. cit.*, 983).
[2] *Treatise of the Three States* (above, p. 92, n. 2), 33–7.   [3] *Ibid.*, 38.
[4] *Ibid.*, 43–50.   [5] *Ibid.*, 157–8.
[6] *Ibid.*, 98–128, 137–9, 145–8.   [7] Cf. above, p. 54.

medieval chronicles to support his conclusions. His subtle distinctions were much in contrast with the broader, and more simplistic, generalizations of the *Francogallia*.

At the time of the publication of Zampini's *Degli stati di Francia* Hotman left Geneva for Basel. He suffered from financial privation and family cares in the years that followed. He visited the landgraf of Hesse at Cassel on several occasions, but he could no longer rely upon the patronage he had received from the elector palatine. After the death of Frederick III in 1576 the palatinate experienced a Lutheran reaction for eight years, and Hotman received little tangible reward for his endeavour to negotiate a settlement between the Calvinist and Lutheran factions there. He refused the offer of a chair of jurisprudence at Leyden in 1579, but he had no substitute in Basel for the post he had enjoyed as professor of law at Geneva. The *Francogallia* continued to bring him notoriety. With the three printings of the work in Goulart's *Mémoires de l'Estat de France* in the years 1576-8, the *Francogallia* had appeared four times in French and thrice in Latin. Hotman might not have considered another revised edition had not political events in France taken a new turning. In 1580 he became the political agent of the Protestant Bourbon princes Henry of Navarre and Henry of Condé, the successors of their fathers, whom Hotman had served in the early 1560's.[1] In 1584 the death of Anjou, the last of the sons of Catherine de Medici, precipitated a succession crisis. Henry III had no other close male heirs and was known to be impotent. Upon his death the throne would pass to the only other surviving descendants of a king of France by exclusively male inheritance, his cousins twenty degrees removed, the Bourbons. Representing the senior Bourbon line were Henry of Navarre, the leader of the Huguenot faction, and his uncle the cardinal de Bourbon, a candidate who was soon to be supported by the revivified Catholic League.

Huguenot political attitudes within the court of Navarre changed overnight, and some of the opinions expressed in the *Francogallia* became a considerable embarrassment. It may well be that Hotman began at once to consider the revision of his treatise,

[1] Dareste, 'Hotman, sa vie et sa correspondance', 395.

but, if so, he was obliged to put it aside to deal with a more pressing commission from Henry of Navarre. On Saint Bartholomew's day 1584 Henry wrote to Hotman with praise of his past writings and a request to compose a legal treatise on *représentations* that would answer the Leaguer case for preferring the uncle before the nephew.[1] In November Hotman asked for details of the points he was required to answer, and in the following month received a reply from Mornay itemizing the heads of the Guisard thesis and stressing the need to avoid offending Henry III. Mornay suggested the use of every legal system: ancient and modern; civil and canon; Roman, French and any other nationality.[2] Just before Christmas Hotman submitted a plan to Mornay, which doubtless followed the lines of discussion Hotman had recently conducted with Paul Choart, sieur de Buzanval, another of Navarre's agents, who had visited him in Basel. On 30 December Buzanval wrote that the enemy was now using Hotman's earlier works against their cause. They were reciting the *Francogallia*'s arguments about the election of kings and the opinion expressed in the *Quaestionum illustrium liber* that the claims of the uncle were better than those of the nephew.[3]

Both Navarre and Mornay welcomed the manuscript of Hotman's *Disputatio de controversia successionis regiae inter patruum et fratris praemortui filium* when it reached them in April 1585.[4] However, Hotman was soon to receive contradictory instructions. Navarre's chancellor, Armand du Ferrier, wrote expressing his agreement that the royal succession 'n'a rien de commun avec les feudes et encores moings avec les autres choses héréditaires et divisibles'. It should proceed, he said, down the line of eldest males in the senior line of the dynasty.[5] In June, at the very time when the king of Navarre wrote to urge publication, Mornay sent Hotman a letter contradicting both his own earlier advice and the comments

[1] Blok, *Correspondance inédite de Hotman*, 204.
[2] *Ibid.*, 207–8. [3] *Ibid.*, 209–11.
[4] *Ibid.*, 212–13. The editor of this correspondence is grievously in error when he annotates this letter and confuses the *Disputatio* with Hotman's *De iure successionis regiae*. He is also mistaken in thinking Hotman is replying to the treatise of Jean de Terre Rouge (see below, p. 97). [5] *Ibid.*, 213–14.

of Du Ferrier. Mornay told Hotman to base his argument upon the law of the kingdom rather than upon general juridical considerations (*a justa re*), and to use feudal rather than ancient law.[1] These instructions were too late, for the *Disputatio* was already in the press. Mornay repeated his remarks with some acerbity when a published copy reached him in July.[2] What he required was evidently an historical treatise in the manner of the *Francogallia*. The *Disputatio* does, at least, assume an air of detachment similar to that of the first edition of that notorious work, and nowhere mentions the contemporary succession problem. Hotman was to take Mornay's wishes into account when he published a revised edition of the *Disputatio* in Geneva in 1586. The correspondence reveals the extent to which it was a *livre de circonstance* and how Hotman was willing to apply his supple legal skills to whatever would best serve the Huguenot cause.

In the *Francogallia* Hotman had rejected the Salic Law as applying to the succession because it was private law governing the inheritance of allodial land. He rejected the claim for inheritance through the distaff side just as vehemently as did the supporters of the Salic Law, but on the grounds that it was long-established French custom. Although the Salic Law was not an issue in the respective claims of Navarre and his uncle, Mornay wanted an argument in terms of custom to justify the throne-worthiness of his master. Hotman had provided more than this in his *Disputatio*.[3] The second edition was published together with a treatise on royal succession composed in 1418–19 by the French jurist Jean de Terre Rouge. Hotman drew heavily upon Terre Rouge's arguments supporting the right of the dauphin Charles VII to succeed despite his public repudiation by his father. Terre Rouge used Roman Law principles, but not those of inheritance, since the paterfamilial power to disinherit ran counter to his purpose. Instead, he extracted from diverse sections of the *Corpus juris civilis* the con-

---

[1] *Ibid.*, 215–16. [2] *Ibid.*, 216–17.
[3] The legal arguments of the *Disputatio*, and their relationship to the thought of Terre Rouge outlined in the passage that follows, are discussed in detail by Giesey, *Juristic Basis of Dynastic Right*, 32–7.

cept of a filiational right which provided the son with some kind of natural law claim to succeed.

Terre Rouge's cause was limited to a son's right. Hotman extended Terre Rouge's arguments and developed a general law of succession which covered all degrees of relationship. His key concept was *suitas*, a neologism of fifteenth-century Roman Law jurists which designated something like 'his-own-ness', and referred to the state of heir-worthiness that the successor held in his own right, which no one could deny him. Terre Rouge's treatise had dealt explicitly with a celebrated crisis in the succession to the French throne 170 years earlier, and this tended to obscure the essentially abstract nature of the *ius filiationis*. Hotman's *ius suitatis* was not only abstract and complicated but was contrived from words that had no place in older literature on the problem. His concern with abstractions is not surprising in the light of the confused instructions he received. The same tendency to deal with the abstract and the universal in Roman Law terms is noticeable in his new revision of the *Francogallia*. In the early editions it was the authority of the public council, as demonstrated by their control of the succession in ancient times, that was of importance. After 1584 the royal succession became the paramount issue, and the *Francogallia* needed to brought up to date.

From 1584 until the year 1589, when the murder of Henry III made the royal succession a direct conflict of armed strength between the first Bourbon king and the League, Hotman remained an active propagandist in the cause of Henry of Navarre. In the interval between the two printings of the *Disputatio* he published *Brutum fulmen*, his celebrated defence of Navarre and Condé against their excommunication by Pope Sixtus V. When Zampini went over to the League and issued a treatise supporting the rights of the cardinal de Bourbon to the succession, Hotman answered him anonymously with *Ad tractatum Matthaei Zampini, de successione praerogativae primi principis...responsio* (1588), a tract which reproached Zampini for failing to see the problem as essentially concerned with French public law, and which was expressed with all the vigour of his replies to Matharel and Masson. Zampini, however, appears to have had the last word with his *Pro successionis praerogativae primi principis, per legem regni, Cardinali Borboni delatae confutatio*... (Paris, 1589; licence dated 30 November 1588). In 1588 Hotman also published a straightforward statement of the principles of the royal succession as he then saw them, *De jure successionis regiae in regno Francorum* In the midst of this activity Hotman published his third and final edition of the *Francogallia* in 1586. Many of the revisions can be explained only through his overriding preoccupation with the cause of the future Henry IV.

11. *The edition of 1586*

The expansion of the *Francogallia* from twenty-one chapters in 1576 to twenty-seven in 1586 seems to indicate that Hotman added six new chapters. Of these, however, only two (XXIV and XXV) are actually new. They are concerned with the French quarrel with Benedict XIII in the early fifteenth century and a new list of fundamental laws. The other additional four chapters come from the division of existing sections. The old chapter VI, on the appointment of kings, becomes chapters VI and VII, on the election and deposition of kings respectively. The new chapters VIII and IX are constructed from the original chapter VII, divided between the question of the inheritance where a king leaves several sons on the one hand and issues concerning the royal domain and appanages on the other. The former chapter X, on the form of the Francogallican constitution, is converted into chapters XII and XIII, of which the first deals with general aspects and the second with matters of procedure in the ancient assembly and with the terms *placitum, curia* and *parlamentum*. Chapters XVIII and XIX emerge from the old chapter XV by the separation of the discussion of the difference between king and kingdom from the demonstration of the continued authority of the public council under the Carolingians. Many of the 1573 chapters had already been unbalanced by new matter, and the insertion of several long passages in the 1586 version necessitated these changes in general arrangement.

In itself the rearrangement of chapters neither strengthened nor attenuated the argument of the *Francogallia*. Nor, in general, do the new stylistic alterations produce such an effect, although some instances of more highly coloured language, such as new references to the sanctity of the ancient council ('the most august and holy temple of justice', 'the august shrine'),[1] do tend to add greater persuasive force. This is also the effect of the increased number of scholarly citations inserted to support points which are already adequately protected with authorities. Thus on the use of the name of the Franks, Saint Jerome, the abbot of Ursperg, Zosimus, Johannes Aventinus, Géronimo Zurita and Albert Krantz are added to an already formidable list.[2] All of these authors, with the exception of the abbot of Ursperg and Albert Krantz, are not cited anywhere in previous editions. Other new authorities in the 1586 edition are Ivo of Chartres, the Burgundian chronicler Besuensis, and the Englishmen Thomas of Walsingham and Sir John Fortescue. There are also several new historical examples adduced to support existing propositions. Thus a report of an address by Louis the Pious to an assembly is quoted on two occasions from Ansegius' collection of Carolingian capitularies to strengthen the claims that the Francogallican constitution was a mixture of the three forms and that government proceeded by consent.[3] Similarly, the new chapter on the insults offered the emissaries of Benedict XIII is introduced, albeit in an incongruous position, to strengthen the point made in the chapter on Boniface VIII, namely that the public council was the controlling authority in matters of religion.

The author's change of front on the royal succession appears in several passages in the 1586 edition. Although Hotman had admitted in his controversy with Matharel and Masson that the method of succession had been altered, and that the *Francogallia* did not advocate the election of modern kings, he did not include a similar statement in the 1576 version.[4] In the section on the royal domain in the 1586 edition, a passage is added saying that when the crown of France became hereditary by custom, it passed through

[1] See below, pp. 322, 402.   [2] See below, pp. 182, 200, 202, 212.
[3] See below, pp. 294, 346.   [4] See above, p. 89.

the eldest sons by male descent, and the domain went with it.[1] The use of the word 'hereditary' in this context is strange, since Hotman accepts Terre Rouge's opinion that succession to the French crown was neither hereditary nor patrimonial but simply established by custom. Then, in his new chapter on the fundamental laws limiting the authority of kings, Hotman sets out as the second, third and fourth of such laws his view of the succession. The fourth law concerns the exclusion of women and does not require comment. The second law asserts that the king has no power to dispose of his kingdom, since it is an 'established and ancient custom' that succession goes to the eldest son alone. He cites Terre Rouge to the effect that kings cannot bequeath the realm by testament.[2] He also inserts a denial of the validity of royal wills in an earlier section, but there it is said that they can become valid if they are confirmed by the public council. This discussion occurs in the account of the authority of the public council, where Charlemagne's will has already been mentioned.[3] In his description of the second fundamental law, however, the council does not so much decide upon the successor as proclaim the appropriate custom. The example of the succession crisis of the early fifteenth century is adduced to support the point, and the action of the public council is interpreted as a judicial ruling on the illegality of Charles VI's repudiation of his son.[4]

Hotman cannot easily escape contradiction in this matter, for in yet another new passage on the succession he introduces the opinions of Gaguin and Thomas of Walsingham on the rivalry of Edward III of England and Philip of Valois for the French crown in 1328. His actual quotation from Gaguin refers to a judicial process before the estates, in which the rights of both kings were considered, and it can thus be interpreted, once again, as a declaration of custom.[5] Yet the original context of the section of the Francogallia to which the new passage is added is clearly designed to show that the public council had the power to choose the claimant

[1] See below, p. 256.   [2] See below, pp. 462, 466.
[3] See below, p. 334.   [4] See below, p. 462.
[5] See below, p. 418.

it preferred. Custom had not proved a completely satisfying argument in the original *Francogallia* and Hotman had introduced *a priori* considerations of choice into the royal succession. Now a more conservative and less flexible attitude to custom dominated his mind, and with it, as we have seen, came new *a priori* opinions of the right of the nephew before the uncle in terms of natural law. Thus in his discussion of the third fundamental law, succession by male primogeniture, Hotman reproduces the argument of the *Disputatio* concerning abstract filiational right, and cites canonists and civilians to support his view, together with Terre Rouge's assertions about the overriding force of the national custom.[1] This shift cannot but undermine the rôle in which Hotman originally cast the Francogallican assembly, and, while he may disclaim the desire to revive the election of kings, his stress upon the need to return to the original model, and his failure to say precisely when the new custom of succession by blood right of the eldest son had become established, must inevitably confuse the reader.

In two new sections of the 1586 edition Hotman appears to be responding to Bodin's *République*.[2] One very long addition consists of corroborative evidence for the supposed Aragonese oath.[3] Bodin had doubted the verisimilitude of the oath, arguing in part from the silence of the sources. He had consulted the *Speculum principis* of the Aragonese jurist Pierra Belluga and found no trace of the oath. Hotman, meanwhile, had read Zurita's *Indices rerum aragonensium*, where he found, if not direct evidence of the oath itself, at least solid proof of the authority in other respects of the justicia of Aragon, the protector of the subject against possible royal injustice, and supposedly the main actor in the ceremony of administering the oath to the king. Hotman is among the first of many to be seduced by the demonstrable authority of the justicia into believing in the existence of the oath, which seems to be a fiction. He quotes about one hundred lines from Zurita, together with a short passage from the early sixteenth-century humanist,

---

[1] See below, p. 464.   [2] See above, p. 94.

[3] See below, pp. 308–16. The Aragonese oath is the main subject of Giesey, *If Not, Not*.

Vasaeus, describing medieval examples of the justicia's rôle. This large amount of material unbalances the chapter in which it is inserted (on the form of the Francogallican constitution), and gives further stress to universal principles at the expense of French historical experience. This tendency is aggravated by the introduction of further new passages in the same chapter, citing Fortescue on the power of the English parliament, Cicero on the mixed form, Aristotle on the necessity to limit monarchical authority, and Aristotle and Herodotus together on public councils in ancient Greece.[1] The chapter, in short, comes to resemble sections of the *De jure magistratuum* and, more particularly, the *Vindiciae contra tyrannos*, with its emphasis upon the power of magistrates to restrain the ruler.[2]

Such is also the trend of the new chapter on the fundamental laws circumscribing the authority of the crown, which may also be regarded as a reply to Bodin, especially to those passages in the *République* listing the attributes of sovereignty and maintaining that all are incorporated within the legislative power.[3] As we have seen, the 1576 edition made some attempt to resolve the contradiction between the survival of the authority of the public council until Louis XI, and the earlier usurpation of its powers by the parlement. The 1586 chapter on the fundamental laws, however, adopts the attitude of Beza and Mornay that the restraints upon monarchy embodied in French public law are still operable. Three of these laws, concerning the succession, have already been mentioned. The first law, regarding the inability of the king to decide anything affecting the condition of the whole commonwealth without the public council, appears at first sight to be a restatement of the original theme of the *Francogallia*.[4] However, it is phrased in a negative manner and contains no flavour of the superiority of the estates to the monarch. The proposition is demonstrated by the necessity for all royal ordinances to be registered by the parlement before they become law. Although the parlement is stated to have

[1] See below, pp. 306, 294, 286, 302.
[2] See Giesey, 'Monarchomach Triumvirs', 54–5.
[3] *République*, I, viii and I, x. See above, p. 93.
[4] See below, p. 458.

usurped some of the prerogatives of the estates, this practice is declared to be a remnant of the ancient constitution, and the judges are said to act in the same capacity as the tribunes of ancient Rome. The fifth fundamental law concerns the familiar restriction of the inalienability of the royal domain. In this respect Hotman quotes Seyssel to show that it is the chambre des comptes and the parlement who police this law.[1] The sixth law forbids the king to remit the punishment for a capital crime, and the seventh prevents him from dismissing a magistrate or officer of state without investigation by the official's peers.[2] Finally, the eighth law denies the king the right to tamper with the coinage without permission from the public council, and cites the research of Du Moulin in the records of the chambre des comptes to demonstrate the antiquity of this practice.[3] A parallel insertion is made in the list of the powers of the public council where that body is described in the original chapter XI (now chapter XIV).[4]

Hotman's constitutionalism in his discussion of these fundamental laws is at times strikingly like that of Seyssel, whom he quotes in this chapter so extensively and with such approbation. The implications of an active sovereignty in the estates general have almost disappeared. It is the parlement and the chambre des comptes that are cited beside the public council as enforcing the laws against the king. The whole tenor of the chapter allows the ruler initiative in most governmental matters, and the constitutional laws are merely barriers against abuse. Moreover, in other new additions to the 1586 *Francogallia*, Hotman mentions other constitutional institutions, which, taken together with the rôle now permitted the parlement and the chambre des comptes, suggest that the public council is much less important than it was earlier thought to be. He describes how an assembly of notables gave the consent of the nation for the raising of the money to ransom Francis I from Spanish captivity, and he discusses a compact between the provincial estates of Languedoc and the crown which guaranteed the preservation of local liberties.[5] Although Hotman

[1] See below, p. 472.   [2] See below, pp. 474–6.
[3] See below, p. 476.   [4] See below, p. 332.   [5] See below, pp. 450, 416.

refuses to omit the passages in the 1576 *Francogallia* where he intensified the argument, and although there are many instances of his strengthening the original text with further examples and more colourful language,[1] the author has clearly become more conservative in outlook.

Perhaps the most striking change in the 1586 edition is the introduction of non-historical arguments, especially the use of Roman and Canon Law as a source of political precepts. Some Roman Law citations had been made in 1573 and 1576 for their historical content;[2] now they comport themselves as bearers of truths of political philosophy. For example, the Julian law of treason is used to show the difference between the king and the kingdom;[3] the canonist Panormitanus (as seen through the eyes of Connan) is cited beside the *Digest* and the *Code* to support the exclusion of women;[4] the *Digest* is quoted to define law as an agreement of the people and resolution of the commonwealth in the public interest;[5] the legality of trusts in any language is shown from Ulpian;[6] and the invalidity of a royal testament on the succession without confirmation by the public council is likened to the appointment of a trustee in Roman Law without confirmation by the praetor.[7] The opinions of the decretalists, and of Baldus and Durand, are cited beside that of Guy Pape to show that a French king is independent of the emperor,[8] and Hostiensis is quoted on the issue of the French king's right to alter the coinage.[9] Reference is made to the *Digest* to support the right of a son to an inheritance, and the succeeding remarks on the succession are buttressed with the opinions of Johannes Andreae, Jason de Maino, Panormitanus and Baldus (on feudal usage), as well as with those of Terre Rouge.[10] A rare instance of the omission of part of the existing text occurs in the chapter on royal inheritance of property, when a short survey of the four kinds

---

[1] In addition to the examples already mentioned, we may cite new references to the valour of the Gauls, to Louis XI, and to venality of office (below, pp. 178, 440, 520).　　[2] See below, pp. 162, 300, 344, 398.

[3] See below, p. 398.　　　　　　[4] See below, p. 482.

[5] See below, p. 346.　　　　　　[6] See below, p. 158.

[7] See below, p. 334.　　　　　　[8] See below, p. 244.

[9] See below, p. 476.　　　　　　[10] See below, p. 464.

of property supposedly at the disposal of a king is replaced by a much longer and more coherent passage, bespattered with references to the *Corpus juris civilis*.[1]

The casual reader would find it difficult to conceive from the 1586 edition that the *Francogallia* came from the same pen as did the *Antitribonian*. Yet, while the contrast between abstract legal generalization and concrete French historical example is patent, Hotman is using Roman and Canon Law in terms of the natural law they contain, and this is not inconsistent with his attack upon the methods of Tribonian and upon the application of specific Roman public laws to modern France. After all, most of Hotman's published work concerned Roman Law, and much of it dealt with the theory of public authority. That he had tried to compose a purely French theory of the public law of the state in the original *Francogallia* does not mean that the universal, natural law ideas associated with the philosophical basis of Roman Law were necessarily invalid. It might have been better to avoid the possibility of confusion by continuing to limit the intrusion of Roman Law into the *Francogallia*. Hotman's failure to do so may be seen as a further consequence of his overriding concern with the claims of Henry of Navarre in 1586.

The 1586 *Francogallia* has become a kind of patchwork quilt in which Hotman is unwilling to leave out or replace any pieces of material, however garishly the colours appear to clash. Beside the mixture of motives that went to the making of the first edition, we now have a series of revisions widely separated in time and influenced by the changing political attitudes of the author. To the vehemence and the more abstract argument of the 1576 modifications are added the more conservative stand upon custom and the rôle of the estates, together with universal principles derived from Roman Law. On the whole Hotman shows remarkable technical skill in sewing the pieces together. Sometimes, however, his needle slips, and he repeats passages he has used elsewhere.[2] These instances

---

[1] See below, pp. 246–52.

[2] Hotman sometimes transferred passages to new positions in later editions. For example, in 1576 he moved his explanation of the name 'Frank' as being connected

of repetition may in themselves suggest to the unprepared reader how the *Francogallia* was put together and subsequently adapted. But without an extensive knowledge of the methods used in compilation, it is easy to read the book with one particular political theme in mind. This is, in fact, what happened to the *Francogallia* in the centuries following its first publication.

12. *The tradition of the 'Francogallia'*

Whatever Hotman's intentions in making the revisions of 1586, it was in the spirit of the 1573 and, more particularly, of the 1576 editions that the *Francogallia* was remembered. As Buzanval had feared late in 1584, the Catholic League began to make new adaptations of Hotman's ideas and methods. In his *Avertissement des Catholiques Anglois aux Catholiques François* (1587), one of the most

with the refusal to pay tribute to Valentinian and with a pun on the German for 'fierce' and 'free' (below, pp. 202, 206). Sometimes, however, he forgot to delete the passage in its original position. Thus in 1576 he quoted the lines of Sidonius Apollinaris on the Franks' and Sicambri's inhabiting the swamps and left the same passage standing where it had appeared in the 1573 edition a few pages earlier (below, pp. 192, 206). He was also capable of using the same passage twice in the one edition. At times this practice is the result of a slip, as with his citation of Cato's condemnation of women, which appears on successive pages in all editions until the second instance was eliminated by the editor in the 1600 version (below, pp. 482, 486). Similarly he inserted his quotation from Saint Jerome's letters on the advantage of completing one's education in Rome twice in the 1586 edition (below, pp. 159, 168). Of course, he often used the same passage more than once for quite deliberate reasons. The most obvious example of this is the repetition of Cicero's maxim, 'Let the welfare of the people be the supreme law' (see above, p. 89). Another example is his use of the celebrated quotation from Tacitus that the Germans chose their kings by reason of their nobility and their military leaders for their valour (see above, p. 67). This was employed in the 1573 version at the beginning of the chapter on the practice of election among the Franks, and was inserted again in 1586 in the chapter concerning the transfer of the monarchy to the Capetians (below, p. 406). He often deliberately repeated the same episode in a different context and with different wording. An example of this practice is the story of Clothild and the murder of her grandsons, used once in the chapter on the regal right to long hair and again in the chapter against the participation of women in government (below, pp. 278, 482). Some quotations from the chroniclers appear at first sight to be repetitions, since similar or identical wording is given, but in fact these are often the result of conflation of sources in their accounts of the same incident.

capable of Leaguer propagandists, the *avocat* Louis Dorléans, took advantage of the reversal in the political situation of the Huguenots to suggest that, since the *Francogallia* maintained it was lawful to choose a king to one's own taste, the Protestant faction should realize that the heretical king of Navarre was not to the taste of the Catholic majority.[1] A series of pamphlet exchanges followed Dorléans' tract. In one of his replies Dorléans listed the *Francogallia* for refutation side by side with the *Apologie catholique* of Pierre de Belloy, who had answered the papal excommunication and deprivation of Henry of Navarre with the theory of the divine right of the Bourbon claim to the succession.[2] Dorléans used the doctrine of fundamental constitutional law to assert that the law concerning the necessity for the king to be Catholic took precedence over the Salic Law. Assuming that Hotman had defended the Salic Law, he subtly began to undermine its validity in terms of the transfer of the kingdom to the Carolingians and the Capetians. Not content with leaving the door ajar for the house of Lorraine, he reproduced Hotman's list of kings deposed by the estates and declared that the reasons for their deposition were far less heinous than heresy.[3]

There were times when Dorléans was ensnared by his own paradoxes, for he was obliged to declare the supremacy of the estates as the source of royal authority. Other Leaguer propagandists said so more directly. A tract composed in the summer of 1586 called for annual meetings of the estates general, and tried to demonstrate from Gregory of Tours and Aimon of Fleury that the estates had played an active and determining rôle in government.[4] A Leaguer declaration in 1588 promised free and regular assem-

---

[1] Cf. Allen, *Political Thought in the Sixteenth Century*, 346. Pierre Bayle also took a wry delight in quoting this passage: *Dictionary Historical*, III, 522.

[2] *Responce des Vrays Catholiques François à l'Avertissement des Catholiques Anglois, pour l'exclusion du Roy de Navarre de la Couronne de France* (n.p., 1588), list of 'Libels diffamatoires confutez en ce livre' on reverse of title-page.

[3] *Ibid.*, 199, 203, 212, 233.

[4] *Discours sur les Estats de France, et si seroit plus expedient que les Estats de France fussent annuels* by 'I.L.P.I.C.D.' (Paris, 1587; approved by the Sorbonne, May 1586), 2–5.

blies.[1] In the following year a direct attack upon Henry III by André de Rossant pointed out that there were precedents in early times for dealing with miscreant rulers.[2] Soon afterwards, at the time when Henry III was assassinated by a Leaguer fanatic, there appeared one of the most powerfully argued of all the works of the League, Jean Boucher's *De justa Henrici Tertii abdicatione*. Boucher not only proclaimed the deposition of the king by papal fiat and the sovereignty of the people; he also provided an historical exposition of the election and deposition of kings by the estates from Pharamond to Philip of Valois.[3] Boucher did not acknowledge his debt to his Calvinist predecessors, and in fact his conclusions were far more explicit than theirs. He did, however, mention the views of Seyssel, which he distorted to fit his own radical purpose.[4] An equally notorious work by the English Catholic member of the League, William Reynolds ('Rossaeus'), provided instances of the popular deposition of early kings and quoted Du Haillan's history.[5] If any of these later tracts owed a debt to the *Francogallia* in those sections where they relied upon early French history, they did not acknowledge it. Nor is it likely that Hotman would have seen the least resemblance. He was to die at Basel in 1590, when the fury of the League was still at its height.

Hotman was fortunate in his literary executors. Foremost among them was his eldest son Jean, the friend of Sir Philip Sidney[6] and a secretary to the latter's uncle, the Earl of Leicester, during his campaign to aid the rebels in the Netherlands in 1586.

[1] *Declaration des Estats qui ont meu Monseigneur le Cardinal de Bourbon, et les Pairs, Princes, Seigneurs, Villes et Communautez Catholiques de ce Royaume de France, de s'opposer à ceux qui par tous moyens s'efforcent de subvertir la Religion Catholique et l'Estat* (n.p., 1588), 10.

[2] *Les Meurs, Humeurs et comportemens de Henry de Valois* (Paris, 1589), 121.

[3] *De iusta Henrici Tertii abdicatione e Francorum regno, libri quatuor* (2nd edition: Lyon, 1591), 30–1, 46–8.   [4] *Ibid.*, 46.

[5] *De iusta reipublicae Christianae in reges impios et hereticos authoritate* (2nd edition: Antwerp, 1592), 71–7.

[6] See Sidney's letter to Jean Hotman, praising François, in *The Prose Works of Sir Philip Sidney* (Cambridge, 1962), 134. Cf. William D. Briggs, 'Political Ideas in Sidney's *Arcadia*', *Studies in Philology*, XXVIII (1931), 137–61, and Irving Ribner, 'Sir Philip Sidney on Civil Instruction', *Journal of the History of Ideas*, XIII (1952), 257–65.

Jean Hotman had lived in the house of Sir Amyas Paulet, the English ambassador in Paris, and remained in touch with influential circles at the English court, where his book, *The Ambassador* (1603), was well received. In 1592 he left England for Basel and Geneva, where he was in touch with Pierre Nevelet, who had undertaken to write a biography of François, and with Jean Lect, a professor at the Genevan University, who was to be the third editor responsible for the publication of Hotman's works in 1600.[1] Opinion within the circle of those Protestants attached to the court of Henry of Navarre, now Henry IV, still looked askance at the *Francogallia*. When in 1595 Jacob Bongars, the king's diplomatic agent in Strasbourg, read the biography which Nevelet had dedicated to him, he wrote to the historian Jacques-Auguste de Thou, son of président de Thou, and commented on the *Francogallia*. The book, he said, was unseasonable for present times. It had been written under the stress of the emotions of 1572, and was grievously mistaken in its thesis, which would have reduced government to anarchy.[2] In *Historiarum sui temporis* De Thou himself described the *Francogallia* as designed to show that the kingdom was not hereditary, and that the power of electing and deposing kings had rested in an ancient council of the nation. The book even provided examples in the fourteenth and fifteenth centuries, ending with Louis XI. The author, De Thou observed, insisted on the exclusion of women, not just from the succession, but also from all participation in government.[3] This summation of the *Francogallia* was to exert great influence in later times.

[1] *Franc. Hotmani iurisconsulti operum tomus primus* [*–tertius*] (Geneva, 1599–1600). Lect identifies himself as the author of the dedicatory letter in the first volume, and is clearly the author of those in the other two volumes. In the last of them (*ibid.*, III, p. iii) he testifies to the importance of Jean Hotman's ability to read his father's handwriting. Jean also has an introduction to this volume. Pierre Nevelet's eulogy of Hotman is printed in the front of the first volume. His help in preparing various texts is shown in his correspondence with Jean Hotman over several years. Cf. Schickler, 'Hotman', 108 ff.

[2] Quoted by Bayle, *Dictionary Historical*, III, 520.

[3] *Historiarum sui temporis*, II, lvii (ed. Frankfurt, 1614, 1261–2). This opinion is also quoted by Bayle (*loc. cit.*) under the impression that it is that of the Huguenot Teissier.

The editors of Hotman's publications did not wish him to be remembered in terms of hostile reactions to the *Francogallia*, and they grouped together similar works under new collective titles. The *Francogallia* was not placed beside the *Antitribonian*, which Pierre Nevelet did not publish until 1603: instead, it was matched with the two tracts on the succession commissioned by Henry IV in 1585. The three appeared under the title of *De jure regni Franciae, libri III*. The *Francogallia* does not carry its famous name but is called *De auctoritate comitiorum*. Introducing the trilogy, Jean Hotman makes clear his intention to attenuate the radical reputation of the first item. The worst of calumnies, he says, is to hold that his father wanted to transform an hereditary kingdom into an elective one. No one who reads the book to the end can commit this error, for François Hotman was unrivalled in his strict observance of the laws of the fatherland.[1]

Some four score textual variations are introduced in the *Francogallia* of 1600. A few, including a reference to a work by his brother, Antoine,[2] are scholarly modifications, presumably left by Hotman as marginalia in his personal copy of the 1586 edition. His posthumous editors recognized these. But the rest of the changes in the 1600 edition – and especially the gross suppression of words, sentences and whole chapters – are much more likely to have been the work of the editors alone. Many represent a significant softening of radical sense and expression in earlier editions. Most noticeable of these latter changes is the omission of the two chapters directed against Boniface VIII and Benedict XIII, intended to demonstrate the control of religious matters by the public council. Also, the section on the rôle of the papacy in the election of Pepin is attenuated, although the pope's inability to appoint and depose kings is restated in unequivocal terms.[3] Hotman had had no cause to vary his antipapal attitude before his death. A decade

---

[1] 'Praecipua horum criminatio haec fuit, quod ex hereditario, ut vocant, regno electivum facere conatus sit. Verum qui non libri principum, sed finem etiam legere volet, facile animadvertet; non fuisse hoc auctori propositum, nominem vero hoc seculo acriorem patriarum legum vindicem extitisse.' *Opera* (above, p. 110, n. 1), III, p. vii.

[2] See below, p. 284.   [3] See below, p. 368.

later Henry IV had accepted Catholicism and been granted absolution at Rome, and it seemed politic to suppress these polemical
sections. Further, several vehement passages added in 1576 are
deleted or attenuated in the 1600 version. This was the fate of one
of the most vigorous passages against tyranny repeating Cicero's
'Let the welfare of the people be the supreme law', and asserting
there could be no kingdom on earth, save that of the Turks, where
true men could tolerate oppression.[1]

The passage where Hotman had added the words 'by force' to
justify armed resistance to Louis XI was weakened by a parenthetical remark that this was not a practice the author would recom-
mend.[2] A comment that some seditions might be necessary,
originally in the 1573 edition, was elided, as also was Hotman's
reference to the understandable reluctance of writers to criticize
queen mothers.[3] Just as Hotman's anti-papalism and his indictment
of tyranny were softened, so too was his attack upon the parlement in the concluding chapter. The first three paragraphs and
the last three pages, together with two sections in the body of the
chapter, disappeared.[4] Most of this virulent material had been
added in 1576. Finally, a subtle but most significant alteration was
the deletion of references to royal deposition from many of those
passages which spoke of the power of the public council to unmake kings as well as to make them.[5] Where it was impossible
to suppress the fact that the *Francogallia* proclaimed the legality of
the practice in times past, a new passage was inserted stating that
it had no present application.[6]

It is difficult to avoid the inference that changes of this sort were
the work of Jean Hotman. The father may have begun the conversion of the *Francogallia* into a temperate pro-monarchical tract
in 1586; the son continued the process to the extent of rebaptizing
it. With its new title, its 1586 material drawn from Terre Rouge and
the succession controversy, and its association with Hotman's own

---

[1] See below, p. 412. See also pp. 204, 316, 342, 414.
[2] See below, p. 441.   [3] See below, pp. 444, 492.
[4] See below, pp. 496, 512, 514, 516.
[5] See below, pp. 234, 246, 286, 332, 360, 362, 458, 480.
[6] See below, p. 234.

tracts on the right of Henry IV to the throne, the *Francogallia* assumed a conservative hue. But its history was such that few could accept it in these terms. In the very year that Hotman's son published his revised version, William Barclay branded the work with the name 'monarchomach'.

Hotman's *Francogallia* had been directly attacked by royalist writers before Barclay, notably by Adam Blackwood in his *Pro regibus apologia* (1581), where Hotman was accused of destroying the 'authority of kingly majesty', and linked with the *Vindiciae contra tyrannos*.[1] Blackwood's main target in this work, however, was Buchanan's *De jure regni apud Scotos*. Similarly the main thrust of Barclay's *De regno et regali potestate* was directed, not against Hotman, but against the author of the *Vindiciae contra tyrannos*, Buchanan and Boucher – the author of the *Francogallia* being relegated to the category of 'reliqui monarchomachi'. Barclay considered the question of whether Hotman might be the author of the *Vindiciae*, and rejected the possibility because Hotman was too good a civilian to be guilty of the errors in Roman Law committed in the *Vindiciae*, and because the *Francogallia*, in Barclay's estimation, ridiculed many of the propositions defended in that work.[2] Nevertheless, Barclay's *De regno* alluded critically to the *Francogallia* on several occasions.[3]

During the first two decades of the seventeenth century the issue of the relationship between pope and king continued to be a matter of European controversy. It had been debated at the time of Sixtus V's excommunication of Henry of Navarre, and in the following decade it had been at stake between the ultramontane theories of the League, with their Jesuit champion, Robert Bellarmine, and Gallican writers such as Louis Servin and the brothers François and Pierre Pithou. The debate gained fresh impetus from the oath of allegiance which James I imposed upon English Catholics, from the return of the Jesuits to France, from the assassi-

[1] *Adversus Georgii Buchanani dialogum de iure regni apud Scotos: pro regibus apologia* (2nd edition, Paris, 1588), 14, 16.

[2] *De regno et regali potestate: adversus Buchananum, Brutum, Boucherium et reliquos monarchomachos* (Paris, 1600), 107.

[3] E.g., *ibid.*, 1, 299, and lib. IV, cap. xv. *passim.*

nation of Henry IV, and from the attempt of the third estate in 1614–15 to promote a declaration of royal independence against Rome in the estates general. Barclay himself was a leading protagonist of the royalist cause, but the *Brutum fulmen* of Hotman also played some part. In 1613 it was published in the third volume of Melchior Goldast's collection of tracts against ultramontanism, beside Barclay's *De potestate papae*, Du Moulin's *Tractatus de origine, progressu et praestantia monarchiae regnique Francorum* and Louis Servin's *Vindiciae secundum libertatem ecclesiae gallicanae et regii status Gallofrancorum.*[1] The *Brutum fulmen* was also quoted in Jean Bédé's tract against Bellarmine, which appeared in an English translation in 1612.[2] The deposition of Childeric III and the respective rôles of Pepin and Pope Zachary in that event were a constant debating point in this literature, but few quoted the appropriate pages of the *Francogallia* in this context. It was almost as if there were two François Hotmans, the monarchomach and the defender of Henry IV. Indeed, there was a third image in Hotman's posthumous reputation, for his fame as a civilian was not easily forgotten.

In the Netherlands and Germany Hotman was constantly quoted by the jurists of the seventeenth century. Grotius respected him as both an historian and a jurisconsult. In the introduction to his most celebrated work, *De jure belli ac pacis*, he paid tribute to Hotman and Bodin together as the leading representatives of the French school of jurists who had made law intelligible through history.[3] But Grotius never quoted the *Francogallia* in this respect. He referred, instead, to Hotman's discussion of inheritance and of the respective claims of uncle and nephew in the *Quaestionum illustrium liber*. Hotman had reversed his earlier opinion upon this issue in a later edition of that work, but Grotius pointed out that the first view was upheld by the practice of several German principalities.[4] In contrast with Grotius, Althusius treated the *Francogallia* in the

---

[1] In M. Goldast, *Monarchiae S. Romani Imperii, sive tractatuum de jurisdictione imperiali seu regia ac pontificia seu sacerdotali* (Frankfurt, 1613), vol. III.

[2] *The Right and Prerogative of Kings against Cardinall Bellarmine and other Jesuites*, transl. Robert Sherwood (London, 1612), 154.

[3] *De jure belli ac pacis* [1625] (Oxford, 1925 – the 1646 edition), I, Prolegomena.

[4] *Ibid.*, 59, 186, 187.

manner in which he used the second dialogue of the *Reveille-Matin*, the *Vindiciae contra tyrannos*, the *De jure magistratuum*, and the *De jure regni apud Scotos* (and, for that matter, the works of Mariana and Rossaeus too). His *Politica methodice digesta* was a subtle blend of monarchomach theory to produce a more explicit and coherent doctrine of popular sovereignty than that of any French theorist of resistance. Citing the 1600 edition, Althusius ignored its conservative aspect, and quoted it on such issues as the superiority of the nation to the ruler, the right of the people to dispose of the crown and to appoint magistrates, the rôle of ephors, and the fundamental laws binding the king as part of a contract of government.[1]

Another jurist of great European reputation, Heningus Arnisaeus, set out to refute Althusius and his sources and in so doing interpreted the *Francogallia* as the work of one of his enemies. Indeed, he described Hotman, together with Buchanan, Boucher, Rossaeus and the author of the *Vindiciae contra tyrannos*, as 'sworn enemies of royal sovereignty'.[2] On the other hand, an equally well-known German constitutional theorist, Johannes Limnaeus, quoted the *Francogallia* with a measure of objectivity in his erudite discussion of whether the French crown was hereditary or elective.[3] It was in Germany, moreover, that the last Latin edition of the *Francogallia* was published in 1665.[4]

In seventeenth-century England Hotman's name was respected without political bias by a number of antiquaries and civilians. Selden praised his learning as a jurist in the preface to his *Titles of Honour*, and must have disturbed Hotman's ghost by citing from the *Francogallia* the opinion he had subsequently discarded on the association of the peers with King Arthur.[5] Sir Henry Spelman admired Hotman's work as a feudist, and cited the *Francogallia* in his

---

[1] *Politica methodice digesta* [1603], ed. C. J. Friedrich (Harvard, 1932 – the 1614 edition), 91, 146, 149, 162, 185.

[2] *De jure majestatis libri tres* (Strasbourg, 1635), 6. The phrase used by Arnisaeus is 'regiae majestatis jurati hostes.' See also p. 32, where the author attacks the *Francogallia*'s use of history.

[3] *Notitiae regni Franciae* (Strasbourg, 1655), 325–6.

[4] See below, p. 129.   [5] *Titles of Honour* (London, 1614), 349.

essay *Of Parliaments* as though Hotman had seen his public council simply as an assembly of feudal magnates.[1] Among civilians Sir Thomas Smith, Elizabeth's ambassador to France in the years 1562–6 and author of *De republica Anglorum* (1583), is said to have been favourably impressed by Hotman's *Francogallia*,[2] while in the next generation John Cowell, who, like Smith, was professor of Roman Law at Cambridge, attacked that work in his dictionary, *The Interpreter* (1607), under the heading of 'Parliament'. Cowell, in the eyes of the house of commons at least, was by no means free of absolutist prejudice. His contemporary, the Scottish jurist Sir Thomas Craig, was deeply indebted to Hotman for his views on feudalism, and quoted the *Francogallia* on several occasions.[3] In the next generation Richard Zouche, professor of Roman Law at Oxford, cited Hotman in his treatise on international law.[4] During the restoration, Robert Brady, who renewed the historical insights of Spelman and other earlier antiquaries, referred to Hotman with respect in his glossary of feudal terms. In his rôle as a defender of the Stuarts, however, Brady attacked Hotman's politics and accused him of being the author of the *De jure magistratuum*, 'a piece so wicked and so destructive of peace and human society that neither papists nor puritans would own it'.[5]

The *Francogallia* was put to polemical use in the English civil war and interregnum. It was cited beside other monarchomach tracts in William Prynne's *Soveraigne Power of Parliaments and Kingdoms*, published in 1643 to demonstrate the authority of the Long Parliament against Charles I. Prynne provided his own demonstration from French history of the similar supremacy of the estates general, but he quoted the *Francogallia* on such issues as the right of resistance, the oath of Aragon, the superiority of the kingdom to the king, and

---

[1] *Of Parliaments*, in *English Works* (London, 1727), 58. The *Francogallia* is also cited on p. 63 of this work.

[2] *De republica Anglorum*, ed. L. Alston (Cambridge, 1906), xlii.

[3] See Smith, 'Hotman', 328, 348.

[4] *Juris et judicii fecialis sive juris inter gentes* (Oxford, 1650).

[5] 'Glossary', in *An Introduction to the Old English History* (London, 1684), 39; 'A True and Exact History of the Succession of the Crown of England', in *ibid.*, 346.

the rôle of kings as guardians.[1] Milton's *Defence of the People of England* referred to Hotman as 'a very learned man' and cited him on French history to support the monarchomach thesis against the condemnation of the execution of Charles I by the Huguenot Claude de Saumaise.[2] A less celebrated justification of the regicide, by the Fifth-Monarchist John Canne, buttressed its views with reference to the *Francogallia* (under its 1600 title), the *Vindiciae contra tyrannos*, the *De jure regni apud Scotos* and the *Politica methodice digesta*.[3] Defenders of the Stuart cause often retorted by associating their enemies with French doctrines of resistance from the sixteenth century, Calvinist as well as Leaguer,[4] and occasionally the *Francogallia* was included in the condemnation of such works. In his *Sacro sancta regum majestas* (1644) John Maxwell, archbishop of Tuam, blamed the political corruption of English sectaries on the *Francogallia*, together with the works of Boucher, Rossaeus and Mariana.[5] Similarly, Peter Heylyn, in his *Aerius Redivivus, or the History of the Presbyterians – from 1536 to 1647*, a book composed during the interregnum, associated the *Francogallia* with the supposedly uniform and invariably seditious political doctrines of Calvin, Beza, Knox, Buchanan and the authors of the *Vindiciae contra tyrannos* and the *Reveille-Matin*.[6] The theme of French Calvinist political subversion was a venerable tradition among Anglican writers. Archbishop Bancroft had mentioned the *Francogallia* in this respect, beside other Huguenot tracts, in his *Survay of the Pretended Holy Discipline* in 1593,[7] and so had David Owen in

[1] *Soveraigne Power of Parliaments and Kingdoms*, III (ed. London, 1643, 10, 79, 150, 163, 173, 194).

[2] *A Defence of the People of England* (n.p., 1692 – Latin edition 1650), 111, 180.

[3] *The Golden Rule* (London, 1649), 12.

[4] This practice was given greater force by the frequent drawing of parallels between the English political situation and that of the French wars of religion. Cf. Salmon, *French Religious Wars, passim.*

[5] *Sacro sancta regum majestas, or the Sacred and Royal Prerogative of Christian Kings* (2nd edition, London, 1680), 18.

[6] *Aerius redivivus* (Oxford, 1670), 23. Heylyn also suggested that Hotman might have composed the *De jure magistratuum* (ibid., 78). In his *Cosmographie* [1621] (2nd edition, London, 1657), 177, however, he praised Hotman for his attack upon Sixtus V.

[7] *A Survay of the Pretended Holy Discipline* (London, 1593), 15.

Herod and Pilate Reconciled in 1610.[1] On the whole, however, the *Francogallia* was cited far less frequently in English seventeenth-century polemics than were the comparable works of Beza, Mornay and Buchanan, and there was no seventeenth-century English version to compare with the English dress of the *Vindiciae contra tyrannos*, which appeared in 1648 and 1689.[2]

While the *Francogallia* appears to have been widely known in England and Germany in the seventeenth century, it is seldom mentioned in the country which inspired it. During the Fronde opposition to the crown within the parlement took its stand upon constitutionalism and fundamental law, and on two occasions during the conflicts there were promises to convoke the estates general. But frondeur propaganda made no mention of Hotman's work. This is understandable since the Fronde was by no means as long drawn out or intense a crisis as the wars of religion, and the earlier stuggles, like the *Francogallia* itself, were generally regarded with abhorrence, as models of sedition and unsuitable precedents for the situation in the years 1648–53. Moreover, leading constitutional theorists were Catholic, and connected with the parlement. The one sustained work which seemed to reproduce a number of the ideas of the *Francogallia*, the *Recueil des maximes véritables et importantes pour l'institution du Roy*, was composed by Claude Joly, a canon of Notre-Dame who had no desire to quote a heretic and

[1] *Herod and Pilate Reconciled, or the Concord of Papist and Puritan – for the Coercion, Deposition and Killing of Kings* (London, 1610), 42. This tract was republished as *A Persuasion to Loyalty* (London, 1642); see p. 24 for a new reference to the *Francogallia* and other monarchomach works. It was also the policy at times of moderate English Catholic writers to expose Calvinist political doctrine. For example, *A Treatise Tending to Mitigation towards Catholicke Subiectes in England*, by 'P.R.', possibly Robert Parsons (n.p., 1607), 164, attacked the *Francogallia* and praised Barclay's criticism of it. Another English Catholic tract condemning the *Francogallia* was the anonymous *Image of Bothe Churches, Hierusalem and Babel* (Tournai, 1623), by Charles I's physician, Matthew Patteson. This was republished in 1669 under a false title, *The Jesuites Policy to Suppress Monarchy*; the references to Hotman and the *Francogallia* appear on pp. 131, 137 and 142 of this edition. An abbreviated version of the tract appeared in 1663 under another false title, *Philanax Anglicus*, and provoked a reply by a Huguenot supporter of the Stuarts, Pierre du Moulin the younger.

[2] *A Defence of Liberty against Tyrants*, ed. H. J. Laski (London, 1924 – the 1689 edition).

critic of the parlement. Joly placed particular reliance upon the works of Seyssel and Du Haillan, and never cited the *Francogallia*.

A generation after the Fronde, the persecution of the Huguenots by Louis XIV did provide incentive for the revival of the doctrines of the 1560's and 1570's. Before the revocation of the edict of Nantes the most aggressive of the Huguenot writers, Pierre Jurieu, was cautious not to defend monarchomach tradition with any vigour,[1] and after the revocation, when he came close to the doctrines popular among Protestants in the aftermath of the massacre of Saint Bartholomew, he did not choose to identify his opinions with those of the *Francogallia*. It was common enough, of course, for French critics of the Huguenots to make such identifications. This was the practice of the historian Antoine Varillas, who repeated the libel that Hotman was the author of the *Vindiciae contra tyrannos*.[2] Pierre Bayle, himself a refugee from Louis XIV's persecution of French Protestantism, was also a critic of resistance theorists, hoping to dissuade his fellow exiles from following their example. In the *Avis important aux réfugiez*, if indeed he was the author of that anonymous work, he too suggested the possibility of Hotman's authorship of the *Vindiciae*.[3] His attitude to the *Francogallia* in his *Dictionary*, however, was not wholly condemnatory. He remarked that 'it is a commendable work in point of learning, but very unworthy of a French civilian'. In another place in the same article he wrote: 'Of all his writings, his *Franco-Gallia*, which he so much valued, is least approved, and has persuaded some persons that he was the author of the *Vindiciae contra tyrannos*, which is a book intirely agreeable to republican notions.'[4]

A tract by another Huguenot exile, which in some respects resembled the early editions of Hotman's book, was Michel le

---

[1] E.g., *Histoire du Calvinisme et celle du Papisme mises en parallèle* (Rotterdam, 1683), III, 286–92, where Jurieu discusses the Calvinist monarchomachs in response to Maimbourg's *Histoire du Calvinisme*.

[2] *Reflexions on Dr. Gilbert Burnet's Travels* (London, 1688), 102. This tract by Varillas was part of a series of exchanges caused by the criticism of his history of Calvinist rebellion in Burnet's *Reflections on Mr Varillas's History of the Revolutions that have happened in Europe* (Amsterdam, 1686).

[3] *Avis important aux réfugiez* (Amsterdam, 1690), 205.

[4] *Dictionary Historical*, III, 519, 520–1.

Vassor's *Les Soupirs de la France esclave qui aspire après la liberté*. This work relied upon much early French history, and cited the chronicle sources used by Hotman to demonstrate the superiority of the estates to the crown.[1] Le Vassor used the prerogative of the parlement to register ordinances, as Hotman had done in a 1586 modification of the *Francogallia*, to suggest that the power to withhold registration was a surviving remnant of the ancient authority of the estates.[2] But he, like Jurieu, made no specific mention of the *Francogallia*, and his argument, like Joly's, expressed neither a particular admiration for the Franks nor the kind of fundamentalism that appraised all constitutional history by its conformity with a pristine model. He spoke of the Franks as a barbarous race of nomads, and denied that it was necessary to discuss their origins 'pour prouver que la Monarchie Françoise a été fondée avec le Droit du Peuple d'élire ses rois'.[3] Yet, if Huguenot theorists of resistance to Louis XIV did not choose explicitly to resurrect the *Francogallia*, their Whig associates of the 1680's[4] were to do so in a novel and unexpected form.

When Grotius had adapted Hotman's vision of the liberty-loving Franks and their method of governing by election and common consent to the early history of the Netherlands, he had claimed these attributes for all the Germanic peoples, and applied the observations of Tacitus upon their customs to all the primitive kingdoms established after the fall of the Roman empire.[5] It became common practice among critics of Stuart monarchy in the 1640's to quote Tacitus in reference to the political institutions of the Saxon conquerors of England, and even to suggest that the parallels between English parliaments, French estates, and German diets

[1] G. H. Dodge, *The Political Theory of the Huguenots of the Dispersion* (New York, 1947), 68, believes Jurieu to be the author of *Les Soupirs*, but this attribution is improbable.

[2] *Les Soupirs de la France esclave qui aspire après la liberté* (n.p., 1689), 109. On this modification in the 1586 *Francogallia*, see above, p. 103.

[3] *Les Soupirs de la France esclave*, 82.

[4] For the association of Huguenot and Whig propaganda at this time see Salmon, *French Religious Wars*, 148–55.

[5] See above, p. 6. On Gothicism in general see S. Kliger, *The Goths in England, a Study in Seventeenth and Eighteenth Century Thought* (Harvard, 1952).

were not fortuitous but the result of common origins.[1] In the later years of the reign of Charles II the opposition still made use of Tacitus and the Saxons, as in William Petyt's *Antient Right of the Commons of England Asserted*,[2] but there was also a growing habit among more radical and republican writers to see the Saxons as but one instance of the model of a Gothic polity. Perhaps the most notorious example was Henry Neville's *Plato Redivivus*, where an explicit theory was advanced that the Germanic Goths had imposed standard principles of government involving limited monarchy, or a mixture of forms, and representative assemblies. 'The governments of France, Spain, England and all other countries where these people settled', Neville wrote, 'were fram'd accordingly.'[3] In comparatively recent times decay had set in. Louis XI had subverted the French constitution; the Aragonese cortes and the oath administered by the justicia had been destroyed by Castile; the Austrian Hapsburgs had subverted the liberties of Germany and eastern Europe; and, most recently of all, Denmark had experienced a revolution in 1660 which transferred authority to the king.[4]

In 1684 a supporter of the future James II, Thomas Goddard, published a lengthy refutation of Neville's Gothic constitution in his tract, *Plato's Demon*.[5] In the previous year Algernon Sidney had been executed for treason on Tower Hill. His *Discourses concerning Government*, an answer to the patriarchal theories of Sir Robert Filmer, contained an account of the Gothic polity even more explicit than Neville's, and clearly related to the political thought of the *Francogallia*.

All the northern nations [he wrote] which, upon the dissolution of the Roman empire, possessed the best provinces that had composed it, were under that form which is usually called the Gothic polity. They had

---

[1] For example, Sir Roger Twysden, *Certaine Considerations upon the Government of England* [composed after 1648] (London, 1849), 118–19; Nathaniel Bacon, *An Historical Discourse of the Uniformity of the Government of England* (London, 1647), 14–15, 46–7. Bacon concentrates upon the Saxons and, unlike Twysden, offers few parallels. His book is an English counterpart of the *Francogallia*.

[2] *The Antient Right of the Commons of England Asserted* (London, 1680), 6.

[3] *Plato Redivivus* (London, 1681), 92–8.   [4] *Ibid.*, 143, 153, 139.

[5] *Plato's Demon or the State-Physician Unmaskt* (London, 1684), 212–94.

king, lords, commons, diets, assemblies of estates, cortes and parliaments, in which the sovereign powers of these nations did reside, and by which they were exercised.[1]

In another place he referred to the decay of the constitution in Sweden, Hungary, Bohemia and Denmark, cited the supposed oath of Aragon, and gave an account of how the Goths, Franks, Vandals and Saxons had originally elected their kings as military leaders and raised them upon a shield. Later, when their numbers increased, they had exercised their authority through representative assemblies.[2] Sidney quoted the same passages from Tacitus as Hotman had quoted.[3] He followed Hotman through Frankish history, and specifically admitted his debt.[4] On several occasions he referred to the betrayal of the French constitution by Louis XI.[5] His opinion of the *Francogallia* provided the formula inherited by Whig theory in the eighteenth century:

Hottoman, a lawyer of that time and nation, famous for his learning, judgment and integrity, having diligently examined the ancient laws and histories of that kingdom, distinctly proves, that the French nation never had any kings, but of their own choosing; that their kings had no power, except what was conferred upon them; and that they had been removed, when they excessively abused, or rendered themselves unworthy of that trust.[6]

With the creation of the Gothic myth, the *Francogallia* and its themes returned to fashion. Locke's friend, James Tyrrell, cited the book in his *Bibliotheca politica*.[7] John, first Baron Somers, described the spread of the Gothic race over Europe, including England, and referred to the views of Hotman, Craig and Le Douaren on the development of the feud.[8] His friend, the antiquary Thomas Rymer, quoted Tacitus in *Of the Antiquity, Power and Decay of Parliament* and explained that 'when the English and French came

---

[1] *Discourses concerning Government* [1698], in *Works* (London, 1772), 139.
[2] *Ibid.*, 80.   [3] *Ibid.*, 81, 422, 425.   [4] *Ibid.*, 255.
[5] *Ibid.*, 254, 445, 506.   [6] *Ibid.*, 253.
[7] *Bibliotheca politica* (London, 1694), 91.
[8] *Jus regium or the King's Right to grant forfeitures and other revenues of the crown* (London, 1701), 40–1.

from Germany to people Britain and Gaul, the German liberty and moderate sway were transplanted with them; and still the Common Council had the main stroke in all weighty affairs; for to that policy they had been educated'.[1] He went on to discuss Frankish history with copious references to the chroniclers, commented on the use of diets in Germany, and concluded: 'All this seems but a paraphrase upon the passage afore-cited out of Tacitus, as to the form of government.'[2] There followed a discussion of the growth of arbitrary power with the Hapsburgs and the cunning of Louis XI.[3] In the same year as Rymer's piece (1714), a descendant of Sir John Fortescuc published a new edition of his ancestor's *De dominio regali et politico*, which he entitled *The Difference between an Absolute and Limited Monarchy*. In the preface the editor referred to the views of Grotius on the expansion of the Germans at the fall of Rome, and the establishment of similar bodies of law and similar institutions all over Europe by 'Lombards, Burgundians, Franks, Swevians and Vandals, and other Brothers and Kinsmen of the Saxons'.[4]

Of all the authors who discussed the Gothic policy, none publicized it more effectively than Viscount Molesworth, the first English translator of the *Francogallia*. It was he who assimilated the *Francogallia* to the Old Whig school in the eighteenth century. Robert Molesworth was a disciple of Algernon Sidney. He visited Denmark as an English envoy from 1689 to 1692, as Sidney had done in 1659, and published an account of that country in which he stressed the fall of the ancient 'Gothic' constitution in 1660. His preface included the remark that 'all Europe was in a manner a free country till very lately, insomuch that the Europeans were, and still are, distinguish'd in the Eastern parts of the world by the name of Franks', and ended with Cicero's maxim: 'Salus populi

[1] *Of the Antiquity, Power and Decay of Parliaments. Being a General View of Government, and Civil Polity, in Europe: with other Historical and Political Observations Relating Thereunto* (London, 1714), 12.

[2] *Ibid.*, 20. [3] *Ibid.*, 22–35, 61.

[4] *The Difference between an Absolute and Limited Monarchy, as it more particularly regards the English Constitution, being a treatise written by Sir John Fortescue, Kt...Publish'd with some remarks by John Fortescue-Aland* (London, 1714), xxx.

suprema lex esto.'[1] The first English version of the *Francogallia* was completed in 1705. It was published in 1711 with a brief preface stating that it was the translator's intention to show Englishmen their true liberties, and with a short account of Hotman's life based on the article in Bayle's *Dictionary*. The translation itself was fairly free and followed the text of the 1574 Latin edition. Molesworth subsequently became aware of Hotman's 1576 version, and when the second English edition appeared in 1721 it contained an additional three-page section as chapter XIX, which corresponded to chapter XVIII of the 1576 text. As has been indicated, this was the only new chapter added by Hotman in 1576, and concerned the authority of the public council in the dispute with Boniface VIII. Molesworth carelessly assumed that there was no other change in the 1576 edition. He made no attempt to consult the editions of 1586 and 1600.

The most striking aspect of the 1721 edition was the new preface Molesworth had composed. It began with a comment that much had been written to justify the revolution of 1688 as a return to the 'solid foundations of our *Constitution*: Which, in truth, is not ours only, but that of almost all *Europe* besides; so wisely restor'd and establish'd (if not introduced) by the *Goths* and *Franks*, whose Descendants we are'.[2] Such justifications of the revolution, Molesworth continued, had been disputed by those who supported the divine right of hereditary monarchy and held resistance to be a sin, and also by those who, denying that any authority could be produced for resistance, held it to proceed from dissidence and antimonarchical principles. It was to refute the last kind of objection that the translator had prepared his version of the *Francogallia*, the work of 'that most Learned and Judicious *Civilian, Francis Hoto-*

---

[1] *An Account of Denmark as it was in the Year 1692* [1694] (London, 1738), xiv–xvi. Chapter VI ('Of their Form of Government', p. 27) begins: 'The ancient form of Government here was the same which the *Goths* and *Vandals* established in most, if not all, Parts of *Europe* whither they carried their Conquests, and which in *England* is retained to this day for the most part.' On Molesworth's *An Account*, and its connexion with his interest in the *Francogallia*, see Caroline Robbins, *The Eighteenth-Century Commonwealthman* (Harvard, 1959), 98 ff.

[2] *Franco-Gallia; or an Account of the Ancient Free State of France and Most other Parts of Europe, before the Loss of their Liberties* (London, 1721), i.

man; a Grave, Sincere and Unexceptionable Author, even in the Opinion of his Adversaries'.[1] A few pages later Molesworth felt the impulsion 'to appear in my own Colours, to make a publick Profession of my *Political* Faith'. He went on to state:

My Notion of a *Whig*, I mean of a real *Whig* (for the Nominal are worse than any Sort of Man) is, that he is one who is exactly for keeping up to the Strictness of the true old *Gothick Constitution*, under the *Three Estates* of *King* (or *Queen*) *Lords* and *Commons*; the *Legislature* being seated in all Three together, the *Executive* entrusted with the first, but accountable to the whole Body of the People, in Case of Male Administration.[2]

The thirty subsequent pages of the preface set out the doctrines of English Whiggery, which, the reader was induced to believe, were contained in a tract composed over 150 years earlier in the context of the first phases of the French wars of religion. The *Francogallia* was represented in this way in another English edition of 1738, while Molesworth's preface appeared separately in 1726,[3] and again in 1775 under the title of *The Principles of a Real Whig*.[4]

While the English were re-interpreting Hotman in the early eighteenth century as the progenitor of Gothic constitutionalism, the French resumed the debate on the relevance of Frankish history to contemporary politics, but without any mention of the *Francogallia*. Under Louis XIV historians such as Mézeray had treated the original Franks as Gallic colonists east of the Rhine, much as Bodin, Connan and Forcadel had done in the sixteenth century. As the party of aristocratic reaction to the autocracy of Louis XIV gathered strength, the *thèse nobiliaire* of Henri de Boulainvilliers, comte de Saint-Saire, provided it with a new historical vision. Instead of Hotman's Francogallican partnership, Boulainvilliers depicted the Franks as the founders of the nobility, and the Gauls as

---

[1] *Ibid.*, iii.   [2] *Ibid.*, vii.

[3] With the exception of the first six pages, Molesworth's preface was printed in *Memoirs and Secret Negotiations of John Kerr, of Kersland, Esquire* (London, 1726), II, 191–221.

[4] *The Principles of a Real Whig contained in a preface to the famous Hotoman's Franco-Gallia written by the late Lord-Viscount Molesworth and now reprinted at the request of the London Association* (London, 1775).

the ancestors of the *roturier* class. After the Capetians had usurped the throne, this line of kings had undermined the liberties of the aristocracy and subverted the aristocratic council of the ancient constitution. Louis XI had advanced commoners to positions of importance, and Louis XIV had completed the process with his intendants. It has been said that Boulainvilliers' historical vision was essentially that of Hotman,[1] but they were fundamentally opposed on the relationship of the Franks to the Gauls. Moreover, it seems certain that Boulainvillers never read the *Francogallia*, for in his *Etat de la France* he wrote that all historians, 'sans en excepter aucun', had regarded Clovis as a personal conqueror, instead of seeing him merely as the captain of an army of free men, and had regarded conquered Gaul as the patrimony of kings, instead of the property of the Frankish warriors who had embarked in common upon their glorious enterprise.[2] It is true, of course, that Hotman's view of the rôle of the crown in the nation had not been so very dissimilar from the way in which Boulainvilliers saw the position of the king vis-à-vis his *Frankish* subjects, 'tous libres et parfaitement égaux et independans, soit en général, soit en particulier'.[3]

Against this aristocratic thesis the abbé Dubos set forth a monarchical one in his *Histoire critique de l'établissement de la monarchie françoise dans les Gaules*. The kings of the conquering Franks, he

[1] Franklin L. Ford, *Robe and Sword, the Regrouping of the French Aristocracy after Louis XIV* (New York, 1965), 227.

[2] *Etat de la France* [1737] (London, 1752), I, 53 (in a chapter headed 'Etat de la Nation Françoise – c'est à cette époque que nous devons rapporter l'ordre politique, suivi depuis par la Nation, et le droit essentiel et primordial de tous ses Ministres').

[3] *Ibid.*, 54. This passage is certainly reminiscent of Hotman, for it continues: 'Les Rois François n'étoient à proprement parler que des Magistrats Civils, choisis et nommés par les Cantons pour juger les différends des particuliers: de sorte qu'encore qu'il y ait lieu de soutenir que l'Emploi en étoit successif, ou du moins attaché à une certaine famille, on ne laisse pas de voir par les exemples de Merouée et de Childeric son fils, que le peuple jouissoit d'une liberté effective dans le choix personnel de ses Rois. Les François avoient aussi des chefs pour les conduire à la guerre, et ils les choisissoient indifféremment ou dans la Famille Royalle, ou dans toute autre, ne s'attachant à cet egard qu'à la valeur, qu'à la capacité dans l'art de la guerre et à la réputation du bonheur. Reges ex nobilitate, Duces ex virtute sumunt; nec Regibus infinita nec libera potestas; et Duces exemplo potius quam imperio praesunt (Tacitus).'

maintained, were merely the clients and allies of the Roman emperors and their authority was based upon commissions from Rome. Dubos, like Boulainvilliers, made no mention of Hotman. He was aware of the scholarship of Hotman's time, however, for he brushed aside sixteenth-century historians with the remark that they were too involved in the religious disputes of their age to embark upon the serious study of the remote past.[1] Nor did Montesquieu, when he criticized Dubos in De l'Esprit des Lois, refer to the Francogallia, despite his parallel belief in the birth of liberty in the forests of Germany.[2] Finally in this dialectical process, the abbé de Mably produced a democratic interpretation of Frankish history, and he too had no wish to cite the Francogallia. He accepted Tacitus on primitive German democracy, but he argued that the principles of popular government brought from the Teutonic woods began to decay almost as soon as Gaul was conquered. Charlemagne had restored national assemblies, but the social divisions within them reflected the exploitation of sections of the Gallic population and were very different from the Champs de Mai under the first successors of Clovis.[3] Mably's ideas were not without force in the period of the revolution. In 1787 the abbé Brizard delivered Mably's éloge at the Academy, and remarked:

Deux idées neuves et brilliantes ont frappé tous les esprits. La première est le tableau d'une république des Francs, qui, quoi qu'on en ait dit, n'est nullement imaginaire. On y voit la liberté sortir avec eux des forêts de la Germanie, et venir arracher les Gaules à l'oppression et au joug des Romains. Clovis n'est que le général et le premier magistrat du peuple libérateur, et c'est sur une constitution libre et républicaine que Mably place, pour ainsi dire, le berceau de la monarchie...La seconde est la législation de Charlemagne:...Charles reconnoît les droits imprescriptibles de l'homme, qui étoient tombés dans l'oubli.[4]

---

[1] Histoire critique de l'établissement de la monarchie françoise dans les Gaules (Paris, 1734), I, 45.

[2] De l'Esprit des Lois, lib. XI. cap. vi (ed. Gonzague Truc, Paris, n.d., I, 174).

[3] Observations sur l'Histoire de France [1765], ed. François Guizot (Paris, 1823), 5, 26, 103, 127.

[4] Quoted by Augustin Thierry, Considérations sur l'Histoire de France, published with Récits des Temps Mérovingiens (Paris, 1894), I, 98.

Until the final phrases of this eulogy are reached, it is possible to see an affiliation, however distant and distorted, between Mably's democratic warriors and Hotman's standard-bearers of liberty.

The era of the revolution itself experienced a few more tangible instances of the influence of the *Francogallia*. Indirectly, this influence was expressed through the republication of Le Vassor's *Soupirs de la France esclave* (*Les Voeux d'un patriote*, 1788), of Milton's *Defence of the People of England* (*Théorie de la Royauté d'après la doctrine de Milton*, 1789, preface by the younger Mirabeau) and even, at least by way of association, of an extract from Du Haillan's *Histoire générale* (*Conditions sous lesquelles les François se sont donné un Roi*, 1789). Directly, the *Francogallia* itself appeared relevant to the revolutionary situation. Among the many fragments and fugitive pieces from the past referring to French representative institutions and published in 1788 in the multi-volumed work entitled *Etats-Généraux et autres assemblées nationales*, there appeared four chapters of the *Francogallia*.[1] Remote from the motives that inspired it, and oblivious of the modifications in later sixteenth-century editions, the tradition of the *Francogallia* played a significant part in European thought for over two centuries, and parts of the book were reprinted in the context of both the English and the French revolutions.

SECTION II — TECHNICAL ASPECTS OF THIS EDITION

1. *The Latin text*

Of the six previous printings of the Latin *Francogallia* only three represent distinct editions, and each of these was prepared by Hotman during his lifetime: 1573, 1576, and 1586. Two of the remaining three were simply copies of earlier editions: 1574 of that of 1573, 1665 of that of 1586. The status of the posthumous text of 1600 is problematical, but for reasons given on p. 111 of the

[1] *Etats-Généraux et autres assemblées nationales* (Paris, 1788), VI, 259–304.

introduction this edition will be viewed here as a reprint of the 1586 edition.

The six earlier editions will be identified in the present variorum text by the following bold-faced italic letters:

a 1573   *Franc. Hotomani Iurisconsulti, Francogallia.* Genevae, Ex officina Iacobi Stoerii. The title-page of this edition is pictured on p. ii. This edition was also issued with a slightly different title-page: another variety of the printer's emblem, and 'Genevae' omitted.

*a*¹ 1574   *Franc. Hotomani Iurisconsulti, Francogallia. Libellus statum veteris Reipublicae Gallicae, tum deinde à Francis occupatae, describens.* Coloniae, Ex officina Hieronymi Bertulphi. As is the case with *a*, *a*¹ was also issued with a slightly different title-page: 'Coloniae' omitted.

b 1576   *Franc. Hotomani Iurisconsulti, Francogallia. Editio tertia locupletior.* Ex officina Iohannis Bertulphi. [Cologne]

c 1586   *Francisci Hotomani Iurisconsulti Celeberrimi, Francogallia: Nunc quartùm ab auctore recognita, & praeter alias accessiones, sex novis capitibus aucta.* Francofurdi, Apud heredes Andreae Wecheli.

*c*¹ 1600   Under the title *De Antiquo Iure Regni Galliae, Praecipue quo ad Auctoritatem Comitiorum,* in *Franc. Hotmani Iurisconsulti Operum Tomus Tertius.* Excudebant Haeredes Eustathii Vignon, & Iacobus Stoer. [Geneva]

*c*² 1665   *Francisci Hotomanni ICti celeberrimi Franco-Gallia juxta editionem Francofurt: adauctam...* Francofurti, Apud Georg Fickwirt. Together with the *Francogallia* the publishers reprinted Matharel's 1575 attack upon it, so that the full title continues (after the word *adauctam*): *Accessit Antonii Matharelli Reginae Galliae à rebus procurandis primarii Responsio,*

> *quae directa ad editionem Genevensem, quae Anno 1573*
> *prodiit, in quâ deficiunt ea capita, quae in indice Aste-*
> *risco notata reperiuntur.*

Textual variations of *a*¹ from *a*, or *c*¹ and *c*² from *c*, have been relegated to the footnotes. The likeness of these 'reprints' to their parent editions is the basic fact to remember, so that the first of the two governing rules of the present variorum edition – the 'intramural' rule – can be stated as follows:

> *References to **a** include **a**¹, and references to **c** include **c**¹ and **c**²,*
> *unless specified otherwise.*

The other rule concerns the relationships between *a* and *b* and *c* as groups. This 'extramural' rule is:

> *All passages marked **a** in the text are also found in **b** and **c**, and*
> *all passages marked **b** are also found in **c**, unless specified otherwise.*

A reader who wishes to follow the text of the 1573 edition should simply ignore the passages beginning with the superscript letters *b* and *c*; if he desires to read the edition of 1576 he should heed only the passages marked *a* and *b*; and if he requires the text of the 1586 edition he must read everything. These conventions may also be summarized as follows: to encounter superscript letter *a* in the text means to return to the first edition after reading a passage inserted in one of the later editions; to encounter *c* means to begin an augmentation not found in either of the earlier editions; and to encounter *b* means to begin an augmentation of *a* or to finish an additional passage inserted in *c*.

There are, however, three instances where Hotman suppressed substantial passages appearing in the first edition. In these instances a departure has been made from the rules described above, and the passages have been omitted from the text and placed in appendix A. The first of them concerns the kinds of property which may be thought to be at the disposal of the ruler. It occurs in both *a* and *b*, but in *c* it was replaced by a longer and more elaborate passage (see above, p. 105). The second example discusses the origin of the peers.

It appears in *a* only, and was replaced in *b* and *c* by a completely different account (see above, p. 90). The third instance takes up certain remarks by Guillaume Budé concerning thirteenth-century judicial assemblies at which members of the clergy were present (see above, p. 86). This passage occurs in *a* only, and in this and the two other cases mentioned the reader who desires to reconstitute the 1573 text must refer to the appendix at the appropriate points.

Bold-faced italic letters, used to identify editions, make it a simple matter for the reader to look back and ascertain what text he has been reading up to the point of a change. It is never necessary, however, to turn back the page, for at the top left of every page will be found, in brackets, the letter appropriate to the text being continued from the previous page.

2. *Latin variorum footnotes*

Since augmentations of the previous text constitute the vast majority of changes made in 1576 and 1586, and these could be embodied in the present variorum text by means of the superscript letters just described, footnotes serve only to show the remainder of the textual variants. These comprise the topmost of the two sets of footnotes below the Latin text. They concern the replacement or deletion in *b* or *c* of words or phrases in the *a* version (except, of course, for the three major suppressed passages placed in appendix A), the alteration in *b* or *c* of the order in which certain passages originally appeared in *a*, and a number of intramural variants. The latter are usually trivial, except for the notices of how c^1 emasculated the text of *c*. The extramural changes are generally intended to achieve syntactical nicety and consistency with some augmentation of the text. Asterisks in the text and corresponding line numbers in the footnotes identify the locus of all variants.

Economy of expression being the general rule, footnotes do not repeat the words of the text above unless there exists some danger of ambiguity about the content of the variant reading. Such turns out to be the case in about one of six instances, where the footnotes begin by citing the exact words of the text to be replaced (or the terminal words of a given passage, separated by ellipsis marks) followed by the appropriate edition mark and exact replacement wording.

Decisions concerning spelling, punctuation, and like matters have had to be made arbitrarily. In *spelling*, the letter 'j' should not be found in any part of the present text labelled *a* or *b*, for the printers of those editions used 'i' where 'j' might be found; but 'u' and 'v' have been rendered throughout the present text according to modern practice, irrespective of the reading in any of the earlier editions. In *punctuation*, the priority of style accorded to *a* in most matters has been violated in order to allow augmentations from *b* and *c* to sit comfortably within the previous text. On the other hand, the *capitalization* style of *a* has been preserved in all *a* passages, without recording variants in the equivalent passages in *b* and *c*; similarly, *b* passages follow *b*'s capitalization without recording variants in *c*. *Paragraphing* was almost entirely absent in all earlier Latin editions, and has been supplied here simply to conform with the way Salmon chose to divide the translation. Lastly, *typographical errors* in earlier editions have not been recorded unless there was a possible ambiguity. Text *c*², of the seventeenth century, was by far the most poorly proofread of earlier editions; but, being the least important, it could be the most casually heeded.

3. *Identification of Hotman's sources*

Italicized portions of the Latin text indicate Hotman's quotations from his sources, but at least half of them are not verbatim. Sometimes Hotman was compelled, when condensing another author's words, to change a word or add one for grammar's sake. Sometimes he employed indirect discourse, rather than direct quotation, but in fact used his authority's exact words except for case and tense endings. Sometimes – indeed, very often – he supplied a word or two in order to have a partial quotation make sense. The present editor, faced with hundreds of decisions involving these kinds of imperfect quotations, has decided whether or not to italicize according to this rule of thumb: if the key words Hotman used when citing an authority are found in the original, and one could believe that he avoided absolutely precise quotation only because of his own literary exigencies, then the passage has been italicized. If the quotation fails to meet this standard, it has not been italicized and the numbered footnote invites the reader to compare Hotman's words with those of his source. The rule about quotations has been applied rigorously in cases involving delicate political notions, and, further, the gap in meaning between Hotman and his source has been spelled out when it could be done so briefly.

When identifying sources, as when giving textual variants, the minimum of material from the text has been repeated in the footnote. If Hotman's book-and-chapter identification conforms to current practice, then the footnote simply gives a page reference from a modern edition. Where Hotman uses now-antiquated names for his sources, especially mediaeval chroniclers, the modern usage will be found in the English translation. Titles of books have been greatly abbreviated, because a complete biographical list of Hotman's sources is given below in Bibliography A.

4. *The English translation*

In general the English translation follows the conventions employed in the Latin for augmentations of the original text in later editions and for variorum readings. It should be noted, however, that, unlike the Latin, the lines of the English text are not numbered, and in consequence the variants are marked by a number of signs in addition to the asterisk (†, ‡, §). It should also be pointed out that many of the Latin variants have no English counterpart. This is because these variants are purely stylistic changes in the Latin, such as an alteration of word order, or the replacement of a word with a synonym, and the English sense is unaffected. In the English version explanatory matter in the variorum footnotes is italicized.

Another departure from the conventions of the Latin is the method used to convey passages where Hotman claims to be citing an author verbatim. The whole of each alleged direct quotation is surrounded by quotation marks. Moreover, the English version omits the detailed references in the text where Hotman identifies his sources. These, of course, are further identified in the lower set of footnotes on the Latin page. Similarly, the *incipit* passages used by Hotman to establish a juristic reference, especially to the *Corpus juris civilis*, have not been translated into English, but are shown simply as 'in the *Code*', 'in the *Digest*', etc.

Square brackets in the English text indicate explanatory matter inserted by the translator; round brackets indicate Hotman's own parentheses. The Latin names of Gallic tribes and places have been preserved in the English, but in later times Latin names have been given in modern French or English versions. The spelling of Frankish names has been standardized in English. Where passages of Greek or Spanish occurring in the Latin text are also provided by Hotman in Latin, these have been given in English alone on the facing pages. The word *parlamentum* has been rendered by 'parliament' where Hotman uses it to refer to his alleged representative assemblies, and by 'parlement' where the author refers, usually in derogatory fashion, to the law court of that name instituted in the thirteenth century. The translation has endeavoured to preserve the pedantic flavour of the Latin while, at the same time, providing a measure of fluency.

TEXT

^aPRAEFATIO

Illustrissimo et Potentissimo Principi ac Domino, Domino Friderico Comiti Palatino ad Rhenum, Bavariae Duci, etc. Romani Imperii Electori primario, Domino suo clementissimo. S. P.*

5 Vetus verbum est, Illustrissime Princeps, *Patria est ubicunque est bene,*[1] Teucro Telamonis filio attributum, multisque seculis comprobatum. Nam fortis animi excelsique videtur esse, ut coetera incommoda, sic etiam exilium, aequo animo ferre, ingrataeque patriae, tanquam novercae, iniurias contemnere.
10 Verum, ego longe esse arbitror secus; nam si parentum mores, atque adeo asperitatem iniquius ferre, sceleratum, ac prope impium videtur, quanto magis patriae, quam sapientes omnes, una et mente et voce, semper parentibus anteposuerunt? Est quidem hominis securi, et de suis tantum commodis cogitantis,
15 patriae caritatem suis opportunitatibus metiri; sed illa tanta securitas, pars quaedam eius immanitatis videtur, quae propria, vel Epicureorum, vel Cynicorum fuit, unde vox illa furialis profecta est, *Me mortuo, terra misceatur incendio.*[2] A qua ne illud quidem vetus Tyrannicum abhorret: *Pereant amici, dum una inimici*
20 *intercidant.*[3] Est in mansuetis ingeniis caritas quaedam innata patriae, quae deleri, nisi cum reliquis humanitatis sensibus, non potest. Qualem caritatem Homerus in Ulysse describit,[4] qui patriam Ithacam saxis praeruptis et asperis, tanquam nidulum, affixam, omnibus tamen deliciis, atque adeo Regno sibi a
25 Calypsone oblato anteposuit.

---

4 **c²** 'Olim ad Illustrissimum Principem ac Dominum, Dominum Fridericum, Comitem Palatinum ad Rhenum, Ducem Bavariae, S. R. I. Electorem, annis sc. hinc 91 perscripta, et primae illius opusculi editioni praefixa.'

[1] Cicero, *Tusc. disp.*, 5, 37, 108; Loeb, 532.   [2] Ἐμοῦ θανόντος γαῖα μιχθήτω πυρί: *Frag. Adespota*, 513; ed. Nauck, *Tragicorum Graecorum fragmenta*² (Leipzig, 1889), 940. Quoted (in Greek) by Suetonius, *Nero*, 38 (Loeb, II, 154), from whom Hotman could have drawn this translation out of an early all-Latin edition.
[3] Cicero, *Pro rege Deiotaro oratio*, 25; Loeb, 522.   [4] *Odyssey*, V, *passim* – e.g., 219ff.; Loeb, I, 184.

*a*PREFACE

To the most illustrious and mighty Prince and Lord, Lord Frederick, Count Palatine of the Rhine, Duke of Bavaria etc., First Elector of the Roman Empire, the author's most gracious Lord, in health and prosperity.*

Most illustrious Prince, it is an ancient saying attributed to Teucer son of Telamon and attested by many generations, that 'a man's country is wherever he finds content'.[1] For it seems to be the mark of a strong and excellent character to endure with equanimity such inconveniences as exile, and to despise the injuries inflicted by an ingrate fatherland that has assumed the rôle of step-mother. And yet I hold a very different opinion. For, if it seem a crime and all but blasphemy to bear impatiently the humours, and even the asperity, of family elders, how much greater is it an offence to resent our native country, which the wise have always unanimously preferred to natural parents. He is a foolish man who would calculate his affection for his country in proportion to the advantages it brings him. Yet such was the careless disregard, seemingly part of a monstrous doctrine of indifference, attributed to the Epicureans and Cynics, and from it was derived that abominable saying: 'When I am dead, I care not if the world be consumed in flame.'[2] The latter is not inconsistent with an old tyrannical adage: 'Let my friends perish so long as my enemies fall with them.'[3] In those of gentle nature there is a certain inborn love of country which can no more be renounced than any other human attribute. Such was the love Homer described in Ulysses,[4] who preferred his native land of Ithaca, fixed like some tiny nest to its harsh and jagged rock, to all the delights, and to the very kingdom, which Calypso offered him:

---

* *c*[2] Ninety-one years ago this preface was addressed to the most illustrious Prince and Lord, Lord Frederick, Count Palatine of the Rhine, Duke of Bavaria and Elector of the Roman Empire, and prefixed to the first edition of the work.

Nescio qua natale solum dulcedine cunctos
Afficit, immemores nec sinit esse sui,[5]

ut vere Poeta vetus cecinit, cum et coeli, unde primum spiritum duximus, et soli in quo prima vestigia posuimus, et cognatorum,
5 propinquorum, aequaliumque nobis in mentem venit.

Verumenimvero, dicet aliquis, delira interdum patria est, mentisque errore afficitur, ut Plato de sua locutus est.[6] Interdum etiam furore amens crudeliter bacchatur, atque in sua viscera saevit. Primum cautio est, ne alienam culpam innocenti patriae
10 ascribamus. Multi Romae, multi aliis in locis Tyranni immanes fuerunt, hi non modo bonos viros, verumetiam benemeritos de patria cives omnibus cruciatibus afficiebant. Continuone verum fuit, illorum insanias patriae acceptas ferre? Memoratur Imperatoris Macrini crudelitas, quem Iulius Capitolinus Macel-
15 linum nominatum scribit,[7] propterea quod domus eius, ut macellum sanguine pecudum, sic illa hominum sanguine cruentabatur. Complures alii passim ab historicis commemorantur, quorum alius (ut idem Capitolinus scribit[8]) ab eadem crudelitate Cyclops, alius Busiris, alius Siron, alius Typhon,
20 alius Gyges nominatus est. Cum illi sic animum induxissent, regna et imperia nisi crudelitate retineri non posse. Idcircone cura omnis et solicitudo patriae, civibus bonis abiicienda fuit? imo vero tanquam oppressae et miserae et natorum opem imploranti succurrendum, remediaque modis omnibus conqui-
25 renda. Quamquam, ô fortunatas bonis et mansuetis Principibus regiones! ô beatos cives, quibus Principum suorum benignitate, tranquille licet in patriis avitisque sedibus, cum coniugibus et liberis consenescere! Nam plerunque certe usuvenit, ut remedia malis ipsis, quibus ea quaeruntur, deteriora sint.

---

[5] Ovid, *Ex Ponto,* I, iii, 35–6; Loeb, 282.   [6] Probably a reference to *Axiochus,* 368 D; this dialogue, supposedly by Plato, was translated and published many times in the late 15th and 16th centuries.   [7] *Scr. hist. Aug.,* Apel. Macrinus, XIII, 3; Loeb, II, 76.   [8] *Scr. hist. Aug.,* Maximiani, VIII, 5; Loeb, II, 328.

'I know not how the charm of natal soil holds them all firm,
And does not let them be unmindful of their origin.'[5]

So sang the ancient poet in all truth. Nor can his sentiment be
denied when we recall the air where we drew our first breath, the
soil where we took our first step, and the friends, neighbours and
contemporaries we knew.

Yet one may also say that one's country sometimes loses its
reason, and is afflicted by illusions, as Plato said of his.[6] Sometimes,
indeed, it raves in cruel and frantic frenzy, and vents its rage upon
its own offspring. We must first take care that we do not ascribe to
any country the blame that others deserve, when it in fact be guilt-
less. There were many monstrous tyrants in Rome and elsewhere
who afflicted ordinary men, as well as those citizens deserving well
of their fatherland, with all kinds of torments. Does it follow that
the madness of these tyrants must be held against their country?
Such cruelty is remembered as that of the Emperor Macrinus, who,
as Julius Capitolinus writes,[7] was named Macellinus, because his
dwelling was like a butcher's shop [*macellum*], stained with the blood
of cattle, from the manner in which he had bespattered it with the
blood of men. Historians record many other similar tyrants, of
whom, as the same Capitolinus writes,[8] one was called Cyclops,
another Busiris, another Sciron, another Typhon and another
Gyges because of like savagery. These men were led to think that
kingdoms and empires could not be retained without cruelty.
Should good citizens reject all care and solicitude for their country
on that account? On the contrary, they should care for her as one
who is oppressed and unfortunate, and implores the aid of her
native-born. They should seek remedies in all ways possible. How
fortunate are those countries that have good and gentle rulers!
How blessed are those citizens who, through the benevolence of
their princes, are permitted to grow old in the tranquillity of the
homes of their fathers and ancestors with their wives and children
round them! Certainly, it very often happens that the measures by
which one seeks to procure these things are worse than the evils
themselves.

Anni sunt, ut opinor, sexdecim, Princeps illustrissime, ex quo
Deus optimus maximus partem Germaniae Rhenanae non exi-
guam fidei ac potestati C. T. commendavit. Vix dici potest,
quantam ex eo tempore tranquillitatem, et tanquam in pacato
5 mari malaciam toto Palatinatu videre licuerit, quam pacata
semper sedataque omnia, quam pie, sancte, et religiose con-
stituta. Macte igitur ista mansuetudine ^cesto, ^aclementissime
Princeps, quod ego, quantum et animi et corporis viribus con-
tendere possum iterum exclamo: Macte ista virtute ^cesto!
10 ^aplacida et mansueta, non quemadmodum Seneca memoriae
prodidit moris apud Romanos fuisse,[9] ut sanguinolentis et ex
acie redeuntibus, Macellinis denique cruore madentibus dicere-
tur, Macte virtute ^cesto! ^aSed macte ista mansuetudine animi,
clementia, pietate, iustitia, facilitate, et imperii ac ditionis tuae
15 tranquillitate. Atque hic cum fere sit vestrae Germaniae status,
quemadmodum qui navigationem instituunt, freta turbulenta,
et tumultuosa devitant, sedatos ac tranquillos cursus quaerunt,
similiter quamplurimi hodie regiones latrociniis infestas fugi-
unt, tranquillas et pacatas quaerunt.
20   Ac fuit tempus, cum in Francogalliam nostram undique ex
omnibus terrarum oris, sese studiosi adolescentes effunderent, et
ad nostras Academias, tanquam ad bonarum artium merca-
turam conferrent; nunc illas quasi maria pyratis infesta horrent,
neque secus quam Cyclopicam barbariam* execrantur. Cuius rei
25 meum pectus memoria exulcerat, cum cogito miseram et in-
fortunatam patriam duodecim iam fere annorum spatio
incendiis civilibus exarsisse. Sed multo me acerbior excruciat
dolor, cum considero non modo tam multos esse otiosos incendiorum spectatores, (qualem olim Neronem Romae confla-
30 grantis fuisse memorant) verumetiam flammas illas impiorum
quorundam vocibus ac libellis, tanquam flabellis, excitari, ad eas
autem extinguendas perpaucos ac fere nullos accurrere. Mea
quidem quam sit tenuis, quamque humilis conditio, non sum
ignarus; sed tamen ut in communi incendio si quis quantumvis

24 *bc* 'barbariem'.
[9] *Epist.* LXVI, 50; Loeb, II, 32.

I believe, most illustrious Prince, that it is now sixteen years since Almighty God committed to your trust and authority a considerable part of the German Rhineland. During this time it is difficult to conceive the tranquillity and calm which can be seen to have existed throughout the Palatinate, as though it were a smooth, unruffled sea. It is difficult to conceive how peaceful and quiet all things have remained, and how they have been controlled with such piety and holy sanctity. May you, most gracious Prince, rule with gentle moderation, and while strength of mind and body remain to me I shall say once again: Well done! [*Macte ista virtute* *°esto!*] *°*May you rule with a placid and gentle virtue, and not in the manner which, as Seneca reminds us, was the custom of the Romans[9] when their leaders returned bloodied from the battle-array, covered in gore like Macellinus, and were saluted with these same words, *Macte virtute esto!* Rather, may you rule with gentleness of mind, clemency, piety, justice and courtesy, and with the peaceful exercise of your sovereign authority. There are those who, when plotting a voyage, avoid turbulent and tumultuous waters and seek a quiet and tranquil course, and there are many today who will flee from countries infested with brigands, and seek quiet and peaceful places. May such be the condition of your lands in Germany.

There was a time when young men, anxious to learn, poured into our Francogallia from all the ends of the earth to attend the academies, coming, as it were, to sample the wares available in the arts. Now they shun them, as if they were seas infested with pirates, and curse them as though they were the lair of some barbarous Cyclops. The thought of this circumstance wounds me deeply when I consider that for nearly twelve years my miserable and unfortunate country has been scorched by the fires of civil war. My sorrow is even more bitter when I reflect that so many have stood by unconcerned, observing the flames (as Nero once watched Rome burning), and some have wickedly blown upon these fires with the bellows of their speeches and libels, while few, if any, have hastened to extinguish them. I know well enough my own slight and humble condition. Nevertheless, in a general

abiecta fortuna sitellam aquae deferat, studium credo eius nemo repudiet, ita spero neminem patriae communis amantem meam hanc in quaerendis remediis operam aspernaturum.

^c(Anno 1572 et 1573.)^{* a}Superioribus quidem mensibus in tan-
5 tarum calamitatum cogitatione defixus, veteres Francogalliae nostrae historicos omnes* et Gallos et Germanos evolvi, summamque ex eorum scriptis confeci eius status, quem annos amplius mille in Republica nostra viguisse testantur, ex qua incredibile dictu est quantam maiorum nostrorum in consti-
10 tuenda Republica nostra sapientiam cognoscere liceat; ut mihi quidem nequaquam dubium esse videatur, quin ab illa certissimum tantorum malorum remedium petendum sit. Nam mihi attentius in istarum calamitatum caussam inquirenti, sic videbatur, sicuti corpora nostra vel externo impulsu atque ictu,
15 vel intestinis humorum vitiis, vel senio intereunt, ita Rerumpublicarum alias hostili impetu, alias domesticis dissensionibus, alias vetustate confici. Nostrae autem Reipublicae incommoda etsi vulgo ex intestinis dissidiis nata existimantur, tamen hanc non caussam, sed principium malorum esse animadverti, quod
20 principium a caussa plurimum discrepare, gravis auctor imprimis Polybius demonstrat.¹⁰ Caussam autem confirmo esse plagam quam annis abhinc circiter centum ab illo accepit, quem constat primum omnium praeclara maiorum nostrorum instituta labefactasse. Quemadmodum autem corpora nostra
25 externo aliquo ictu luxata sanari, nisi membris suum quibusque in locum et naturalem sedem restitutis, non possunt, ita Rempublicam nostram tum denique sanatam iri confidimus, cum in suum antiquum et tanquam naturalem statum divino aliquo beneficio restituetur. Et quia C. T. patriae nostrae semper se

---

4 *c* has this as marginalia; *c*¹ omits it; *c*² puts it in the text, as here; see above, p. 51. **6** *c* omits 'omnes'.

¹⁰ VI, 5; Loeb, III, 274. Hotman had published this passage in 1563 – cf. below, ch. XII, n. 12 (p. 292).

conflagration I believe that anyone, however low his station, who can throw on a bucket of water makes a welcome contribution. In this spirit I hope that no one who loves our country will disdain the service I would render in seeking salve for its affliction.

In reflecting upon these great calamities I have, for several months past ^c(in the year 1572 and in 1573),* ^afixed my attention on what is revealed by all† the old French and German historians of our Francogallia, and from their writings I have compiled a summary of its constitution. They show that our commonwealth flourished in this form for more than a thousand years. From this review it is astonishing to find how great was the wisdom of our ancestors in constituting our commonwealth, and it does not seem possible for me to doubt in any way that the most certain remedy for our great afflictions should be sought in the constitution. For, as I gave increasing attention to the cause of these calamities, it seemed to me that, even as our own bodies decay (whether by external blows and shocks, or by the inward corruption of humours, or by old age), so, too, do commonwealths perish, some by hostile attack, some by internal dissensions, and some by senescence. Although the troubles that afflict our commonwealth are commonly thought to proceed from internal conflicts, these should be seen not as the cause but as the beginning of our troubles. That weighty writer Polybius[10] shows in his works how important it is to distinguish between the beginning of a thing and its cause. Now I assert that the cause was the blow delivered against our constitution about one hundred years ago by one who certainly was the first to undermine the excellent institutions designed by our ancestors. Just as our bodies, when dislocated by some external blow, cannot be repaired unless each member be restored to its natural seat and place, so we may trust that our commonwealth will return to health when it is restored by some act of divine beneficence into its ancient and, so to speak, its natural state. And, because Your Highness has always proved himself to be the

* *c has this in marginalia; c¹ omits it; c² puts it in the text as here; see above, p. 51.*
† *c omits all.*

amicissimam praebuit, optimum factu iudicavi, summam hanc
historiae nostrae illustrissimo tuo nomini inscribere, quasique
consecrare, ut eius patrocinio atque auctoritate tutior in hominum manus pervenire possit. Vale Illustrissime Princeps, et
5 Salve. Deum Opt. Max. oro, ut illustrissimum genus vestrum
perpetuo beatissimum ac florentissimum esse patiatur. XII
Kalendas Septemb. MDLXXIII.*

Illustriss. C. T.
obsequentissimus
10   Franc. Hotomanus.

7 *a*[1] 1574 – probably the typographer's doing.

greatest friend of our country, I judged it to be the best thing I could do to inscribe, if not to consecrate, this summary of our history to your most illustrious name, so that your patronage and authority will enable it to pass more safely into the hands of its readers. Hail and farewell, most illustrious Prince. I beseech Almighty God to suffer your illustrious house to live for ever in all blessedness and prosperity. Dated this 21st day of August, 1573.*

> I am, Your Illustrious Highness,
> Your most obedient servant,
> François Hotman.

* *a*¹ 1574.

FRAN. HOTOM. IURISC. FRANCOGALLIA*

ᵃCAPUT I

De statu Galliae priusquam a Romanis in provinciam redigeretur

---

Cogitanti mihi de Francogalliae nostrae institutis, quantum ad usum Reipublicae nostrae, et horum temporum opportunitatem satis esse videbitur, conscribere, principio exponendum videtur, qui Galliae status fuerit, antequam a Romanis in Provinciae
5 formam redigeretur. Nam quae de* gentis origine et antiquitate, de bellicis laudibus ᶜeloquentiae studio, ᵃde regionis situ et natura, privatorumque moribus apud Caesarem, Polybium, Strabonem, Ammianum et reliquos scripta extant, nota sunt omnibus, mediocriter quidem eruditis. ᶜ*Pleraque Gallia* (in-
10 quibat M. ille Cato Censorius in Originibus¹) *duas res industrio-sissime persequitur: rem militarem, et argutissime loqui.*

ᵃIntelligendum est igitur, eo tum statu Galliam fuisse, ut neque universa unius imperio regeretur, neque singulae civitates vel in populi, vel in Optimatum potestate essent, sed ita divisam in
15 Civitates Galliam universam fuisse, ut pleraeque Optimatum consilio regerentur, quae Liberae dicebantur, ceterae Reges haberent; omnes quidem hoc institutum tenerent, ut certo anni tempore publicum gentis concilium agerent, quo in concilio quae ad summam Reipublicae pertinere videbantur, constituerent.
20 *Civitates autem quatuor et sexaginta* Corn. Tacitus numerat lib. 3,² hoc est, ut ex Caesare³ intelligitur, Regiones, quae non modo

---

Cap. **c¹** instead of 'Francogallia' entitles the work 'De antiquo iure regni Galliae, praecipue quo ad auctoritatem comitiorum.' See above, p. 111. **5 c¹** omits 'de'.
¹ II, 31; ed. Peter, I, 61, which reads just 'argute loqui'. ² *Annales*, III, 44; Loeb, 590. ³ Cf. *B.G.*, I, 1; Loeb, 2.

FRANCOGALLIA

BY FRANÇOIS HOTMAN, JURISCONSULT[*]

*a*CHAPTER I

The condition of Gaul before the Romans reduced it to a province

---

I have it in mind to examine the institutions of our Francogallia with the aim of serving our own commonwealth, and in present circumstances this may not seem inopportune. Let us first consider the condition of Gaul before the Romans reduced it to the form of a province. Anyone of even modest education knows what Caesar, Polybius, Strabo, Ammianus and the rest wrote about the origin and antiquity of that people, their military exploits, *c*their skill in oratory, *a*the geography of the country and the personal customs of its inhabitants. *c*'Most of Gaul', wrote Cato the Censor in his *Origins*,[1] 'energetically follows two pursuits: waging war and making speeches.'

*a*It should be realized that in those days the whole of Gaul was not ruled by a single man, nor were particular regions under the control of populace or aristocracy. Rather was the entire country so divided that many regions were ruled by a council of nobles, and were termed free, while the other regions had kings. All, indeed, accepted the general practice of holding a public council of the nation at a fixed time of the year, and there they decided whatever seemed appropriate for the greatest good of the commonwealth.

According to Cornelius Tacitus,[2] there were 'sixty-four *civitates*', or regions, as they are known in Caesar's account.[3] They

---

* *c*[1] *instead of 'Francogallia' entitles the work 'The ancient law of the kingdom of France and especially that pertaining to the authority of its assemblies'; see above, p.* 111.

147

lingua, moribus, et institutis, verum etiam iisdem magistratibus
utebantur, quales ipse multis locis Aeduorum, Arvernorum, et
Rhemorum civitates praecipue commemorat. Itaque cum
Aeduum Dumnorigem Caesar interficiendum curaret, *resistere*,
5 inquit, *ac se manu defendere, suorumque fidem implorare coepit, saepe*
clamitans, liberum se, liberaeque civitatis esse: lib. 5, cap. 3.[4] Quapropter in candem sententiam Strabo lib. 4, ita scribit:[5] ἀριστο-
κρατικαὶ δ᾽ ἦσαν αἱ πλείους τῶν πολιτειῶν, ἕνα δ᾽ ἡγεμόνα
ᾑροῦντο κατ᾽ ἐνιαυτὸν τὸ παλαιόν, ὡς δ᾽ αὕτως εἰς πόλεμον εἷς
10 ὑπὸ τοῦ πλήθους ἀπεδείκνυτο στρατηγός. *Pleraeque*, inquit,
civitates Optimatum consiliis regebantur, unum autem magistratum
olim quotannis deligebant, sicut et ad bellum gerendum unus a populo
imperator creabatur. Eodem pertinet quod Caesar lib. 6, cap. 4,
his scribit verbis:[6] *Quae civitates commodius suam Rempublicam*
15 *administrare existimantur, habent legibus sancitum, si quis quid de*
Reipublicae a finitimis rumore aut fama acceperit, ut ad Magistratum
deferat, neve cum quo alio communicet; Magistratus quae visa sunt,
occultant, quaeque esse ex usu iudicaverint, multitudini produnt. De
Republica nisi per concilium loqui non conceditur.
20   De communi vero totius Gentis concilio pauca haec ex Caesare
testimonia proferemus. *Petierunt* (inquit lib. 1, cap. 12),[7] *uti sibi*
concilium totius Galliae in diem certam indicere, idque Caesaris
voluntate facere liceret. Item lib. 7, cap. 12:[8] *Totius Galliae con-*
cilium Bibracte indicitur; eodem conveniunt undique frequentes multi-
25 *tudines.* Et lib. 6, cap. 1:[9] *Caesar concilio Galliae primo vere* (*ut*
instituerat) *indicto, cum reliqui praeter Senones, Carnutes, Trevi-*
rosque venissent, concilium Lutetiam Parisiorum transfert. Et lib. 7,
cap. 6:[10] *Quae ab reliquis Gallis civitates dissentiebant, has sua*
diligentia (de Vercingentorige loquitur) *adiuncturum, atque unum*
30 *concilium totius Galliae effecturum, cui concilio ne orbis quidem*
terrarum possit obsistere.
    Iam vero de regibus, qui civitatibus quibusdam praeerant, loca

---

[4] *B.G.*, v, 7; Loeb, 242.   [5] *Geog.*, IV, 4, 3; Loeb, II, 242.   [6] *B.G.*, VI, 21;
Loeb, 344.   [7] *B.G.*, I, 31; Loeb, 44.   [8] *B.G.*, VII, 63; Loeb, 468.   [9] *B.G.*, VI,
3; Loeb, 318   [10] *B.G.*, VII, 29, 6; Loeb, 422. Hotman's 'cui consilio' should
read 'cuius consensui'.

not only observed the same language, customs and laws but also recognized the same magistrates. In many passages Tacitus singled out the states of the Aedui, Arverni and Rhemi for mention in this respect. When Caesar ordered the killing of Dumnorix the Aeduan, the latter, as Caesar puts it,[4] 'began to resist, to take steps to defend himself, and to call for the support of his own people, often declaiming that he was a free man and a member of a free state'. Strabo writes to the same effect:[5] 'Most of these regions were ruled by councils of the nobility, but in former times they chose a single magistrate annually, and in like manner, the people appointed a single general to wage war.' In this context Caesar writes:[6] 'Those states are thought to administer their government more effectively when they have it inviolably established by laws that, if anyone receive any report concerning the lands bordering the commonwealth, whether by rumour or repute, he should inform the magistracy and no one else. The magistrates keep secret what they deem should be concealed, and communicate to the public what they think proper. No one may speak on an issue concerning the commonwealth unless he does so in a council.'

We offer these few supporting passages from Caesar regarding the common council of the whole people. In the first Caesar states:[7] 'They asked whether it was permitted to proclaim a council of the whole of Gaul for a certain day, and whether it might be done by the will of Caesar.' In another passage he writes:[8] 'A council of all Gaul was summoned at Bibrax, and there a great multitude assembled.' And elsewhere he says:[9] 'Caesar summoned a council of Gaul to meet early in the spring, as he had earlier arranged, and when all had arrived, save for the Senones, Carnutes and Treviri, he moved the council to Paris.' Of Vercingetorix Caesar writes:[10] 'When some of the Gallic states differed from the rest, he hoped that he (that is, Vercingetorix) would inspire them to join together in creating a single council for all Gaul, which no other power on earth could withstand.'

The same author refers very frequently indeed to the kings who

sunt apud eundem auctorem prope innumera, ex quibus illud
memoria dignum intelligitur, moris fuisse Romanis, ut quos
Regulos ad suas rationes accommodatos, id est, ad res novas,
conturbandasque civitates et inimicitias cum aliis exercendas
5 idoneos iudicabant, eos sibi amicitia et societate adiungerent,
summique honoris ac beneficii loco, socios atque amicos suos
honorificentissimis decretis appellarent; eumque verborum
honorem reges exteri complures magnis largitionibus a civitatis
Romanae principibus comparabant. Reges autem vel Regulos
10 potius, Galli eos nominabant, qui non ad tempus, ut civitatum
magistratus, sed in perpetuum, regium imperium quantumvis
exiguis finibus obtinebant, quos immutata temporum consuetudo, Duces, Comites, Marchiones appellavit.

Earum porro civitatum aliae aliis potentiores erant, quarum se
15 in fidem et clientelam, quae minus per se poterant, studiose conferebant. Has Caesar superiorum stipendiarias, vectigales, et
earum imperio subiectas appellat.[11] Plerunque tamen in fide
aliarum esse scribit. *Regnante Romae Prisco Tarquinio* (inquit
Livius lib. 5[12]) *Celtarum penes Bituriges summa imperii fuit; ii Regem*
20 *Celtis dabant.* Adventu Caesaris in Galliam (qui fuit annus ab
urbe condita DCXCV), *Galliae totius factiones erant duae. Harum*
alterius principatum tenebant Aedui, alterius, Arverni, multosque annos
de potentatu inter se contenderant.[13] Sed illa contentio ea re magnopere augebatur, quod Bituriges Arvernorum finitimi, in fide et
25 imperio Aeduorum erant. Sequani contra, Aeduorum finitimi,
in Arvernorum fide: lib. 1, cap. 12;[14] lib. 6, cap. 4.[15] Cum has
Gallorum contentiones Romani ad suas rationes, id est, ad suam
potentiam amplificandam aptissimas iudicarent, studiose illas
alebant. Itaque Aeduos in societatem asciverunt, eosque exquisito
30 verborum honore Fratres consanguineosque suos appellarunt.

---

[11] *E.g., B.G.,* II, 8; Loeb, 148 (as below, p. 152, n. 21).   [12] v, 24, 1; Loeb, III,
116.   [13] *B.G.,* I, 31; Loeb, 46.   [14] *Ibid.*   [15] Cf. *ibid.,* VI, 11–12; Loeb, 332.

ruled over certain of these states, and his remarks suggest a most significant point: that it was the practice of the Romans to associate themselves in friendship and alliance with those kinglets whom they found adaptable to their own thinking and to the novelties they introduced, because they thought them likely to embroil the states with one another and occupy them with local enmities. With the most flattering of public declarations the Romans bestowed the titles of friend and ally upon such rulers, rather than giving them any tangible honour or favour. Many foreign kings obtained these prodigally bestowed honorifics from the leaders of the Roman republic. Moreover the kings, or rather kinglets, as the Gauls called them, were not appointed for a set term, as were the civil magistrates, but in perpetuity. They acquired as much regal authority as they wished within their small territories, and by the fixed custom of the times became known as dukes, counts and marquesses.

Then again, some of the states were more powerful than others, and those which were less able to look after themselves eagerly became allies and clients of the stronger. Caesar calls them hirelings and tributaries of the greater states, and subservient to their authority.[11] In general, however, he prefers to say that the weak were under the protection of the strong. Livy states in his history[12] that 'when Tarquinius Priscus reigned in Rome the Bituriges held the supreme authority among the Celts and gave them a king'. When Caesar entered Gaul, which was in the year 695 after the founding of Rome, 'there were two factions in Gaul: the Aedui controlled one, and the Arverni the other, and the two had struggled for the supremacy for many years'.[13] But what exacerbated this rivalry was the fact that the Bituriges, who bordered on the Arverni, were under the protection and authority of the Aedui; whereas the Sequani were the neighbours of the Aedui and the allies of the Arverni.[14, 15] Since the Romans saw the dissensions of the Gauls in the light of their own advantage, that is, as a most convenient means of extending their own power, they eagerly fanned the flames of conflict. Thus they took the Aedui into partnership, and styled them their blood-brothers with a host of pretty compliments.

In Aeduorum fide et clientela reperio fuisse primum Senones, quibuscum Parisii paulo ante suam civitatem foedere et societate coniunxerant: lib. 6, cap. 1;[16] tum Bellovacos, *quorum tamen erat civitas magna, et plurimum inter Belgas et virtute, et auctoritate, et* 5 *hominum multitudine valebat*: lib. 2, cap. 4[17] et lib. 7, cap. 7.[18] Sub imperio Nerviorum Caesar numerat Centrones, Grudios, Laevacos, Pleumosios, Gordunnos: lib. 5, cap. 11.[19] Trevirorum clientes idem numerat Eburones, et Condrusos: lib. 4, cap. 2.[20] *Venetorum autem civitatis* (hi sunt in Armorica) *longe amplissimam* 10 *auctoritatem idem fuisse* scribit *omnium orae maritimae regionum earum, omnesque fere qui eo mari uti consueverant, illius fuisse vectigales*: lib. 3, cap. 2.[21] Arvernorum autem tanta erat amplitudo, ut non modo se Aeduis adaequarent, verumetiam paulo ante Caesaris adventum *magnam clientum partem ab illis ad se traduxis-* 15 *sent*: lib. 6, cap. 4;[22] lib. 7, cap. 10.[23] Itaque Strabo lib. 4 scribit,[24] eos quadringentis hominum millibus duce Vercingentorige bellum adversus Caesarem gessisse.

Hi ab regio imperio abhorrebant. Itaque *cum Celtillus Vercingentorigis pater summae potentiae atque auctoritatis esset, eoque totius* 20 *Galliae principatum obtineret, ob eam causam, quod Regnum appetebat, ab civitate interfectus fuerat*: lib. 7, cap. 1.[25] Sequani contra Catamantaledem Regem habebant, quem Romani amicum ac socium appellarant: lib. 1, cap. 2.[26] *Suessiones quoque qui latissimos feracissimosque agros possidebant, oppidaque habebant* 25 *numero XII, et armatorum L. millia conficere poterant, Divitiacum totius Galliae potentissimum Regem paulo ante habuerant, qui non tantum magnae partis Belgarum, verumetiam Britanniae imperium obtinuerat. Caesaris adventu Regem Galbam habebant*: lib. 2, cap. 1.[27] *In Aquitania Pisonis cuiusdam Aquitani avus regnum obtinuerat, et* 30 *a Romanis amicus appellatus fuerat*: lib. 4, cap. 3.[28] *Senones quoque,*

---

[16] Cf. *ibid.*, VI, 3; Loeb, 320.   [17] *Ibid.*, II, 15; Loeb, 108.   [18] Cf. *ibid.*, VII, 59; Loeb, 464.   [19] Cf. *ibid.*, V, 39; Loeb, 284.   [20] Cf. *ibid.*, IV, 6; Loeb, 186. [21] *Ibid.*, III, 8; Loeb, 146f.   [22] *Ibid.*, VI, 12; Loeb, 332; the words quoted apply to the Sequani, not the Arverni.   [23] Cf. *ibid.*, VII, 38; Loeb, 434; here, the Arverni are indeed the subject.   [24] *Geog.*, IV, 2, 3; Loeb, II, 218.   [25] *B.G.*, VII, 4; Loeb, 384.   [26] Cf. *ibid.*, I, 3; Loeb, 6.   [27] Cf. *ibid.*, II, 4; Loeb, 94. [28] *Ibid.*, IV, 12; Loeb, 192.

The first people to have been the allies and clients of the Aedui were the Senones, with whom the Parisii had shortly before associated themselves by treaty and alliance.[16] Then, says Caesar, 'came the Bellovaci, despite the fact that their own state was an important one and among the Belgae was esteemed foremost in courage, power and number of warriors'.[17, 18] Caesar numbers the Centrones, the Grudii, the Laevaci, the Pleumosii and the Gorduni under the rule of the Nervii.[19] He also lists the Eburones and the Condrusi as clients of the Treviri.[20] He remarks: 'The power of the state of the Veneti in Armorica was by far the most extensive over all the coastal regions in that area, and nearly all those peoples who were accustomed to make use of the sea were their tributaries.'[21] Yet so great was the power of the Arverni that they not only equalled that of the Aedui but, shortly before the arrival of Caesar, 'they had won over a large proportion of the Aeduan client states'.[22, 23] Thus Strabo writes[24] that, under the leadership of Vercingetorix, they made war against Caesar with 400,000 men.

These people abhorred kingly rule. According to Caesar,[25] 'when Celtillus, the father of Vercingetorix, held the supreme power and authority and obtained control of the whole of Gaul, his people put him to death for seeking to acquire a crown'. By way of contrast, the Sequani had Catamantales as king, whom the Romans called a friend and ally.[26] Caesar writes: 'Also the Suessiones, who possessed most extensive and fertile lands, with twelve towns and a fighting strength of 50,000 men, had Divitiacus, the strongest king in all Gaul, who had gained dominion not only over a great part of the Belgae but also over Britain. At the time of Caesar's coming they had Galba as king.[27] The grandfather of Piso the Aquitainian won a kingdom in Aquitaine, and had been called friend by the Romans.[28] Also, the Senones, who formed one of the strongest

quae fuit civitas in primis firma, et magnae inter Gallos auctoritatis, quodam tempore Moritasgum Regem habuerant, *cuius etiam maiores regnum in eadem civitate obtinuerant*: lib. 5, cap. 13.[29] Item Nitiobriges Olloviconem Regem habuerat, *Amicum a Senatu* 5 *Romano appellatum*: lib. 7, cap. 6.[30]

In illis porro regnis illud observatione dignum, neque leviter praetereundum videtur: primum quod haereditaria non erant, sed a populo propter iustitiae opinionem deferebantur; deinde quod Reges non infinitum, solutum et effrenatum imperium 10 habebant, sed certis legibus ita circunscriptum, ut non minus ipsi in populi, quam populus in ipsorum ditione ac potestate esset,[31] ut fere illa regna nihil aliud, nisi magistratus perpetui viderentur. Nam multos Caesar nominat privatos, quorum tamen parentes ac maiores regnum obtinuerant: *in his Casticum* 15 *Catamantaledis filium, cuius pater in Sequanis multos annos regnum obtinuerat*: lib. 1, cap. 2.[32] Item Pisonem Aquitanum: lib. 4, cap. 3.[33] Item *Tasgetium, cuius maiores in Carnutum civitate cum Regio imperio fuerant*: lib. 5, cap. 8.[34] De imperii vero et potestatis modo, Ambiorix Rex Eburonum apud eundem auctorem 20 ita loquitur (lib. 5, cap. 8):[35] *Sua esse eiusmodi imperia, ut non minus haberet in se iuris multitudo, quam ipse in multitudinem.* Quam optimam ac praestantissimam Reipublicae formam esse, propterea Plato et Aristoteles, et Polybius, et Cicero iudicarunt,[36] quod Regalis dominatus, si sine freno (ut ait Plato[37]) relinquatur, 25 ubi in tantam omnium rerum potestatem, tanquam in lubricum locum, venerit, facillime in tyrannidem delabitur; qua de caussa, *c*inquit, *a*optimatum et delectorum auctoritate, quibus eam potestatem populus permittit, tanquam freno coercendus est.

---

[29] *Ibid.*, v, 54; Loeb, 304f.   [30] *Ibid.*, vii, 31; Loeb, 424.   [31] These sentiments are largely Hotman's; all that Caesar said is given below, in n. 35.   [32] *Ibid.*, i, 3; Loeb, 6.   [33] *Ibid.*, iv, 12; Loeb, 192.   [34] *Ibid.*, v, 25; Loeb, 264.   [35] *Ibid.*, v, 27; Loeb, 268.   [36] See below, ch. x [xii], nn. 10–13 (p. 292), where these four authors are mentioned in the same context and the likely passages in their writings are cited.   [37] Certainly not Plato verbatim, any more than the clause that follows it (*qua de caussa* etc.) which becomes attributable to Plato by the addition of the word *inquit* in the 1586 edition; for a discussion of this passage, see above, p. 63.

tates and had great authority among the Gauls, had Moritasgus as
their king at one time, whose ancestors had also acquired regal
authority in the same state.[29] Similarly, the Nitiobriges had
Ollovico as their king, who was styled friend by the Roman
senate.'[30]

It is to be noted, and this is not a point to be lightly passed over,
that, in the first place, these kingdoms were not hereditary but
conferred by the people on someone who had a reputation for
justice; and, in the second place, the kings did not possess an unlimited, free and uncontrolled authority, but were so circumscribed by specific laws that they were no less under the authority
and power of the people than the people were under theirs.[31]
These kingdoms, then, appear to have been no other than permanent magistracies. Indeed Caesar names many private men whose
fathers and ancestors had held kingly rank: 'Among these were
Casticus, the son of Catamantales, whose father ruled over the
Sequani for many years,[32] Piso the Aquitainian[33] and Tasgetius,
whose ancestors were endowed with regal authority in the region
of the Carnutes.'[34] Ambiorix, king of the Eburones, told Caesar of
the nature of his government and his method of exercising power
in these terms:[35] 'That their form of government was such that the
populace had no less jurisdiction over him than he over them.' This
is the best and most excellent kind of government according to the
judgment of Plato, Aristotle, Polybius and Cicero,[36] because, as
Plato puts it,[37] if a regal authority is left unfettered, it can attain
such great power over all things that it stands, as it were, upon
slippery ground, and very easily falls into tyranny. For this reason,
ᶜhe argues, ᵃit ought to be controlled by the nobility and men of
distinction, authorized by the people to exercise what may be
described as a bridle upon power.

Quae priscis temporibus Gallorum
lingua fuisse videatur

Hoc loco non praetermittenda quaestio videtur, multorum eruditorum hominum tractata disputationibus quinam, priscis illis temporibus* Gallorum sermo fuerit. Nam quae ad religiones, et privatorum mores, ceteraque instituta pertinent, Caesar (ut 5 ante diximus) copiose exposuit. Primum autem meminisse oportet, quod idem auctor initio Commentariorum scribit, cum Gallorum alii Belgae, alii Aquitani, alii Celtae essent, omnes non modo institutis, verumetiam lingua inter se discrepasse. Quod etiam* Strabo lib. 4 testatur,¹ ubi ait eos ὁμογλώττους non 10 fuisse, ἀλλ᾽ ἐνίους μικρὸν παραλλάττοντας ταῖς γλώτταις. Idemque Ammianus Marcellinus lib. 15² testatur.*

Quod vero doctissimi complures, ac praesertim nostri populares, disputant, Gallos Graeca lingua usos fuisse, vel ex eo solo refelli potest, quod Caesar lib. 5, cap. 12³ commemorat, cum 15 Q. Cicero a Gallis obsessus suis in castris teneretur, epistolam ei se Graecis literis scriptam misisse, ne, si interciperetur, sua consilia a Gallis cognoscerentur. ᶜItem lib. 1, cap. 4,⁴ ubi scribit, se cum Divitiaco Dumnorigis fratre, per C. Valerium Troacillum, principem Galliae provinciae, familiarem suum, remotis quoti- 20 dianis interpretibus, locutum esse. Nam Troacillus civis Romanus factus et Latinae et Gallicae linguae usum habebat. Quod si Divitiacus Graecae linguae notitiam habuisset, quid Caesari ad colloquium cum eo instituendum interprete opus fuisset? Eodem etiam illud Ciceronis pertinet in Orat. pro Fonteio,⁵ ubi de 25 Gallis loquens: *Hi vagantur*, inquit, *laeti atque erecti, passim toto*

---

3 *c*² omits 'quinam...temporibus'. **9** *c* 'aperte'. **11** *c* 'confirmat'.

¹ *Geog.*, IV, 1, 1; Loeb, II, 162. ² XV, 11, 1; Loeb, I, 188. ³ Cf. *B.G.*, V, 48; Loeb, 296. ⁴ Cf. *ibid.*, I, 19; Loeb, 30. ⁵ §33; Loeb, 340.

The probable language of the Gauls in early times

This may be the appropriate place to deal with that unavoidable question which has been debated by many learned men, namely, what was the language used by the Gauls in those early times.* As we have already stated, Caesar provided a full account of their religion, private customs and other institutions. First, it should be remembered that Caesar himself writes at the beginning of his *Commentaries* (where he divides the Gauls into the Belgae, the Aquitani and the Celtae) that they all differed from one another in their speech as well as in their institutions. Strabo† says the same thing,¹ where he observes that they were not of one tongue but differed slightly from one another in their speech. Ammianus Marcellinus also testifies to this effect.‡²

But the view that the Gauls used Greek, which is supported by many learned men and especially by our fellow-countrymen, can be refuted from a single passage in Caesar. Caesar recalls³ that when Quintus Cicero was besieged by the Gauls in his camp he sent him a letter, written in Greek so that, if the Gauls intercepted it, they would not discover his plans. ᶜAnd again, Caesar writes⁴ that when he spoke with Divitiacus, the brother of Dumnorix, he did so through C. Valerius Troacillus, his intimate friend and the ruler of provincial Gaul, because the usual interpreters were unavailable. Troacillus was a Roman citizen and had both Latin and Gallic. If Divitiacus had known the Greek tongue, what could Caesar have been doing arranging a discussion with him by means of an interpreter? A remark made by Cicero in his speech on behalf of Fonteius⁵ is also pertinent. Speaking of the Gauls he says: 'Happy and proud, they wander about from place to place in the country-

---

* *c²* omits in those early times. † *bc* add plainly. ‡ *bc* testifies to this effect *becomes* confirms this.

foro, cum quibusdam minis, et barbaro atque immani terrore ver-
borum. Nam Graecam linguam Ciceroni barbaram atque
immanem fuisse, nemo, opinor, existimarit. Ulpianus in l.
Fideicommissa, 11 D. de Legat. 3 :⁶ *Fideicommissa** *quocunque*
5 *sermone relinqui possunt: non solum Latina vel Graeca, sed etiam*
Punica, vel Gallicana, vel alterius cuiuscunque generis lingua.

ᵃSed occurritur ab nonnullis, proferentibus Strabonis locum
ex eodem lib. 4 ubi scribit, *omnium optimarum artium, ac praesertim*
Graecarum literarum, studia Massiliae viguisse, usque eo ut Galli
10 *eorum exemplo Graecae linguae studio caperentur, ut iam pacta et*
*conventa** *Graece scriberent* :⁷ καὶ φιλέλληνας (inquit) κατεσκεύαзε
τοὺς Γαλάτας ὥστε καὶ τὰ συμβόλαια 'Ελληνιστὶ γράφειν. Verum
ad hanc obiectionem* facilis et expedita responsio est. Primum
enim si Galli Massiliensium exemplo Graecam linguam disc-
15 ebant, annon perspicuum est, vernaculam illam eorum linguam
non fuisse? Deinde Strabo eodem loco non obscure ostendit
morem illum pacta et contractus Graece scribendi, suo demum
tempore initium cepisse, cum iam universa Gallia Romanis
parere didicisset. Praeterea de iis tantum praecise loquitur, qui
20 Massiliensibus erant finitimi, quibus in locis non modo privati
complures, verumetiam *civitates* (inquit⁸) *doctos viros Massilia*
publico consilio propositis honorariis ad iuventutem suam insti-
tuendam evocabant. ᶜCum tamen aliis plerisque in Galliae locis
Academiae florerent, in quibus sermone Gallico artes ac
25 disciplinae iuventuti tradebantur, quod Hieronymus ad Rusticum scribens his ostendit verbis :⁹ *Mater post studia Galliarum quae*
florentissima sunt, misit te Romam, ut ubertatem, nitoremque Gallici
sermonis gravitas Romana condiret.

ᵃSuperest locus ille apud Caesarem, ubi ait,¹⁰ *Gallos in publicis*
30 *privatisque rationibus Graecis literis usos fuisse.* Sed videamus ne vox
GRAECIS eo loco non modo ᵇut ᵃsupervacanea, verumetiam

---

4 *c*¹ 'Eodem quoque pertinet quod ait, fideicommissa...'   11 *b* '*ut iam pacta*
et conventa'; *c* '*et iam pacta conventaque*'.   13 *c* 'Verum huic obiectioni'.

⁶ *Dig.* 32, 1, 11; Mommsen, I, 484.   ⁷ *Geog.*, IV, 1, 5; Loeb, II, 178.   ⁸ *Ibid.*
⁹ (Letter CXXV [alias IV]) *PL*, XX, 1075; cf. below, n. 45, p. 168.   ¹⁰ *B.G.*, VI,
14; Loeb, 338.

side, uttering threats in words of fierce and barbarous dread.' No one will assume, I believe, that the Greek language was fierce and barbarous to Cicero. According to Ulpian's law of trusts:[6] 'Trusts can be bequeathed by any kind of oath: not only in Latin or Greek but also in Carthaginian, Gallic or any other kind of language whatsoever.'

[a]But some will suggest reference to a passage in Strabo's *Geography* where he writes:[7] 'Schools of all the best of the arts, and especially of Greek literature, flourished at Marseille, and the Gauls were so impressed by this that they learnt Greek and used it for their contracts and agreements.' There is, however, a quick and ready reply to this objection. In the first place, if the Gauls learnt Greek by imitating the people of Marseille then it is perfectly clear that Greek was not their native tongue. Further, Strabo makes it plain in the same passage that the custom of writing their covenants and contracts in Greek began precisely at the time when the whole of Gaul had accepted the rule of the Romans. Moreover, he speaks with assurance only about those who lived near the people of Marseille, and he observes[8] that in those regions not only many private men but also 'local governments officially solicited the learned men of Marseille and offered them rewards to teach their youth'. [c]However, schools flourished in many other places in Gaul which passed on the arts and sciences to the young in the Gallic tongue, and Jerome reveals this when he writes:[9] 'After studying in the Gallic schools, which are in a most flourishing state, your mother sent you to Rome, so that Roman severity might temper the richness and splendour of the Gallic mode of expression.'

[a]There remains that passage in Caesar where he says that[10] 'the Gauls used Greek letters in public and private transactions'. But let us consider whether that word 'Greek' ought not to be deleted,

ut importuna et adulterina tollenda sit, quippe, cum ad Caesaris sententiam exprimendam satis fuisset dixisse, Gallos in sola Druydum disciplina literis et scriptione usos non esse, in caeteris omnibus, et privatis et publicis rationibus, literis usos esse. Nam
5 Uti literis, pro Scribere, locutio est Latinis auctoribus crebro usitata. ᶜFabius lib. 11, cap. 2:[11] *Quanquam invenio apud Platonem,*[12] *obstare memoriae usum literarum.* ᵃPraeterea repugnant, Gallos linguae Graecae imperitos fuisse (quod Caesar illo superiore loco dixerat) et ᶜvulgo ᵃtabulas rationesque suas
10 publicas ac privatas Graecis literis conscripsisse. Quod autem plerique existimant, Graecas literas eo loco non pro scriptione, sed pro formis literarum usurpari, nobis propterea minus probatur, quod locis innumeris (ut modo dicebamus) veteres scriptores Uti literis dixerunt pro Scribere; at pro, formas
15 literarum ducere, quantum adhuc observare licuit, nusquam.

Neque enim illos adiuvat, quod idem Commentario primo scripserat,[13] *repertas in Helvetiorum castris tabulas, literis Graecis conscriptas*; quasi vero qui Graecis literarum notis scribere didicerat, non idem eadem opera Graeco sermone scribere didicisset,
20 aut non esse potuerint in Helvetia vel sacerdotes, vel adolescentes nobiles, qui, ut hodie tam multi sunt qui Latine didicerunt, ita literas Graecas, quae tum in honore et pretio erant, perdiscere potuerint. Quam opinionem vel unica Massiliensis scholae vicinitas refellit. Itaque idem Caesar lib. 5, ubi de illa sua ad
25 Ciceronem epistola loquitur:[14] *Hanc,* inquit, *Graecis conscriptam literis mittit, ne intercepta epistola, nostra ab hostibus consilia cognoscantur.** Justinus lib. 20:[15] *Facto S. C. nequis postea Carthaginensis aut literas Graecas, aut sermonem studeret, ne aut loqui cum hoste, aut scribere sine interprete posset.* Tacitus de moribus Germanorum:[16]

---

27 cᴵ adds here 'Cic. Ver. vi. [IV, 48, §103; Loeb, II, 410] *Itaque in his* (loquitur de dentib. a Masinissa, ex Africa, in insulam Melitam remissis) *inscriptam litteris Punicis fuit, regem Masinissam imprudentiam accepisse; recognita reponendos restituendosque curasse.*'

[11] Quintilian, XI, ii, 9; Loeb, IV, 216.   [12] *Phaedrus*, 275A; Loeb, 562.   [13] *B.G.*, I, 29; Loeb, 42.   [14] *Ibid.*, IV, 48; Loeb, 296.   [15] XX, 5; Teubner, 126.   [16] Cap. 3; Loeb, 268.

not just as superfluous, but also as unfitting and false. It was enough for Caesar's meaning to say that only in Druidic lore did the Gauls avoid writing, whereas they used writing for all other business, private and public. For the term 'use of letters' is often employed by Latin authors to mean 'write'. ^cThus Quintilian says:[11] 'I find Plato[12] claims writing hinders the memory.' ^aMoreover, it is contradictory to say both that the Gauls were ignorant of Greek, as did Caesar in the remark above, and that Greek letters were ^ccommonly ^aused in recording public and private accounts and transactions. However, many suppose 'Greek letters' in the passage cited means the use of Greek characters rather than writing in Greek. This will scarcely do, because, as mentioned, ancient writers in countless instances said 'use letters' to mean 'write', but never, so far as can be seen, to refer to the form of the characters.

Nor is this opinion supported by Caesar's remark in his first commentary[13] that 'tablets written in Greek letters were found in the Helvetian camp', for surely one who had learnt to write Greek characters would also have learnt to write in Greek, and there would have been priests or young noblemen who had learnt Greek, which was then valued and esteemed, just as today many learn Latin. The unique situation of the Marseille academy refutes this view. Hence, when Caesar refers to the letter he sent Cicero, he writes:[14] 'It was written in Greek letters so that, if intercepted, our plans would not be understood by the enemy.'* Justin states:[15] 'The senate forbade any Carthaginian thereafter to study written or spoken Greek, so as to prevent him, without an interpreter, from speaking or writing to the enemy.' In *Customs of the Germans* Tacitus says:[16] 'In Germany and south Switzerland

---

* *c*[1] *adds* Cicero states in his impeachment of Verres: 'So it was written in Carthaginian letters on these objects (he refers to the tusks sent from Africa by Masinissa to Melos) that King Masinissa had received them unwittingly, and, after discovering this, had had them sent back and restored.'

Monumenta et tumulos quosdam Graecis literis inscriptos in confinio
Germaniae Rhetiaeque adhuc extare. Livius lib. 9:[17] *Vulgo tum*
Romanos pueros, sicut nunc Graecis, ita Hetruscis literis erudiri
solitos. Idem lib. 28:[18] *Ibique aram Annibal condidit, dedicavitque*
5 *cum ingenti rerum ab se gestarum titulo, Punicis Graecisque literis*
insculpto. Item lib. 40:[19] *Literis Latinis Graecisque utraque ara*
inscripta erat. [b]Ulpianus iurisconsultus tit. de institor. act.:[20]
Proscribere sic accipimus, claris literis, utrum Graecis, an Latinis? Puto
secundum loci conditionem, ne quis causari possit ignorantiam liter-
10 *arum.* Trebell. Pollio in Aemiliano:[21] *Fertur enim apud Memphim*
in aurea columna Aegyptiis literis scriptum, tunc demum, etc.

[a]Denique non arbitror isto sensu dicturum Caesarem fuisse,
Graecis literis scribere, sed potius Graecarum literarum forma,
[b]vel figura, [c]vel notis. [a]Velut apud Tacitum lib. 11:[22] *Novas*
15 *literarum formas addidit, comperto Graecam literaturam non simul*
coeptam absolutamque. Et mox:[23] *Et formae literis Latinis quae*
veterrimis Graecorum. [b]Item apud Paulum Iurisc. sub tit. De oblig.
& actionibus:[24] *Non figura literarum, sed oratione quam exprimunt*
literae, obligamur. [c]Item apud Ciceronem, Tuscul. 1:[25] *Aut qui*
20 *sonos vocis, qui infiniti videbantur, paucis literarum notis terminavit.*
[a]Ac ne quis nimiopere admiretur vocem GRAECIS apud Cae-
sarem irrepsisse, proferam similem casum apud Plinium lib. 8,
cap. 57,[26] ubi sic scriptum est: *Gentium consensus tacitus primum*
omnium conspiravit, ut IONUM *literis uterentur.* Et mox,[27]
25 *Sequens gentium consensus in tonsoribus fuit.* Et mox:[28] *tertius con-*
sensus est in horarum observatione. Nam vocem IONUM tolendam
esse, quis non videt? non tam quia plane supervacanea est (nam ad
Plinii institutum satis fuit dicere, primum Gentium consensum
fuisse in scriptione et literatura) quam quia falsum est, IONUM

[17] IX, 36, 3; Loeb, IV, 302.   [18] XXVIII, 46, 16; Loeb, VIII, 198.   [19] XI, 39; Loeb, XII, 88.   [20] *Dig.* 14, 3, 11; Mommsen, I, 222.   [21] *Scr. hist. Aug.*, Trig. Tyran.: Aemilianus, XXII, 13; Loeb, III, 120.   [22] *Annales*, XI, 13; Loeb, 268.   [23] *Ibid.*, XI, 14; Loeb, 270.   [24] *Dig.* 44, 7, 28; Mommsen, I, 767.   [25] I, 25, 62; Loeb, 72.   [26] *Nat. Hist.*, VIII, 27; Loeb, II, 648.   [27] *Ibid.*, VII, 59; Loeb, II, 648.   [28] *Ibid.*, VII, 60; *loc. cit.*

there still stand monuments and tombs inscribed in Greek letters.' Livy writes:[17] 'At that time Roman boys were generally accustomed to learn Etruscan, as now they learn Greek.' And in another passage:[18] 'Hannibal there erected an altar, and dedicated it with a large inscription of all his achievements, carved in Carthaginian and Greek.' Elsewhere he states:[19] 'Each altar had been inscribed in both Latin and Greek letters.' [b]Ulpian the jurist writes in the Digest:[20] 'Should we then agree that a thing is published if it be in plain letters, whether they be Greek or Latin? I believe it depends upon local conditions and whether anyone can allege ignorance of letters.' Trebellius Pollio in his life of Scipio Aemilianus writes:[21] 'It is said that at Memphis it was written on a golden pillar in Egyptian letters that etc.'

[a]Finally, I do not think Caesar would have said 'writing Greek letters' in the sense attributed to him, but meant rather the shape, [b]form [c]or characters [a]of Greek letters. It is in this sense that Tacitus writes:[22] 'Finding that Greek modes of expression were not fixed from the moment of their inception, he added new forms of letters.' And, a little further on:[23] 'The forms of the Latin letters were the most ancient letters of the Greeks.' The same usage may be found in the jurist Paulus in the Digest:[24] 'We are placed under an obligation not by the shape of the letters but by the sense they express.' [c]It is also conveyed in the first of Cicero's Tusculan Disputations:[25] 'He ended the vocal sounds he had been emitting in a seemingly endless fashion with a few written characters.' [a]And lest anyone should be greatly puzzled how the word 'Greek' crept into this passage from Caesar, I offer a similar instance from Pliny where this is written:[26] 'At first the tacit agreement of all the people conspired to have them use the letters of the Ionians.' And, soon afterwards, appear the words:[27] 'The next agreement of the people concerned the manner of wearing their hair.' And then:[28] 'The third agreement was the manner of their reckoning time.' Now surely it is obvious that the words 'of the Ionians' should be deleted. They are quite superfluous, for all that Pliny wanted to say was that the first thing the people agreed upon was the form of their writing. And, what is more, it is an error to say that the first letters

primas fuisse literas, ut ipse Plinius superiore primo capite docuit,[29] et Tacitus lib. 11.[30]

Animadverti tamen apud Gregorium Turon. lib. 5, et Aimoinum lib. 3, cap. 41, locos duos, quibus significari videtur, 5 Gallos Graecarum literarum notis usos fuisse; nam ubi de Chilperico Rege loquuntur: *Addidit* (inquiunt[31]) *et literas literis nostris, id est* ω, ψ, ȝ, φ, *et misit epistolas in universas civitates regni sui, ut sic pueri docerentur.* Apud Aimoinum[32] autem tres tantum ponuntur χ, θ, φ. Verum intelligendum est, Francos istos fuisse, 10 non Gallos, vel potius Francogallos, qui Germanica lingua, id est, patria et nativa, non illa veterum Gallorum, quae Romanorum dominatu obsoleverat, utebantur; deinde si Francogalli Graecis literis usi fuissent, quid ita reliquas omnes, his solis exceptis, usurpassent? Verum haec quidem plus satis.

15 Superest eorum opinio, qui putant Gallos Germanica lingua usos fuisse, quos vel unus ille Caesaris [c]lib. 1 [a]refellit locus, in quo scribit,[33] *Ariovistum propter** longinquam in Gallia consuetudinem lingua Gallica usum esse.* [c]Eo accedat Taciti locus ille ex lib. De moribus Germanorum:[34] *E quibus Marsigni et Burii sermone* 20 *cultuque Suevos referunt, Gothinos Gallica, Osos Pannonica lingua coarguit non esse Germanos.* Planius autem hoc confirmat Suetonius in Caligula:[35] *conversus hinc*, inquit, *ad curam triumphi, praeter captivos et transfugas Barbaros, Galliarum quoque procerissimum quemque, et (ut ipse dicebat)* ἀξιοθρίαμβητον, *ac nonnullos* 25 *ex principibus legit, ac seposuit ad pompam, coegitque non tantum rutilare, et submittere comam, sed et sermonem Germanicum addiscere, et nomina Barbarica ferre.* Ubi planius contrariae sententiae testimonium Glareanus,[36] et alii Glareanum secuti protulerint, fidem illis habendam existimabo.

---

17 *c*[1] '*Ariovistum* Germanum *propter*'.

[29] This could be either *ibid.*, v, 13 (Loeb, II, 27) or VII, 56 (Loeb, II, 634) where Pliny attributes the invention of letters to the Phoenicians.   [30] As above, p. 162, n. 22.   [31] Greg. Tours, v, xliv; *MGH SS Mer.*, I:1[2], 254, 3 – also Aimon (next note) with the variant noted by Hotman.   [32] Cf. *PL*, CXCIII, 721. [33] Cf. *B.G.*, I, 47; Loeb, 78.   [34] Cap. 43; Loeb, 322.   [35] Cap. 47; Loeb, I, 476. [36] Loriti, *Commentariolus*, ed. 1579, 27–8.

were those of the Ionians, as Pliny himself earlier revealed,[29] and as Tacitus also said.[30]

However, I have noticed two passages, one from Gregory of Tours and the other from Aimon, which seem to indicate that the Gauls used the characters of the Greek letters. Of King Chilperic they say:[31] 'He added some letters to our own, namely, Ѡ, Ѱ, Z, Φ, and sent missives to all parts of his kingdom requiring boys to be taught them.' Aimon, on the other hand, mentions only three letters, X, Θ, Φ.[32] But it should be understood that these were Franks, not Gauls, or, rather, Francogauls, who used the native tongue of their fatherland, that is, the German language, not that of the ancient Gauls, which had fallen into disuse under the domination of the Romans. So if the Francogauls made use of Greek letters, how did they come to appropriate all the rest of the Greek alphabet while omitting only these particular characters? We have said more than enough on this issue.

There remains the opinion of those who think the Gauls used the German tongue, but there is a single passage in Caesar which refutes it, where he writes:[33] 'Ariovistus* spoke Gallic because of his long intimacy with Gaul.' ᶜA reference in Tacitus' *Customs of the Germans* agrees with this:[34] 'The Marsigni and Burii declared that the Suevi were Gallicised Goths in language and culture, and that likewise the Osi, who spoke the tongue of Pannonia, were not Germans.' Moreover, Suetonius confirms this with even greater clarity in his account of Caligula:[35] 'He turned his attention to arranging the triumphal procession, and, besides the prisoners and deserters among the barbarians, he chose all the tallest among the leading Gauls and some picked from the chiefs who (as he said himself) were ἀξιοθριάμβητον [worthy of the triumph], and he set apart for the procession some whom he not only had redden and grow their hair but also learn the German language and assume barbarian names.' Glareanus gives clearer evidence to the contrary[36] and there are some who have taken his opinion even further. I am inclined to think they should be believed.

---

* cᶦ Ariovistus the German.

Interea*a* duabus autem* de causis mihi eorum probabilis
opinio videtur,* qui scribunt, veterum Gallorum linguam
peculiarem, neque a Britannica* dissimilem fuisse: primum,
quia Caesar scribit[37] moris fuisse, ut qui Druydum disciplinam
5 diligentius cognoscere volebant, plerunque in Britanniam pro-
ficiscerentur. Cum autem libris nullis uterentur, consentaneum
est, eos* eodem quo in Gallia sermone usos in docendo fuisse.
Deinde quia Corn. Tacitus in Agricolae vita scribit[38] Britannorum et Gallorum sermonem haud multum diversum fuisse.
10 Neque mihi Beati Rhenani coniectura displicet,[39] qui sermonem
eorum qui hodie Britones Britonantes appellantur, veteris
nostrae linguae reliquias* fuisse arbitratur, iis de caussis, quas
satius est ex ipsius commentario cognosci, quam a nobis
describi,* *b*tum praecipue quia constat Britannos ab Anglis
15 Saxonibus patria pulsos in eam regionem profugisse. Unde illa
Eduardi I. Anglorum Regis lex vetus:[40] *Britones Armorici, cum*
venerint in Regno isto, suscipi debent et protegi, sicut probi cives de
corpore regni huius. Exierunt enim quondam de sanguine Britonum
*regni huius. a*Atque haec quidem de prisca Gallorum lingua dicta
20 sint.

Nostram autem qua iam utimur, non difficile intellectu est, ex
variis variarum gentium sermonibus conflatam esse. Ac, si
breviter dilucideque dicendum est, is quo iam utimur sermo,
quadripartito distribuendus est, ac dimidia eius pars Romanis
25 accepto ferenda; quemadmodum *b*Otto Frisingensis testatur
lib. Chronic. 4, cap. pen.[41] et *a*quivis Latinis literis tinctus potest
animadvertere. Nam praeterquam quod ita natura fert,* ut Galli
Romanis subiecti ad eorum se mores et linguam lubenter

1 *c* omits 'autem'; *ab* begin new sentence with 'Duabus'.   2 *c* 'videbitur'.
3 'peculiarem...Britannica': *bc* 'propriam, atque ab aliarum gentium, praeter
quam a Britannorum, sermone'.   7 *bc* 'illos'.   12 *c*[2] 'linguae relinguae
reliquias' [!].   14 'iis de caussis...nobis describi': *bc* 'cum aliis de caussis'.
27 *c* 'ferebat'.

37 Cf. *B.G.*, VI, 13; Loeb, 336.   38 Cap. 11; Loeb, 188.   39 *Rer. Germ.*, I,
'Britanni in Galliam'; ed. 1551, 77.   40 APXAIONOMIA, *sive de priscis Anglorum*
legibus libri, ed. Wm. Lambard (London, 1568), 136[v]–137.   41 *Chron.*, IV, 32;
MGH SS, XX, 213.

*a*Yet* for two reasons it seems to me very likely that there is truth in the view that the ancient Gauls had a particular language of their own, not very different from that of the Britons.† First, because Caesar writes[37] that it was very often the custom for those who wished to study closely the art of the Druids to journey to Britain. Since the Druids did not make use of books it is obvious that they taught in the same language employed in Gaul. Second, because Cornelius Tacitus writes in his *Life of Agricola*[38] that there was not much difference between the languages of the Gauls and the Britons. Moreover, I am inclined to accept the conclusion of Beatus Rhenanus[39] that the language of those who today call themselves Bretons is thought to be the remnant of our‡ ancient tongue. His arguments to this effect should be studied in his own commentary rather than set out here§ – *b*particularly since he maintains that when the Britons were expelled from their own country by the Anglo-Saxons they fled to that region. From this circumstance was derived that ancient law of Edward I, king of the English,[40] requiring that when the Bretons of Brittany visited England they should be supported and protected as though they were true citizens from the community of the kingdom, since they once stemmed from the blood of the Britons. *a*The same point may be made for the ancient language of the Gauls.

It is not difficult to perceive that the tongue we now speak is a mixture of the languages of several peoples. To put it succinctly, the tongue we now use should be classified under four heads. Half of it was constructed from borrowing from the Romans, *b*as Otto of Freising testifies in his chronicle,[41] *a*and as anyone familiar with Latin can observe. For, apart from the fact that it was natural for the Gauls, as subjects of the Romans, willingly to adapt themselves

---

* *c omits* Yet. † *bc* that the ancient Gauls...Britons *becomes* that the language peculiar to the ancient Gauls was different from the tongue of other peoples, though not from that of the Britons. ‡ *c²* *adds* abandoned. § *bc* His arguments... set out here *becomes* There are various reasons for this.

accommodarent, satis constat, Romanos ferendi sermonis Latini
studiosissimos fuisse, ut per omnes gentes venerabilior dif-
funderetur; quemadmodum Valerius Maximus testatur:[42]
eaque de causa ludos literarios passim instituisse, veluti Augusto-
5 duni, Vezontione, Lugduni, quod vel ex Tacito[43] et Ausonio[44]
cognosci licet. *c*Hieronymus ad Rusticum:[45] *Ac post studia
Galliarum, quae florentissima sunt, misit Romam, ut ubertatem
Gallici nitoremque sermonis gravitate Romana condiret.**

*b*Itaque tantum in Gallia Latinae linguae consuetudo valuit, ut
10 non modo leges ad summam Regni et Reipublicae pertinentes
Latinis literis conscriberentur (cuius rei cum vetustissima quaeque monimenta testimonio sunt, tum etiam Regum antiquorum
constitutiones, quarum quaedam extant in libro inscripto Stilus
curiae parlamenti[46]), verum etiam Latine et litigaretur, et
15 sententiae pronuntiarentur, ac praesertim litigandi rabiosa
quadam* consuetudine atque arte ex Pontificum Romanorum*
curia in Galliam introducta, potissimum autem ubi de sacerdotiis et eorum opimis vectigalibus litigari coeptum est; quod
institutum ad nostram usque aetatem servari solitum. Edictum
20 Francisci primi documento est, qui anno 1539 florescentibus
bonis in Gallia literis iussit,* ut Gallico sermone iudicia exercerentur.[47] Eodem* accesserat religionis disciplina et ratio; nam
cum Latinis ab initio literis tradita fuisset, cuius rei veteres
ecclesiastici testimonio sunt: Irenaeus, episcopus Lugdunensis;
25 Hilarius, Pictaviensis; Sidonius, Bituricensis; Salvianus, Massiliensis; Gregorius, Turonensis; postea Romanis ritibus ac cere-
moniis in Christianorum ecclesias introductis, multum ea consuetudo crevit; ac praesertim posteaquam Carolus Magnus

8 'Hieronymus ad...Romana condiret'. *c*[1] 'Augustin. de civit. [non invenio]
imperiosa non solum iugum, verum etiam linguam suam per pacem societatis
imponeret.' 16 *c*[1] omits 'rabiosa quadam'. 16 'Pontificum Romanorum':
c[1] 'Romana'. 21 *c* 'edixit'. 22 *c*[1] omits the long passage from here through
p. 170, l. 20.

42 Non invenio.   43 *Ann.* III, 43; Loeb, 590.   44 Cf. xx, 7; Loeb, II, 236.
45 (Letter cxxv [alias IV]) *PL*, xx, 1075; cf. above, p. 158, n. 9.   46 Cf. *Ordinationes* [or *Constitutiones*] *regiae antiquae* (see bibliography under Du Breuil,
Stilus), *passim*; ed. 1551, 157-232.   47 Cf. *Ordonnance royaulx sur le faict de la
justice* (6 Sept. 1539), cap. cxi; ed. Isambert, XII, 622.

to Roman customs and language, it is clear enough that the Romans were most assiduous in disseminating their tongue and inducing greater respect for it among all peoples. Valerius Maximus supports this view when he says[42] that for this purpose they established literary competitions everywhere, as, for instance, in Autun, Besançon and Lyon. This is established in Tacitus[43] and Ausonius.[44] cWe read in St Jerome's *Rural Letters*:[45] 'After studying in the flourishing academies of the Gauls he went to Rome to temper the richness and lustre of the Gallic tongue with Roman severity.'*

bThe use of the Latin tongue was much valued in Gaul, and in addition those laws concerning the welfare of the kingdom and the commonwealth were written in Latin (the oldest monuments bear witness to this practice, and so, too, do the enactments of the ancient kings, which still exist, in part, in the written records of the court of the parlement).[46] It is also true that Latin was used in legal pleadings and the promulgation of decisions, and especially in the vicious and fraudulent† legal practices introduced into Gaul from the court of the popes‡ of Rome. Before all else, this was the source of litigation about religious issues, with the copious fees that it involved. This practice had endured right up to our own age, as shown in the edict of Francis I, who in the year 1539 promoted the literary development of our language by requiring judgments to be given in French.[47]§ Religious learning and doctrine had come to resemble litigation, for doctrine had been expounded in Latin from the beginning, as the early clerics testify, including Irenaeus bishop of Lyon, Hilary of Poitiers, Sidonius of Bourges, Salvianus of Marseille, and Gregory of Tours. The usage became much more widespread when the Roman rites and ceremonies were later introduced into the Christian churches. It was especially so when, after obtaining the kingdom of Gaul by the influence and advice of

---

* c¹ We read...Roman severity *becomes* Augustine in his *City of God* says that the imperial power imposed not only its yoke but also its own language under pretext of general peace. † c¹ *omits* vicious and fraudulent. ‡ c¹ *omits* of the popes. § c¹ *omits remainder of paragraph.*

Galliae regnum Papae Zachariae ope consilioque adeptus, in tanti beneficii gratiam edixit, ut Romano more ritus ecclesiae servarentur, et cantiones haberentur, quae lex ipsius cum in Capitulari tum ᶜin ᵇlegibus Francicis his extat verbis:[48] *Ut*
5 *cantum Romanum pleniter discant, ordinaliter per nocturnalia, vel graduale officium peragatur, secundum quod beatae memoriae genitor noster Pipinus Rex decretavit, ut fieret, quando Gallicanum tulit, et ob unanimitatem Apostolicae sedis, et sanctae Dei Ecclesiae pacificam concordiam*; quod idem etiam Sigebertus sub anno 774 memoriae
10 prodidit,[49] quae res dici non potest, quantam et Gallicis ecclesiis caliginem offuderit, et pontificibus Romanis auctoritatem in negotiis religionis tribuerit, qua auctoritate cum illi adversus Galliae Reges mirandum in modum abuterentur, repertus est Rex Carolus quintus, cognomento Sapiens, qui circiter annum
15 MCCCLXX tyrannidi Pontificum infensus sacra Biblia in linguam Gallicam convertenda curavit, quam translationem multis etiam nunc locis in Gallia nostra videre licet, cum hac inscriptione: DE MANDATO ET IUSSU REGIS CAROLI QUINTI, eamque memini me in Regia bibliotheca Fontaneblaei
20 ᶜanno 1563, iterumque anno 1567 ᵇvidisse.[50]

ᵃAltera vero ᵇeius qua nunc utimur linguae ᵃdimidia pars ita distribuenda est, ut partem unam priscis Gallis attribuamus, alteram Francis, postremam Graecorum literis. Nam Francorum, id est (ut paulo post docebimus) Germanorum, innumeras in
25 quotidiano sermone nostro voces occurrere, iampridem a multis demonstratum est. Ex Graecorum vero lingua complura vocabula ad usum traducta nostrum fuisse, multi iam pridem* eruditi viri ostenderunt; cuius rei causa non Druydibus (quos Graece loquutos non arbitror*) sed Massiliensium consuetudini
30 ac disciplinis, de quibus* superius diximus, tribuenda est. ᶜUnde sensim ea consuetudo in reliquas Galliae regiones manavit.

---

27 'iam pridem': *c* 'quoque iam dudum'.   **29** *bc* 'quos Graece non loquutos docuimus'.   **30** 'consuetudini...quibus': *c* 'institutis ac disciplinae, de qua'.

[48] Ansegius, I, 74; *MGH LL*, II:I, 415.   [49] *MGH SS*, VI, 334, 23f.
[50] Undoubtedly the Raoul de Presles translation; see Berger, *Bible fran. au M.-A.*, 244f.

Pope Zachary, Charlemagne repaid so great a favour by declaring that both the rites of the church and the chants to be used should follow the Roman custom. This very law is expressed, first in the capitulary and then in the Frankish laws, in these words:[48] 'The Roman incantations shall be fully intoned, successively throughout the night: or, if desired, the ceremony shall be carried out alternatively in the way laid down by our parent King Pepin of blessed memory who, when he supported the Gallican practice, acted for the concord of the Apostolic See and the peaceful agreement of God's holy church.' Sigebert also published the same decree in the year 774.[49] This is a matter one can hardly bear to mention, so great was the darkness it spread over the Gallic churches. It conceded authority to the Roman pontiffs in religious matters, and its authors wronged the kings of France in a manner scarcely to be credited. Their own authority was regained by King Charles V, known as the Wise, who, in about the year 1370, became so incensed against the tyranny of the popes that he arranged the translation of the holy scriptures into French. This version of the Bible may now be seen in many places in the France of our own time, bearing the inscription BY ORDER AND COMMAND OF KING CHARLES V, and I myself can recall having seen it in the royal library of Fontainebleau, *c*once in the year 1563 and again in the year 1567.[50]

*a*The other half of the language *b*we now use *a*should be analysed as follows: we may credit a third to the ancient Gauls, a third to the Franks and a third to Greek influence. For it has long ago been shown by many writers that innumerable words occur in our daily speech which descend from the Franks, or rather from the Germans, as we shall shortly indicate. Many learned men have also long since revealed that a great many terms have been introduced for our use from the Greek tongue. As we have said earlier, this is not to be attributed to the Druids, who, I believe,* did not speak Greek, but rather to the practice and the learning of the people of Marseille. *c*From Marseille the practice spread gradually to other parts of Gaul.

---

* *bc* who, I believe, *becomes* because we have shown that they.

De statu Galliae a Romanis in provinciae formam redactae

Galliam a Romanis diu magnis saepe cladibus tentatam, tandemque a C. Caesare decenni prope bello, praeliisque compluribus domitam ac subactam fuisse atque ad extremum in provinciae formam redactam, eruditis omnibus notum est. Hoc
5 fortissimae et bellicosissimae gentis fatum fuit, ut Magnae Belluae (quemadmodum in sanctis literis appellatur[1]) tandem aliquando pareret; cum qua tamen ita per annos octingentos (ut Josephus testatur[2]) de imperio certarat, ut illa nullius alterius nationis armis aeque terreretur. Itaque Plutarchus in Marcello et
10 Camillo,[3] Appianus in lib. de civilibus bell. 2,[4] Livius lib. 8 et 10,[5] memoriae prodiderunt, Gallos Romanis usque eo formidolosos* fuisse, ut lege sancitum haberent, ne vacationes a militia, quae sacerdotibus et senibus permittebantur tumultu Gallico valerent, quod idem et Cicero Philippi. 2[6] commemorat
15 *b*itaque Salustius in Iugurth. scribit[7] Romanos omnibus temporibus ita statuisse, *alia omnia virtuti suae prona esse, cum Gallis pro salute, non pro gloria certasse.* *a*Quinetiam Caesar lib. 6 testatur,[8] atque ex eiusdem auctoritate Tacitus in lib. de moribus Germanorum commemorat,[9] *fuisse tempus cum Germanos Galli virtute*
20 *superarent, et ultro bella inferrent, ac propter hominum multitudinem trans Rhenum colonias mitterent.*

Tantae autem virtutis amissae iacturam, idem Tacitus amissae libertati tribuit, in libro de vita Agricolae:[10] *Nam Gallos,*

12 *bc* 'formidabiles'.

[1] The 'beast' of *Revelations*, 13ff., was identified with Rome.   [2] Quoted exactly below, p. 176, n. 18.   [3] Marcellus, IV, 2; Loeb, V, 440. Camillus, *passim* – *e.g.*, XX, 1; Loeb, II, 140.   [4] Cf. II, 120; Loeb, III, 504.   [5] Cf. VIII, 20, 3 & X, 16, 6; Loeb, IV, 78 & 416.   [6] Cf. VIII, 1, 3; Loeb, 366.   [7] CXIV, 2; Loeb, 378. [8] *B.G.*, VI, 24; Loeb, 348.   [9] Cap. 28; Loeb, 301 – referring to Caesar (previous note).   [10] Cap. 11; Loeb, 188.

^aCHAPTER III

The condition of Gaul after the Romans reduced it to a province

---

It is well known that the Romans made many attempts to conquer Gaul, and often suffered disastrous setbacks, until, after nearly ten years of war and many battles, Caesar at last totally subdued and tamed the country and reduced it to the status of a province. It was the fate of this, the strongest and most warlike of peoples, to submit in the end to the Great Beast, to use the holy words of scripture.[1] Nevertheless, as Josephus tells us,[2] for eight hundred years they had striven so hard with Rome for supremacy that the Romans feared the armed strength of no other nation as they did that of Gaul. Plutarch in his lives of Marcellus and Camillus,[3] Appian in his account of the civil wars,[4] and Livy in his history[5] all recorded that the Romans regarded the Gauls with such dread* that they had it enshrined in law that all exemptions from service in the militia, which were granted to priests and old men, were no longer valid in the event of a threat from the Gauls. Cicero records this in his *Second Philippics*,[6] ^band Sallust in his account of the Jugurthine Wars writes[7] that the Romans established it as a permanent rule that 'all other things were subordinated to the danger they presented, since a contest with the Gauls was not for glory but simply for preservation'. ^aEven Caesar writes to the same effect,[8] and Tacitus accepts his judgment in his *Customs of the Germans*.[9] They write that 'there was a time when the Gauls exceeded the Germans in valour, and carried war to their furthest boundaries, sending colonies across the Rhine because of the pressure of their own numbers'.

In his *Life of Agricola*[10] Tacitus attributes the decline of their great valour to the loss of their liberty. 'We accept the fact', he

---

* ***bc*** with such dread *becomes* as so formidable.

inquit, *in bellis floruisse accepimus; mox segnitia cum otio intravit,*
amissa virtute pariter ac libertate. Et quoniam amori patriae non-
nihil indulgendum est, age, praeclarum insuper illud de Gallorum virtute, Iustini testimonium proferamus, ex lib. 24:[11]
5 *Namque Galli,* inquit, *abundanti multitudine cum eos non caperent*
terrae, quae genuerant, trecenta millia hominum ad sedes novas
quaerendas velut peregrinantem miserunt. Ex his portio in Italia
consedit, quae et urbem Romam captam incendit, et portio Illyricos
sinus per strages barbarorum penetravit, et in Pannonia consedit; gens
10 *aspera, audax, bellicosa, quae prima post Herculem, cui ea res virtutis*
admirationem et immortalitatis fidem dedit, Alpium invicta iuga, et
frigore intractabilia loca transcendit. Ibi domitis Pannoniis per multos
annos cum finitimis varia bella gesserunt. Hortante deinde successu,
divisis agminibus alii Graeciam, alii Macedoniam, omnia ferro pro-
15 *terentes, petivere, tantusque terror Gallici nominis erat, ut etiam*
Reges non lacessiti ultro pacem ingenti pecunia mercarentur. Item lib.
sequen.:[12] *Quanquam Gallorum ea tempestate tantae foecunditatis*
iuventus fuit, ut Asiam omnem velut examine aliquo implerent.
Denique neque Reges Orientis, sine mercenario Gallorum exercitu,
20 *ulla bella gesserint, neque pulsi Regno ad alios quam ad Gallos con-*
fugerint. Tantus terror Gallici nominis, sive armorum invicta felicitas
erat, ut aliter neque maiestatem suam tutam, neque amissam recuperare
se posse, sine Gallica virtute, arbitrarentur. Atque haec quidem de
Gallorum bellicis laudibus et virtute dicta sint, quae tamen
25 (quemadmodum ex Tacito[13] modo dicebamus) amissa libertate
interiit. Nonnullas tamen civitates post formam provinciae a
Romanis constitutam libertati suae relictas, testis est Plinius
lib. 4, cap. 17,[14] veluti Nervios, Suessiones, Ulbanesses,
Leucos, nonnullos etiam foederatos: in iis, Lingones, Rhemoss
30 Carnutos, Aeduos; ^cquod etiam Tranquillus in Iulio hi,

---

[11] XXIV, 4, 1; Teubner, 142.   [12] XXV, 2, 8; Teubner, 147.   [13] As above, n. 10
[14] *Nat. Hist.,* IV, 17–18; Loeb, II, 200ff.

writes, 'that the Gauls distinguished themselves in warfare; but after a time sloth became the concomitant of leisure, for they lost their valour with their liberty'. In addition, patriotism may allow us to offer that celebrated tribute to the valour of the Gauls stated by Justin:[11] 'The Gauls', he writes, 'found their population to be so great that their lands no longer supported them, and so they sent three thousand men to wander in foreign lands in search of new dwelling places. Some of these settled in Italy and seized and burnt the city of Rome. Others penetrated the lands on the gulf of Dalmatia, massacred the opposing barbarians, and established themselves in Pannonia. They were a tough, bold and warlike people, the first after Hercules (who gained a reputation for valour and a promise of immortality for the deed) to cross the unconquered peaks and rough, freezing domain of the Alps. There they conquered the Pannonians and for many years waged various wars with neighbouring peoples. Then, encouraged by their success, they split into several bands, and, while some invaded Greece, others attacked Macedonia, destroying everything in their path. Such was the terror of their name that kings who were in no way threatened by them bought peace with vast sums of money.' In the following section he writes:[12] 'At that time the young men of Gaul bred so rapidly that they filled all Asia like a swarm of bees. No king in the eastern lands would make war without a mercenary army of Gauls, nor would a ruler seek refuge with any save the Gauls when he was driven from his kingdom. Such was the terror of the Gallic name, and so unbroken was Gallic military success, that no king felt secure on his throne, nor was any king able to recover his lost dominions, without the valour of the Gauls.' Such are the praises of the warlike nature and valour of the Gauls, and yet, as we have already explained in the words of Tacitus,[13] it all disappeared when they lost their liberty. However, some Gallic states retained their liberty after the Romans had converted Gaul into a province, as Pliny relates.[14] Such were the Nervii, the Suessiones, the Ulbanesses and the Leuci. Some of the confederate states were also free, as the Lingones, the Rhemi, the Carnutes and the Aedui. *c*This is confirmed by Suetonius in his *Julius* as

confirmat verbis:[15] *Omnem Galliam quae saltu Pyrenaeo, Alpi-*
busque, et monte Gebenna, fluminibusque Rheno et Rhodano
continetur patetque circuitu ad bis et tricies centena millia passuum,
praeter socias ac bene meritas civitates, in provinciae formam redegit,
5 *eique in singulos annos sestertium quadringenties stipendii nomine*
imposuit.

[a]Quae vero carum civitatum, quae in provinciae formam
redactae fuerant, forma et ratio extiterit, facile ex Critognati
Arverni verbis intelligi potest, apud Caesarem lib. 7:[16] *Quod si ea,*
10 inquit, *quae in longinquis nationibus geruntur ignoratis, respicite*
finitimam Galliam, quae in provinciam redacta, iure et legibus com-
mutatis, securibus subiecta, perpetua premitur servitute. [b]Itaque
Cicero pro Fonteio,[17] *Referta,* inquit, *Gallia negotiatorum est,*
plena civium Romanorum nemo Gallorum sine cive Romano quic-
15 *quam negotii gerit; numus in Gallia nullus sine civium Romanorum*
tabulis commovetur. [a]Triplex autem erat servitus: primum ut
imposito praesidio firmarentur, quanquam quae pacatae satis et
sedatae provinciae videbantur, in eas non magnae copiae
mittebantur. Galliam certe Josephus lib. belli Iud. 2 scribit,
20 Imperatoris Titi tempore mille tantum et ducentorum militum
praesidio firmatum fuisse: *quanquam,* inquit,[18] *annos fere octin-*
gentos de libertate cum Romanis pugnarint, et pene plures civitates,
quam Romanos milites praesidiarios habeant.

Alterum servitutis genus fuit, ut Provinciae Romanis sti-
25 pendiariae ac vectigales essent, eoque nomine publicanos apud se
habere cogerentur, id est harpiyas et hirudines, quae provincialium sanguinem exugebant. [c]Suetonius autem eo quem modo
protulimus loco,[19] itemque [a]Eutropius autem* lib. 6[20] memoriae [c]prodiderunt,* [a]Caesarem subactae Galliae tributi nomine
30 imperasse [c]in annos singulos [a]HS. quadringenties, hoc est,
scutatorum, ut nunc loquimur, decies centena millia. Tertia

---

28 *c* omits 'autem'.   **29** *ab* 'prodidit'.

[15] Suetonius, *Caesar*, 25; Loeb, I, 32.   [16] *B.G.*, VII, 78; Loeb, 494.   [17] §11;
Loeb, 316.   [18] *De bello Judaico*, II, 373; Loeb, II, 468.   [19] As above, n. 15.
[20] Cf. 6, xvii; *MGH AA*, II, 104, 4–6.

follows:[15] 'He reduced the whole of Gaul to the status of a province, that is the area bounded by the forests of the Pyrenees, the Alps and Mount Gebenna, and by the Rhine and Rhône rivers, and extending in a circumference of 3,200 miles. He imposed in the form of a tribute a tax of four hundred sesterces to be paid every year. The only exceptions he made were those states which were allies and had deserved well of him.'

[a]It is easy to understand the condition of those states which had been reduced to the position of a province from the words of Critognatus the Arvernian, as given by Caesar:[16] 'If you do not know what is being done by the Romans in distant lands, you need only examine neighbouring Gaul, which has been reduced to a province, its system of justice and laws altered, and its people subjected to Roman authority and oppressed by perpetual servitude.' [b]Thus Cicero in his speech on behalf of Fonteius declares:[17] 'Gaul is crammed with Roman merchants, and is so full of Romans that no Gaul conducts any business except through a Roman citizen. No silver coin circulates in Gaul without going through the accounts of Romans.' [a]Moreover, this servitude was threefold. First, they were held down by a garrison quartered upon them, although it is true that large forces were not sent into provinces which seemed peaceful and quiet. Josephus writes in his *History of the Jewish War* that in the time of the Emperor Titus Gaul was held by a garrison of no more than twelve hundred soldiers.[18] 'Although', he says, 'they fought for their liberty against the Romans for nearly eight hundred years, and had nearly as many states as the Romans had soldiers in garrison.'

There was another kind of servitude under which the provinces were obliged to pay taxes and tributes to the Romans. For that purpose they were obliged to receive tax-gatherers, or, rather, harpies and leeches, who sucked out the blood of the provinces. [c]We have quoted Suetonius[19] to the same effect, [a]and also* Eutropius, who recorded[20] that, when Caesar had conquered Gaul, he imposed an [c]annual [a]tribute of forty millions of sesterces, that is a million crowns in modern currency. The third form of

* *c omits* also.

provincialium servitus erat, ut ne legibus suis patriis uterentur, sed magistratus a populo Romano cum imperio et securibus mitterentur, qui in iis* ius dicerent. Hanc triplicem servitutem cum omnes fere provinciales, tum vero Galli nostri aegerrime
5 molestissimeque tulerunt. Itaque non longo post Caesaris victorias intervallo, imperante Tiberio, Cornel. Tacitus auctor est, *Galliae civitates ob continuationem tributorum, saevitiam foenoris, et superbiam praesidentium* (haec enim lib. 3 illius verba sunt[21]) *rebellionem fecisse*. Post etiam Nerone imperante, Suetonius
10 scribit, Gallos illius imperium pertaesos, ab ipso defecisse. *Talem Principem* (inquit cap. 40[22]) *paulo minus per XIII annos perpessus terrarum orbis tandem destituit, initium facientibus Gallis*. ᶜQuam maiorum nostrorum laudem eximiam satis pro dignitate praedicare non possumus, quod primi omnium in orbe terrarum tam
15 potentis Tyranni dominatum a suis cervicibus amoliri seseque ex immanis Tyranni servitute in libertatem vindicare coeperunt.

ᵃDivisae autem sunt a Romanis Galliae omnes in sexdecim provincias: Viennensem, Narbonensem primam, Narbonensem secundam, Aquitaniam primam, Aquitaniam secundam, No-
20 vempopulanam, Alpes maritimas, Belgicam primam, Belgicam secundam, Germaniam primam, Germaniam secundam, Lugdunensem primam, Lugdunensem secundam, Lugdunensem tertiam, Maximam Sequanorum, et Alpes Graecas, quemadmodum Antoninus in Itinerario,[23] et Sextus Ruffus tradunt.[24] Subtilius
25 autem singulas enumerat Ammianus Marcellinus lib. 15.[25]

Nunc, ut ad institutum revertamur, incredibile dictu est, quam indigne atque acerbe Galli Romanorum latrocinia tulerint, quamque crebrae ab iis defectiones rebellionesque numerentur; quanquam cum per se satis virium ad depellen-
30 dam Romanorum tyrannidem non haberent, vetus institutum tenebant, ut Germanos mercede conductos ad suum auxilium evocarent. Unde Francicarum coloniarum semina primum

---

3 'in iis': **c** 'apud eos'.
[21] *Ann.*, III, 40; Loeb, 586.   [22] Suetonius, *Nero*, 40; Loeb, II, 160.   [23] Cf. *Itinerarium Antonini Augusti, ad finem*; ed. Venice, 1518, fol. 187.   [24] Ed. 1845, 899.   [25] xv, 11, 7–15; Loeb, I, 190.

servitude was the prohibition of native provincial laws and the imposition of magistrates bearing the authority and insignia of the Roman people, with the power to declare law in the provinces. Nearly all the provinces, and, indeed, our Gallic people as a whole, endured this triple servitude with the utmost misery and resentment. Cornelius Tacitus relates that when Tiberius was Emperor, not so very long after Caesar's conquests, the states of Gaul rebelled against the continuation of the tribute moneys, the ferocity of the extortioners, and the proud insolence of the soldiery (and these are the actual phrases used by Tacitus[21]). Suetonius writes that later, during the reign of Nero, the Gauls became so disgusted with his rule that they threw off his authority. 'The entire world', writes Suetonius,[22] 'endured such a ruler for rather less than thirteen years before the Gauls gave the signal for a general renunciation of him.' *c*We cannot offer sufficiently high praise for the worth of our ancestors because they were the first in the world to begin to remove from their necks the yoke of so powerful a tyrant, and to claim for themselves release from their servitude under so monstrous an oppressor.

*a*All Gaul was divided by the Romans into sixteen provinces: Viennensis, Narbonensis Prima, Narbonensis Secunda, Aquitania Prima, Aquitania Secunda, Novempopulana, the Maritime Alps, Belgica Prima, Belgica Secunda, Germania Prima, Germania Secunda, Lugdunensis Prima, Lugdunensis Secunda, Lugdunensis Tertia, Maxima Sequanorum, and the Greek Alps. This is set out by Antoninus in his *Itinerary*[23] and by Sextus Rufus,[24] but it is Ammianus Marcellinus who lists them separately in greater detail.[25]

To return to our main theme, it is difficult to conceive both the shame and bitterness with which the Gauls endured the plundering of the Romans and the frequency with which they rebelled against them. Since they had not enough of their own men to throw off the Roman tyranny, they took to that ancient custom of hiring German mercenaries to come to their aid. In this way the first Frankish colonies began. For the Germans, who were either conquered by

exorta sunt. Nam Germani sive a Romanis victi, sive (quod probabilius videtur) pretio empti, coepere sensim in Galliae finibus sedes collocare. Hinc illud Suetonii in Augusto:[26] *Germanos ultra Albim fluvium summovit, ex quibus Suevos et Sicambros*
5 *dedentes se traduxit in Galliam, atque in proximis Rheno agris collocavit.* Idem in Tiberio:[27] *Germanico bello quadraginta millia dedititiorum traiecit in Galliam, iuxtaque ripam Rheni sedibus assignatis collocavit.* Neque vero praetereundum est, quod Flavius Vopiscus de Probi Caesaris imperio memoriae prodidit, quo tempore uni-
10 versa prope Gallia, hoc est, sexaginta civitates, ab imperio Romano desciverunt, armaque communi consilio libertatis recuperandae caussa ceperunt: *His gestis,* inquit,[28] *cum ingenti exercitu Gallias petit, quae omnes occiso Postumo turbatae fuerunt, interfecto Aureliano a Germanis possessae. Tanta autem illic praelia*
15 *feliciter gessit, ut a Barbaris sexaginta per Gallias nobilissimas reciperet civitates. Et cum iam per omnes Gallias securi vagarentur, caesis prope quadringentis millibus, qui Romanum occupaverant solum, reliquias ultra Nicrum fluvium et Albim removit.* Quam crudelis autem et immani Romanorum dominatus fuerit, quam
20 acerba latrocinia, quam tetra, et obscoena vitae consuetudo, quantoque illa odio atque acerbitati Gallis hominibus, sed praesertim Christianis fuerit, nullius opinor ex scriptis, melius quam ex Salviani Massiliensis Episcopi libris de providentia,[29] cognosci potest. Itaque incredibile dictu est, quantae Ger-
25 manarum gentium copiae Gallis non modo faventibus, verumetiam adiuvantibus, sese in Gallias effuderint. Unde illud Latini Pacati ad Theodosium:[30] *Unde igitur exordiar, nisi a tuis Gallia malis, quae ex omnibus terris, quas illa pestis insederat, haud iniuria tibi vindicas privilegium miseriarum?* Earum autem Ger-
30 manicarum gentium partem Francos nostros fuisse, cum ex Sidonio Apollinari,[31] tum vero praesertim ex illius Salviani locis compluribus[32] planissime intelligitur.

[26] Cap. XXI; Loeb, I, 150. [27] Cap. IX; Loeb, I, 304. [28] *Scr. hist. Aug.,* Probus, XIII, 5–6, 7; Loeb, III, 362f. [29] Esp. VII, xv (§62); *MGH AA,* I:1, 95.
[30] *Latini Pacati Depanii panegyricus Theodosio Augusto dictus,* xxiv; ed. Galletier, III, 91. [31] Quoted below, ch. IV, n. 40 (p. 192) and ch. v, n. 17 (p. 206).
[32] See above, n. 29.

the Romans or, as seems more probable, were bought off by them, began gradually to establish settlements within the boundaries of Gaul. Suetonius remarks on this in his life of Augustus:[26] 'He drove the Germans beyond the River Elbe, except for the Suevi and the Sicambri, who had accepted his authority. These he sent into Gaul and provided with land near the Rhine.' In his life of Tiberius Suetonius writes:[27] 'He transferred to Gaul forty thousand of those who had surrendered during the German war, and settled them on the banks of the Rhine.' Nor should we pass over what Flavius Vopiscus recorded concerning the rule of the Emperor Probus. In his time nearly the whole of Gaul, that is, sixty states, disavowed the authority of Rome and with one mind took up arms to recover their liberty. 'When Probus had done these things', Vopiscus writes,[28] 'he attacked Gaul with a huge army. The country had been thrown into anarchy at the slaying of Posthumus, and when Aurelian was killed it was occupied by the Germans. Probus successfully fought so many battles there that he recovered from the barbarians sixty of the noblest states in Gaul. For a time the Germans wandered at will throughout the whole country, but he slaughtered nearly four hundred thousand of those who had occupied Roman territory, and removed the survivors beyond the Neckar and Elbe Rivers.' The works which Salvianus, the bishop of Marseille, wrote on providence[29] best enable us to understand how cruel and oppressive was the rule of the Romans, how violent were their exactions, how abominable and obscene was the manner of their living, and how bitterly they were hated by the men of Gaul, and especially by the Christians. Thus it is far from surprising that such multitudes of Germans should pour into Gaul and that the Gauls, far from hindering the flood, should actively encourage it. Latinus Pacatus addressed these words to Theodosius:[30] 'How, therefore, should I begin unless it be with your wrongs, O Gaul! Of all the countries which that plague has infected, surely you may claim the greatest suffering.' It is abundantly clear from the writings of Sidonius Apollinaris,[31] and especially from the many passages in the works of Salvianus,[32] that our Franks were part of that influx of German peoples.

*a*CAPUT IV

De ortu Francorum, qui Gallia occupata, eius nomen in Franciam vel Francogalliam mutarunt

Quare instituti nostri ratio postulat, ut hoc loco de Francorum ortu, primisque sedibus et tanquam incunabulis inquiramus. Qua in disquisitione illud summe admirandum videtur, quod cum Francorum nomen per tot annos magnam totius Europae
5 partem occuparit, eamque Germaniae gentem fuisse constet, tamen eorum mentio neque apud Ptolemaeum, neque apud Strabonem, aut Plinium, ac ne apud Cornelium quidem Tacitum ulla reperiatur, qui tamen Germanicarum omnium gentium situs et nomina mira diligentia persecutus est. Nam de Francici quidem
10 nominis amplitudine pauca haec ex multis testimonia proferemus.

Primum ex *c*Hieronym. in vita Hilarionis Heremitae:[1] *Namque*, inquit, *candidatus Constantii Imperatoris, rutila coma, et candore corporis, indicans provinciam; inter Saxones quippe et Alemannos gens est non tam laeta, quam valida, apud historicos*
15 *Germania, nunc vero Francia vocatur.* Et paulo post:[2] *Et qui Francam tantum et Latinam linguam noverat.* Item ex *a*Iohan. Nauclero, Generat. 27, ubi sic loquitur:[3] *Carolus Magnus Rex Francorum dicebatur, quod idem erat ac si nominatus fuisset Rex Germaniae et Galliae. Nam clarum est, quod eo tempore omnis Gallia*
20 *Transalpina, et etiam Germania, a montibus Pyrenaeis usque in Pannonias, Francia dicebatur: illa, id est, Germanica, Francia Orientalis; alia, id est, Gallica, Francia Occidentalis.*[*] In quo verae historiae consentiunt omnes. *c*Haec ille. Itaque Abbas Urspergensis in Carolo Calvo Franciam Orientalem Ostrofranciam
25 appellat;[4] Occidentalem autem Neustriam appellatam fuisse,

---

22 *c²* omits 'alia...Occidentalis'.

[1] *PL*, XXIII, 40.   [2] *Ibid.*, 41.   [3] Ed. 1579, 683.   [4] Ekkehard, *Chronicon*, A.D. 887; *MGH SS*, VI, 173, 14.

^aCHAPTER IV

The origin of the Franks, who, when they had
occupied Gaul, changed its name to France or
Francogallia

Our argument now requires us to inquire into the place of origin of
the Franks, into their original settlements and the cradle of their
race. It is certain that the people who bore that name occupied a
large part of Europe for many years and that they were German.
Hence it is very surprising that no mention is made of them by
Ptolemy, Strabo and Pliny, and especially that no reference is to be
found in Cornelius Tacitus, who traced the locations and names of
all the German peoples with extraordinary diligence. We offer some
few examples from the many references which attest the importance of the Frankish name.

First, ^cSt Jerome in his *Life of Hilary the Hermit* remarks:[1] 'The
man whom the Emperor Constantine supported had red hair and
a white skin, indicating that he was a provincial. Among the Saxons
and Alemanni that people is strong rather than agreeable, and used
to be called Germans by the historians, though now they are called
Franks.' A little further on Jerome writes:[2] 'He had known a good
deal of the Frankish tongue as well as Latin.' Another example is
from ^athe chronicle of Johannes Nauclerus, where he says:[3]
'Charlemagne was called king of the Franks, which is the same
thing as saying he had been declared king of Germany and Gaul.
It is well known that at that time the whole of Transalpine Gaul
and Germany, stretching from the Pyrenees as far as Pannonia, was
called France [*Francia*]. The latter was called Germany or Eastern
France, the former Gallica or Western France.'* All historians agree
as to the truth of this statement. ^cAgain, the abbot of Ursperg in his
Life of Charles the Bald[4] calls Eastern France Ostrofrancia, whereas

---

* *c omits* the former Gallica or Western France.

quasi Wcstriam, annotavit Rhenanus.[5] Unde Sigebertus
in Chronico:[6] *Ebroinum*, inquit, *maiorem domus Neustriae*. Et
mox:[7] *Pipinus sibi Neustriam subiugat.* Sic etiam Aimoinus lib. 4,
cap. 27,[8] et alibi pcrsaepe. Chronicum vero Maioris Monasterii[9]
5 sic habet: Neustria est quicquid a Parisiis et Aurclianis interiacet
inter Ligerim et Sequanam inferius usque ad Oceanum. Sic
enim Abbas Ursperg.[10] Et hac de caussa Otto Frising. duo
Francorum regna numerat. Nam lib. 4, cap. 3, de donatione
Constantini sic scribit:[11] *Ex hinc Romana Ecclesia Occidentalia*
10 *regna tanquam sui iuris a Constantino sibi tradita affirmat, in argu-*
mentumque tributum, exceptis duobus Francorum regnis usque hodie
exigere non dubitat. ᵃEguinarthus in vita Caroli Magni:[12]
ᵇ*Carolus*, inquit, *regnum Francorum quod post patrem Pipinum*
magnum quidem et forte susceperat, ita nobiliter ampliavit, ut pene
15 *duplum illi adiecerit. Nam cum prius non amplius quam ea pars*
Galliae, quae intra Rhenum et Ligerim, Oceanumque et mare
Balearicum iacet, et pars Germaniae, quae intra Saxoniam et Danu-
bium, Rhenumque ᵃ*ac Salam fluvium qui Thoringos et Sorabos*
dividit,* *postea a Francis, qui Orientales dicuntur, incolitur,* ᵇ*et*
20 *praeter haec Alemanni atque Baioarii ad regni Francorum potestatem*
pertinerent, ipse per bella memorata primo Aquitaniam, etc.

    ᵃOtto Frising. Chron. lib. 5, cap. 9:[13] *Erat autem Francorum iam*
terminus (loquitur de Dagoberti Regno) *ab Hispania usque in*
Pannoniam, duos nobilissimos ducatus, Aquitaniam et Baioariam. Sed
25 multo copiosius postea lib. 6, cap. 17,[14] eumque imitatus
Godefridus Viterb. Chron. parte 17, sub anno 881:[15] *Porro*,
inquit, *Arnulphus totam Orientalem Franciam, quae hodie Teu-*

---

19 bc drop '*qui Thoringos et Sorabos dividit*'.

[5] *Rer. Germ.*, I, 'Nortmanni in Galliam'; ed. 1551, 77.   [6] A.D. 688; *MGH SS*,
VI, 327, 63.   [7] A.D. 691; *MGH SS*, VI, 328, 6.   [8] Cf. *PL*, CXXXIX, 786.
[9] I cannot find this in the writings of Abbot Majoris Monasterii, eds. 1610 or
1854; I know of no edition in Hotman's time.   [10] Ekkehard, *Chronicon*, cf.
A.D. 743; *MGH SS*, VI, 158, 45.   [11] *Chron.*, IV, 3; *MGH SS*, XX, 196, 42.
[12] C. 15; *MGH SS*, II, 450, 30–6. The 1573 quotation is maladroit, suggesting that
part of it (i.e., what was later added) was accidentally dropped by the compositor
in 1573.   [13] *Chron.*, V, 9; *MGH SS*, XX, 220, 2.   [14] *Ibid.*, VI, 17; *loc. cit.*,
234, 5.   [15] Partic. XXIII, 24; *MGH SS*, XXII, 230, 33ff.

Western France was called Neustria, or Westria, as Rhenanus[5]
commented. Thus Sigebert writes in his chronicle:[6] 'Ebroinus was
the Neustrian mayor of the palace', and, in a latter passage:[7]
'Pepin subdued Neustria.' Aimon has the same usage in one
particular passage[8] and also employs it on many other occasions.
The *Chronicle of the Greater Monastery* has this to say:[9] 'Neustria is
the land of the Parisii and the Aureliani and extends from the Loire
and the lower Seine to the Great Ocean.' The abbot of Ursperg
says the same,[10] and Otto of Freising in this context lists two
Frankish kingdoms. Concerning the donation of Constantine he
writes:[11] 'Hence the Western Roman Church maintains that the
kingdoms were legally transferred to it by Constantine, and its
right to exact tribute even today is not doubted, except for the
two Frankish kingdoms.' [a]Einhard in his *Life of Charlemagne*
writes:[12] [b]'Charles had received the mighty kingdom of the
Franks from his father Pepin the Great, and he so nobly extended its
boundaries that he nearly doubled its size. Formerly it was not
larger than that part of Gaul which lies between the Loire and the
Rhine, the ocean and the Balearic Sea, and included a part of
Germany between Saxony and the Danube and between the Rhine
[a]and the River Sala, which divides the Thuringians from the
Sorabi.* Later this area was inhabited by the so-called Eastern
Franks. [b]Beyond these the Alemanni and the Bavarians passed
into the power of the Frankish kingdom. Through various
memorable wars he first conquered Aquitaine, etc.'

　　[a]Otto of Freising writes in his chronicle concerning the kingdom
of Dagobert:[13] 'The land of the Franks now extended from Spain
as far as Pannonia, including two most noble duchies, Aquitaine
and Bavaria.' He gives much greater detail in a later passage.[14]
Godfrey of Viterbo follows him in his chronicle for the year 881:[15]
'Arnulf ruled all Eastern France, which today is called the kingdom

---

* **bc** *omit* which divides the Thuringians from the Sorabi.

tonicum regnum vocatur, id est Bavariam, Sueviam, Saxoniam,
Turingiam, Phrigiam, et Lotharingiam rexit. Occidentalem vero
Franciam Odo tenuit. Idem sub anno 913:[16] *Mihi ex multis*
scriptorum auctoritatibus patuit, regnum Teutonicorum, quod Im-
5 *perator Fridericus nostro tempore possidet, partem esse regni Fran-*
corum. Ibi enim primi Franci fuerunt, cis citraque Rhenum, quae hodie
Francia Orientalis usque ad terminos Bavariae appellatur. Francia vero
Occidentalis, est regnum illud, quod est cis citraque Sequanam et
Ligerim fluvios. Et mox:[17] *Tempore Caroli Magni regis Francorum,*
10 *tota Gallia, id est Celtica, Belgica, Lugdunensis, omnisque Germania,*
quae est a Rheno usque ad Illyricum, una Francia fuit; quae omnia
ex Ottone, ut dixi, fere descripta sunt.

*b*Vitichindus Saxo lib. 1:[18] *Ultimus Carolorum apud Orientales*
Francos imperantium Lothovicus etc. *a*Notandum etiam est, quod
15 Regino in Chron. anni DLXXVI ita scribit:[19] *Mortuo Pipino Rege,*
Ludovicus eius filius, qui ad patris obitum fuerat, et funeris eius
obsequia celebraverat, apud Francofurt, Orientalis regni principalem
sedem, residebat. *c*Abbas Ursperg.:[20] *Carolus Magnus duas habuit*
filias, de Foestrada uxore, quae de Orientalium Francorum, scilicet
20 *Germanorum gente erat.* Idem de orig. Sax.:[21] *Theodoricus, cum*
Austrasiam accepisset, cuius regni sedes apud Metensem fuit civitatem.
*a*Liutprandus Ticin. lib. 1, cap. 6:[22] *Simul ut Wido, quam Ro-*
manam dicunt Franciam, Berengarius Italiam obtineret. Et paulo
post:[23] *Cumque Burgundionum regna transiens, Franciam, quam*
25 *Romanam dicunt, ingredi vellet,* etc. Romanam autem Franciam
iccirco appellabant, primum quia Galliam quae Romanis paru-
erat, Franci occuparant; deinde quoniam Romana lingua in ea
regione usitata erat, quemadmodum superius diximus; unde
vetus nata locutio, Loqui Romanum, de iis qui Germanice sive
30 Francice non loquebantur. *b*Indidemque factum est, ut eadem
Gallia Romana diceretur. Regino lib. 2, sub anno 939:[24]

---

[16] Partic. XXIII, 27; *MGH SS*, XXII, 232, 12ff.　　[17] *Ibid.*; lines 22ff.　　[18] Widukind, I, 16; *MGH SS*, III, 425, 12.　　[19] (A.D. 876) *MGH SS*, I, 588, 28ff.
[20] Ekkehard, *Chronicon*, A.D. 783; *MGH SS*, VI, 167, 6.　　[21] *Ibid.*, A.D. 919 'De
Origine Saxonum'; *MGH SS*, VI, 176, 52.　　[22] (I, 14) *MGH SS*, III, 280, 20.
[23] I, 16; *ibid.*, 280, 40.　　[24] *MGH SS*, I, 618, 12ff.

of the Teutons, namely Bavaria, Suabia, Saxony, Thuringia, and Lorraine. Odo held Western France.' There is another passage for the year 913 :[16] 'It is clear from many authorities that the kingdom of the Teutons, which the Emperor Frederick possessed in our own day, was a part of the kingdom of the Franks, for the Franks were the first to inhabit the area on both banks of the Rhine, which, as far as the boundaries of Bavaria, is now called Eastern France. Western France is that kingdom which extends on both banks of the Seine and Loire Rivers.' And later he writes:[17] 'When Charlemagne was king of the Franks, the whole of Gaul, that is Celtica, Belgica and Lugdunensis, and all Germany from the Rhine to Illyria, composed the single kingdom of France.' As I have said, a description of all these matters is given by Otto of Freising.

*b*Widukind the Saxon writes in his first book:[18] 'The last of the Carolingian emperors of the Eastern Franks was Lothar etc.' *a*It is also to be noted that Regino of Prüm writes in his chronicle for the year 576:[19] 'After the death of King Pepin, his son Louis, who had been present at his father's death and had celebrated his funeral obsequies, resided in Frankfurt, the principal centre of the eastern kingdom.' *c*The abbot of Ursperg writes:[20] 'Charlemagne had two daughters by his wife Foestrada, who was one of the Eastern Franks or Germans.' The same author says in his treatise on Saxon origins:[21] 'Theuderic had accepted Austrasia, and the centre of this kingdom lay in the district of Metz.' *a*Liutprand of Tessino observes:[22] 'Thus Guido was to obtain what is termed Roman France, and Berengar was to have Italy.' A little further on he remarks:[23] 'Passing through the kingdom of the Burgundians, he wished to enter what men call Roman France etc.' They called France 'Roman' because, in the first place, the Gaul which the Franks occupied had earlier been seized by the Romans, and, secondly, because the Roman language had been used in that country, as we have said before. From this was derived that old expression 'speaking Roman' used to distinguish those who did not speak either the German or the Frankish tongue. *b*Another usage is the expression 'Roman Gaul', as in Regino's second book under the year 939:[24] 'Meanwhile Louis, the king of

Interim Ludovicus Rex Galliae Romanae, filius Caroli, consilio ini-
micorum Regis Alsatiam invadit. Hinc illud *ᵃ*Ottonis Frising.
Chron. 4, cap. pen.:[25] *Videtur mihi inde Francos, qui in Galliis*
morantur, a Romanis linguam eorum, qua usque hodie utuntur, ac-
5 *commodasse. Nam alii qui circa Rhenum, ac in Germania reman-*
serunt, Theutonica lingua utuntur. Et hunc *ᵇ*nimium familiariter
*ᵃ*imitatus *ᶜ*multis locis *ᵃ*Godfridus Viterb. parte 17, cap. 1:[26]
Videntur, inquit, *mihi Franci in illis temporibus linguam Romanam,*
qua usque hodie utuntur, ab illis Romanis, qui ibi habitaverant,
10 *didicisse.* His ex locis perspicuum est, miram Francorum nominis
amplitudinem atque auctoritatem fuisse, quippe, cum magnam
Europae partem occuparet.

Quinetiam videmus Germanos in Neapolitanum et Siculum
regnum ab Imp. Friderico II traductos, ibique tanquam colonos
15 praesidio collocatos, Francorum nomine appellatos fuisse. Petrus
de Vineis libro Epist. 6, cap. 25:[27] *Vivens iure Francorum, in eo*
videlicet, quod maior natu, exclusis minoribus fratribus, in castro ipso
succedat. Imp. Fridericus II, Neapol. const. lib. 2, tit. 32:[28]
Ingerentes se casus praesentis materiae circa Francos, qui personarum
20 *suarum, plurimarumque rerum suarum omnium fortunam in mono-*
machiam, quae Duellum vulgariter dicitur, reponebant. Et mox:[29]
Praedictum igitur probationis modum, quo iure Francorum viventes
utebantur. Item lib. 2, tit. 33:[30] *Quod ius inter omnes tam Francos,*
quam Longobardos in caussis omnibus volumus esse commune.

25   Haec cum ita sint, tamen Gregorius Turon. Episcopus, qui de
Francorum ortu octingentis ab hinc annis scripsit, initio historiae
suae testatur,[31] se, cum accurate de Francorum ortu quaesivisset
nihil tamen certi comperisse, quamvis veterem quendam illorum

---

[25] *Chron.,* IV, 32; *MGH SS,* XX, 213, 8.   [26] Partic. XXII, 40; *MGH SS,* XXII, 202, 7–8.   [27] Ed. 1740, II, 197.   [28] Ed. 1534, fol. 67.   [29] *Ibid.*   [30] *Ibid.,* fol. 68ᵛ. [31] Cf. II, 9; *MGH SS Mer.,* 1:1², 52, 9 (Sulpitius Alexander does not survive outside Gregory's citation).

Roman Gaul and the son of Charles, invaded Alsatia by the advice of the king's enemies.' In this sense *a*Otto of Freising writes in his fourth chronicle:25 'It seems to me that the Franks who lived in Gaul adapted their language as a result of their contact with the Romans and so produced the tongue they speak today, while others who remained near the Rhine and in Germany employed Teutonic speech.' *c*In many passages *a*this opinion has been *b*closely *a*followed by Godfrey of Viterbo:26 'The Franks seem to me', he writes, 'to have learnt in those times the Roman language they still use today, and to have learnt it from those Romans who had once lived there.' It is perfectly clear from these references that both the Frankish name and the breadth of their authority were widely recognised, which one might expect, since they held a large part of Europe.

Furthermore, we read that those Germans, who were moved into the kingdom of Naples and Sicily by the Emperor Frederick II and established in colonies there as a garrison, were described as Franks. Thus Petrus de Vinea writes in his *Letters*:27 'The Frankish law that the eldest son should succeed to an inheritance to the exclusion of his younger brothers applied even within the garrison camp itself.' The Emperor Frederick II refers to the Franks by name in his *Neapolitan Constitutions*:28 'Those who were anxious to press some existing grievance against the Franks soon laid it aside, because the Franks were wont to venture their persons and all their goods in a trial by ordeal, or as it is commonly called, in a duel.' A little later the emperor writes:29 'They used, therefore, the aforesaid manner of trial appropriate to those observing Frankish law.' Or again:30 'It is our will that the law observed by the Franks and the Lombards shall be generally applied to all legal causes.'

These matters seem clearly established, and yet Gregory bishop of Tours, who wrote about the origin of the Franks eight hundred years earlier, declares at the beginning of his history that, though he had conducted detailed researches into the problem, he had found nothing at all that was certain.31 Gregory possessed an ancient work by one of their historians, Sulpicius Alexander, but he had nothing

historicum habuerit Sulpitium Alexandrum, qui neque de primis
illorum sedibus, neque de Regni primordiis quicquam affirmarit.
At nos ex ea regione Francos primum ortos animadvertimus,
quae inter Albim et Rhenum interiecta, Oceano alluitur, ubi fere
5 Chauci maiores et minores collocantur, *populus* (ut ait Tacitus[32])
inter Germanos nobilissimus, quique magnitudinem suam iustitia
tuetur, et Batavorum regioni finitimus erat. Nam primum
omnium satis constat, Francos in ora maritima sedes habuisse,
locis admodum palustribus, reique nauticae peritissimos, et in
10 bellis maritimis exercitatissimos fuisse. Quarum rerum docu-
menta haec extant, primum apud Claudianum, qui Stiliconi
victorias gratulans, ita scribit:[33]

> *Ut iam trans fluvium non indignante Chayco,*
> *Pascat Belga pecus mediumque ingressa per Albin*
15 > *Gallica Francorum montes armenta pererrent.*

Quo loco Chaycos poetice appellavit, quos Geographi Chaucos
nominarunt.

De maritima vero illorum regione Panegyricus Constantino
Magno dictus, testimonio est, ubi Rhetor ita loquitur:[34] *Quid*
20 *loquar rursus intimas Franciae nationes, non iam ab his locis quae olim*
Romani invaserunt, sed a propriis ex origine suis sedibus, atque ab
ultimis Barbariae litoribus avulsas, ut in desertis Galliae regionibus
collocatae, pacem Romani imperii cultu iuvarent, et arma delectu.
Rursus in altero Eumenii Rhetoris Panegyrico, ubi sic loquitur:[35]
25 *Aut haec ipsa, quae modo desinit esse Barbaria, non magis feritate*
Francorum, velut hausta desederat, quam si eam circumfusa flumina et
mare alluens operuisset. Eodemque pertinet Procopii testimonium
belli Gottici lib. 1, nam ubi eum locum describit, quo Rhenus in
Oceanum influit:[36] *His,* inquit, *locis non mediocres sunt paludes, ubi*
30 *antiquitus Germani habitabant, natio barbara nec magnae tum existi-*

---

[32] *Germ.,* 35; Loeb, 312.   [33] *De consulatu Stilichonis,* 225–7; Loeb, 380.
[34] *Panegyr. Constantino Aug.,* vi; Galletier [No. VII (6)], II, 58.   [35] *Oratio de*
scholis, ed. 1570, 24ʳ.   [36] v, xii, 8; Loeb, III, 110.

to say about their first place of origin nor about the origins of their kingdom. Nevertheless, we have noted that the original Franks came from that area lying between the Elbe, the Rhine and the sea, close to the country where the greater and lesser Chauci were settled, 'a people', as Tacitus says,[32] 'who were the most noble among the Germans, and who maintained their greatness by following the path of justice'. This was the region which bordered on the country of the Batavi, for it is generally agreed that the Frankish settlements were on the sea coast among the marshes, and that the Franks excelled in seamanship and in naval warfare. There is evidence to support this, first in the work of Claudian, who wrote a poem to celebrate the victories of Stilicho:

> 'Beyond the river Belgian cattle feed;
> Gone are the Chayci who resisted them.
> The Gallic herds that pass across the Elbe
> Roam onwards o'er the mountains of the Franks.'[33]

In this passage the author uses poetic licence to call Chayci the people whom the geographers name Chauci.

The panegyric to Constantine the Great provides evidence of the fact that the Franks lived near the sea. The panegyrist declaims:[34] 'Let me speak again of the most remote peoples of Francia, who were forcibly removed, not from the places which the Romans had formerly annexed, but from their pristine settlements on the furthest shores of the barbarian lands, and who were established in the wastelands of Gaul to help keep the peace of Roman authority by cultivating the soil and by levying arms.' Again, in another panegyric by the orator Eumenius the following statement appears:[35] 'Where once the savagery of the Franks seemed to engulf all things, this barbarity now ceases to exist, as if it had been drowned by their rivers pouring in upon it, or by the sea washing it away.' The testimony of Procopius in the first book of his *Gothic War* is to the same effect, for he describes how, at the point where the Rhine enters the sea,[36] 'there exist extensive marshes which were inhabited by the Germans in ancient times, when they were a barbarous people of slight renown – the same who now are called

mationis homines, qui nunc Franci nominantur. Eumque* Procopii locum Zonaras commemorat* Annal. tom. 3 [37] ^cretulit; Zosimus autem in Gothici belli librum primum.[38] ^aItemque ille* Flav. Vopisci locus, in vita Probi Imp. ubi scribit, Francos a Probo
5 inviis paludibus profligatos: *Testes sunt,* inquit,[39] *Franci, inviis strati paludibus.* Item illud Sidonii Apollinaris,[40]

> *Francorum et penitissimas paludes*
> *Intrares venerantibus Sicambris.*

Iam vero quod de Chaucorum vicinitate diximus, ea planis-
10 sime ex collatione locorum, et utrorumque sedium descriptione perspicitur. Chaucorum quidem apud Plin. lib. 16, cap. 1. Francorum vero, apud illum Rhetorem Panegyristem.[41] Nam Plin. quidem ita loquitur:[42] *Sunt in Septentrione visae nobis Chaucorum gentes, qui maiores minoresque appellantur, vasto ibi*
15 *meatu, bis dierum noctiumque singularum intervallis effusus in immensum agitur Oceanus, aeternam operiens rerum naturae contro-versiam, dubiumque terrae sit, an parte in maris.* At Panegyristes:[43] *Quanquam,* inquit, *illa regio divinis expeditionibus tuis Caesar vindicata, atque purgata, quam obliquis meatibus callidis* (sic legen-
20 dum, ut in libris vulgatis, non SCALDIS, ut quidam reposuit[44]) *interfluit, quamque divortio sui Rhenus amplectitur, pene, ut verbi periculo loquar, terra non est, ita penitus aquis imbuta* permaduit, ut non solum quae manifeste palustris est, cedat adnixum, et hauriat pressa vestigium, verumetiam ubi paulo videtur firmior, pedum pulsu*
25 *tentata quatiatur, et sentire se procul moto pondus testetur.*

Patefactum igitur arbitramur esse locum, unde propagata in Gallias Francorum natio est,* palustris videlicet ea regio, quae inter Albim et Rhenum Oceanum attingit. Quod eo etiam argu-

---

1 *bc* 'Quem'.   2 'commemorat': *c* 'in suum'.   3 *bc* 'Eodem etiam pertinet ille'.   22 *bc* omit '*imbuta*'.   27 *c* 'unde Francorum in Galliam natio pro-pagata est'.

37 *Epit.*, XV, 4, 2; Bonn, III, 261.   38 I, 68; Bonn, 58.   39 *Scr. hist. Aug.*, Pro-bus, XII, 3; Loeb, III, 360   40 *Carmen* XXIII, vv. 245–6; *MGH AA*, VIII, 255–6; cf. next chapter, p. 206, n. 17.   41 See below, n. 43.   42 *Nat. Hist.*, XVI, 1, 2; Loeb, IV, 386ff.   43 *Panegyr. Constantio Caes.*, viii; ed. Galletier [No. IV], I, 88. 44 Correcting the bad reading in the edition of Aimon, 1567, 416.

Franks'. In the third volume of his annals Zonaras refers to this passage,[37] ^cand Zosimus also quotes Procopius' first book of the *Gothic War*.[38] ^a*Flavius Vopiscus tells us in his life of the Emperor Probus that the Franks were defeated by Probus among their inaccessible marshes.[39] 'The mutilated Frankish corpses', he writes, 'were scattered about among the trackless swamps.' Sidonius Apollinaris also remarks:[40] 'Enter, if you will, the innermost Frankish marshes revered by the Sicambri.'

What we have said about the Franks living near the Chauci becomes clear when one compares the places inhabited by the Chauci with accounts of the Frankish settlements. Pliny describes the former and the panegyrist the latter.[41] Pliny observes:[42] 'In the north we have seen the Chauci peoples, called the greater and the lesser Chauci. There the ocean is moved by a vast disturbance, and twice every night and day pours in regularly in a great wave through an immense channel, creating an everlasting conflict in nature, so that it is difficult to know whether it be part of the land or part of the sea.' The panegyrist remarks:[43] 'That region, Caesar, has been delivered and cleared by your Heaven-blessed armies. It is a country through which the Rhine flows with crafty (the word is *callidis*, not *scaldis* as in imperfect versions)[44] sideways movements and entwines in its coils a substance scarcely to be called land, so thoroughly soaked and† permeated it is with water. Not only do those parts which are clearly marsh yield to pressure, but, even when the ground seems firmer, the mark of a footstep fills with water, and the earth quakes beneath the tread and trembles as if it felt an oncoming weight.'

We believe that we have disclosed the place whence the nation of the Franks spread into Gaul, namely from that swampy region along the coast between the mouths of the Elbe and the Rhine. This

---

* **bc** *add* It is also worth noting that.　† **bc** *omit* soaked and.

mento confirmari potest, quod Franci maritimarum rerum usum maximum habebant, lateque per eam oram vagabantur. Nam Eutrop. lib. 9, ubi Gallieni Imperatoris historiam percurrit:[45] *Post haec tempora, inquit, Carausius cum per tractum Belgicae et**
5 *Armoricae pacandum mare accepisset, quod Franci et Saxones infesta- bant.* Qua eadem de re Paulus quoque Orosius lib. 7,[46] com- memorat. Eodem pertinet alter in illo, quem aliquoties iam protulimus Panegyrico, locus, ubi Rhetor ita loquitur:[47] *Franci, inquit, praeter caeteros truces quorum vis cum ad bellum effervesceret,*
10 *ultra ipsum Oceanum aestu furoris evecta, Hispanorum etiam oras armis infestas habebat.* Itaque Iustinianus Imper. [b]lib. Codic. 2,[48] [a]ubi Praefecti praetorio Africae officium exponit, mentionem facit Francorum, qui in parte quadam Galliae finitima His- paniae consederant.

15   Memorabile est autem, et ad bellicae laudis gloriam insigne, quod alio Panegyrici loco narratur, exiguas Francorum copias, quos Imperator Probus bello superatos in Pontum captivos ab- duxerat, navibus aliquot interceptis, usque in Graeciam et Asiam vagatos esse, Siciliam invasisse, Syracusas cepisse, post onustos
20 praeda et spoliis per fretum Herculeum in Oceanum revertisse. *Recursabat, inquit,*[49] *in animos, sub divo Probo, et paucorum ex Francis captivorum incredibilis audacia, et indigna felicitas, qui a Ponto usque correptis navibus, Graeciam, Asiamque populati, nec impune plerisque Lybiae littoribus appulsi, ipsas postremo navalibus quondam*
25 *victoriis nobiles ceperant Syracusas, et immenso itinere permensi Oceanum, qua terras rupit, intraverant, atque ita eventu temeritatis ostenderant, nihil esse clausum piraticae desperationi, quo navigiis pateret accessus.* [c]Quam eandem historiam Zosimus sub finem Histor. 1, his verbis commemorat:[50] *Cum Franci ad Imperatorem*
30 *accessissent, et ab eo sedes obtinuissent, pars eorum quaedam defec- tionem molita, magnamque navium copiam nacta, totam Graeciam*

---

4 *bc* omit '*et*'.
[45] 9, xxi; *MGH AA*, II, 162, 18-20.   [46] VII, 25; *PL*, XXXI, 1125.   [47] *Naz. panegyr. Const. Aug.*, xvii; Galletier [No. X (4)], II, 180.   [48] *Cod.* I, 27, 2; Mommsen, II, 79.   [49] *Panegyr. Constantio Caes.*, xvii; ed. Galletier [No. IV], I, 96ff.   [50] I, 71; Bonn, 61.

can be confirmed by the argument that the Franks were very much a seafaring people, and travelled extensively along the coast. Eutropius mentions this when he surveys the history of the Emperor Gallienus:[45] 'Carausius', he writes, 'had later been given the task of patrolling the sea off Belgica and Armorica, which was infested by the Franks and Saxons.' Paulus Orosius records the same thing.[46] The remarks of the panegyrist, to which we have already referred, are also relevant.[47] 'When the passions of the Franks turn to war', he observes, 'their strength exceeds that of other peoples, and it propels them onward with a surge of fury beyond the narrow seas, so that they have even infested the coasts of Spain with their armed might.' Thus the Emperor Justinian, [b]in that second part of the *Code* [a]where he sets out the duties of the praetorial prefect of Africa,[48] mentions the Franks who were established in a certain part of Gaul near the Spanish frontier.

There is another memorable passage, reflecting great glory on the warlike deeds of the Franks, in the oration of the panegyrist, where he recounts that a small force of Franks, who had been defeated in war by the Emperor Probus and led captive into Pontus, seized some ships, sailed all round Greece and Asia, invaded Sicily, captured Syracuse, and returned to the Atlantic through the straits of Hercules, laden with booty and plunder. 'It used to be remembered', he writes,[49] 'how in the reign of the divine Probus a small band of captive Franks, with incredible daring and a good fortune they scarcely deserved, sailed from Pontus in vessels they had surreptitiously acquired as far as Greece and Asia, plundering as they went, and voyaged along much of the coast of Libya, though not without some loss. Finally, after several naval victories, they even took the noble city of Syracuse, and, having sailed on for a vast distance, entered the Great Ocean where it surges between the continents. By that foolhardy deed they showed that no place on earth where ships might sail was safe from the curse of piracy.' [c]Zosimus records the same story in his history:[50] 'When the Franks had approached the emperor and obtained lands from him, a group of them tried to desert, acquired a large fleet of ships and spread confusion throughout the whole of Greece. They sailed also

conturbavit. In Siciliam quoque delata, et urbem Syracusas adorta,
magnam in ea caedem edidit. Tandem cum et in Africam appulisset, ac
reiecta fuisset, adductis Carthagine copiis, nihilominus domum redire,
nullum passa detrimentum potuit. Hoc quoque Probo imperante
5 *contingit.*

^aEt ad hanc disputationem ea quoque auctorum loca re-
ferenda sunt, ex quibus intelligitur, Francorum sedes Batavorum
finibus propinquas fuisse. Nam Rhetor ille Maximianum et
Constantinum alloquens:[51] *Multa, inquit, ille Francorum millia,*
10 *qui Bataviam aliasque cis Rhenum terras invaserant, interfecit,*
depulit, abduxit. Praeterea insignis extat locus apud Corn.
Tacitum in lib. 20, ubi de Bataviae et Frisiae vicinitate commemorans, Caninefates quoque admiscet, quorum eam scribit
consuetudinem in Rege creando fuisse, quam posterius vere
15 Francicam fuisse ostendemus: *Missi, inquit,*[52] *ad Caninefates, qui*
consilia sociarent. Ea gens partem insulae colit, origine, lingua,
virtute par Batavis, numero superantur. Et mox:[53] *Brinnio impositus*
scuto, more gentis, et sustinentium humeris vibratus, dux deligitur.
Quae verba haud exigui esse ad nostram disputationem mo-
20 menti, posterius, cum ad eum locum ventum erit, intelligetur.
Quae cum ita se habeant, satis equidem admirari Adr. Turnebi[54]
doctissimi viri iudicium non possum, qui tam multis veterum
auctorum locis pro nihilo habitis, scripsit videri sibi Francos ex
Scandinavia oriundos, propterea quod apud Ptolemaeum in illa
25 insula Phirassi[55] collocantur. Quam vocem corruptam, et
FRANCI reponendum censet. Neque tamen praeter meram
divinationem ullam huius opinionis suae rationem affert; quae
tamen opinio a veterum scriptorum omnium auctoritatibus
apertissime dissidet.
30 De caeteris vero prope omnibus, qui fabulis delectati, Francorum originem ad Troianos et Priami filium Francionem nescio
quem retulerunt,* tantum dicimus, Poëtis illos, non historicis

---

32 c 'ad Troianos, et Francionem nescio quem Priami filium retulerunt'.

[51] *Panegyr. Maxim. et Const.*, iv; ed. Galletier [No. vi (7)], II, 19.   [52] *Hist.*, IV,
15; Loeb, 26.   [53] *Ibid.*, Loeb, 28.   [54] Cf. *Adversariorum*, XXIV, 37; ed. 1564,
II, 297.   [55] Φιραῖσοι in Ptolemy, *Geographia*, II, 11, 16; ed. Nobbe, 124, 12.

to Sicily, attacked the town of Syracuse, and caused great slaughter there. Although, when they reached Africa, they were thrown back by forces gathered at Carthage, nevertheless they were able to overcome every obstacle and to return home. This happened in the reign of Probus.'

*There are also various passages which should be consulted to show that the settlements of the Franks were close to the borders of the Batavi. The panegyrist remarks in his address to Maximianus and Constantine:[51] 'He slew, expelled and captured many thousands of Franks, who had invaded Batavia and other lands on this side of the Rhine.' Moreover, there is an important passage in Cornelius Tacitus where, remarking that Batavia and Frisia were neighbouring countries, he names also the Caninefates among those whose custom it was to elect their kings, which we shall later show to have been actually the Frankish custom: 'Envoys', he writes,[52] 'were sent to the Caninefates to persuade them to join the alliance. That people lived upon part of an island, and in origin, language and valour were like the Batavi, though less than they in number.' A later passage reads:[53] 'According to local custom, Brinnio was hoisted upon a shield, shaken to and fro on the shoulders of those who supported him, and chosen as leader.' These words will be of no small moment in our argument when we come later to the appropriate point. Such being the state of the matter, I cannot avoid astonishment at the opinion of that very learned author Adrian Turnebus,[54] who, discounting so many passages from the ancient writers, declared that it seemed to him that the Franks had come from Scandinavia, because Ptolemy had supposed the Phirassi[55] to be located in that area. He thought the word Phirassi had been corrupted, and should be replaced by the word Franks. Yet he provides no reason for his opinion beyond mere guesswork, and his view differs manifestly from that of all the ancient authors.

As to nearly all those others who take delight in fables and would relate the origin of the Franks to the Trojans and to a certain hypothetical Francion, son of Priam, we can only say that such an argument provides material for the work of poets, not of his-

scribendi argumentum praebuisse, eoque in numero primum
merito locum Guillielmo Bellayo tribuimus, qui cum omnium
optimarum artium doctrina, summaque ingenii laude prae-
staret, tamen in libello de Galliae et Franciae antiquitatibus,[56]
5 non Francogallicae historiae, sed Amadisicarum fabularum
instituisse tractationem videtur.

---

[56] Du Bellay, *Epitome de l'antiquité des Gaules de France*, 1; ed. 1556, 19ff.

torians. Among them pride of place should go to Guillaume du Bellay, who, although he stood foremost in his knowledge of all the higher arts and deserved great praise for his ingenuity, yet in his book[56] on the antiquities of Gaul and France would seem to have composed a work of fabulous deeds, after the manner of the *Amadis de Gaule*, rather than a history of Francogallia.

^aCAPUT V

De Francorum nomine, variisque excursionibus, et quo tempore regnum sibi in Gallia constituerint

Sed ratio postulat, ut de hoc Francorum nomine paulo attentius consideremus, quod nusquam in Germaniae descriptione reperiri superius diximus. Ne diutius teneam, necesse est vel Francorum gentem tenuem obscuramque fuisse, a qua tamen tantarum
5 rerum gerendarum initia nata sunt; quemadmodum in Suittis tenuissimo Helvetiorum pago usuvenit, a quo cum recuperandae libertatis auctores orti primum fuissent, Suicerorum* nomen in Helvetios omnes propagatum est, vel, quod mihi verisimilius videtur, fictam ex re et occasione appellationem fuisse, cum ii,
10 qui se libertatis recuperandae principes atque auctores profiterentur, FRANCOS se nominassent, qua voce liberos, et servitutis expertes, apud Germanos intelligi, satis inter eruditos et literatos Germanos constare video; indeque Francum populari lingua, pro libero et immuni, et Francisiam, pro asylo usurpamus, et
15 Francisare, ^bvel affrancire ^apro in libertatem asserere.
^bItaque rectissime ^cIohan. Aventinus lib. 4,[1] *Francorum nomen,* inquit, *crebrum est in fastis nostris antiquis, deductum a libertate, quae Teutonum lingua Freyghait, et Freyghun dicitur, quod cognomen adhuc Franconibus nostris tribui solet. Vocitantur enim vulgo, die freyen*
20 *Francken, hoc est liberi Franci.* Item Hieronymus Surita de regibus Aragon. sub anno DCCCXLIV:[2] *Carolus Calvus Francorum Rex Barcinonensibus sive Hispani, sive Gothi essent, immunitatem libertatemque elargitur, qua Franci uti assueverant, permittitque, ut Gothicis legibus iura inter se foraque constituant. Immunitas ea a*

---

7 *bc* 'Switzerorum'.

[1] *Ann. Boiorum,* IV, I, 7; ed. 1710, 279.   [2] Zurita, *Indices,* Bk. I, an. 844; ed. Schott, III, 8, 1ff.

^aCHAPTER V

Concerning the name of the Franks, their various forays, and when it was they made a kingdom for themselves in Gaul

---

It seems necessary to consider a little more closely this word 'Frank', which, as we have already said, is not to be found in early accounts of Germany. To come directly to the point, there can be only two possibilities. First, the Frankish people, who were destined for such great deeds, may have had very obscure beginnings. In such a way it chanced that the word 'Swiss' originated in the meanest canton of the Helvetii, for the breath of liberty was first secured there, and the name 'Swiss' spread to all the Helvetians. Alternatively – and this explanation seems more probable to me – the name was created from a particular event and occasion. It was when those who declared themselves foremost in the recovery of liberty called themselves FRANKS, by which they were understood among the Germans to mean free men, exempt from servitude. This explanation satisfied those who possessed learning and literacy in Germany, and thus in popular speech the word 'Frank' came to mean free and immune, the word 'franchise' a sanctuary, and the verb 'to enfranchise' to set at liberty.

^cThus Johannes Aventinus is assuredly correct when he writes:[1] 'The name of the Franks occurs frequently in our old legal records. It is derived from the Teutonic words for liberty, *Freyghait* and *Freyghun*, and was then customarily given as a family name to our Franconian people. They were vulgarly called *die freyen Francken*, that is free Franks.' Jerome of Zurita in his work on the kings of Aragon writes for the year 844:[2] 'Charles the Bald, king of the Franks, bestowed immunity and freedom on the Barcinonenses, whether they were Spanish or Gothic – a status which the Franks had been accustomed to enjoy. He allowed their ordinances and business transactions to be drawn up according to Gothic law. In

Francis in Hispania FRANKITAS *dicta. Francorum enim nationem Germanicam Carolus Magnus Germanis reliquis et Frisiis commodiore immunitatis conditione antetulerat.* Item sub anno MCX:[3] *Iulio mense, ut oppidum frequentissime coleretur, habitareturque,*
5 *civibus Exeanis Frankitatis (id est, ingenuitatis) ornamenta ab Imperatore praestantur.* Item Albert. Krantz. lib. 4 metrop. cap. 13:[4] *Nam ex Theutonico vocabulo ortum est: Franck enim Germanica lingua liber dicitur, nulli obnoxius servitutis.* [b]Ant. Sabellicus Ennead. x, lib. 3:[5] *Francos,* inquit, *Itali liberos appellant,*
10 *quippe cum Itali ex Germanorum eluvionibus promanarint.*

[a]Eius autem rei primum argumentum est, quod Procopius lib. Gott. bell. I, memoriae prodidit,[6] Francos antiquitus generali nomine Germanos appellatos fuisse, post vero quam e finibus suis excesserunt, Francorum nomen obtinuisse. In eadem sententia
15 video et Gregorium Turonensem, et Abbatem Urspergensem, et Sigebertum, et Adonem Viennensem, et Godfridum Viterbiensem esse, ut Franci a libertate, et (ut illi ad vocem illam alludentes scribunt) a ferocitate nomen invenerint, quod Valentiniano Imper. stipendiarii esse, tributumque aliarum
20 nationum more, pendere recusarent.* Alterum est, quod Corn. Tacitus lib. 20, ubi de Caninefatibus loquitur (quos Francorum finitimos, vel potius populares, atque adeo Francos ipsos nativos fuisse ostendimus) eorumque primam adversus Romanos victoriam describit, his utitur verbis:[7] *Clara ea victoria in praesens*
25 *in posterum usui, armaque et naves quibus indigebant adepti, magna per Germanias Galliasque fama,* LIBERTATIS AUCTORES *celebrabantur. Germaniae statim misere legatos, auxilia offerentes.* Valeat igitur omen, ut FRANCI vere proprieque dicantur, qui Tyran-

---

20 *bc* alter the sentence 'In eadem...pendere recusarent.' and move it down in the text; see the seventh note after this (p. 206).

[3] *Ibid.,* Bk. I, an. 1110; *ed. cit.,* III, 33, 38ff.   [4] Ed. 1568, 110.   [5] Ed. 1517, 296ʳ.   [6] V, xi, 29; Loeb, III, 116.   [7] *Hist.,* IV, 17; Loeb, II, 30.

Spain this freedom, as granted by the Franks, was called "*Fran-kitas*". For Charlemagne had preferred the Frankish part of the German nation to the rest of the Germans and to the Frisians in according this more pleasant form of freedom.' Under the year 1110 the same author writes:[3] 'In July the special privilege of *Frankitas* (that is, to be styled of noble birth) was offered to the citizens of Exea by the Emperor, so that the town would remain populous and inhabited.' Again, Albert Krantz in his chronicle writes:[4] 'The word is of Teutonic origin. "*Franck*" means free in the German tongue, that is submission to no form of servitude.' *b*And Antonius Sabellicus writes in his *Tenth Ennead*:[5] 'The Italians call the Franks free, and this was surely because the former continued to exist under the inundations of the Germans.'

*a*As further proof of this matter let us remember that Procopius in his *Gothic War* recounted[6] that in ancient times the Franks were called by the general name of Germans, but that after they had expanded beyond their own lands they were given the name of Franks. Gregory of Tours, the abbot of Ursperg, Sigebert, Ado of Vienne and Godfrey of Viterbo are all of the opinion that the Franks acquired their name from their freedom and their ferocity (the latter being a play upon words by these authors), because they refused to be hired by the Emperor Valentinian and to pay tribute, as was the custom with other nations.* Support for this view is also provided in a passage where Cornelius Tacitus writes about the Caninefates, whom we have shown to have been near neighbours of the Franks, if not fellow-countrymen and therefore themselves native Franks. Tacitus describes their first victory against the Romans in these words:[7] 'That victory proved to be a very famous one at the time, and of great use later, for it enabled them to obtain the arms and ships they had lacked, and they were celebrated with great renown throughout Germany and Gaul as the AUTHORS OF LIBERTY. The Germans at once sent envoys to offer assistance.' It was surely a valuable omen for the future when they were truly and properly named FREE [*Franci*]. When they had thrown off the

* *bc the sentence* Gregory of Tours. . . with other nations *altered and inserted below as indicated on p. 207.*

norum servitute depulsa,* honestam, etiam sub regum auctoritate, libertatem sibi retinendam putarunt. Non enim Regi
parere servitus est, neque qui Regi parent, continuo servi
habendi sunt, sed qui Tyranni libidini, aut* latroni, aut* carnifici,
5 tanquam pecudes lanioni sese subiiciunt, ii demum vilissimo
servorum nomine appellandi sunt.

Itaque Reges semper Franci habuerunt, etiam tum, cum
assertores se ac vindices libertatis profitebantur, et cum sibi Reges
constituerunt, non tyrannos, aut carnifices, sed* libertatis suae
10 custodes, praefectos, tutores sibi constituerunt; quemadmodum
ex Francogallicae Reipublicae forma posterius intelligetur. ᶜSic
Claudianus lib. 3 cecinit:[8] *Nusquam libertas gratior ulla est, Quam
sub Rege pio.* ᵇSic Salustius; Regem primis temporibus a
Romanis habitum scribit:[9] *conservandae libertatis atque augendae*
15 *Reipublicae caussa.* Ubi vero suam libertatem labefactari Regum
insaniis senserunt, tum iis pulsis suam sibi tutandam libertatem
iudicarunt.*

ᵃNam quae* vero Iohannes Turpinus[10] nescio quis, monachus
certe stolidus atque imperitus, qui Caroli Magni, non vitam, sed
20 fabulam conscripsit, de Francorum vocabulo nugatur, ut qui
pecuniam ad Dionysianum templum aedificandum contulisset
Francus, id est, liber diceretur, quasi ᵇnomen illud ᵃRegis illius
Caroli tempore demum natum sit, ne memoratu quidem dignum
est, non magis quam reliqua illius omnia, fabulis anilibus ac
25 deliriis referta. ᵇNostram porro de Francorum nomine con-
iecturam adiuvat, quod Gregorius Turon.,[11] Ado Viennensis,[12]
Sigebertus,[13] Abbas Ursperg.,[14] Godfridus Viterbiensis[15] scribunt, Francos a libertate, et (ut illi ad vocis notionem alludentes
loquuntur) a ferocitate nomen invenisse, propterea quod

---

1 *c*¹ omits 'qui Tyrannorum servitute depulsa'.   4 *c* 'qui'.   4 *c* 'qui'
9 *c*¹ omits 'non tyrannos, aut carnifices, sed'.   17 *c*¹ omits this sentence.
18 *bc* omit 'Nam', begin sentence with 'Quae'.

[8] *De consulatu Stilichonis*, 114–15; Loeb, 50.   [9] *Catiline*, VI, 7; Loeb, 12.
[10] Ed. *Ger. rer. script.*, 1566, 12ᵛ.   [11] Non invenio.   [12] PL, CXXIII, 95.
[13] *Roberti de Monte cronica* (Continuator of Sigebert), A.D. 1167; MGH SS, VI,
516, 22. Hotman had the passage, attributed to Sigebert, from *Germ. rer. quat.*,
150, under the year 1168.   [14] Cf. Ekkehard, *Chronicon*, A.D. 367 'De Origine
Francorum'; MGH SS, VI, 115, 55.   [15] Partic. XXII, 40; MGH SS, XXII, 201,
25–6.

servitude imposed by tyrants,* they considered it their duty to keep their honest liberty, even when they were under the authority of kings. For obedience to a king is no servitude, nor do those who obey a king take on the status of slaves in consequence. But those who subject themselves to a lustful tyrant, as to a brigand or an executioner, become like cattle under the butcher's knife. Such men should indeed be called by the vilest name appropriate to slaves.

Thus the Franks always had kings, even at the time when they declared themselves protectors and defenders of liberty. When they appointed kings for themselves, they were not appointing tyrants and butchers, but rather† guardians, governors and tutors for their liberty, in the very same form as will later be shown to have applied to the commonwealth of Francogallia. cThus Claudian the poet sang:[8] 'No other form of freedom is ever so agreeable as that which exists under a devout and pious king.' bThus Sallust writes that in ancient times the Romans had kings[9] 'so that liberty might be preserved and the commonwealth prosper'. And when they felt that their freedom was being imperilled by the madness of the kings, then they judged that their liberty would be safeguarded by driving them out.‡

aFor§ as to the opinion of some monk or other called Johannes Turpinus (who was as stupid as he was ignorant and wrote not a biography but a fairy-story of Charlemagne) that the word 'Frank' came from some trifling play upon words, wherein a man who contributed money to the building of the church of Saint-Denis was called 'Frank' or free[10] (as if the word could conceivably have originated in the time of that King Charles!) – such an opinion is not worth remembering, any more than all the rest of his compendium of old wives' tales and crazy fables. bMoreover, our own conjecture as to the name of the Franks is sustained by the opinion of Gregory of Tours,[11] Ado of Vienne,[12] Sigebert,[13] the abbot of Ursperg[14] and Godfrey of Viterbo[15] that the name was derived from Frankish freedom and ferocity, since these authors play upon

---

*c[1] *omits preceding clause.* † c[1] not appointing tyrants and butchers, but rather *becomes* appointing. ‡ c[1] *omits preceding sentence.* § *bc omit* For.

Valentiniani Imperatoris stipendiarii esse, tributaque aliarum
nationum more pendere recusarent;* non quo Francorum
nominis mentio non multo antiquior sit Valentiniani Imp. aetate;
nam (ut superius demonstratum est) amplius centum ante annis
5 sub Gallienis Impp. usurpata est, sed quia finitimi populi cum
Francorum exemplum virtutemque imitarentur, seseque ex
Romanorum tyrannide in libertatem vindicarent, eorundem
etiam nomen usurpandum putarunt.

Nam quod Hunibaldus[16] ait nominatos a Franco Antharii
10 Sicambrorum Regis filio, idque factum addit Octaviano Augusto
imperante, primum ab omnium Romanorum et Graecorum
historiis alienum est, apud quos nulla tam antiquis temporibus
Francorum mentio reperitur, ut superius demonstratum est.
Deinde cum illi populi Regem sibi crearent (sicuti et iam prius
15 dictum est, et postea dicetur), perabsurdum est, existimare
populum a Rege potius, quam Regem a populo denominatum.
Multo vero absurdius est, eosdem dicere Francos et Sicambros
fuisse, propter hemistichium a divo Remigio in Clodoveo
baptisando usurpatum: Mitis depone colla Sicamber. Nam alios
20 Francos, alios Sicambros fuisse, versus illi Sido. Apollinaris
declarant:[17]

> *Francorum et penitissimas paludes*
> *Intrares, venerantibus Sicambris.*

*c*Item illi Claudiani ad Honorium:[18]

25
> *Ante ducem nostrum flavam sparsere Sicambri*
> *Caesariem, pavidoque orantes murmure Franci*
> *Procubuere solo.*

*b*Quare ut illud a Remigio usurpatum hemistichium conce-
damus, tamen alludendi potius quam veri nominis designandi
30 caussa, id factum esse probabile est.

---

2 As noted above, most of this sentence occurred earlier in *a*.

16 Ed. Schard, I, 308.   17 *Carmen* XXIII, *vv.* 245–6; *MGH AA*, VIII, 255–6; cf.
previous chapter, p. 192, n. 40.   18 *Panegyricus de quarto consulatu Honorii
Augusti*, 446–8; Loeb, 318.

words in arriving at the concept. It was because, as they say, the Franks refused to become the hirelings of the Emperor Valentinian and to pay the tributes customary for other nations.* It is not that there was scarcely any mention of the Frankish name before the age of the Emperor Valentinian, for, as we have shown earlier, it was employed fully a hundred years before under the Emperor Gallienus, but rather that neighbouring peoples, who copied both the courage and the example of the Franks and claimed their freedom from Roman tyranny, thought that they should also use their name.

Hunibaldus[16] states that they were named by Francus, the son of King Antharus of the Sicambri, and that this occurred in the reign of Octavian Augustus, but this view is quite contrary to all the Greek and Roman accounts, among which, as we have already shown, there is not to be found the slightest mention of the Franks in early times. And, since those peoples used to make themselves a king, as has been said earlier and will be said again, it is quite ridiculous to think that a king named the people rather than that the people named a king. It is even more absurd to say that the Franks and the Sicambri were the same people because of some fancy form of words used in baptising Clovis by Saint Rémi: 'Yield yourself to subjection, gentle man of Sicamber.' For some were Franks and others Sicambri, as the lines by Sidonius Apollinaris proclaim:[17] 'Enter, if you will, the innermost depths of the Frankish swamps, which the Sicambri hold in awe.' *c*The lines of Claudian addressed to Honorius support the point:[18] 'The Sicambri bowed their yellow hair before our leader, and the Franks prostrated themselves in entreaty with nothing more than a timid murmur.' *b*Even if we were to grant that the expression was used by Saint Rémi, it is probable that it was a play upon words rather than a deliberate act of designation.

---

* **bc** *the two preceding sentences taken from context in* **a** *and inserted here, as shown in the note on p. 203.*

Verum, ut ad institutum redeamus. *a*Nunc* illud verissime dici ac praedicari potest, omen Francorum nominis, hoc est (ut Cornelius Tacitus interpretatur) auctorum libertatis ita faustum, felix, fortunatumque fuisse, ut ex eo victoriae prope innumer-
5 abiles consecutae sint. Nam postea quam illo consilio Franci e suis finibus excesserunt, non modo Germaniam, patriam communem, verumetiam Galliam, ad extremum etiam Alpes transgressi, partem Italiae non mediocrem a Romanorum tyrannide liberarunt. Prima autem et antiquissima huius illus-
10 trissimi nominis mentio reperitur apud Trebellium Pollionem in vita Imper. Gallieni, hoc est, circiter annum Christianae salutis CCLX.* *Cum ludibriis* (inquit de Gallieno loquens[19])* *et helluationi vacaret, neque aliter Rempublicam regeret, quam cum pueri fingunt per ludibria potestates, Galli, quibus insitum est luxuriosos*
15 *principes ferre non posse, Postumum ad imperium vocarunt,* qui tum Gallieni legatus Galliae cum imperio praeerat. Et paulo post:[20] *Contra Postumum igitur Gallienus bellum incoepit, et cum multis auxiliis Postumus iuvaretur, Celticis ac Francicis, in bellum cum Victorino processit.* Quibus ex verbis intelligitur, Gallos ad depel-
20 lendam Gallieni Tyranni servitutem, Francorum, id est, auctorum libertatis, auxiliis usos fuisse. Quod idem breviter Zonaras significans in Gallieni vita,[21] ἐπολέμησε δὲ inquit, φράγγοις etc.

Altera eorundem mentio rursus occurrit apud Flav. Vopiscum,
25 in Aureliani vita, his verbis:[22] *Apud Moguntiacum Tribunus legionis sextae Gallicanae, Francos irruentes, cum vagarentur per totam Galliam, sic afflixit, ut trecentos ex his captos septingentis interemptis, sub corona vendiderit.* Non enim Franci nostri

---

1 *bc* omit 'Nunc'.   12 *bc* rearrange and expand last part of this sentence to read '. . . mentio reperitur non sub Imperatore Decio, ut quosdam nimium confidenter affirmare video, sed sub Imp. Gallieno, hoc est circiter annum Christianae salutis CCLX. Nam Trebellius Pollio in eius vita'.   12 *bc* omit 'de Gallieno loquens'.

[19] *Scr. hist. Aug.*, Gallieni, IV, 3; Loeb, III, 22. Hotman's Romanophobia shows by his omission of some words from this quotation.   [20] *Ibid.*, VII, 1; Loeb, III, 30.
[21] *Annal.*, XII, 24; Bonn, II, 596.   [22] *Scr. hist. Aug.*, Aurelian, VII, 1; Loeb, III, 204.

However, to return to our purpose, *a*it can be truly declared and proclaimed that the name of Franks, or, as Cornelius Tacitus interprets it, authors of liberty, proved so auspicious, happy and fortunate an omen that from that triumph followed innumerable others. When the Franks had left their own territories with this intent, they freed Gaul as well as their own German fatherland from Roman tyranny, and, after crossing the Alps, liberated a large part of Italy as well. The first and most ancient mention of this illustrious name is to be found in Trebellius Pollio's life of the Emperor Gallienus, that is approximately in the year A.D. 260.* Speaking of Gallienus, he† writes:[19] 'While he indulged in lewd sports and gluttony, and ruled the commonwealth after the fashion of small boys at play who create titles for themselves, the Gauls, who had an instinctive aversion to luxury-loving princes, elected Posthumus as their ruler.' Posthumus at that time was the viceroy of Gallienus in Gaul, bearing the imperial authority. In a later passage Pollio writes:[20] 'Gallienus therefore declared war against Posthumus, but Posthumus, who was supported by many auxiliaries, including the Celts and the Franks, took the field against Victorinus.' From these words it is clear that the Gauls had been accustomed to call upon the forces of the Franks, that is, of the authors of freedom, to cast off their servitude under the tyrant Gallienus. This is also what Zonaras briefly indicates in his life of Gallienus[21] with the phrase: 'He fought against the Franks.'

Another mention of the Franks occurs in the life of Aurelian by Flavius Vopiscus:[22] 'At Metz the tribune of the sixth Gallic legion brought ruin to the Franks, who had erupted into Gaul and traversed the country at will. Having slaughtered seven hundred of their number, he sold a further three hundred of them into slavery.' For in that war our Franks did not always have a favour-

---

* *bc this sentence altered to read* The first and most ancient mention of this illustrious name is not to be found under the Emperor Decius, as I note some too confidently assert, but rather under the Emperor Gallienus, that is about A.D. 260. For in his life of Gallienus Trebellius Pollio... † *bc omit* Speaking of Gallienus, he.

in illo bello, non magis quam alii in aliis, quantumvis iustis, semper secundos praeliorum eventus habuerunt. Quinetiam a Constantino, qui postea Magnus dictus est, duo ipsorum Reges capti, et bestiis in spectaculo quodam obiecti memo-
5 rantur, quam historiam Eutropius lib. 9,[23] et Rhetor in Panegyrico,[24] quem superius aliquoties protulimus, attingunt. Et quoniam alio loco de bellis in Batavorum finibus gestis idem Rhetor commemorat, quos a nostris non longe abfuisse ostendimus, verba eius subscribemus. *Multa*, inquit Rhetor,[25]
10 *Francorum millia qui Bataviam, aliasque cis Rhenum terras invaserant, interfecit, depulit, abduxit.* Et alio loco:[26] *Terram Batavorum sub ipso quondam alumno suo a diversis Francorum Regum gentibus occupatam omni hoste purgavit, nec contentus vicisse, ipsos in Romanas transtulit nationes, ut non solum arma, sed et feritatem ponere*
15 *cogerentur.* Quo ex loco non obscure intelligitur, Constantinum Francorum vi atque armis coactum, sedes illis in Romani imperii finibus concessisse. Quinetiam Ammianus lib. 15 scribit,[27] Francos exorto inter Constantinum et Licinium civili bello, pro Constantini partibus saepenumero fortiter decertasse. Sed
20 et alio eiusdem libri loco, imperante Constantino, Constantini filio, Francos in Regia quam plurimos fuisse memorat, magnaque apud Caesarem in gratia atque auctoritate fuisse:[28] *Post haec*, inquit, *Malarichus subito nactus, adhibitis Francis, quorum ea tempestate in palatio multitudo florebat.*
25 Iam vero imperante Iuliano, qui Apostata dictus est, iidem Franci coloniam Agrippinam Romanorum servitute oppressam in libertatem vindicare conati sunt, eamque longa obsidione pressam, deditionem facere coegerunt, quemadmodum idem Ammianus lib. 12 commemorat.[29] Cumque ad flumen Salam

---

[23] X, 3, 2; *MGH AA*, II, 170, 21ff.   [24] Meant here, most likely, is the passage cited in the previous chapter, p. 196, n. 51, which is the same as that which is quoted in the next note.   [25] *Panegyr. Maxim. et Const.*, iv; ed. Galletier [No. VI (7)], II, 19.   [26] *Panegyr. Constantino Aug.*, v; ed. Galletier [No. VII (6)], II, 58. [27] Probably a reference to Sylvanus the Frank; Ammianus, XV, 5, 1; Loeb, I, 132ff.   [28] *Ibid.*, XV, 5, 11; Loeb, I, 138ff.   [29] *Ibid.*, XV, 8, 19; Loeb, I, 174.

able outcome to the battles they fought, and in this respect they were no different from other peoples in other wars, no matter how just their cause. Indeed two of their kings were captured by Constantine, afterwards called the Great, and exposed to wild beasts in a public spectacle, as is recounted by Eutropius[23] and by the author of that panegyric[24] which we have quoted on several occasions. Since the same panegyrist describes in another passage the wars waged in the lands of the Batavi, which, as we have shown, were close to those of our Franks, we shall cite his words:[25] 'He slaughtered, expelled, or led away into captivity many thousands of Franks, who had invaded Batavia and other territories on this side of the Rhine.' In another place the panegyrist writes:[26] 'The land of the Batavi, which had been under his personal control and formerly under that of his adopted son, was occupied by various peoples led by Frankish kings. He drove all hostile elements out of the district, and, not content with his victory, he made them accept Roman ways, so that they were obliged not only to lay down their arms but also to renounce their savage disposition.' This passage makes it manifest that Constantine was compelled by the armed strength of the Franks to allow them to settle within the boundaries of the Roman Empire. Moreover, Ammianus writes[27] that from the beginning of the civil war between Constantine and Licinius the Franks fought bravely and often on Constantine's behalf. Elsewhere in the same book he records that in the reign of Constantine, the son of Constantine the Great, great numbers of Franks attended the court and were in high favour and authority with the Emperor. He continues:[28] 'After these events Malarichus suddenly seized power through the support of the Franks, and a great number of them achieved significant positions in the palace at that time.'

In the reign of Julian, the so-called Apostate, these same Franks tried to set free the colony of Cologne, which was oppressed by the servitude imposed by the Romans, and forced it to surrender after a long siege, as is recorded by Ammianus in his twelfth book.[29]

aliquot e Francis consedissent, ea re, Salii dicti sunt, de quibus idem Ammianus eodem libro :[30] *Quibus paratis,* inquit, *petit primos omnium Francos, eos videlicet quos consuetudo Salios appellavit, ausos olim in Romano solo, apud Toxiandriam locum, habitacula* 5 *sibi figere praelicenter.* [c]Item Zosimus lib. 3 :[31] *Saliorum nationem, profectam a Francis, et vi Saxonum in hanc insulam* (de Batavia loquitur) *suis sedibus expulsam, eiecerunt. Haec insula, prius Romanis in universum subiecta, a Saliis hoc tempore possidebatur.* [a]Rursus [c]Ammianus [a]libro 20, Regionem a Francis ultra 10 Rhenum occupatam, et Franciam dictam, commemorat :[32] *Rheno,* inquit, *transmisso, regionem subito pervasit Francorum, quos Attuarios vocant, inquietorum hominum, licentius etiam tum percursantium extima Galliarum.* Et lib. 30, ubi de Rege Macriano loquitur, quo cum Valentinianus Imperator ad ripam Rheni, 15 prope Moguntiacum pacem fecerat :[33] *Periit autem,* inquit, *in Francia, postquam dum internecine vastando perrumpit avidius, oppetiit Mellobaudis bellicosi Regis insidiis circumventus.* Hunc autem Francorum Regem Mellobaudem idem auctor lib. seq. fortem et bellicosum fuisse scribit,[34] et ob virtutem militarem ab 20 Imp. Gratiano Comitem domesticorum, et Legatum cum Nannieno factum fuisse, ut exercitum adversus Lentiates Germanos educeret. Post vero imperante Honorio, propter pactam cum illo Imperatore societatem, Galliae Romanae fines adversus Stiliconem tutati sunt. Nam Orosius libro. ult. :[35] 25 *Excitatae,* inquit, *per Stiliconem gentes Alanorum, Suevorum, Vandalorum, multaeque cum his aliae Francos proterunt, Rhenumque transeunt, Gallias invadunt.*

    Post Honorii Imperatoris aetatem perexigua de Francorum rebus gestis extat memoria, nam ad illa tempora referendum est, 30 quod D. Ambrosius epistola 29 ad Imper. Theodosium scribit, Francos et in Sicilia et aliis locis compluribus Maximum Ro-

---

[30] *Ibid.,* XVII, 8, 3; Loeb, I, 350ff.   [31] *Ibid.,* III, 6; Bonn, 130.   [32] *Ibid.,* XX, 10, 2; Loeb, II, 68.   [33] *Ibid.,* XXX, 3, 7; Loeb, III, 316.   [34] *Ibid.,* XXXI, 10, 6–7; Loeb, III, 448.   [35] VII, 40; *PL,* XXXI, 1165.

Some of the Franks had settled near the River Sala, and in consequence were called Salians. Ammianus writes of them in the same
book:[30] 'After these preparations he sought out the leading people
among all the Franks – those whom custom had designated the
Salians and who had formerly been bold enough to settle with
wilful impudence in Roman territory near a place named Tox-
andria.' [c]Zosimus writes of them in his third book as follows:[31]
'They expelled the nation of the Salians, who had been pushed
forward by the Franks, and driven by the might of the Saxons from
their own settlements to this island (that is, Betuwe). The island,
which was once generally under the control of the Romans, was
held by the Salians at this time.' [a]Again, [c]Ammianus [a]relates how
the region beyond the Rhine was occupied by the Franks and called
'Francia'.[32] 'Having crossed the Rhine', he writes, 'he came
suddenly upon the land of those Franks termed the Attuarii, a
restless people who were then making unrestrained forays on the
Gallic borders.' When Ammianus discusses King Macrianus, with
whom the Emperor Valentinian had made peace on the banks of
the Rhine near Metz, he observes:[33] 'He met his death in Francia,
when, after bursting savagely into the district with the intention
of laying it waste, he was surrounded and fell into an ambush laid
by the warlike king Merobaudes.' Now the same author writes[34]
that this Merobaudes, king of the Franks, was strong and warlike,
and that, because of his military valour, he was made master of the
household by the Emperor Gratian, and joint commander, with
Nannienus, of an army he was to lead against the German Lentiates.
Later, in the reign of Honorius, the Franks made a treaty of alliance
with that Emperor, whereby they defended the frontiers of Roman
Gaul against Stilicho. For Orosius writes:[35] 'Stilicho stirred up the
Alans, Suevi, Vandals, and many other peoples besides, to break
through the Franks, cross the Rhine and invade Gaul.'

There is very little information about the deeds of the Franks in
the period following the age of the Emperor Honorius, and for
those times we are obliged to refer to a letter written by Saint
Ambrose to the Emperor Theodosius, where he states that the
Franks had overcome Maximus, the commander of the Roman

manarum copiarum ducem superassc:[36] *Ille igitur* (inquit, de
Maximo commemorans) *statim a Francis, et a Saxonum gente, in
Sicilia, Siciae, Petavione, ubique denique terrarum victus est.* Verum
imperante Valentiniano III, hoc est, circiter annum salutis
5 Christianae CCCCL, illud auctorum omnium consensu constat,
Childericum Merovei Francorum Regis filium, post annorum
amplius ducentorum contentionem, Galliam e Romanorum
servitute in libertatem vindicasse, in eaque Regni sui sedem
primum* certam stabilemque constituisse. Nam etsi nonnulli
10 primos Francorum Reges Faramundum et Clodiocrinitum
numerant; tamen nemini dubium est, alios antea complures
Francorum reges fuisse, qui etiam transmisso Rheno in Galliam
irruperunt, quorum nemo pacatum in Galliae finibus imperium
obtinuerit. Meroveus autem, quem vulgo tertium numerant,
15 Francorum quidem Rex fuit, sed advena, et peregrinus, non in
Gallia factus, non denique Francogallorum, hoc est, gemellae et
consociatae gentis iudicio et voluntate creatus. Francorum
denique Reges illi omnes fuerunt, non Francogallorum. Primus
Childericus, Merovei (ut diximus) filius, a Francis et Gallis,
20 publico gemellae gentis concilio,* Rex Francogalliae creatus est,
posteaquam Meroveus pater, Attilino praelio interfectus est,
imperante Valentiniano III, perdito ac libidinoso principe. Quo
tempore Angli et Scoti, Britanniam; Burgundi, Sequanorum,
Aeduorum, et Allobrogum fines; Gotti, Aquitaniam; Wandali
25 Africam atque Italiam, urbemque ipsam Romam occupabant.
Hunni vero, Attila duce, Galliam caedibus, atque incendiis
vastabant.* Hic cum exercitum haberet hominum circiter quin-
gentorum millium, late per Galliam, Tholosam usque vagatus
est. Erat tum Galliae Praeses Aetius, qui Attilae potentiam
30 veritus, Gottos sibi foedere ac societate adiunxerat. Horum
auxiliis instructus, praelium cum Attila commisit, cecidisseque
dicuntur eo praelio non minus centum et octoginta hominum

9 *bc* 'primumque in ea Regni sui sedem'.   20 *bc* 'consilio'.   27 *bc* put
next the sentence 'Quam rei...urbes occupavit.' (see next note) followed by
'Attila autem', but dropping 'Hic', so as to give 'Attila autem cum exercitum...'
[36] *Epist.*, XL, 23; *PL*, XVI, 1110.

armies, in Sicily and many other places.[36] He writes of Maximus:
'And so he was soon defeated by the Franks and by the Saxon
people in Sicily, at Siscia and Pettau in Pannonia, and finally
throughout the known world.' However, it is the view of all
writers that in the reign of Valentinian III, that is about 450 A.D.,
Childeric, son of Merovech, king of the Franks, finally won
freedom for Gaul from Roman servitude after a struggle lasting
more than two hundred years, and was the first to establish there a
firm and stable base for his kingdom. For, although some list
Pharamond and Chlogio Longhair as the first kings of the Franks,
it cannot be doubted that there were many earlier Frankish kings,
who broke into Gaul after crossing the Rhine but in no case won
unchallenged authority within the borders of Gaul. Merovech,
commonly numbered as the third of the kings, was certainly king
of the Franks. Yet he was a foreigner and stranger who was not
made king in Gaul, not, at least, by the Francogallians through the
choice and will of their joint and associated peoples. All these early
kings were kings of the Franks, not of the Francogallians. The first
to be created king of the Franks by both Franks and Gauls in a public
council of the twin peoples was Childeric, son of Merovech, as we
have said. He was made king soon after his father, Merovech, was
killed in battle with Attila during the reign of that corrupt and
libidinous prince Valentinian III. At that time the Angles and the
Scots took possession of Britain, the Burgundians occupied the
lands of the Sequani, the Aedui and the Allobroges, and the
Vandals seized Africa and Italy and even the city of Rome itself.
The Huns laid Gaul waste with fire and sword under the leadership
of Attila.* The latter,† who had an army of about five hundred
thousand men, overran Gaul as far as Toulouse. Aetius, who was
responsible for the defence of Gaul at the time, was so alarmed at
the strength of Attila that he made an alliance with the Goths. With
the support of their forces he gave battle to Attila, and in that battle
reputedly slew at least one hundred and eighty thousand men.

* **bc** *insert the two sentences* Merovech...for action *and* He crossed...the country
as shown in the note following the next note. † **bc** The latter *becomes* Moreover,
Attila.

millibus. At victor Actius, cum apud Imperatorem Valentinianum in regni appetendi suspicionem adductus esset, ipsius iussu necatus est. Aliquanto post Imperator ipse quoque opera Maximi, de quo superius mentionem fecimus, est interfectus.

5   Quam rei gerendae facultatem Meroveus Francorum Rex non aspernatus, magnis coniunctis copiis, Rhenum transmisit, civitatibusque compluribus ad eum recuperandae libertatis caussa confugientibus, tandem interiores Celtarum urbes occupavit.* Eo mortuo, unaque iam e duabus Gallorum et Francorum
10 gentibus civitate facta, universi coniunctis animis,* Childericum Merovei filium Regem sibi deligunt, scutoque de more impositum, atque in humeros sublatum, ter circum comitia deportant, et plausu undique excitato, summisque omnium gratulationibus, regem Francogalliae consalutant. Quarum rerum omnium
15 auctores habemus Sidonium Apollinarem, *b*Paulum Diaconum, *a*Gregorium Turonensem, Ottonem Frisingensem, Aimoinum, et ceteros; quorum testimonia, nec ita multo post ubi de Regis inaugurandi more dicendum erit, proferemus. De urbium quidem occupatione, Ottonis, lib. 4, cap. pen. verba haec sunt:[37]
20 *Franci Rheno transmisso, Romanos qui ibi habitabant, primo fugant; post captis Tornaco et Cameraco, Galliae urbibus, ac inde paulatim progredientes, Rhemos, Suessionem, Aurelianum, Agrippinam, Treverim subiugant.* *b*Neque vero praetermittendus est insignis Hunibaldi locus, apud quem scriptum ita est:[38] *Merovei tempore*
25 *Franci pene totam Galliam suo regno adiecerunt, Romanorum iam viribus imminutis, ac deficientibus, praesertim post Aetii mortem, quem Valentinianus ex invidia occiderat. Franci ergo Gallis commixti de ipsorum filiabus sibi acceperunt uxores, genuerunt filios et filias, qui omnes didicerunt linguam eorum, simul et mores, cum quibus sunt*

---

8 *bc* put this sentence earlier, as stated in the previous note.   **10** *bc* begin this sentence differently: *b* 'Meroveo mortuo, unaque iam e duabus Gallorum et Francorum gentibus civitate facta, universi coniunctis animis...'; *c* 'Meroveo mortuo, cum duae iam Gallorum et Francorum gentes, dispari genere, dissimili lingua, alio atque more viventes in unam civitatem coaluissent, coniunctis animis...'

[37] *Chron.*, IV, 32; *MGH SS*, XX, 212, 44.   [38] Ed. Schard, I, 329.

However, the Emperor Valentinian came to suspect that the victorious Aetius was aspiring to the crown, and had him put to death. Shortly afterwards the Emperor was himself slain by Maximus, to whom we have earlier referred.

Merovech, king of the Franks, did not disdain the opportunity for action. He crossed the Rhine with the large force he had assembled, and, when many of the states turned to him for help in recovering their liberty, he took possession of the Celtic towns in the centre of the country.* By the time of his death a single state had been created by the two peoples, the Gauls and the Franks, and with a common mind they all elected Childeric, the son of Merovech, as king.† They placed him upon a shield according to their custom, bore him thrice upon their shoulders round the assembly, and saluted him as king of Francogallia with enthusiastic applause and the greatest rejoicing of all present. The following authors testify to these facts: Sidonius Apollinaris, *b*Paul the Deacon, *a*Gregory of Tours, Otto of Freising, Aimon and others whose evidence we shall shortly produce when we come to discuss the way in which a king was inaugurated. The occupation of the towns is described by Otto of Freising:[37] 'When the Franks had crossed the Rhine they first chased out the Romans who lived there, and then took the Gallic towns of Tournai and Cambrai. Thence they moved steadily forward to take Reims, Soissons, Orléans, Cologne and Trèves.' *b*Nor should we neglect the relevant observations of that eminent writer Hunibaldus:[38] 'In the time of Merovech the Franks added nearly the whole of Gaul to their kingdom. The Roman forces were either much weakened or had withdrawn, and their weakness was accentuated after the death of Aetius, whom Valentinian had slain in his jealousy. Thus the Franks intermingled with the Gauls and took their daughters to wife. The children of these unions assimilated both their language and their customs, with

---

* *bc* the two sentences Merovech...for action *and* He crossed...the country *are removed from their context in* **a** *and inserted above as shown.* † *c the sentence altered to read* By the time of the death of Merovech the two peoples of the Gauls and the Franks, though disparate in race, dissimilar in language and living under different customs, had coalesced into a single state, and with a common mind they all elected Childeric, the son of Merovech, as king.

deinceps conversati usque in praesentem diem. Haec ille, quibus
consentanei sunt ii auctorum loci, in quibus per illa tempora Galli
et Franci promiscuo nomine appellantur; velut apud Paul.
Diaconum, lib. de gest. Langob. 3, cap. 13:[39] *Galli autem vehe-*
5 *menter afflicti, etsi multi capti, plurimi tamen per fugam elapsi vix ad*
patriam revertuntur, tantaque strages facta est de Francorum exercitu,
quanta nunquam alibi commemoratur; [c]indeque nata vul-
garis Francigenarum appellatio est, iis proprie attributa, qui ex
illis Francis suscepti in Gallia fuerant, velut in Syn. Triburicensi,
10 etc. I, ext. De sponsal.:[40] *De Francia quidam nobilem mulierem de*
Saxonia duxit, verum quia non iisdem utuntur legibus Saxones et
Francigenae, etc.

[a]Atque haec quidem de primo Francogalliae Rege, summatim,
quibus illud subiungendum est: Cum hoc Francogalliae Regnum
15 annos fere mille ducentos durarit, tres tantum per id omne
tempus Regum familias numerari; Merovingiorum, qui orti a
Meroveo stirpem ad annos ducentos octoginta tres propagarunt;
Carlovingiorum, qui orti a Carolo Magno, sobolem in annos
trecentos triginta septem produxerunt; et Capevingiorum, qui ab
20 Hugone Capetto prognati, quingentesimo iam et octogesimo
anno* Regnum obtinent.

---

21 'quingentesimo...anno': **bc** 'per quingentos iam et octoginta annos'.

39 III, 29; *MGH SS Lang.*, 108. 'Franci' not 'Galli' is the proper reading.
40 *Corp. iur. can.*, c. I X 4, 1; Friedberg, II, 661.

which they have become increasingly familiar down to the present day.' In this way, as various writers agree, the Gauls and the Franks came to be called in those times by a mixed name. Thus Paul the Deacon writes in his *Deeds of the Lombards*:[39] 'The Gauls were in great distress, and, though many of them had been taken captive, more yet managed with difficulty to make their escape. However, they returned to their native land, and, great as was the victory of the Frankish army, it was to be remembered only in Gaul.' [c]Hence originated the common term of Francigenians, which was properly applied to those Franks who had been brought up in Gaul. This usage is employed in the proceedings of the council of Triburicum concerning betrothal:[40] 'A certain man from Francia brought a noble woman from Saxony, but because the Saxons and the Francigenians did not make use of those laws...etc.'

[a]In brief, these further observations may be added to what has been said of the first king of Francogallia: although this kingdom of Francogallia has endured for nearly twelve hundred years, in all that time there have been only three dynasties of kings; the Merovingians, who from their ancestor, Merovech, continued their line for two hundred and eighty-three years; the Carolingians, descended from Charlemagne, whose line lasted three hundred and thirty-seven years; and the Capetians, derived from Hugh Capet, who today are in the five hundred and eightieth year of their reign.[*]

---

[*] *bc final clause becomes* who have now reigned throughout five hundred and eighty years.

Regnum Francogalliae utrum haereditate,
an suffragiis deferretur, et
de regum creandorum more

Sed hoc loco praeclara quaestio exoritur, et ad maiorum
sapientiam cognoscendam aptissima, utrum Francogalliae
regnum haereditario iure, an vero populi iudicio et suffragiis deferretur. Germaniae quidem Reges (quo ex genere Francos nos-
5 tros fuisse, superius demonstratum est) suffragiis creari solitos,
Cornelius Tacitus in libello de moribus Germanorum testatur.[1]
Reges, inquit, *ex nobilitate, Duces ex virtute sumunt.* Quod institutum etiam nunc Germani, et Dani, et Suevi, et Poloni retinent,
ut Reges quidem in Concilio gentis eligant; filii tamen *c*demor-
10 tuorum regum *a*praerogativam habeant, et (ut Tacitus memoriae
prodidit[2]) ceteris praeferantur. Quo instituto, haud scio, an
quicquam sapientius aut Reipublicae salutarius excogitari
potuerit. Nam (ut Plutarchus in Sylla luculenter monet[3]) quemadmodum venatores non quod ex generoso cane natum est,
15 sed canem ipsum generosum quaerunt; equites non quod ex
equo generosissimo natum, sed equum ipsum expetunt; eodem
modo qui Rempublicam constituunt, magno errore ducuntur,
si quis Princeps sibi agnaturus* sit, potius quam qualem habituri
sint, exquirant. *b*Eo accedebat, quod parentes successionis illius
20 spe ad suos filios praeclare instituendos adducebantur, ne
tanquam paterna successione indigni a populo repudiarentur.

*a*Atque hanc maiorum nostrorum in Francogalliae regno
constituendo sapientiam fuisse, documento est, primum Caroli
Magni testamentum, apud Ioan. Nauclerum,[4] et Hen. Mutium

---

18 *c* 'nasciturus'.

[1] Cap. 7; Loeb, 274. [2] *Ibid.* [3] II, 2; Loeb, IV, 446ff. (comp. of Lysander and
Sulla). [4] *Chron.*, II, gen. 28; ed. Mutius, 1579, 701.

Whether the kingdom of Francogallia was hereditary or elective, and the custom appropriate to the creation of kings

A celebrated issue arises here which most fittingly reveals the wisdom of our ancestors: whether the kingdom of Francogallia was transmitted by hereditary right or by the decision and the votes of the people. Cornelius Tacitus shows in his book on the *Customs of the Germans* that kings in Germany (and as we have proved earlier, our kings were of the same kind) were created by suffrage only. 'Kings', he said,[1] 'are chosen by reason of their nobility, dukes because of their valour.' This is an institution which the Germans, Danes, Swedes and Poles retain even at this day, for they elect their kings in an assembly of the nation. However, the sons *c*of deceased kings *a*had prior claims, and, as Tacitus recorded,[2] they were preferred to others. I cannot conceive that anything could be devised which is more prudent than this practice, or more healthy for a commonwealth. As Plutarch so rightly notes in his life of Sulla,[3] just as hunters prefer a dog or a horse that is itself a fine animal to one that is of fine breeding, so those who constitute a commonwealth make a great mistake if they seek birth before quality in a prince. *b*There was a further consideration that parents were induced by hope of their children's succession to have their sons clearly invested with authority, in case they might later prove unworthy of taking the place of their fathers and be repudiated by the people.

*a*As an example of this wise decision on the part of our ancestors in constituting the kingdom of Francogallia, we may take first the will of Charlemagne, according to the chronicle of Johannes Nauclerus[4] and as published by Henricus Mutius,[5] which contains

editum,[5] in quo clausula haec extat: *Quod si filius cuilibet horum trium filiorum meorum natus fuerit, quem populus eligere velit, ut patri suo in regni hereditate succedat, volumus ut consentiant patrui ipsius, et regnare permittant filium fratris sui in portione Regni paterni.*

5 *b*Quinetiam memorabile est, quod Regino libro Chron. 2 scribit, sub anno DCCCVI, cum Carolus Magnus tres filios haberet, quibus mature in vita sua consulere volebat:[6] *Cum primoribus (inquit) et optimatibus Francorum de partitione sui regni inter filios suos placitum habuit; et divisione facta inter* tres partes*

10 *testamentum de illa fecit, quod per sacramentum interpositum a Francis confirmatum est.* Sic Eguinarthus in eiusdem Caroli vita:[7] *Evocatum ad se Ludovicum Aquitaniae regem, qui solus filiorum Hildegardis supererat, congregatis solenniter de toto Francorum regno primoribus, cunctorum consilio consortem sibi totius regni fecit;**

15 *c*quem locum totidem verbis scriptor Chronici Besnensis[8] de quo supra commemoravimus, in suum librum transcripsit.

*b*Sed superiores videamus. *a*Item illud quod Aimoinus* lib. 1, cap. 4, de Pharamundo, quem vulgo (ut dixi) primum Francorum Regem numerant, ita loquitur:[9] *Regem vero caeterarum more*

20 *nationum Franci sibi eligentes, Pharamundum solio sublimant regio.* *b*Sed multo copiosius Hunibaldus, scriptor vetustissimus:[10] *Anno, inquit, CCCCV, omnes Duces, proceres et nobiles Francorum in mense Martio convenerunt apud Neopagum, pro novi Regis electione facienda.* Et mox:[11] *Hi omnes cum ceteris uno consensu*

25 *Faramundum de regio genere ortum unanimiter in Regem elegerunt.* Rursus Aimoinus *a*et* lib. 4, cap. 51:[12] *Franci autem Danielem quendam clericum caesarie capitis crescente, in regnum stabiliunt, atque Chilpericum nuncupant.* Item. lib. 4, cap. 67:[13] *Mortuo rege*

---

9 *c* 'in'.   **14** *a* has this sentence later; see below, p. 224, l. 7 ff.   **17** *bc* 'Nam Aimoinus quidem'.   **26** *bc* omit 'et'.

[5] *De Germ. orig.*, VIII; ed. 1539, 65.   [6] *MGH SS*, I, 563, 64 ff.   [7] C. 30; *MGH SS*, II, 459, 5–7.   [8] *PL*, CLXII, 797 (should say: '*infra* commemoravimus'). [9] *PL*, CXXXIX, 640.   [10] Ed. Schard, I, 322.   [11] *Ibid.*   [12] Ed. 1567, 388; cf. below, p. 230, n. 44.   [13] *Ibid.*, ed. 1567, 414.

this clause: 'If any son be born of these three sons of mine, whom the people may wish to elect as succeeding his father to the kingdom by heredity, it is our will that his uncles should consent to it and allow the son of their brother to reign over that part of the kingdom that was his father's.' *b*Moreover, the words of Regino in his chronicle for the year 806 should not be forgotten. Charlemagne then had three sons, with whom he wished to take counsel at the appropriate point in his own life. 'In conjunction with the leading men and the nobles among the Franks', Regino writes,[6] 'he decided upon the division of his kingdom among his sons, and, when the division into three parts had been effected, he made a will concerning it, which was confirmed by a solemn oath taken by the Franks.' To this effect Einhard writes in his life of Charlemagne:[7] 'He summoned Louis king of Aquitaine, who alone of the sons of Hildegard still survived, and, when the leading men throughout the whole kingdom of the Franks had been gathered together, he made him his consort over the entire realm with the united advice of those present.'* *c*This has been described in as many words by the chronicler of Dijon,[8] whom we have mentioned below.

*b*But let us look at earlier examples. *a*This is what Aimon writes concerning Pharamond, who, as I have said, is commonly ranked as the first king of the Franks:[9] 'The Franks elected themselves a king according to the custom of other nations, and they placed Pharamond upon the royal throne.' *b*But there are many further references in Hunibaldus, the earliest writer of them all.[10] 'In the year 405', he writes, 'all the leading men, chiefs and nobles of the Franks met together in the month of March at Dieuze in order to elect a new king.' A little further on he says:[11] 'All these men, and others besides, by common consent unanimously chose Pharamond as king and originator of royalty.' Referring again to Aimon:[12] *a*'The Franks took a certain clerk called Daniel and when the hair upon his head had grown they established him as ruler and named him Chilperic.' He also writes:[13] 'At the death of King Pepin, his

---

* *a* has the preceding quotation from Einhard appear at a later point as shown in the note following the next note.

Pipino filii eius Carolus et Carolomannus consensu omnium Fran-
corum Reges creati sunt. Et alio loco:[14] *Mortuo Pipino, Franci facto*
solenniter conventu, ambos sibi eius filios Reges constituunt, ea condi-
tione praemissa, ut totum regni corpus ex aequo partirentur.* Et rursus
5 post alterius e vita excessum:[15] *Carolus autem fratre defuncto*
consensu omnium Francorum Rex constituitur. Item sub finem
historiae Caroli Magni:[16] *Evocatum ad se Ludovicum Aquitaniae*
Regem, qui solus filiorum Hildegardis supererat, congregatis solenniter
de toto Regno Francorum primoribus, cunctorum consilio consortem
10 *sibi totius Regni et Imperialis nominis heredem constituit.** Atque
haec quidem ex Aimoino.

Similia autem apud Gregorium Turonensem testimonia
complura extant, e quibus pauca haec proferemus. Nam lib. 2,
cap. 12:[17] *Franci, inquit, eiecto Childerico Eudonem sibi unanimiter*
15 *Regem asciscunt.* Item lib. 4, cap. 51:[18] *Tunc Franci, qui quondam ad*
Childebertum aspexerunt seniorem, ad Sigebertum legationem mit-
tunt, ut ad eos veniens, derelicto Chilperico, ipsum per se Regem
stabilirent. Et aliquanto post:[19] *Collectus est ad eum omnis exercitus,*
impositumque super clypeo sibi Regem statuunt. Item alio loco:[20]
20 *Sigebertus Francis consentiens, more gentis impositus clypeo,*
Rex constitutus est, ac Regnum fratris sui Chilperici adeptus. Et
non ita multo post:[21] Burgundiones et Austrasii cum reliquis
Francis pace facta, Clotharium in tribus totis Regnis super se
Regem levaverunt. Quod idem Abbas Urspergensis confirmat:[22]
25 *Burgundiones, inquit, et Austrasii facta pace cum Francis, Clotharium*
in monarchia totius Regni Regem sublimaverunt. Et paulo post:[23]

---

4 c repeats this quotation below; see p. 226, n. 27.   **10 bc** move the sentence
'Item sub...*heredem constituit.*' to an earlier location; see above, p. 222, l. 11 ff.

[14] Besuensis, as below, p. 226, n. 27; here the word 'generali' is omitted, but in
n. 27 it appears (as is proper).   [15] Non invenio; but for a similar passage see
Aimon, IV, 67–8; ed. 1567, 414f.   [16] Einhard, *Vita Caroli,* c. 30; *MGH SS,* II,
459, 5–7. See textual variant note to line 10.   [17] *MGH SS Mer.,* I:I², 61, 16.
[18] *Ibid.,* V, 51; *loc. cit.,* 188, 3. 'Ipsum per se' should read 'super se ipsum', which
emasculates the argument.   [19] *Ibid.; loc. cit.,* 188, 11.   [20] See next note.
[21] Neither this nor the previous quotation are from Gregory, judging from the
extremely well indexed *MGH* second edition of the *Historia Francorum.*
[22] Ekkehard, *Chronicon,* A.D. 367 'De origine Francorum'; *MGH SS,* VI, 118, 8.
[23] *Ibid.; loc. cit.,* 118, 37.

sons Charles and Carloman were made kings by the consent of all the Franks.' And in another passage he says:[14] 'At the death of Pepin the Franks solemnly met together and constituted both his sons as their kings on the condition, agreed in advance, that they should divide the whole body of the kingdom equally.'* A further instance is Aimon's comment on events after the death of Carloman:[15] 'At the death of his brother Charles was constituted king by the consent of all the Franks.'† Such is the evidence in Aimon.[16]

There are many similar passages in Gregory of Tours, and we offer these few examples. In one instance he writes:[17] 'When the Franks had deposed Childeric they unanimously adopted Eudo as their king.' Again, he states:[18] 'Then the Franks, who had formerly considered inviting Childebert the Elder, sent an embassy to Sigebert asking him to come to them so that, when Chilperic had been deserted, they might establish him as king on their own account.' A little later occurs the passage:[19] 'The whole army was ranged before him, and, placing him upon a shield, they chose him for their king.' And in another reference:[20] 'Sigebert accepted the offer from the Franks, and according to the custom of the nation he was placed upon a shield and elected king, thus acquiring the kingdom from his brother Chilperic.' Soon afterwards one reads:[21] 'When the Burgundians and Austrasians had made peace with the rest of the Franks, they raised up Lothar as king with jurisdiction over them in all the three kingdoms.' The abbot of Ursperg confirms this.[22] 'The Burgundians and Austrasians', he says, 'made peace with the Franks and elevated King Lothar as ruler over the whole kingdom.' A little further on he writes:[23] 'The Franks

---

* *a This sentence is repeated below in* c, *where it is taken from the Dijon chronicle. See the note following the next note.* † *a a quotation from Einhard was given here in* a *and attributed to Aimon. In* bc, *as shown in the note preceding the last note, it was moved to an earlier place and correctly attributed. It has not been given a second time in the translation, as it has been in the Latin.*

Franci alterum eius fratrem Hildericum, qui Austrasiis iam imperabat, super se Regem constituunt.

^cNuper etiam incidi in Chronica manuscripta monasterii Besnensis in Burgundia, ubi sub anno DCLVIII haec reperio:[24]
5 *Clotarius Rex immatura praeventus morte, regnum sine herede reliquit* (id est, sine filio, more Feudistico) *cuius obitum dolentes Francorum principes, germanum eius Childericum Regem Austrasiorum, in omni sublimant Francorum regno.* Et mox,[25] *Childericus ergo Rex paucis annis quibus regnum Francorum obtinuit, defunctus*
10 *est, et germanus eius Theodoricus in regno fratris loco sublimatus.* Item alio loco et multo ante:[26] *Dagobertus Metis urbem veniens cum consilio Pontificum et Procerum, sed et omnibus primatibus regni sui consentientibus Sigebertum filium suum in regnum sublimavit, sedemque Metis civitate habere permisit.* Item sub anno DCCLXVIII:[27]
15 *Franci facto solemniter generali conventu, ambos sibi constituunt Reges, ea conditione praemissa, ut totum regni corpus ex aequo partirentur.*[*]

^aEodem pertinet quod Luitprandus Levita Ticinensis lib. 1, cap. 6 ita scribit:[28] *Cumque Burgundionum Regna transiens, Franciam, quam Romanam dicunt, ingredi vellet, Francorum nuntii*
20 *ei occurrunt, se redire nuntiantes, eo quod longa expectatione fatigati, cum sine Rege diutius esse non possent, Odonem cunctis petentibus elegerunt. Fertur autem hac occasione Francos Widonem sibi Regem non assumpsisse,* etc. Sed de hoc Odone memorabilis[29] ^bet Reginonis[30] ^aet Sigeberti[31] narratio est, ex qua planius etiam de
25 Regis filio repudiato, et alieno ascito cognoscitur. ^bNam Regino quidem lib. 2 sic loquitur, sub anno 888:[32] *Interea Galliarum populi in unum congregati, Ottonem Ducem filium Rudperti, cui prae*

---

16 bc have this sentence twice, here and above at p. 224, l. 3ff.
[24] PL, CLXII, 786.   [25] Ibid.   [26] Ibid., 779.   [27] Ibid., 788–9.   [28] Antapodosis, I, 16; MGH SS, III, 280, 40.   [29] See below, n. 37.   [30] See below, n. 32. [31] See below, n. 36.   [32] MGH SS, I, 598, 35ff.

constituted as their king his other brother Childeric [Childeric II], who already ruled over the Austrasians.'

^cI recently made an extract from the manuscript chronicle of the monastery near Dijon in Burgundy where I found these observations under the year 658:[24] 'Since King Lothar met an early death, the kingdom remained without an heir (that is, without a son according to feudal custom), and at his passing the sorrowing chiefs of the Franks raised up his half-brother King Childeric of the Austrasians to authority over the entire kingdom of the Franks.' A subsequent passage states:[25] 'King Childeric held the kingdom of the Franks for a few years, and when he died, his half-brother Theuderic was elevated to the throne in his place.' A similar point is made in a much earlier passage:[26] 'Dagobert arrived at the town of Metz with a council of bishops and nobles, and with the agreement of all the leading men of his kingdom, he endowed his son with authority and allowed him to have his capital in the province of Metz.' Another entry occurs for the year 768:[27] 'The Franks made a solemn general agreement to constitute two kings, on the condition, agreed in advance, that they should divide the whole body of the kingdom equally.'*

^aIt is appropriate to quote here the words written by Liutprand of Tessino:[28] 'Crossing the kingdoms of the Burgundians, he was about to enter that part of Francia which was described as "Roman", when the Frankish ambassadors met him. They told him they were returning to their country because they had been tired by their long expectation of his coming, and, as they could not wait any longer without having a ruler, they had joined together in soliciting and electing Odo as king. However, it is reported that on this occasion they did not take Odo [Wido] as their king etc.' There is an important account of this Odo[29] ^bby Regino[30] and another^a by Sigebert,[31] from which a fuller understanding can be derived of the way in which the son of a king might be rejected and another adopted. ^bFor under the year 888 Regino states:[32] 'Meanwhile the peoples of France gathered together in a single place, and by their deliberation and decision they created as

* See the note preceding the last note.

caeteris formae pulchritudo et proceritas corporis et virium sapientiae-que magnitudo inerat, Regem super se pari consilio et voluntate creant. Sed et Annalium Rhemensium scriptor:[33] *Quum quotidie,* inquit, *copiis Roberti crescentibus decrescerent Caroli, clam tandem* 5 *secedens cum Haganone trans Mosam proficiscitur. Franci Robertum seniorem eligunt, ipsique sese committunt. Itaque Rex, Rhemis apud S. Remigium, ab Episcopis et primatibus regni rex constituitur.* [c]Rhegino vero sub anno DCCL:[34] *Pipinus,* inquit, *secundum morem Francorum electus in Regem, et unctus per manum Bonifacii* 10 *Mogontinensis urbis Archiepiscopi, et elevatus est a Francis in regno in Suessionis civitate.* [a]Nam sub anno 890 ita loquitur:[*35] *Franci vero neglecto Carolo Ludovici Balbi puero, vix decenni, Regem sibi praeficiunt Odonem filium Roberti Ducis, quem a Nortmannis occisum supra diximus.* Item Otto Frising. Chron. lib. 6, cap. 10:[36] 15 *Occidentales,* inquit, *Franci, Odonem Roberti filium, virum fortem, consensu Arnolphi Regem creant.*

[b]Quae testimonia eo magis notanda atque observanda sunt, quod populi ius demonstrant summum fuisse, non modo in Regibus deligendis, verumetiam in Regum filiis repudiandis, et 20 alienis asciscendis,[*] quod etiam post Caroli Simplicis mortem usu venit. Nam Rhegino sub anno DCCCCXXV:[37] *Carolus Rex,* inquit, *in custodia, qua tenebatur, obiit, qui fertur vir hebetis esse ingenii, et minus aptus utilitatibus regni. Omnes etiam a filio eius deficientes, quendam Rodulphum sibi Regem eligunt.* Filium autem 25 Aimoinus[38] Ludovicum appellat, qui minus commode illud narrans, scribit Carolum in custodia praecepisse de Francorum procerum consilio, ut Rudolphus Richardi Burgundionum Ducis filius in regem ordinaretur. Sed Annalium Rhemensium scriptor planius id exponit:[39] *Audito,* [c]inquit, [b]*Franci, quod*

---

11 *bc* begin this sentence 'Sigebertus vero sub anno 890, hoc modo'.   20 'populi ius...asciscendis': *c* 'perspicue ac dilucide demonstrant, summum penes populum ius arbitriumque fuisse, non modo Regum deligendorum, verum etiam, repulsis ac repudiatis demortuorum Regum filiis, alienorum asciscendorum'.

33 Frodoard, A.D. 922; Bouquet, VIII, 178 D. The penultimate word 'rex' does not belong.   34 *MGH SS*, I, 556, 14ff.   35 Sigebert; *MGH SS*, VI, 343, 52f. 36 *MGH SS*, XX, 233, 43.   37 *MGH SS*, I, 616, 12ff.   38 Cf. IV, 42; ed. 1567, 733.   39 Frodoard, A.D. 923; Bouquet, VIII, 179 D.

king over them Duke Odo, the son of Robert, who surpassed all others in his beauty, size and wisdom.' But in the annals of Reims the writer says:[33] 'As the forces of Robert increased daily while those of Charles diminished, he finally withdrew in secret and set out across the Meuse with Hagano. The Franks elected Robert the Elder and engaged themselves to follow him. In this way he was constituted king at Reims in the church of Saint Rémi by the bishops and leading men of the kingdom.' cAnd then for the year 750 Regino writes:[34] 'Pepin was elected to the throne according to the custom of the Franks. He was anointed by the hand of Boniface the archbishop of Metz, and in the state of Soissons was granted by the Franks authority throughout the kingdom.' aFor the year 890 Sigebert remarks:[35] 'The Franks passed over Charles, the son of Louis the Stammerer, who was then scarcely ten years old, and appointed as their king Odo the son of Duke Robert, who, as we said earlier, was killed by the Normans.' Otto of Freising states in his chronicles:[36] 'With the consent of Arnulf the Western Franks made Odo, the son of Robert, king, who was a man of strength.'

bThese quotations should be the more carefully noted and observed, because they show that the right of the people was supreme, not only in choosing kings but also in repudiating the sons of kings and adopting strangers,* a practice which came into fashion after the death of Charles the Simple. For Regino writes for the year 925:[37] 'King Charles, who was reported to be slow-witted and of very little skill in government, died in the custody in which he was held. All abandoned his son and elected a certain Rudolph as king.' Aimon gives a less satisfactory account of the episode.[38] He calls the son Louis and writes that Charles was taken into custody in advance by the decision of the Frankish nobles so that Rudolph, the son of Duke Richard of Burgundy, might be declared king. But the writer of the annals of Reims explains the matter more fully.[39] 'When the Franks heard the rumour', che observes,

---

* c because they show...adopting strangers *becomes* because they very clearly and plainly show that the supreme right of choice lay with the people, not only in selecting kings but also in rejecting and repudiating the sons of deceased kings and in adopting strangers.

Carolus Normannos ad se venire mandasset, ne illi coniungerentur,
inter Carolum atque Normannos cum Rodulpho medii resederunt;
tumque Carolo trans Mosam refugiente, Rodulphum cuncti Regem
eligunt. ᵃItem* in Appendice Gregor. Turon. lib. 15, cap. 30:⁴⁰
5 *Post Dagoberti decessum, filius suus Clodoveus sub tenera aetate*
regnum patris ascivit, omnesque leudes (id est, subiecti) eum in
Masolano villa sublimant in regnum.

Item Sigebert. in Chron. anno 987:⁴¹ *Ludovico Francorum*
Rege mortuo, Francis Regnum transferre volentibus ad Carolum
10 *fratrem Lotharii Regis, dum ille rem ad concilium defert, regnum*
Francorum usurpat Hugo, etc. Multa eiusdem generis apud
Adonem testimonia sunt, velut anno 686:⁴² *Clodoveus Rex decessit,*
Franci Clotarium filium eius Regem constituunt. Et mox:⁴³ *Clotarius*
quatuor annos regnans obiit, cuius loco Franci Theodoricum fratrem
15 *eius erigunt.** Item anno 669:⁴⁴ *Franci Danielem quendam clericum*
post abiectionem tonsurae, in regno stabiliunt, atque Chilpericum
nuncupant. Et mox:⁴⁵ *Franci Theodoricum Dagoberti filium Regem*
super se constituunt. Item apud Ottonem Frising. Chron. 6,
cap. 13:⁴⁶ *Ottone,* inquit, *Francorum rege mortuo, Carolus voluntate*
20 *omnium rex creatur.* Item Appendix Gregor. Turon. lib. 11,
cap. 101:⁴⁷ *Mortuo Theodorico Rege, Franci Clodoveum filium eius*
parvulum elegerunt in regnum. Et cap. 106:⁴⁸ *Franci vero Chil-*
pericum quendam Regem constituerunt. ᵇEt cap. 107:⁴⁹ *Quo mortuo*
Theodoricum regem statuerunt in sedem regni. ᵃItem Godfrid.
25 Viterb. Chron. parte 17, cap. 4:⁵⁰ *Pipinus vero per Papam Za-*
chariam ex electione Francorum factus est Rex Francorum, Hilderico
ignavo Rege per Francos in monasterium misso.

His ex locis, aliisque similibus quamplurimis ᶜdilucide ᵃpatere
arbitror, Reges Francogalliae populi potius, ᵇhoc est ordinum,
30 et (ut nunc loquimur) statuum ᵃiudicio ac studio quam

4 *a*¹ 'Itaque'.
15 *bc* '*eligunt*' (but '*erigunt*' is correct).

⁴⁰ XI, 79; ed. 1568, App., 62.   ⁴¹ *MGH SS*, VI, 353, 2f.   ⁴² *PL*, CXIII, 116.
⁴³ *Ibid.*   ⁴⁴ *Ibid.,* an. 718; *loc. cit.,* 120; this passage was quoted earlier from
Aimon: see above, p. 222, n. 12.   ⁴⁵ *Ibid.; loc. cit.,* 121.   ⁴⁶ *MGH SS*, XX,
234, 42.   ⁴⁷ Ed. 1568, App., 79.   ⁴⁸ *Ibid.,* 81.   ⁴⁹ *Ibid.,* 83.   ⁵⁰ Partic. XXII,
43; *MGH SS*, XXII, 204, 11ff.

b'that Charles had summoned the Normans to his aid, they, together with Rudolph, remained inactive between the two for fear they might unite; and, when Charles fled across the Meuse, the Franks joined together to elect Rudolph king.' *a*Also in the appendix to Gregory of Tours we read:[40] 'After the death of Dagobert, his son Clovis [Clovis II], who was of tender age, received the kingdom, and all his subjects raised him to the throne in the country estate of Masolanum.'

Sigebert writes to the same effect in his chronicle for the year 987:[41] 'After the death of Louis, king of the Franks, they wished to transfer the royal authority to Charles, the brother of King Lothar, but, while Charles was reporting the matter to the council, Hugo usurped the Frankish throne etc.' There are many instances of this kind in Ado of Vienne, as, for example, under the year 686:[42] 'At the death of King Clovis the Franks made his son Lothar king.' Or, soon afterwards:[43] 'Lothar died after a reign of four years, when the Franks raised up* his brother Theuderic [Theuderic III] to his place.' Or, again, for the year 669:[44] 'The Franks established in authority a certain clerk called Daniel, after removing his tonsure, and they named him Chilperic.' Or, in a following passage:[45] 'The Franks made Theuderic, son of Dagobert, king over them.' The same custom is reported in Otto of Freising.[46] 'At the death of Odo, king of the Franks', he writes, 'Charles was made king by the will of all.' Also in the appendix to Gregory of Tours:[47] 'At the death of King Theuderic the Franks appointed his little son Clovis to the royal authority.' And also:[48] 'The Franks made a certain Chilperic king.' *b*And in another passage:[49] 'Upon his death they installed Theuderic on the throne as king.' *a*In Godfrey of Viterbo we read:[50] 'The Franks sent their wretched king Childeric to a monastery, and Pepin was made king of the Franks through Pope Zachary and by the election of the Franks.'

I think it is *c*abundantly *a*clear from these references and from many other similar ones that the kings of Francogallia were constituted by the authoritative decision and desire of the people, *b*that is, of the orders, or, as we are now accustomed to say,

* *bc* elected.

hereditario iure constitutos fuisse; cuius rei magno etiam argumento est ritus, quo maiores in Regibus inaugurandis utebantur.
Quod enim paulo superius diximus, Cornel. Tacitum de
Caninefatibus,[51] Francorum popularibus, testari, ut designa-
5 tum Regem scuto imponerent, sublimemque humeris ges-
tarent, idem in Regibus nostris usurpatum animadvertimus.
Nam qui populi suffragiis delectus fuerat, hunc scuto impositum
sublevabant, humerisque sustentatum ter circum populi comitia,
vel, *b*si in castris id acciderat, *a*circum exercitum, plaudentibus
10 atque acclamantibus universis, gestabant. Gregor. lib. 2, ubi de
Clodovei Regis electione commemorat:[52] *At illi,* inquit, *ista
audientes, plaudentes tam palmis, quam vocibus, eum clypeo evectum,
super se regem constituunt.* Item lib. 7, cap. 10, ubi de Gondebaldo
loquitur:[53] *Ibique,* inquit, *parmae superpositus Rex est levatus; sed
15 cum tertio gererent, cecidisse fertur, ita ut vix manibus circumstantium
sustentari posset.* Qua de re Aimoinus lib. 3, cap. 6 ita scribit:[54]
*Evocatum Gondobaldum more antiquorum Francorum Regem pro-
clamantes esse suum, elevaverunt eum clypeo; cumque tertio totum
cum eo circuissent exercitum, repente ruens cum Rege vix a terra
20 elevari potuit.* Item Ado Viennensis Aetat. 6:[55] *Sigebertus,*
inquit, *Francis consentiens, more gentis impositus clypeo, rex
constitutus est.* Ac nimirum ex eo factum constat, ut scriptores
illi ubi de Rege creato commemorant, libenter* hanc locu-
tionem usurpent, ut eum in regem elevatum dicant.

23 *bc* 'plerunque'.

[51] *Hist.,* IV, 15; Loeb, 26. [52] II, 40; *MGH SS Mer.,* 1:1², 91, 4. [53] *Ibid.,*
VII, 10; *loc. cit.,* 332, 5. [54] Cap. 61; *PL,* CXXXIX, 735. [55] *PL,* CXXIII, 110.

of the estates, *a*rather than by any hereditary right. The custom employed by our ancestors in the installation of kings is another powerful argument to the same effect. We may observe that the custom we have remarked a little earlier, which Cornelius Tacitus reported of the Caninefates,[51] the fellow-countrymen of the Franks – namely, the placing of the designated king upon a shield and his elevation upon the shoulders of those present – this was the custom practised among our kings. For he who had been chosen by the votes of the people was placed upon a shield, lifted up, and borne three times round the assembly of the electors, or, *b*if the ceremony occurred in a military camp, *a*round the ranks of the army amid general applause and acclamation. Gregory of Tours describes the election of King Clovis.[52] 'As soon as they heard these things', he writes, 'they applauded with both clapping and shouting, and, lifting him upon a shield, made him king over them.' Later he says the same thing of Gundovald.[53] 'And there', he states, 'the king was placed upon a shield and elevated. But it is said that he fell as they were carrying him round for the third time, so that those around him were scarcely able to hold him up with their hands.' Aimon writes about this incident as follows:[54] 'They called forth Gundovald and proclaimed him king in accordance with the custom of the early Franks. They hoisted him on a shield, and, as they marched with him for the third time round the entire army, they fell suddenly with the king and were barely able to lift him from the ground.' Another reference is in Ado of Vienne:[55] 'Sigebert accepted the offer of the Franks, and according to the custom of that people was placed upon a shield and proclaimed king.' Hence doubtless derives the practice of some writers who, when they refer to the creation of a king, make free* use of the expression and speak of his being elevated to kingship.

* *bc* frequent.

^cCAPUT VII [^{ab}VI cont.]

De summa populi potestate in regibus caussa cognita condemnandis et abdicandis*

---

^aSed nunc ad tertium huius disputationis argumentum acceden-
dum est, ut intelligatur, quantum in Regibus constituendis, reti-
nendisve, ^bordinum ac ^apopuli ius potestasque fuerit; siquidem
ex omnibus nostris Annalibus constat, Regum abdicandorum
5 summam potestatem penes populum* fuisse. Cuius potestatis*
insigne documentum is qui primus Francogalliae Rex creatus
fuit, nobis praebet, quem cum populus comperisset flagitiis ac
libidini deditum, aetatem in stupris* et scortationibus consu-
mere, publico consilio removerunt, Galliaeque finibus excedere
10 coegerunt; quod anno CCCCLXIX factum nostri testantur.
Quinetiam is quem ipsius in locum suffecerunt, Eudo, cum sua
potentia ad superbiam et crudelitatem abuteretur, pari severitate
iudiciorum exauctoratus est. Cuius rei testes sunt ^bHunibaldus
sub anno 467;[1] ^aGregor. Turon. lib. 2, cap. 12;[2] Aimoin. lib. 1,
15 cap. 7;[3] Godfrid. Viterbiens. parte 17, cap. 1;[4] Sigebert. sub
anno 461 et 469.[5] *Childericus vero* (inquit Gregorius[6]) *cum esset
nimia in luxuria dissolutus, et regnaret super Francorum gentem, coepit
filias eorum stuprose detrahere. Illique ob hoc indignantes, de regno eum
eiiciunt. Comperto autem, quod etiam eum interficere vellent, Thorin-*
20 *giam petiit.* ^bHunibaldus autem:[7] *Anno*, inquit, *regni sui sexto
conspirantes contra eum principes et proceres Francorum, propterea
quod impotenter et nimis luxuriose vivens uxores et filias nobilium
plures vitiasset, voluerunt eum occidere; quod cum ei innotuisset, cum
paucis occulte fugit in Thoringiam.* Post Franci quendam Aegidium

Cap. c[1] 'De summa antiqui populi Gallici severitate in condemnandis et abdicandis Regibus'. 5 'populum': *bc* 'ordinum comitia'. 5 'Sed nunc...Cuius
potestatis': *c*[1] 'Huius severitatis, quae iam exsolevit'. 8 *bc* 'ganeis'.

[1] See below, n. 7. [2] See below, n. 6. [3] Cf. *PL.* CXXXIX, 641. [4] Partic.
XXII, 40; *MGH SS*, XXII, 201. [5] II, 12; *MGH SS Mer.*, I:1², 61, 7.
[6] *MGH SS*, VI, 310 and 311. [7] Ed. Schard, I, 329.

The supreme power of the people in condemning and deposing kings for known cause*

---

^aBut now we come to the third argument in this disputation. It is to be understood that, in as much as it was the right and power of ^bthe estates and ^athe people to constitute and maintain kings, so, if at least all our annals do not lie, the supreme power of deposing kings was also that of the people.† The very first man to be made king of Francogallia offers us a remarkable proof of this power.‡ When the people discovered that he was given to shameful acts and libidinous behaviour, spending his time in debauchery§ and fornication, they removed him by public consent and expelled him from Gaul. Our annals show this to have happened in the year 469. Even Eudo [Aegidius], whom they put in his place, abused his authority through his pride and cruelty and was dethroned with similar severity on the part of his judges. The evidence of this is contained in ^bHunibaldus under the year 467,[1] ^aGregory of Tours,[2] Aimon,[3] Godfrey of Viterbo,[4] and Sigebert for the years 461 and 469.[5] 'Childeric', writes Gregory,[6] 'became licentious through too much luxury while he was reigning over the nation of the Franks and began to seduce their daughters. They became so indignant at this behaviour that they ejected him from his office. Discovering that they also planned to kill him, he escaped to Thuringia.' ^bHunibaldus writes:[7] 'In the sixth year of his reign the princes and leading men of the Franks conspired against him because, in his intemperate and excessively luxurious way of life, he had violated many of the wives and daughters of the nobility. When he found out that they wished to slay him, he fled secretly to Thuringia with a few retainers.' Later the Franks made a certain Aegidius king over

---

* c¹ 'The extreme severity of the ancient French people in condemning and deposing kings'. † *bc* the assembly of the estates. ‡ *c¹ omits the first two sentences and alters* this power *to read* this severity, which is now set aside. § *bc* feasting.

sibi constituerunt in regem, qui regnavit annis octo; quem
Franci denuo nimis tyrannisantem, et proceres quosque crudeliter occidentem, tolerare diutius non valentes, eiecerunt.
*ª*Abbas autem Urspergensis:[8] *Quem* (inquit) *luxuriose viventem,*
5 *et cum filiabus populi fornicantem, interficere nolentes, abiecerunt.* Et
Sigebertus:[9] *Hildericum* (inquit) *insolenter et luxuriose se agentem
Franci de regno deturbant, et Aegidium Regem sibi praeficiunt.* Atque
hoc quidem praeclarum ac singulare maiorum nostrorum
facinus eo diligentius notandum est, quod in primordiis ac prope
10 incunabulis regni gestum, quasi quaedam testificatio fuisse
videtur, ac denuntiatio, Reges in Francogallia certis legibus
creari, non Tyrannos cum* imperio soluto, libero, et infinito
constitui.

Itaque cum hoc idem institutum posteri retinerent, anno
15 DCLXXIX,[10] Childericum Regem undecimum insolentius se
in imperio gerentem abdicarunt, cumque nobilem quendam,
nomine Bodilonem ad palum alligari, atque indicta caussa virgis
caedi iussisset, ab eodem Bodilone paucis post diebus interfectus
est; auctoribus Aimoino, lib. 4, cap. 44;[11] Adone, Aetate 6;[12]
20 Tritenhemio anno 673;*[13] itemque Sigeberto anno 667.[14] Eiusdemmodi maiorum nostrorum severitas aliquanto post extitit
adversus Theodoricum Regem XII, qui cum iniquo et avaro
imperio Regnum administraret, *Franci* (inquit Aimoinus[15])
super eum insurgunt, ac eum de regno eiiciunt, crinesque capitis eius vi
25 *abstrahentes incidunt*: lib. 4, cap. 44; Ado, Aetat. 6, anno 696,[16]
Sigebertus autem sub anno 667, magnam illius culpae partem in
praefectum Regium Ebroinum conferunt:[17] *Theodoricus,* inquit, *Rex propter insolentiam Ebroini a Francis repudiatur, et frater
eius Hildericus a cunctis ad regnum evocatur.* Et Ado:[18] *Franci,* in-
30 quit, *Theodoricum de regno abiiciunt; Ebroinum Lexovio monasterio*

---

12 *c*² omits 'certis legibus creari, non Tyrannos cum'.   **20** *c* '687'.

[8] Ekkehard, *Chronicon*, A.D. 367 'De origine Francorum'; *MGH SS*, VI, 116, 14.
[9] A.D. 461; *MGH SS*, VI, 310, 58.   [10] Sigebert, *MGH SS*, VI, 326; 54.
[11] See below, n. 15.   [12] Cf. *PL*, CXXIII, 116.   [13] *De orig. Franc.*; ed. 1539,
106 – identical to Hunibaldus, below, n. 20.   [14] A.D. 679; *MGH SS*, VI, 326, 7.
[15] Ed. 1567, 380.   [16] Below, n. 18.   [17] *MGH SS*, VI, 326, 7.   [18] *PL*,
CXXIII, 116.

them, who reigned for eight years. He also proved a great tyrant who put several nobles cruelly to death, and when the Franks were not able to endure his tyranny any longer, they drove him out. ªThe abbot of Ursperg states:[8] 'He lived luxuriously and debauched the daughters of the people, and, not wishing to kill him, they cast him out.' Sigebert says:[9] 'Childeric conducted himself with insolence and luxury, so that the Franks deposed him and appointed Aegidius as their king.' And this celebrated and remarkable deed of our ancestors should be noted all the more carefully because it was done near the beginning and in the infancy of the monarchy, as if it were a witness and declaration that in Francogallia kings were created by fixed laws and were not constituted as tyrants with unbridled, free and unlimited authority.*

The later Franks preserved this custom, and in the year 679[10] they deposed Childeric [Childeric II], their eleventh king, for the insolent manner of his rule. He had ordered that a certain nobleman named Bodilo be tied to a stake and flogged without being accused of an offence, and a few days later he was slain by the same Bodilo. This is recounted by Aimon,[11] by Ado,[12] by Trithemius for the year 673†[13] and by Sigebert for the year 667.[14] Sometime later the severity of our ancestors was expressed in the same way against Theuderic [Theuderic III], the twelfth king, who administered the government with a wicked and covetous hand. 'The Franks', writes Aimon,[15] 'rose up against him, and cast him out from the kingdom, pulling out the hair from his head by force and cutting it off.' Ado, describing the matter under the year 696,[16] and Sigebert, writing of the year 667, impute a great part of the blame to the royal general Ebroinus.[17] 'King Theuderic', he says, 'was deposed by the Franks because of the insolence of Ebroinus, and his brother Childeric [Childeric II] was enthroned by a united assembly.' Ado writes:[18] 'The Franks deposed Theuderic, cropped the hair of Ebroinus in the monastery of Lisieux, and elevated

---

* c² kings were created by fixed laws and were not constituted as tyrants with unbridled, free and unlimited authority *becomes* kings were constituted with unbridled, free and unlimited authority. † c 687.

237

tondent; Childericum super se Regem levant. Item Appendix Greg.
Turon. lib. 11, cap. 64:[19] *Franci contra Theodoricum insurgunt,
eumque a regno deiiciunt, crines capitis eius abscindentes totonderunt,
Ebroinumque ipsum tondent.* ^bSed optime omnium Hunibaldi
5 appendix:[20] *Theodoricus* (inquit) *otio et inertiae deditus omnia
negotia regni per Comitem Palatii, quem Maiorem domus nuncupa-
bant, disponere coepit. Huius maior domus fuit Ebruvinus, homo
sceleratus et impius, qui multa fecit mala, quibus commoti proceres
Francorum, Theodoricum a regno deiiciunt, et tam ipsum quam*
10 *Ebruvinum, separatos ab invicem ad duo monasteria intrudunt.* Et
mox:[21] *Hildericus duorum praecedentium frater medius, et Clodovei
filius, deiecto a regno Francorum Theodorico fratre iuniore, procerum
electione ad regnum de Austragia vocatus, regnavit annis paucis, qui
cum esset moribus asper, et multis nobilibus Francorum odiosus, in*
15 *venatione occisus est.* Eodem accedat Chronologia Idalii nondum
in lucem edita sub anno Christi DCIII.[22] Post Lotharium,
inquit, Theodoricus subrogatur in regnum, sed hoc post paucum
tempus, cum Ebroino maiore domus expulso, Childericum
Regem Austrasiorum fratrem eius minorem Franci in toto
20 sublimaverunt regno.

^aSimilis eorundem virtus* extitit in Chilperico Rege XVIII,
quem cum propter inertiam tanto imperio indignum censuis-
sent, Regno se abdicare coegerunt, atque in* monachatum
redegerunt,* auctoribus Aimoino lib. 4, cap. 61;[23] Sigeberto[24]
25 et Tritemio[25] anno 750; et Godfrid. Chron. part. 17, cap. 4.[26]
Sextum rursus eiusdem severitatis exemplum extitit in Carolo
Crasso Rege XXV, quem* propter similem ignaviam, et quod
Nortmannis Galliae partem concessisset, Regnumque imminui
passus esset, *ab optimatibus Regni* (ut Sigebertus loquitur[27])
30 *repudiatus est anno,* ut idem scribit, *890;* quod idem Godfridus

---

21 *c*[1] 'facinus'.   **23** *c* 'ad'.   **24** *bc* 'relegarunt'.   **27** *bc* 'qui'.

[19] XI, 94; ed. 1568, App., 14.   [20] Ed. Schard, I, 338.   [21] *Ibid.*   [22] Non
recognosco.   [23] Cf. ed. 1567, 404f.   [24] A.D. 750; *MGH SS*, VI, 332, 8.
[25] *De orig. Franc.*, ed. 1539, 118–19.   [26] Cf. Partic. XXII, 43 & 46; *MGH SS*,
XXII, 204, 10ff. & 205, 10ff.   [27] *MGH SS*, VI, 343, 49.

Childeric to the throne.' Gregory of Tours states in the sixty-fourth chapter of the eleventh book of his appendix:[19] 'The Franks rose up against Theuderic, drove him from the throne, and cut off his hair, as well as that of Ebroinus.' *b*But the best account of all is given in Hunibaldus' appendix:[20] 'Theuderic gave himself to idleness and sloth and began to dispose of all the business of government through the count of the household, who was called the mayor of the palace. This mayor of the palace was Ebroinus, a wicked and impious man who did many evil things. Roused by these actions, the Frankish nobility deposed Theuderic, and thrust both Theuderic and Ebroinus, one after another, into different monasteries.' A little further on he writes:[21] 'When Theuderic, a younger brother, was deposed from the Frankish throne, Childeric, son of Clovis [Clovis II] and middle brother of the two already mentioned, was called from Austrasia to the throne by the election of the leading men. He reigned for a few years, which were marked by the harshness of his conduct and the hatred it inspired among many of the Frankish nobles, and then was killed while hunting.' The same point is made in the chronologies of Idalius, which have not yet been published, for the year 603.[22] 'After Lothar', he writes, 'Theuderic was elected to the throne in his place, but after a little time, when Ebroinus the mayor of the palace had been expelled, the Franks elevated his younger brother Childeric, king of the Austrasians, to rule the entire kingdom.'

*a*Similar virtue was displayed* by our ancestors concerning Chilperic [actually Childeric III], the eighteenth king, whom they regarded unworthy of governing because of his sloth. They obliged him to resign the throne, and sent† him to a monastery. The authorities for this are Aimon,[23] Sigebert[24] and Trithemius[25] for the year 750, and Godfrey of Viterbo in his chronicle.[26] Charles the Fat, the twenty-fifth king, provides a sixth example of this same severity. Because of his like cowardice and the fact that he allowed the kingdom to be diminished, conceding part of France to the Normans, he was, to quote Sigebert,[27] 'deposed by the leading men of the realm' in the year (again according to Sigebert) 890. Godfrey

---

* *c*[1] Similar virtue was displayed *becomes* There was a similar act.   † *bc* despatched.

part. 17 testatur;[28] sed uberius Otto Frising. Chron. 6, cap. 9,[29] ubi memorabile illud adscribit: *hunc cum post Carolum Magnum inter omnes Reges Francorum maximae fuerat* auctoritatis, in brevi ad tantam tenuitatem venisse, ut panis quoque egens, ab Arnolpho iam* 5 *Rege facto stipendia miserabiliter exigeret, ac* ab ipso paucos fiscos* ^b*gratanter* ^a*susciperet; unde humanarum rerum status miserrimus cognoscitur, quod is qui tam Orientalia, quam Occidentalia regna cum Romano susceperat Imperio, ad tantam postremo deiectionem venit, ut panis quoque egeret.** Septimi etiam exempli memoria extat in 10 Odone rege XXVI, quem cum Franci repudiato Ludovici Balbi filio Carolo, Regem sibi delegissent, quarto post anno in Aquitaniam amandarunt, ibique considere iusserunt, eiusque in locum Carolum eiusdem Balbi filium suffecerunt: auctoribus Sigeberto sub anno 894;[30] Aimoino lib. 5, cap. 42;[31] Godfrid. 15 part. 17.[32] ^bSed et Regino lib. 2:[33] *Ottone,* inquit, *rege in Aquitania commorante, Francorum Principes ex maxima parte ab eo deficiunt, et in Rhemorum civitate Carolus filius Ludovici in regnum elevatur.*

    ^aIn eundem quoque numerum ascribitur Carolus Rex XXVII, propter stuporem in genii, Simplex cognomento dictus, qui cum 20 stultitia sua regnum pessundaret, Lotharingiamque quam prius recuperaverat, amisisset, captus atque in carcerem coniectus est, eiusque in locum Rodolphus suffectus: auctoribus Aimoino lib. 5, cap. 42;[34] Sigebert. anno 926.[35]

    ^bEt de eodem Annal. Rhemens. auctor, anno 920:[36] *Pene* 25 *omnes,* inquit, *Franciae Comites regem suum Carolum Simplicem apud urbem Suessionicam, quia Haganonem consiliarium suum, quem de mediocribus potentem fecerat, dimittere nolebat, reliquerunt.* ^cItem Rhegino lib. 2, Chr. anno 838:[37] *Ludovicus,* inquit, *a suis imperio privatur, regnique monarchia Lothario filio eius per electionem* 30 *Francorum datur.* ^bItem sub anno 922:[38] *Et cum quotidie copiis*

3 *bc* 'fuisset'.   5 *bc* 'atque'.   9 *c*¹ adds 'Haec ille.'.

[28] Cf. Partic. xxiii, 24; *MGH SS,* xxii, 230, 20–2.   [29] *MGH SS,* xx, 233, 21. [30] *MGH SS,* vi, 344, 6.   [31] v, 41; ed. 1567, 727–8.   [32] Cf. Partic. xxiii, 22–4; *MGH SS,* xxii, 229–30.   [33] A.D. 892; *MGH SS,* i, 605, 12ff.   [34] Cf. ed. 1567, 733.   [35] *MGH SS,* vi, 347, 8.   [36] Frodoard, A.D. 920; Bouquet, viii, 176c.   [37] *MGH SS,* i, 567, 18ff.   [38] Frodoard, A.D. 922; Bouquet, viii, 178D.

of Viterbo supports this account.[28] Otto of Freising gives more re-
warding detail in his chronicle,[29] where he writes these memorable
words: 'The man who after Charlemagne held the most extensive
power of all the kings of the Franks was in a brief space reduced to
such misery that he even lacked bread to maintain himself and had
to beg a pension from Arnulf, who had been made king in his place,
and was grateful to receive a pittance from him. From this we may
learn the wretched uncertainty of all human affairs, for here was
one who had ruled the western as well as the eastern kingdoms with
the authority of the Roman imperium, and yet he came in the end
to so abject a condition that he was in want of bread.' A further
memorable example, the seventh, concerns Odo, the twenty-sixth
king, who was chosen as king by the Franks after Charles, the son of
Louis the Stammerer, had been set aside. After he had reigned for
four years they removed him to Aquitaine and ordered him to
remain there, and elected the same Charles, son of the Stammerer,
in his place. Authorities are Sigebert for the year 894,[30] Aimon,[31]
and Godfrey of Viterbo.[32] [b]However, Regino writes:[33] 'While
Odo lingered in Aquitaine most of the Frankish princes defected
from his services, and Charles the son of Louis was elevated to the
throne in the city of Reims.'

[a]Charles, the twenty-seventh king, who was named the Simple
because of his dullness of wit, is also be numbered among these
examples. He ruined the kingdom through his stupidity, and he
lost possession of Lorraine, which he had earlier regained. He was
taken and cast into prison, and Rudolph was elected in his place.
The authorities are Aimon[34] and Sigebert for the year 926.[35]

[b]The compiler of the annals of Reims writes on this matter
under the year 920:[36] 'Nearly all the nobility of Francia abandoned
their King Charles the Simple in the town of Soissons because he
would not dismiss his counsellor Hagano, to whom he had entrusted authority in day-to-day affairs.' [c]In the second book of his
chronicle under the year 838 Regino states:[37] 'Louis was deprived
of his authority by his own followers, and the royal title was
bestowed on his son Lothar by the election of the Franks.' [b]The
chronicler of Reims writes for the year 922:[38] 'As the forces of

*Roberti crescentibus, decrescerent Caroli, clam tandem secedens cum
Haganone trans Mosam proficiscitur. Franci Robertum* SENIOREM
ELEGERUNT, *ipsique sese committunt. Robertus itaque rex Rhemis
apud Remigium ab Episcopis et primatibus regni constituitur.*
5 Item* sub anno 923:[39] *Auditoque Franci, quod Carolus Nortmannos ad se venire mandasset, ne illi coniungerentur inter Carolum
atque Nortmannos, super Isaram flumen; tumque Carolo trans Mosam
refugiente, Rodolphum cuncti* REGEM ELIGUNT. *Rodolphus ergo
frater Richardi rex apud urbem Suessionicam constituitur.* Atque
10 haec quidem post Francogalliae regnum constitutum Maiorum
nostrorum virtus fuit, cuius exemplum ipsi a suis quoque
maioribus acceperant. Nam Hunibaldus antiquissimus Francorum historicus, apud Iohannem Tritenhemium de Francis et
Heleno ipsorum Rege ita scribit:[40] *Anno eius regni* XIIII *congre-
15 gati apud Neopagum Sicambri Helenum regem inertem et inutilem
communi omnium sententia deposuerunt a regno, et ad privatam redire
vitam compulerunt; in cuius locum elegerunt fratrem eius minorem.*

Quae cum ita se habeant, perspicuum est, Agathium, qui
lib. 1 scribit,[41] regum Francorum* filios a parentibus regnum
20 successione excipere solitos, vel eorum instituti minus peritum
fuisse, utpote Graecum hominem et alienigenam; vel ita intelligendum esse, ut superius diximus, moris fuisse, ut regum filii,
regaliter educati atque instituti, praerogativam in commitiis
haberent, praesertim cum ea spe parentes adducti summum in
25 filiis bene honesteque instituendis studium collocarent. Sed
multo imperitius et absurdius est, quod Theo. Nehemius in
Nemore unionis tract. 6 scribit, Carolum Magnum constituisse,
ut deinceps Franci ex parentum successione reges haberent; cum
superius demonstratum sit, eundem Carolum in suo testamento
30 ius regum constituendorum populo Francico integrum illi-
batumque servasse.* Verba Nehemii haec sunt:[42] *Porro quia ipse*

---

5 *c* 'Idem'. 19 *c*^I adds 'illo seculo'. 31 *c* 'reliquisse'.

39 *Ibid.*, A.D. 923; Bouquet, VIII, 179D. This passage was quoted earlier: previous
chapter, p. 228, n. 39. 40 Ed. Schard, I, 304. 41 1, 3, §19; *PG*, LXXXVIII, 1284.
42 Dietrich von Nieheim, *De schismate*, IV (*Nemus unionis*), 6; ed. 1566, 363.

Robert increased daily while those of Charles diminished, he finally withdrew in secret and set out across the Meuse with Hagano. The Franks elected Robert the Elder and engaged themselves to follow him. In this way he was constituted king at Reims in the church of Saint Rémi by the bishops and leading men of the kingdom.' For the year 923 the same author says:[39] 'When the Franks heard the rumour that Charles had summoned the Normans, they were unwilling to be caught between Charles and the Normans beyond the River Isara. When Charles fled across the Meuse, they joined together to ELECT Rudolph KING. Thus Rudolph, the brother of Richard, was established as king in the town of Soissons.' Such was the excellent practice of our ancestors after the kingdom of Francogallia had been constituted, and they were in turn following the example of their own ancestors. For Hunibaldus, the earliest historian of the Franks, is recorded in Johannes Trithemius as writing of the Franks and their King Helenus as follows:[40] 'In the fourteenth year of his reign the Sicambri gathered together at Dieuze and deposed him as a king whom they all regarded as inactive and ineffective. They forced him to return to private life and elected his younger brother in his place.'

This was the established practice and when Agathias writes[41] that the sons of the Frankish kings* customarily followed their parents in succession to the kingdom, he clearly has little knowledge of their ways, being a Greek and a foreigner. Alternatively, it should be realised that it was the custom, as we have said earlier, that the sons of kings, who were brought up and provided for in royal fashion, had the right of voting first in councils. The parents were moved by ambition for their sons and took the greatest trouble to see that their sons might be comfortably and honourably established. It is even more crass and absurd to say, as does Dietrich von Nieheim, that Charlemagne enacted that thereafter the Franks should have kings who succeeded their fathers. It has already been shown that Charlemagne's will preserved† whole and unimpaired the right of the Frankish people to constitute their kings. These are the words of Nieheim:[42] 'Furthermore, because Charles was him-

---

* c¹ *adds* in that age.   † c left.

*Carolus Rex Francorum extitit, istud regnum fuit ad eum ex succes-
sione devolutum* (Hoc vero quid absurdius dici potuit?), *et videns
quod ipse factus Imperator, suos haeredes dignitate propria, scilicet
regno Francorum penitus denudasset* (Et hoc quoque perabsurde
5 scriptum apparet) *statuit, ut Francigenae cum quadam regni Francorum portione regem haberent de regali semine, iure hereditario
successorem, qui in temporalibus superiorem non recognosceret, videlicet ut Imp. posteritati** *ad homagium, vel aliquod obsequium teneretur.* Haec ille; quae, ut vera essent, tamen illud confirmarent,
10 usque ad Carolum Magnum Francogalliae regnum non haereditate, sed populi arbitrio delatum fuisse.

^cSed haec a Nehemio scripta esse apparet, ad tollendam quo-
rundam veterum Iuris Doctorum disputationem, his verbis
conceptam, 'An Rex Galliae Imperatorem aut alium superiorem
15 recognosceret?' de qua tractatur a Decretalistis in c. per venerabilem, Qui fil. sint legit.;[43] Bald. in consil. 49, vol. 1;[44] Specul.
tit. de feud. § Super homagiis;[45] Guid. Pap. quaest. 239.[46]

---

8 *c* '*potestati*'.

[43] c. 13 X 4, 17; Friedberg, II, 714ff.   [44] Baldus, *Consiliorum volumen tertium,*
cons. 159, §4; ed. 1575, III, 45ᵛ.   [45] Durandus, *Spec. Iuris,* Lib. IIII, Partic. III,
Rubr. *De feudis,* 'De homagiis et fidelitatibus' §29; ed. Venice, 1602, IV, 321.
[46] *Decis. Gratianop.* q. 239, §2, gl. *a*; ed. 1609, 164.

self king of the Franks, the kingdom had come to him by way of succession (what could be more absurd than this statement?), and, seeing that he himself after becoming emperor had gravely reduced his heirs in their own rank within the kingdom of the Franks (and this also seems a ridiculous thing to write), laid it down that the Francigenians in a certain part of the Frankish kingdom should have a king from the royal stock, who would succeed by hereditary right and who would not recognize any superior in temporal matters, neither by way of homage nor by any form of obedience to the descendants* of the emperor.' These are his words and in so far as they may contain any truth they confirm the fact that before Charlemagne the kingdom of Francogallia was not hereditary but was transferred by the choice of the people.

cBut it seems that this opinion expressed by Nichcim has to be accepted in the disputation of certain ancient doctors of the law when they conceive the issue, 'whether the king of France recognizes the emperor or any other superior'. This matter is traversed by the decretalists,[43] by Baldus,[44] by Durandus,[45] and by Guy Pape.[46]

* c authority.

^aCAPUT VII [^cVIII]

Pluribus extantibus regis demortui liberis, quid iuris in haereditate observaretur

Atque haec quidem eo pertinent,* ut doceamus, regnum Francogalliae antiquitus non hereditatis iure, ut privata patrimonia, sed
^bordinum ac ^aPopuli iudicio et suffragiis deferri solitum fuisse,
quo minus illi relictum quaestioni videtur loci: Si plures regis
5 demortui liberi extarent, quae in illorum iure ratio* teneretur.
Nam cum penes populi Comitia, et publicum Gentis concilium
non modo deferendi, verumetiam adimendi* regni summa
potestas esset, illud necessario consequitur, in eiusdem arbitrio
fuisse, utrum omnibus aequaliter, an uni tantum regni succes-
10 sionem deferret.

Quanquam hoc loco quaestio exoritur, si populus filio repudiato alium eligeret, ecquid tamen illi ad suam dignitatem
tuendam relinqueretur. Quare intelligendum est,* ^ciure quidem
Romano earum rerum, quae in Principis imperio ac ditione
15 sunt, quatuor tantum esse species: aliae namque ipsius Principis
patrimoniales sunt; aliae Fiscales; aliae publicae; aliae privatae.
Patrimoniales posteriorum Imperatorum Romanorum aetate
appellatae sunt, quae propriae ipsius Principis erant, non Principatus, sed patrimonii iure, quae idcirco de propria Principis
20 substantia esse dicuntur: L. 3, § 1, C. de quadr. praescriptione;[1]
veluti, si cui e proceribus Imperium a populo delatum esset,

---

1 *b* 'Quae omnia eo pertinent'; *c* 'Haec autem omnia eo pertinent'.   5 'quae
...ratio': *c* 'quae nam in cuiusque iure constituendo ratio'.   7 *c*[1] omits 'non
modo' and 'verumetiam adimendi'.   13 *c* from here to p. 258, l. 7, replaces
a suppressed *ab* passage which will be found in Appendix A, p. 528.

[1] *Cod.* 7, 37, 3; Krueger, II, 310.

^aCHAPTER VII [^cVIII]

The legal practice observed concerning the inheritance
of a deceased king when there were
several surviving sons

It is relevant* here to point out once more that the kingdom of
Francogallia was not subject to the law of inheritance as if it were a
private patrimony, but was habitually transferred by the votes and
decision of the ^bestates and the ^apeople. It follows that there is less
substance in the problem of what legal argument† applied when
there were several surviving sons of a deceased king. For, since the
supreme power not only of transferring but also of taking away‡ the
kingdom lay within the competence of the assembly of the people
and the public council of the nation, it is a necessary consequence
that the same authority must have decided whether the succession
should be shared equally among all the sons or bestowed upon one.

Nevertheless a question does arise here: whether any right to
preserve his rank remains with a son when the people have repudiated him and elected another. In this context it should be understood
that§ ^cby Roman law there are as many as four kinds of property
which are within the authority and at the disposal of the prince:
there is that which comprises the patrimonial estate of the prince
himself; there is fiscal property; public property; and private
property. In the age of the later Roman emperors patrimonial
property was described as that which belonged personally to the
prince, and not to the principality, and by the law of patrimony
this property was therefore said to comprise the particular goods of
the prince. See the relevant section of the *Code*.¹ If, for example, the
people transferred the sovereignty from the nobles to the prince,

* **b** All these matters make it relevant; **c** *adds* Moreover *to* **b**. † **c** what should
be the appropriate legal argument to be. ‡ **c**¹ *omits* not only *and* but also of taking
away. § **ab** *The ensuing* **c** *passage replaces the* **ab** *text, which is in Appendix A.*

247

certum est, ea bona quae ante delatum illum honorem propria
ipsius erant, in ipsius dominio mansisse, non qua Imperator erat,
sed qua Valens, aut Honorius, aut Theodosius, idque in libris
nostris Sacrum patrimonium passim appellatur: L. ult. C. de
5 vectig.;[2] L. 1, C. de indiction.[3] Pari ergo ratione, si Dagoberto,
puta, vel Lothario Francogalliae regnum ab ordinibus regni
delatum erat, quod ante adeptam illam dignitatem in bonis
habuerat, pleno iure ipsius manebat.

Fiscus autem, sive Fiscalia bona dicuntur, quae Principi ad
10 tuendam dignitatem suam populi voluntate attributa sunt; sive
ea in pecunia numerata; sive in praediis; sive in iure constitant.
Quamvis enim Fisci nomen stricte proprieque ad thesauros
pertineat: d. L. 3, C. de quadr. praescript.[4] (quod etiam origo
appellationis ostendit), tamen etiam ad fundos et praedia pro-
15 ductum est, quae in fisci patrimonio esse dicuntur: L. 2, § 2, D.
ne quid in loc. pub.;[5] L. 49, D. locat.;[6] L. 38, §1, D. ad municip.[7]
Quin etiam iura vectigalia, mulctae pecuniariae, privilegiaque
omnia Principi concessa, eo nomine continentur, uti patet ex
tot. tit. D. et C. de iur. fisc.[8] Magna igitur inter Patrimonium
20 Principis et Fiscum differentia est, multisque locis inter se
distinguuntur, veluti d. L. 3, § 1, C. de quadr. praescript.;[9]
L. 6 et L. ult. C. de vectigal.;[10] d. L. 49, D. locat.;[11] L. 6, D. de
iur. fisc.;[12] L. ult. D. qui pot. in pign. hab.[13]

Nam rerum patrimonialium commercium non est, nisi
25 voluntate Principis: L. cum servus, 39, § ult. D. de legat. 1.[14]
Fiscalium autem usitatum ac legitimum commercium est: L. si
procurator, 5, d. iur. Fisc.;[15] L. pacta, 72, § ult. D. de contr.
empt.;[16] illae ad Principis heredes transmittebantur, quamvis
imperii successores non essent: L. quod principi, 56, D. de legat.

---

[2] Cod. 4, 61, 13; Krueger, II, 187.   [3] Cod. 10, 17, 1; Krueger, II, 403.   [4] Cod.
7, 37, 3; Krueger, 310.   [5] Dig. 43, 8, 2, 2; Mommsen, 431.   [6] Dig. 39, 2, 49;
Mommsen, 442.   [7] Dig. 50, 1, 38; Mommsen, 895.   [8] Dig. 49, 14 and Cod.
10, 1; Mommsen, 879ff., and Krueger, 395ff.   [9] Cod. 7, 37, 3, 1; Krueger, 310.
[10] Cod. 4, 61, 6 & 13; Krueger, 187.   [11] Dig. 49, 2, 49; Mommsen, 442.   [12] Dig.
49, 14, 6; Mommsen, 880.   [13] Dig. 20, 4, 21; Mommsen, 301.   [14] Dig. 30, 39,
10; Mommsen, 459.   [15] Dig. 49, 15, 5; Mommsen, 880.   [16] Dig. 18, 1, 72, 1;
Mommsen, 268.

it is certain that those goods which were his before the transfer of that distinction remained under his control, not in his capacity as emperor, but because he was Valens, or Honorius or Theodosius. In our records this is described as the sacred patrimony. (See the *Code*.[2, 3]) For the same reason consider, therefore, whether, if the kingdom of Francogallia were transferred from Dagobert to Lothar by the estates of the realm, he would not retain an entire right to the goods he possessed before being deprived of his authority.

It is otherwise with the fisc, whether it consist of fiscal property made available to the prince for the maintenance of his rank by the will of the people, whether it be specified in money, whether it consist of lands, or whether it be established in law. For, although the word fisc concerns treasure in any proper and precise sense (as in the *Code*[4] which also shows the origin of the term), nevertheless it was applied additionally to farms and landed estates, which were said to be in the patrimony of the fisc (see the *Digest*[5, 6, 7]). Indeed the taxatory laws, together with many monetary matters and all the privileges conceded to the prince, are included within that term, as is evident from the use of the many headings concerning fiscal laws in the *Digest* and the *Code*.[8] Therefore there is a very great difference between the patrimony of the prince and the fisc, and they are distinguished one from another in many instances in the *Code*[9, 10] and the *Digest*.[11, 12, 13]

For no trafficking in goods that belong to the patrimony may take place unless the prince wills it (*Digest*[14]). However it is the legitimate practice for trade to take place within the fiscality (*Digest*[15, 16]). The patrimony was passed on to the heirs of the prince, although they were not his successors in the government

2.[17] Haec vero quia magis Principatus sunt, quam Principis, ad eum solum, cui principatus defertur, una cum principatu transferuntur. Qua de caussa Ulpianus dixit, res Fiscales, quasi proprias et privatas ipsius Caesaris esse: d. L. 2, § 2. Ne quid in
5 loc. public.;[18] id est, non vere, proprie ac pleno iure, quamvis interdum illud *quasi*, omittatur, ut in L. 3, D. de his quae pro non script. hab.[19]

Publicas autem res appellamus, quae civitatis cuiusque et proprietate et usu communes sunt, quales sunt curiae, fora, arcae
10 communes, agri publici, veluti compascua et sylvae communes: L. 1, § 1. Quod cuiusque univers.[20] Item (ut ex aetatis nostrae statu exemplum sumamus) tormenta muralia, unde illa controversia, quam And. Tiraquellus quodam loco commemorat,[21] cum civitas quaedam Galliae Regi sua tormenta muralia certum
15 ad usum commodasset, ille autem inter homines esse desiisset, civitas ab ipsius successore sua tormenta repetebat. Cui assentatores aulici stolidissime respondebant, novum Regem ex sui decessoris contractibus et obligationibus non teneri, quod absurdissimum esse constat, neque in Francogallia usurpatum,
20 ut Paponius testatur lib. 20, tit. de testam., art. 14,[22] ubi Oldradi consilium 94[23] in suam sententiam commemorat. Verum est igitur, civitates quamplurimas res proprias habere, a Fiscalibus rebus plane alienas L. 2, § publicae, Ne quid in loc. publ.;[24] L. 2, ubi omnes Doctores late hoc tractant; C. de divers. praed.
25 urb.;[25] L. civitatibus, 122, D. de legat. 1;[26] L. 1, C. de vend. reb. civit.;[27] L. 14, § ult. D. de servitut.;[28] L. 72, § ult. D. de contr. empt.[29]

Privatae autem res dicuntur, quae in cuiusque patrisfamiliae fortunis ac facultatibus censentur: L. 1, D. De rer. divis.[30] cum

---

[17] *Dig.* 31, 56; Mommsen, 474.   [18] *Dig.* 38, 8, 2, 2; Mommsen, 731.
[19] *Dig.* 34, 8, 3; Mommsen, 537.   [20] *Dig.* 3, 4, 1, 1; Mommsen, 72.   [21] Not found in the indexed ed. of Tiraqueau's *Opera omnia*, 1597.   [22] *Recueil*, lib. 20, tit. 1, art. 17; ed. 1574, 1081.   [23] Ed. 1583, 42^vff.   [24] *Dig.* 43, 8, 2, 3; Mommsen, 731.   [25] *Cod.* 11, 70, 2; Krueger, 451.   [26] *Dig.* 30, 122; Mommsen, 469.   [27] *Cod.* 11, 32, 1; Krueger, 436.   [28] *Dig.* 8, 1, 14, 2; Mommsen, 143.   [29] *Dig.* 18, 1, 72, 1; Mommsen, 268.   [30] *Dig.* 1, 8, 1; Mommsen, 39.

(*Digest*[17]). However, the status of the principality surpasses that of the prince, and so, when a patrimony is passed to a single person, to whom the principality has also been transferred, then the patrimony is united to the principality. Ulpian observed in this respect that fiscal matters are like the private property of the ruler himself (*Digest*[18]): that is to say, they are not regarded as truly property by full legal right, although they may be temporarily classified as similar to property, as in the third book of the *Digest*.[19]

We call those matters public which are common both by ownership and use of the state. Such are the courts, the markets, the common coffers, the public fields and common woods used for pasturage (*Digest*[20]). Or again, to take an example from our early history, there is the controversial issue of the battering rams, which André Tiraqueau records in a particular reference.[21] When the commonwealth had offered its battering rams for the use of a certain king of Gaul, the latter had retired into seclusion, and the commonwealth sought to recover its siege machines for his successor. The court commissioners replied in a most stupid fashion that a new king was not bound by the contracts and obligations of his predecessor. This is patently absurd and was never a practice observed in Francogallia, as Papon bears witness in a passage[22] where he includes the advice of Oldradus[23] within his judgment. Accordingly it is clear that commonwealths have the ownership of many things quite separate from fiscal matters (see the *Digest*,[24] the reference in the *Code* which all the doctors of the law discuss,[25] and four other rulings in the *Digest*[26, 27, 28, 29]).

Those things are called private property which are listed as the wealth and possessions of every head of a household (*Digest*)[30].

similibus quae latiore interpretatione, aeque ut res publicae,
Principis esse dicuntur, sed (ut ex Seneca in Quaest. Illustribus
docuimus[31]) imperio, non dominio; ditione, non proprietate;
universe, non singulatim; sola iuris fictione, non possessione et
5 usu. Itaque vendi, donari, legari a privatis res suas videmus
Principi, aut Imperatori, aut Regi, quae si antea ipsius propriae
fuissent, iterum ipsius fieri non possent.

---

[31] Hotman, *Quaest. illust.*, q. 1; ed. 1567, 1 (where he cites Seneca, *Lib. de benef.*,
VII, iv, 2 & v, 1 & vi, 3; Loeb, III, 464ff.).

Similarly, though by a wider interpretation, one may say of public property that in a sense it belongs to the prince – although (as we have shown from Seneca in our book of *Famous Questions*[31]) it is under his government, not in his domain. It is at his disposal but it is not his property, and it is so in general, not in particular. It is only his by a legal fiction, not in his possession and for his use. So we see that private men may sell, donate or bequeath their possessions to the prince, emperor or king, and even though such property was formerly private, it cannot become so again.

^cCAPUT IX [^{ab}VII cont.]

De regis domanio et fratrum ipsius appannagio

Nunc ut ad institutum, et quaestionem propositam revertamur, sciendum est, antiquitus institutum fuisse, ut Francorum Regibus non modo Fiscalia illa iura, qualia Romanis Imperatoribus concessa erant, verumetiam certa quaedam fruenda praedia ad
5 regiam suam dignitatem tuendam assignarentur, quae barbaro vocabulo DEMANIUM Regium appellantur, plerumque autem DOMANIUM. Est enim Domanium regium quasi *dos regni*, quomodo veteres dicebant Vatem* praedii, sive (ut planius loquamur) quasi quidam ususfructus certarum possessionum, Regi ad
10 tuendum dignitatis suae splendorem attributus. Dixi QUASI ususfructus propterea quod earum possessionum proprietas penes populum manet, neque ulla eius pars alienari a Rege potest, sine populo auctore, hoc est sine Ordinum et publici Concilii consensu, quemadmodum posterius commodiore loco doce-
15 bimus; ius tantum utendi fruendi ei conceditur. Addidi autem particulam QUASI, quia permultis in rebus ius illud ab usufructu discrepat; veluti, ut cautio* de fruendo boni viri arbitrio praestetur, ut ne forma et species praediorum mutetur, et quae sunt in eodem genere.
20   Utcunque sit, magnam ex illa definitione patet esse differentiam inter Patrimonium et Domanium Regale. Nam Patrimonium, ipsius Regis proprium est; Domanium vero, Regni, atque (ut vulgus loquitur) ipsius Coronae. Illud pleno iure, Regis est, atque ideo plenam et summam ipsius pro sua voluntate alienandi
25 potestatem habet. Huius nuda proprietas est penes universitatem populi, sive Rempublicam, ususfructus autem penes Regem;

---

8 c¹ 'Dotem'.   17 c¹ adds 'de restituendo cautio'.

The king's domain and the appanage
of his brothers

Let us return to the question we have posed as to what the law was
in ancient times and whether those rights in fiscal matters, possessed
by the kings of the Franks in the same manner as they had been
granted to the Roman emperors, did not also comprise the produce
of those estates which were assigned to them for the maintenance of
their kingly status. These estates were known in the barbaric
speech as the royal demesne [*Demanium*], but generally as the
domain [*Domanium*]. For the royal domain is like the kingdom's
dowry, the marriage portion in ancient usage, or, to be more
explicit, as if it were the usufruct of defined estates granted the king
to maintain the splendour of his rank. I have said 'as if it were the
usufruct' because the ownership of that property remains with the
people, and no part of it can be alienated by the king without
popular authority, that is, without the consent of the estates and
the public council. As we shall show later in a more appropriate
place, such a right of making use and profit is conceded to the king.
Moreover I have added these particular words 'as if it were'
because that right differs in many respects from a usufruct. For
instance, it is important to choose a reliable man to have the usufruct of a piece of land so that the shape and type of that land will
not be altered, and all such matters preserved in the same form.

However this may be, it is clear from this definition that there is
a great difference between the patrimony and the royal domain.
For the patrimony belongs to the king himself, but the domain
belongs to the kingdom, or, as it is commonly put, to the crown
itself. The king has full right over the former and he has the
supreme and entire authority to alienate it by his own will. The
simple ownership of the latter is that of the body of the people as
a whole, or of the commonwealth, while the usufruct is the king's,

qua de causa nullam, ut iam diximus, illius alienandi potestatem
habet. Ac plane verissima est Doctorum hac de re sententia:
Par idemque esse ius Regis in suum domanium, quod est viri,
in dotem suae uxoris; quemadmodum praeter caeteros tradunt
5 Lucas de Penn. in L. quocunque, C. de ann. agr. desert.;[1] Paris
de Put., de syndicat., sub Rub. de excessibus Imper.;[2] And. Isern.
in tit. Feud., quae sint regal.[3] Inter Domanium autem et Fiscum
hoc interest, quod illud ad usum ipsius Regis, hoc est ad anno-
nam, et victum cultumque Maiestatis Regiae consentaneum
10 institutum est; hic, ad statum Regni et Reipublicae tuendum
atque conservandum, qui si forte propter bellorum et aliarum
eiusmodi necessitatum rationem sufficere non videatur,
tum demum in subsidium tributa de communi ordinum
sententia in publico Concilio universae genti indicuntur.
15 Praeterea domanii commercium nullum est, Rerum Fiscalium
usitatum ac legitimum, ut paulo ante demonstravimus. Illud
certum ac definitum est, harum modus incertus, atque infinitus,
quia Fisci nomine non modo ea omnia quae vulgo praecise
Regalia, plene autem Iura regalia vocantur, verum etiam alia
20 innumera, quae Regiae Maiestati ad Rempublicam tuendam
concessa sunt, complectitur. Ac de Domanio quidem illud ac-
cipiendum est, quod Eguinarthus in eo libello, quem ad Caroli
Magni et Carlovingorum gratiam, et ad imminuendam Merovingorum existimationem conscripsit, his verbis tradidit:[4] *Cum*
25 *praeter inutile Regis nomen et precarium vitae stipendium, quod ei*
Praefectus aulae exhibebat, nihil aliud proprii possideret, quam unum
perparvi redditus villam, in qua domum, ex qua famulos sibi necessaria
ministrantes, atque obsequium exhibentes paucae numerositatis
habebat. Haec ille.
30   Itaque postquam, recepta sensim consuetudine, Francogalliae
corona hereditaria esse coepit, et vel filio, vel proximo agnato
deferri, quamvis plures eiusdem gradus vel filii vel agnati essent,
tamen uni tantum, seniori scilicet, ac natu maximo domanium

---

[1] (= *Cod.* 11, 58, 7) *Lectura super tribus libris*, ed. 1544, 184–185^v.   [2] §11; ed.
1578, 78.   [3] §§54–6; ed. 1568, 767–8.   [4] C. 1; *MGH SS*, 11, 444, 7–10.

and for this reason the king, as we have said already, has no power whatever to alienate it. This is quite explicit in the opinions of the learned in the matter, the king having the same share and right in his domain as a husband has in the dowry of his wife. This is the way in which Lucas de Penna, before all others, treats the issue in his commentary on the *Code*.[1] See also Paris de Puteo in his views on corporations, under the heading of the limits of imperial authority,[2] and Andreas de Isernia on the titles of royal fiefs.[3] There is a difference between the domain and the fisc, since the former is for the king's own use and was created for his sustenance and for the mode of living appropriate to kingly majesty, while the latter is for the safety and preservation of the kingdom and commonwealth. If it does not seem adequate because of the necessity of wars and other affairs of this kind, then contributions in the form of a subsidy are proclaimed following the common decision of the estates in a public council of the whole people. Moreover the domain cannot be used for commercial purposes, whereas trade is allowed and employed in fiscal property, as we have shown a little earlier. The domain is well known and clearly defined, whereas the extent of the fisc is unknown and unlimited, because within the term fisc is included not only all those things called in the common abbreviation the regalia, or, more fully, the regalian rights, but also countless other things which are granted to the royal sovereignty for the security of the commonwealth. The nature of the domain may be understood from Einhard's description in the book he wrote to exalt Charlemagne and the Carolingians and to diminish the reputation of the Merovingians:[4] 'Apart from the useless title of king and the uncertain salary the court prefect offered him, he had nothing else of his own, except for a small country house, where, out of necessity, he had attendants to wait upon him and a few who showed him servility.'

Later, when the custom had been clearly established, the crown of Francogallia began to be hereditary, and was passed to a son or to the nearest cousin, and although many of that rank were either sons or cousins, the crown passed to only one such, namely to the eldest. The domain was accorded to the eldest by birth, and all the

illud attributum fuit reliquis omnibus eiusdem gradus vel filiis
vel agnatis ab illo exclusis, quorum tamen habita ratio est diligenter. Nam ad vitae cultum et decus familiae pro dignitate tuendum, institutum fuit, ut iis possessiones quaedam assignarentur,
5 quae vulgo *appannagia* dictae sunt, ab antiquo et Francico (ut mihi
persuasi) vocabulo *Abbannem*, quod Latine valet, excludere; item
ut *Ausbannen* et *Forbannen*, quasi ea portione accepta exclusos se
a Regni succesione intelligerent; ^aquemadmodum Otto Frising.
Chron. 5, cap. 9,[5] et Godfridus Viterbiensis[6] scribunt, Dago-
10 bertum Lotharii filium, Regem constitutum, fratri Heriberto
urbes et pagos aliquot prope Ligerim fruendos dedisse; quod
idem Aimoinus lib. 4, cap. 17 commemorans, ita subiungit:[7]
*Pactum cum ipso pepigit, ut privato contentus habitu, nil amplius de
paterno sperare deberet regno.* ^bEt Regino lib. 1:[8] *Dagobertus,*
15 inquit, *monarchiam totius imperii obtinuit, excepto quod fratri suo
Heriberto contra Ligerim et limitem, quo tenditur partibus Vasconiae,
pagum scilicet Tholosanum, Caturcinum, Aganensem, Petragorium,
et Sanctonicum, vel quod ab his versus Pyranaeos montes excluditur,
concessit.* Ex quibus intelligitur, quod Aimoinus illo loco scribit,[9]
20 Heribertum consortem regni factum, non de regni iure intelligendum esse, sed de regni ditionibus. Itaque paulo post scribit,[10]
eundem Heribertum illa ditione non contentum, vi et armis regis
nomen sibi sumpsisse, bellumque fratri contra pactionem in-
tulisse. Similiter autem idem Aimoinus eo libro quarto, ^aItem*
25 cap. 61 de Pipino scribens,[11] *Grisonem fratrem,* inquit, *more Ducum
XII comitatibus donavit.* Atque huc illud pertinet quod Greg.
Turonen. lib. 7, cap. 32 ita scribit:[12] *Misit Gondobaldus duos
legatos ad Regem, cum virgis consecratis iuxta ritum Francorum, ut
scilicet non contingerentur ab ullo. Et mox,*[13] *Gondobaldus dicit se*
30 *filium esse patris nostri Regis Clotarii, et misit nos ut debitam por-
tionem regni sui recipiat.*

---

24 *bc* omit 'Item'.

[5] *MGH SS*, xx, 219, 46.   [6] Cf. Partic. xxii, 28; *MGH SS*, xxii, 196, 32.
[7] *PL*, cxxxix, 778.   [8] A.D. 576; *MGH SS*, i, 551, 50ff.   [9] Non invenio.
[10] Non invenio.   [11] Ed. 1567, 403.   [12] *MGH SS Mer.*, i:1², 352, 7.   [13] *Ibid.*,
352, 12.

rest of that same rank, whether sons or cousins, were excluded from the domain, despite the fact that their claim was carefully considered. To preserve their way of life and maintain the dignity and splendour of the family, it became the practice to assign certain properties to them, which were commonly called appanages, or, as I believe, by the ancient Frankish word *Abbannem*, the Latin equivalent for which is *excludere* [to exclude]. Thus they were known as *Ausbannen* and *Forbannen*, as if, by the acceptance of that portion, they had excluded themselves from the succession to the kingdom. [a]Otto of Freising[5] and Godfrey of Viterbo[6] record that when Dagobert, the son of Lothar, had been made king he gave certain towns and villages near the Loire for the use and enjoyment of his brother Charibert. Aimon records the same thing, and adds these words:[7] 'He made a pact with him that he should be content to live as a private person and hope for nothing more from his father's kingdom.' [b]Regino also states:[8] 'Dagobert secured the monarchy's full authority, except for the lands he granted his brother, Charibert, on the other side of the Loire, including parts of Gascony and the towns of Toulouse, Quercy, Agen, Périgueux and Saintes, but excluding the territory towards the Pyrenees.' It can be understood from this, as Aimon remarks in the passage cited,[9] that, although Charibert was given a share in the kingdom, this was not done because of any established law but because the kingdom had authorized it. Aimon writes in a passage a little later[10] that the same Charibert was not content with the authority given him, and assumed the title of king by force and in arms, and made war against his brother contrary to their pact. Moreover Aimon says the same thing [a]when, writing about Pepin, he states:[11] 'He granted some counties to his brother Grifo at the wish of the twelve dukes.' It is appropriate here to quote the observations of Gregory of Tours:[12] 'Gundovald sent two envoys to the king carrying staffs which had been consecrated according to Frankish rites so that no one would place a hand upon them.' Gregory of Tours continues:[13] 'Gundovald said that he was the son of their father King Lothar, and sent the envoys to receive that part of the kingdom that was his due.'

Nunc ut ad propositam quaestionem redeamus, quantum ad regni successionem attinet: certum hac de re ius Francogalliae nullum reperio, quippe, cum hereditaria, ut dixi, non esset; ceteris autem in patrimoniis nobilibus, quae feuda nominantur,
5 Otto Frising. lib. Frid. 2, cap. 29:[14] *Mos est*, inquit, *in Burgundia, qui pene in omnibus Galliae provinciis servatur, quod semper seniori fratri, eiusque liberis, seu maribus, seu foeminis, paternae haereditatis cedat auctoritas, ceteris ad illum tanquam ad dominum respicientibus.*
^cQuibus omnibus ex locis intelligendum est, res eas, quae Apan-
10 nagii titulo filiis natu minoribus attribuuntur, neque regni, neque regiae hereditatis partes esse,* non magis, quam res certas legati aut hereditatis titulo relictas, hereditatis partes esse intelliguntur: L. pen. C. de hered. instit.;[15] L. quoties, 9, § heredes, D. eod.;[16] L. qui fundum, 87, § 3, D. ad l. Falcid.;[17] L. quaedam,
15 9, § 1, D. de edend.;[18] non enim hereditas pars proprie in una re intelligitur: L. quamvis, 14, D. si quis omiss. causs. test.[19]
^aAtque hoc idem iuris in gente Francorum universa ^bfuisse, ^amultis verbis traditur a Petro de Vineis, lib. Epistol. 6, epist.* 25,[20] et aliis nonnullis locis.
20   Sed in regni successione aliud iuris fuit. ^bNam primum vetus lex fuit, ut quamvis deferendi regni iudicium arbitriumque summum penes Ordinum comitia, publicumque gentis totius Concilium esset, tamen si Regis defuncti filii annis XXIIII minores essent, eos creari ius non esset, atque adeo alium aetatis
25 legitimae creari necesse esset. Qua ex re de Maiorum nostrorum sapientia existimare licet, qui Reipublicae suae gubernacula ei aetati committenda non existimarunt, quae alieni consilii, etiam in privatis rebus suis administrandis, indigeret. Verba autem Hunibaldi apud Iohann. Tritenhemium haec sunt:[21] *Anno*
30 *Christi CCCIX, cum Rex Francorum Clogio incautius dimicaret, a Romanis interfectus et occisus est, duos relinquens filios, quorum natu*

11 *c*² omits 'esse'.   18 *c*² omits '6, epist.'.

[14] *Gest. Fred.*, II, 29; *MGH SS*, XX, 413, 2.   [15] *Cod.* 6, 24, 13; Krueger, II, 258.   [16] *Dig.* 28, 5, 9, 12; Mommsen, I, 419.   [17] *Dig.* 35, 2, 87, 3; Mommsen, I, 558.   [18] *Dig.* 2, 13, 9; Mommsen, I, 56.   [19] *Dig.* 29, 4, 14; Mommsen, 449.   [20] Ed. 1740, II, 197 (quoted above, ch. IV, n. 27, [p. 188]).   [21] Ed. Schard, I, 314.

Let us return to the question we have postulated, so far as it concerns the succession to the kingdom. I find no certain law of Francogallia in the matter, since, as I have already remarked, the kingdom was not hereditary. But for other noble patrimonies described as fiefs Otto of Freising writes:[14] 'In Burgundy it is the custom, as it is in nearly all the provinces of France, that the control of the paternal inheritance always descends to the elder brother and his children, whether they be male or female, the others regarding him as if he were their lord.' cFrom all these references it should be understood that property which, under the name of an appanage, is attributed to sons who are younger by birth, is neither part of the kingdom nor of the royal inheritance. It is no more so than those things bequeathed under the name of a legacy or inheritance are actually parts of that inheritance (see the *Code*[15] and the *Digest*[16, 17, 18, 19]). aPetrus de Vinea in various passages in his letters[20] shows this bwas athe general legal practice among the Frankish people.

But the law was otherwise concerning the succession to the kingdom. bFor in the first place it was an ancient law that, although the supreme decision and choice in the transfer of the kingdom lay with the assembly of the estates and the public council of the whole people, the sons of a deceased king who were younger than twenty-four years in age had no right to be made king. In these circumstances it became necessary to appoint someone else who was of legal age. One may well praise the wisdom of our ancestors in this respect. They did not believe that the government of their commonwealth should be committed to one of tender age who might desire foreign counsel, especially in the administration of his private affairs. These are the words of Hunibaldus, as conveyed by Johannes Trithemius:[21] 'In the year 309 A.D. Chlogio, the king of the Franks, very rashly made war and was slain by the Romans. He left two sons, of whom the elder, Helenus, was then aged twenty,

maior Helenus annum tunc agebat XX, minor vero natu Richimer
XVIII. Lege autem Francorum erat interdictum, ne quis promoveretur
in Regem, nisi XXIIII aetatis annum complesset. Hinc factum est,
quod neuter filiorum Clogionis ad regnum potuit pervenire, sed patruus
5 *eorum Clodomer, electione principum, fuit in Regem coronatus.*

Haec ille, ex quibus perspicuum est, quod superius dicebamus,
quod Agathius scribit,[22] Regum filios regnum a parentibus
excepisse, nequaquam simpliciter et absolute intelligendum
esse, sed ita, si caussa eorum, Ordinum comitiis, publicoque
10 gentis Concilio probata esset, in cuius caussae cognitione caput
hoc fuit, An XXIIII annorum maiores essent. Quam aetatem si
compleverant, *aNam** memoriae proditum est, antiquis temporibus persaepe Francogalliae Regnum Rege mortuo non uni
filio a populo* attributum, sed in viriles partes divisum,
15 atque assignatum fuisse. Itaque defuncto Clodoveo Rege
secundo, anno DXV, qui liberos IIII reliquerat, Theodoricum,
Clodoveum, Childebertum, et* Chlotarium, satis constat,*
Regnum inter eos ita divisum fuisse,* ut Theodoricus Metarum,
Clodoveus Aureliae, Chlotarius Suessionum, Childebertus
20 Lutetiae regnum obtineret: auctoribus Agathio lib. histor. 1;[23]
Greg. Turon. lib. 3, cap. 1;[24] Aimoin. lib. 2, cap. 1;[25] Rheginone
sub anno 421.[26] Rursus post Chlotarii Regis IIII excessum,
Regnum inter quatuor ipsius filios ita partitum fuit, ut Chere-
bertus Lutetiae, Guntrannus Aureliae, Chilpericus Suessionum,
25 Sigebertus Rhemorum regnum obtineret:* auctoribus Greg.
lib. 4, cap. 22;[27] Aimoin. lib. 3, cap. 1;[28] Rheginone sub anno
498.[29] Contra vero anno circiter DCXXX, mortuo Lothario
Rege VII, Otto Frising. Chr. 5, cap. 9,[30] et Godfrid. Viterb.[31]
ita scribunt: *Dagobertus Clotarii filius solus in Francia regnabat, sed*

---

12 *bc* 'tum'.   **14** 'a populo': *bc* 'ab Ordinum comitiis'.   **17** *bc* omit 'et'.
17 *c*¹ omits 'satis constat'.   **18** *c*¹ 'fuit'.   **25** 'Suessionum...obtineret':
bc 'Suessionibus, Sigebertus Rhemis regni sui sedem arcemque collocaret'.

[22] I, 3, §19; *PG*, LXXXVIII, 1284 (as above, ch. VI [VII], n. 41 [p. 242]).   [23] *Ibid.*
[24] *MGH SS Mer.*, I:I², 97.   [25] Cf. *PL*, CXXXIX, 661.   [26] *MGH SS*, I, 547,
41ff.   [27] *MGH SS Mer.*, I:I², 155, 2.   [28] *MGH SS*, I, 548, 9ff.   [29] *PL*,
CXXXIX, 691.   [30] *MGH SS*, XX, 219–20.   [31] Partic. XXII, 28; *MGH SS*,
XXII, 196, 32.

and the younger, Richemer, was actually eighteen. But by the law of the Franks it was forbidden for anyone to be advanced to the kingship if he had not completed his twenty-fourth year. So, since neither of the sons of Chlogio could become king, their paternal uncle Chlodomir was chosen by the leading men and crowned as king.'

From all this it is clear, as we have already said, what Agathias[22] means when he writes that the sons of kings were withdrawn from the succession by their parents. This should in no sense be understood simply and absolutely in the terms in which it is expressed, but rather in terms of the reasons behind the parents' action. The issue had been examined by the assemblies of the estates and the public council of the people, in whose jurisdiction the determination of the matter lay, that is whether the sons were more than twenty-four years of age. *^aFor** it is recorded that in ancient times the kingdom of Francogallia often was not granted by the people† to a single son upon the death of a king, but was divided, and each part assigned to adult rulers. So it was that when Clovis, the second king, died in the year 515, leaving his four sons, Theuderic, Clovis [actually, Chlodomir], Childebert, and‡ Lothar, it was convenient to divide the kingdom among them, Theuderic taking Metz, Clovis Orléans, Lothar Soissons and Childebert Paris. This is related by Agathias in his history,[23] Gregory of Tours,[24] Aimon,[25] and Regino under the year 421.[26] After the death of Lothar, the fourth king, the kingdom was again divided between his four sons, Charibert taking Paris, Guntram Orléans, Chilperic Soissons and Sigebert Reims.§ This is recorded by Gregory,[27] Aimon,[28] and Regino for the year 498.[29] However, Otto of Freising[30] and Godfrey of Viterbo[31] describe the situation about the year 630, on the death of Lothar, the seventh king, as follows: 'Dagobert,

---

* *bc* omit For. † *bc* by the assembly of the estates. ‡ *bc* omit and. § *bc* Charibert taking...Sigebert Reims *becomes* so that Charibert established the capital and stronghold of his kingdom at Paris, Guntram his at Orléans, Chilperic his at Soissons and Sigebert his at Reims.

fratri suo Heriberto circa Ligerim fluvium paucas urbes et pagos dimi-
serat; a Clodoveo enim usque ad id tempus regnum Francorum inter
filios, filiorumque filios, multifarie diviso confuse regnatum est.
Terminus autem Regni Francorum erat iam ab Hispania usque Pan-
5 *noniam. Dagobertus itaque unicus Rex Francorum leges Bavaris dedit.*
Haec Godefridus; neque, ut multi sapientes saepe iudicarunt,
iniuria. Nam (ut est apud Iustinum libro 21)[32] *firmius est futurum*
regnum, si penes unum remanserit, quam si portionibus inter plures
fratres dividatur.

10   Aliquot tamen interiectis annis, cum Francorum Regnum
longe lateque propagatum esset, Pipino rege mortuo, alia
publico Gallorum concilio* sententia placuit, quod valet ad
confirmandum* quod superius diximus, penes ^bOrdinum et
^aConcilii arbitrium, totum illud ius fuisse. Nam Eguinarthus in
15 vita Caroli Magni, sic loquitur:[33] *Mortuo Pipino, Franci facto*
solenniter generali conventu, ambos sibi eius filios Reges constituunt,
ea conditione, ut totum Regni corpus ex aequo partirentur, et Carolus
eam partem, quam pater eorum Pipinus tenuit, Carolomannus eam,
cui patruus eorum praeerat, regendam susciperat. Item Abbas
20 Ursperg.:[34] *Mortuo Pipino, Carolus et Carolomannus filii eius,*
omnium Francorum consensu ambo reges creati sunt, ea conditione, ut
totum Regni corpus ex aequo partirentur. Simillima post Caroli
Magni excessum in partiendo regno ratio fuit, quemadmodum
ex ipsius testamento apud Iohan. Nauclerum,[35] et Eguinarthi
25 libello de ipsius vita,[36] cognosci licet, ubi tota prope Europa inter
tres ipsius filios ita dividitur, ut tamen filiabus nihil dotis, aut
legitimae portionis caussa tribuatur; sed earum collocandarum,
dotisque constituendae potestas summa* fratrum fidei, ^bchari-

---

12 *bc* 'consilio'.   **13** *c*[1] adds 'id'.   **28** *bc* omit 'summa'.

[32] XXI, 1, 2; Teubner, 127.   [33] C. 3; *MGH SS*, II, 445, 2–5.   [34] Ekkehard,
Chronicon, A.D. 768; *MGH SS*, VI, 161, 18.   [35] *Chron.* II, gen. 28; ed. 1579,
701.   [36] Cf. cap. 2; *MGH SS*, II, 460–1.

the son of Lothar, ruled alone in France, but he had given up to his brother Charibert a few towns and villages near the River Loire. Indeed from the reign of Clovis until this point the kingdom of the Franks was subjected to endless subdivisions ruled over in confusion by a number of sons, and the sons of sons. Moreover, the boundaries of the kingdom of the Franks at this time stretched from Spain to Hungary, and as Dagobert was the sole king of the Franks he gave laws to the Bavarians.' This was a sound opinion of Godfrey, as many wise men have often pointed out. For, as Justin remarks,[32] 'the kingdom will in future be much stronger if it remains under the sway of a single ruler than it would be if divided into segments between many brothers'.

Yet after a number of years, when the kingdom of the Franks had expanded far and wide and King Pepin had died, another attitude became popular – a circumstance which validates and confirms the remarks we made earlier to the effect that the entire authority in the matter lay in the choice of *b*the estates and *a*the council. For in his life of Charlemagne Einhard writes as follows:[33] 'At the death of Pepin the Franks summoned a general assembly with all due solemnity and appointed both his sons as their kings, with the condition that they should divide the whole body of the kingdom equally between them: so that Charles should rule over that part which their father Pepin held and Carloman over that part which their uncle controlled.' The abbot of Ursperg writes on the same matter:[34] 'After Pepin's death his sons, Charles and Carloman, were both appointed as kings by the agreement of all the Franks on the condition they should divide the whole body of the kingdom equally between them.' There was very much the same purpose behind the division of the kingdom after the death of Charlemagne, which can be seen from his will as represented by Johannes Nauclerus,[35] and from Einhard's book about his life.[36] Therein one can see how nearly the whole of Europe was divided between his three sons in such a way that nothing was provided as a dowry or as a recognized portion for his daughters. Complete* authority in arranging their marriage and dowry was left to the

* *bc omit* Complete.

tati ^aet prudentiae permittatur. ^bNeque iniuria, cum principes, et proceres quibus illae nuptum collocantur, non tam dotis spe, et magnitudine, quam generis et familiae dignitate ad earum matrimonium adducantur.

5   ^aEandem in Orientali Francia partitionem post Ludovici mortem anno DCCCLXXIIII* fuisse, testatur Otto Frisingensis Chron. 6, cap. 6,[37] et Rhegino in Chron. anno 877.[38] Rursus annis aliquot interiectis, post Ludovici Balbi Regis XXIII excessum, anno DCCCLXXX, eadem quoque partiendi ratio
10 servata est, quam tamen non in Regum* ipsorum, sed in ^bOrdinum ac ^apublici Concilii arbitrio fuisse, facile, ex his Aimoini verbis cognosci licet, lib. 5, cap. 40:[39] *Filii*, inquit, *Ludovici quondam Francorum Regis profecti sunt Ambianos, et sicut fideles eorum invenerunt, Regnum paternum inter se diviserunt.* Ex quibus
15 ita disputatis, perspicuum est, nullum antiquitus certum hac de re ius in Francogallia fuisse, sed totam eius rei potestatem in ^bOrdinum et ^apublico gentis consilio* positam fuisse. Postea vero Philippo III, Rege XLI auctore constitutum est,[40] ut ditio aliqua minoribus fratribus attribueretur, sed eius quoque iuris variae
20 interpretationes fuerunt, multaeque natae contentiones, propter filiarum rationem, ut plane nihil certi hac de re tradi a nobis possit, nisi, si res ad antiquum Maiorum nostrorum institutum revocetur, totum eius rei ius publico Gentis ^bet Ordinum ^aConcilio committendum esse, ut* pro liberorum numero certae illis
25 ditiones ad victum et cultum ^bet dignitatem generis tuendam ^afruendae attribuantur.

---

6 *bc* 'DCCCLXIIII'.   **10** *ab* 'Regnum' (erroneously).   **17** *bc* 'concilio'.
24 'res ad antiquum...esse, ut': *c*¹ 'ex more veteri'.

[37] *MGH SS*, xx, 232.   [38] A.D. 876; *MGH SS*, I, 588, 28ff.   [39] Ed. 1567, 718.
[40] Cf. Isambert, II, 646 (Philip III, No. 139).

good faith, *b*affection *a*and prudence of their brothers. *b*Nothing unjust could follow from this since the princes and leading men with whom marriages might be arranged would not be encouraged to wed the daughters in expectation of a large dowry or in hope of added status for their house and family.

*a*Otto of Freising,[37] and Regino in his chronicle under the year 877[38] record that the same thing occurred in eastern France when it was partitioned after the death of Louis in 874.* Some years later, in 880, after the death of this twenty-third king, Louis the Stammerer, the same method of dividing the kingdom was employed. The decision was not, however, that of the kings themselves, for it was made by *b*the estates and *a*the public council. This would appear to be the meaning behind the observations of Aimon:[39] 'The sons of Louis, late king of the Franks, proceeded to Amiens, and, as they found their faithful subjects there, divided their father's kingdom among them.' From this it is clear that there was no clearly defined ancient law in Francogallia concerning this issue, and that the complete authority was vested in the public council of *b*the estates and *a*the nation. Indeed in a later period it was enacted by Philip III,[40] the forty-first king, that a certain grant might be assigned to younger brothers, but there were also various interpretations of this law and many disputes arose out of the position of the daughters. Hence it is not possible for us to convey fully anything certain in the matter, except that, if what is at stake concerns the practice followed by our ancient ancestors, the entire right in the matter belongs to the public council of the nation *b*and the estates, *a*and† they should act on behalf of the various children to grant them certain territories for the maintenance of their status *b*and the safeguarding of the dignity of their line.

* *bc* 873. † *c¹ omits* the entire...estates, and.

^aCAPUT VIII [^cX]

De lege salica, et iure mulierum in regum parentum haereditatibus

Quoniam de Regalis hereditatis iure dicere instituimus non praetermittenda legis Salicae commemoratio videtur, quae cum
assidue nostris hominibus in ore est, tum vero maiorum nostrorum memoria maximam et periculosam de Regni successione
5 contentionem sedavit. Nam cum anno 1328 Rex Carolus
Pulcher, Philippi Pulchri filius moriens uxorem praegnantem
reliquisset, paucis intermissis mensibus agnata filia, Eduardus
Angliae Rex, ex Isabella Philippi Pulchri filia Caroli Regis sorore
natus, hereditatem aviti Regni ad se pertinere contendit. At ex
10 contrario* Philippus Valesius Regis Caroli Pulchri frater patru-
elis exortus est,* qui diceret, antiquam esse legem Regiam,
Salicam nominatam, qua lege mulieres a Regni haereditate
arcerentur. Hanc porro legem Gaguinus et eiusdem generis
scriptores a Pharamundo scriptam tradunt: *Ad nostram*, inquit,[1]
15 *usque aetatem nominatissimam.* Et in vita Philippi Valesii: *Eduardo,*
inquit,[2] *obstabat lex Salica, quae a Pharamundo Francis data in illos*
usque dies observantissima habebatur. Ea lege soli virilis sexus Reges
a maioribus Regibus orti regnum administrant, nec ad eam dignitatem
foeminae admittuntur, cuius legis haec sententia est: Nulla hereditatis
20 *portio de terra Salica ad mulierem venito. Terram autem Salicam,*
Francorum Iureconsulti eam dicunt, quae solius Regis est, et a lege
Alodii distat, quae subditos comprehendit; quibus datur per hanc legem
rei alicuius liberum dominium, non exclusa Principis maiestate. Haec
Gaguinus. In eandem autem sententiam Francogalli omnes non
25 modo Historici, verumetiam Iurisconsulti et pragmatici usque

---

10 *bc* 'adverso'.   11 *c* move 'exhortus est' up after 'Philippus Valesius'.

[1] Gaguin, *Rerum Gallicarum annales*, Bk. 1 (under Pharamond); ed. 1577, 3.
[2] *Ibid.*, Bk. 8; ed. 1528, fol. cxlii.

The Salic Law and the right of women in the
inheritance of the kings, their fathers

Since we undertook to deliver some comments on the law of regal
inheritance, we must not neglect to make mention of the Salic Law.
This matter is constantly on the tongues of our contemporaries, and
in the memory of our elders it settled an intense and very dangerous
dispute as to the succession of the kingdom. In the year 1328, when
Charles the Fair, son of Philip the Fair, died, he left his wife bearing
a daughter who was born a few months later. Edward king of
England, whose mother was Isabella, daughter of Philip the Fair
and sister of King Charles, claimed for himself the succession to the
inheritance of his grandfather's kingdom. But Philip of Valois, a
cousin on his father's side to King Charles the Fair, opposed him,
and asserted that there was an ancient regal law named the Salic
Law by which women were excluded from inheriting the kingdom.
Gaguin and writers of his kind relate that this law was written down
by Pharamond. He describes it as 'a most celebrated law enduring
even to our own time'.[1] In his life of Philip of Valois he writes:[2]
'The Salic Law was an obstacle to Edward's claim. It was a law
given by Pharamond to the Franks as one to be scrupulously
observed even in those times. By that law only kings of male sex,
descended from kings, govern the kingdom, and females may not
be admitted to that dignity. This is the substance of that law: No
part of the inheritance of Salic land shall come to a woman. Moreover French jurists define Salic land as that which belongs to the
king alone, as distinct from allodial law, which applies to subjects.
By the latter law subjects are given free ownership of anything
not excluded by the authority of the prince.' These are the
words of Gaguin. Not only the historians of Francogallia but
also the jurists and practising lawyers have subscribed to this
opinion even to the present day – as, for example, Papon in his

ad hoc tempus scripserunt: teste Paponio Arest. lib. 4, cap. 1,[3]
ut iam *b*communis *a*error propemodum ius fecisse videatur.

    Verum illud meminisse oportet, quod superius attigimus, Fran-
corum duas sedes, duoque regna fuisse. Unum in Gallia, quod ad
5 hunc usque diem permansit, alterum ultra Rhenum ad flumen
Salam, unde Salii et Salici Franci coniuncte, plerunque autem
Salici praecise appellati, quorum et regnum et iam prope nomen
obsoletum est. De Saliis superius ex Ammiani Marc. historia
dictum est, demonstratumque, illos Orientales, hos Occidentales
10 appellatos fuisse.[4] Quemadmodum autem duo Francorum
regna fuerunt, ita duae Francorum leges: Salica, quae ad Salios;
Francica, quae ad Francogallos pertinebat. Eguinarth. in Carolo
Magno:[5] *Post susceptum Imperiale nomen, cum animadverteret,*
multa legibus populi sui deesse (nam Franci duas habent leges, plurimis
15 *in locis valde diversas) cogitavit quae deerant addere.* Auctor prae-
fationis in Legem Salicam:[6] *Gens Francorum inclita, antequam ad*
fidem catholicam converteretur, dictavit Salicam legem per Proceres
ipsius gentis, qui tunc temporis apud eandem erant rectores. Sunt autem
electi de pluribus viri quatuor, Wisogast, Arbogast, Salogast, et
20 *Windogast, qui per tres mallos (id est comitia) convenientes, omnes*
causarum origines solicite discurrendo, tractantes de singulis, iudicium
decreverunt hoc modo, etc. Ac fere iisdem verbis utitur Sigebertus
in Chron. anni 422;[7] Otto Frisin. lib. 4, cap. pen.:[8] *Leges quoque*
Wisigastaldo et Salagasto auctoribus ex hinc habere coepere. Ab hoc
25 *Salagasto legem, quae ex nomine eius Salica usque hodie vocatur,*
inventam dicunt. Hac nobilissimi Francorum, qui Salici dicuntur,
adhuc utuntur. Atque haec quidem veteres Chronographi, ex
quibus eorum errorem coargui licet, qui Salicam legem vel a sale,
id est, prudentia dictam, vel corruptam vocem tradiderunt, pro
30 Gallicam,[9] quo dici absurdius nihil potuit.

---

[3] *Recueil*, lib. 4, tit. 1, art. 2; ed. 1574, 212.   [4] See above, ch. v, n. 30 (p.
212); not literally true, though Ammianus does imply different groups of Franks.
[5] C. 29; *MGH SS*, II, 458, 10–12.   [6] *Lex Salica*, praefatio; ed. Eckhardt, 82ff.
[7] *MGH SS*, VI, 307, 13f.   [8] *Chron.*, IV, 32; *MGH SS*, XX, 212, 35.   [9] See,
e.g., Postel, *La loy Salique* (1552), ch. 7.

decrees[3] – so that this [b]common [a]mistake seems virtually to have become law.

It is necessary to recall the fact on which we have touched earlier, namely that the Franks had two capitals and two kingdoms. One was in Gaul, which has remained to this day, while the other was beyond the Rhine near the River Sala. Hence they were jointly called Salian and Salic Franks, and generally Salic for short, though their kingdom, and, now, virtually their name, have become extinct. We have already mentioned that the history of Ammianus Marcellinus reveals that some were called the eastern Salians and others the western.[4] Just as there were two Frankish kingdoms, so there were two bodies of Frankish law: the Salic, belonging to the Salians, and the Frankish, belonging to the Francogauls. Einhard writes in his life of Charlemagne:[5] 'He noticed after assuming his imperial title that his people lacked much in their laws, for the Franks had two bodies of law which differed exceedingly from each other in many respects. He gave much thought to the addition of what was lacking.' The author of the preface to the Salic Law has this to say:[6] 'Before it was converted to the Catholic faith, the celebrated nation of the Franks enacted the Salic Law by medium of their leading men, who were then their governors. Four men were chosen out of many – Wisogast, Arbogast, Salogast and Windogast – and in the course of three harmonious meetings they carefully examined all the original causes and investigated all matters separately before finally giving judgment to this effect...' Sigebert in his chronicle for the year 422,[7] and Otto of Freising in his fourth book[8] employ nearly the same words: 'From this point the laws prepared by Wisigastald and Salagast began to apply. It is said that the law set forth by Salagast, which even today is called the Salic Law, was so-called because of his name, and the most noble men of the Franks, who are called Salic, make use of it still.' The ancient chronographers express these opinions, which allow us to refute the error of those who would either derive the name of the law from the word *sal*, that is to say 'prudence' or 'good sense', or would claim the name has been corrupted from 'Gallic',[9] which is more absurd than anything that can be imagined.

Sed longe maiores ex eodem fonte nati sunt errores. Primum quod illis auctoribus* creditum est, Salicam legem ad ius publicum civitatis atque* Imperii, et hereditariae Regni successionis pertinuisse. Nam illius legis Salicae tabulae non multis ab
5 hinc annis repertae, et* in lucem editae sunt, ex quarum inscriptione cognoscitur, eas primum circiter aetatem Pharamundi Regis scriptas editasque fuisse, deinde omnia et Salicae legis et Francicae capita non de publico Regni et civitatis* iure, sed de privato tantum constituta fuisse. In iis autem unum hoc caput
10 extat tit. 62 *b*qui inscriptus est DE ALODIS, hoc est, de iis rebus, quae non feudi, sed patrimonii iure a privatis possidentur, quod summe notandum est:¹⁰ *a*DE TERRA SALICA IN MULIEREM NULLA PORTIO HEREDITATIS TRANSIT, SED HOC VIRILIS SEXUS ACQUIRIT; *hoc est, filii in ipsa* hereditate succedunt;* SED
15 UBI INTER NEPOTES AUT PRONEPOTES POST LONGUM TEMPUS DE ALODE TERRAE CONTENTIO SUSCITATUR, NON PER STIRPES, SED PER CAPITA DIVIDATUR.* Cuius legis similis extat apud Ripuarios tit. 58.¹¹ Itemque apud Anglos tit. 7,¹² ubi tantum abest, ut de Regnorum hereditatibus
20 sanciatur, ut ne ad feudorum quidem, sed tantum ad allodiorum successiones eae leges pertineant, quanquam dos quidem mulieribus ex iisdem allodiis assignabatur;* *b*ut facile illorum imperitia arguatur,* qui lege illa aut nunquam lecta, aut non intellecta affirmare ausi sunt, lege Salica cautum fuisse, ne regia
25 potestas ad mulieres transferatur.

*a*Utcunque sit, primum illud constat, etsi nullum nec Salicae, nec Francicae legis caput extet, quo mulieres a Regni hereditate

---

2 *bc* omit 'illis auctoribus'.   **3** *bc* omit 'civitatis atque'.   **5** *bc* 'atque'.
8 *bc* 'Imperii'.   **14** *bc* omit '*ipsa*'.   **17** *bc* render the Salic Law text in caps as here; *a* in lower-case letters.   **22** *bc* omit 'quanquam...assignabatur'.
23 *c* 'coarguatur'.
¹⁰ Usually tit. 59; ed. Eckhardt, p. 234.   ¹¹ §57 [56], 'De alodibus', 4; *MGHLL Sect. I*, III:2, 105.   ¹² Ed. Herold, *Orig. Germ. antiq. lib.* (1557), 128–9.

Over the centuries, however, there are yet greater errors born from the same source. In the first place from these authors* it has come to be thought that the Salic Law was a part of the public law of the commonwealth and† empire, and the law of hereditary succession to the kingdom. Not many years ago the tables of this Salic Law were discovered and brought to light, and it is known from these records that they were first written down and published about the time of King Pharamond. Moreover it is clear that all the main elements of the Salic and Frankish Law were enacted in the context of private law, and not of the public law of the kingdom and commonwealth.‡ One chapter among them has this heading *b*(which has been inscribed *De alodis*, that is, concerning property which is possessed by private men by the law of patrimony and not of the fief – a point which must be particularly noted[10]): *a*'NO PART OF INHERITANCE IN THE SALIC LAND PASSES TO A WOMAN BUT IS ACQUIRED ONLY THROUGH ONE OF THE MALE SEX (which means that sons succeed to the inheritance itself);§ BUT IN A CASE WHERE, AFTER A LONG PERIOD OF TIME, A DISPUTE ARISES BETWEEN THE GRANDSONS AND GREAT-GRANDSONS CONCERNING ALLODIAL LAND, IT SHALL BE DIVIDED NOT AMONG THE LESSER SHOOTS BUT AMONG THE HEADS OF THE FAMILY.' The like provision exists within the Ripuarian Law[11] and also within the law of the Angles,[12] which is so far removed from approval of anything concerning the inheritance of kingdoms that it does not even apply to the succession to fiefs, but only to the succession to allodial lands. At the same time those laws allowed marriage portions for women to be assigned from the same allodial lands.¶ *b*So it is easy to establish the stupidity of those who are bold enough to affirm from the Salic Law, which they have either never read or have failed to understand, that it was a prudent provision to prevent regal power being transferred to women.

*a*However this may be, it is plain in the first place that, even if no article of the Salic or Frankish law, by which women were

---

* *bc omit* from these authors. † *bc omit* commonwealth and. ‡ *bc* empire. § *bc omit* itself. ¶ *bc omit this sentence.*

arceantur, tamen instituta et mores gentis tanto seculorum consensu conservatos, *b*ac praesertim contradictoriis iudiciis confirmatos *a*legis scriptae vim obtinere. Nam Childiberto tertio*
rege mortuo, duabus filiabus superstitibus fratri eius Clothario
5 Regnum, illis exclusis, delatum est. Rursus Chereberto quinto
Rege mortuo, tribus filiabus superstitibus, Sigeberto ipsius fratri
successio delata est. Item, Gontranno Burgundiae et Aureliae
Rege mortuo, non Clotildae filiae ipsius, sed fratri Sigeberto
regnum delatum est.

10   Deinde* multo consideratius et cautius *b*illos *a*Philippi Valesii
consiliarios ex feudali iure disputaturos fuisse, quo iure feudorum
hereditates liberis posterisque virilis sexus tantummodo deferuntur, neque ad eas mulieres admittuntur. Ubi autem in ea
stirpe, in qua feudum versatur, mares defecerunt, tum ad alteram
15 stirpem feudum revocatur, ut illo casu acciderat. Quae vero
feuda depravato iure ad mulieres deferuntur, ea non proprie
feuda, sed feudastra potius appellanda esse, aliis libris *c*quos de
illo iure scripsimus,[13] abunde *a*demonstravimus.

3 *bc* 'Childericus 3.'.   **10** *bc* 'Constat praeterea'.

[13] *De feudis disputatio* (Part i of *De feudis commentatio tripertita*), ii, *ad finem*;
ed. 1573, 18.

excluded from hereditary right in the kingdom, be extant, nevertheless the practices and customs of the nation have acquired the force of written law. This is to be expected since they have been preserved for so long by the consent of succeeding generations *b*and especially since they have been confirmed through acceptance by those who had denied them. *a*Thus, after the death of Childebert* the third king, his two surviving daughters were excluded and the kingdom was transferred to his brother, Lothar. Again, at the death of Charibert the fifth king, the succession was passed to his brother Sigebert, although there were three surviving daughters. Similarly, when Guntram the king of Burgundy and Orléans died, the kingdom was bestowed upon his brother Sigebert, and not upon his daughter Clothild.

Furthermore the supporters of Philip of Valois would have been much better advised had they argued on the basis of feudal law, by which the inheritances of fiefs are passed to the subsequent children of the male lines only, and women are excluded. When that line in which a fief descends lacks male heirs, the fief reverts to the other line in the circumstances that happen to apply. Indeed those fiefs which, by some distortion of the law, are passed to women are not really fiefs at all, but should rather be called quasi-fiefs, as we have amply shown in other books *c*we have written about that law.[13]

---

* *bc* Childeric.

^aCAPUT IX [^cXI]

De iure regalis capillitii

Hoc loco non alienum videtur, aliud Maiorum nostrorum institutum commemorare, de Regio capillitio; nam memoriae proditum est singulare quoddam ius capillitii apud maiores nostros
fuisse, ut qui Reges a populo creati, aut regio genere prognati
5 essent, comam alerent, eamque a fronte discriminatam, un-
guentisque delibutam, decus atque insigne regium, regiaeque
stirpis haberent; reliqui cives omnes quamvis illustri loco nati,
tamen capillitii ius non haberent, sed propter assiduos (ut credi
par est) in re militari labores, raso vel detonso capite incederent,
10 quemadmodum de Iulio Caesare et plerisque aliis, Romanae
historiae commemorant. Aimoinus lib. 1, cap. 4:[1] *Regem vero*
ceterarum more nationum Franci sibi eligentes, Pharamundum solio
*sublimant regio, cui filius successit Clodiocrinitus; illo enim in**
tempore Francorum Reges criniti habebantur. Item lib. 3, cap. 61:[2]
15 *Hic Gundoaldus more Regum a matre sua enutritus (uti consuetudo*
antiquis fuit Franciae Regibus) capitis comam gerebat profusam.
Similiter Agathius lib. de bell. Goth. 1, ubi Clodoveum Regem
nostrum (quem tamen Clodamirum appellat)* a Burgun-
dionibus in bello captum commemorat:[3] *Ut primum,* inquit, *ex*
20 *equo lapsus est, Burgundiones conspicati capillitium, quod illi a tergo*
propendebat, ducem esse hostium animadverterunt; neque enim Fran-
corum regibus coma carere licet, sed a pueris intonsi permanent, et
profusum capillitium, atque in tergum reiectum habent.
Quinetiam multis ex locis licet animadvertere, maioribus

---

13 *bc* omit '*in*'.   18 'ubi Clodoveum...(...appellat)': *bc* 'ubi Regem
Francorum Clodamirum [*c* Clodomirum]'.

[1] *PL*, cxxxix, 640.   [2] *PL*, cxxxix, 733.   [3] I, 3, §19; *PG*, lxxxviii, 1284.

^aCHAPTER IX [^cXI]

The regal right to long hair

It may not be inappropriate here to mention our ancestors' practice of having their kings wear long hair. It is recorded that there was a certain remarkable law among them to the effect that those who were appointed kings by the people, or who belonged to the royal dynasty, varnished their hair, parted it on the forehead, besmeared it with oils, and adorned it with royal insignia and the ornaments peculiar to the royal family. All the other citizens, however illustrious their rank by birth, did not possess the right to long hair, but because of their zealous occupation in military affairs (and this seems credible enough) cut or shaved off their hair in the manner recorded in Roman histories concerning Julius Caesar and many others. For instance Aimon relates:[1] 'According to the custom of several peoples the Franks elected a king for themselves, and elevated Pharamond to the royal throne. He was succeeded by his son Chlogio Longhair, so called because at that time the kings of the Franks wore their hair long.' He mentions the practice again in a later passage:[2] 'Gundovald was brought up by his mother according to the manner of kings and wore a great mane of hair, as was customary with the ancient kings of France.' Agathias writes in similar terms in his account of the Gothic wars of our King Clovis (whom he calls Clodamir)* when he was captured in battle by the Burgundians:[3] 'As soon as he fell from his horse the Burgundians noticed from the conspicuous head of hair trailing down his back that he was the leader of their enemies; for the kings of the Franks may not cut off their hair, but remain with their hair untrimmed even from their boyhood, and always have a great mane of hair hanging behind them.'

Indeed one may infer this from many references to the custom of

---

* **bc** our King Clovis (whom he calls Clodamir) *becomes* Chlodomir, king of the Franks.

nostris in more fuisse, ut si cui vel Regnum abrogarent, vel ad-
ipiscendi Regni spem adimerent, ei capillitium abscinderent.
Aimoinus illo eodem loco:[4] *Ille intuitus in eum, incidi eius prae-*
cepit capillos, hunc suum negans filium fuisse. Item:[5] *Iterum incisis*
5 *crinibus Coloniae in custodiam traditur, unde fuga elapsus succres-*
centibus capillis, ad Narsetem transiens, etc., quam histor. Gregor.
Turonen. lib. 6, cap. 24 commemorat.[6] Item cap. 44, ubi de
Theodorico Rege loquitur:[7] *Franci,* inquit, *super eum consur-*
gunt, ac eum de regno eiiciunt, crinesque capitis eius vi abstra-
10 *hentes incidunt.* *b*Item lib. 7, cap. 36:*[8] *Tu ne es ille, qui plerumque*
a regibus Francorum propter has praesumptiones quas profers,
tonsoratus, et exilio datus es? Et mox:[9] *Quod me Chlotarius pater*
meus exosum habuerit, nulli est incognitum, quod autem ab eo, et
deinceps a fratribus sim tonsoratus, manifestum est omnibus. *a*Memor-
15 abilis autem ac potius horribilis historia extat apud Gregor.
Turon. de Regina matre Crotilde,* quae duobus filiis* caput
abscindi, quam comam maluit. Locus est lib. 3, cap. 18:[10] *Mater*
nostra (inquibat rex fratri suo) *fratris nostri filios secum retinuit, et*
vult eos regno donari. Communi consilio pertractare oportet, quid de
20 *his fieri debeat, utrum incisa caesarie, ut reliqua plebs habeantur, an his*
interfectis regnum germani nostri inter nos dividatur. Et mox:[11] *Tunc*
misere Archadium cum forcipe, atque evaginato gladio, qui veniens
ostendit Reginae utrunque, dicens: Voluntatem tuam, ô gloriosissima
Regina, filii tui domini nostri expetunt, quid de pueris agendum
25 *censeas, utrum incisis crinibus eos vivere iubeas, an utrumque iugulari.*
Maluit autem illa interfectos videre, quam tonsos. *b*Quam historiam
Aimoinus lib. 2, cap. 12 ennarans,[12] Chrotildem ita loquentem
inducit: *Sed utcunque se res habeat, nullatenus clericos fieri patiar,*
quasi ad clericatum tonsura puerorum quaereretur. Quod cum a
30 Gregorii verbis alienum est, tum etiam ab illa consuetudine

---

10 *c*² 'cap. 37'.   **16** *bc* 'Chrotilde'.   **16** *bc* 'nepotibus'.

[4] I.e., III, 61; *PL*, CXXXIX, 734.   [5] *Ibid.*   [6] Cf. *MGH SS Mer.*, I:I², 291.
[7] Non invenio.   [8] Greg. Tours, VII, 32; *MGH SS Mer.*, I:I², 357, 8.
[9] *Ibid.*; *loc. cit.*, 357, 15.   [10] *MGH SS Mer.*, I:I², 118, 1.   [11] *Ibid.*, 118, 13.
[12] *PL*, CXXXIX, 674.

our ancestors of cutting off the hair of anyone from whom they wished to withdraw either the kingdom or the hope of acquiring it. Aimon says in the same passage:[4] 'He looked closely at the man and ruled that his hair should be cut, denying that he was his son.' And again, he writes:[5] 'When his hair had once more been cut off he was sent under guard to Cologne, whence he escaped and, allowing his hair to grow again, made his way to Narses...' Gregory of Tours also records this incident,[6] and in a later chapter he remarks of King Theuderic:[7] 'The Franks rose up against him, cast him out of the kingdom and forcibly cut off his hair.' *b*Elsewhere he writes:[8] 'Are you he who because of the claims you make have been frequently shaven and sent into exile by the kings of the Franks?' Gregory continues:[9] 'It is known to everyone that my father Lothar detested me, and it is clear to all men that I have been tonsured successively by him and my brothers.' *a*Gregory of Tours also tells a remarkable or, perhaps I should say, horrible story concerning the queen mother, Clothild, who preferred to cut off the heads of her two sons* rather than their hair. The reference is as follows:[10] 'Our mother (said the king to his brother) has kept our brother's sons beside her and wants them to be given the kingdom. The matter should be the subject of general deliberation to see what should be done; whether their hair should be cut off so that they would be like ordinary people, or whether they should be slain and the kingdom of our full brother divided between us.' A little further on he writes:[11] 'Then they sent Arcadius with scissors and a naked sword, and he showed each to the queen, saying: "Most glorious queen, my lords your sons seek to know your will as to what you judge should be done about your young boys, and whether, by cutting off their hair, you will let them live, or whether you prefer their throats to be cut." Yet she chose that they should be slaughtered rather than shorn.' *b*Aimon tells the same story,[12] and represents Clothild as saying: 'Whatever happens, I could not suffer their being made priests' – as if what was being sought was the tonsuring of the boys preparatory to their entering the priesthood. This account differs from the words given

---

* *bc* sons *becomes* grandsons.

usitata, ut tonsura quasi quaedam* abdicatio, et a regni hereditate
exclusio quaedam esset. ^aQuinetiam moris fuisse animadverto, ut
cum Reges praelio decertarent, nodatum capillitium in galeam,
quasi cristam erigerent, idque insigne in praeliis haberent.
5 Itaque, Aimoinus* lib. 4, cap. 18,[13] ubi de Dagoberti Regis cum
Bertoaldo Saxonum Duce acerrimo, praelio commemorat: *Rex,*
inquit, *ense percussus in caput, decisos cum parte galeae crines patri per*
armigerum mittit, ut sibi in auxilium properet.

Huius autem instituti caussam cum apud me considero, hanc
10 fere reperio, quod cum et Gallorum et Francorum nationes
comatae essent (item ut Sicambrorum, ac fere regionum illarum
institutum fuisse constat) maioribus nostris visum est, hoc
proprium Regiae dignitati decus atque insigne tribuere. Nam de
Gallis quidem (unde Comata Gallia dicta est) nemo mediocriter
15 eruditus testimonium quaerit: memor praesertim illius Claudiani
ex lib. in Ruffinum 2:[14]

> *Inde truces flavo comitantur vertice Galli,*
> *Quos Rhodanus velox, Araris quos tardior ambit,*
> *Et quos nascentes explorat gurgite Rhenus.*

20 De Francis autem, quos ex Chaucis, sive Chaycis ortos demonstravimus, vel unus ille ex Lucani primo locus, testimonio esse
potest:[15]

> *Et vos crinigeros bellis arcere Chaycos*
> *Oppositi petitis Romam, etc.*

25 Quod cum ita esset, animadvertimus, exteros qui animo in
nostros inimico essent, Reges capillatos, non modo contumelioso
nomine Setatos appellasse, verum cum setae leonum, equorum,
et suum communes essent (qui omnes propterea Setosi et Setigeri
appellantur) etiam ad suillas setas nominis contumeliam pro-

---

1 *c* omits 'quaedam'.   5 *a* 'Ammianus', already corrected in *a*¹.
[13] *Ibid.*, 779.   [14] *In Rufinum II*, 110–12; Loeb, 66.   [15] *Bel. civ.*, I, 463–4;
Loeb, 36.

by Gregory, who refers to that customary practice whereby the tonsure was a certain* kind of abdication and involved exclusion from inheritance of the kingdom. *a*Moreover, I see it was the custom that when the kings went into battle they knotted their hair upon their helmet like a kind of crest, which served as their distinguishing mark in combat. This is mentioned by Aimon† in a passage[13] where he describes the bitter struggle between King Dagobert and Bertoald, duke of the Saxons. 'The king', he writes, 'had his hair and part of his helmet cut off by a sword blow he received on the head, and sent them by a servant to his father so that he might come swiftly to his aid.'

When I ponder the reason behind this practice I find merely this: that, because the nations of the Gauls and the Franks wore long hair (and this was also the practice of the Sicambri and of nearly all those regions), our ancestors thought it appropriate to assign it as the proper ornament and distinction of royal rank. No one of the slightest learning needs any proof that the Gauls wore long hair (whence the expression *Comata Gallia*, Hairy Gaul, is derived), and especially when he recalls the lines of Claudian addressed to Rufinus:[14]

'Thence follow the hirsute Gauls, yellow-crowned,
Whom the swift Rhône and the tardy Saône surround
While the Rhine seeks out their watery origins.'

A single passage from the verse of Lucan proves that the custom was the same with the Franks, who, as we have shown, were derived from the Chauci or Chayci:[15]

'On Rome's behalf you boldly sought to check
The long-haired Chayci from their warlike course...'

This being so, we may note that foreigners who disliked our long-haired kings not only insulted them by calling them the 'bristled ones' but also said their bristles were a thing they had in common with lions, horses and swine (which for this reason are all called *Setosi* and *Setigeri*, 'bristlers'), and they even extended the insult by

* *c omits* certain. † *a has* Ammianus; *a¹bc correct to* Aimon.

duxisse. Unde et obscoena conficta fabula, et spurcum nomen
τριχοραχάτον, de quo Georgius Cedrenus in historia ita scribit:[16]
Ἐλέγοντο δὲ οἱ ἐκ τοῦ γένους ἐκείνου καταγόμενοι κριστάτοι,
ὃ ἑρμηνεύεται τριχοραχάτοι· εἶχον γὰρ κατὰ τῆς ῥάχεως
5 αὐτῶν τρίχας ἐκφυομένας ὡς χοῖροι, id est, *Qui regio erant pro-*
gnati genere, dicebantur Cristati, quod interpretatur, Tergisetosi.
Habebant enim in spina dorsi pilos enascentes, quasi porci. Quem
tamen locum mendosum, ac depravatum esse arbitror, ac pro
ΚΡΙΣΤΑΤΟΙ vel reponendum ΣΕΤΑΤΟΙ, vel utrunque certe
10 coniungendum, ut a nonnullis festive Cristati, propter erectum
in galeam crinium flocculum, a malevolis etiam contumeliose
Setati, vel Setigeri appellarentur. Quod si clausulam illam tam
aperte Cedrenus non apposuisset, et Cristatorum nomen reti-
nendum fuisset, dicendi potius τριχοχάρακτοι fuissent, ut cuivis
15 perspicuum esse arbitror, pro, Crinibus insignes. ^cQuanquam
totum illum Cedreni locum animadverti iam ab auctore Historiae
Miscellae ad verbum ita conversum, lib. xxii:[17] *Dicebantur sane ex*
genere illo descendere Cristati, quod interpretatur Trichorachati, pilos;
enim habebant natos in spina, veluti porci. ^bUtcunque sit, ne illud
20 quidem praetermittendum videtur, circiter Caroli Magni
aetatem, consuetudinem quandam increbuisse, ut regis filius ad
exterum aliquem principem amicum ac foederatum mitteretur,
qui honoris caussa capillos ei praecideret, eoque facto Pater
ipsius honorarius diceretur. Nam Paulus Diaconus lib. 6, cap. 15,
25 de Carolo Magno scribens:[18] *Carolus,* inquit, *Francorum princeps*
filium suum ad Liutprandum Longobardorum regem misit, ut eius,
iuxta morem, capillum susciperet, qui eius caesariem incidens, ei pater
effectus est, multisque regiis muneribus donatum genitori remisit; quam
historiam Regino libro 1, sub anno DCLV, commemorat,[19] apud
30 quem pro SUSCIPERET, commodius legi videretur, INCI-
DERET.[20]

---

[16] §794; *PG*, cxxi, 872 (which has however a faulty reading of αριχοραχάτοι
for τριχοραχάτοι). [17] Land. Sagax, lib. 22; ed. 1569, 691. [18] vi, 53; *MGH*
SS Lang., 183, 15. The passage refers to Charles Martel, not Charlemagne:
'Pipinum' should be inserted before 'filium suum'. [19] *MGH SS*, i, 553, 74ff.
[20] True: *ibid.*, 554, 2.

saying they had pig's bristles. Hence arose that foul and fictitious story and disgusting name τριχοραχᾶτον ('hairycrests'), on which Georgius Cedrenus writes as follows in his history:[16] 'They who sprang from royal stock were called *Cristati*, that is "tufted", because they had hair growing down their backbone like swine.' I regard this passage as faulty and corrupted, and instead of the word ΚΡΙΣΤΑΤΟΙ should be read ΣΕΤΑΤΟΙ, or perhaps both words should appear together. For some called them *Cristati*, in the pleasant sense of the word, because of the lock of hair rising above their helmet, while others, who wished them ill, insultingly called them *Setati* or *Setigeri*. If Cedrenus had not made his meaning so clear in this passage, and the name *Cristati* had not to be retained, they should rather have been called τριχοχάρακτοι, which would convey the meaning I prefer, that is, distinguished by their long hair. *c*But I now notice that Cedrenus' whole passage has been changed by the author of the *Historical Miscellany* to read as follows:[17] 'Indeed from that stock were said to descend the *Cristati* or *Trichorachati*, who were born like pigs with hair growing on their spine.' *b*However this may be, I should not like anyone to think I have omitted the fact that near the age of Charlemagne a custom prevailed by which a king's son was sent to some allied and friendly foreign prince, who out of respect would cut short the son's hair, and after this act would be called the honorary father of the youth. Paul the Deacon writes about Charlemagne in these terms:[18] 'Charles, the ruler of the Franks, sent his son to King Liutprand of the Lombards so that the latter, according to the custom, would lift up his son's hair. When the hair was cut he was made the boy's father, and he sent back the youth with many royal gifts to the real father.' This story is recorded by Regino under the year 655,[19] who, instead of the term used by Paul the Deacon, *susciperet* [lift up], employs the word *incideret* [cut off],[20] which seems to read more easily.

Verum haec quidem de regalis capillitii iure, hactenus[*]. Quod
vero nonnulli fabulantur, regnante Ludovico VII Petri Lom-
bardi Parisiensis Episcopi consilio atque hortatu institutum
fuisse, ut discrimen inter Gallos et Francos tolleretur, cum illi
5   comam tantum hi et comam et barbam colerent, indignum
hominibus doctis videtur, quasi vero per annos amplius octingentos (totidem enim a Francogallici regni origine ad Ludovicum
VII numerantur) discrimen ullum inter Gallos et Francos
durarit, ac non superius demonstratum sit, post Francogalliae
10   regnum constitutum, unam e duabus quasi gemellam gentem,
et unius linguae et eorundem institutorum ac morum conflatam fuisse.

---

1 *c*[1] adds 'praesertim cum Antonii fratris mei extet libellus de Coma [Antoine
Hotman, Πωγωνίας, *sive de barba dialogus* (Antwerp, 1586)] eruditus simul &
elegans'.

So far, so good as to the right of kings to wear long hair*. But there are some who say that in the reign of Louis VII it was enacted on the advice and exhortation of Peter the Lombard, bishop of Paris, that the difference between Gauls and Franks should be abolished, since the former cultivated their hair and the latter both their hair and their beard. Such a story is unworthy of learned men, for it suggests that this distinction between Gauls and Franks lasted for more than eight hundred years (such being the span between the origin of the kingdom of Francogallia and Louis VII). On the contrary, we have shown above that after the founding of the kingdom of Francogallia one nation was formed from the two as if they had been a twin-born people, and through their intermingling there was one language and one set of institutions and customs.

* *c*¹ *adds* especially in the light of an erudite and elegant book on hair by my brother, Antoine.

Qualis regni Francogallici constituendi forma fuerit

His ita breviter expositis, deinceps qualis Regni Francogallici constituendi forma fuerit, exponendum videtur. Ac superius quidem populum *b*in comitiis *a*non modo creandi, verumetiam abdicandi* Regis potestatem sibi omnem reservasse,* docuimus.
5 Quam eandem regnandi formam constat Gallos nostros, priusquam in Romanorum potestatem redigerentur, habuisse, ut populus non minus (inquit Caesar) in Regem, quam Rex in populum imperii ac potestatis retineret.¹ Quanquam non a Gallis, sed a popularibus suis Germanis eam Reipublicae constituendae formam Francos nostros sumpsisse, consentaneum est,
10 de quibus Tacitus in lib. de moribus German. ita scribit:² *Regibus non est infinita aut libera potestas.* Hac autem forma nullam a Tyrannico dominatu remotiorem esse constat. *c*Nam ut ait Aristoteles lib. Polit. v, cap. 11,³ *quanto pauciorum rerum penes*
15 *Regem potestas est, tanto diutius regnum maneat necesse est.* *a*Quinetiam e tribus tyrannidis notis, quas philosophi veteres indicarunt, nullam in regni nostri forma constituenda licet animadvertere. Primum enim quantum ad coactum imperium *b*attinet, *a*hoc est, ut Rex invitis dominetur, docuimus iam antea,
20 summam populi* tum in deligendis, tum in abdicandis Regibus potestatem fuisse. Quantum ad* peregrinam corporis custodiam, quam secundam tyrannidis notam numerant, tantum abest, ut Francogalliae reges peregrinis et alienigenis mercenariis ad praesidiariam cohortem uterentur, ut *b*plerunque *a*ne cives
25 quidem et indigenas ad corporis custodiam adhiberent, quippe, cum omnem in clientum suorum fide et benevolentia praesidii

---

4 *c*¹ omits 'non modo' and 'verumetiam abdicandi'.　4 *c* 'retinuisse'.
20 'populi': *bc* 'ordinum publicique Concilii'.　21 *c*¹ omits 'coactum imperium...Quantum ad'.

¹ Cf. *B.G.*, v, 27; Loeb, 268.　² Cap. 7; Loeb, 274.　³ v, ix, 1; Loeb, 456.

The form in which the kingdom of Francogallia was constituted

Now that these matters have been briefly set forth, it seems necessary to explain the form in which the kingdom of Francogallia came to be constituted. We have shown earlier that the people *b*in their assemblies *a*reserved* all power to themselves in creating and also in deposing† a king. Our Gauls possessed that same form of government before they were brought under the power of the Romans, for, as Caesar says,[1] the people had no less power and authority over a king than a king had over the people. It is agreed, nonetheless, that our Franks assumed this form of constituting their commonwealth from the German peoples rather than from the Gauls. In this respect Tacitus writes in his *Customs of the Germans*:[2] 'The power of their kings is neither unlimited nor free.' It is clear that no form of government is more remote from tyranny than this. *c*For, as Aristotle says in his *Politics*:[3] 'The fewer the things over which the authority of the king extends, the longer will the kingdom endure.' *a*It may be observed that not one of the three signs of tyranny defined by the ancient philosophers is to be found in the form in which our kingdom was constituted. First, in so far as the government *b*involved *a*compulsion, that is to say, where a king rules over his subjects against their will, we have already indicated that the highest authority in both electing and deposing kings lay in the people.‡ As to the second mark of tyranny, the existence of a foreign bodyguard, so far were our kings of Francogallia from employing foreigners and alien mercenaries for their guards that they *b*generally *a*did not even make use of citizens or local people as their bodyguard, but placed their whole trust in the

---

* *c* retained. † *c*¹ *omits* and also in deposing. ‡ *bc* the estates and the public council: *c*¹ *omits the preceding sentence.*

sui fiduciam collocarent. Cuius rei argumento est, quod Gregor. Turon. lib. 7, cap. 18,[4] et Aimoinus lib. 3, cap. 63[5] scribunt, Regem Gontrannum ab homine quodam tenui Lutetiae admonitum, ut insidias sibi a Faraulpho paratas vitaret, continuo se
5 armis et custodiis munivisse: ut nusquam, inquit Gregorius,[6] ac ne *ad loca quidem sacra, nisi vallatus armatis atque custodibus procederet.* Quinetiam extat Ludovici cognomento Divi praeclara historia, et ab illustri viro Ioanne Ionvillaeo scripta, qui cum illo Rege perfamiliariter multos annos versatus est: qua in historia
10 nullam plane satellitum, aut stipatorum, aut praesidiariae cohortis mentionem licet animadvertere, sed tantum Ianitorum, quos populari lingua Husserios, ^cid est, Hostiarios, ^aappellat.[7]

   ^bVerum, quid haec tenuia et minuta dilucidae rei argumenta conquirimus? cum perspicuum eius documentum extet, apud
15 Wilhelmum Neunbrigensem, libro Rerum Anglicarum 4, cap. 2, quod iccirco subscribemus, ne tam insignis Maiorum nostrorum sapientiae memoria intercidat, et canibus aulicis, qui nobis antehac allatrarunt, ora obturemus. Scribit autem Neunbrigensis de rege Philippo, Ludovici filio, qui cum Richardo
20 Anglorum rege ad recuperandas Hierosolymas profectus est, circiter annum MCXC:[8] *Sane,* inquit, *postquam percrebuit apud regem Francorum, quod Marchioni acciderat, de amici quidem indigno exitu doluit; sed mox hunc dolorem suscepta cum ingenti gaudio suggillandi regem Anglorum occasio compensavit. Cumque in propriis*
25 *esset tam longe finibus a Syria constitutus, illius in Oriente consistentis vel frustra timebat, vel potius se ad augendam invidiam, timere fingebat insidias, et tanquam ab eo subornati imminerent sicarii, praeter morem Maiorum suorum non nisi firmata vallatus custodia procedebat, adeo ut quidam familiari ausu propius accedentes, non sine periculo hoc ausi*
30 *dicantur. Mirantibus hanc novitatem regiam plurimis, ut pro ea satisfaceret, gentemque suam in regem Anglorum accenderet, Praesulum*

---

4 See below, n. 6.   5 Cf. *PL*, cxxxix, 737.   6 *MGH SS Mer.*, 1: 1², 338, 18.
7 Seems true enough, judging from the well-indexed Wailly edition of Joinville.
8 William of Newburgh, IV, xxv; ed. 1884, 75.

good faith of their dependants and the good will of their troops. Gregory of Tours[4] and Aimon[5] support this view when they describe how King Guntram was warned by a common Parisian fellow to beware the wicked plans of Faraulph who was at that very time gathering arms and men. Gregory says[6] that he went nowhere, 'not even to holy places, without being surrounded by armed men and guards'. There still exists the famous history of Saint Louis written by that illustrious man Jean de Joinville, who spent many years on terms of familiarity with that king. It may be remarked that throughout this history there is no mention of escorts, retinues or bodyguards but only of janitors and those he calls in the popular speech *Husserii*, [c]that is *Hostarii* [ushers].[7]

[b]But what is the use of searching for these slender and paltry proofs in so obvious an issue when there is an irrefutable source for it in the second chapter of the fourth book of the writings of William of Newburgh on English affairs? We shall quote it here in order to preserve an outstanding instance of our ancestors' wisdom, and to muzzle the jaws of those sycophantic curs who have barked at us on earlier occasions. William of Newburgh writes of King Philip, the son of Louis, who in about the year 1190 set out with King Richard of England to recover Jerusalem:[8] 'When the news of what had happened to the marquis was heard in the camp of the French king, he was grieved at the unworthy death of his friend. But soon afterwards an opportunity to taunt the English king, which was received with great joy, compensated for this sorrow. Although he was established in his own territories at so great a distance from Syria, he was either in needless fear of Richard, who remained in the east, or else he pretended to fear conspiracies in order to increase ill-will against him. He pretended that assassins whom King Richard had supposedly suborned were a threat to him, and he refused to move without being surrounded by a strong guard. This was contrary to the custom of his ancestors, and those who came near him on some friendly errand were said to have achieved something daring and fraught with danger. This novelty in royal affairs startled many, and in consequence he tried to justify his policy by inflaming the people against the English king. To this

Procerumque suorum Concilium Parisios convocavit. Ubi allegans
contra eundem regem plurima, tanquam certa, atque inter cetera, quod
virum illum nobilissimum nequiter per diros satellites peremisset,
literas quoque protulit a quibusdam potentibus sibi (ut dicebat) trans-
5 *missas, quibus monebatur propensiorem suimet habere cautelam; sciens*
quod rex Anglorum insidiaturus animae suae ab Oriente iam direxisset
sicarios: 'Quamobrem', inquit, 'nemo debet mirari, quo praeter
solitum diligentiorem mei ipsius curam habeam, quam tamen si repu-
tatis vel indecentem, vel superfluam, decernite amovendam.' Adiecit
10 *etiam, cordi sibi esse de manifesto proditore proprias mature ulcisci*
iniurias. Adhaec plurimi adulatorie responderunt, bonum honestumque
esse, quod pro cautela faciebat, et quod pro ultione disponebat. Pru-
dentes vero dixerunt: 'Cautelam quidem tuam, Rex, qua tibi contra
incertos casus forte abundantius prospicis, non culpamus; praematurae
15 *vero ultionis propositum minime approbamus. Nam etsi vera sint quae*
de rege Anglorum dicuntur, non tamen est petulanter et praemature
agendum, sed respectum honesti sustinendum, quousque ad propria
revertatur, qui propter Christum peregrinari noscitur.' Haec Neunbrigensis. Deinceps alteram Maiorum nostrorum in regno
20 constituendo sapientiam consideremus.

Nam ^aQuae vero* tertia tyrannidis nota numeratur, ut non ad
civitatis et subiectorum, sed ad ipsius dominantis commodum
atque arbitrium omnia referantur, ^beius nullam in nostra Republi-
lica merculam* multas per aetates haesisse, ex eo intelligetur,
25 quod ^apaulo posterius docebimus, summam regni Francogallici
administrationem penes publicum et solenne gentis Concilium
fuisse, quod posterior aetas Conventum trium Statuum appel-

---

21 *bc* omit 'vero'.   24 *c* 'maculam'.

end he summoned a council of his supporters and nobles at Paris. There he made a great many accusations against King Richard as though they were established truth, and among them he claimed that the king had basely killed that most noble marquis by means of his detestable soldiers. He produced letters supposedly sent by certain authorities to himself, in which he was warned to take greater precautions for his safety, as the king of the English had a most treacherous disposition and was at that very time arranging for assassins to be sent against him from the east. "Why should anyone wonder", he said, "that I take such zealous care of myself? But, if you regard it as improper or unnecessary, then order the guard to be abolished." He added also that he had it in mind to avenge himself at the appropriate time for particular wrongs he suffered from such a manifest traitor. A great many greeted this with an adulatory response, and agreed that it was wise and honest for him to take precautions and to plan his revenge. However those who were prudent observed: "We do not blame you for your caution when you make such secure provision against the unexpected, but we are much less favourably inclined towards your proposal for an untimely revenge. Even if what is said about the king of the English be true, it is unwise to attempt a petulant and premature action. It is better to maintain the respect due to an honest man who is known to have undertaken a pilgrimage for the cause of Christ, until such time as he may return to deeds appropriate to his reputation.'" Such are the words of William of Newburgh. Now let us consider another aspect of our ancestors' wisdom in setting up the form of the government.

*a*Now* it has been observed that the third mark of tyranny occurs when all matters are judged by the comfort and will of him who governs rather than by the ease and desire of the commonwealth and the subjects. *b*Through many ages no such blemish became established in our commonwealth, and hence it may be seen, *a*as we shall explain a little later, that the highest administrative authority in the kingdom of Francogallia lay in the formal public council of the nation, which in later times was called the assembly of the three

* *bc omit* Now.

lavit. *b*Cuius appellationis rationem Claudius Seyssellus in libello quem Franciae monarchiam inscripsit, ad tres Civium ordines referendam putat, quorum summum nobilitati, medium iuridicis et mercatoribus, tertium opificibus et agricolis attribuit.
5 Verba illius cap. 13 haec fere sunt:9 *Est in hoc regno forma quaedam Reipublicae magnopere et laudanda et retinenda, quoniam plurimum in ea momenti est ad ordinum omnium concordiam constabiliendam, neque dubium est, quin quandiu suum cuique ordini ius suaque dignitas servabitur, difficile sit regnum labefactari. Nam cuiusque ordinis certa*
10 *est praerogativa, neque, ea servata, potest alter alterum evertere, ac ne tres quidem simul in Principem et Monarcham conspirare possunt. Horum porro in ordinum trium numerum nequaquam repono Ecclesiasticos, qui per illos mixti* sunt, sed tres status sive ordines numero: primum Nobilitatem, tum medium populum, qui dici Opimus potest,*
15 *postremo plebem infimam.* Haec Seyssellus.

Sed videamus, ne cum haec tripartita distributio non ad vitae communis rationem, sed ad publicum gentis Concilium referatur (qua de caussa Concilium illud vulgo Trium Statuum appellatur) ecquid commodius, ad illa tria genera referri possit, quibus id
20 Concilium constat: hoc est, ad regalem, optimatum et popularem, quippe, cum *a*Huius enim* regni status is fuerit, quem Philosophi veteres, (in his Plato10 et Aristoteles,11 quos Polybius *b*et Tullius12 imitati sunt*) *a*optimum ac praestantissimum iudicarunt, nimirum qui e tribus generibus Regali, Optimo,* et
25 Populari mixtus ac temperatus esset; quam Reipublicae formam Cicero* in suis de Republica libris13 unam ex omnibus comprobavit.* Nam cum Regius et popularis dominatus natura inter se

---

13 *c* '*permixti*'. **21** *bc* omit 'enim'. **23** *a* 'imitatus est'. **24** *bc* 'Optimatum'.
26 'Cicero': *bc* 'idem Tullius'. **27** 'comprobavit': *bc* 'potissimam [*c*1 & certissimam] esse duxit'.

9 I, 13; ed. 1961, 120f.   10 Cf. *Laws*, III, 693D & VI, 756E; Loeb, I, 222f. & 410f.
11 Cf. *Politics*, II, iii, 11ff. (1266a); III, v, 1ff. (1279a); IV, vii, 1ff. (1294a) – Loeb, 106f., 205f., 318f.   12 Polybius, VI, 3, ff.; Loeb, III, 272ff. (The Cicero passage is the same as in the next note.) Hotman had published Pompilius Amasaeus' Latin translation of this part of Polybius in the appendix to his *Novus Commentarius de verbis iuris* (Basel, 1563), 499ff.   13 Cf. *De re pub.*, II, xxiii, 41; Loeb, 150.

estates. *b*In the book entitled *The Monarchy of France* Claude de Seyssel considers that this assembly is named after the three orders of citizens. He regards the first of these as the nobility, the second as comprising the lawyers and merchants and the third the artisans and farmers. This is virtually what he writes in the thirteenth chapter:[9] 'In this kingdom there is a certain aspect of the commonwealth which is greatly to be admired and ought to be preserved, because it is of great influence in establishing the harmony of all the orders. For it is indubitable that, so long as the legal right and dignity of each order is preserved, it is difficult for the kingdom to be overthrown. Each order has its fixed prerogative, and, while that is maintained, one order cannot subvert another, and the three cannot conspire together against the prince and the monarchy. There should be but three estates or orders, and the clergy should not be added to them, since they are already a mixture* of the existing orders. The first estate is the nobility; the middle estate consists of those among the people who are said to be well-off; and the last is the lowest common people.' So says Seyssel.

However, this division into three orders is not intended as a description of the basis of ordinary society but rather is related to the public council of the nation (wherefore the council is commonly called the council of the three estates). Let us see, then, whether it would not be more convenient if it could correspond to the three kinds of government embodied in the council – that is to the regal, the aristocratic and the popular types. *a*For† such indeed was the form of government which the old philosophers (including Plato[10] and Aristotle,[11] whom Polybius *b*and Cicero[12] *a*imitated) considered the best and most excellent, a form which was mixed and tempered from the three elements of monarchy, aristocracy and democracy. This was the form of commonwealth approved before‡ all others by Cicero§ in his book of the *Republic*.[13] For, since a kingly and a popular government are by nature at variance with

---

* *c* a complete mixture. † *bc omit* For. ‡ *bc* approved before *becomes* vastly preferred to. § *bc* the same Tully.

dissideant, adhiberi tertium aliquem oportet intermedium, et
utriusque communem, qui est Principum, sive Optimatum, qui
propter splendorem generis* et antiquitatem ad Regiam dignitatem accedit, propter clientelam, et (ut vulgo loquimur)
5 subiectionem a plebeio genere minus abhorret. Unum enim
eundemque cum plebe populi universi Magistrum agnoscunt.
De hac autem praeclara Reipublicae temperatione insignis* extat
Ciceronis laudatio, ex Platonis de Republica libris expressa,[14]
quam propter singularem elegantiam subscribemus:[15] *Ut in*
10 *fidibus, inquit, ac tibiis, atque cantu ipso, ac vocibus concentus est*
quidam tenendus ex distinctis sonis, quem immutatum ac discrepantem
aures eruditae ferre non possunt, isque concentus ex dissimillimarum
vocum moderatione concors tamen efficitur, et congruens; sic ex summis
et mediis, et infimis ᵇ*et* ᵃ*interiectis ordinibus, ut sonis, moderata ratione*
15 *civitas, consensu dissimillimorum concinit, et quae harmonia a musicis*
dicitur in cantu, ea est in civitate concordia, arctissimum atque opti-
mum in Republica vinculum incolumitatis, quae sine iustitia nullo
pacto esse potest.
   ^cHaec Cicero, de Optimo Reipublicae statu, quem ex tribus
20 permixtis generibus temperatum, Maiores nostri in Francogalliae regno constituendo tenuerunt, quod cum aliis argu-
mentis demonstrari potest, tum vero vel maxime ex Oratione
Regis Ludovici cognomento Pii, ad omnes Francogalliae ordines
habita, et ab Ansegiso in lib. Franc. leg. secundum relata, cuius
25 cap. 3 verba haec extant:[16] *Sed quanquam summa huius ministerii*
Regii in nostra persona consistere videatur, tamen et divina auctoritate,
et humana ordinatione ita per partes divisum esse cognoscitur, ut unus-
quisque vestrum in suo loco et ordine partem nostri ministerii habere
cognoscatur; unde apparet, quod nimirum vestrum admonitor esse debeo,
30 *et omnes vos nostri adiutores esse debetis. Nec enim ignoramus, quid*

---

3 *bc* put 'generis' after 'antiquitatem'.　　**7** *bc* 'Huius autem praeclari Reipublicae status insignis'.

[14] Cicero does not refer to Plato; see above, p. 69, on this passage.　　[15] Cicero,
De re pub., II, xlii, 69; Loeb; 180ff.　　[16] II, 3; *MGH LL*, II: 1, 415.

each other, it is necessary to add some third or intermediate element common to both. Such is the rôle of the princes or nobles, who, because of the splendour and antiquity of their stock, approach the status of royalty, and who, because of their position as dependants (or, as it is commonly put, subjects), have less dislike for those of plebeian birth. For, like the common sort, they recognize one and the same person as magistrate of the whole people. There is a fine passage from Cicero in praise of the remarkable symmetry* of this type of commonwealth. He follows Plato's *Republic*,[14] and we repeat the passage because of its singular elegance:[15] 'With lyres and flutes, and also with voices raised in song, a certain harmony should emerge from the individual sounds, but a trained ear cannot endure an altered or discordant note. This harmonious and agreeable concord is produced, however, from the regular arrangement of dissimilar sounds. In the same way a commonwealth which is regulated by reason produces harmony through the consent of dissimilar elements, drawn, like the sounds, from the highest and the middling orders, from the lowest *b*and *a*the intermediate estates. What is called harmony in song by musicians, is called concord in a commonwealth. In such a state concord provides the narrowest and best assurance of security, which no general agreement can embody unless it is accompanied by justice.'

*c*In constituting the kingdom of Francogallia our ancestors accepted Cicero's opinion that the best form of a commonwealth is that which is tempered by the mixture of the three kinds of government. This can be shown by a variety of proofs, especially from the speech of King Louis, known as the Pious, delivered to all the estates of Francogallia, and also from Ansegius' book on Frankish law, where an official report is quoted as follows:[16] 'Yet, however mighty this royal office may seem to be in our person, our office is known by both divine authority and human ordinance to be so divided throughout its parts that each one of you in his own place and rank may be recognized as possessing a piece. Hence it seems that we should be your counsellor, and all of you should be our deputies. And we are aware that it is fitting for each one of you

* *bc* form.

unicuique vestrum in sibi commissa portione conveniat. Item cap. 12:[17]
*Et sicut diximus, unusquisque vestrum partem ministerii nostri per
partes habere dignoscitur.* Item cap. 6:[18] *Monemus vestram fideli-*
5 *tatem, ut memores sitis fidei nobis permissae, et in parte ministerii vestri
vobis commissi.*

   ^aHanc igitur mixtam a tribus generibus Reipublicae tempera-
tionem Maiores nostri secuti, sapientissime constituerunt, ut
quotannis publicum totius regni concilium Kalendis Maii
10 haberetur, quo in concilio de summis quibusque Reipublicae
negotiis communi Ordinum omnium consilio ageretur; ^bsic, ut
vetus illa aurea lex valeret: SALUS POPULI SUPREMA LEX
ESTO.[19] ^aCuius instituti sapientia et utilitas tribus maxime rebus
cernitur. Primum quod in magno prudentium numero magni-
15 tudo consilii ^cac propterea salus populi ^aversatur, ^cProverb. 11
et 15,* ^aut Salomoni[20] et aliis sapientibus placuit. Deinde quia
libertatis pars est, quorum periculo res geritur, ut ^billa ^aeorum
consilio atque auctoritate administretur, et, quemadmodum
vulgo dici solet,* quod omnes tangit, ab omnibus approbetur.[21]
20 Postremo ut qui apud Regem in magna potentia sunt, et magnis
imperiis praesunt, eius concilii metu, in quo Civitatum postulata
libere audiuntur, in officio contineantur. Nam quod Regna quaedam unius Regis arbitrio ac nutu gubernantur, ^bquale hodie
Turcicum esse constat, ^arectissime Aristoteles lib. Polit. 3 anim-
25 advertit,[22] non hominum liberorum et lumine ingenii* utentium,
sed pecudum potius et brutorum consilii expertium eam guber-
nationem esse. Sic enim se res habet, ut pecudes, non ab uno e suo
genere, ut pueri aut adolescentes, non ab uno e suis aequalibus, sed
a praestantiore aliquo reguntur.

---

16 *c* has 'Proverb. 11 et 15' in the margin; *c*[1] omits; *c*[2] has in text.   **19** 'vulgo
dici solet': *c* 'Imp. Iustinianus dixit'.   **25** 'ingenii': *bc* 'mentis et rationis'.

[17] *Ibid.*, II, 12; *loc. cit.*, 416.   [18] *Ibid.*, II, 6; *loc. cit.*   [19] Cicero, *De legibus*,
III, iii, 8; Loeb, 464f.   [20] Cf. *Prov.* 14 & 22.   [21] *Cod.* 5, 59, 5, 2; Krueger,
231.   [22] III, xi; Loeb, 263ff.

to have a piece of authority vested in you.' Later Ansegius writes to the same effect:[17] 'And as we have said, each one of you is distinguished by having your part among the many segments of our office.' Again, he says:[18] 'We urge your loyalty so that you may recall both your desire for the trust placed in us and the office which in part has been entrusted to you.'

[a]For this reason our ancestors accepted this mixed and tempered commonwealth embodying the three kinds of government, and very wisely laid it down that every year there should be a public council of the whole kingdom on the first of May, and that at this council the greatest affairs of the commonwealth should be dealt with through the general advice of all the estates. [b]In this manner that ancient and golden law prevailed: 'LET THE WELFARE OF THE PEOPLE BE THE SUPREME LAW.'[19] [a]The wisdom and utility of this practice is very apparent in three respects. First, the large number of men of prudence ensured that there would be an amplitude of advice, [c]and advice of a kind to procure the welfare of the people, [a]such as might satisfy Solomon[20] [c](Proverbs 11 and 15)* [a]and other wise men. Next, because it is an attribute of liberty that those at whose peril a thing is done should have some say and authority in arranging it, or, as it is customarily and commonly said,† what touches all should be approved by all.[21] Lastly, those who have great influence with the king, and are foremost in great affairs of government, should, in the performance of their office, be held in fear of this council, in which the requests of the provinces are freely heard. When certain kingdoms are governed by the will and pleasure of a single king [b] – as today the Turks are ruled – [a]their government would lack the advice of free men and enlightened opinion‡ and would be like that of cattle and beasts, as Aristotle rightly observes in his *Politics*.[22] For in such circumstances they are like cattle who are not controlled by one of their own kind, or like boys and youths, who are governed by someone of superior status rather than by one of their own age.

* **c** *has* (Proverbs 11 and 15) *in the margin;* **c¹** *omits it;* **c²** *has it in the text.* † **c** *as it is customarily and commonly said becomes* as the Emperor Justinian said. ‡ **bc** *and enlightened opinion becomes* of intelligence and good sense.

Sic hominum multitudo non ab uno e suo numero, qui minus fortasse, quam alii complures videret, sed a probatis delectisque omnium consensu praestantioribus, et coniunctis consiliis, et quasi mente ex multis conflata,* regenda et gubernanda est. Nam
5 quod Senatum assiduum et ordinarium plerique habent reges, cuius consilio in administranda Republica sese uti dicunt: primum aliud est Regni, aliud Regis consiliarium esse. Ille Reipublicae universae, et in commune consulit, hic unius hominis commodis atque utilitatibus servit. Deinde cum illi Senatores
10 assidui vel uno in loco, vel certe in aula Principis perpetuo maneant, longinquarum civitatum nosse, ac videre statum commode non possunt. Praeterea Regalis et aulicae vitae illecebris inducti, facile ad libidinem dominandi, ad ambitionem, et opes amplificandas depravantur, ut ad extremum non regni,
15 et Reipublicae consiliarii, sed Regis unius assentatores, et ministri cupiditatum et Regiarum, et suarum quoque appareant.

Qua de re extat insigne Imp. Aureliani elogium apud Fl. Vopiscum, quod subscribemus:²³ *Ego* (inquit) *a patre meo audivi, Diocletianum principem, iam privatum dixisse, nihil esse difficilius,*
20 *quam bene imperare. Colligunt se quatuor vel quinque, atque unum consilium ad decipiendum Imperatorem capiunt, dicunt quid probandum sit. Imperator qui domi clausus est, vera non novit; cogitur hoc tantum scire, quod illi loquuntur. Facit iudices, quos fieri non oportet. Amovet a Republica quos debebat retinere; quid multa? ut Diocletianus*
25 *ipse dicebat, Bonus, cautus, optimus venditur Imperator.* ᶜHactenus Vopiscus apud quem tamen haud scio, an non rectius IN-CAUTUS legeretur.

ᵇItaque* haec incommoda veteres Romani metuentes, Regi quidem Senatum ordinarium attribuerunt; sed, ut salus populi

---

4 'probatis...conflata': **bc** 'mente ex multis conflata, hoc est, coniunctis probatorum virorum consiliis'.   **28 c** 'Utcunque sit'.
²³ *Scr. hist. Aug.*, Aurelian, xlⅢ, 2–4; Loeb, Ⅲ, 280.

In the same way a multitude of men ought not to be ruled and governed by one of their own number, who, peradventure, sees less than others do when taken together, but rather by proven men of excellence, selected with the consent of all,* who act by combined advice as if they possessed one mind composed from many. Although kings customarily have an attendant senate, whose advice, they say, is used in governing a commonwealth, the counsellor of a kingdom is something other than the counsellor of a king. The former cares for the whole commonwealth and gives his advice in public, whereas the latter serves the profit and convenience of a single man. Moreover, since senators of the latter kind either attend at one place only or are for ever attached to the court of the prince, they cannot easily see and be acquainted with the condition of remote provinces. Besides, they are seduced by the allurements of life at the royal court, and are easily depraved by a lust to dominate others, by ambition and by avarice. Ultimately they seem not to be counsellors of the kingdom and commonwealth, but rather flatterers of a single king and servants of his and their own appetites.

This is apparent in a remarkable saying of the Emperor Aurelian, reported by Flavius Vopiscus, which we quote:[23] 'I have heard my father say that Diocletian, when still a private man, declared that nothing was more difficult than to rule well. Four or five persons conspire together to take a common resolution to deceive the emperor, and tell him what should be approved. The emperor, shut up in his palace, does not know the truth, and knows only as much as they tell him. He appoints unsuitable persons as judges. He dismisses from the government those whom he should retain. What a multitude of errors he may commit! As Diocletian himself said, however well-intentioned, prudent and excellent a man may be, he is always betrayed as an emperor.' cThus far Vopiscus, although I am inclined to think he would have been more correct if he had written 'imprudent'.

bAnd so,† fearing these difficulties, the ancient Romans provided the king with a senate in the customary way. So that the welfare

---

* bc *omit* of excellence, selected with the consent of all.   † c It may be that.

suprema lex esset,[24] summam Reipublicae non regi, aut eius senatui, sed ipsi populo et comitiis reservarunt. Quare sub omnibus Regibus haec lex fuit: ut populus in comitiis magistratus crearet, leges scisceret, bella decerneret, quemadmodum
5 Dionysius Halic. lib. 2 testatur.[25] Pomponius quidem Iurisconsultus memoriae prodidit,[26] populum Romanum primis temporibus in triginta partes divisum, quae Curiae dictae sunt, propterea quod Rex Reipublicae curam (ut ipse ait) per sententias partium earum expediebat, unde leges Curiatae dictae,
10 et antiquissima omnium comitia, Curiata.

Quinetiam Seneca lib. Epistol. 19 scribit,[27] se ex Ciceronis de Republica libris[28] didicisse, PROVOCATIONEM AD POPULUM ETIAM A REGIBUS FUISSE, quod etiam Tullius initio libri Tusculanarum disputationum IV his demonstrat verbis:[29] *Nam*
15 *cum a primo urbis ortu regiis institutis, partim etiam legibus, auspicia, cerimoniae, comitia, provocationes, et cetera tota res militaris divinitus esset constituta,* etc. Sed et in Oratione quam pro domo sua habuit:[30] *Nego,* inquit, *potuisse iure publico, legibus iis quibus haec civitas utitur, quenquam civem ulla eiusmodi calamitate affici sine*
20 *iudicio hoc iuris in hac civitate etiam tum cum Reges essent, dico fuisse, ut nihil de capite civis, aut de bonis sine iudicio senatus, aut populi, aut eorum qui de quaque re constituti iudices sunt, detrahi possit.* Quibus ex locis perspicuum est, Romanos, etiam tum cum regibus parebant, hanc tamen sacrosanctam legem habuisse, quam
25 superius commemoravimus: SALUS POPULI SUPREMA LEX ESTO.[31] Neque unquam regnum ullum fuisse arbitror, praeter Turcicum, ^caut Turcici simile, ^bin quo cives non aliquam libertatis imaginem retinerent, quae in unico comitiorum habendorum iure posita est.
30 ^aHaec igitur incommoda maiores nostri in Republica consti-

---

[24] See above, n. 19. [25] II, xiv; Loeb, 352. [26] *De Rom. mag.*, c. 1; ed. 1552, 7. [27] *Epist.*, cviii, 31; Loeb, III, 250. [28] II, xxxi, 54; Loeb, 164. [29] IV, I, I; Loeb, 326. [30] 13, §33; Loeb, 172f. [31] See above, p. 296, n. 19.

of the people might be the supreme law,[24] they reserved the highest authority neither for the king nor for his senate, but for the people themselves and their assemblies. For this reason it was an established law under all the kings that the people should appoint the magistrates in their assemblies, that they should enact the laws and determine matters concerning war, as Dionysius of Halicarnassus bears witness.[25] The jurist Pomponius records[26] that the Roman people in early times were divided into thirty sections which were called *curiae*, because the king of the commonwealth paid attention [*cura*] to the opinions expressed by the sections. Hence are derived the terms 'curial laws' and *curiata*, the most ancient of all assemblies.

In his letters Seneca[27] gives an opinion he had himself learnt from the books of Cicero's *Republic*,[28] namely that APPEALS AGAINST THE AUTHORITY OF THE KINGS WERE MADE TO THE PEOPLE. Cicero further supports this in his *Tusculan Disputations* as follows:[29] 'From the origin of the city, when the ordinances of the kings, and in part also the laws, regulated the auguries, rites, assemblies, appeals to the people...and the entire military organisation...' But in his speech on behalf of hearth and home he said:[30] 'I do not believe that it was possible by any public right for the commonwealth as such to have made use of these laws, although I do say that within the commonwealth a citizen could not be affected by any misfortune of this kind without a judgment being delivered under the law, and this applied even in the time of the kings. Hence nothing could be done against the life and goods of a citizen without the judgment of the senate, or of the people, or of those who had been made judges in a particular case.' From these references it is clear that the Romans, even in the age when they submitted to kings, held this law we have mentioned above as inviolable: 'LET THE WELFARE OF THE PEOPLE BE THE SUPREME LAW.'[31] And I do not think there has ever been any kingdom other than that of the Turks, *c*or those like them, *b*in which the citizens have not retained some concept of liberty based upon the unique right of holding assemblies.

*a*In constituting the commonwealth our ancestors, therefore,

tuenda, tanquam scopulos vitantes, decreverunt,* Rempublicam
communi omnium ordinum consilio gerendam esse, cuius
consilii habendi caussa certo anni tempore Rex, et principes et
delecti ex singulis provinciis conventum agerent. Quod idem
5 institutum, videmus etiam multis aliis in* gentibus observatum
fuisse. Primum in Gallia nostra antiqua, *b*et libera, *a*quam
superius *b*ex Caesaris commentariis³² *a*ostendimus communi
Delectorum Concilio administratam fuisse.

Sed quoniam de Regno instituta commemoratio est, satis
10 constat, antiquitus in Graecia Amphyctionum Concilium fuisse
ab Rege Amphyctione (ut Suidas³³ et alii testantur) Deucalionis
filio institutum, ut e XII Graeciae civitatibus certo anni tempore
delecti ad Thermopylas convenirent, ibique de Regni et Reipublicae summis rebus communi consilio deliberarent; qua de
15 caussa Cicero *Commune*,³⁴ Plinius *Publicum* illud *Graeciae Concilium*³⁵ appellat. ^cSic Aristoteles lib. Ethicorum III scribit,³⁶
Homericis temporibus, quae Reges suscipiebant, de iis prius ad
populi Concilium referre solitos fuisse. Sic Herodotus memoriae
prodidit, duodecim Ioniae civitates commune plerunque Con-
20 cilium habuisse, quod idcirco πανιώνιον³⁷ appellabant, sicuti
Aetoliae quoque civitates suum παναιτώλιον³⁸ habuere, quorum
nominum exemplo Budaeus³⁹ noster Francogalliae nostrae
Concilium πανκέλτικον appellat.*

*a*Simillimam Germanorum in Imperio Germanico consti-
25 tuendo sapientiam fuisse apparet, ubi Imperator, Monarchiae;

---

1 'Haec igitur...decreverunt': *bc* 'Itaque legem illam Maiores nostri summa
sapientia secuti decreverunt'.   5 'aliis in': *c* 'in aliis'.   23 *bc* insert here 'Sic
Populus Lacedaemonius, etsi regem habebat, tamen de summa Republica quidnam esset utile et honestum deliberat, ut ex Aeschine scribit Gellius lib. 18, cap.
3 [Loeb, 302], quinetiam Regibus suis Ephoros, tanquam custodes atque observatores, imponebat'; these words take the place of those dropped from *a* as
indicated in the note after next.

³² Above, ch. 1, nn. 7ff. (p. 138), and *passim*.   ³³ *Ad verb*. 'Αμφικτυόνες; ed.
Bernhard, 1:1, 302.   ³⁴ *De inventione*, II, 23; Loeb, 234.   ³⁵ *Nat. hist.*,
XXXV, 59; Loeb, IX, 304.   ³⁶ Cf. *Nicom. Ethics*, III, 3, 18 [1113a8]; Loeb, 140.
³⁷ I, 148; Loeb, I, 188.   ³⁸ Not in Herodotus; in Latin, however, Livy uses
the term *Panaetolium*: XXXI, 29, 1; Loeb, IX, 82.   ³⁹ *Annot.*, §Ex titulo, De
officio Praefecti praetoris; *Opera*, 1557, III, 108.

reduced these difficulties as if they were avoiding dangerous precipices, and arranged* that the commonwealth should be administered by a general council of all the estates. In order to hold this council the king, the nobility and those chosen from individual provinces met at a fixed time of the year. We note that this same practice was also observed by many other nations. We have shown above *b*from the commentaries of Caesar[32] *a*that this was first effected in our *b*free and *a*ancient Gaul by a general council of notables.

But since we are concerned with recounting the constitutional practices of a kingdom it may suffice to say that in Greece in ancient times the council of Amphictyon was instituted by King Amphictyon, the son of Deucalion (as Suidas[33] and others testify), who arranged that at a fixed time of the year delegates from twelve states of Greece should meet at Thermopylae and should there deliberate in a general council about the most important matters in the kingdom and commonwealth. For this reason Cicero calls it the 'common council' of Greece,[34] and Pliny the 'public council' of Greece.[35] *c*Thus Aristotle writes in the third book of his *Ethics* that in the time of Homer, when kings were recognized, it was the custom for them first to refer such matters to a council of the people.[36] Similarly Herodotus records that the twelve states of Ionia frequently held a common council, which for that reason they called πανιώνιον,[37] just as the states of Aetolia had their παναιτώλιον.[38] Consequently Budé calls the council of our Francogallia πανκέλτικον.[39]†

*a*It seems that the Germans exercised a like wisdom in the establishment of the German empire. There the emperor represents monarchy, the princes aristocracy and the deputies of the

---

* *bc* In constituting...and arranged *becomes* And so in their supreme wisdom our ancestors decreed the law.   † *bc add* And, although the Spartan people had a king, they deliberated on whatever was useful and proper to the greatest good of the commonwealth, as Gellius writes in his *Attic Nights*, and, moreover, they imposed their ephors over the kings as watchdogs and supervisors. *The passage takes the place of part of the sentence dropped from a, as shown in the note following the next note.*

Principes, Aristocratiae; civitatum vero legati, Democratiae
speciem obtinent, neque quicquam quod ad summam Reipublicae Germaniae pertinet, nisi in trium illorum ordinum
conventu constitutum sit, ratum et firmum habetur.* Eodemque
5 vetus illud et praeclarum Lacedaemoniorum institutum perti-
nuit,⁴⁰ ut Ephoros suis Regibus attribuerent,* qui (quemadmodum Plato scribit⁴¹) Regibus freni instar essent, quorumque
consilio atque auctoritate Reges Rempublicam administrarent.
Quam eandem in insula Taprobone Regni rationem Plinius
10 commemorat lib. 6, cap. 22,⁴² ut ei* XXX Rectores attribu-
erenter a populo, quorum consilio in gubernanda Republica
uteretur, ne si infinita* Regibus in cives potestas permitteretur,
eodem loco ac numero* suos cives,* quo vel mancipia vel pecudes,
haberent. ᵇquod in Turcico imperio accidisse constat, ubi non
15 modo privatos quosque cives quasi pecudes mactare Tyranno ius
est, verum etiam cognatos, propinquos, affines, fratres denique
consanguineos.*

ᵃQuinetiam eandem apud Anglos Regni administrandi formam esse, testis est Polyd. Virg. lib. Ang. Hist. 11, ubi sic
20 scribit:⁴³ *Ante haec tempora* (Regis autem Henrici I vitam exponit)
Reges non consueverant* populo conventum consultandi causa, nisi

4 *bc* move this sentence ('Simillimam Germanorum...firmum habetur') down
after the word 'consanguineos' (below, l. 17), and change the last half of it to
read '...neque quicquam quod ad summam Rempublicam Germanicam pertineat, nisi in Ordinum conventum constitutum, atque complacitum sit, ratum et
firmum habetur'.   5 'Eodemque...attribuerent': *bc* transform and move this
sentence, as remarked in the note before last.   9 *bc* 'Regi'.   11 'infinita': *bc*
'immensa interminataque'.   13 *c*¹ adds 'non modo'.   13 *c*¹ adds 'sed etiam
propinquos & consanguineos, quos [for 'quo']'.   17 *bc* (as said six notes earlier)
put here the sentence 'Simillimam Germanorum...firmum habetur'. To sum
up the scramble of sentences affected in *bc*, be it noted that they observe this
order: after '...παυκέλτικον appellat' (p. 302, l. 23) comes the sentence 'Sic
Populus...observatores, imponebat', (see seventh note above); then '...qui
(quemadmodum...)...denique consanguineos' (above, l. 6ff., with variants as
noted); then 'Simillimam Germanorum...firmum habetur' (see sixth note
above); finally, with 'Quinetiam eandem...' (l. 18) the several editions fall back
in stride.   20 *bc* '*consuerant*'.

⁴⁰ Gellius, 18, 3, 2: Loeb, 302 (specifically identified in editions of 1576 and 1586;
see textual variant note at the end of the previous sentence).   ⁴¹ *Laws*, III, 692;
Loeb, 219.   ⁴² *Nat. Hist.*, VI, 24; Loeb, II, 406 – but this applies only to capital
punishment cases.   ⁴³ Ed. 1641, 245.

cities the democratic element. And nothing which has to do with the welfare of the German commonwealth may be constituted, established and made permanent unless it be done in a meeting of those three estates.* This was also the purpose of that celebrated law of the Spartans[40] associating the ephors with the kings† so that, as Plato records,[41] they acted as restraints on the kings and the latter governed the commonwealth by their advice and authority. Pliny finds the same motive in the island kingdom of Ceylon,[42] where thirty rectors were assigned to the king by the people, and their counsel was employed in governing the commonwealth. For, if an unlimited‡ power over the citizens were allowed the kings, they would have treated their citizens§ as if they were slaves or cattle. *b*This happens to have been the practice in the Turkish empire, where the law requires the veneration of the tyrant not only by private men and citizens, who are treated like cattle, but also by all relatives by blood or marriage, and even by the tyrant's brothers.¶

*a*Indeed the same form of government is to be found in the kingdom of England, as Polydore Virgil indicates in his *History of England*, where he states:[43] 'Before these times (he was writing on the life of King Henry I) the kings did not maintain the assembly of

---

* *bc move the two preceding sentences to the end of this paragraph.* of those three estates *becomes* of the estates.   † *bc* This was also...with the kings *becomes the passage shown as added at the end of the preceding paragraph and the whole sentence is moved to that point.*   ‡ *bc* vast and unbounded.   § *c¹ adds* and their associates and relatives.   ¶ *bc the passage on the German Empire beginning* It seems that the Germans... *is inserted here as shown in the note preceding the last two notes. See corresponding note for the Latin text for the general order of sentences. The reference to Budé is followed by the account of Sparta. Then come the comments on Ceylon and the Turks, followed by the passage on Germany.*

perraro, facere, adeo ut ab Henrico id institutum manasse, iure dici possit quod tam altis defixum, uti* etiam nunc, radicibus semper stetit, ut deinceps quicquid ad Rempublicam bene gerendam, eiusque conservationem deliberandum foret, illud ad concilium deferretur, et siquid aut
5 *Regis aut populi iussu decretum factumque esset, id totum pro nihilo haberetur, nisi eiusmodi concilii auctoritate foret comprobatum. Ac ne imperitae vulgi multitudinis, cuius proprium est nihil sapere, iudicio Concilium impediretur, certa lege exceptum fuit ab initio, qui ex Sacerdotum coetu, quive, quotve ex reliquo populo vocari deberent ad*
10 *concilium. More Gallico, vulgo Parlamentum appellant, quod unusquisque Rex initio sui Regni habere solet, qui et deinde, quoties res postulat, suo arbitratu illud ipsum convocat.* Haec Vergilius. ^cEt in eandem sententiam vetus quidam scriptor Angliae Concellarius in libello cui titulus est, A learned commendation, cap. 36:⁴⁴
15 *Neque Rex, inquit, ibidem per se aut ministros suos tallagia, subsidia, aut quaevis alia onera imponit legiis suis, aut leges eorum mutat, vel novas condit, sine concessione vel assensu totius Regni sui, in Parlamento suo expresso.*

    ^aSed ex his gentium fere omnium institutis nullum aeque
20 insigne memoratur, ut illud Hispanorum, qui cum in communi Arragoniae concilio Regem creant, rei memoriaeque consignandae caussa fabulam peragunt, hominemque inducunt, cui Iuris Arragonici nomen imponunt, quem Rege maiorem ac potentiorem esse communi populi decreto sanciunt, tandemque
25 Regem certis legibus et conditionibus creatum his affantur verbis, quae propter eximiam ac plane singularem gentis illius in frenando Rege fortitudinem proferemus:⁴⁵ NOS QUI VALEMOS TANTO COME VOS, Y PODEMOS MAS QUE VOS, VOS ELEGIMOS REY, CON ESTAS Y ESTAS CONDITIONES:
30 INTRA VOS Y NOS, UN QUE MANDA MAS QUE VOS. Id est,

---

2 *bc* '*ut*'.
⁴⁴ Fortescue; ed. 1567; fol. 84ʳ.   ⁴⁵ On the source of this quotation, see above, p. 102.

the people, which existed to give advice but seldom met. Hence it
can be said with certainty that, while that institution was ordered
by Henry, it was so fashioned in earlier times and always had such
deep roots that it has survived to the present day. This was because
whatever had to be considered relating to the welfare and preservation of the commonwealth was submitted to the council, and, if any
decree was issued by command either of the king or the people, it
was entirely without force unless it were approved in this way by
the authority of the council. Lest the council be hindered by the
judgment of an inexperienced and vulgar multitude which was
incapable of judging anything wisely, it was made clear from the
beginning by a specific law who from the convocation of clergy,
and who and how many from the rest of the people, should be
summoned to this council. They commonly call it parliament
according to the French usage. Each king customarily calls it at
the beginning of his reign, and thereafter he convokes it by his
own decision as often as occasion may demand.' Such are the words
of Polydore Virgil. [c]A certain ancient writer [Fortescue] who was
chancellor of England offers the same opinion in a work entitled
A Learned Commendation:[44] 'A king', he says, 'may not himself or
through his ministers impose tallages, subsidies or any other
burdens whatsoever upon his subjects, nor may he change their
laws, nor make new laws without the agreement and consent of his
whole kingdom expressed in his parliament.'

[a]Yet from these laws of nearly all nations none is as remarkable
as that of the Spanish, who, when they appoint a king of Aragon in
their general council, enact a kind of play to keep the issue constantly in mind. They lead in a man whom they name 'the Law of
Aragon', and by a decree of the people declare him to be greater
and more powerful than the king. Then they harangue the king,
who is appointed with fixed laws and conditions, using words,
which, because of the extraordinary and most singular fortitude of
that people in disciplining the king, we shall here repeat:[45] 'WE,
WHO ARE WORTH AS MUCH AS YOU AND CAN DO MORE
THAN YOU, ELECT YOU AS KING UPON SUCH AND SUCH
CONDITIONS; BETWEEN YOU AND US THERE IS ONE WHOSE

Nos qui tanti sumus, quanti vos, et plusquam vos possumus, Regem vos eligimus, his atque his conditionibus. Inter vos et nos unus maiore cum imperio est, quam vos. ^cEoque illud pertinet Iohannis Vassci in Chronicis Hispan. sub anno 839:[46] *Ermicus*
5 *populari suffragio electus Rex, unctus, et coronatus, sed certis condi-tionibus, nimirum, ut in eos aequis legibus uteretur, atque ut unus iudex esset medius inter Regem et populum, si quid controversiae oriretur,* ISQUE ARAGONIAE IUSTITIA *appellaretur.* Item Lucius Marinaeus lib. 8 :[47] *Princeps,* inquit, *eligitur, propositis tamen*
10 *nonnullis conditionibus, ut in eos aequis legibus uteretur, a quibus etiam iudex qui medius inter eos esset, petebatur, et* ARAGONIAE IUSTITIA *vocabatur.*

Item Hieronymus Surita, sub anno DCCCXLIX :[48] *Iohannes Simenius Cerdanus, qui praefecturam, quam vocant Iustitiae Ara-*
15 *gonum, plures annos avorum aetate gessit, cuius praestantissimi viri magna est apud omnes, et in primis gravis auctoritas, prodit eundem Magistratum, cui nostri summam rerum deferunt, initio regni consti-tutum, ut quemadmodum apud Lacedaemonios Ephori Regibus oppositi fuerant, sic apud Aragonios is magistratus vim maiorem, atque im-*
20 *potentiam Regiae potestatis coerceret, et quodammodo praeses atque custos libertatis haberetur. Inde enim magistratum introductum ferunt, praesidia communi libertati suppeditantem, cuius vis in libertate retinenda emineat, ut nemo ius suum amittere posset, nisi qui eum gerat auctor sit factus, et in posterum certum mansisse perfugium aut intermis-*
25 *sae aut retentae libertatis, adeoque integrum purumque esse voluerunt, ut ipsius* IUSTITIAE *nomine insignitum produxerint. Aragonensium certe legum atque institutorum serie liquido constat, magnis inter-dictorum praesidiis eam praefecturam septam fuisse, atque communitam, cum, regno latius patente de libertate retinenda maiores paulatim*
30 *cautum sibi decrevere, ne in posterum extraordinariis potestatibus libertas adimeretur, neve quid de eius dignitate minueretur.*

---

[46] Ed. Schott, I, 710, 17ff.   [47] Ed. Bel, II, 823, 50.   [48] Zurita, *Indices*, Bk. I, an. 845; ed. Schott, III, 8, 38ff.

AUTHORITY IS GREATER THAN YOURS.' ᶜWhat Johannes
Vasseus writes in his chronicle of Spain for the year 839[46] is relevant
to the point: 'Ermicus was elected king by the votes of the people,
and was anointed and crowned on certain fixed conditions, such
as that he should apply the laws with equity and that there should
be a judge to mediate between king and people if any dispute
should arise. This judge was called the "Justicia of Aragon".'
Lucius Marinaeus writes:[47] 'Although the prince is elected, some
conditions are proposed, such as that he should apply the laws
equitably to the people. Under these laws a judge was also required
whose rôle was to mediate between them. He was called the
"Justicia of Aragon".'

Jerome of Zurita writes for the year 849:[48] 'Johannes Simenius
Cerdanus administered the office known as the justiciarship of
Aragon for many years until he was a very great age. This excellent
man, who held great authority among all other men and stood in
the foremost rank, declared that this same magistracy to which the
greatest affairs are submitted was established at the founding of the
kingdom. And just as the ephors stood in opposition to the kings
with the Spartans, so with the Aragonese this magistrate confines
the force and violence of the power of kings, and in a certain manner
acts as the superintendent and guardian of liberty. They introduced
the office as providing protection for free men in general, and its
power became pre-eminent in the defence of liberty, so that no one
could lose his legal right unless he deliberately renounced it. In
later times the office remained a certain refuge for those who had
lost their liberty or had it withheld, and, as they wished it to be
whole and undefiled, they advanced its remarkable status with the
name of "Justicia". It became clearly established by a succession of
Aragonese laws and decrees that the office was hedged about and
fortified by the strong protection of interdicts. Since the kingdom
suffered many instances of restraint of liberty, the statesmen of
ancient times gradually came to determine it should be made
secure, lest in later years liberty might be undermined by extraordinary powers, or lest its status might be diminished in any
way.'

Item sub anno MCXIV:[49] *Petrus Simenius praefectus Iustitiae Aragonum. Is magistratus primo Maior Iustitia appellatus fuit, quod supremum ius ac potestatem a Regibus obtineret; postea vero legibus ita septus fuit, atque munitus, ut libertatis, a supremo dominatu vindi-*
5 *candae atque tuendae commune perfugium atque praesidium esset.*

Item sub anno MCCCXLIV:[50] *Rex proventus omnes et vectigalia Athonis Foccii militariaque beneficia notari describique decernit, et Foccius Garciae Ferdinandiae Castrensis Iustitiae Aragonum prae-fecti intercessione atque interdicto notationem eam abrogandam con-*
10 *tendit, summaque de iurisdictione controversia suboritur. Regii enim advocati eo actionem intenderunt, ut praefectum Iustitiae Aragonum reiectione interposita, iudicem aspernentur, atque repudient, id ius esse asseverantes, ut in generali conventu, de iis controversiis diiudicet, atque definiat, quae cum Rege haberentur, neque illi ius fasque esse,*
15 *extra conventum Regem in iudicium deducere, neque adversus regiam dignitatem, pro aliquo iudicium accipere, nisi, in ingenuitatis actioni-bus, aut in eis litibus, quibus Rex tanquam auctor obstrictus esset, et in his quaestionibus, quae adversus Regios magistratus, et iudices constituerentur.*

20 Item sub anno MCCCXLVIII:[51] *Ex eo magistratus et Praefectura Iustitiae Aragonum stabiliendae communis libertatis caussa, antiquitus legibus septa, atque munita, in eo vires suas exercere coepit, ne quis contra regiorum ministrorum extraordinariam potestatem iussa, atque imperia, auxilii egeret, aut potentiorum iniuria premeretur, ac fere de*
25 *omnibus controversiis publicis, privatisque ne vis inferatur, constituit. Si quis aut privatus aut publicus eius decreto non steterit, gravissima poena afficitur, neque petenti ius redditur, aut ullus honos communi-catur, eiusque auctoritas e civitate exterminatur, idque legibus habent sancitum. Institutum vero eius praefecturae interdictis tale tempera-*

---

[49] *Ibid.,* Bk. I, an. 1114; *ed. cit.,* III, 36, 32ff.   [50] *Ibid.,* Bk. I, an. 1144; *ed. cit.,* III, 189, 43ff.   [51] *Ibid.,* Bk. III, an. 1348; *ed. cit.,* III, 199, 15ff.

For the year 1114 Zurita states:[49] 'Petrus Simenius was the justicia of Aragon. At first this office was called "the major justice". Later it was so hedged in and fortified by laws that it was a general refuge and protection to vindicate and preserve liberty from the supreme authorities.'

Again for the year 1344 he writes:[50] 'When all had come forth the king decreed that the rents and military offices of profit in the hands of Athonis Foccius be listed and set in writing. Foccius argued for this process to be set aside through the intervention and interdict of Garcia Ferdinand, the justicia of Aragon, and a controversy arose concerning jurisdiction. The royal advocates brought an action to repudiate the justicia of Aragon, who had interposed a stay. They refused to accept the claim that it was the law which, as in a general assembly, determined and defined such matters as were in dispute with the king. Nor would they agree that it was just and right to bring the king to judgment outside the assembly, and that it was not contrary to the royal dignity to receive a judgment on behalf of someone else, except in actions concerning nobility of birth, or in those suits where the king was hampered by being the instigator, or in such charges as might be brought against the royal magistrates and judges.'

Under the year 1348 Zurita writes as follows:[51] 'In order to establish the general liberty, which had been determined and protected by the ancient laws, the justicia of Aragon began to exercise his powers to that end, lest anyone might need aid against the extraordinary power, the orders and commands of royal ministers, or might be oppressed by the wrongful acts of the powerful, and generally lest force might be employed in public or private quarrels. So inviolate is his decree that if any private or public person will not accept it, the gravest punishment is applied, and no right is granted a petitioner, nor is any honour bestowed, and such a man's influence is removed from the commonwealth. Indeed the design of this office was hedged with prohibitions in

mentum fuit, ut tenuiores et qui locum infimum civitatis tenent, cum
principibus viris aequari se arbitrentur, et eam sciscendarum legum
rationem nostri secuti videntur, in eo magistratu muniendo, ut regiis
iudicibus opponeretur, quemadmodum Lacedaemone Ephori a Theo-
5 pompo Spartanis Regibus oppositi fuerant, et apud Romanos Con-
sulibus Tribuni plebis.

Sed ne existimatio atque auctoritas eius magistratus unquam
imminui posset, aut popularis fieret, atque omnes iussis supremae legis
obtemperarent, et cum omnibus ea lex semper una atque eadem voce
10 personaret, ut vere populi salus suprema lex esset, ac vinculum et
firmamentum libertatis, atque omnes quod dici solet, quasi sacrae legis
cathenis constringerentur, ea cautio adhibita est, ne ex infimo ordine,
aut populari suffragio, quispiam eum magistratum adipisceretur, sed
militari decore cohonestatus, et a Rege ascitus, atque suffectus. Modera-
15 tione quoque ea praefectura, non ad popularem auram provecta, sed
temperatior a maioribus instituta est, quam Ephororum magistratus a
Lacedaemoniis fertur introductus, qui se adeo insolenter efferre consueverant, ut in more institutoque positum esset, ut in tribunali
sedentes Regibus ne assurgerent, neve eos venerarentur, et singulis
20 mensibus iurisiurandi religione obstringerentur, Reges se patriis
legibus obtemperaturos, Ephori vero se Regum imperio obedientes fore,
dum leges, ac scita institutaque maiorum ab illis observarentur. Inde
evenit ut non dissensione ac dissidio, sed more institutoque in unius
Praefecturae magistratu Respublica regiis magistratibus opposita non
25 imbecilla esset, sed magnum applausum assentiente populo conse-
queretur, et turbidi concitatique motus in posterum comprimerentur,

such a way that more humble men and those who hold the lowest place in the commonwealth may regard themselves as equal to the great, and our descendants may see the purpose of seeking out the laws and of strengthening that office so that it may stand against the royal judges, just as the ephors of Sparta were opposed by Theopompus and the Spartan kings, and as the tribunes of the people among the Romans were opposed by the consuls.

'So that the reputation and authority of that office could never be diminished or become vulgar, all men had to comply with the commands of the supreme law, while the law had always to speak to all with one and the same voice. Then indeed the welfare of the people would be the supreme law and the bond and chief support of liberty, while all men, as it is said, would be constrained as if bound by the sacred chain of the law. This prudent restriction has been added lest anybody from the lowest order, or someone who used the popular vote, might acquire the office in question, or lest a person showered with military honours and enjoying the favour of the king might be elected. The office was established by our elders as a moderating force – one not subjected to the breath of popular opinion, but rather something steadier than the magistracy of the ephors introduced by the Spartans. The latter had so habituated themselves to speak insolently that it became the established custom to remain in their seats in the tribunal, and neither to stand up in the presence of the kings nor to offer them any respect. In particular months the Spartan kings were bound under a religious oath to comply with the laws of their fathers, but the ephors themselves should have shown obedience to the command of the kings so long as the latter were observing the laws and known decrees of their ancestors. So it happened that the commonwealth of Aragon avoided dissension and dissidence, and through the office of the single justicia proceeded according to custom and law, without instances of unreasoned opposition to the royal magistrates. The approval and assent of the people was the natural consequence of this practice. Tumults which were later excited and stirred up were

*atque intestinae dissensiones sine ullo tumultu, aut motu
sedarentur.*

Item anno MCCCLXXXVI:⁵² *Rex Iohannem filium procuratione Regni privat, imperatque atque edicit, nequis primogenio pareat.*
5 *Iohan. anxius exploratis in se patris novercaeque odiis, ut adversus
regiam potestatem iuris imploraret auxilium, Dominicum Cerdanum
summo Iustitiae Aragonum magistratui Praefectum appellat, atque ad
eum provocat, eoque perfugio et legum praesidio adversus maiorem vim
regiae potestatis munitur. Praefectus, ut est consuetudo, de vi inter-
10 dicit. Tantum communi libertati tribuitur, ut Princeps de suo iure, et
de legibus disceptaturus ad eum potius magistratum venire, necesse
habuerit, cum is magistratum gerat, qui a Rege creatus sit. Eius namque magistratus interdictis appositis, nihil Regii imperii, aut summae
potestatis fit reliqui, quoad magistratus suum de interdicti iure iudicium
15 pronunciet, et sententiam ferat, ne dignitatis Regiae praestantia
aequabilitatem communis iuris transeat, aut vi oppressos extra-
ordinario imperio coërceat.*

*Cerdanus in caussa populari, maximeque plausibili perpetua
constantia in proposito, susceptoque consilio permansit. Eam enim vim
20 intercessionum, inhibitionemque Praefecturae Iustitiae Aragonum
maiores esse voluerunt, ut nihil inviolabilius, sanctiusve ducant, et ad
eam summam omnia referri velint, ut ii restituantur, qui vi compressi,
constricti aut depulsi deiective fuerint, eaque religione observant, et in
ea positum fuit semper ratione atque sententia, ut eius magistratus ea vis
25 sit, ut praescribat Regiis iudicibus, ne quid adversus interdicta inter-
cessionemque attentent, molianturve. Inde id perfugium, quasi praesidium communis salutis, legum, et institutorum venerantur, observant,*

⁵² *Ibid.,* Bk. III, an. 1386; *ed. cit.,* III, 248, 54ff.

suppressed, and internal dissensions were settled without riot or disturbance.'

Another passage from Zurita occurs for the year 1386:[52] 'The king deprived his son John of the kingdom by procuration, and commanded that no one should obey his first-born. John was perplexed by this decision, and when he had ascertained the animosity of his father and step-mother against himself, he sought the aid of the law against the royal authority, and appealed to Dominicus Cerdanus, the justicia of Aragon. He asked him for the refuge and protection afforded by the laws against the greater strength of the royal power. According to the usual practice, the justicia forbad the use of force. The general principle of liberty was so respected that the king found it necessary to go to that officer so that he might debate the issues concerning his oath and the laws, since he who has been appointed by the king assumes the magistracy. When the justicia's prohibitions had been applied, nothing seemed to remain of the royal authority or the supreme power until the justicia gave his own judgment on the law of the interdict, and pronounced his opinion that the pre-eminence of the king's rank should not transgress the equity of the common law, and that he should not coerce the oppressed by force under his extraordinary authority.

'In this popular and most praiseworthy cause Cerdanus continued to show an unyielding constancy in making his view known and in maintaining it. For our forefathers wished the power of intercession and prohibition possessed by the justicia of Aragon to be exercised in a more sacred and inviolable way than anything else. It was their wish that everything should be submitted to that supreme authority, so that those who were oppressed, constrained, deprived, or thrown down by force, should be restored. Religion should be respected, and always should dependence upon it proceed through reason and opinion. Thus the power of the justicia relies upon what he prescribes for the royal judges, to inhibit their attacking or undertaking anything against his interdicts or his intervention. Hence they reverence that bastion as if it were the safeguard of the common welfare, the laws and the

*arcte tenent, accurateque tuentur, ac primigenium regni heredem ad ea
legis praesidia decurrisse, civitates omnes gloriantur.**

^aQuae cum ita se habeant, cum, inquam, gentium ac nationum
omnium commune hoc institutum semper fuerit, quae quidem
5 regio ac non tyrannico imperio uterentur, ^but SALUS POPULI
SUPREMA LEX ESSET,[53] ^aperspicuum est, non modo praeclaram
illam communis concilii habendi libertatem partem* esse iuris
gentium, verumetiam Reges qui malis artibus illam sacrosanctam libertatem opprimunt, quasi iuris gentium violatores, et
10 humanae societatis expertes, iam non pro Regibus, sed pro
tyrannis* habendos esse.

^bQuanquam quid eos tyrannos appellemus, ac non etiam
atrociore vocabulo utamur?* cum Fl. Constantinus tyrannus, qui
iuniore Honorio imperante tyrannidem in Gallia occupavit,
15 vetus istud Galliae nostrae institutum violare ausus non sit, sed
tanquam sacrosanctum conservarit. Nam cum Arelate regni sui
sedem fixisset, eamque propterea Constantinam urbem vocari
statuisset, publicum gentis Concilium quotannis ex vetere
instituto haberi solitum,* in ea urbe haberi statuit, hoc est,
20 septem provinciarum conventus, Viennensis, utriusque Narbonensis, utriusque Aquitaniae, Novempopulaniae, et Alpium
maritimarum. Quod ex ipsius Constitutione nuper duorum
clarissimorum virorum beneficio in lucem edita, cognoscere
licebit:[54] *IMP. CONSTANTINUS AD AGRICOLAM PRAE-*
25 *FECTUM PRAETORIO GALLIARUM. Saluberrima magnificentiae
tuae suggestione inter reliquas Reipublicae utilitates evidenter
instructi, observanda provincialibus nostris, id est, per septem Provincias mansura in aevum auctoritate decernimus, quod sperari plane ab
ipsis provincialibus debuisset. Nam cum propter privatas et publicas
30 necessitates de singulis civitatibus, non solum de singulis Provinciis vel
Honoratos confluere, vel mitti legatos aut possessorum utilitas, aut*

2 c¹ adds 'Hactenus Hispaniensium historicorun testimonia copiose protulimus,
ut omnes intelligant nihil a nobis fingi, nihilve novi & inusitati in medium
adferri.'   7 c² omits 'partem'.   11 c¹ omits 'iam non...pro tyrannis'.
13 c¹ omits this sentence.   19 c 'solutum'.

53 See above, p. 296, n. 19.   54 Hänel, *Corpus legum*, 238; dated 17 April 418.

customs. They hold to it narrowly and safeguard it with precision, and all the cities in the commonwealth boast that the first-born heir of the kingdom had recourse to those guardians of the law.'*

*a*Since this is the way things are, and since, as I say, there has always been this common law among all peoples and nations who practise regal rather than tyrannical government, *b*namely, that 'THE WELFARE OF THE PEOPLE WAS THE SUPREME LAW',[53] *a*it is obvious not only that this celebrated liberty of holding a common council is a part† of the law of nations but also that kings who oppress that sacred liberty with their evil arts, as if they were violators of this international law and beings set apart from human society, should not be regarded as kings but rather as tyrants.‡

*b*Although we call them tyrants, should we not use some word that is even harsher?§ When Flavius ruled as a tyrant in Gaul in the reign of the young Honorius, he did not dare to abuse our ancient Gallic constitution, but preserved it inviolate. With his capital at Arles, thenceforth named Constantina, he decided that the public council of the nation should be held there annually, as by ancient practice. The assembly included the seven provinces of Vienne, the two Narbonenses, the two Aquitaines, Novempopulana and the Maritime Alps. This is known from the edict itself, which was recently brought to light through the kindness of two most celebrated men. It runs as follows:[54] 'THE EMPEROR CONSTANTINE TO AGRICOLA, PRAETORIAN PREFECT OF THE GAULS. We know of the excellent proposal from your magnificence as to the remaining services of the commonwealth, and under our authority we issue this decree for all eternity concerning the establishments to be observed in our seven provincial governments knowing it will be most welcome to the governments themselves. The private and public needs of individual cities and provinces, as well as the benefit of landowners and the interests of public administration, all require distinguished officers to assemble

---

* *c*[1] *adds* Thus far we have offered all this evidence from Spanish histories so that all men may know we have invented nothing, and nothing novel or unusual has been introduced. † *c*[2] *omits a part.* ‡ *c*[1] not be...tyrants *becomes* be so regarded. § *c*[1] *omits preceding sentence.*

publicarum ratio exigat functionum; maxime opportunum et con-
ducibile iudicavimus, ut servata posthac quotannis consuetudine, in
constituto tempore, in Metropolitana, id est, in Arelatensi urbe incipiant
septem Provinciae habere concilium. In quo plane tam in singulis quam
5 *in commune consulimus: primum, ut optimorum conventus sub*
illustri praesentia praefecturae, si id tamen ratio publicae dispositionis
obtulerit, saluberrima de singulis rebus possint esse consilia. Tum
quicquid tractatum fuerit, et discussum ratiociniis constitutum, nec
latere potiores Provincias poterit, ut parem necesse est inter absentes
10 *aequitatis formam, iustitiaeque servari.*

Hinc plane praeter necessitates etiam humanae conversationi non
parum credimus commoditatis accedere, quod in Constantina urbe
iubemus annis singulis esse concilium. Tanta est enim loci oppor-
tunitas, tanta est copia commerciorum, tanta illic frequentia commean-
15 *tium, ut quicquid usquam nascitur, illic commodius distrahatur. Neque*
enim ulla Provincia fructus sui facultate laetatur, ut non nisi haec
propria Arelatensi, soli credatur esse foecunditas. Quicquid enim dives
Oriens, quicquid odoratus Atalis, quicquid delicatus Assyrius, quod
Africa fertilis, quod speciosa Hispania, quod foecunda Gallia potest
20 *habere praeclarum, ita illi exhibetur affatim, quasi sibi nascantur*
omnia, quae ubique constat esse magnifica.

Iam vero de cursu Rhodani, et Turoni recursu, necesse est, ut
vicinum faciant, et pene conterminum, vel quod iste praeterfluit,
vel ille quod circuit. Cum ergo huic serviat civitati quicquid habet terra
25 *praecipuum, ad hanc vel navi, vel vehiculo, terra, mari, flumine*
deferatur quicquid in singulis nascitur, quomodo non multum sibi
Galliae nostrae praestitum credant, cum in eadem civitate praecipiamus
esse conventum, in qua divino quodam munere commoditatum et

or deputies to be sent. We have judged it extremely seasonable and expedient, and trust that the custom may annually be preserved hereafter, for them to begin to hold a council of the seven provinces at the appropriate time in the principal town, that is at Arles. So that there may be full individual, as well as general, participation we consider, first, that, provided the public disposition be conducive to it, there should be a meeting of the leading men, convened in the presence of the illustrious prefect, which may engage in the most useful deliberations concerning particular matters. Next, whatever will have been discussed there may be considered and decided proportionately among the more powerful provinces, but not too widely, for it is necessary to maintain an appearance of equity and justice among those provinces which are not represented.

'We believe that apart from the need for discussion it will prove of considerable convenience for us to order that the council should be held in the town of Constantina in particular years. For it is a place so full of opportunity, so plentifully supplied with merchants, and so often frequented by travellers, that no matter where anything is produced it may be easily distributed there. No other province so rejoices in its productive capacity as does that of Arles, and its plenitude of goods suggests an unparalleled fecundity. Whatever wealth be found in the Orient, whatever sweet odours be known in Arabia, whatever luxuries exist in Assyria, whatever the products of fertile Africa, whatever the treasures of Spain, whatever excellence bountiful Gaul can bring forth – all this will be found there in abundance, as if all things of magnificence everywhere were produced there.

'Now as to the course of the Rhône and the valley of the Loire, wherever these rivers flow the land beside or between them should become neighbouring or bordering districts. Therefore, whenever the land has any special quality let it be put to the service of the city, and let whatever is produced in particular places be brought by ship or cart, by land, sea or river, so that men will believe that few countries surpass our Gaul when we enjoin that an assembly be held in that same city. Could there be any place so divinely blessed

commerciorum opportunitas tanta praestatur? Siquidem hoc rationa-
bili plane, probatoque consilio iam et vir illustris Petronius observari
debere praeceperit.

Quod interpolatum vel iniuria temporum, vel desidia Tyrannorum
5 *reparari solita prudentiae nostrae auctoritate decernimus, Agricola*
Parens charissime, atque amantissime. Unde et illustris magnificentia
tua et hanc praeceptionem nostram, et priorem sedis suae dispositionem
per septem provincias in perpetuo faciet custodiri, ut ab Idibus Augusti
quibuscunque mediis diebus in Idus Septembris in Arelatensi urbe
10 *noverint Honorati, vel Possessores iudices singularum Provinciarum*
annis singulis Concilium esse servandum, ita ut de Novempopulania,
et de secunda Aquitania, quae Provinciae longius constitutae sunt, si
eorum Iudices occupatio certa detinuerit, sciant legatos iuxta consue-
tudinem esse mittendos. Qua provisione plurimum et provincialibus
15 *nostris nos intelligimus, utilitatisque praestare, et Arelatensis urbis,*
cuius fidei secundum testimonia atque suffragia Patritii parentisque
nostri multa debemus, non parvum adiicere nos constat ornatum. Sciat
autem magnificentia tua, quinis auri libris Iudicem mulctandum esse,
ternis Honoratos, vel Curiales, qui ad constitutum locum intra
20 *definitum tempus venire distulerint.*

where so great an opportunity offers for trade and commerce? Although this clearly reasonable plan has now been approved, that much esteemed man Petronius should give instructions as to what should be done.

'Agricola, our most dear and well-beloved kinsman, we hereby decree that whatever may have been corrupted by the passage of time or the sloth of tyrants shall be restored by the sole authority of our wisdom. Your illustrious magnificence is required by this our injunction to arrange a better establishment for your capital in the seven provinces and ensure that it be protected in perpetuity. Throughout the days between the thirteenth of August and the thirteenth of September the leading men and the judges of individual provinces should learn that a council is to be held in the town of Arles every year. Where business is likely to detain the magistrates from the remoter provinces, that is from Novempopulana and Aquitaine II, they should know that, according to the custom, deputies must be sent. By this provision we may learn a great deal from our provincial governments, which will serve a distinguished purpose, while it shall be our intent to add considerably to the splendour of the town of Arles, to whose loyalty, as related by the reports and opinions of our patrician and kinsman, we owe much. May your magnificence know that any judge is to be fined five pounds of gold, and any lesser officials or magistrates three pounds of gold, should they fail to attend at the established place within the time we have fixed.'

^cCAPUT XIII [^{ab}X cont.]

De regia maiestate et annuo gentis Francogallicae conventu, placito, curia, parlamento

---

^aVerum ut ad institutum redeamus,* cum illa, quam superius exposuimus forma, Respublica nostra ^csapientissimo ^amaiorum instituto temperata e tribus generibus fuisset, constitutum est,* ut quotannis, atque adeo quoties maior aliqua res incideret,
5 solenne et publicum concilium indiceretur, quod propterea Trium statuum Parlamentum appellatum est, cum eo vocabulo colloquium et conventus hominum intelligeretur, variis ex locis unum in locum communi de re deliberandi caussa coeuntium; itaque* colloquia inter hostes pacis aut induciarum causa insti-
10 tuta, semper in Chronicis nostris ^cvetusto ^aillo Parlamenti nomine appellantur. Huic porro concilio Rex in aureo tribunali sedens, praeerat, cui primum Principes Regnique magistratus, tum inferiore loco Legati* ex singulis civitatibus subsidebant, quos populari lingua Deputatos appellamus. Nam ubi dies
15 Concilii venerat, Rex ea pompa in constitutum atrium* ^cquasi in augustissimum et religiosissimum Iustitiae Gallicae templum, ^adeducebatur, quae magis ad popularem moderationem, quam ad Regalem magnificentiam accommodata videbatur.

Quam etsi perditis hisce temporibus aulicis assentatoribus
20 irrisui fore non dubitamus, tamen quoniam pietatis pars est, Maiorum sapientia delectari, ex antiquis monimentis exponemus. Carpento igitur Rex in atrium vehebatur bubus tracto, quos auriga stimulo agebat. Ubi vero in atrium* ac potius in Rei-

---

1 <i>c</i>¹ begins 'Perspicuum est igitur,'.   3 'constitum est': <i>c</i>¹ 'idcirco institutum fuisset'.   9 <i>c</i> 'Nam'.   13 <i>c</i> 'Delecti'.   15 <i>c</i> redistribute these six words: 'Rex in atrium constitutum' remain here, 'ea pompa' go below after 'templum'.   23 'in atrium': <i>c</i> 'in eum locum'.

^cCHAPTER XIII [^{ab}X cont.]

The royal majesty and the annual assembly of the
Francogallican people, also known as the
'*Placitum*', '*Curia*' and '*Parlamentum*'

---

^aTo return to the main issue,* our commonwealth, as we have
shown above, was established ^con the most praiseworthy foundation ^aby our ancestors as a mixed state incorporating the three
forms. Every year, and more often than this if occasion so demanded, a solemn and public council was convened. The assembly
was called the parliament of the three estates, since this phrase
implies a conference and convention of men, gathered together
from many districts in one place in order to deliberate on the
general welfare. In this way[†] meetings called to establish a peace
or a truce among enemies are always given that ^cancient ^aname
of parliament in our chronicles. Sitting on his golden throne, the
king presided at this council. Below him were the princes and
magistrates of the kingdom, while beneath them came those
representing[‡] individual provinces, who were described as
deputies in the common speech. On the day appointed for the
council the king was escorted to the meeting place, ^cas if it were
the most august and holy temple of Gallic justice, ^awith a ceremony
which seemed more appropriate to popular moderation than to
regal magnificence.

Although in these profligate times of ours it is doubtless a
matter for the ridicule of obsequious courtiers, we shall, nevertheless, provide an account drawn from our ancient records, because it
is a kind of piety to take delight in the wisdom of our ancestors.
The king was taken to the meeting-house in a carriage drawn by
oxen, which were driven by a waggoner with a goad. When he
had arrived at the hall,[§] or, rather, the holy place of the common-

---

* ^{c1} *begins* It is therefore clear that.   † *bc* In this way *becomes* For.   ‡ *c* chosen
from.   § *c* there.

publicae sacrarium* ventum erat, tum Principes Regem in aureo
solio collocabant, reliquique (ut iam diximus) suo quisque loco
atque ordine subsidebant. Eoque, demum *b*in *a*statu atque
sacrario Regia Maiestas dicebatur, cuius rei etiam nunc insigne
5 monimentum animadvertere licet in typo Regio, quo Sigillum
Cancellariae* vulgo nominamus, ubi Rex non equo militari
insidens, aut triumphali more quadrigis invehens, sed togatus et
coronatus, sedens in solio, dextraque sceptrum regale, sinistra
sceptrum Iustitiae tenens, solennique concilio praesidens con-
10 spicitur. Et profecto ita est, ut ibi* demum Regalis maiestas vere
proprieque dicatur, ubi de summa Reipublicae consilium agitur,
non, ut imperitum vulgus *c*hodie *a*usurpare solet, sive Rex ludat
*b*pila,* *a*sive saltet *b*ac tripudiet, *a*sive cum mulierculis garriat *b*ac
nugas agat, denique, *a*ut semper Maiestatem Regiam nominet.
15   Harum autem rerum omnium testimonia e multis pauca proferemus. Primum ex historia Eguinarthi,[1] qui Caroli Magni
Cancellarius fuit, eiusque vitam conscripsit, *b*et Hunibaldi
Appendice apud Iohannem Tritenhemium:[2] *a* *Quocunque*, inquit,
eundum erat, carpento ibat, quod bubus iunctis et bubulco rustico more
20 *agente trahebatur. Sic ad palatium, sic ad publicum populi sui con-*
ventum, qui *c*ad Kalendas Maii *a*annuatim ob Regni utilitatem cele-*
brabatur, ire, sic domum redire solebat. Quod idem totidem prope
verbis Iohannes Nauclerus in Chronologia Generat. 26 commemorat.[3] Itemque auctor Magni Chronici sub initium vitae
25 Caroli Magni, fol. 177.[4] Neque vero nimiopere admirandum id
videtur, nam hunc temporum illorum morem fuisse, ut et
Reges et Reginae, et Regii liberi bubus veherentur, argumento

---

1 *c* move 'ac potius in Reipublicae sacrarium' to the previous sentence, before
'vehebatur'.   6 *b* 'quod Sigillum Cancellariae'; *c* 'quod Magnum Cancellariae
sigillum'.   10 *c*[1] 'ita'.   13 'ludat pila': *c* 'pila ludat'.

[1] See next note.   [2] The following quotation is from Einhard, c. 1 (*MGH SS*,
II, 444, 11–15), and although Hotman added the reference to Hunibaldus in 1576,
not until 1586 did he make his text conform to Hunibaldus by adding the phrase
'ad Kalendas Maii'; cf. ed. Schard, I, 340.   [3] *Chron.*, II, gen. 28; ed. 1579, 669.
Nauclerus expands upon Einhard's words to claim that this was the *institutio
parlamenti* by Charlemagne.   [4] *Grandes chroniques*, ed. 1514, I, fol. 177ʳ.

wealth,* the nobles led the king to a golden throne, and the remainder, as we have already said, took their seats according to their place and rank. This was the shrine and these the precise circumstances where royal majesty was said to exist, and even today we may notice a remarkable record of this on the royal seal, or the chancery† seal, as it is commonly called. There the king is not shown in military guise on horseback, or riding on a four-horse chariot in the manner of a triumph, but robed and crowned, seated on his throne, with the royal sceptre in his right hand and the sceptre of justice in his left, presiding at the solemn council. Hence it can be truly and properly said that royal majesty resides in that place where counsel is taken for the welfare of the commonwealth, and not *c*as today, *a*when it is the common and ignorant usage to misapply the word in circumstances where the king plays *b*at ball, *a*or dances *b*and capers about, *a*or prattles with women *b*and jests about trifles *a* – such circumstances as commonly prompt a reference to 'Royal Majesty'.

We shall offer a few proofs of these matters, selected from the many available. The first is from the history of Einhard,[1] who was Charlemagne's chancellor and wrote the life of his king, *b*and also from the appendix of Hunibaldus according to Johannes Tri-themius:[2] *a*'Wherever the king went, he travelled on a waggon drawn by yoked oxen and driven by a waggoner in rustic fashion. In this way he was wont to proceed to the palace and to the public assembly of his people, which was held annually *c*on the first of May *a*for the profit of the kingdom, and to return to his own dwelling.' Johannes Nauclerus uses almost the same words to describe this in his chronicles.[3] So, too, does the author of the *Great Chronicle* in the section at the beginning of the life of Charlemagne.[4] This should not be the cause of any great surprise, for it was the custom in those times for kings and queens and their children to be

---

* *c* or, rather, the holy place of the commonwealth *is moved to the previous sentence after* meeting-house. † *c adds* great.

est etiam ille Gregorii Turon. locus lib. 3, cap. 26:[5] *Deuteria vero*
(haec Childeberti regis uxor erat) *cernens filiam suam* ex superiore
marito susceptam, *adultam valde esse, timens ne eam concupiscens
Rex sibi adsumeret, in basterna positam indomitis bobus coniunctis eam*
5 *de ponte praecipitavit.* Iam vero de Tribunali aureo Aimoinus
lib. 4, cap. 30[6] ita scribit, ubi de Rege Dagoberto commemorat:
Generale indixit PLACITUM, *in loco nuncupato Bigargio; ad quod
propere convenientibus cunctis Franciae Primoribus Kal. Maiis Rex
solio residens aureo hoc apud eos habuit orationis exordium.* Item
10 cap. 41, ubi de Clodoveo Rege loquitur:[7] *Medius inter eos solio
residens aureo hoc habuit orationis exordium.* Item Sigebertus in
Chron. anni 662:[8] *Francorum* (inquit) *Regibus moris erat, Kal. Maii
praesidere coram tota gente, et salutare, et salutari, obsequia et dona
accipere.* Quod Georg. Cedrenus totidem prope verbis sic
15 exponit:[9] κατὰ δὲ τὸν Μάϊον μῆνα προκαθέζεσθαι ἐπὶ παντὸς
τοῦ ἔθνους, καὶ προσκυνεῖν αὐτοῖς καὶ ἀντιπροσκυνεῖσθαι ὑπ'
αὐτῶν, δωροφορεῖσθαί τε κατὰ συνήφειαν καὶ ἀντιδιδόναι
αὐτοῖς.

Iam vero de popularium, qui ad Concilium convenerant,
20 auctoritate, testimonium hoc extat apud Aimoinum lib. 4,
cap. 41, ubi de Clodoveo secundo loquitur:[10] *Quanquam* (inquit
Rex) *Francigenae cives, terreni nos cura principatus admoneat, publicis vos consultores rebus advocare.* Idem eodem lib., cap. 74:[11] *Aes-
tatis initio in Saxoniam eundum,** *et ibi* (*ut** *in Francia quotannis
25 solebat) generalem conventum quotannis habuit.* Item lib. 4, cap. 13,
ubi de Carolo Magno loquitur:[12] *Peracta venatione Aquisgrani,
rediens generalem populi sui conventum more solenni habuit.* Cap.
116:[13] *Imperator autem duobus conventibus habitis, uno apud Novio-
magum, altero apud Compendium, in quo et annua dona suscepit.* Item
30 cap. 117:[14] *Mense Augusto Wormaciam venit, atque habito generali
conventu, et oblata sibi annua dona more solenni suscepit, et legationes*

---

24 *bc* 'eundem'.   24 *bc* omit '*ut*'.

5 *MGH SS Mer.*, 1:1², 123, 19.   6 *PL*, cxxxix, 788.   7 *Ibid.*, 795.   8 *MGH
SS*, vi, 325, 55ff.   9 §794; *PG*, cxxi, 869–72.   10 *PL*, cxxxix, 795.   11 Ed.
1567, 430.   12 Cap. 113; *ibid.*, 526.   13 Cap. 115; *ibid.*, 534.   14 Cap. 117;
ibid., 539.

drawn by oxen. There is an instance of it in Gregory of Tours:[5] 'Deuteria (who was the wife of King Childebert) perceived that her daughter (who had been fathered by an earlier husband) had reached maturity and feared that the lustful king might seduce her. So she placed her in a cart, to which untamed oxen were yoked, and had her thrown off the side of a bridge.' Aimon writes as follows about the golden throne, where he speaks of King Dagobert:[6] 'He issued a general order of convocation in Bigargium, the place he had appointed. The nobility of France hastily proceeded there and assembled on the first of May, when the king, sitting on his golden throne among them, began his speech.' Aimon says of King Clovis:[7] 'Sitting in the midst of them on his golden throne he delivered the first part of his oration.' Also, Sigebert in his chronicle for the year 662 writes:[8] 'It was the custom of the kings of the Franks to preside in the presence of the entire nation on the first of May, to greet their people and be greeted by them, and to receive their obedience and their gifts.' Georgius Cedrenus describes the ceremony in almost the same words.[9]

There is evidence of the authority of the people assembled at the council in another passage from Aimon, where he speaks of Clovis II:[10] '"Although", proclaims the king, "the care of our earthly principality requires us, Francigenian citizens, to seek your advice in public affairs..."' In a later chapter Aimon writes:[11] 'At the beginning of the summer he proceeded to Saxony and there he summoned a general assembly, just as he did annually in France.' And elsewhere, when writing of Charlemagne, he states:[12] 'He returned from the hunting at Aix-la-Chapelle to hold a general assembly of his people according to the solemn custom.' He gives another example when he says:[13] 'The Emperor held two assemblies, one at Lisieux and the other at Compiègne, at which he received the annual gifts...' Similarly in the following passage:[14] 'In the month of August he came to Worms, held the general assembly, received the gifts tendered to him according to the

plurimas audivit. Item lib. 5, cap. 31:[15] *Generale* PLACITUM
Idibus Iuniis in villa Duziaco tenuit, ubi et annua dona sua suscepit.

Atque haec quidem de solenni Concilio, quod Historici et
Galli et Germani depravata Latini sermonis consuetudine modo
5 Curiam, modo Conventum generalem, plerunque autem
PLACITUM appellarunt. Grego. lib. 7, cap. 14:[16] *Igitur adveniente*
PLACITO *directi sunt a Childeberto rege,* etc., *b*et lib. 8, cap. 21:[17]
Sed cum ad PLACITUM *Childebertus cum proceribus suis con-*
venisset, etc. *a*Aimoinus lib. 4, cap. 109:[18] *Medio mense Conventus*
10 *generalis apud Theodonis villam magna populi Francorum frequentia*
celebravit. Et mox:[19] *Eminuit in hoc* PLACITO *piissimi Impera-*
toris misericordia singularis.

Nam moris fuit, ut in illo Concilio munera undique Regi
mitterentur, quod et aliis multis locis traditur, quibus Concilium
15 illud, Conventus generalis appellatur. Aimoinus lib. 4, cap. 64,[20]
ubi de Pipino Rege loquitur: *Coëgit ut promitterent se omnem*
voluntatem illius esse facturos et annis singulis honoris caussa ad
generalem conventum equos trecentos pro munere daturos. Item
cap. 85:[21] *Saxonum perfidiae non immemor, conventum generalem*
20 *trans Rhenum in villa Cuffenstein* more solenni habuit.*

Iam vero Concilium illud alio quoque vocabulo Curia dicebatur, unde nata popularis locutio, cum ad aulam et Regiam itur,
ut, iri ad Curiam dicatur, propterea quod raro ad Regem, nisi
indicto *b*publico gentis *a*concilio *b*et parlamento, *a*et de magnis
25 rebus adibatur.* *c*Ivo Carnotens. epist. 206:[22] *Rex concessit, ut*
eum ad Curiam suam, quae Aurelianis in Natali domini congreganda
erat, secure adduceremus, et ibi cum eo, et cum Principibus regni de hoc
negotio, quantum fieri posset salva regni integritate tractaremus.
Factum est, ut condictum erat, et convenientes in Curiam petitionem
30 *nostram replicavimus. Sed reclamante Curia plenariam pacem im-*
petrare nequivimus, nisi praedictus Metropolitanus per manum et

20 bc '*Cuffensten*'.   **25** 'et de magnis rebus adibatur': **bc** 'magnisque de rebus
adibatur'.

[15] *Ibid.,* 671.   [16] *MGH SS Mer.,* I:I², 334, 21.   [17] *MGH SS Mer.,* I:I²,
388, 9.   [18] Ed. 1567, 510.   [19] *Ibid.*   [20] *Ibid.,* 409.   [21] *Ibid.,* 451.
[22] Epist. 190; *PL,* CLXII, 196.

solemn custom and gave audience to many ambassadors.' Again, in a further reference:[15] 'He held the general assembly on the first of June in the town of Dusiac, where he received his annual gifts.'

So much then for this solemn council which, through a corrupted usage of the Latin tongue, French and German historians sometimes call *curia*, sometimes *conventus generalis* and, more often, *placitum*. This latter usage is that of Gregory of Tours, as in the following instance:[16] 'Therefore, as the time for the *placitum* approached, they were directed by King Childebert...'[b]Or, again:[17] 'But since Childebert and his nobles had joined the *placitum*...' [a]Aimon writes:[18] 'In the middle of the month a *conventus generalis* was held in the town of Thionville, which was thronged with the Frankish people.' He goes on:[19] 'The remarkable compassion of this most pious emperor was manifest at this *placitum*.'

It was the practice in that council to send gifts to the king from all corners of the kingdom. This is referred to in many passages where the council is called the *conventus generalis*. Writing of King Pepin, Aimon states:[20] 'He obliged them to promise to comply with his will in every way and to give him annually at the *conventus generalis* a present of three hundred horses as a mark of respect.' In a later chapter he says:[21] 'He was not unmindful of the treachery of the Saxons, and held a *conventus generalis* across the Rhine in the town of Kostheim according to the solemn custom.'

The council was also called by another name, the *curia* or court. Thence arose the common expression to say that one was going to court when one went to the royal palace, because the king was seldom approached except at a specially proclaimed council [b]and parliament of the people, [a]and then only concerning great affairs. [c]Ivo of Chartres writes in one of his letters:[22] 'The king allowed us to conduct him safely to his *curia*, which should have been assembled in his native province of Orléans, and there to treat with him and the princes of the kingdom as to how far the unity of the kingdom might be preserved. What had been agreed was indeed carried out, and, having assembled in the *curia*, we unrolled our petition. But as the *curia* did not agree we were unable to procure a complete peace, until the aforesaid metropolitan had made the

*sacramentum eam fidelitatem Regi faceret, quam praedecessoribus suis
Regibus Francorum antea fecerant omnes Remenses Archiepiscopi, et
ceteri regni Francorum episcopi. Quod persuadentibus omnibus Curiae
optimatibus factum est.*

5   ^aAimoinus lib. 5, cap. 50:[23] *Carolus, inquit, Danorum Regis
filius Flandriae Proceres quosdam iudicio Curiae convenienter petebat.*
Item cap. sequenti:[24] *Defuncto Henrico Romanorum Rege, in ea
quae maxima et generalis est habita Maguntiae Curia.* Item Otto
Frising. lib. Frider. 1, cap. 40:[25] *Post haec Princeps Bavariam in-*
10 *greditur, ibique mense Februario generalem Curiam celebravit.* Item
cap. 43:[26] *Conradus Romanorum Rex, Principes convocans in
oppido Orientalis Franciae Franconofurt generalem curiam celebrat.*
^bPosterioribus autem seculis dicta est Franciae Curia, interdum
Curia Parlamenti trium statuum, ^cinterdum curia Regis Fran-
15 ciae, ^binterdum praecise Parlamentum statuum, ut posterius
docebimus. Hinc illud Speculatoris Iuriscon. sub titulo De feriis,
ad finem:[27] *Potest excusari consuetudo* CURIAE REGIS FRAN-
CIAE, *quae tempore* PARLAMENTORUM *omni die ius reddit,
ut venientes de longinquis partibus citius expediantur.* Item illud
20 Ioannis Fabri in Auth. hoc nisi, C. de solut.:[28] *Curia Franciae
consuevit statuere, quod quando rex monetam debilitat, recipitur pro
forti, quando fortificat, habetur respectus ad tempus contractus.*
^cThomas Walsingham Historiae Angl. sub anno 1275:[29] *Sub
iisdem diebus Gasco de Bierna a Rege Anglorum obsessus, super eo
25 negotio quod inter Regem Eduardum et ipsum vertebatur, appellationem
interponit ad curiam Regis Francorum, cui deferens Rex Eduardus,
nolens Regem Francorum (quem nuper dominum suum pro terris in
Francia recognoverat) contra se partem facere, ministris suis commisit,
ut in curia Regis Franciae caussam prosequerentur contra Gasconem.*

---

[23] Ed. 1567, 764.   [24] *Ibid.,* 771.   [25] *Gest. Fred.,* I, 40; *MGH SS,* xx, 373, 16.
[26] *Ibid.,* I, 43; *loc. cit.,* 374, 10.   [27] Durandus, *Spec. iuris,* lib. II, Partic. I 'De
Feriis': *quod sunt genera feriarum,* 9 (ed. 1602, II, 506).   [28] (Jean de Faure de
Roussines) *Annot. codicis,* in Cod. Lib. VIII, Tit. 43, ad authen. 'Hoc nisi'; ed. 1594,
408.   [29] Ed. 1863, I, 13.

sign and taken the oath of loyalty to the king, which in earlier times all the archbishops of Reims and other bishops of the kingdom of the Franks had also taken to the kings his predecessors. All were persuaded by this act, and the nobility of the *curia* did likewise.'

*a*Aimon provides another example.[23] 'Charles, the son of the Danish king', he writes, 'found it appropriate to seek the judgment of the *curia* against certain nobles of Flanders.' Again in the following chapter he states:[24] 'At the death of Henry, King of the Romans, a supreme and general *curia* was held at Mainz about the matter.' And Otto of Freising writes in his book on Frederick I:[25] 'Subsequently the prince entered Bavaria, and there he held a general *curia* in the month of February.' Later the same author says:[26] 'Conrad, King of the Romans, calls the princes together and celebrates a general *curia* for East Francia in the town of Frankfort.' *b*In later times the *curia* of France was sometimes called the *curia* of the parliament of the three estates, *c*sometimes the *curia* of the king of France, *b*and sometimes, with precision, the parliament of the estates, as we shall show at a later point. Hence the comment of the jurisconsult known as Speculator:[27] 'One can understand the custom of the *curia* of the king of France, where the right of determining the length of the session on each day is surrendered to the parliaments themselves, in order to shorten proceedings for those coming from distant parts.' The same usage occurs in the work of Jean de Faure on commerce:[28] 'The *curia* of France habitually laid it down that, when the king debased the coinage, it should be received in place of the stronger coin, and, when he increased its value, the period of existing contracts should be taken into account.' *c*Another example occurs in Thomas of Walsingham's *History of England* for the year 1275:[29] 'At this time Gasco de Bierna was besieged by the English king and, over and above the arrangement made between King Edward and himself, he appealed to the *curia* of the French king. King Edward accepted the jurisdiction of the latter, for he had recently recognized him as his overlord for his lands in France, and he did not wish to cause the French king to side against him. So King Edward instructed his ministers to prosecute his cause against Gasco in the *curia* of the French king.'

^aCAPUT XI [^cXIV]

De sacrosancta publici concilii auctoritate,
et quibus de rebus in eo ageretur

Deinceps locus postulat, ut quibus de rebus in ^cillo ^asolenni concilio ageretur, consideremus, Maiorumque nostrorum in constituenda Republica sapientiam admiremur. Summatim autem has fere observavimus. Primum de creando vel abdicando* Rege;
5 tum de pace et bello; de legibus publicis; de summis honoribus praefecturis, et procurationibus Reipublicae; de assignanda patrimonii parte liberis defuncti Regis, vel dote filiabus constituenda, quod Germanico verbo Abannagium, quasi exclusоriam partem, appellarunt;* ^cde re numaria, et monetae rationi
10 bus; ^adenique de iis rebus omnibus, quae vulgus etiam nunc Negotia Statuum populari verbo appellat, quoniam ^csummo multarum aetatum consensu ^ade nulla (ut dixi) Reipublicae parte, nisi in statuum sive Ordinum concilio agi ius esset.

Ac de creandis quidem aut abdicandis Regibus superius, tum
15 ex Caroli Magni testamento, tum etiam ex aliis auctoribus satis multa testimonia protulimus. Neque tamen unum* illud praetermittemus, ex ^bReginonis lib. 2, sub anno DCCCVI, ubi de Carolo Magno scribens:[1] *Cum primoribus*, inquit, *et optimatibus Francorum de pace constituenda et conservanda inter filios suos, et de*
20 *partitione regni placitum habuit.* Quo eodem modo ^aAimoin. lib. 5, cap. 17, ubi de rege Carolo Calvo commemorat:[2] *Generali* (inquit) *conventu in Carisiaco habito filium suum Carolum armis virilibus, id est, ense, cinxit, corona Regali caput insignivit, et Neustriam ei attribuit; Pipino, Aquitaniam.* ^bNam (ut superius
25 dictum est) praerogativam quidem regis filii magnam in illis

---

4 *c*¹ omits 'vel abdicando'.   **9** *c* omits 'quod Germanico...appellarunt'.
16 *bc* omit 'unum'.

[1] *MGH SS*, I, 563, 64ff.   [2] Ed. 1567, 621.

*a*CHAPTER XI [*c*XIV]

The sacred authority of the public council, and what was done there

This is now the appropriate place for us to consider the matters transacted in *c*that *a*solemn council and to admire the wisdom of our ancestors in constituting the commonwealth. In brief, they were generally these: first, the appointing and deposing* of kings; next, matters concerning war and peace; the public laws; the highest honours, offices and regencies belonging to the commonwealth; assigning part of the patrimony of a deceased king to his children, or constituting the dowry of his daughters, which they described by the German word appanage, or a 'part separated from the rest'; *c*monetary matters; *a*and, lastly, all those issues which in popular speech are now commonly called affairs of state, since *c*by the highest authority of many generations *a*there was, as I have said, no right for any part of the commonwealth to be dealt with except in the council of estates or orders.

On the appointing and deposing of kings we have offered enough evidence above, including Charlemagne's will and the views of other authors. However, we should not omit this one† further reference *b*from the second book of Regino under the year 806, where he writes of Charlemagne:[1] 'He called a meeting with the leading men and nobility of the Franks to establish and maintain peace between his sons and to partition the kingdom.' In the same sense *a*Aimon remarks of Charles the Bald:[2] 'At a general assembly held in Crécy he girded his son Charles with the insignia of manhood, that is, with the sword, placed the royal crown on his head, and assigned him Neustria, while he gave Pepin Aquitaine.' *b*For, as already mentioned, the sons of a king enjoyed a great privilege

---

* *c*¹ *omits* and deposing. † *bc omit* one.

comitiis habebant, sed tamen etiam si a parentibus in suo testamento designati heredes erant, a populo tamen confirmandi
erant,* ^cex quo intelligitur, nullam Regibus de suo Regno testamenti factionem fuisse, neque ipso iure illam patris institutionem
5 valuisse, sed a populo in communi Ordinum conventu confirmandam fuisse, quemadmodum in iure Romano dicere
solemus, quia curator testamento patris inutiliter datur,
iccirco datum a Praetore confirmandam esse. Hunc autem
^bquem* morem non modo Occidentales nostri, sed etiam
10 Orientales Franci retinuerunt; eiusque* rei cum alia pleraque
apud alios testimonia extant, tum illud singulare apud Viti-
chindum Sax. lib. 2, ubi cum paulo ante scripsisset Henricum
Imp. filium suum Oddonem regni sui successorem designasse,
ita infert:[3] *Defuncto Henrico, omnis populus Francorum atque*
15 *Saxonum iam olim designatum regem a patre, filium eius Oddonem,*
elegit sibi in principem, universalisque electionis notantes locum,
iusserunt ad Aquisgrani palatium. Et mox, ubi Magontini Episcopi,
qui cum infulis illius in pompa et processione occursum*
expectabat, orationem ad populum exponit:[4] *En*, inquit, *adduco*
20 *vobis a domino Henrico olim designatum, nunc vero a cunctis Principi-*
bus regem factum Oddonem. Si vobis ista electio placeat, dextris in
coelum levatis significate. Ad haec omnis populus dextras in excelsum
levans, cum clamore valido imprecati sunt prospera novo Regi.

Quibus et similibus aliis permultis* ex locis facile intellectu est,
25 idem Francorum Orientalium et Occidentalium institutum in
suis regibus deligendis fuisse; quippe, qui et unis ex sedibus
patriaque olim profecti, et perquandiu sub iisdem regibus ac
principibus iisdem legibus ac moribus uterentur.

^aIam de regni procuratione, insigne illud testimonium apud

---

3 *c* 'a populo tamen eos confirmari oportebat'.   **9** *c* omits 'quem'.   **10** *c*
'cuius'.   **18** *c* puts 'occursum' after 'infulis'.   **24** *c* omits 'permultis'.
[3] Widukind, ii, 1; *MGH SS*, iii, 437, 16f.   [4] *Ibid.*, 30ff.

in those assemblies, and yet, even if they had been designated heirs by their father's will, they had to be confirmed by the people. cIt follows that the kings did not make a will disposing of their kingdom, nor could such an arrangement have any validity through the individual right of a father, without the necessary confirmation by the people in a general assembly of the estates, just as we customarily say in Roman law that the nomination of a trustee in a father's will is invalid without confirmation by the praetor. Moreover this* bwas a custom retained by our western Franks, as well as the eastern Franks. While there is a great deal of very full evidence of this practice among a variety of authors, a remarkable instance is provided by Widukind in his book on the deeds of the Saxons, where, having written that the Emperor Henry had designated his son Otto as the successor to his kingdom, he goes on to remark:[3] 'At the death of Henry his son, Otto, who had already been designated king by the emperor, was elected as their ruler by all the people of the Franks and the Saxons, and those responsible for nominating the place for the general election ordered that it should be at the palace at Aix-la-Chapelle.' And a little further on Widukind gives the speech with which the bishop of Mainz, robed in splendour and with all pomp and ceremony, addressed the people while awaiting the appearance of Otto:[4] '"Behold, I present to you him who was formerly nominated by the Lord Henry and who has now truly been made king by the united princes of the realm. If you are satisfied with this election, raise your right hand to indicate your approval." At these words all the people raised high their right hands and with a shout of approbation invoked prosperity for the new king.'

From these and very many† other similar references it is clearly to be understood that the same practice in choosing their kings was common to the western and eastern Franks, and in fact those who formerly originated from one centre and fatherland, and who for long continued to be ruled by the same kings and princes, employed identical laws and customs.

aNow as to the regency of the kingdom, there is that important

* b And this. † c omits very many.

eundem auctorem extat, lib. 5, cap. 35,[5] ubi de eodem Carolo
Calvo loquitur: *Carolus, inquit, Romam proficiscens, Compendii
Placitum generale Kalend. Iunii habuit, ubi per Capitula, qualiter
Regnum Franciae filius suus Ludovicus cum fidelibus eius et regni*
5 *primoribus regeret, usque dum ipse Roma rediret, ordinat.* Idem eodem
lib., cap. 42:[6] *Cuius aetatem* (de Carolo Simplice loquitur)
*Franciae primores incongruam, ut erat, exercendae dominationi arbi-
trati, consilium* de summis ineunt rebus Franci, Burgundiones,
Aquitaniensesque proceres congregati in unum, Odonem tutorem
10 *Caroli, regnique elegere gubernatorem.*

Iam vero de legibus et constitutionibus, vel unus ille Gaguini
locus in vita Ludovici cognomento Sancti, testimonio esse
potest:[7] *Cum Parisium*, inquit, *Ludovicus venisset, conventu
generali habito, Rempublicam reformavit, statutis optimis legibus de*
15 *iure a iudicibus dicendo, et de officiis non emendis, etc.*

Porro de summis honoribus, et praefecturis ad probatos viros
deferendis, testimonium apud Aimoinum extat, lib. 5, cap. 36,[8]
ubi de Carolo Calvo loquitur, qui cum ante inaugurationem
Regni praefecturas arbitratu suo tribuisset,* Proceres solenne
20 Concilium indicere coeperunt, legatosque ad Regem mittere,
neque prius Regem coronari passi sunt, quam illorum Concilio
atque auctoritate in illis mandandis magistratibus usus esset:
Regni primores, inquit, *indignati, quia quibusdam honores dederat
sine illorum consensu, et ob id adversum ipsum conspirarunt, et con-*
25 *ventum suum in villam Witmarium conduxerunt, indeque legatos suos
ad Ludovicum direxerunt; sed et Ludovicus legatos suos ad illos
direxit, etc.* Item ^bRegino lib. 2:[9] *Carolus placitum habuit in Com-
pendio, ibique cum optimatum consilio Rodiberto comiti ducatum inter
Ligerim et Sequanam commendavit.* Item ^aAppendix Grego. Turon.
30 lib. 11, cap. 54:[10] *Eo anno*, inquit, *Clotharius cum proceribus et*

---

8 *c* '*concilium*'.   **19** *c* '*distribuisset*'.

[5] Aimon; ed. 1567, 696.   [6] Cap. 41; ed. 1567, 727 (quoted more fully below,
ch. xv [xviii], n. 4 [p. 392]).   [7] Bk. 7; ed. 1528, fol. cxiii^v.   [8] Ed. 1567, 700.
[9] A.D. 861; *MGH SS*, I, 570–1.   [10] Ed. 1568, App., 39–40.

testimony in the chronicle of Aimon,[5] where the author writes as follows concerning Charles the Bald: 'When Charles was about to depart for Rome, he held a general assembly at Compiègne on the first of June, where in several decrees he laid down the manner in which his son Louis, together with his vassals and the leading men of the kingdom, should rule France until he returned from Rome.' A few chapters later he writes of Charles the Simple:[6] 'Since the leading men of France considered that he was too young to govern (as indeed he was), the nobility of France, Burgundy and Aquitaine decided to take counsel about great affairs, and met together in one body to elect Odo, the guardian of Charles, as governor of the kingdom.'

We can offer this single passage from Gaguin's life of Saint Louis as evidence of the nature of the laws and constitution:[7] 'When Louis had arrived in Paris, he held a general assembly and reformed the commonwealth, enacting excellent laws concerning legal pronouncements by judges and the prohibition of the sale of offices', etc.

And as to the conferring of the highest honours and offices upon worthy men, there is proof of the practice in Aimon,[8] where he speaks of Charles the Bald. As Charles had allocated* the governorships of the kingdom by his own decision before his inauguration, the nobility began to proclaim a solemn council and sent envoys to the king, and would not allow him to be crowned until he had made use of their council and authority to authorize those officers. 'The chief men of the kingdom', he states, 'were indignant that he should have bestowed honours on certain men without their consent, and for this reason they conspired against him and conducted their own assembly in the town of Witmar, whence they sent envoys to Louis. But Louis sent his own envoys to them', etc. [b]Another example occurs in Regino:[9] 'Charles held an assembly at Compiègne, and there he took the advice of the nobility to appoint Rodibert to the dukedom of the district between the Loire and the Seine.' [a]There is also an instance in the appendix to Gregory of Tours:[10] 'In that year', he writes, 'Lothar joined with the nobility

* c distributed.

337

*leudibus Burgundiae Trecassinis coniungitur, cum eos solicitasset, si
vellent, mortuo iam Warnhario alium in eius honoris gradum sublimare;
sed omnes unanimiter denegantes, se nequaquam velle Maiorem domus
eligere, Regis gratiam obnixe petentes, cum Rege transegere.* ^bEt

5   cap. 101:¹¹ Mortuo Theodorico rege, Franci *Clodoveum filium
eius parvulum elegerunt in regnum,** *quo non multos post annos
mortuo, Childebertus frater eius in regnum resedit; Grimoaldus autem
cum Childeberto rege Maior domus palatii super Francos electus est.*

^aAd eundem numerum referendae sunt Principum conten-
10   tiones, quae Reipublicae perniciosae futurae videbantur, de
quibus in eodem illo Concilio disceptabatur. Nam Aimoinus
lib. 4, cap. 1,¹² ubi de Clotario Chilperici filio commemorat, a
quo Brunechildis Austrasiae regnum postulabat, ita loquitur:
*Clotarius respondit, conventum nobilium debere eam aggregare
15   Francorum, et communi tractatu de communibus consulere rebus, se
vero iudicio illorum in omnibus pariturum, nec praeceptis promisit
obstaturum.* Quod idem Appendix Gregor. lib. 11, commemo-
rans:¹³ *Clotarius,* inquit, *respondebat, iudicio Francorum electorum
quicquid procedente domino a Francis inter eosdem iudicabitur,
20   pollicitum esse implere.*

^bEodemque modo apud eundem Gregorium lib. 8, cap. 21,
Boso Gunthrannus sepulchri violati in publico Francorum Concilio accusatus damnatusque dicitur:¹⁴ *Cum ad placitum,* inquit,
*Childebertus cum proceribus suis convenisset, et Gunthranus de his
25   interpellatus clam aufugisset, ablatae sunt ei omnes res, quas in
Arverno de fisci munere promeruerat.* ^aItem Aimoinus lib. 5, cap. 12,
ubi de Rege Ludovico Pio loquitur, quem filii ^codiis et ^acon-
tentionibus exagitabant:¹⁵ *Cum autem instaret Autumnalis
temperies, ii qui Imperatori contraria sentiebant, alicubi in Francia*

---

6   c '*regem*'.
¹¹ *Ibid.*, 79.   ¹² *PL*, cxxxix, 765.   ¹³ xi, 39; ed. 1568, App., 27.   ¹⁴ *MGH
SS Mer.*, I:1², 388, 9.   ¹⁵ Ed. 1567, 589.

and freemen of Burgundy at Troyes, where he solicited them to say whether they wished him, now that Warnarchar was dead, to raise another man to the status he had held. But all denied unanimously that it was in any way their wish to elect a mayor of the palace, and they besought the king's grace with such resolution that they came to an agreement with him.' *b*In a later chapter Gregory states:[11] 'At the death of King Theuderic the Franks elected Clovis, his young son, as king, and, after the latter's death a few years later, Theuderic's brother, Childebert, was reestablished in the kingdom. However Grimoald was elected as mayor of the palace over the Franks, with Childebert as king.'

*a*In the same context should be seen those disputes between princes which appeared to have pernicious effects upon the commonwealth, for these were determined in that same council. Aimon writes of Lothar, the son of Chilperic, from whom Brunhild demanded the kingdom of Austrasia:[12] 'Lothar replied that she ought to convoke an assembly of the nobility of the Franks, and through general discussion take counsel on matters of common concern. He undertook to obey their decision in all respects, and promised not to impede their commands.' This is also mentioned in the appendix to Gregory of Tours:[13] 'Lothar replied that he would execute any undertaking given in the form of a ruling by the deputies of the Franks, concerning anything that might be adjudged between them by the Franks in favour of a particular ruler.'

*b*The same principle is exemplified by Gregory when he describes how Boso Guntram was tried and condemned in the public council of the Franks for violating a tomb:[14] 'When Childebert and his high officers had joined the assembly, and Guntram, who had been deeply troubled by these accusations, had secretly fled, all those perquisites which he had acquired in Auvergne through his fiscal office were taken away from him.' *a*Aimon provides another instance when he writes of King Louis the Pious, who was harassed by the *c*animosities and *a*quarrels of his sons:[15] 'As autumn began to set in those who felt differently from the emperor wished a general assembly to be convened

conventum fieri generalem volebant. Item cap. 13 :[16] *In Theodonis villam convenire generaliter suum populum praecepit.* Et paulo post :[17] *Sed post paucum tempus idem ad festum Sancti Martini populum convocavit, filiumque Pipinum fugientem ad se quoquomodo* 5 *revocare voluit, sed ille id refugiebat.* Eademque ipsa de re Gaguinus commemorans :[18] *At coniurati,* inquit, *cum intelligerent absque procerum conventu Regem se deiicere non posse, magnis viribus eni-tuntur concilium in Francia habere. Repugnabat tamen Ludovicus quod sciret Francos ab inimicis adversum se persuasos esse, Maguntiae* 10 *propterea conventum indixit, mandatque neminem in concilio cum armis admitti.* At ne publico auctoramento coniurati adversus patrem filii destituerentur, coacto apud Compendium ex toto regni Episcoporum Procerumque concilio, Lotharius eductum de custodia patrem Compendium perduxit. Rursus Aimoinus 15 lib. 5, cap. 38, ubi de rege Ludovico Balbo scribit, qui concilium Marsuae agebat, et de pace cum suo consobrino referebat :*[19] In ipso quidem placito,* inquit, *haec quae sequuntur inter eos, consensu fidelium suorum servanda convenerunt.*

Nunc cetera videamus. Nam illud praeterea reperio moris 20 fuisse, ut siquis Princeps atque illustriore loco natus criminis alicuius insimularetur, in iudicium ad illud concilium vocaretur, ibique caussam dicere cogeretur. Itaque Regis Clotarii tempore cum Brunechildis multorum capitalium criminum accusata et damnata est, Rex concilio Francogalliae indicto, ita cum ordini- 25 bus loquitur, apud Aimoinum lib. 4, cap. 1 :[20] *Vos dulcissimi com-militones, et praeeminentes Franciae primores, decernite cui subiaceat supplicio tanti obnoxia sceleris.* Et Ado Aetat. 6, sub anno 583 :[21] *In praesentia,* inquit, *Regis iudicantibus Francis, indomitis equis religata discinditur.*

---

16 bc 'conferebat'.

[16] *Ibid.,* 592.　　[17] *Ibid.,* 594.　　[18] Bk. 4; ed. 1528, fol. lviii[v].　　[19] Ed. 1567,
708.　　[20] *PL,* cxxxix, 767.　　[21] *PL,* cxxiii, 112.

somewhere in France.' Again, in his next chapter he states:[16] 'He ordered his people to meet in general assembly in the town of Thionville.' A little further on he says:[17] 'After a little time he called together his people on Saint Martin's day, and wished to recall to his side his exiled son, Pepin, but the latter would not come.' Gaguin remarks on that very same issue:[18] 'But when the conspirators discovered that they could not depose the king without an assembly of the nobles, they strove with great force to have the council held in France. However Louis frustrated this endeavour because he knew that the Franks had been suborned against him by his enemies, and on this account he fixed Mainz as the place for the assembly. Moreover he ordered that no one should be admitted to the council bearing arms. But his sons, who had conspired against their father, feared that they might lack public authority, and so they enforced the holding of a council at Compiègne consisting of the bishops and nobility drawn from the entire kingdom. Lothar released his father from custody and brought him to Compiègne.' Or, again, there is a reference in Aimon where he describes how Louis the Stammerer held a council at Marsua and referred to it* the question of making peace with his cousin:[19] 'In that very assembly', he says, 'the following matters were agreed upon with the consent of all their vassals, which was intended to preserve the treaty.'

We may now consider other functions of the council. For in this respect I find it to have been the custom that, if any prince or man born to an illustrious place should be accused of any crime, he was called before that council sitting in judgment and was there obliged to plead his case. Thus in the time of King Lothar when Brunhild was accused and condemned for many capital crimes, she was indicted by the council of Francogallia, and, according to Aimon, the king spoke these words before the estates:[20] 'May you pronounce judgment, most gentle comrades and foremost noblemen of France, to whom this guilty woman submits herself in supplication for her wicked crime.' Under the year 583 Ado writes:[21] 'The Franks passed sentence upon her in the presence of the king, and condemned her to be torn apart by wild horses.'

bc * referred to it *becomes* consulted with it about.

De Regalis vero patrimonii partitionibus et abannagiis,*
testimonium extat apud Aimoinum* lib. 5, cap. 94, ubi de Carolo
Magno commemorans, ita loquitur:[22] *Illis absolutis conventum*
habuit Imperator cum primoribus et optimatibus Francorum de pace
5 *constituenda, et conservanda inter filios suos, et divisione Regni*
facienda in partes tres, ut unusquisque illorum quam* partem tueri et
regere debuisset, si superstes illi eveniret. Item eo loco ubi de
partitione inter Ludovici liberos facta loquitur, lib. 5, cap. 40:[23]
Profecti Ambianos, et sicut fideles illorum invenerunt, regnum
10 *paternum inter se diviserant.** Item cap. 41,[24] ubi de Carolomanno
scribit, qui Wormaciae concilium agebat: *Ad quod Placitum Hugo*
profectus pro petitione partis Regni, quam frater suus Ludovicus in
locarium acceperat.

Quinetiam ex aliis locis licet animadvertere, si quando Rex
15 maiores sumptus facere instituisset, velut in templis aedificandis
et monasteriis fundandis, Rex ordinum concilium inquirebat.*
Nam Aimoinus lib. 4, cap. 41, ubi de Clodoveo secundo loquitur,
qui in tribunali pro solenni concilio sedebat:[25] *Hoc habuit*, inquit,
sermonis exordium. Quanquam Francigenae cives, terreni nos cura
20 *principatus admonet, publicis vos consultores rebus advocare.*

Atque haec quidem hactenus. Ex quibus perspicuum esse
arbitramur, quod initio diximus, *b*Maiores nostros, qui vere
Franci ac libertatis custodes fuerunt, *c*non Tyrannum sibi aut
carnificem imposuisse, qui suos cives in pecudum loco ac
25 numero haberet, sed ab omni tyrannica et *b*a* Turcica dominandi
tyrannide* abhorruisse, divinumque illud praeceptum arcte
retinuisse: SALUS POPULI SUPREMA LEX ESTO,[26] quippe, qui
*a*omnem plane Regni administrandi potestatem penes publicum
Concilium fuisse,* quod,* ut ante diximus, Placitum appella-

---

1 *c* 'appannagiis'.   2 *aa*¹ read 'eundem' for 'Aimoinum', an error listed
in the corrigenda of *b* and rectified in *c*.   6 *c* '*suam*'.   10 *c* '*diviserunt*'.
16 'Rex...inquirebat': *b* 'Rex ordinum consilium exquirebat'; *c* 'his de rebus
ordinum consilium exquirebat'.   25 *c* omits 'a'.   26 *c* 'libidine'.   29 'penes...
fuisse': *bc* 'penes maximum comitiatum, et ordinum Concilium collocarint
[*c* collocarunt]'.   29 *c*¹ omits the nine lines of this paragraph, to this point, and
begins here 'Porro Concilium hoc, ut ante diximus...'.

[22] Ed. 1567, 469.   [23] *Ibid.*, 718.   [24] *Ibid.*, 724.   [25] *PL*, CXXXIX, 795.
[26] See above, ch. x [XII], n. 19 (p. 296).

As to the partitions of the regal patrimony and the provision of appanages, there is a passage in Aimon,* where he speaks of Charlemagne in these terms:[22] 'At the conclusion of these matters the emperor held an assembly with the magnates and nobility of the Franks in order to establish peace, to preserve it among his sons, and to divide the kingdom into three parts, so that each of them should safeguard and rule his portion in the event of their surviving him.' In an earlier chapter Aimon writes as follows on the partition of the kingdom between the children of Louis:[23] 'They proceeded to Amiens and, as they found their faithful subjects there, they divided their father's kingdom between them.' Aimon in his next chapter writes of Carloman, who had convened the council at Worms:[24] 'Hugo set out for this council to present his demand for that part of the kingdom which his brother Louis had obtained on lease'.

Moreover, it may be observed from other passages that, when a king intended to incur major expenditure, such as the construction of churches or the founding of monasteries, he asked for the advice of the estates.† Aimon gives an instance when he writes of Clovis II, who was seated on his throne before the solemn council.[25] 'This', says Aimon, 'was the way he began his speech: "Francigenian citizens, although the responsibility of our authority on earth requires us to summon you in consultation in matters of public concern..."'

So much, then, for these examples. We believe that they clearly show, as we said at the beginning, *b*that our ancestors who, as Franks, were truly the guardians of liberty, *c*did not place themselves under any tyrant or executioner who might treat his subjects as if they were cattle, but rather did they *b*abhor *c*all tyranny and especially *b*the domination of any Turkish tyrant,‡ and they held strictly to that divine precept:[26] 'LET THE WELFARE OF THE PEOPLE BE THE SUPREME LAW.' Indeed our examples prove *a*that the whole power of administering the kingdom clearly lay with the public council,§ which,¶ as we said earlier, was called the

---

* *a* in the same writer.　　† *c adds* in such matters.　　‡ *c* lecher.　　§ *bc* lay with the public council *becomes* was established in the supreme assembly and the council of the estates.　　¶ *c*¹ *omits the preceding part of this paragraph and begins* The public council, as we said earlier...

bant, ^cvelut apud scriptorem Chronici Besnensis:[27] *Anno DCCLXIIII Pipinus Rex placitum magnum habuit cum Francis apud villam Carisiacum.* Huius autem vocabuli origo hinc fluxit, ^apropterea* quod Latina consuetudine Placitum id proprie
5 dicitur, quod re in multorum consilio quaesita et deliberata, tandem inter ipsos convenit, unde Placita philosophorum apud Ciceronem, et alios antiquos,* dicta sunt. ^bGellius lib. 18, cap. 3:[28] *Populus*, inquit, *Lacedaemonius de summa Republica quidnam esset utile et honestum deliberabat.* Et mox:[29] *Consilium quod*
10 *dabat acceptum ab universis et complacitum est.* Sic Romae quae Senatus de maioris Senatorum partis sententia decreverat, his perscribebantur verbis: PLACERE SENATUI, ut cum ex aliis veteribus S. C. cuivis notum est, tum etiam ex iis quae in libris nostris extant, velut in l. item veniunt, 20, § praeter haec, D. de
15 hered. petit.,[30] et l. 2, D. ad Velleian.[31] neque quicquam in iisdem libris frequentius est, quam Placitum appellari, quod inter aliquos convenit; velut in l. ult. C. de pignorib.[32] Pro tenore communis militantium placiti unde Placitum, pro conventione in l. 33, C. de transact.;[33] l. i, C. de pact.;[34] l. 4, D. de servitut.[35]
20 et aliis sexcentis locis.

 ^aQuod* cum ita se habeant, non absurda, opinor, coniectura nostra videbitur, quam aliis iam quibusdam in libris nostris exposuimus,[36] vulgatam formulam, qua etiam nunc Regii scribae in legum et constitutionum clausulis utuntur, ex illo PLACITI
25 vocabulo, natam esse: QUIA TALE EST NOSTRUM PLACITUM. Nam cum illae Latinis literis scriberentur (quod ex Aimoino et Capitulari Caroli Magni,[37] et aliis eiusmodi, monimentis satis

---

4 *c* omits 'propterea'. **7** *bc* 'auctores'. **21** *bc* 'Quae'.

[27] *PL*, CLXII, 788. [28] Loeb, 302. [29] *Ibid.*, Loeb, 304. [30] *Dig.* 5, 3, 20, 6; Mommsen, I, 113. [31] *Dig.* 16, 1, 2; Mommsen, I, 238. [32] *Cod.* 8, 13, 27; Krueger, II, 341. [33] *Cod.* 2, 4, 33; Krueger, II, 96. [34] *Cod.* 2, 3, 1; Krueger, II, 92. [35] *Dig.* 8, 2, 4 [30?]; Mommsen, I, 144 [146]. [36] Non invenio. [37] Aimon, see below, n. 41; Capitularies, see next note.

placitum. ᶜSuch is the term used by the anonymous chronicler of Dijon in this passage:²⁷ 'In the year 764 King Pepin held a great *placitum* among the Franks in the town of Carignan.' But the origin of this word was lost, ᵃand the reason for this was that* by strict Latin usage the term meant something which had been questioned and debated by many men in consultation, and a thing upon which they had finally reached agreement among themselves, whence the expression *placita* among philosophers, as employed by Cicero and other men of ancient times.† ᵇAn example is given by Gellius:²⁸ 'The Spartan people used to deliberate on anything that was useful and honourable and for the greatest good of the commonwealth.' He goes on:²⁹ 'The advice they gave was accepted and approved [*complacitum*] by all the citizens.' Thus at Rome those matters which the senate decreed as being the opinion of the majority of the senators were announced with these words: 'Placere senatui' ['the senate determines']. This is known for certain from many other writers of those times, as it is also from passages in our own records (see the *Digest*³⁰, ³¹). Few terms occur more often in those books than what is called a *placitum*, meaning a decision agreed upon by several persons, as, for instance, concerning the general assembly of knights, whence the use of the term *placitum* as a summons (see the *Code*³², ³³, ³⁴ and the *Digest*³⁵ and in six hundred other places besides).

ᵃThis being so I believe the conjecture I have already set forth in certain other books will not seem unreasonable,³⁶ that is that the common phrase, 'For such is our *placitum*', which royal clerks even today employ at the foot of laws and ordinances, was derived from the word *placitum*. All these ordinances used to be written in Latin (which we regard as clearly enough established from Aimon, the *Capitulary* of Charlemagne³⁷ and other records of this

---

* *c* and the reason for this was that *becomes* because. † *bc* men of ancient times *becomes* authors.

constare arbitramur*) postea scribae Regii, ubi populari sermone
uti coeperunt, ita vel inscientia,* vel malitia potius converterunt:
Car tel est nostre plaisir, Quoniam ita nobis placet.

    Nam de populi quoque potestate argumentum in Caroli
5 Capitulari hoc extat:³⁸ Ut populus interrogetur de capitulis, quae
in lege noviter addita sunt, et postquam omnes consenserint,
subscriptiones et manufirmationes suas in ipsis capitulis faciant.
Quibus ex verbis patet, populos Franciae, iis demum olim legibus
astringi solitos quas in comitiis suffragiis suis sanxerant. ^cQuod*
10 ei legis definitioni consentaneum est, quam iuris consultus
Marcianus ex Demosthene protulit in l. 2, D. de Legibus,³⁹
νόμος ἐστὶ πόλεως συνθήκη κοινή: lex est pactio et conventio
civium, Reipublicae bonoque publico consulentium. Eodemque
illud pertinet ^aEt* in fine Legis Alemann.:⁴⁰ *Hoc decretum*
15 *est apud Regem, et Principes eius, et apud cunctum populum*
Christianum, qui infra Regnum Merovingorum consistunt. Item apud
Aimoin. lib. 5, cap. 38:⁴¹ *In ipso Placito haec quae sequuntur, inter*
eos consensu fidelium suorum servanda convenerunt. Conventio quae
inter gloriosos Reges etc., ^bet ^a*ipsis et communibus fidelium ipsorum*
20 *faventibus et consentientibus facta est.* ^cSed nullum certius eius rei
documentum est, quam quod superius ex libro Legis Francicae II
protulimus, ubi Ludovicus Pius universos Regni sui Ordines sic
affatur:⁴² *Quanquam summa ministerii Regii in nostra persona*
consistere videatur, tamen et divina auctoritate, et humana ordinatione
25 *ita per partes divisum esse dignoscitur, ut unusquisque vestrum in suo*
loco et ordine partem ministerii nostri habere cognoscatur. Item cap.
12:⁴³ *Unusquisque vestrum partem ministerii nostri per partes habere*
dignoscitur. Item cap. 22:⁴⁴ *In nostro Capitulari de hac re communi*

---

1 'aliis...arbitramur': *bc* 'et omnibus archiis, monimentisque Gallicis satis
constat'.   2 *c* 'ignorantia'.   9 *c*¹ adds 'institutum'.   14 *c* omits 'Et'.
38 Non invenio.   39 *Dig.* 1, 3, 2; Mommsen, 1, 33.   40 *MGH LL Sect. 1*, 5:
1, 157.   41 Ed. 1567, 708.   42 Ansegius, II, 3; *MGH LL*, II:1, 415.   43 *Ibid.*,
II, 12; *ed. cit.*, 416.   44 *Ibid.*, II, 22; *ed. cit.*, 419.

kind),* but later, when the royal clerks began to use the vernacular, they unwittingly,† or, rather, maliciously, translated the expression as 'Car tel est nostre plaisir' ['For such is our pleasure'].

There is this further evidence of the power of the people in Charlemagne's *Capitulary*:[38] that, if any new clauses be added to the law, the people should be consulted about them and, when all consented to the additions, they should sign their names in confirmation on these clauses. It is manifest from these words that the people of France were formerly bound only by those laws which they had approved by their own votes in the assemblies. cThis practice is expressed in terms of legal definition by the jurist Marcianus in the *Digest*, using the words of Demosthenes:[39] 'The law is a pact and agreement of the citizens and a resolution of the commonwealth in the public interest.' This statement applies to our own constitution. aMoreover, the law of the Alamans concludes with the words:[40] 'This is decreed by the king, his princes, and the united Christian people who are settled in the area below the Merovingian kingdom.' There is another example in Aimon:[41] 'At this assembly they agreed among themselves, and with the consent of their supporters, that the following matters would be upheld. This agreement was made between these most celebrated kings with the approval and consent of their subjects in general.' cThere is no more positive proof of this matter than the reference from the second book of the Frankish law, which we have already cited.[42] It concerns the address of Louis the Pious to all the estates of his kingdom: 'Although the highest authority in the government of the kingdom seems to reside in our person, it may be discerned that by divine authority and human ordinance it is so divided into parts that each one of you in his own place and rank may be recognized as possessing a share in our government.' The same point is made in the twelfth chapter:[43] 'Each one of you is seen to possess one share among many in the government of the kingdom.' Or, again, in a later chapter:[44] 'We have issued a decree in our capitulary concerning this matter with the common consent of our loyal

* *bc* and other records of this kind *becomes* and all the archives and records of France.   † *c* through ignorance.

consultu fidelium nostrorum ordinavimus; et cap. 24:[45] *Volumus etiam, ut capitula quae nunc et alio tempore consultu fidelium nostrorum a nobis constituta sunt, a Cancellario nostro Archiepiscopi et Comites accipiant.*

5   ^aPostremo ne illud quidem praetermittendum est, tantam huius Concilii apud exteras gentes auctoritatem fuisse, ut etiam Principes exteri si quid controversiae haberent, id interdum illius Concilii iudicio permitterent. Appendix Gregor. Turon. lib. 11, cap. 37:[46]*Anno XII regni Theodorici cum Alsaciones, ubi*
10 *fuerat enutritus, praecepto patris sui Childeberti tenebat, ad Theodebertum barbarico ritu pervaditur, unde placitum inter hos duos Reges, ut Francorum iudicio finiretur, Saloisso castro instituunt.*

---

[45] *Ibid.*, II, 24; *loc. cit.*   [46] Ed. 1568, App., 23.

subjects.' And finally :[45] 'We also desire that the ordinances which now and at any other time are established by us with the advice of our faithful subjects may be received through the chancellor by the archbishops and magnates.'

ᵃLest any point be overlooked, it may be said, in conclusion, that such was the authority of this council among other peoples that even foreign princes sometimes applied for the judgment of the council on an issue in dispute between them. This is shown in the appendix to Gregory of Tours :[46] 'In the twelfth year of his reign, the district of Alsatia, where Theuderic had been brought up and which he held by command of his father, Childebert, was passed to Theudebert according to a barbarous custom. Accordingly it was agreed by the two kings to hold an assembly in the fortress by the River Sala, so that the matters might be resolved by the judgment of the Franks.'

349

^aCAPUT XII [^cXV]

De praefectis regiis, qui maiores
domus dicebantur

Priusquam de continuata Publici Concilii auctoritate plura exponamus, non praetermittenda commemoratio est de Regiis Praefectis, qui Merovingicis temporibus Maiores domus, hoc est, Magistri Palatii dicebantur, qui cum regiam potestatem
5 aliquandiu obsedissent, aliquando tandem facultatem nacti, eam pro sua occuparunt. Eorum video eandem prope apud Reges nostros dignitatem fuisse, qualis quondam apud Imperatores Romanos erat Praefectorum Praetorio, qui etiam Aulae praefecti dicebantur. Eodem autem in concilio et conventu, quo
10 Reges ipsi designabant, publicique consilii auctores ac principes esse solebant.* Itaque passim apud Historicos nostros illa occurrunt: In principatum Maiores domus elegerunt. Item: Herchinoldo Maiore domus defuncto, Franci Ebroinum in hac dignitate, ut Maior esset in Aula Regia, constituunt. Item:
15 Hilderichum super se regem levant, Maiorem domus, Wolfoldum. Quod ad superiorem proximam tractationem pertinet, ubi ^cdocuimus ^amaiores quosque magistratus non a Rege ^cpro suo arbitrio ^amandari, sed in solenni concilio fidelissimis et probatissimis viris deferri solitos demonstravimus.*
20 Verum in hoc magistratu idem plane usuvenit, quod Plutarchus in Lysandri vita tum accidisse scribit, cum Agesilaus a Lacedaemoniis ad exercitum Imperator missus est, Lysander

---

11 'Eodem...solebant': *b* changes last part of sentence to read '...designabantur publicique consilii auctores ac principes erant'; *c* change whole sentence to read 'Creari autem eodem in Concilio et conventu, quo reges ipsi solebant, publicique postea consilii auctores ac principes erant.'.   19 *c* 'fuisse'.

^aCHAPTER XII [^cXV]

The royal officials known as the mayors of the palace

There are many further points to be made about the continuing authority of the public council, but, before we do so, we should not fail to mention those royal officials who, in the period of the Merovingians, were termed mayors or masters of the household or palace. For some time they had laid claim to the royal power, and at last the opportunity occurred for them to take possession of it on their own behalf. Their official status close to the person of our kings seems to have been much the same as that once held beside the Roman emperors by the commander of the Praetorian guards, who was also called the Aulic prefect. They were nominated in that same council and assembly which elected the kings, and they were customarily the instigators and directors of public policy.* Thus passages such as these are to be found throughout the writings of our chroniclers: 'They elected him to the sovereign position of mayor of the palace'; 'At the death of Herchinold, the mayor of the palace, the Franks appointed Ebroinus to that office, so that he would be the controller of the royal court'; 'They raised up Childeric as their king over them and Wolfold as mayor of the palace'. These references are as immediately relevant to our preceding chapter, where ^cwe maintained that ^athe mayors and other high officers were not appointed by the king ^cby his own decision ^abut, as we have shown, such offices were usually conferred upon men of outstanding loyalty and probity in the solemn council.

However, the same thing clearly happened to this office as Plutarch describes in his life of Lysander, when the Spartans sent to the army Agesilaus as its commander and Lysander as second-in-

---

* *b* customarily the instigators and directors of public policy *becomes* the authors and directors of public policy. *c has the same sense as b except that* customarily *is inserted before* elected *and subsequently* is added before the authors.

autem legatus:[1] *Ut in tragoediis,* inquit, *plerunque usuvenit histrionibus, ut qui nuncii vel servi* personam sustinent, pluris fiant, primasque partes agant, illius vero qui sceptrum et diadema gestat, ne vox quidem exaudiatur; sic penes legatum Lysandrum maiestas*
5 *imperii versabatur, penes Regem vero, nudum atque inane nomen manebat.* Quod eodem modo in Francogallia nostra tum accidit, oblata videlicet occasione, et crescendi facultate ex Regum aliquot inertia, desidiaque, in quibus Dagobertus, Clodoveus, Clotarius, Childericus et Theodoricus numerari possunt. Nam
10 ^bPaulus Diaconus libro de gestis Langobardorum 6, cap. 5:[2] *Hoc tempore,* inquit, *apud Gallias Francorum regibus a solita fortitudine et scientia degenerantibus, ii qui Maiores domus regalis esse videbantur, administrare regis potentiam, et quicquid regibus agere mos est, coeperunt.* Et in eandem sententiam ^aauctor historiae
15 Francorum, quem Venericus Vercellensis aliquoties sine nomine tamen profert, ita scribit:[3] *Tempore Clotarii patris Dagoberti regnum Francorum regi coeptum est, et administrari ab his, qui Provisores aulae Regiae, vel Maiores domus esse videbantur.* Quod idem Godfridus Viterbien. parte Chronic. 16 testatur.[4] ^cItemque
20 scriptor Chronici Besnensis monasterii:[5] *In illo tempore,* inquit, *deficientibus iam a pristino vigore Regibus, cura totius regni administrabatur per duces et Principes domus.*

  ^aItaque dum illi Magistri Palatii omnia Reipublicae munera obirent, et si quod gerendum esset bellum, exercitibus prae-
25 essent, hi domi nudo atque inani Regum nomine contenti, propter desidiam in otio vivebant. Tandemque eo progressa res est, ut Childerico Rege XVIII regnum obtinente, Pipinus Magister palatii, qui Regis nomine magna diuturnaque bella gesserat, Saxones devicerat, suamque in potestatem redegerat,
30 oblatam Regii nominis occupandi facultatem non repudiarit, exercitu praesertim, eoque victore et glorioso instructus.

---

2 *bc* 'famuli'.

[1] XXIII, 4; Loeb, IV, 296.   [2] VI, 16; *MGH SS Lang.*, 170, 5.   [3] Walramus, *De unit. eccles.*, I, 16; *MGH Lib. Lit.*, II, 209, 20ff.   [4] Cf. Partic. XII, 28; *MGH SS*, XXII, 196, 31.   [5] *PL*, CLXII, 786.

command:[1] 'It often happens in tragedies and dramatic per-
formances', he writes, 'that they who play the rôles of messengers
and servants have more to do, and play better parts, than one who
bears a sceptre and a diadem but has scarcely a line to speak in the
play. Likewise, the real power to command was reposed in the
lieutenant-general, Lysander, while there remained to the king only
the bare and empty title.' The very same thing happened in our
Francogallia, and the opportunity was offered because of an
increasing bent towards idleness and sloth on the part of some of
our kings, among whom Dagobert, Clovis, Lothar, Childeric and
Theuderic can be mentioned in this respect. *b*For we read in the
book of Paul the Deacon on the deeds of the Lombards:[2] 'Within
France at this time the Frankish kings became degenerate and lost
their accustomed strength and craft, while those who appeared to
be the mayors of the royal palace began to administer the authority
of the king and to do whatever it was customary for kings to do.
*a*In the same sense the author of the history of the Franks, whom
Venericus Vercellensis often quotes anonymously, writes as
follows:[3] 'In the time of Lothar, the father of Dagobert, the
kingdom of the Franks began to be ruled and administered by those
who were known as controllers of the royal court or mayors of the
palace.' Godfrey of Viterbo provides further evidence in his
chronicle.[4] *c*So, too, does the compiler of the chronicle of the
monastery near Dijon.[5] 'At the time', he writes, 'the kings lacked
their pristine vigour, and responsibility for the government of the
entire kingdom passed to the dukes and princes of the household.'

*a*Thus, while those mayors of the palace took possession of all the
public offices of the commonwealth, and commanded the armies if
any war had to be waged, those who were satisfied with the bare
and empty title of king lived at leisure in their palace because of their
sloth. At last matters went so far that, when Childeric [Childeric
III], the eighteenth king, acquired the kingdom, Pepin, the mayor
of the palace, who had waged long and great wars in the king's name
and had crushed the Saxons, concentrated power in his own hands
and did not let slip his opportunity to seize the royal title, especially
since the conquering and glorious army was still in its array. These

Quarum rerum apud Auctores testimonia haec extant. Primum apud Ottonem Frisingensem Chronic. 5, cap. 12,[6] et imitatorem ipsius Godfridum Viterbiensem, part. 16,[7] ubi sic scribunt: *Reges Franciae ante tempora Pipini Magni, qui Maior domus erat, expertes*
5 *omnis administrationis et regiminis, solo nomine regnabant, sed Maiores domus universam Regni administrationem habebant.* In eandem sententiam Sigebertus sub anno 662 et Lothario Clodovei filio ita loquitur:[8] *Abhinc Francorum Regibus a solita fortitudine et scientia degenerantibus, regni potentia disponebatur per*
10 *Maiorem domus, Regibus solo nomine regnantibus, quibus moris erat principari quidem secundum genus, et nil agere vel disponere.*

    Quanquam in hac commemoratione cautio adhibenda est; nam cum et Pipinus et eius filii ob ereptum Regi Childerico regnum invidia (ut credi par est) laborarent, reperti sunt homines
15 ingeniosi, qui et Childerici, et superiorum regum desidiam verbis maiorem facerent, inertiamque gravius accusarent. In his Eguinarthus Caroli Magni Cancellarius, qui suo Imperatori strenuam in ea re operam navavit. Nam initio sui libri ita scribit:[9] *Gens Merovingorum, de qua Franci Reges sibi creare soliti*
20 *erant, usque in Hildericum Regem, qui iussu Stephani Romani Pontificis depositus ac detonsus, atque in monasterium trusus est, durasse putatur, quae licet in illo finita possit videri, tamen iamdudum nullius vigoris erat, nec quicquam in se clarum, praeter inane Regis vocabulum, praeferebat. Nam et opes et potentia Regni penes Palatii*
25 *Praefectos, qui Maiores domus dicebantur, et ad quos summa imperii pertinebat, tenebantur, neque aliud Regi relinquebatur, quam ut Regio tantum nomine contentus, crine profuso, barba submissa, solio resideret, ac speciem dominantis effingeret, legatos undecunque venientes audiret, eisque abeuntibus responsa, quae erat doctus, vel etiam iussus,*
30 *ex sua velut potestate redderet, cum praeter inutile Regis nomen et*

---

[6] Cf. *MGH SS*, xx, 223, 44 – and see next note.   [7] Partic. xxii, 34; *MGH SS*, xxii, 199, 38; Hotman's quotation is a kind of mélange of Godfrey and Otto (see previous note).   [8] *MGH SS*, vi, 325, 55ff.   [9] C. 1; *MGH SS*, ii, 443, 40 – 444, 11.

are the proofs of these matters from various authors. First from the chronicle of Otto of Freising[6] and its transcription in that of Godfrey of Viterbo,[7] where they write as follows: 'Before the time of Pepin the Great, who had been mayor of the palace, the kings of France had no part in the administration and government, ruling in name alone while the mayors of the palace conducted the entire government of the kingdom.' Under the year 662 Sigebert writes to the same effect of Lothar [Lothar III], the son of Clovis [Clovis II]:[8] 'From this time the kings of the Franks degenerated from their accustomed strength and craft, and the power of the kingdom was disposed of through the mayor of the palace. Meanwhile the kings reigned in name only, for it was the custom for them to rule in appearance as belonging to the royal stock, although they actually did nothing and controlled nothing.'

Yet caution should be used in reading these records. Since it seems likely that both Pepin and his sons incurred much envy for seizing the kingdom from Childeric, they sought out men of ingenuity to exaggerate the inactivity of Childeric and the sloth-fulness of the earlier kings. Among these historians we may rank Charlemagne's chancellor, Einhard, who devoted himself diligently to this end on his emperor's behalf. At the beginning of his book he writes as follows:[9] 'The Merovingian line, from which the Franks were wont to elect their kings, is supposed to have lasted down to King Childeric, who by order of Stephen, the Roman pontiff, was deposed, tonsured and thrust into a monastery. Yet, although it may seem to have terminated with Childeric, it had long been lacking in vigour, and bore in itself no claim to any glory except through the empty title of king. For both the wealth and power of the kingdom were held by the governors or mayors of the palace, who exercised supreme jurisdiction. Nothing else remained to the king save that he should rest content with the royal title, sit upon the throne with his long hair and beard to represent the person of the ruler, and there give audience to incoming ambassadors and provide those envoys who were departing with answers which he had been taught, or instructed to give as if he had himself authorized them. Apart from the useless title of king and an

*precarium vitae stipendium, quod ei praefectus aulae, prout videbatur,
exhibebat, nihil aliud proprii possideret, quam unam praeparvi reditus
villam, in qua et domum, ex qua famulos sibi necessaria ministrantes,
atque obsequium exhibentes, paucae numerositatis habebat.*

5   His Eguinarthi verbis, *b*quae in Appendice quoque Hunibaldi
apud Trithenhemium reperio,[10] *a*inductus Sigebertus sub anno
662, eadem prope verborum contumelia superiores Reges
insectatur:[11] *Quibus,* inquit, *moris erat principari quidem secundum
genus, et nihil agere vel disponere, quam irrationabiliter edere et bibere,*
10 *domique morari.* Quasi vero haec eadem Regum superiorum ratio,
atque inertia fuerit, *c*ac non potius virtus ac fortitudo animi
singularis, qualem scriptores omnes *a*in his Clodovei* *c*commemorant, *a*qui non modo innumerabiles Germanorum copias,
in Galliam irrumpentes, praelio prope Tolbiacum commisso,
15 profligavit, verum etiam Romanorum reliquias e Galliae finibus
propulsavit.

    Iam vero quid de Childeberto et Clothario dicemus, qui
Wisigothos et Ostrogothos e Provincia et Aquitania, ubi sedes
fixerant, exterminarunt? Quorum omnium in historiis nulla
20 Magistri Palatii, ne minima quidem mentio fit, nisi forte cursim
atque obiter, et tanquam unius e Regii Imperii administris, velut
apud Grego. lib. 5, cap. 18,[12] ubi de Gucilio loquitur; et lib. 6,
cap. 9 et cap. 45;[13] et lib. 7, cap. 29.[14] Itaque honos ille non
tantum in Regis, verum etiam in Reginae aula et comitatu
25 versabatur. Nam idem Grego. lib. 7, cap. 27,[15] Wadonem quendam nominat Maiorem domus in aula Reginae Rigunthae, aliisque locis compluribus idem Gregor. et Aimoinus[16] Magistros
aulae domusque Regiae commemorant.

    Tantae autem illorum Regiorum praefectorum potentiae
30 initium (ut modo diximus) coepit tempore Clotharii II circiter
annum *b*Christi *a*DLXXXVIII, id est, circiter CXXX annis post

---

12 'in his Clodovei': *c* 'in Clodoveo'.

[10] Ed. Schard, I, 343.   [11] *MGH SS*, VI, 325, 56.   [12] *MGH SS Mer.*, I:1²,
224, 18.   [13] *Ibid.*, 279, 17 & 319, 1.   [14] Non invenio.   [15] *MGH SS Mer.*,
I:1², 346, 8.   [16] Ed. 1567: the index gives many synonyms for *Maior domus
regis*, but *Magister aulae domusque regis* is not one of them.

uncertain allowance for his expenses, which the governor of the court gave him, he possessed no other property but one country seat of slight revenue, where he had a house and the few servants he needed to look after him and show him deference.'

Under the year 662 Sigebert employs Einhard's words, *b*which I find also in the appendix to Hunibaldus in the version of Johannes Trithemius,[10] *a*and rails against the earlier kings with the same kind of invective:[11] 'It was the custom for them to rule in appearance as belonging to the royal stock, although they actually did nothing and controlled nothing. They merely lived in their palace, eating and drinking, as if they were creatures who lacked the ability to reason.' This is as much as to say that such mindlessness and sloth is to be imputed to all the earlier kings, whereas *c*they often possessed a unique courage and fortitude of mind, such as that which all writers record *a*in the case of Clovis, who not only conquered the vast forces of the Germans invading Gaul at the battle near Tolbiac, but also expelled the remaining forces of the Romans from the boundaries of Gaul.

And what, indeed, shall we say of Childebert [Childebert I] and Lothar [Lothar I] who rooted out the Visigoths and Ostrogoths from Provence and Aquitaine, where they had established themselves? In the histories of all these kings there is not the slightest mention of a mayor of the palace, unless it be a cursory and oblique reference to one of the administrators of the royal sovereignty, as in the instance where Gregory of Tours mentions Gucilius,[12] or in two similar passages from the same author.[13, 14] Moreover, this dignity existed within the court and council of the queen as well as within that of the king. For in another reference Gregory names a certain Waddo as mayor of the palace in the court of Queen Rigunthis,[15] and in many other passages Gregory and Aimon[16] refer to the masters of the royal court and household.

As we have said, the origin of this authority among these royal governors began in the time of Lothar II, about the year A.D. 588, that is, about one hundred and thirty years after the founding of the

Regnum Francogalliae constitutum. Quod ex eo, quem Venericus aliquoties profert,[17] historico licet cognoscere. Sunt tamen
duo alii* historici, sed nequaquam tantae auctoritatis, Sigebertus[18] et Tritenhemius,[19] qui tantae potentiae initium ad Clotharii
5   III Regnum referunt, cuius Magister Palatii Ebroinus nominatur,
homo nequitia et crudelitate insignis. Utcunque sit, Historici
aliis quoque nominibus Magistros illos Regii palatii appellabant,
*b*item *a*Comites domus Regiae, Praefectos aulae, Comites
Palatii,* *c*Duces et Principes domus, *b*quinetiam aliquot post
10   seculis Seneschalli Franciae appellati sunt; Sigebertus sub anno
MCLXX:[20] *In purificatione beatae Mariae fuit filius Regis Anglorum
Parisiis, et servivit Regi Francorum ad mensam, ut Seneschallus
Franciae. Hanc Senescalciam, vel (ut antiquitus dicebatur) Maioratum
domus Regiae Robertus Rex Francorum dedit Gaufrido,* etc.

---

3 'duo alii': *c* 'alii duo'.   **9** *c* 'Utcunque sit, Historici aliis quoque nominibus
praefectos illos appellabant, nimirum Magistros Regii palatii, Comites domus
Regiae, Praefectos aulae, Comites Palatii'.

[17] Walramus, as above, p. 352, n. 3.   [18] *MGH SS*, VI, 325, 53f.   [19] *De orig.
Franc.*; ed. 1539, 91.   [20] *Roberti de Monte cronica*, A.D. 1169; *MGH SS*, VI, 518,
11ff.; Hotman had this as Sigebert from *Germ. rer. quat. chron.*, 1566, 151.

kingdom of Francogallia. This may also be ascertained from the historian so frequently quoted by Venericus.[17] However, there are two other historians lacking this kind of authority, Sigebert[18] and Trithemius,[19] who place the origin of this greater power in the reign of Lothar III, whose mayor of the palace was called Ebroinus, a man notorious for his wickedness and cruelty. However this may be, historians also call those mayors of the royal palace by other names, such as counts of the royal household,* governors of the court, and counts of the palace, *c*as well as the dukes and princes of the household, *b*and after the passage of time they were even called seneschals of France. Sigebert writes for the year 1170:[20] 'The son of the English king came to Paris on the fête of the purification of the blessed Virgin, and waited at table on the French king, as if he were the seneschal of France. Robert, king of the Franks, gave Gaufridus this office of seneschal, or, as it was called in ancient times, mayor of the royal palace' etc.

---

* c mayors of the royal palace by other names such as counts of the royal household *becomes* officials by other names, such as mayors of the royal palace, counts of the royal household.

^aCAPUT XIII [^cXVI]

Utrum Pipinus papae, an Francogallici concilii auctoritate rex factus fuerit

Quoniam superius dictum est, Pipinum ex Magistro Palatii Regem esse factum, exacto Childerico Rege stupido, in eoque Childerico Merovingiorum stirpem defecisse, non alienum est, hoc loco exquirere, cuiusnam auctoritate Regnum illi delatum
5 fuerit. Nam Gelasius Papa in can. alius, 15, quaest. 6:[1] *Alius,* inquit, *Romanus Pontifex, Zacharias scilicet, Regem Francorum non tam pro suis iniquitatibus, quam pro eo quod tantae potestati erat inutilis, a regno deposuit, et Pipinum Caroli Imperatoris patrem in eius locum substituit, omnesque Francigenas a iuramento fidelitatis abso-*
10 *lvit.* Neque fere quisquam est, qui non illud Papae de semetipso testimonium approbarit: Ado,[2] Lambertus,[3] Regino,[4] Sigebertus,[5] Aimoinus,[6] Landulphus.[7] Quinetiam Venericus Vercellensis, in eo quem superius protulimus libro, verba haec ex epistola Gregorii Papae VII ad Hermannum Metensem Epi-
15 scopum profert:[8] *Quidam Romanus Pontifex Regem Francorum non tam pro suis iniquitatibus, quam pro eo quod tantae potestati non erat utilis, a Regno deposuit, et Pipinum in eius loco substituit, omnesque Francigenas a iuramento fidelitatis, quam illi fecerant, absolvit.* Haec ille. Quod idem Otto Frising. commemorans lib. Chron. 5,
20 cap. 23,[9] itemque Godfrid. Chron. parte 17,[10] ita exclamant: *Ex hoc facto Romani Pontifices Regna mutandi auctoritatem trahunt.*

Sed videamus, ne huius historiae veritas non satis constet, nam primum omnium ex tanto Regum Francorum numero, quos vel creatos vel abdicatos docuimus,* neminem esse constat, Papae

---

24 c¹ omits 'quos vel creatos vel abdicatos docuimus,'.

[1] *Corp. jur. can.,* c. 3, C.xv, q. 6; Friedberg, I, 756.   [2] See below, p. 362, n. 15.
[3] *Hist. Germ.,* an. 748; ed. 1566, 179ᵛ.   [4] A.D. 749; MGH SS, I, 556, 3ff.
[5] See below, p. 364, n. 18.   [6] See below, p. 364, n. 16.   [7] Ed. 1569, 690–1.
[8] Walramus, *De unit. eccles.,* I, 2: *MGH Lib. Lit.,* II, 186, 26ff.   [9] *MGH SS,*
XX, 224, 12.   [10] Partic., XXII, 49; MGH SS, XXII, 207, 16.

"CHAPTER XIII [^cXVI]

Whether Pepin was made king by the authority of
the pope or by that of the Francogallican council

We have described above how, when the doltish king Childeric,
with whom the Merovingian line came to an end, had been
driven out, Pepin was raised from his office as mayor of the
palace to the throne. Accordingly it is here appropriate to inquire
by whose authority the kingdom was passed to him. For Pope
Gelasius states one opinion, as recorded in the Canon Law:[1]
'A Roman pope, namely Zacharias, deposed the king of the
Franks, not so much on account of his misdeeds, but rather
because he was incapable of exercising such great responsibility;
and he replaced him with Pepin, father of the Emperor Charles,
absolving all the Franks from their oath of allegiance.' Scarcely
anyone fails to agree with the opinion offered by this particular
pope, including Ado,[2] Lambert,[3] Regino,[4] Sigebert,[5] Aimon[6] and
Landulphus.[7] And even Venericus Vercellensis, in the book we
have already cited, quotes the following words from a letter of
Pope Gregory VII to Herman, the bishop of Metz:[8] 'A certain
pope of Rome deposed the king of the Franks, not so much on
account of his misdeeds, but rather because he was incapable of
exercising such responsibility; and he put Pepin in his place, absolving all the Francigenians from the oath of allegiance they had
sworn to him.' Such are his words. Otto of Freising[9] and Godfrey
of Viterbo[10] observe: 'From this deed the Roman pontiffs derive
authority to dispose of kingdoms.'

But let us see whether or not the truth of this story may be
satisfactorily established, for in the first place no one can deny that
out of the very great number of kings of the Franks whom we have
shown to have been either elected or deposed,* there was not one

---

* c¹ *omits the preceding clause.*

auctoritate vel creatum vel abdicatum; contra vero docuimus, ius illud omne et creandorum et abdicandorum Regum penes solenne gentis concilium fuisse, ut plane incredibile videatur, Francos in hoc uno ius illud suum neglexisse.* Quid verbis opus
5 est? Venericus ille Vercellensis testimonium profert historici veteris,[11] qui de gestis Francorum conscripserat, quo tota illa narratio mendacii coarguitur,* dilucideque affirmatur, et Childericum et Pipinum usitato Francorum more, veterumque* instituto, illum abdicatum. Hunc autem in illius locum
10 suffectum fuisse, hoc est, solenni gentis concilio, cuius solius tantum fuisse potestatem superius demonstravimus. Illius autem historici verba haec sunt:[12] *Quod una cum concilio* et consensu omnium Francorum missa relatione ad sedem Apostolicam, et auctoritate percepta, praecelsus Pipinus electione totius gentis sublimatus sit in*
15 *sedem Regni, cum consecratione Episcoporum, et subiectione Principum.* Quibus ex verbis satis patet, Pipinum non a Papa, sed a populo ipso et Ordinibus ac Statibus Regni delectum, inauguratumque fuisse. Quod etiam paulo ante dilucidius idem Venericus ex eodem Historico sic exponit:[13] *Pipinum Maiorem Palatii*
20 *cum ad illum spectaret summa Regiae potestatis et officii, electum fuisse primum ex praefectis palatii in Regem, atque ordinatum fuisse, prius super hoc experto Zachariae Papae iudicio, quia consensus et auctoritas Romani Pontificis necessaria huic videbatur negotio.* Et mox:[14] *Quorum legatorum postulationem cum aequam atque utilem*
25 *Zacharias Papa iudicasset, ad ea quae postulabant consensit, et Pipinus factus est Rex communi suffragio Principum.*

In eandem sententiam Ado Viennensis Aet. 6, sub anno 727, ita scribit:[15] *Missi legati ad Zachariam, ut interrogarent eum, si ita manere deberent Reges Francorum, cum pene nullius potestatis essent,*
30 *iam solo Regio nomine contenti. Quibus Zacharias Pontifex respon-*

---

4 *c*[I] omits 'contra vero...suum neglexisse'.   7 *c*[I] omits 'mendacii coargitur'.
8 *c* 'veterique'.   12 *bc* 'consilio'.

[11] See next note.   [12] Walramus, *De unit. eccles.,* I, 16; *MGH Lib. Lit.,* II, 209, 16ff.   [13] *Ibid.,* I, 2; *ed. cit.,* II, 185, 41ff.   [14] *Ibid.; ed. cit.,* II, 186, 13ff. [15] *PL,* CXXIII, 123.

appointed or deprived of his kingdom by the authority of the pope. On the contrary, we have truly shown that the entire right to make and unmake kings lay with the solemn council of the people, so that it can scarcely be believed that the Franks would have neglected to exercise their right in this single instance.* But why should we waste words on this issue? Venericus Vercellensis offers the testimony of an ancient historian[11] who wrote about the deeds of the Franks, and whose work reveals the whole account to have been false. It is affirmed† with clarity that Childeric was deposed and replaced by Pepin according to the usual custom of the Franks and the practice of their ancestors.‡ Pepin was substituted for him by the solemn council of the nation, which alone possessed such power, as we have shown above. These are the very words used by that historian:[12] 'With the advice and consent of all the Franks, a report had been sent to the apostolic see, and the papal opinion had been received, and then that most distinguished man, Pepin, was elevated to the throne by the choice of the entire nation, and with the consecration of the bishops and the submission of the princes.' It is quite obvious from these words that Pepin was not instituted by the pope, but was chosen by the people, the orders and the estates. In a preceding passage Venericus explains the matter very clearly in his comments on that same historian:[13] 'As mayor of the palace Pepin was seen to exercise the authority and office of the king, and, as the first among the officers of the court, he was chosen and appointed to the throne. In addition, the opinion of Pope Zacharias was first ascertained, because the consent and advice of the Roman pontiff was thought to be necessary in the matter.' In a following passage he writes:[14] 'Pope Zacharias had adjudged the proposal of these envoys to be just and advantageous, and agreed with what they suggested. Accordingly, Pepin was made king by the general vote of the princes.'

Ado of Vienne writes to the same effect for the year 727:[15] 'Envoys had been sent to Zacharias to seek his advice as to whether the kings of the Franks should remain in office when they held virtually no power at all and had to be content with the regal title

---

* c¹ *omits the preceding sentence.*   † c¹ have been false...affirmed *becomes* affirm.
‡ c practice of their ancestors *becomes* ancient practice.

sum dedit, Regem potius illum debere vocari, qui Rempublicam regeret. Reversis legatis, abiectoque Childerico, qui tunc Regium nomen habebat, Franci per consilium legatorum et Zachariae Pontificis electum Pipinum Regem sibi constituunt.

5   Praeter illos superiores extat Aimoini testimonium in eandem sententiam lib. 4, cap. 61, ubi ad extremum ita concludit:[16] *Hoc anno Pipinus Rex Francorum appellatus est, et more Francorum elevatus in solium Regni, in Suessionum civitate.* Sed et Godfrid. Viterb. Chron. parte 17, cap. 4:[17] *Pipinus, inquit, per Papam*
10 *Zachariam ex electione Francorum rex factus est Francorum, Hildrico ignavo Rege per Francos in monasterium misso.* Horum similia dilucide scripserunt Sigebertus sub anno 752,[18] auctores historiae miscell. lib. 22.[19] Item Otto Frising. lib. 5, cap. 21, 22, 23;[20] et auctor libri, cui titulus est, Fasciculus temporum;[21] ex quibus
15 omnibus facile intellectu est: Non si Franci Pipinum exquisita Papae sententia Regem crearunt, iccirco illum Papae imperio atque auctoritate creatum fuisse. Aliud est enim Regem creare, aliud creandi consilium dare; aliud ius creandi habere, aliud ius consilii dandi; quanquam consilii in huiusmodi rebus dandi ius
20 nemo habet, nisi is a quo petitur.

^cProferam etiam testimonium insigne, quod mihi ex veteri quodam manuscripto incerti auctoris libro missum est, in quo haec Archiepiscopi Maguntinensis ad Pipinum oratio profertur:[22]*Galli omnium ordinum consensu hoc diadema regium cum oneris,*
25 *tum honoris insigne capiti tuo mea manu inferunt, teque spoliis Childerici exornant, cuius non familiam aut maiorum memoriam, sed perditissimos mores oderunt, tuae virtutis lucem suspiciunt et amant. Quod si tantum lumen in te extingui superbia, aut obscurari ignavia senserint, quid de te illos facturos putas, quorum beneficio stabis, qui in eum, qui*

---

[16] Ed. 1567, 403f.   [17] Partic. XII, 43; *MGH SS*, XXII, 204, 11–12.   [18] A.D. 750; *MGH SS*, VI, 332, 8ff.   [19] Land. Sagax; ed. 1569, 691.   [20] *MGH SS*, XX, 223ff.   [21] Rolevinck; ed. 1480, 46^r.   [22] Non invenio.

alone. Pope Zacharias replied to them that he who ruled the commonwealth ought rather to be called the king. When the envoys returned and Childeric, who held the title of king at that time, had been deposed, the Franks acted on the advice of the envoys and the decision of Pope Zacharias, and made Pepin their king.'

In addition to the authors cited above, we have the similar testimony of Aimon, who concludes in this fashion:[16] 'In this year Pepin was named king of the Franks, and in accordance with the Frankish custom he was raised to the throne in the city of Soissons.' And even Godfrey of Viterbo in his chronicle says:[17] 'Pepin was made king of the Franks by Pope Zacharias through the choice of the Franks, the slothful King Childeric having been sent by the Franks to a monastery.' Similar accounts of this matter are set forth by Sigebert for the year 752,[18] by the authors of the *Historical Miscellany*,[19] by Otto of Freising,[20] and by the author of the book entitled *An Historical Collection*.[21] From all these authors it is easy to conclude that, although the Franks created Pepin king after seeking the opinion of the pope, he was not created so by the sovereignty and authority of the pope. For it is one thing to create a king and another to give counsel about creating him. It is one thing to have the right of creation and another to have the right of giving advice – although no man has the right of giving advice in matters of this kind unless his advice is first sought.

cI shall also offer a remarkable piece of evidence which was sent to me from a certain ancient manuscript of undetermined authorship, and which contains this address to Pepin by the archbishop of Mainz:[22] 'By my hand the French, with the consent of all the estates, place upon your head this crown of kings bearing with it both the honour and the burden of the office, and they adorn you with the accoutrements of Childeric, whose family and the memory of whose ancestors they respect but whose abandoned habits they abhor, whereas they love and esteem the light of your virtue. For if they should perceive that pride extinguishes this great light in you, or that sloth obscures it, what do you imagine they would do about you? It is by their favour that you will endure, and since you are

suo iure, non alieno beneficio regnum obtinebat, tam severum exercu-
erunt iudicium? Disce igitur Pipine, alieno exemplo, atque periculo,
Regem agere, hoc est omnem curam et cogitationem in salute populi tui
collocare.

5   ^aDenique nemo dilucidius totam hanc rem explicat Marsilio
Patavino, qui imperante Ludovico Bavaro librum de trans-
latione imperii conscripsit, in quo, cap. 6, ita loquitur:²³ *Pipinus*
filius Caroli Martelli, vir in rebus bellicis strenuus, legitur a Zacharia
Papa in Regni Francorum excellentiam sublimatus. Sed Aimoinus in
10   *Gestis Francorum scribit,*²⁴ *et verius, Pipinum per Francos legitime in*
Regem electum, et per Regni Proceres levatum. Childericus vero, qui
tum sub nomine Regio in delitiis marcescebat, fuit in monachum ton-
soratus. Unde non illum Zacharias deposuit, sed deponentibus (ut
quidam aiunt) consensit. Nam talis depositio Regis, et alterius insti-
15   *tutio, propter rationabilem caussam, non ad Episcopum tantummodo,*
neque ad clericum aliquem, aut clericorum collegium pertinet, sed ad
universitatem civium inhabitantium regionem, vel nobilium, vel ip-
sorum valentiorem multitudinem.

      ^bHaec Marsilius. Quibus consentaneum postea reperi locum
20   in Appendice Hunibaldi, apud Iohann. Tritenhemium, ubi
scriptum ita est:²⁵ *Eodem anno proceres totius Regni convenientes in*
unum super abrogatione Regis Hilderici inutilis, coeperunt habere con-
silium. Placuit autem in commune omnibus, ut Regem Hildericum
nullam regnandi vel peritiam, vel potestatem habentem deponerent, et
25   *Pipinum, penes quem totius regni summa manebat auctoritas, in regem*
sublimarent. Sed Pipinus in hanc rem consentire noluit, nisi prius
consilium Romani Pontificis Zachariae inquiratur, caussas allegans se
monentes. ^cHaec ille.

      ^aPaparum igitur commentum ^cimpudens ^ade iure* Regum vel

---

29 c¹ begins this sentence differently: 'Qua ex re perspicuum satis est'.
²³ Ed. 1554, 230.   ²⁴ As above, p. 364, n. 16.   ²⁵ Ed. Schard, I, 343.

one who acquired the kingdom by their oath, and not through favour of anyone else, do you not think that the judgment they would exercise would be just as severe? Learn, therefore, Pepin, to act the king by avoiding that example and its contingent danger, learn to employ all care and thought for the welfare of your people.'

*a*Lastly, no one has explained this whole matter more clearly than has Marsiglio of Padua, who during the reign of Lewis of Bavaria wrote a book about the translation of the empire. His view of the matter is as follows:[23] 'Pepin, the son of Charles Martel and a man of energy in military affairs, is said to have been raised to supremacy in the kingdom of the Franks by Pope Zacharias. But Aimon writes more truly in his work on the deeds of the Franks[24] that Pepin was lawfully elected king by the Franks, and raised up by the nobility of the kingdom. Indeed Childeric, who at that time exhausted his energies in wanton pursuits while holding the royal title, was tonsured as a monk. Thus Zacharias did not depose him, but, as some say, merely agreed with those who did. For such a deposition of a king and the institution of another for proper reasons does not belong to any bishop in any way whatever, nor to any clerk or college of clerics, but rather to the whole body of the citizens living in a particular region, or to the whole body of the nobles, or the majority of them.'

*b*These are the words of Marsiglio, and we may later find agreement with them expressed in a passage in the appendix to Hunibaldus, in the version of Johannes Trithemius, where it is written:[25] 'In the same year the nobles of the entire kingdom, meeting together in one body about the deposition of the ineffective King Childeric, began to take counsel. They all decided together to depose King Childeric, who had neither the skill nor the strength to rule, and to raise up Pepin, in whose possession the highest sovereignty of the entire kingdom remained, to be king. But Pepin was unwilling to consent to this step without first seeking the counsel of Zacharias, the Roman pontiff, and stating the appropriate reasons.' *c*These are his words.

*a*I therefore believe it to be obvious to all men that the claim of

creandorum, vel abdicandorum,* perspicuum omnibus esse
arbitror; sed praeter commentum, quod improbitatis et malitiae*
documentum est ^ccertissimum, ^aoperae pretium est, insignem
quandam Stephani Papae epistolam ad hanc fabulam accommo-
5 datam proponere, ex qua de veteratoris illius stoliditate et
vesania existimare liceat. Extat autem apud Rheginonem,
monachum ordinis Benedictini, Abbatem Pruniacensem, testem
in hoc genere irrefragabilem, in Chronic. anni DCCLIII:²⁶
STEPHANUS Episcopus, servus servorum Dei. Sicut nemo se debet
10 *iactare de suis meritis, sic non debent opera Dei, quae in illo per suos*
sanctos fiunt, sine suis meritis sileri, sed praedicari, sicut angelus
admonet Thobiam. Unde ego pro oppressione sanctae Ecclesiae a Rege
atrocissimo et blasphemo et nec dicendo Haistolpho, ad optimum et
Sancti Petri fidelem Dominum Pipinum, Christianissimum Regem, in
15 *Franciam veni, ubi aegrotavi usque ad mortem, et mansi aliquod*
tempus apud pagum Parisiacum, in venerabili monasterio Sancti
Dionysii martyris, quem, cum iam medici desperarent, fui sicut in
oratione in Ecclesia eiusdem beati martyris subtus campanis, et vidi ante
altare Dominum Petrum, et Magistrum gentium Dominum Paulum,
20 *et tota mente illos recognovi de illorum surcariis, et tunc Beatum Do-*
minum Dionysium ad dextram Domini Petri, subtilem et longiorem,
dixitque bonus Pastor, Dominus Petrus: 'Hic frater noster postulat
sanitatem'; et dixit beatus Paulus: 'Modo sanabitur'; et appro-
pinquans misit manum suam ad pectus Domini Dionysii amicabiliter,
25 *respexitque ad Dominum Petrum, et dixit Dominus Petrus ad Do-*
minum Dionysium hilariter: 'Tua gratia est sanitas eius.' Et statim
Dominus Dionysius thuribulum incensi, et palmam in manu tenens
cum presbytero et diacono, qui in parte stabant, venit ad me, et dixit:
'Pax tecum frater, noli timere, non morieris donec ad sedem tuam

---

1 *c*¹ omits all hereafter in this chapter, ending it instead with 'ius penes Pontifices
R. nec esse nec unquam antea fuisse'.   **2** *c* 'impudentiae'.
²⁶ *MGH SS*, I, 556, 27ff.

the popes to a right to appoint or depose kings is an ᶜimpudent ᵃfabrication.* But besides this fabrication, which in itself is the ᶜmost certain ᵃproof of dishonesty and malice,† it is worth the trouble to cite a certain remarkable letter of Pope Stephen, which has been tailored to fit this fiction. By it one may judge the stupidity and madness of that old fox. The letter is contained under the year 753 in the chronicle of Regino, a monk of the Benedictine Order and abbot of Prüm, and it is an irrefutable piece of evidence in the matter.²⁶ It reads: 'Stephen the bishop, the servant of the servants of the Lord. No man should boast of his own merits, but the works of God, which are accomplished through the saints without their merits being concealed, should be openly preached, as the angel commanded Tobias. Because of the oppression of the holy church by that most wicked, blasphemous and unmentionable king, Aistulf, I fled to France to the best and most faithful servant of Saint Peter, the Lord Pepin, the most Christian king, and there I sickened near to death and remained for some time in the area of Paris in the venerable monastery of Saint Denis the martyr. Since they then despaired of a cure, I was one day in prayer beneath the bells in the church of that same blessed martyr, and I saw before the altar the Lord Peter together with the Lord Paul, master of the gentiles, whom I recognized with all my understanding because of their robes. And then I saw the blessed Lord Denis standing slender and tall on the right hand of the Lord Peter. And that good pastor, the Lord Peter, said: "This, our brother, asks to be restored to health." And blessed Paul said: "He shall even now be made well." And, coming close, he placed his hand gently on the breast of the Lord Denis, and looked toward the Lord Peter. And the Lord Peter said gaily to the Lord Denis: "By your grace is he healed." And the Lord Denis took a censer of incense, and, holding a palm frond in his hand and accompanied by a presbyter and a deacon, who stood at his side, he came to me and said: "Peace be with you, brother. Have no fear. You will not die until you return safely to

---

* cᴵ *omits the remainder of this chapter and replaces the preceding sentence with* From this it is quite obvious that the right to appoint and depose kings does not lie, and never has lain, with the Roman Pontiffs. † *bc* impudence.

prospere revertaris. Surge sanus, et hoc altare in honorem Dei et Apostolorum Petri et Pauli, quos vides, dedica, missas gratiarum agens.' Moxque factus sum sanus, et volebam implere, quod mihi praeceptum erat, et dicebant, qui ibi aderant, quod dementabam. Quapropter retuli
5 *illis et Regi, suisque omnibus ex ordine quae videram, et quomodo sanatus fuerim, et implevi quae visa sunt mihi omnia. Gesta sunt autem haec anno ab incarnatione Domini DCCLIII, V. Id. Aug. quo Christi roboratus virtute, inter celebrationem consecrationis praefati altaris, et oblationem sacrificii, unxi in Reges Francorum Regem Pipinum et*
10 *duos filios eius Carolum et Carolomannum. Sed et Bertrandam coniugem ipsius Regis, indutam cycladibus regiis, et gratia spiritus sancti septiformis consignavi in Dei nomine, atque Francorum proceres Apostolica benedictione sanctificans, auctoritate S. Petri sibi a Christo tradita obligavit, et obtestatus est, ut nunquam de altera stirpe per*
15 *succedentium temporum curricula, ipsi vel quique ex eorum progenie orti, Regem super se praesumant aliquo modo constituere, nisi de eorum progenie.*

    ^bHaec Papa Stephanus, cuius cum ridicula bonis omnibus vesania videri debet, tum etiam detestanda illa execratio, qua in
20 eorum caput utitur, qui non ex Caroli Magni stirpe prognati regnum obtinerent, ut vel unicus ille locus eius libelli quem Matharellus²⁷ nescio quis, rabula impudens et impurus, adversus hanc nostram Francogalliam ^cnuper ^bedidit, et in quo stultissimam illam Papae Stephani epistolam comprobat, stoliditatem
25 insignem coarguat* dignissimumque et illum et alterum nescio quem Papirium Massonum,²⁸ Iesuitam Bardocucullum, ^cet ^bSycophantam mercede conductum ostendat, qui in Mathurini Parisiensis fano, ubi eiusmodi fanatici curantur, flagris ad necem cedantur.

---

25 c relocate the three words 'stoliditatem insignem coarguat' earlier in the sentence: '. . . ut vel unicus ille locus insignem eius libelli stoliditatem coarguat, quem Matharellus. . .'

²⁷ Ed. 1575, 94 (end of ch. 12); see above, p. 77, for a discussion of this work.
²⁸ Ed. 1575, 6–9; on this work, see above, p. 79.

your see. Arise in health, and dedicate this altar to the honour of God and the apostles Peter and Paul, whom you see before you, celebrating masses of thanksgiving." Within a brief space I was cured, and I wished to fulfil what I had been instructed to do. At which those who were present said I was mad. Accordingly I related all the things I had seen one after another to the king and his court, and how I had been healed. And I carried out all things I had been told. This happened in the year 753 A.D. on the 9th of August, and, as I was made strong by the virtue of Christ, I anointed Pepin and his two sons, Charles and Carloman, as kings of the Franks between the time when I celebrated the consecration of the said altar and the time when I offered the sacrifice. Moreover in the name of God I vouched for Bertranda, the wife of Pepin, who was clad in her royal robes and sanctified by the grace of the sevenfold Holy Spirit. And I blessed the Frankish nobles with the apostolic benediction, and under the authority bestowed by Christ upon Saint Peter himself they were obliged and adjured, themselves and their descendants, never to take upon themselves in any way the constituting of a king from any other stock through all subsequent ages.'

*b*So wrote Pope Stephen, and, while his absurd folly ought to be apparent to us all, so too should we abhor the curse he placed upon the head of those who might acquire the kingdom without being descendants from the stock of Charlemagne. A unique instance of such madness is a passage in a book *c*recently *b*published to refute this our *Francogallia* by some writer called Matharel,[27] a noisy, impudent and unclean fellow, who approves of that most fatuous letter by Pope Stephen and thereby demonstrates his remarkable stupidity.* So it is also with some worthy fellow or other called Papire Masson,[28] a renegade Jesuit and hired sycophant, who should be taken to the asylum of Saint Mathurin in Paris, where maniacs are cared for, and put to death by whipping.

---

* *c omits* and thereby demonstrates his remarkable stupidity; *adds* and demonstrating a remarkable stupidity *after Francogallia.*

De comestabulo, et paribus Franciae

Praeter illam Magistri Palatii dignitatem, de qua superius diximus, fuit et altera de qua iccirco dicendum hoc loco est, quoniam haec,* Maiorum nostrorum memoria videtur in illius locum successisse. Erant enim Comites stabuli Regii, unde Comestabuli,
5 ad extremum Connestablii postea, corrupto nomine, dicti sunt. Comites autem *posteriorum Imperatorum Romanorum aetate *vulgo dicebantur omnes, qui amplissimos quosque honores in Regia obtinebant, et Rempublicam pro parte administrabant, a qua consuetudine veteres non abhorruisse, aliis quibusdam libris
10 nostris docuimus.[1] Sic enim Cicero *Callisthenem Alexandri Magni Comitem* non uno loco appellat.[2] Erat autem Comes stabuli, fere is, qui apud Romanos Magister equitum dicebatur, hoc est, qui equitatui praeerat, cui custodes *regiorum *equorum suberant, quos vulgo Scutieros appellamus; Gregor. Turon. lib. 5, cap. 39:[3]
15 *Thesaurarius Clodovei a Cuppane Stabuli comite de Biturigo retractus, vinctus Reginae transmissus est.* Et rursus cap. 48, ubi de Leudaste loquitur:[4] *Quae libenter eum colligens provocat, equorumque meliorum deputat esse custodem. Hinc iam obsessus vanitate, et superbiae deditus, Comitatum ambit stabulorum, quo accepto, cunctos*
20 *despicit ac postponit.*

Quibus ex locis apparet, custodiam equorum praefecturam fuisse honestissimam, sed multo ampliorem Comitatum Stabulorum. Cuius rei Aimoinus quoque auctor est, lib. 3, cap. 43, ubi de eodem Leudaste loquitur:[5] *Reginae familiarissimus factus, custos*
25 *equorum efficitur. Inde Comitatum super ceteros nactus custodes, post mortem Reginae Comitatum Thuronicum a Chariberto percepit.* Et

---

3 'quoniam haec': *c* 'quia non multis ab hinc seculis, sed prope'.

[1] Cf. *Commentarius verborum iuris* [ed. prin., 1558], *s.v.* 'Comites'; ed. *Opera*, I, 590.   [2] *Pro C. Rabirio Postumo oratio,* [IX] 23; Loeb, 388.   [3] *MGH SS Mer.,* I: I², 247, 14.   [4] *Ibid.,* 257, 27.   [5] *PL,* CXXXIX, 722.

^aCHAPTER XIV [^cXVII]

The constable and the peers of France

There was another high office we should here discuss in addition to that of mayor of the palace, of which we have spoken above. This is necessary because, according to the historical records of our ancestors, it seems* to have replaced the latter office. For there used to be royal counts of the stable, whence, through the corruption of the term, were derived the words *comestabuli* and later constables. Now ^cin the age of the later Roman emperors ^aall those who acquired the highest honours at court and played their part in the administration of the commonwealth were commonly called counts. This was a practice which the ancients accepted, as we have shown in certain of our other books.[1] Thus in several places Cicero calls Callisthenes the 'count of Alexander the Great'.[2] This constable was very like what the Romans called the master of the horse, that is, the commander of the cavalry, who was responsible for the maintenance of the royal horses and is commonly called the shield-bearer or equerry. Thus Gregory of Tours writes:[3] 'Clovis' treasurer was removed from Bourges by Cuppa, the count of the stable, and was sent in chains to the queen.' He also refers to Leudast in these terms:[4] 'She summoned him willingly to her side, and appointed him the keeper of the best horses. He soon became obsessed with vanity and puffed up with pride, and solicited the countship of the stables. When he had acquired this post, he despised and looked down upon everyone else.'

From these examples it appears that, while the custodianship of the horses was a very honourable office, it was much inferior to that of constable. Aimon also provides evidence of this where he writes as follows of the same Leudast:[5] 'He became very intimate with the queen, and was made keeper of the horses. Then he became constable over the rest of the keepers, and after the queen's death

* *c adds* not so very much later.

rursus cap. 70:[6] *Leudegisilus Regalium praefectus equorum, quem
vulgo Conestabilem vocant, quemque Rex ei praefecerat expeditioni,
machinamenta deduci imperat.* Item lib. 4, cap. 95, ubi de Carolo
Magno loquitur:[7] *Eodemque anno Burchardum Comitem Stabuli sui*
5 *cum classe misit in Corsicam.* Quod Regino lib. 2 commemorans:[8]
Eodem anno, inquit, *Burchardum Comitem Stabuli sui, quem cor-
rupte Constabulum appellamus, cum classe misit in Corsicam.* Hunc
autem Appendix Gregorii Comestabulum appellat, lib. 11:[9]
Brunechildis, inquit, *ab Erporre Comestabulo de pago producitur.*
10   Quod cum ita esset, Albert. Krantzius lib. Suet. 5, cap. 41
ausus est Connestablium affirmare, eundem esse, quem Germani
Marschalcum* appellant:[10] *Gubernatorem,* inquit, *appellavere ex
optimis militem, qui convocandis Regni coetibus, et omnia vice
Principis gerendi habeat potestatem. Mareschalcum nostri vocant, Galli*
15 *Connestabulum.* Haec ille. Quae fortassis eo probabiliora videri
possunt, quod Mareschallorum nullam in Francogallia nostra
mentionem antiquitus animadverto, ut verisimile sit, Regum
posteriorum institutum illud fuisse, ad Germanorum consuetudinem accommodatum. ^cUtcunque sit, vetus hoc verbum esse
20 patet etiam ex Annalib. Anglicis Thomae Walsinghamii, ubi
sub anno 1293 ita scribit:[11] *Moxque Rex Francorum praecepit
constabulario Franciae, ut in manu armata ducatum Aquitaniae regis
Francorum nomine occuparet.*
    ^aHunc autem stabulorum Comitatum non dubito a Roman-
25 orum Imperat. instituto natum fuisse, etsi ex parvis initiis tandem
moribus nostris ad praefecturae praetoriae dignitatem excrevit.
Erat autem per illa tempora dignitas haec tanquam militaris
Tribunatus. Ammianus lib. 26, ubi de Imperatore Valentiniano
loquitur:[12] *Nicomediam itineribus certis ingressus, Kalendis Martiis*
30 *Valentem fratrem stabulo suo cum Tribunatus dignitate praefecit.* Eius
dignitatis in Cod. Iustiniani mentio fit l. 1, Cod. de comitibus et
tribunis schol.,[13] ubi magni honoris loco illis tribuitur, ut

---

12 *bc* 'Marschallum'.

[6] *Ibid.*, 744.   [7] Ed. 1567, 473.   [8] A.D. 807; *MGH SS*, I, 564, 67ff.   [9] XI, 41,
ed. 1568, App., 29.   [10] Krantz, *Chronica*, V, 41; ed. 1546, 580.   [11] Ed. 1863,
I, 44.   [12] XXVI, 4, 2; Loeb, II, 589.   [13] *Cod.* 12, 11, 1; Krueger, II, 457.

Charibert made him count of Tours.' In a later chapter Aimon writes:[6] 'Leudegisilus, the prefect of the royal horses who was commonly called the constable, was placed in command of that mission by the king, and ordered the war-machines to be brought forth.' Or again, he writes of Charlemagne:[7] 'In the same year he sent Burchard, his constable, with a fleet against Corsica.' Regino describes this incident as follows:[8] 'In the same year he sent Burchard, his count of the stable (a term which we have corrupted to constable), against Corsica with a fleet.' In the appendix to Gregory of Tours this officer is termed the constable.[9] 'Brunhild', he writes, 'was brought out of the village by Erpor, the constable.'

In these circumstances Albert Krantz has dared to affirm in his book on the Swedes that the office of constable is identical with the German office of marshal.[10] 'They named as governor', he writes, 'a prominent soldier who had authority to convoke the assembly and to conduct all affairs in place of the prince. We call him marshal, whereas the French call this officer the constable.' Such are his words, and this seems to be the more probable because I notice no mention of marshals in our Francogallia, and it may well be that it was the practice of the later kings to make use of the German convention. ᶜHowever this may be, there is this ancient piece of evidence taken from the English annals of Thomas of Walsingham, who under the year 1293 writes as follows:[11] 'Presently the king of the Franks instructed the constable of France to seize the dukedom of Aquitaine by armed force in the royal name.'

ᵃI have no doubt that the countship of the stables was derived from the practice of the Roman emperors, even if it grew from small beginnings within our customs until it became the office of a praetorian prefect. But in early times that office was a kind of military tribunate. Ammianus, writing of the Emperor Valentinian, states:[12] 'Having entered Nicomedia in the course of the journeys he had arranged, at the beginning of March he named his brother Valens to his stable with the rank of tribune.' This rank is mentioned in Justinian's *Code*[13] where it is considered a great

Imperatoris epulis praeesse, et purpuram eius adorare possint.
Itemque in l. 3, Cod. Theodos. de annon. et tribut.;[14] et l.
perpensa, 29, Cod. Theodos. de equor. collat.;[15] et l. 1, Cod.
Theodos. qui a praebit. tyron.,[16] ubi ius illis conceditur sportulas
5 exigendi a provincialibus, qui militares equos ad usum Imperatoris conferebant.

Superest, ut de iis magistratibus differamus, qui vulgo PARES
FRANCIAE nominantur, quanquam nobis quidem non studium,
sed monimentorum facultas deest. Nam ex tanto librorum
10 numero, qui Francogalliae Annales et Chronica dicuntur,
ne unus quidem extat* in quo probabilis aliqua illius instituti ratio proferatur. Quod enim Guaguinus[17] et ᶜItalus quidam ᵃPaulus Aemilius[18] non tam ᵇRegum ᵃGallorum, quam
Paparum historicus, et alii pervulgati scribunt,* magistratus illos
15 vel a Pipino, vel a Carolo Magno institutos fuisse, id plane absurdum esse, vel hinc ᵇlicet ᵃintelligatur, quod ex tam multis
Germanis Historicis, qui regum illorum aetate, aut paulo infra
eorum aetatem historias scripserunt, nullus plane Magistratuum
illorum mentionem vel tenuissimam interponit. Quinetiam
20 Aimoini de Francorum institutis et rebus gestis historia, usque ad
Ludovici Pii, eiusque Appendix ad Ludovici Iunioris Regis 37
aetatem perducta, nusquam horum Parium mentionem facit.[19]

Quare tantisper dum certius aliquid afferatur,* ᵇinstitutum
illud ad* Hugonis Capetti regnum referendum arbitror, qui
25 cum remoto herede legitimo regnum occupasset, proceres
aliquot novo aliquo* honore ac beneficio sibi devinciendos
putavit; nam eiusmodi aliquid ab illo factum omnes consentiunt.
Eius autem instituti exemplum facile intelligitur ex Feudali iure
sumptum fuisse, quo iure Vassalli qui ab eodem Seniore ac

---

11 'extat': c 'adhuc editus est'.   14 'non tam...scribunt': c 'non tam Regum
Galliae historicus, quam Paparum assentator mercenarius, et alii nescio qui vulgo
scribunt'.   23 *bc* from here to p. 378, l. 14, replace a suppressed *a* passage which
will be found in appendix A, p. 530.   24 'illud ad': *c* 'ad illud'.   26 *c* 'quodam'.

[14] *Cod. Theodos.*, 11, 1, 29; Mommsen, 1:2, 578, 4.   [15] *Ibid.*, 11, 17, 3; *ed.
cit.*, 605, 3.   [16] *Ibid.*, 11, 18, 1; *ed. cit.*, 605, 10.   [17] Cf. Bk. 3; ed. 1528, fol. 50.
[18] Non invenio.   [19] Cf. ed. 1567, where 'Peers' are not in the index nor
found at likely junctures in the text.

honour to be able to preside at the emperor's banquets and to worship the purple. The same point is contained in three passages in the Theodosian *Code*.[14, 15, 16] The last of these occurs in the context of authority to demand contributions from the provinces which provided war horses for the use of the emperor.

It remains for us to consider those magistrates who are commonly called the PEERS OF FRANCE, although, despite our researches, we can find no record of them. For from the great number of books described as annals or chronicles of Francogallia there is not one* which provides any convincing account of this institution. What is said by Gaguin,[17] by ^ca certain Italian writer ^aPaulus Aemilius,[18] who is more an historian of the popes than he is of the French ^bkings, ^aand by other common authors,† namely that those officers were instituted either by Pepin or by Charlemagne, is quite clearly absurd. Their view is not easy to understand, since not one of the many German historians who wrote their histories in the age of those kings, or shortly after them, makes any clear mention or gives the least hint of such magistrates. Even Aimon, whose history of the customs and deeds of the Franks extends to the reign of Louis the Pious, and whose appendix reaches the age of Louis the Younger, the thirty-seventh king, never makes mention of these peers.[19]

Thus until someone may inform me better,‡ ^bI shall regard the institution as associated with the reign of Hugh Capet, who had taken possession of the kingdom without any lawful hereditary claim, and who considered that a few nobles who received new honour and favour should be bound in loyalty to him. For in this way all would agree with what he had done. Moreover it was easy enough to understand how this institution had arisen out of the feudal law, whereby those vassals who received fiefs from their

---

* *c adds* so far published. † *c* an historian...common authors *becomes* a mercenary flatterer of the popes than he is an historian of the kings of France, and a motley crew of other publicists. ‡ *a The ensuing bc passage replaces the a text, which will be found in appendix A.*

patrono feuda receperunt, Pares inter se, hoc est, quasi ὁμότιμοι,
appellantur, quorum triplex haec potestas est: primum, ut qui in
vassallorum ordinem cooptantur, pro eorum collegio coop-
tentur, lib. Feud. 2, tit. 2;[20] tum ut rogati testimonium de investi-
5 tura dicant, lib. 2, tit. 19;[21] postremo, ut si qua vel inter
ipsos, vel inter Seniorem et ipsos controversia exoriatur, ipsi
iudicium et civile et criminale exerceant, lib. 2, tit. 46 et tit. 52
et tit. 55.[22] Et profecto ita est, ut Pares Franciae hoc iure sint,
primum ut neque inaugurari, nisi pro collegio, neque abdicari,
10 nisi caussa in consilio cognita, neque ad aliud ullum nisi ad
collegarum iudicium, vocari possint. Quanquam Parisiensis
Senatus hanc sibi auctoritatem ascivit, ut Pares caussam apud se
dicere iubeat.

Ac *a*Budaeus autem* vir longe doctissimus, Pares illos Patri-
15 tiorum nomine appellat,[23] scribitque videri sibi ab uno aliquo
Rege institutos, ex eorum numero, qui Germanicum Imperium
obtinuerunt; propterea quod Iustinianus Patres eos ab Imperatore
delectos esse ait, quasi Reipublicae patronos, tutoresque. Ego
*b*vero *a*doctissimi viri sententiam non aspernor, praesertim a
20 Parium dignitate non alienam. Fuit enim Romanorum Imperat.
posteriorum aetate Patritiatus, dignitas ab illa Parium non admodum dissimilis, partim quod Reipublicae quodammodo
patres erant, ut Suidas testatur,[24] et de summis quibusque rebus
ab Imperatore consulebantur, insignibusque iisdem, quibus
25 Consules, utebantur, ac maiorem quidem Praefecto Praetorio,
minorem autem Consule, honorem atque auctoritatem habebant. Quod ex Iustiniani Novellis,[25] et Sidonio Apollinari,[26] et
Claudiano,[27] et Cassiodoro[28] praesertim cognosci potest.

Sed translato in Germanos Imperii nomine usurpatum hunc

---

14 *bc* 'quidem'.

[20] *Lib. feud.*, II, 2; ed. 1562, 746.   [21] *Ibid.*, II, 19; *ed. cit.*, 760.   [22] *Ibid.*, 100,
106, 121.   [23] *Annot.*, §Ex lege ultima de Senatoribus; *Opera*, 1557, III, 73.
[24] *Ad verb.* Πατρίκιος; Bernhard, II: 2, 144.   [25] Cf., *e.g.*, *Nov.* XIII; Schoell-Kroll,
II, 99ff.   [26] *Carmen* II, *vv.* 90f. & 205f.; *MGH AA*, VIII, 176 & 179.   [27] XXV
(*De bello Gothico, praefatio*), 8; Loeb, II, 124.   [28] See index of *MGH AA*, XII,
s.v. patricius.

overlord and patron were called peers among each other, that is, as if they were ὁμότιμοι [with an equal share of honour]. According to the *Book of Feuds* such vassals have this threefold authority: first, that those who are admitted into this rank of vassalage may be admitted on behalf of their own collegiate body;[20] second, that those who are asked may give testimony concerning investiture;[21] and, last, that, if any dispute arise either among themselves or between themselves and their overlord, they themselves may exercise civil and criminal jurisdiction.[22] And certain it is that the peers of France are subject to this law, first in that they cannot be appointed except through their college, nor deposed unless the cause be shown in their council. Neither can they be indicted by any other judgment than that of their colleagues, so that the peers enjoy the privilege of pleading their cause among each other.

But* ᵃBudé, who is a man of the widest learning, calls these peers by the name of patricians,[23] and writes that it seems to him they were instituted by one of those of our kings who acquired the German empire, because Justinian says that those *patres* were chosen by the emperor as patrons and guardians of the commonwealth. I do not reject the opinion of this most learned man, especially since it enhances the status of the peers. For in the age of the later Roman emperors the rank of patrician was in a way not unlike that of the peers, because, as Suidas testifies,[24] the patricians were in a sense the fathers of the commonwealth. They were consulted by the emperor on matters of the gravest import; they employed the same symbols of rank as did the consuls; and they had greater honour and authority than the praetorian prefect possessed, although less than those of a consul. This can be established in particular from Justinian's *Novellae*,[25] Sidonius Apollinaris,[26] Claudian,[27] and Cassiodorus.[28]

However, when the title of the empire was transferred to the

---

* **bc** *omit* But.

honorem non putamus;* neque verisimile est, ullos eiusmodi*
Patritios ab aliquo Germanico Imperatore, qui idem Francogalliae Rex esset, institutos fuisse, ut non aliquis ex Germanicis
historicis eius mentionem fccisset. Denique idem Budaeus,
5 eodem loco haesitans,[29] commemorat eiusmodi Parium dignitatem apud ceteras quoque vicinas gentes fuisse, atque in Regiis
Commentariis scriptum esse, anno MCCXXIIII, Ioannem
quendam Nigellanum Flandrum, cui controversia in Flandria
illata esset a Comitissa Flandriae, ^cad ^aPares Franciae appellasse,
10 quod se* aequo iudicio apud Pares Flandriae certare se non posse
iurasset, cumque a Comitissa ad Parium Flandriae iudicium
revocaretur, tandem certis de caussis decretum ^cfuisse, ^aut ea
controversia ad Pares Franciae introduceretur. Caussa autem
translati iudicii cuiusmodi fuerit, neque Budaeus exponit:[30]
15 et, qui in iure feudali versatus esset,* nunquam praetermisisset.

^bVerum ut iam huius magistratus institutum paulo planius ac
certius exponamus, primum omnium, ut iam ante dixi, constare
inter omnes arbitror, nullam Parium nominis, neque apud
Germanos, neque apud Gallos historicos ante Capevingiorum
20 regum mentionem inveniri. Sed quoniam eruta quaedam nuper
vetustatis monimenta video, atque in lucem edita, in quibus
illorum Parium iura non minima ex parte designantur, operaepretium esse arbitror, quae ex illis commentariis observavimus,[31]
breviter exponere, idque eo lubentius, quod ab eo ipso, a quo illi
25 commentarii nuper evulgati sunt, in aliam partem ac veritas et
ratio postulat, contorquentur. Ergo eorum quidem instituen-
dorum caussam duplicem video fuisse: primum, ut regis in-
augurationi atque (ut tum loquebantur) investiturae prae-
essent, hoc est, ut regem imperii sui insignibus, atque infulis,
30 solenniter in Principum atque Optimatum conventu exornarent;
deinde ut siquis e Potentium et Principum Franciae numero
fraudis capitalis reus fieret, iudicium illud exercerent. Nam cum

---

1 *bc* 'arbitror'.   1 *c*¹ 'huiusmodi'.   10 *bc* omit 'se'.   15 *c* 'fuisset'.
29 Cf. *Annot.*, §Ex lege ultima de Senatoribus; *Opera*, 1557, III, 97.   30 *Ibid.*
31 René Choppin, *De domanio Franciae* (1572); see above, p. 90.

Germans we do not believe that this honour was taken into use, nor is it probable that none of the German historians would have mentioned it if any patricians of that sort had been established by the German emperor, who was then also the king of Francogallia. Lastly, the same Budé remarks in the passage already cited,[29] though with some hesitation, that the rank of peer was also used in other neighbouring nations, and that it is written in the royal commentaries under the year 724 that a certain Johannes Nigellanus of Flanders, who was involved in a dispute there, appealed from the countess of Flanders [c]to [a]the peers of France. He had first sworn that he could not be sure of a just hearing before the peers of Flanders, and when the countess revoked the hearing to the peers of Flanders, it was at length decreed for well-established reasons that the dispute should be heard before the peers of France. Budé does not, however, explain the reason for the transference of the case,[30] and one who was so well versed in the feudal law should never have omitted to do so.

[b]Let us now expound somewhat more fully and clearly the origin of this magistracy, and first let me repeat what I believe to be established among all writers, namely that no mention of the name of peers is to be found among the German historians nor among the French before the age of the Capetian kings. But since I notice that certain records of antiquity have recently been discovered and made known through publication, and that these records contain some partial mention of the rights of the peers, I believe it worth while to offer some brief comments on the issues we have noted in these writings.[31] I do this the more willingly since these issues have been distorted by the author who recently made the records known to the public, and truth and reason suggest something quite otherwise. Thus I note that there were two reasons for the instituting of the peers: first, that they presided at the inauguration of the king, or, as it was then called, his investiture, that is to say, they solemnly bedecked the king with the symbols and badges of his sovereignty at the assembly of the princes and leading men; second, that, if any one of the nobles and princes of France was accused of a capital crime, they judged the case. For since in ancient

antiquitus ea iudicia in publico Gentis Concilio exercerentur (ut superius copiose demonstratum est) atque is mos Maiorum paulatim Capevingiorum instituto ad iuridiciale parlamentum (de quo posterius dicemus) traduci coepisset, neque Principes
5 regni facile illi parlamento suas fortunas committendas putarent, Regibus illis ad suas rationes commodissimum fore visum est, praeter illius parlamenti curiam, suum hunc Parium consessum instituere, quae Parium curia vocitata est, quorum tamen ordo ac numerus aliquandiu varius fuit.

10 Neque enim Duodecim viri semper fuerunt, ut eos ipsos a quibus haec monimenta prolata sunt, ariolari video, sed interdum plures, interdum pauciores erant, prout Regi, a quo in summi honoris ac beneficii loco magistratus ille deferebatur, commodum videbatur. Id quod ex infrascriptis monimentis cognoscere
15 licebit, quorum antiquissimum est sub anno 1216, hoc est sub Rege Ludovico Crasso:[32] *Iudicatum est a Paribus Regni nostri, videlicet a Rhemensi Archiepiscopo, Wilel. Lingonen., Guillelmo Cathalaunensi, Ph. Beluacensi, Stephano Noviomensi episcopis, et Odone Duce Burgundiae, et a multis aliis Episcopis et Baronibus*
20 *nostris, videlicet Altisiod., R. Carnot., G. Silvanect. et I. Lexoviensi Episcopis, et Comite Pontivi, R. Comite Drocarum, B. Comite Britanniae, G. Comite S. Pauli, Wil. de rupibus, Senesc. Andeg., Wil. Comite Iuvigniaci, I. Comite Bellimontis, et R. Comite Alencon., nobis audientibus, et iudicium adprobantibus,* etc. Quibus ex verbis
25 cognosci potest, non eosdem fuisse per id tempus Pares Franciae, qui posterioribus temporibus fuerunt, magnamque illorum partem, pro illorum temporum superstitione, Archiepis. et Episcopos fuisse. Nam cum Episcopales sedes iis in locis constituerentur, quibus opima et fructuosa praedia et tanquam satrapiae
30 attributae Regum liberalitate fuerant, facile cum illis opibus superbia Sacerdotum crevit, ac tum praesertim cum sacerdotia et Episcopatus non propter muneris Ecclesiastici functionem, sed propter opum et potentiae magnitudinem ad homines illustri familia natos deferri coepti sunt. Hinc illud Sigeberti sub anno

[32] *Ibid.*, 3, 7, 4; ed. 1621, 330.

times such trials were conducted before the public council of the nation (as we have shown at length above), and since the custom had begun shortly after the institution of the Capetian mayors of the palace of referring jurisdiction to the parlement (on which we shall have something to say later) and the princes of the kingdom were unwilling that their fate should be placed simply at the disposal of the parlement, it seemed to the kings that it would be very much to their own convenience to institute, in addition to the court of the parlement, a special jurisdiction for the peers, which was called the court of peers, whose rank and number, however, changed from time to time.

For there were not always twelve peers, as I see it foolishly stated by those who have cited the records in question. Sometimes there were many and sometimes few, as it might seem convenient to a king who was responsible for awarding that magistracy in place of the highest honour and distinction. It is relevant to quote from the records cited, of which the earliest is for the year 1216 in the reign of Louis the Fat:[32] 'This is the judgment of the peers of our kingdom, to wit the archbishop of Reims, bishops William of Langres, William of Châlons, Philip of Beauvais, and Stephen of Noyon, Odo duke of Burgundy, together with many other bishops and barons, namely the bishops of Auxerre, Chartres, Senlis and Lisieux, the counts of Pontheiu, Dreux, Brittany, Saint-Paul, des Roches, Juvigny, Beaumont, and Alençon, together with the seneschal of Anjou. This judgment was given in our presence and with our approval.' From these words we can ascertain that at that time these were not the same as those peers of France of later ages, and that many of them were archbishops and bishops because of the superstition of the time. For when the episcopal sees were created in these places, and the generosity of the kings had resulted in the distribution of rich and fruitful estates and satrapies, if we may use the term, the pride of the priesthood readily increased with such wealth, and then, especially, clerical benefices began to be handed out to men of high birth, not because they would fulfil the functions of ecclesiastical office but because of the amount of wealth and power it brought them. In this respect we cite the words of Sigebert for the

D:[33] *Collatis a Clodoveo rege multis praediis Ecclesiae Rhemensi, Remigius multa eorum parte data Ecclesiae Laudunensi sedum Episcopatus ibi esse constituit.*

Sed ad Parium institutum redeamus. Nam ex aliis commen-
5 tariis aliud Parium iudicium adversus Petrum Mauclerum, id est, Maledoctum, Armoricae Britanniae principem, his profertur verbis:[34] *Ex anno* MCCXXX. *Galterus Dei gratia Senonensis Archiepiscopus, Galterus eadem gratia Carnotensis et Guillelmus Parisiensis Episcopi, Comes Flandriae, Th. Comes Campaniae, Comes*
10 *Nivernensis, Comes Blesensis, Comes Carnotensis, Comes Montisfortis, Comes Vindocinensis, Comes Rociacae, Matthaeus de Montmorencio Franciae Constabularius, Iohannes Suessionensis, Stephanus de Sacrocaesare, Vicecomes Bellimontis, etc., notum facimus quod nos coram charissimo domino nostro Ludovico Rege Franciae iudicavimus*
15 *unanimiter, quod Petrus quondam Britanniae Comes, propter ea quae eidem domino Regi fors fecerat, Baillium Britanniae per iustitiam amisit, et quod Barones Britanniae et alii qui ei fecerunt fidelitatem vel homagium ratione illius Baillii, sunt penitus absoluti, et quicti ab illa fidelitate et homagio, etc.*
20 Sed aliud insignius profertur, ex anno MCCCXV, sub Rege Ludovico Hutino, ex quo intelligitur, primum quam saepe Parium dignitas variis Principibus attributa sit;* deinde ad illorum iudicia nonnullos insuper alios e Franciae proceribus et satrapis Episcopis adhiberi solitos; postremo in illorum numero
25 interdum etiam Reges ac principes exteros fuisse, siquidem satrapiam aliquam ex iis, quibus Pariatus dignitas attributa fuerat, possidebant. Verba autem illius Commentarii haec sunt;[35] *Nos Pares supradicti ad requestam et mandatum Regis venimus in suam curiam Parisiis, et fecimus et tenuimus curiam cum duodecim aliis*
30 *personis, praelatis, et aliis altis hominibus, Archiepiscopo Rothomagi, Episcopis Briocensi et Macloviensi, Philippo filio Regis Franciae, Comite Pictaviensi, Ludovico Ebroicarum Comite, Carolo Comite Marchiae, Guydone Comite S. Pauli, Gaucherio dom. Castellionis et*

22 c 'fuerit'.

[33] *MGH SS*, VI, 313, 56f.   [34] Choppin, *De dom. Fran.*, 3, 19, 10; ed. 1621, 405.   [35] *Ibid.*, 3, 7, 16; ed. 1621, 337.

year 500:[33] 'King Clovis had bestowed many estates on the church of Reims, and Saint Rémi decided that many of them should be given to the church of Laon and the episcopal seat established there.'

But let us return to the origin of the peers. From the various commentaries the judgment of the peers against Peter Mauclerc or Maledoctus, the ruler of Brittany, may be cited as follows:[34] 'In the year 1230. We, Gautier by the grace of God archbishop of Sens, Gautier by the same grace bishop of Chartres and Guillaume similarly bishop of Paris, the count of Flanders, Thomas count of Champagne, the count of Nevers, the count of Blois, the count of Chartres, the count of Montfort, the count of Vendôme, the count of Roissy, Matthieu de Montmorency constable of France, Jean de Soissons, Etienne de Sancerre, the viscount of Beaumont etc., give notice in the presence of our dearest lord Louis, king of France, that we unanimously judge that Peter, formerly count of Brittany, has justly lost the office of bailiff of Brittany because of the deeds he has committed against the said lord king, and that the barons of Brittany and all others who had pledged him fealty or homage on account of the said office of bailiff are entirely absolved from that said fealty and homage.'

There is a yet more remarkable passage for the year 1315 in the reign of Louis Hutin, from which it can be understood that at first the rank of peers was often bestowed at will upon various princes; that, later, the names of some rather than others of the French nobility and episcopal satraps were customarily added to the judgments; and that in the end there were sometimes foreign kings and princes among the number of peers, if perchance they happened to possess some satrapy among those to which the status of being a peer was attached. Now these are the words of that commentary:[35] 'We the aforesaid peers have assembled at the royal court at Paris at the request and command of the king, and we have established and held a court with twelve other persons, being prelates or men of high rank; the archbishop of Rouen, the bishops of Saint-Brieu and Saint-Maclou, Philip the son of the king of France, the count of Poitiers, Louis count of Evreux, Charles count of Marche, Guy count of Saint-Paul, Gaucher lord of

Portiani, Comestabili Franciae, primogenito Comitis Claromontis,
Io. dom. Claromontis et Carolesii, dom. de Marcueil, et Milone dom.
de Noyers, a nobis electis ad iudicandum nobiscum, tanquam curia
Paribus munita regis auctoritate, qui dixit se non posse plures Pares
5 *habere, quia Dux Aquitaniae, nempe rex Angliae, qui vocatus fuerat,*
se excusavit ob bellum Scotorum, Dux Burgundiae quoque excusavit
se propter certam exoniam, Episco. Novioduni mortuus erat, et
Cathalaunen. Episco. pro certis caussis in carceribus detinebatur, etc.

His insignibus vetustatis testimoniis accedat etiam illud, quod
10 ex commentariis anno MCCCLX prolatum est, unde intelligi
potest, primum quod iam aliquoties diximus, certum quidem ac
definitum Parium numerum fuisse, sed eius arbitrium summum
penes regiam potestatem fuisse, deinde honorem illum non
Patriciatus, ut Budaeus[36] et Budaeum secuti crediderunt, sed
15 *Pariatus* nomine appellatum fuisse, quanquam posterioribus
seculis *Paritatis* quoque et ex Gallicae linguae consuetudine
Perriae nomen illi tributum est. Verba autem illius commentarii
haec sunt:[37] *Et cum huiusmodi Ducatus dignitatis nomine, honorem*
superaddentes honori, parem Franciae ipsum fecimus, statuentes auctori-
20 *tate praedicta ut ipse, quamdiu vixerit in humanis, et dicti eius heredes*
masculi de matrimonio legitimo procreati, post eius obitum Duces
Bituricenses et Arverniae ac Pares Franciae nominentur, omnique
Ducatus et Pariatus honore cum nomine, iure, et quacunque alia
praerogativa laetentur, etc. Eiusdemmodi fere illud diploma est
25 regis Iohann. sub anno 1363, ubi honos ille non *Patriciatus* sed
Pariatus appellatur:[38] *Ducatum Burg. in Pariatu, et quicquid iuris et*
proprietatis habemus in eodem, nec non in Comitatu Burg. ex succes-
sione Philippi ultimi, ducis consanguinei nostri, charissimo Philip.
filio nostro concessimus tenenda et possidenda per eum et heredes suos
30 *in legitimo matrimonio, ex proprio corpore procreandos perpetuo,*
hereditarie, pacifice et quiete.

Sed posterioribus temporibus *Paritatis* et *Perriae* verbum (ut

---

[36] Cf. *Annot.* §Ex lege ultima de Senatoribus; *Opera,* 1557, III, 97.   [37] Choppin,
De dom. Fran., 3, 7, 9; ed. 1621, 333.   [38] *Ibid.,* 2, 11, 7; ed. 1621, 230.

Châtillon and Portian, the constable of France, the eldest son of the count of Clermont, Jean lord of Clermont and Charolais, the lord of Marcueil and Milon, the lord of Noyers. These men have been chosen by us to sit in judgment with us as peers in the court under the protection of the king's authority. The court has declared that it cannot consist of a larger number of peers because the duke of Aquitaine, to wit the king of England, who had been summoned, has made his excuses on account of the Scottish war, and the duke of Burgundy has excused himself because of other business, while the bishop of Noyon has died, and the bishop of Châlons has been held in prison for proven reasons.'

This remarkable evidence from antiquity also confirms the point contained in the commentaries for the year 1360, which indicate, as we have already said several times, that at first there was a fixed and defined number of peers, although the supreme power of deciding it lay with the crown. Moreover that honour was not that of being a patrician, *patriciatus*, as Budé[36] and those who follow Budé believe, but rather it was known by the word *pariatus*, although in later times both the word *pariatus*, and a word derived from Gallic linguistic usage, *perria*, were attributed to it. The actual wording of the commentary is as follows:[37] 'By adding honour to honour we accompanied this ducal title with that of peer of France, laying it down under the aforesaid authority that, as long as he, and after him his male heirs born from legitimate marriage, should survive, they should be named dukes of Berry and Auvergne and peers of France, and should enjoy the status of duke and peer with all title, right and every other prerogative.' To much the same effect is the certificate given by King John in the year 1363, where the honour is called not *patriciatus* but *pariatus*:[38] 'We grant the dukedom of Burgundy as a peerage [*in pariatu*] with whatever right and ownership we have in the same, while not excluding from final succession to the countship of Burgundy our cousin Duke Philip, to our very dear son Philip, to be held and possessed by him and his heirs legitimately procreated from his own body in marriage for ever, in hereditary right, peace and security.'

However, in later times the words *paritas* and *perria* began to be

superius diximus) ex popularis linguae consuetudine usurpari
coepit, ut ex commentariis anni MCCCCXIIII cognosci potest,
in quibus ita scriptum est:³⁹ *Eundem Iohannem consanguineum*
nostrum ampliori volentes fulgere dignitate, et Comitis titulum supra-
5 *dictum in maiorem excelsioremque mutantes, dictum Iohannem con-*
sanguineum nostrum, in Ducem tenore praesentium sublimamus, dic-
tumque Comitatum Alenconii erigimus in Ducatum, volentes ut prae-
dictus Ducatus in Perria seu Paritate nobis teneatur, sub forma tamen
et modis quibus antea idem Iohannes saepedictum tenebat Comitatum.
10   Atque haec quidem ex Commentariis Gallicis, ut dixi, prolata sunt, in quibus illud quoque notatione dignum est, quod dici
et commemorari video, sed tamen sine teste, cum Dux Armoricus
laesae maiestatis reus factus esset, magnopere quaesitum, a
quibus iudicium illud exerceretur, ac tandem cum Philippus
15 Audax Burgundus idem ex Rege quaesisset, Regem de consilii
sententia pronunciasse, Parem nonnisi in Parium iudicium
adduci posse, VI Non. Mart. ann. MCCCLXXXVI,⁴⁰ ac rursus
Regi Carolo septimo quaerenti a Senatu Parisiensi, apud quos
Pares rei capitalis rei fieri possent, idem responsum ᶜfuisse, ᵇXII
20 Kal. Maii, anno MCCCCLVIII,⁴¹ quod (ut superius dictum
est*) iuri feudali ᶜplane ᵇconsentaneum est. ᵃSed iam tempus
est ad institutum nostrum redire.

---

³⁹ *Ibid.*, 3, 7, 14; ed. 1621, 336.   ⁴⁰ *Ibid.*, 3, 7, 15; ed. 1621, 336–7; Hotman
miscopied the date as MCCCXXXVI.   ⁴¹ *Ibid.*, immediately following.

adopted from the vulgar tongue (as we have said above), as can be
seen in the commentaries for the year 1414, where this passage
occurs:[39] 'Wishing to enhance the said John our cousin with
greater honour, and transforming the aforesaid title of count to
one that is more excellent, we hereby raise the said John our cousin
to be duke under the conditions here stipulated, and we elevate the
said county of Alençon to be a dukedom, desiring that the aforesaid dukedom may be held from us as a peerage [*in Perria seu
Paritate*] in the form and mode, however, in which the same aforesaid John formerly held the county.'

These examples are set forth in the French commentaries, as
I have said, and there is also one among them worth remarking
which seems to be stated and recounted, although without
corroboration. Since the duke of Brittany was declared a traitor,
it may well be asked by whom that trial was really conducted, and,
when at length Philip the Bold of Burgundy asked this question
of the king, the king declared in terms of the opinion of the council
that a peer could not be accused save by the judgment of the
peers (declaration of 2 March 1386).[40] Again, the question was
addressed to King Charles VII by the Parisian senate [the parlement],
before whom the peers could be indicted of a capital offence, and
the reply ᶜwas ᵇmade on 20 April 1458[41] that (as it is said* above)
the practice was ᶜentirely ᵇacceptable under feudal law. ᵃBut now
it is time to return to our main topic.

* ᶜ we have said.

^aCAPUT XV [^cXVIII]

De continuata sacrosancti concilii auctoritate
sub Carlovingiorum regno

Cuiusmodi regnantibus Merovingiis Reipublicae nostrae forma
fuerit, quantaque Concilii publici auctoritas, satis iam explicatum arbitramur, nunc consequens est, ut qualis sub Carlo-
vingiis fuerit, exponamus. Quantum enim ex omnibus et nostris
5 et Germanicis historiis existimare licet, eadem prorsus Ordinum,
sive Statuum auctoritas conservata est, ut non penes Pipinum
aut Carolum, aut Ludovicum, sed penes Regiam maiestatem
summum rerum omnium iudicium arbitriumque esset, cuius
Maiestatis veram propriamque sedem ^csummo multarum
10 aetatum consensu ^ain solenni concilio fuisse, superius demonstravimus.

Huius autem rei documento est, primum, ^bRegino lib.
Chron. 2, sub anno DCCCVI, ubi de Carolo Magno loquens:[1]
Imperator, inquit, *cum primoribus et optimatibus Francorum, de pace*
15 *constituenda et conservanda inter filios suos et de partitione regni*
placitum habuit. Et mox:[2] *De hac divisione testamentum interposi-*
tum fecit, quod per sacramentum a Francis confirmatum est. ^aEguin-
arthus,* in eo quem aliquoties iam laudavimus libello, ubi cum
ea quae post Pipini mortem acciderunt exponit, ita loquitur:[3]
20 *Franci siquidem facto solenniter generali conventu ambos sibi Reges*
constituunt, ea conditione praemissa, ut totum regni corpus ex aequo
partirentur, et Carolus eam partem quam pater eorum Pipinus
tenuerat, Carolomannus vero eam cui patruus eorum Carolomannus
praeerat, regendi gratia susciperet, etc.
25 Quibus ex verbis facile intellectu* est, quam potestatem antea

---

18 *bc* 'Eiusmodi est Eguinarthi testimonium, in eo...etc.'.   **25** 'facile intellectu': *c* 'perspicuum'.

[1] *MGH SS*, I, 563, 64ff.   [2] *Ibid.*, 70ff.   [3] C. 3; *MGH SS*, II, 445, 2–5.

^aCHAPTER XV [^cXVIII]

The continued authority of the sacred council under the Carolingians

---

We believe we have said enough to explain both the form of the commonwealth under the Merovingian kings and the extent of the authority of the public council. It follows that we should now explain its nature under the Carolingians. From all our own historians, and the German historians also, it is quite evident that the same authority of the orders or estates was entirely preserved, and that the ultimate judgment and decision on all issues rested not with Pepin or Charles or Louis but with the royal majesty. As we have shown earlier, the true and proper seat of this majesty lay in the solemn council, ^cand this arrangement bore the unvaried consent of many generations.

^bThe first proof of this is contained in Regino's chronicle under the year 806, where the author refers to Charlemagne.[1] 'The emperor', he writes, 'held an assembly of the chief men and nobility of the Franks for the purpose of creating and preserving peace among his sons and of partitioning the kingdom.' A little further on he states:[2] 'He made an addition to his will about this partition, which was confirmed by an oath taken by the Franks.' ^aIn that work which we have praised several times already, Einhard explains* what happened after the death of Pepin in these terms:[3] 'The Franks solemnly convened their general assembly and appointed both his sons as their kings, on the condition that the whole body of the kingdom should be divided and that Charles should rule that part of it which their father Pepin had held, while Carloman should acquire the part controlled by their uncle Carloman.'

It is easy to conclude† from these words that the power which the

---

* *bc sentence begins* Evidence to the same effect is provided by Einhard who explains in that work... † *c* easy to conclude *becomes* clear.

trecentis paulo minus annis sub Merovingiis Regni ordines
habuerant, eandem post illius interitum sibi retinuisse, ut
quamvis defuncti Regis filii extarent, tamen non tam hereditario
iure, quam ordinum iudicio et voluntate ad Regnum per-
5 venirent. *b*Itaque si Regis filius impubes relictus erat, Tutor ei in
populi comitiis creabatur. Aimoin. lib. 5, cap. 42:[4] *Ludovico,
inquit, diem suum obeunte, Carolus filius eius, qui Simplex postea
dictus est, in cunis aevum agens patre orbatus remansit. Cuius
aetatem Franciae primores incongruam (ut erat) exercendae domina-
10 tioni arbitrati, consilium de summis ineunt rebus. Ibi Odonem Franci,
Burgundi Aquitaniensesque proceres congregati in unum, tutorem
Caroli pueri, regnique elegere gubernatorem.*

*a*Iam vero cetera quoque maiora Regni negotia ad illud idem
Concilium referri solita, testimonio est *b*Regino lib. Chr. 2:[5]
15 *Anno, inquit, DCCLXIII Rex Pipinus habuit placitum suum in
Nivernis.* Et mox, Anno 764:[*6] *rex Pipinus habuit placitum suum
in Wormacia.* Item anno 765:[*7] *Rex Pipinus habuit placitum suum
apud Attiniacum.* Et mox:[8] *Habuit placitum suum in Aurelianis
civitate.* Sed et *a*Aimoinus lib. 4, cap. 71, ubi de Saxonum bello
20 loquitur:[9] *Rex, inquit, prima veris aspirante temperie, Novio-
magum profectus est, et ad locum, qui Padabruno vocatur, generalem
populi sui conventum habiturus cum ingenti exercitu in Saxoniam profectus est.* Et rursus cap. 77:[10] *Transacta tandem hyeme publicum
populi sui conventum in loco qui Padabruno vocatur, more solenni
25 habuit.* Item cap. 79:[11] *Et cum uxorem suam Wormaciae invenisset,
generalem populi sui conventum ibi habere statuit.*

Quo loco et aliis superioribus perpetuo de Carolo Rege
loquitur, qui cum Europae fere totius Regnum magnis suis
rebus gestis adeptus esset, Magnique cognomentum gentium
30 omnium consensu consecutus, Francis tamen pristinum illud
suum ius ac libertatem eripere non potuit, ac ne conatus quidem

16 *bc* '864'.   **17** *bc* '866'.

[4] v: 41[2] (i.e., 2nd of 2 chaps. No. 41); ed. 1567, 727.   [5] *MGH SS*, 1, 557, 34ff.
[6] An. 764; *ibid.*, 45ff.   [7] *Ibid.*, 49ff.   [8] An. 766; *ibid.*, 54ff.   [9] Ed. 1567, 424.
[10] *Ibid.*, 436.   [11] *Ibid.*, 440.

estates of the kingdom had held under the Merovingians for nearly three hundred years was still retained by them after the fall of the Merovingians. Thus, although the late king left sons behind him, these did not attain the throne so much by hereditary right as by the choice and will of the estates. *b*In the same way, if the surviving son of a king was under age, a regent was appointed for him through the assembly of the people. Thus Aimon writes:[4] 'When Louis [Louis the Stammerer] met his death, his son Charles, who was later called the Simple, was bereaved while still in the womb. The chief men considered that such an age was too young to govern (as, indeed, it was!), and took counsel on matters of state. The nobles of France, Burgundy and Aquitaine met together in one body, and there chose Odo [Eudes] as the guardian of the boy Charles and the governor of the kingdom.'

*a*Indeed, there were also other major matters of state which were customarily referred to that same council. There is proof of this *b*in Regino's chronicle where he writes:[5] 'In the year 763 King Pepin held his assembly at Nevers.' In a following passage, for the year 764,* he states:[6] 'King Pepin held his assembly at Worms.' For the year 765† he says:[7] 'King Pepin held his assembly at Attigny.' Later he remarks:[8] 'He held his assembly in the city of Orléans.' *a*In his account of the Saxon war Aimon writes:[9] 'At the first breath of spring the king set out for Noyon, and, as he was to hold a general assembly of his people at a place called Paderborn, he marched into Saxony with a vast army.' Another passage contains these words:[10] 'According to the solemn custom, when winter was over he held the general assembly of his people at a place called Paderborn.' Aimon gives a further instance in a later chapter:[11] 'Since he had met his wife at Worms, he decided to hold there a general assembly of his people.'

In this and the other passages cited Aimon is constantly referring to that King Charles who, through his great deeds, had acquired nearly all Europe as his kingdom, and who by the consent of all peoples has consequently been named 'the Great'. Yet Charlemagne was unable to deprive the Franks of their pristine right and

* *bc* 864. † *bc* 866.

unquam est, maiorem ullam rem sine populi iudicio et optimatum auctoritate suscipere. Iam vero post Caroli Magni e vita
excessum, non dubium est, quin Ludovicus eius filius eadem
conditione Regnum administrarit. Nam Appendix Aimoini
5 lib. 5, cap. 10:[12] *Mortuo*, inquit, *Carolo Ludovicus Imperator con-*
cilium populi generale quasi quodam indixerat praesagio, in loco
Theotuadi. Rursus cap. 38, ubi pactionem pacis commemorat
factae inter Ludovicum Regem, et Ludovicum ipsius conso-
brinum:[13] *Condixerunt*, inquit, *placitum, et in ipso placito haec*
10 *quae sequuntur inter eos consensu fidelium suorum servanda con-*
venerunt, in quo placito communi consensu inventum est, ut
ipsi Reges redirent cum scara, etc. Item cap. 41, ubi de Carolomanno Ludovici Balbi filio loquitur:[14] *Et sic*, inquit, *reversus*
Wormaciam placitum suum Kal. Novemb. habiturus a Nortmannis
15 *recessit.* Item cap. seq., ubi de Carolo Simplice loquitur:[15]
Cuius aetatem, inquit, *Franciae primores incongruam exercendae*
*dominationi arbitrati, consilium de summis ineunt rebus.**

ᵇItem auctor Annalium Rhemensium, sub anno DCCCC-
XXXV:[16]*Hoc Rege Rudolpho Laudani degente tumultus ipso die*
20 *sancti Paschae inter Regios et Episcopi milites exoritur; ubi nonnulli non*
*modo laici, verum etiam clerici vulnerati, vel*interempti. Unde Rex pla-*
citum Suessionis cum Regni primatibus habuit. Sed multo planius sub
anno DCCCCXLVI, cum de Rege in Regnum restituendo ageretur:[17] *Edmundus*, inquit, *Anglorum Rex legatos ad Hugonem prin-*
25 *cipem pro restitutione Ludovici Regis dirigit, et idem princeps proinde*
conventus publicos cum nepotibus suis aliisque regni primatibus agit.
Et paulo post:[18] *Hugo Dux Francorum ascito secum Hugone filio*
Richardi, ceterisque regni primatibus, Ludovicum Regem, qui fere per
annum sub custodia detinebatur in regnum restituit. Quin ne illud qui-

---

17 *bc* omit this whole sentence, 'Item...*rebus*'.   **21** *c* 'et'.

[12] *Ibid.*, 573.   [13] *Ibid.*, 708.   [14] v, 41¹ (see above, p. 392, n. 4); *ed. cit.*, 724.
[15] v, 41² (see above, p. 392, n. 4); *ed. cit.*, 727.   [16] Frodoard, A.D. 935;
Bouquet, VIII, 190A.   [17] *Ibid.*, A.D. 946; *ed. cit.*, 200A.   [18] *Ibid.*

liberty, nor did he ever undertake any matter of importance without first obtaining the view of the people and the authority of the nobility. Moreover, it is certain that, when Charlemagne had departed this life, his son, Louis, administered the kingdom on the same conditions. In the appendix to Aimon it is stated:[12] 'At the time of the death of Charles the emperor, Louis, acting as if by a kind of presentiment, had convened a general council at Theotuade.' Again, in the context where the peace made between King Louis and his cousin of the same name is recorded, the author writes:[13] 'They summoned an assembly and there, with the consent of their followers, they agreed to keep the terms which follow.' In this assembly it was devised by common consent that the kings themselves should be accompanied by a guard to watch over them. Another example occurs in a passage where Carloman, the son of Louis the Stammerer, is discussed:[14] 'Thus he left Normandy to return to Worms where his assembly was to be held on 1 November.' Again in the following chapter there is a relevant passage referring to Charles the Simple:[15] 'The chief men of France thought him too young to rule, and took counsel on matters of state.'*

*b*Another reference occurs in the annals of Reims for the year 935:[16] 'While King Rudolph was at Laon a riot occurred there on Easter day itself between the royal troops and the soldiers of the bishop, and in the course of this tumult some priests as well as laymen were wounded or killed. On this account the king held an assembly of the nobility of the kingdom at Soissons.' A much clearer example is given for the year 946, when the issue at stake was the restoration of the king to the kingdom:[17] 'The English king, Edmund,' states the writer, 'sent envoys to Prince Hugh about the restitution of King Louis [Louis IV], and the prince accordingly convoked public assemblies with his nephews and other leading men of the kingdom.' A little further on he writes:[18] 'With the approval of Hugh, the son of Richard, and other leading men of the kingdom, Hugh, the duke of the Franks, restored King Louis to his kingdom after he had been kept in custody for nearly a year.' Let us also cite a

* *bc* omit this sentence.

dem praetermittendum est, quod eorumdem Annalium auctor
PLACITUM REGALE hoc publicum Gentis Concilium appellat,
veluti sub anno 961:¹⁹ *Otto filius Hugonis quondam Principis ad*
Regem Lotharium in ipsis festi paschalis diebus Laudunum venit; sed
5 *et a nonnullis tam Franciae quam Burgundiae PLACITUM REGALE,*
diversorumque conventus principum Suessionis habetur; ad quod
impediendum (si fieri potest) Richardus filius Wilhelmi Nortmanni
accedens, a fidelibus Regis quibusdam pervasus, et interemptis
suorum nonnullis in fugam conversus est.

10   ᵃSed singula testimonia persequi laboris esset infiniti, et, ut
opinor, supervacanei. Nam ex iisquae usque adhuc protulimus
patere cuivis arbitramur, iudicium arbitriumque summae Reipublicae usque ad Carolum Simplicem, hoc est, per annos
amplius quingentos et quinquaginta penes populi comitia, et (ut
15 nunc loquimur) ᶜstatuum sive ᵃOrdinum conventum fuisse,
idque maiorum nostrorum institutum pro sacrosancto habitum
tot seculis fuisse, ut iam Scriptorum quorundam recentium satis
admirari iudicium non possim, quos non est puditum, suis in
libellis tradere, Concilii publici institutum Pipino Regi accepto
20 ferendum esse, cum Eguinarthus,²⁰ Caroli Magni Cancellarius
ita* dilucide testetur, Merovingiorum omnium institutum fuisse,
ut quotannis Kalend. Maii publicum populi sui conventum*
agerent, ad eumque conventum carpento bobus tracto veherentur.

---

21 ᶜ 'tam'.   **22** ᶜ¹ omits 'conventum'.

¹⁹ *Ibid.*, A.D. 961; *ed. cit..* 212B.   ²⁰ Cf. c. 1; *MGH SS*, II, 444, 11–15 –
although the Kalends of May are not mentioned by Einhard, but by Hunibaldus
(see above, ch. XIII, n. 2 [p. 324]).

passage under the year 961, so that nothing concerning what the author of these annals calls the *placitum regale*, or public council of the people, may be omitted:[19] 'Odo, the son of the late Prince Hugh, came to King Louis at Laon during the period of Easter. There were some from both France and Burgundy who desired a *placitum regale*, and an assembly of various princes was held at Soissons. Richard, the son of William the Norman, was marching against this obstacle to his plans (if the assembly can be so described) when his force was surrounded by certain supporters of the king, and, after some of his men had been slain, he turned and fled.'

*a*But it would be an endless task, and, in my view, a superfluous one, to cite every relevant passage. For we believe it is obvious to anyone, from the examples we have so far offered, that until Charles the Simple, that is for more than five hundred and fifty years, the judgment and decision on great matters of state rested with the assembly of the people, or (as we now say) with the assembly of *c*the estates or *a*orders, and that this institution of our ancestors was held as something sacrosanct over so vast a tract of time. Hence I cannot marvel enough at the opinion of those recent writers who have had the effrontery to state in their books that the public council was first instituted through King Pepin, especially since Einhard,[20] Charlemagne's chancellor, shows so decisively that it was the practice of all the Merovingians to hold the public assembly of their people on 1 May every year, and to proceed to that assembly upon a waggon drawn by oxen.

^cCAPUT XIX [^{ab}XV cont.]

De summa inter regem et regnum differentia

^aSed* ut maiore in argumento operam ponamus, atque in illo instituto maiorum nostrorum sapientiam, tanquam in speculo contemplemur, an non ^cex iis quae hactenus dicta sunt ^aperspicuum est, quantam illi inter Regem et Regnum differentiam
5 ostenderint?* Etenim sic se res habet: Rex, princeps est unicus ac singularis, ^bac tanquam caput Reipublicae; ^aRegnum vero ipsa civium ac subiectorum universitas, ^bet quasi corpus Reipublicae, ^aquam distinctionem Iurisconsulti quoque observant. Nam Perduellem Ulpianus definit,[1] *qui hostili animo adversus Rem-*
10 *publicam vel Principem animatus est.* ^cItem in Instit. tit. ult.:[2] *lex Iulia maiestatis in eos qui contra Imperatorem vel Rempublicam aliquid moliti sunt, vigorem suum ostendit.* ^bPaulus lib. Sent. 5:[3] *Qui de salute Principis, vel de summa Reipublicae vaticinatores consulit, cum eo qui responderit, capite punitur.* ^aEt* in legibus Saxonicis titulo 3 :[4]
15 *Qui in Regnum, vel in Regem Francorum consiliatus fuerit, capite punitur.*

Rursus* Rex eandem cum Regno rationem habet, quam Pater cum familia; Tutor, cum pupillo; Curator, cum adolescente; Gubernator, cum navigante ^cet vectoribus onusta ^anavem*;
20 ^cpastor cum grege; ^aImperator, cum exercitu. Ut igitur non pupillus tutoris, non navis gubernatoris, ^cnon grex pastoris, ^anon exercitus imperatoris, sed contra hi caussa illorum instituti sunt, ita non populus Regis, sed Rex populi caussa, quaesitus ac

---

1 ^c'Verum'.   **5** ^c'constituerint'.   **14** ^{bc}'Sic'.   **17** ^c'Praeterea'.
19 ^c'nave'.

[1] *Dig.* 48, 4, 11; Mommsen, I, 845.   [2] *Inst.* 4, 18, 3; Krueger, I, 55.   [3] Julius
Paulus, *Sent. lib.*, 5; ed. 1566, 661.   [4] Tit. 3, §1; ed. 1557, 123.

^cCHAPTER XIX [^{ab}XV cont.]

The main difference between the king and the kingdom

---

^aHowever,* let us pose an issue of greater consequence to our theme, and contemplate the wisdom of our ancestors as reflected in this institution. ^cFrom all that has been said so far, ^ais it not clear that they made† a great distinction between the king and the kingdom? For the matter is so disposed that the king is a unique and individual person in so far as he is the ruler, ^band he is, as it were, the head of the commonwealth; ^awhereas the kingdom is the very totality of the citizens and subjects, ^band is, so to speak, the body of the commonwealth. ^aThis is a distinction which is also noted by the jurists, for Ulpian defines a public enemy[1] as one 'who is moved by hostile intent against either the commonwealth or the prince'. ^cIn the last title of the *Institutes* it is stated:[2] 'The Julian law of treason displays its vigour against those who undertake anything against the emperor or the commonwealth.' ^bThe fifth book of Julius Paulus' judgments reads:[3] 'He who consults soothsayers about the health of the prince or about great matters of state shall be punished by death, together with any man who shall offer him counsel.' ^aAnd‡ among the laws of the Saxons it is said:[4] 'He who takes counsel against the kingdom or against the king of the Franks shall be punished by death.'

Moreover, the king has the same relationship with the kingdom as a father with his family, a tutor with his student, a guardian with his ward, a pilot with the passengers ^cand travellers ^aon a ship, ^cthe pastor with his flock, ^aand a commander with his army. Therefore, just as the pupil is not created for his tutor, nor the ship for the pilot, ^cnor the flock for the pastor, ^anor the army for the commander, but, on the contrary, all these latter are appointed for the former, so the people are not found and procured for the sake of

---

* ^c Indeed.   † ^c established.   ‡ ^{bc} Thus.

repertus est. Potest enim populus sine Rege esse, ut* qui opti-
matum aut suo ipsius consilio paret, ^bitemque in interregno. ^aAt
sine populo ne fingi quidem cogitando Rex potest, ^cnon magis
quam pastor sine grege. *Quamobrem* (inquit apud Xenophontem
5 Socrates ἀπομν. γ.⁵) *existimas Homerum appellasse Agamemnonem*
ποιμένα λαῶν? (id est pastorem populorum) *an non ideo, quia
sicuti pastor curare debet, ut oves suae sint incolumes, neque iis quicquam desit, ita Regis officium est, curare ut sui cives beati ac fortunati
sint.*

10   ^aAge, ceteras differentias videamus. Rex aeque ut quivis
privatus mortalis est, Regnum perpetuum et certe (vel ominis
caussa) immortale, ut ^bIsocrates in Oratione de pace,⁶ de Civitatibus ^clocutus est, ^aIurisconsulti ^bautem ^ade collegiis et uni-
versitatibus loquuntur:* Rex mentis errore, insaniaque affici
15 potest, ut noster Carolus VI qui ^ctemere ^aRegnum suum Anglis
donavit, neque ulli sunt homines, qui facilius voluptatum blandi-
mentis* ^cet muliercularum illecebris infatuentur, atque adeo ^ade
statu mentis deturbentur.* At regnum suam habet in suis Seniori-
bus ^bet Optimatibus ^aet usu rerum peritis propriam certamque,
20 tanquam in capite civitatis, sapientiam. Rex uno praelio, uno
inquam die, vinci, capi etiam, atque in hostium ^cpotestatem
cadere, et vinctus in eorum ^afines abduci potest, quod in Ludovico Sancto, et Iohanne et Francisco primo, usuvenisse nemo
ignorat. Regnum amisso Rege incolume tamen manet continuo-
25 que tanto* accepto incommodo ^crepente publicum ^aConcilium
indicitur, primores conveniunt, et ^bcommuni consilio ^aprae-
sentibus incommodis remedium ^cac subsidium ^aquaerunt, quod
etiam illis casibus factum constat.

     Rex vel ob aetatis infirmitatem, vel ob ingenii levitatem, non
30 modo ab uno et altero consiliario avaro, rapaci, libidinoso, non
modo a lascivis aliquot* adolescentibus aequalibus induci ac

---

1 *bc* 'veluti'.   14 *cc*² omit 'loquuntur'; *c*¹ substitutes for it 'Eo accedit quod'.
17 *bc* 'blanditiis'.   18 *c*¹ omits 'neque ulli...mentis deturbentur'.   25 'con-
tinuoque tanto': *c* 'tantoque'.   31 'a lascivis aliquot': *c*¹ 'ab'.

5 *Memorabilia*, III, 2, 1–3; Loeb, *Xenophon*, IV, 174. The last words, 'ut sui cives
beati ac fortunati sunt', are added by Hotman.   6 §120 (πόλεις διὰ τὴν
ἀθανασίαν ὑπομένουσι); Loeb, II, 82.

the king, but rather the king for the people. For there may be a people without a king, who may obey the counsel of the nobility or of themselves, *b*as they do during an interregnum. *a*But the idea of a king without a people is *c*as *a*inconceivable as a pastor without a flock. 'Why', asked Socrates of Xenophon in the *Memorabilia*,5 'do you think Homer called Agamemnon "pastor of the people" if it were not because, just as the shepherd should take care to see that his sheep are unharmed, and just as he does not fail them in anything, so should the office of a king be such that he promotes the happiness and good fortune of his citizens.'

*a*And we may take note of other differences. A king, like any private man, is mortal; a kingdom is everlasting and known (or foretold) to be immortal, as *b*Isocrates *c*said *b*of states in his oration on peace.6 *a*The jurists, *b*moreover, *a*speak in these terms regarding collegiate bodies and corporations. A king may be simple-minded or afflicted with insanity, as was our Charles VI, who *c*rashly *a*gave away his kingdom to the English. Nor is anyone more easily *c*infatuated *a*by the pleasures of the flesh *c*and the allurements of women, so that *a*the balance of the mind becomes disturbed.* But a kingdom has its true and certain source of wisdom in its senators *b*and nobility, *a*who are experienced in the conduct of affairs and who form, so to speak, the head of the state. A king can be conquered in a single battle – indeed in a single day – or he can be captured by enemies and *c*fall within their power *a*and be taken *c*in chains *a*to their territory. As everyone knows, this was what happened to Saint Louis, to John and to Francis I. But, although a kingdom has lost its king, it may remain unimpaired when, as soon as the news of such a disaster is received, a *c*public *a*council is *c*immediately *a*summoned, and the leading men meet together *b*jointly *a*to seek a remedy and find reserve forces to meet existing problems. And this is exactly what was done in the instances mentioned.

Because of the infirmity of his age or the levity of his character, a king may be seduced and depraved by any greedy, rapacious and libidinous counsellor, or by some lascivious† youths of his own age,

* *c*1 *omits preceding sentence.*   † *c*1 *omits some lascivious.*

depravari potest, verumetiam a muliercula infatuari, sic ut omnem prope administrandi regni potestatem ei committat; cuius mali exempla quam saepe acciderint, pauci, ut opinor, ^cin nostris Annalibus versati ^aignorant. At Regnum, Seniorum
5 suorum consilio et sapientia, perpetuo fretum est. Salomon sapientissimus, tamen a mulierculis, etiam in summa senectute corruptus est; Roboamus ab adolescentibus; Ninus a matre Semiramide; Ptolemaeus, Auletes cognomento dictus, a tibicinibus et citharoedis. Maiores nostri Regibus suis privatos suos consili-
10 arios, qui privata ipsorum negotia curarent, reliquerunt. Seniores, qui Rempublicam administrarent, et in commune consulerent, Regique administrandi Regni rationem ostenderent, ad conventum publicum reservarunt. Anno MCCCLVI, cum Rege Iohanne capto ab Anglis, et in Angliam abducto, publicum
15 Regni Concilium Lutetiae haberetur, eoque nonnulli ex Regis consiliariis convenissent; iussi sunt e conventu exire,* denuntiatumque illis fuit, publici Concilii delectos non amplius conventuros, si ad* ^caugustum ^aillud Regni sacrarium adire pergerent;* cuius rei testimonium extat in Magno Chronico
20 Gallice scripto vol. 2, sub Rege Iohanne, fol. 169.[7]

Neque vero ulla unquam aetas fuit, quae non perspicuam* illam ^catque animadvertendam ^ainter Regem et Regnum differentiam notaret. Rex Lacedaemoniorum (ut Xenophon testatur) et Ephori ^cqui tanquam custodes et observatores ipsius
25 erant, ^asingulis mensibus ^biureiurando fidem ^ainter se iurabant:* Rex, se ex legum praescripto regnaturum; Ephori, se Regium dominatum conservaturos, si ^cmodo ^aipse iusiurandum servasset. Cicero in epist. ad Brutum:[8] *Scis mihi semper placuisse, non Rege solum, sed Regno liberari Rempublicam.* Idem lib. de legibus
30 3:[9] *Sed quoniam Regale Civitatis genus probatum quondam, postea non tam Regni quam Regis vitiis repudiatum est, nomen videbitur*

---

16 *c* 'excedere'.   **18** 'si ad': *bc* 'nisi illi ad'.   **19** *bc* 'desinerent'.   **21** *c* 'certam'.   **25** *bc* 'dabant'.

[7] *Grandes chroniques*; cf. ed. 1514, II, fol. 169.   [8] II, v, 1; ed. Purser, 1902, vol. III.   [9] III, vii, 15; Loeb, 476.

and he may equally well be captivated by some young woman, so that he may pass over nearly all the authority to rule the kingdom to such a person. I should imagine that few ^cwho are versed in our annals ^aare unaware of the many occasions when this evil has occurred. But a kingdom always relies upon the advice and wisdom of its senators. Solomon, the wisest of men, was nonetheless seduced even in his old age by young girls, Rehoboam by young men, Ninus by his mother Semiramis, Ptolemy, named the Piper, by flute-players and harpers. Our ancestors left to their kings the choice of their own private counsellors who looked after their private affairs. The choice of the senators who administered the commonwealth, took counsel in common and showed the king how to govern the kingdom, was reserved to the public council. In the year 1356, when King John was taken by the English and led captive into England, a public council of the kingdom was held in Paris. When some of the king's counsellors appeared there, they were ordered to leave the assembly and were informed that the delegates to the public council would no longer meet if the counsellors continued* to attend that ^caugust ^ashrine of the kingdom. The evidence for this is in the *Great Chronicle*, written in French, in the volume concerning King John.[7]

There has never been any age when that clear† ^cand observable ^adifference between the king and the kingdom was not remarked. As Xenophon bears witness, the king of the Spartans and the ephors, ^cwho were, so to speak, the king's guardians and overseers, ^apledged ^bfaith ^ato each other ^bby a solemn oath ^aevery month. The king swore that he would rule according to the written form of the laws, and the ephors that they would preserve the royal government if, ^cand only if, ^athe king would keep his oath. In his letter to Brutus Cicero says:[8] 'You know that I have always wished our commonwealth to be delivered from both king and kingship.' In his book *Of the Laws* he writes:[9] 'Because the regal form of state was once accepted, and later it was repudiated for the faults of the king rather than the kingship, it may seem that only the title of

---

* **bc** continued *becomes* did not cease.   † **bc** certain.

tantum Regis repudiatum, etc. *^b*Idem Philipp. II :[10] *Si enim affuissem, non solum Regem, sed etiam regnum de Republica sustulissem.*

Sed eius differentiae nullum nobis planius Maiores nostri documentum reliquerunt, quam in Magistratuum iure et appellatione; nam qui a Rege dignitatem aliquam in Regia obtinent, et Regis ministri appellantur, et eo vel mortuo vel abdicato, ^crepente *^b*dignitatem amittunt, Regis denique arbitrio sua illis dignitas, quasi precario tantum concessa, adimitur. Eiusmodi* sunt, qui vulgo Magistri Hospitii REGIS appellantur, et Camerarii REGIS et ^cMagnus venator Regis et *^b*alii aulae regiae officiales. At qui regni et Reipublicae universae magistratus erant, eos Maiores nostri ^cadiecto *^b*amplissimo FRANCIAE nomine designarunt, quem morem etiam nunc retinemus, ut cum dicimus Comestabulum FRANCIAE, Amiralium FRANCIAE, Cancellarium FRANCIAE, et cum antiquitus non a Rege, sed a populo eas dignitates acciperent, neque ipsius morte aut mutatione desinebant, neque ipsius arbitrio abdicabantur. Itaque ne nunc quidem ii* quos vulgus CORONAE OFFICIALES appellat, Rege mortuo magistratus esse desinunt, neque iis adimi dignitas, nisi cum vita, hoc est, nisi rei capitalis damnatis potest.

Quin ne illud quidem summae populi potestatis argumentum praetermittendum est, quod quibus tribus in rebus Reipublicae summa consistit, re militari, iurisdictione, et aerario, iis rebus qui cum summo imperio praefecti sunt, non a Rege, sed a Regno et Francia denominantur; nam, ^cut modo diximus *^b*is ad quem rei militaris summa pertinet, Comestabulus, aut Marescallus, aut (ut Sigebertus testatur[11]) Seneschallus FRANCIAE dicitur; qui vero classi et maritimis copiis praeest, Amiralius FRANCIAE; qui iurisdictioni, Cancellarius FRANCIAE; qui tributis et aerario, Quaestor generalis FRANCIAE.

---

8 *c* 'Cuiusmodi'.   18 'ii': *c* 'magistratus illi summi'.

[10] *Philip.* II, xiv, 34; Loeb, 98.   [11] *Roberti de Monte cronica,* A.D. 1169; *MGH SS,* VI, 518, 9. Hotman had it from *Ger. rer. quat. chron.,* 1566, 161, where it appears as Sigebert, A.D. 1170.

king was rejected, etc.' *b*Again, in his *Second Philippic* Cicero states:[10] 'For had I been present, I should have got rid of kingship as well as the king from the commonwealth.'

But our ancestors left us no clearer proof of that difference than in the law and title of the magistracy. For those who acquire some royal dignity from a king are called his servants or ministers, and if the king should die or be deposed they *c*immediately *b*lose that dignity. Finally, their dignity may be taken away from them at the king's choice, as if it were a thing granted upon request. Among officials of this kind are those commonly called the master of the king's household, the king's chamberlain *c*and the king's master of the chase, *b*together with other officials of the royal palace. But our ancestors designated those who were magistrates of the kingdom and the entire commonwealth by adding to their titles the far more splendid phrase 'OF FRANCE', and this is a custom we retain even today. Thus we speak of the constableship OF FRANCE, the admiralcy OF FRANCE, the chancellorship OF FRANCE. In ancient times these dignities were awarded not by the king but by the people, and hence they did not lapse at the king's death or at some alteration in the affairs of state, nor were their holders dismissed at the king's pleasure. And so today those* who are commonly called OFFICIALS OF THE CROWN do not cease to be magistrates at the death of the king. Nor can they be deprived of their office in their lifetime unless they are convicted of a capital crime.

Lest any aspect of the supreme authority of the people be overlooked, let us note that in the three spheres of government, the military, the legal and the financial, those officers who are given supreme authority in these affairs are named not by the king but by the kingdom of France. For, *c*as we have said, *b*he to whom authority in military matters belongs is called the constable OF FRANCE, or the marshal OF FRANCE, or (as Sigebert testifies[11]) the seneschal OF FRANCE; he who has authority in the law is the chancellor OF FRANCE; and he who controls the taxes and the treasury is the superintendent-general OF FRANCE.

* *c* those *becomes* those supreme magistrates.

De Capevingiorum familia, et regno
Francogalliae in illam translato

Demonstratum est superius, Regnum Francogalliae his mille
ducentis annis in tribus tantum familiarum nominibus versatum
esse, quarum prima Merovingia, altera Carolovingia, ex auctorum et capitum nominibus appellata est. Nam etsi non haere-
5 ditate (ut iam saepe docuimus) sed Concilii iudicio Regni
successio deferretur, libenter tamen Franci Germanorum suorum institutum retinebant, ut *Reges ex nobilitate* (quemadmodum
Tacitus loquitur[1]) *Duces ex virtute sumerent*, ac plerumque Reges
eos sibi deligerent, qui Regali sanguine prognati, regaliter
10 instituti, educatique fuerant, sive illi ex liberorum, sive ex propinquorum numero et gradu essent.

At anno 987, mortuo Ludovico V, Rege Francogalliae XXXI,
et ex Carlovingiorum stirpe XII, migratio sceptri, regnique
mutatio contigit. Nam cum ex illa familia Carolus Lotharingiae
15 Dux superesset, Regis demortui patruus, ad quem instituto
Gentis Regni successio deferenda videbatur, exortus est Hugo
Capetus, Imp. Ottonis I sororis Havuidis nepos, Hugonis
Comitis Parisiensis filius, vir militari laude insignis, qui se praesentem absenti, bene de Regno meritum, alieno, ut ipse loque-
20 batur, praeferri voluit; nam cum inter Germaniae imperium et
regnum Galliae controversiae aliquot extitissent, Carolus
partium se imperii studiosum, et a Galliae regno alieniorem
ostenderat. Qua de caussa Gallorum complurium animos ac
voluntates ab se abalienaverat.

---

[1] *Germ.*, 7; Loeb, 274.

^aCHAPTER XVI [^cXX]

The Capetian family and the transfer to it of the kingdom of Francogallia

It has been shown that for twelve hundred years the kingdom of Francogallia has been held by only three families, of which the first, the Merovingian, and the second, the Carolingian, were named after their founders and heads. For, although the succession to the kingdom was transmitted (as we have by now said many times) not by heredity but by the choice of the council, nevertheless the Franks willingly retained the practice of the Germans in 'choosing their kings for their nobility and their generals for their valour' (to use the words of Tacitus[1]). Thus they usually chose as their kings those who were born of royal blood and were instructed and educated in a royal manner, whether they were actually royal children or cousins in some close degree.

But in the year 987, after the death of Louis V, the thirty-first king of Francogallia and the twelfth Carolingian king, a revolutionary change occurred in the kingdom and the sceptre passed into other hands. Charles, duke of Lorraine, uncle to the late king, alone survived of the family, and by the national custom it seemed that the succession to the kingdom should be passed to him. There then arose Hugh Capet, nephew of Havuidis (the sister of Emperor Otto I) and son of Hugh, count of Paris. He was a man of outstanding military reputation, who wished to be preferred because he was available whereas the others were absent, and, as he put it, he deserved well of the kingdom, in contrast to a stranger. For there had been several disputes between the empire of Germany and the kingdom of France, and Charles had shown himself a zealous supporter of the partisans of the empire and of foreigners to the kingdom of France. For these reasons he had alienated the sympathy and goodwill of a great many Frenchmen.

Itaque Carolus comparato exercitu, vi* in Galliam irrupit,
civitatesque aliquot deditione accepit. Capetus Francogallorum*
Principum favore atque amicitia fretus, ad Laudunum oppidum,
quod est in Campaniae finibus, coactis quibus potuit copiis pro-
5 gressus est; neque ita multo post praelium atrox committitur,
quo Capetus superatus, in interiorem Galliam profugit, bellumque novis coactis copiis redintegrare instituit. Carolus interea in
oppido Lauduno cum uxore, dimisso exercitu, quiescebat.
Anno insequenti circumventus a Capeto, magnisque copiis
10 ibidem circunsessus est. Erat in oppido Anselmus quidam, eius
civitatis Episcopus. Hunc Capetus praemiis et pollicitationibus
ad Regis et oppidi proditionem induxit. Ita oppido et victoria
potitus, Carolum cum uxore comprehensum Aureliam mittit,
custodesque utrique attribuit. Cum biennium in custodia Rex
15 fuisset,* duo ei filii, Ludovicus et Carolus, nati sunt, neque longo
interiecto tempore omnes interierunt. Ita Capetus libere ac sine
controversia totius Galliae Regno potitus, Robertum filium
Regni consortem ascivit, eumque sibi successorem designandum
curavit. Atque hoc facto Carlovingiorum familiae dignitas mem-
20 oriaque interiit, anno ab ipsorum Regni primordio ducentesimo
trigesimo septimo; quam historiam Sigebertus in Chron. ann.
987 commemorat.² Itemque appendix Aimoini lib. 5, ᵇcap. 42³
et ᵃcap. 45.⁴

ᵇEx quibus cognosci potest, Hugonem Capetum, Hugonis
25 magni Francorum Ducis filium, ex Roberto natum, Odonis
illius filio, cui superius diximus Francos Carolo Crasso mortuo,
regnum extra ordinem detulisse, pronepotem Roberti Andium
Ducis fuisse, clari et magni principis. Ex quibus etiam et ex Viti-
chindo Saxone⁵ cognosci potest,* Hugonem Capetum non

---

1 ᵃ¹ 'ut'; ᵇᶜ omit altogether.   2 ᵇᶜ 'Francorum'.   15 'Cum...fuisset':
ᵇ 'Cum biennium in custodia rex fuit'; ᶜ 'Cum in ea custodia Rex biennium
retentus esset'.   29 'cognosci potest': ᶜ 'intelligitur'.

² *MGH SS*, VI, 353, 2ff.   ³ V, 41² (see above, p. 392, n. 4); ed. 1567, 727.
⁴ Cf. *ed. cit.*, 742.   ⁵ Widukind, I, 30; *MGH SS*, III, 430, 16ff.

So Charles raised an army and broke forcibly* into France, receiving the surrender of a number of cities. Capet, who was supported by the favour and friendship of the Francogallican† nobles, proceeded to the town of Laon on the borders of Champagne with what forces he could muster. Soon afterwards a fierce battle took place in which Capet was overcome and fled to the interior of France, where he began to renew the war with fresh forces he had raised. Meanwhile Charles had dismissed his army, and remained quietly in the town of Laon with his wife. In the following year he was surrounded by Capet and besieged there by large forces. In the town was a certain Anselm, who was bishop of the diocese. With rewards and crafty promises Capet induced this man to betray the king and the town. Having thus gained the victory and secured the town, he sent the captured Charles and his wife to Orléans, where he placed them both under guard. During the two years the king spent‡ in prison he had two sons, Louis and Charles, born to him, but before long they all died. Thus Capet acquired the whole of France freely and without dispute, and, making his son Robert his consort in the kingdom, he saw to it that the latter was designated as his successor. After this the rank and memory of the Carolingian family perished in the two hundred and thirty-seventh year from their first establishment on the throne. Sigebert records this history in his chronicle under the year 987.[2] It is also contained in the ᵇforty-second[3] and ᵃforty-fifth[4] chapters of the fifth book of the appendix to Aimon.

ᵇFrom this we may conclude that Hugh Capet was the great-grandson of Robert, duke of Anjou, a great and famous prince. He was the son of Hugh the Great, duke of the Franks, who was the son of Robert, himself the son of that Odo [Eudes] to whom, as we have already said, the Franks transferred the kingdom, as an extraordinary measure, at the death of Charles the Fat. These details and the work of Widukind the Saxon[5] show that Hugh

---

* **bc** *omit* forcibly. † **bc** Francogallican *becomes* Frankish. ‡ **c** spent *becomes* was kept.

sordida et obscura (ut Italici quidam scriptores tradunt⁶) sed
illustrissima familia natum fuisse; nam Roberti Andegavorum
comitis abnepos fuit, quem Aimoinus Saxonici generis fuisse
scribit.⁷ Ex eo natus Odo, sive Otto, tantae virtutis fuit, ut cum
5   a Rege Carolo Crasso Dux Francorum exercitus adversus Danos
creatus, hostium centum millia uno praelio delevisset, Franci ei,
repudiato Crassi filio, Carolo Simplice puero, regnum detu-
lerint, quemadmodum suo loco superius dictum est.* Huius
Odonis filius fuit Robertus, ex quo Hugo magnus Dux quoque
10 Francorum natus est, cuius filius Hugo Capetus dictus, regnum
eo quem superius diximus modo adeptus est. Memorabile est
autem quod idem Vitichindus scribit,⁸ cum Odo Carolo
Simplici regnum restituisset, Arnulphum Imperatorem armis
Galliae regnum occupasse; eique Odoni (sic legendum, non
15 ODA) diadema et sceptrum et cetera regalia ornamenta obtu-
lisse, et Odonem imperium domini sui, gratia Arnulphi Imperatoris obtinuisse. *Unde* (inquit Vitichin.⁹) *usque hodie certamen est de
Regno Carolorum stirpi et posteris Odonis. Nam Hugo, cuius pater
Robertus filius Odonis ab exercitu Caroli occisus est, dolo eum cepit,*
20 *posuitque in custodia publica, donec vitam finiret.*

ᵃNeque vero silentio praetereundum videtur astutum Capeti
in novo Regno constabiliendo consilium. Nam cum Magistratus
et dignitates Regni, quos Ducatus et Comitatus appellant, ita
mandari antiquitus in populi comitiis, certis ac delectis viris
25 solerent, ut in beneficii tantum loco, et (ut Iurisconsulti loquuntur) precario tenerentur (quemadmodum in exponenda Concilii publici auctoritate demonstratum est): *primus Hugo Capetus
ad conciliandos retinendosque sibi procerum animos, has, quae tempo-
rariae erant, dignitates, fecit perpetuas,* constituitque ut qui eas ob-
30 tinebant, patrimonii iure retinerent, atque ad suos liberos pos-

---

8 *c* '...quemadmodum alio loco superius demonstratum est.'.

⁶ *E.g.*, Dante, *Purg.*, xx, 49, 52: 'Chiamato fui di là Ugo Ciapetta.../ Figliuol fui
d'un beccaio di Parigi.' Hotman's sometime student, Etienne Pasquier, defended
Hugh Capet against this libel in his *Recherches*, VI, 1; ed. *Oeuvres*, 1723, I, 511–14.
⁷ As in notes 3 and 4 above.   ⁸ Cf. Widukind, I, 30; *MGH SS*, III, 430, 10ff.
⁹ *Ibid.*, 12ff.

Capet was not born from some sordid and obscure family (as certain Italian writers report[6]), but, rather, from a most illustrious one. For he was the descendant of Robert of Anjou, whom Aimon describes as being of Saxon origin.[7] From him was born Odo, or Otto, a man of such great valour that, when King Charles the Fat appointed him general of the army of the Franks against the Danes, he destroyed one hundred thousand of the enemy in a single battle, and the Franks, who rejected the young Charles the Simple, the son of Charles the Fat, entrusted him with the kingdom in the manner earlier described. The son of this Odo was Robert, from whom Hugh, also great as duke of the Franks, was born, and it was the latter's son who was the said Hugh Capet, and who acquired the throne in the way we have stated above. Moreover, another fact related by the same Widukind is worth remembering,[8] namely that, when Odo restored the throne to Charles the Simple, the emperor, Arnulf, forcibly seized the kingdom of France. The emperor offered Odo (so the name should be read, and not as Oda) the crown, sceptre and other royal emblems, and Odo secured the government for his lord by the grace of Arnulf, the emperor. 'For this reason', writes Widukind,[9] 'to this very day there has been a struggle for the throne between the descendants of the Carolingians and those of Odo. For Hugh, whose father Robert, the son of Odo, was killed by the army of Charles, captured the latter by artifice and placed him in public custody for the rest of his life.'

*a*Nor should we leave unmentioned the astute plan of Capet in establishing his new kingdom. In earlier times the magistracies and offices of the kingdom, which were known as dukedoms and countships, were customarily conferred in the assemblies of the people upon proved and selected men who held their office in place of a benefice and on sufferance, as the jurists say. (This was shown when we explained the authority of the public council.) But 'Hugh Capet was the first who, in order to conciliate the nobles and retain their sympathy for himself, made these offices perpetual where previously they had been temporary', and he laid it down that those who acquired them might retain them with the legal status of a patrimony and transfer them to their children and

terosque, cum reliqua hereditate, transferrent, teste Francisco
Connano Iuriscons. Comment. 2, cap. 9.[10] Quo facinore non
minimam publici Concilii auctoritatem ab ipso imminutam
constat, quam tamen imminui ab ipso, sine Concilii ipsius con-
5   sensu potuisse, temporum illorum rationem consideranti consentaneum non videtur.

---

[10] *Francisci Connani commentariorum*, II, 9, 5; ed. 1557, I, 172. Besides the exact
quotation, Hotman paraphrases Connanus in the preceding passage 'Nam cum
Magistratus...transferrent'.

descendants with the rest of the inheritance. The *Commentaries* of the jurist François Connan support this interpretation.[10] Through this act the authority of the public council was very considerably reduced, yet it does not seem likely, in the context of those times, that Capet would have been able to effect this reduction by himself, without the consent of the council.

De continuata concilii publici auctoritate in Capevingiorum familia

Nam quemadmodum ex Frossardo, Monstrelletto, Guaguino, Cominio, Gillio, et aliis historicis omnibus cognosci licet, nihilo prope minor in Capevingiorum familia, quam in superioribus duabus, publici Concilii auctoritas fuit; *valuitque apud illos
5 praeceptum illud, tam saepe et tam valde, nunquam tamen satis commemoratum: SALUS POPULI SUPREMA LEX ESTO, neque ullum tam tyrannicum dominatum unquam post homines natos fuisse arbitror, praeter unum Turcicum, in quo cives pro pecudibus, non pro hominibus haberentur.* Neque satis* eorum
10 hominum imperitiam admirari possum, qui cum primoribus labris ius civile degustassent, et in libris nostris legissent, lata lege Regia populum Imperatori omne suum imperium et potestatem concessisse, continuo liberam quandam et infinitam Regum *omnium*potestatem commenti sunt, quam Absolutam barbaro
15 et inepto nomine appellant. Quasi vero non etiam Romani Reges Reipublicae curam (ut Pomponius Iurisc. loquitur[1]) per Curiata comitia expedirent; aut, si liberam Imperatores Romani potestatem habuerunt, continuo verum sit, Regibus omnibus eandem a populo potestatem tributam esse; neque enim ex uno
20 particulari recte de universis concluditur, et hac aetate longe dissimillimam esse regum Poloniae, Daniae, Sueciae, Hispaniae rationem, nemo nisi rerum omnium imperitus ignorat. *Regibus Germanorum* (inquit Tacitus[2]) *non est infinita, aut libera potestas.* *Rex Angliae* (inquit lib. 4 Cominaeus[3]) *tributa exigendi nullam*

---

9 *c*[1] omits 'valuitque apud illos...pro hominibus haberentur'.   9 'Neque satis': *c*[1] 'Satis enim'.

[1] *De Rom. mag.*, c. 1; ed. 1552, 7 – quoted above, p. 300, n. 26.   [2] *Germ.*, 7; Loeb, 274.   [3] *Mémoires*, IV, 1; SHF, I, 314.

^aCHAPTER XVII [^cXXI]

The continued authority of the public council under the Capetians

The works of Froissart, Monstrelet, Gaguin, Commines, Gilles and all the other historians indicate that the authority of the public council was in all respects virtually no less under the Capetians than it was under the two preceding dynasties. ^bMoreover that precept which can never be repeated too often or too vehemently – 'LET THE WELFARE OF THE PEOPLE BE THE SUPREME LAW' – continued to be effective under their rule. It is my view that no kind of tyrannical government has ever existed while men have been men, unless it be that of the Turks, where the citizens are treated like cattle rather than human beings.* Nor can I be sufficiently astonished† at the ignorance of those men who had some elementary acquaintance with Roman Law and derived the opinion from our records that under the *lex regia* the people of the Roman empire conceded all its authority and power, and who approve of a perpetual, free and unlimited power in ^call ^bkings, which they call by the barbarous and inappropriate word 'absolute'. As if, indeed, even the Roman kings, as the jurist Pomponius says,[1] were absolved from the guardianship of the commonwealth exercised by the curial assemblies, or, if the Roman emperors did hold unlimited power, this same power was actually granted by the people to all kings in perpetuity. For a universal principle should not be concluded from one particular example, and a very different rule has for a long period applied to the kings of Poland, Denmark, Sweden, and Spain, of which no one is ignorant unless he is completely uninformed. 'The German kings', writes Tacitus,[2] 'do not have a free or unlimited power.' 'The king of England', says Commines,[3] 'has no authority to exact taxes unless he receives the

* ^{c1} *omits the two preceding sentences.* † ^{c1} Nor can I be sufficiently astonished *becomes* For I marvel enough.

415

habet sine Ordinum et Statuum consensu potestatem, quod idem de
ceteris omnibus affirmat lib. 5, cap. 18.[4]

^cDenique, satis constat, nullam esse Galliae regionem, sive (ut
vulgus loquitur) provinciam, quae Regi serva aut dedititia sit,
5 omnemque in se (ut quondam populus Romanus Imperatoribus)
potestatem ei permiserit, quinimo nulla est, quae non iura
quaedam sua propria habeat, iis pactionibus et conditionibus
retenta, quibus se in Regis fidem ac ditionem commisit. Cuius rei
insigne illud argumentum est, quod unaquaeque Regio, cum
10 usus et publicae utilitatis ratio postulat, sua comitia indicit, quae
ad universae provinciae commodum pertinent, publico consilio
provideat. Itaque cum generale universi Regni ac patriae totius
Concilium indictum est, cum ex illo conventu unus aut alter
deligatur, qui cum Provinciae suae mandatis eo ad dicendam
15 sententiam proficiscatur. Exemplo erimus contenti uno, quod ex
celeberrimi Doctoris Tholosani verbis proferemus, Willelmi
nimirum Benedicti, qui in c. Raynutius, ad verbum et uxorem,
num. 499, ita scribit (et laudatur a Nicol. Boerio nobili Iuriscon.
et Praetore Burdegal. Decis. 126[5]) : *De unione*, inquit,[6] *comitatus*
20 *Tholosani, et patriae Occitanae cum Regno Franciae habetur plene in*
documentis inter chartas statuum dictae patriae repositis, in qua unione
tria fuerunt inter Regem et patriam in forma contractus passata: primo
quod omnia privilegia patriae et ius commune illibata servarentur;
secundo, quod nunquam Rex gubernatorem instituet, nisi qui sit de
25 *sanguine regio; tertio quod Rex tallias vel alia subsidia indicere*
patriae non poterit SINE CONSENSU STATUUM EIUSDEM, prout
nunquam fecit, neque facit. Quinimo annis singulis commissarium ad
partes mittit, necessitatem Regni toti patriae explicaturum, ut pro modo
negotiorum Regno pro tempore emergentium subsidium praebeatur.
30 *Quod obediens patria annuere consuevit, in servando per Regem*

---

[4] *Ibid.*, v, 19; SHF, II, 142.   [5] Cf. Dec. 126, §113; ed. 1567, 218.
[6] Benedicti, *In cap. Ray. de test.*, 'Et uxorem nomine Adelasiam', 498–9; ed. 1575,
I, 133^v–134.

consent of the orders and estates.' The same author affirms this principle in respect of other matters in another part of his book.[4]

cFinally, it is clear that no region, or, to use the common term, province, of France was reserved or granted to the king, and in this respect all power was not bestowed upon him in the manner in which the Roman people gave it to the emperors. On the contrary, he had no rights or ownership in anything, but was restrained by those pacts and conditions through which he was entrusted with the loyalty and authority appropriate to a king. A remarkable proof of this is that, when it is to the public advantage, each region summons its assemblies to take public counsel for the benefit of the province as a whole. Thus when a general council is proclaimed for the whole kingdom and the entire region, one or other particular delegate is chosen from the local assembly to proceed to the general council with the mandates of his province and to make known its opinion there. We shall be content to offer one instance of this practice from the words of that celebrated doctor of Toulouse, Guillaume Benedicti, who commented on the words ' *et uxorem* ' in a section of his treatise on Canon Law *Decretalia*, and who is praised by the noble jurist and president of the parlement of Bordeaux, Nicolas Bohier, in one of the latter's judgments.[5] 'As to the union of the county of Toulouse and the province of Languedoc with the kingdom of France,' he writes,[6] 'the issues are fully set forth in the documents deposited among the charters of the estates of the said provinces. There were three matters concerning this union set out in the form of a contract between the king and the province: first, that all provincial privileges and local law will be preserved inviolate; second, that the king will appoint no governor who is not a member of a provincial family; third, that no taxes or other subsidies can be levied on the province by the king without the consent of the provincial estates, and no innovations will be introduced. In particular years a commission will be sent to those concerned to explain to the province the need of the whole kingdom, so that a subsidy may be offered to the kingdom as a proportion of national needs and according to the circumstances. The province has undertaken to remain in obedience while the king preserves its

privilegia patriae, et cetera in dicta unione contenta, et pro illa vice
*duntaxat, ita quod non trahatur in consequentiam.**

^aSed quoniam exempla persequi singula* nimis laboriosum, ac
plane infinitum esset, pauca quaedam illustriora e magno
5 numero, quasi exempli loco, subscribemus. Primum exemplum
sumi licet ex anno MCCCXXVIII, quo tempore, mortuo (ut
superius diximus) Rege Carolo Pulchro, qui sine liberis virilis
sexus, atque postuma filia relicta decesserat, Eduardus Angliae
Rex* natus ex Isabella Caroli sorore, Galliae Regnum ad se
10 hereditate redisse contendebat. Qua controversia nulla neque
maior, neque illustrior ad publicum Concilium deferri potuit.
Quinetiam quod ad publicum Concilium introducta est,
perspicuo argumento esse potest, maiorem Concilii, quam Regis
auctoritatem esse, cum eius se iudicio atque arbitrio ambo illi
15 Reges subiecissent. Quod non modo historici nostri omnes
testantur, verumetiam Polyd. Vergilius Angl. Histor. lib. 19.[7]
Quinetiam Pragmaticus Paponius Arestorum, lib. 4, cap. 1,[8]
scriptum reliquit, bonis (ut opinor) auctoribus fretus,* ^cet Thomas
Walsimgamius in historia Anglic. sub Eduard. 3.[9] *Eduardo et*
20 *Philippo de successione contendentibus* (inquit Guaguinus[10]) *Con-*
ventus Francorum habitus est, quem TRIUM STATUUM COMITIA
vulgo vocant, ibi de contendentium iure diu multumque dis-
ceptatum est, ad extremum ii qui communi auctoritate concilium
habebant, multis rationibus edocti Philippo regnum adiudicaverunt.
25 *Cui iudicio nec Eduardus rex detraxit, fide post paucos annos Philippo*
de Aquitaniae feudo praestita. ^bQuinetiam Claudius Seyssellus,
Massiliensis Archiepiscopus, in libello, quem Franciae Monarchiam inscripsit,[11] affirmat, ^autrumque Regem in eo Concilio
praesentem affuisse. Cum res in contentionem prope adducta
30 esset, Optimatum consilio, populi atque ordinum comitia in-

---

2 *c*[1] '...*in consequentiam.* Haec illi. Sed quoniam...'   3 *bc* 'Sed quoniam
persequi testimonia singula'.   9 *c* 'Angliae Rex Eduardus tertius'.   18 *bc*
omit the sentence 'Quinetiam Pragmaticus...auctoribus fretus.'. The same
reference occurs a few lines below, in all editions.

[7] Ed. 1641, 463–4.   [8] See below, n. 13.   [9] Non invenio.   [10] Gaguin, Bk.
8; ed. 1528; fol. cxliir–v.   [11] Not Seyssel, but the anonymous *La Loy Salique*
often published together with Seyssel; ed. 1557, 83ff.

privileges, and is satisfied with the other matters in the said union so long as in return it is not exploited as a result of the union.'

*a*Since it would be a vast and unending task to trace every individual example,* we shall instead set forth a few of the more celebrated instances selected from the multitude that are available. Our first example is drawn from the year 1328, when, as we have shown earlier, at the death of King Charles the Fair, who had died without male heirs and left a posthumous daughter, the English king, Edward,† who was the son of Isabella, the sister of Charles, claimed the throne of France should revert to him on grounds of heredity. No dispute more important or more celebrated than this could be placed in the hands of the public council. The fact that the dispute was brought to the public council can be regarded as clear proof that the authority of the council was greater than that of the king, since both the kings in question submitted themselves to its judgment and decision. Not only do all our own historians support this but so too does Polydore Virgil in the nineteenth book of his *History of England*.[7] Furthermore the lawyer Papon left this opinion in his book of decrees,[8] and it appears to be based upon reliable authorities.‡ *c*This is also the view expressed by Thomas Walsingham in his *History of England under Edward III*.[9] Gaguin states:[10] ' As Edward and Philip were contending for the succession, a convention of the Franks was held which is commonly called the ASSEMBLY OF THE THREE ESTATES. A long and complex debate concerning the legal rights of the claimants took place there, and when many arguments had been presented the council awarded the kingdom to Philip. Nor did King Edward reject this decision when a few years later he did homage to Philip for the fief of Aquitaine.' *b*Moreover, Claude de Seyssel, archbishop of Marseille, affirms in his *Monarchy of France*[11] that *a*both kings attended the council in person. When the issue in dispute had reached a state of tension, an assembly of the people and the estates was summoned on the

---

* *bc* piece of evidence.   † *c* Edward III.   ‡ *bc* omit this sentence.

dicta sunt. De maioris partis sententia placuit, praeferri agnatum, praegnantisque Reginae custodiam Valesio attribui. Et, si filiam pareret, eidem Valesio Regnum adiudicatum est, quam historiam Frossardus exposuit vol. 1, cap. 22;[12] Paponius Arest. lib. 4,
5 cap. 1, art. 2;[13] Guaguinus in Philippo Valesio;[14] ᵇsed copiosissime omnium Seyssellus, in eo quem modo nominavi libello.[15]

ᵃAlterum exemplum suppeditat annus MCCCLVI quo tempore Rex Ioannes commisso cum Anglis prope Pictavium praelio
10 captus, atque in Angliam abductus fuit. Tanta calamitate accepta, unica in Concilii auctoritate spes erat reliqua. Itaque comitia continuo Lutetiam indicta sunt, et quanquam tres Regis filii extarent, Carolus, Ludovicus, et Ioannes, quorum natu maximus iustam administrandi aetatem haberet, tamen delecti
15 alii sunt, ex uno quoque ordine duodeni probati viri, quibus Regni procuratio mandata est, decretaque in Angliam legatio de pace cum Anglis reconcilianda; auctoribus Frossardo vol. 1, cap. 170;[16] Iohanne Bucheto lib. 4, fol. 118;[17] Nicol. Gillio in Chronicis Regis Iohannis.[18]

20 Tertium suppeditat annus MCCCLXXV, cum Caroli V cognomento Sapientis testamentum prolatum est, quo testamento filiorum suorum tutorem instituerat Philippum ducem Borbonium, uxoris suae fratrem, Regni autem procuratorem, Ludovicum Ducem Andicum, fratrem suum, tantisper dum
25 Carolus ipsius filius in suam tutelam veniret. Concilium enim Lutetiae nihilominus actum est, irritoque habito testamento, decretum est, ut Regni administratio Ludovico pueri patruo committeretur, ea lege, ut eam administrationem de certorum virorum in eo Concilio probatorum sententia gereret, pueri
30 autem tutela et educatio Borbonio permitteretur. Simulque lata Regia lex est, ut qui Regni heres annum aetatis XIIII implesset,

---

[12] Cf. 1, 42; SHF, 1, 84.   [13] Ed. 1574, 212.   [14] This general reference in the first edition is to the same passage quoted at length in the 1586 edition (above, n. 10). [15] See above, n. 11.   [16] Cf. 1, §400; SHF, v, 71.   [17] Bouchet, *Ann. d'Aquit.*, ed. 1557, 118ʳ⁻ᵛ.   [18] Ed. 1551, II, xvᵛff.

advice of the nobility. A majority of the assembly was of the opinion that the claimant on the father's side should be preferred, and the custody of the pregnant queen should be given to the Valois branch. It was also decided that, if she gave birth to a daughter, the throne should pass to the latter family. The matter is related by Froissart,[12] by Papon in his decrees,[13] by Gaguin in his account of Philip of Valois[14] [b]and, in greatest detail, by Seyssel in the book to which I have already referred.[15]

[a]Another example occurs in the year 1356, when King John gave battle to the English near Poitiers, and was captured and carried off to England. When the news of this great disaster was received, the only hope remaining lay in the authority of the council. Hence an assembly was summoned immediately at Paris, and, despite the fact that the king had three sons, Charles, Louis and John, the eldest of whom was at a fit age to govern, nevertheless others were chosen, namely twelve approved men from each estate, to whom the administration of the kingdom was entrusted. It was decreed that an embassy should be sent to England to treat for peace with the English. Accounts of this matter are provided by Froissart,[16] by Jean Bouchet,[17] and by Nicolas Gilles in his chronicles of King John.[18]

The year 1375 provides a third instance when the will of Charles V, named the Wise, was brought forward. By this will his wife's brother, Philip duke of Bourbon, was appointed guardian of his sons, and his brother, Louis duke of Anjou, was to be regent of the kingdom until prince Charles should come of age. Nevertheless a council was held in Paris, and the will was held invalid, while it was decreed that the government of the kingdom should be entrusted to Louis, the boy's uncle. By that enactment it was arranged that Louis should conduct the administration according to the views of certain individuals approved by the council, and the guardianship and education of the boy would be conceded to Bourbon. At the same time a regal law was made by which the heir to the throne should be crowned and offered homage and oaths of fealty when he attained the age of fourteen. Authorities

ei corona imponeretur, hominiaque* et fidelitatum iuramenta praestarentur; auctore Fross. vol. 2, cap. 60;[19] Buchet. lib. 4, fol. 124;[20] Chron. Brit. cap.[21]

5 Quartum suppeditat annus MCCCXCII, cum idem ille Rex Carolus VI repentino mentis errore affectus, primum Cenomanum, tum deinde Lutetiam delatus est, ibique Concilium habitum, Ordinumque auctoritate decretum, ut Bituricae et Burgundiae Ducibus Regni administratio deferretur; auctore Frossardo vol. 4, cap. 44.[22]

10 Neque vero praetermittendum est, quod Paponius Arest. lib. 5, tit. 10, art. 4,[23] nostra memoria in Parlamento Parisiensi commemoratum testatur, cum Rex Franciscus primus dominii sui partem alienare vellet, omnes eiusmodi alienationes a superioribus Regibus factas eo solo nomine irritas fuisse, quod sine Con-
15 cilii et (ut ipse loquitur) trium Statuum auctoritate factae fuissent.

Sextum exemplum extitit anno MCCCCXXVI, cum Philippus Dux Burgundiae, et Hanfredus Dux Clocestrae capitales inimicitias magno Reipublicae detrimento perquandiu exercuissent, tandemque inter eos convenisset, ut controversiis omnibus finem
20 duello commisso imponerent. Nam in ea contentione Concilium se interposuit, decrevitque, ut arma uterque deponeret, deque suis controversiis iure apud se potius, quam ferro disceptarent, quam historiam copiose exponit Paradinus in Chron. Burgund. lib. 3, anno MCCCCXXVI.[24]

25 Septimum exemplum ᵇsuppeditat annus MCCCCLXVIII, cum dissidio inter regem Ludovicum XI et Carolum ipsius fratrem exorto, Concilium publicum indictum est Turones, ad Kal. Decembr. quo in Concilio decretum est, ut rex fratri suo legitimae (ut ita dicam) hoc est Apannagii nomine Ducatum aliquem
30 permitteret,* cuius annui fructus non minoris essent, quam XII

---

1 c² 'homagiaque'.   30 'legitimae ...permitteret': c 'ut rex fratri suo Apannagii nomine Ducatum aliquem cederet'.

19 Cf. II, 173; SHF, x, 12.   20 As above, n. 17; ed. cit., 124ᵛ.   21 Bouchart, in a chapter entitled 'Comment par loy establie par le Roy de France et les estatz l'aisne fils de France peut estre couronne au xiiii an de son aage'; ed. 1541, cxviiiᵛ.   22 Cf. ed. 1559, II, 157.   23 Ed. 1574, 278.   24 Ed. 1566, 697.

for this are Froissart,[19] Bouchet,[20] and Bouchart's *Annals of England and Brittany*.[21]

The fourth example comes from the year 1392 when King Charles VI was unexpectedly seized by delusions of the mind, and was taken first to Le Mans and then to Paris. There a council was held, and it was decreed by the authority of the estates that the government of the kingdom should be passed to the dukes of Aquitaine and Burgundy. This is described by Froissart.[22]

Nor, indeed, should we fail to mention the event that occurred in the parlement of Paris within our own memory, as recorded by Papon in his book on decrees.[23] When King Francis I wished to alienate part of his domain, the parlement declared that all alienations made in this way by earlier kings were invalid when effected in the king's name alone, because they had been made without the authority of the council and, as Papon himself says, without the authority of the three estates.

Our sixth example occurs in the year 1426 when Philip duke of Burgundy and Humphrey duke of Gloucester were incessantly pursuing a deadly enmity against each other to the great harm of the commonwealth. At length they agreed to end their quarrels by fighting a duel. The council then intervened in the dispute, and decreed that they should lay down their arms and submit their differences to the law rather than the sword. This event is fully described by Paradin in his Burgundian chronicles for the year 1426.[24]

A seventh example *b*occurs in the year 1468, when a dispute arose between King Louis XI and his brother Charles and a public council was summoned to Tours on 1 December. In this council it was decreed that the king should lawfully (as I shall put it)* grant his brother some duchy with the status of an appanage and an income of not less than twelve thousand livres a year, and, in

---

* *c omits* (as I shall put it).

millium libellarum, insuperque rex e suo fisco LX libellarum
millia quotannis ei adnumeranda curaret; quam historiam
copiose auctor Chron. Britan. Armor. commemorat, lib. 4,
fol. 200.[25]

5   Octavum exemplum ^aeditum est anno MCCCCLXXXIIII,
cum Ludovico XI mortuo superstite Carolo filio annorum XIII
Concilium Turonis* habitum est, decretumque ut pueri educatio Annae sorori Regis committeretur; Regni vero procuratio
certis viris in eo Concilio probatis et delectis mandaretur, quam-
10 vis Ludovicus Dux Aurelianus proximus agnatus eam postularet. Cuius rei testimonium extat in actis eius Concilii Lutetiae
impressis, et apud ^bPhilipp. Cominaeum lib. 5, cap. 18,[26] itemque in Chron. Britan. lib. 4,[27] et apud ^aIohan. Bucchettum
lib. 4, fol. 167.[28]

15   ^bNeque fortasse ad extremum praetermittendum illud est,
quod Guill. Budaeus libr. de Asse, III et V, memoriae prodidit,[29]
rei nummariae ius, hoc est, potestatis nummorum vel augendae
vel minuendae, semper penes populum Francorum fuisse.
Quinetiam Carolus Molinaeus diligentissimus monetalium
20 ratiociniorum investigator, in extremo Commentario de
contract. et usur. testatur,[30] se in Archivis parlamenti et monetalium praefectorum, quamplurimas leges Francicas reperisse,
quibus sancitum erat, ne qua rei nummariae mutatio sine populi
consensu fieret, semperque in eiusmodi mutationibus populi
25 consensum (quippe, cuius maxime intererat) intervenisse; quemadmodum inter Iurisc. dici solet: Cuius quidque fieri interest,
eius in eo negotio gerendo necessaria est auctoritas. Item, Quod
omnes tangit, debet ab omnibus approbari.*

---

7 *bc* 'Turonibus'.   **28** *b* but not *c* has this 100-odd word paragraph, 'Neque
fortasse...omnibus approbari'. Its contents are given, however, almost verbatim
in the final paragraph of *c*'s chapter xxv, below, p. 478, variant note on l. 8.
The moving around of this passage in successive editions is the subject of Giesey,
'Quod Omnes Tangit: a Post Scriptum', in *Post Scripta: Essays in Honor of
Gaines Post* (= Studia Gratiana, 8: Vatican, 1972), 67–78.

[25] Bouchart, ed. 1541, 188ᵛ–189.   [26] v, 19; SHF, II, 143.   [27] Bouchart, ed.
1541, 199ᵛ–200.   [28] As above, p. 420, n. 17; *ed. cit.*, 166ʳ⁻ᵛ.   [29] Ed. 1532,
lxᵛ & cxlviii; cf. below, ch. xxv, n. 41 (p. 476).   [30] Du Moulin, *Tract. contract.
et usu.*, Quaest. 100 *passim*, esp. §§793–4, 805; ed. *Opera*, 1681, II, 206ff, esp. 320–1.
See also below, ch. xxv, n. 42 (p. 476).

addition, the king should arrange for the annual payment of a specified sum of sixty thousand livres from his own treasury to his brother. This circumstance is described in detail by the author of the Breton chronicle.[25]

An eighth instance [a]may be taken from the year 1484, when, at the death of Louis XI, his son Charles was left at the age of thirteen. A council was held at Tours and it was decreed that the boy's education should be committed to his sister, Anne. Despite the fact that Louis duke of Orléans demanded the government of the kingdom as the nearest cousin by male descent, it was decreed that it would be entrusted to certain individuals approved and chosen by the council. Proof of this matter is contained in the proceedings of that council printed in Paris, [b]in the memoirs of Philippe de Commines,[26] in Bouchart's annals[27] [a]and in Jean Bouchet.[28]

[b]Nor should we neglect to mention in conclusion a most powerful piece of evidence recorded by Guillaume Budé in *De asse*, his work on coinage.[29] He points out that the right of fixing the value of money, that is the power to increase or diminish its worth, has always rested in the French people. Indeed, that most assiduous investigator of monetary matters, Charles du Moulin, declares at the conclusion of his commentary on contracts and usury[30] that in the archives of the parlement and the chambre des comptes he found a great many Frankish laws by which it was forbidden to make any change in monetary values without the consent of the people. He also found that the consent of the people had always been given for changes of this kind in the past (for, indeed, the people were most vitally concerned). In this context it is customarily said by jurists: 'The person whose interest is at stake has authority in handling the affair.' Or again, 'What touches all should be approved by all.'*

---

* *c omits this paragraph at this point but includes it in chapter XXV.*

^{c1}Auffrenium in gloss. pragm. sanct.³¹ & Bened. in verb. Adiectae impuberi, nu. 53.^{32*}

2 c¹ only has this sentence, meant to supplement allegations nos. 26–8; the intermediate paragraph, as just noted, was moved elsewhere in *c*.

³¹ This must be garbled, but in neither case – whether Etienne Aufrier's additions to Du Breuil, *Stilus curiae parlamenti*, or Cosm. Guimier's gloss for the *Pragmatica sanctio* – can I locate it.　　³² Benedicti, *In cap. Ray. de test.*, 'Adiectae impuberi', §53; ed. 1575, I, 219^v.

^cSee the gloss of Aufrier on the pragmatic sanction[31] and Guillaume Benoît's additional observations on the marriage of persons under age.[32]*

---

* *This sentence is in c¹ only.*

*b*CAPUT XVIII [*c*XXII]*

De publici concilii auctoritate in
maximis religionis negotiis

Hactenus demonstratum est, summam in gravissimis quibusque
Reipublicae nostrae negotiis *c*summo permultorum seculorum
consensu *b*Concilii publici potestatem fuisse. Deinceps videamus, ecqua eiusdem in Religionis negotiis auctoritas fuerit.
5 Cuius rei documentum nobis praebent Annales nostri, sub
anno MCCC, quo Bonifacius octavus, Papa Romanus, missis ad
regem Philippum Pulchrum legatis, ei denuntiavit, se non modo
spiritualem (verba haec Historici sunt omnia[1]), verumetiam
temporalem omnium regnorum ac ditionum, quae in orbe
10 Christiano sunt, dominum esse, pro eo iure postulare, ut rex
Philippus eum pro domino ac Principe summo agnosceret, eique
suum regnum acceptum ferret, ac fateretur, se illud ipsius beneficio et liberalitate obtinere; si id facere recuset, futurum, ut
eum haereticum pronunciaret, et sacris suis interdiceret.
15 Qua legatione audita, rex publicum Concilium Lutetiam
indicit; in eo Concilio Papales literae recitantur, his verbis:[2]
Bonifacius Episcopus, servus servorum Dei, Philippo Francorum regi,
Deum time, et mandata eius observa. Scire te volumus, quod in spiri-
tualibus et temporalibus nobis subes, beneficiorum atque praebendarum
20 *ad te collatio nulla spectat; et si aliquorum vacantium custodiam habeas,*
usumfructum earum successoribus reserves; et si quas contulisti, colla-
tionem haberi irritam decrevimus, et quatenus processerit, revocamus.
Aliud credentes, fatuos reputamus. Datum Laterani, IIII Non.
Decemb., pontificatus nostri anno VI. His literis recitatis, auditaque

---

Cap. *c*[1] suppressed this entire chapter.

[1] Most likely Gilles (see next notes), but perhaps Bouchart, ed. 1541, 91ᵛ.
[2] Gilles, *Chroniques*, gives this letter in Latin (ed. 1551, I, cxix) but a better text is
found in Dupuy, *Hist. du differend*, preuves, 44. The date should be 7th year of
Boniface's reign.

428

^bCHAPTER XVIII [^cXXII]*

The authority of the public council in the conduct of high matters of religion

---

So far we have shown that the power of the public council was supreme in the greatest affairs of state concerning our commonwealth ^cand that it was so by general accord throughout many centuries. ^bWe shall now see that there was a parallel authority in religious affairs. Our annals provide us with proof of this for the year 1300, when the Roman pope, Boniface VIII, sent ambassadors to King Philip the Fair, and informed him that he was the temporal as well as the spiritual lord (these are invariably the words used by the historians[1]) of all the kingdoms and powers in Christendom. He demanded that King Philip should acknowledge him as his supreme lord and prince and should offer him the kingdom he had received. Further, the pope required the king to admit he had acquired his kingdom by papal grace and favour. If the king refused to do this, the pope would pronounce him a heretic and place him under interdict.

When the embassy had been heard, the king summoned a public council to Paris, and there the papal letter was repeated as follows:[2] 'Bishop Boniface, servant of the servants of God, to Philip, king of the Franks. Fear God and obey His commandments. We wish you to know, since you submit to us in matters spiritual and temporal, that the accumulation of benefices and prebends is no way appropriate to your authority; and if you have custody of any vacant benefices, you should keep the usufruct for those who will succeed to them. If you have collected any such revenues we decree that the collection of them is to be held invalid, and, in so far as this may have taken place, we hereby revoke it. We consider all men who believe otherwise to be foolishly mistaken. Given at our palace on 2 December in the sixth year of our pontificate.'

* c¹ omits this chapter.

procerum sententia, ac deliberata re, primum decretum est, ut
Epistola Papae in area Palatii Parisiensis coram ipsius legatis et
nuntiis cremaretur, tum ut legati mitellati, turpificati, sordidati,
et a carnifice in illam aream lutulento plaustro advecti, plebis
5 totius ludibrio et conviciis exponerentur, postremo ut regis
nomine literae ad Papam his verbis scriberentur:[3] *Philippus Dei
gratia Francorum rex, Bonifacio se gerenti pro summo pontifice,
salutem modicam, sive nullam. Sciat tua maxima* FATUITAS *in
temporalibus nos alicui non subesse, aliquarum Ecclesiarum et prae-*
10 *bendarum vacantem collationem ad nos iure regio pertinere, et perci-*
*pere, fructus earum contra omnes possessores utiliter nos tueri, secus
autem credentes fatuos reputamus, atque dementes.* Cuius historiae
testes sunt auctor Chronic. Brittan. Armoric. lib. 4, cap. 14;[4] et
Nicol. Gillius in Chron. Gallic.[5] quibus adiungendus est prag-
15 maticus Paponius in lib. Arestorum I, tit. 5, art. 27.[6]

^cSed multo magis Iohannes Tilianus Parisiensis Parlamenti
scriba, homo ceteroqui ab hoc historiarum genere alienissimus:[7]
Cardinalis quidam, inquit, pag. 172, *denuntiavit inducias imperatas a
Papa Bonifacio octavo inter Philippum Pulchrum, et Reges Roman-*
20 *orum atque Anglorum, adiecta poena sive comminatione censurae
Philippus Pulcher anno 1297, consilio suorum Principum et consiliariorum, respondit se paratum esse, Sedi Apostolicae parere, in iis
rebus quae ad suam animam et spiritualitatem pertinerent, sed neminem
praeter Deum agnoscere superiorem se in iis quae ad res sui regni*
25 *temporales pertinerent, neque velle se in rebus sui regni temporalibus
cuiquam mortali subiicere. Quibus rebus cognitis Bonifacius bulla Regi
Philippo missa, denuntiavit eum sibi subiectum esse aeque in temporalibus, ut in spiritualibus, simulque pronunciavit haereticos esse, qui*

---

8 *c*² inadvertently skips '*modicam, sive nullam. Sciat tua maxima*'.

³ Gilles, *loc. cit.* The text of this is even more faulty than the previous quotation:
cf. Dupuy, *loc. cit.*   ⁴ Bouchart; ed. 1541, 91ᵛ.   ⁵ As above, nn. 2 & 3.
⁶ Ed. 1574, 55ᵛ.   ⁷ Du Tillet, *Mém. et rech.,* Bk. II, *in prin.*; ed. 1578, 132.

When these words had been read out, the opinions of the leading men heard and the matter deliberated, it was decreed, first, that the pope's letter should be burnt in the palace square in Paris in the presence of the papal ambassadors and envoys; then that the ambassadors should be blindfolded, defiled and polluted and conveyed to the square by the executioner on a cart covered with mud, and there exposed to the abuse and insults of all the people; and, finally, that a letter would be written to the pope in the king's name as follows:[3] 'Philip, by the grace of God king of the Franks, to Boniface, who conducts himself as though he were the supreme pontiff, a moderate greeting, and preferably none at all. Let it be known to your unparalleled* stupidity that we submit to no one in temporal matters, that the collection of revenues from churches and prebends during a vacancy belongs to us by regal right, and that these revenues may be gathered by us and kept to our advantage against all claimants. We regard all those who think otherwise to be not only foolish but also mad.' Those who describe this matter are the author of the Breton chronicle,[4] and Nicolas Gilles in his French chronicle,[5] to whom should be added the lawyer Papon in his first book of decrees.[6]

^cEven more about this affair is provided by Jean du Tillet, a clerk of the parlement of Paris, who in other respects is a man most averse to this kind of historical narration.[7] 'A certain cardinal', he writes, 'announced the truce ordered by Pope Boniface VIII between Philip the Fair, the king of the Romans and the king of the English. When a penalty was added with a threat of papal censure in 1297, Philip the Fair took the advice of his nobility and legal counsellors, and replied that he was prepared to obey the apostolic see in those things which concerned his soul and his spiritual welfare, but that he would recognise no one beside God as his superior in those things which belonged to the temporal aspects of his kingdom, nor was he willing to subject himself to any mortal man in the temporal affairs of his kingdom. When Boniface heard this he sent a bull to King Philip, and declared that the king was subject to him as much in temporal as in spiritual things. At the

* c² *inadvertently omits the preceding few words.*

431

aliter crederent; cui denuntiationi fortiter reclamatum est, simul bulla
Lutetiae combusta, in praesentia Regis, et Principum, atque consilia-
riorum. Quae, malum, ista est hodie Principum et summorum
Magistratuum, ut ita dicam, Papimania? qui cum tantam ac tam
5 nefariam illius Tyranni superbiam atque arrogantiam videant,
tamen, quasi Circaeo poculo dementati, nihilominus sese ad
illius exosculandos pedes provolvunt, quasi Dcum aliquem de
coelo delapsum intuerentur.

    Sed nemo totam hanc historiam commodius exponit, quam
10 Tho. Walsinghamius, Angl. Historicus, monachus ceteroqui
papisticis superstitionibus addictissimus, et ad tuendam Paparum
amplitudinem praeter ceteros devotissimus. Itaque cum is liber
venalis (ut audio) in Gallia nostra non reperiatur, operae
pretium fore arbitror, totam illam historiam eiusdem illius
15 monachi verbis exponere.[8] Celestinus Papa, vir vitae anachori-
ticae, subdole a Benedicto Caietano inductus est, ut ei Papatum
cederet, et constitutionem ederet, ut Papa quilibet cedere suum
Papatum posset, quam tamen constitutionem Benedictus ille
(postea Bonifacius Papa factus) revocavit, de quo vere Celestinus
20 prophetavit in hunc modum: '*Ascendisti ut vulpes; regnabis ut*
leo; morieris, ut canis.' Bonifacio Papae creato Rex Francorum
Philippus in multis resistebat.[9] Papae favebat Gallus Appa-
mensis Episcopus, qui propterea *de conspiratione contra Regem*
Franciae accusatus, et ad Regis vocatus curiam, in custodia detentus est.
25 *Mense vero Februario ad mandatum Domini Papae liberatus, iubetur*
una cum nuncio domini Papae regnum evacuare. Papa talibus novis
exasperatus, omnes gratias a se, vel suis praedecessoribus Francorum
regibus concessas revocavit, et in eundem Regem cito post excommuni-
cationis sententiam fulminavit. Quam tamen Regi nemo est ausus
30 *nuntiare, vel in regno Franciae publicare. Fecit etiam citari*
praelatos omnes de regno Franciae, necnon et omnes magistros in

---

[8] Everything from here to the end of this chapter is drawn from Walsingham,
mostly quoted, sometimes paraphrased; ed. 1863, I, 49–204.   [9] To this point,
from *ibid.*, I, 49.

432

same time he pronounced all those heretics who believed the contrary. This declaration met with a most vigorous rebuttal, and the bull was at once burnt in Paris in the presence of the king, the princes and the judges.' This, alas, is today a thing I may call 'papimania' among those princes and supreme magistrates who, although they see the heinous pride and arrogance of that tyrant, nevertheless go to such extremes that they act as if they had drunk Circe's potion and prostrate themselves trying to kiss his feet, as though they were worshipping some god cast down from heaven.

But no one gives a better account of these events than does Thomas of Walsingham the English historian, a monk who in other respects is very much given to papist superstitions and who is entirely devoted to the protection of the full authority of the popes before that of other powers. As I understand this book is not to be found for sale in France today, I believe it is worth the trouble to set forth the whole account of the episode in the words of that very monk.[8] 'Pope Celestine, a man who lived like an anchorite, was craftily persuaded by Benedict Cajetan to cede the papacy to him and to enact a law whereby any pope whatever could grant away the papacy to someone else – a law, however, which Benedict, after he had become Pope Boniface, revoked. This was an act which, indeed, Celestine foretold in the following terms: "You have climbed to power like a fox; you will reign like a lion; and you will die like a dog." When Boniface had been made pope, Philip, the king of the Franks, resisted him in many things.[9] The French bishop of Pamiers supported the pope, and for this reason he was accused of plotting against the king of France, and, after being called to the royal court, was detained in custody. Then in the month of February he was released on the demand of the lord pope, and was ordered to leave the kingdom together with the nuncio of the lord pope. As the pope was infuriated by the news of this, he revoked all the concessions granted by him and his predecessors to the kings of France, and soon afterwards thundered forth a sentence of excommunication against the king. But no one was bold enough to tell the king about it, nor to publish it in the kingdom of France. The pope also had all the prelates from the kingdom of France

Theologia, et in iure, tam canonico, quam civili, ut coram eo Romae
Kalend. Novemb. comparerent. Rex vero Franciae publico prohibuit
edicto, nequis aurum, vel argentum seu merces quascunque Romam
asportaret de regno suo, fecit etiam omnes exitus et introitus diligentis-
5 *sime custodiri.*[10] *Praelati Franciae, missis ad Papam tribus Episcopis,*
de non veniendo ad diem citationis praefixum, se per eosdem excu-
sarunt. Papa vero Praelatis Franciae non comparentibus, misit in
Franciam Iohannem Monachum Cardinalem, qui convocatis praelatis
Parisiis, secretum consilium habuit cum eisdem.[11]

10 *Postea circa festum S. Ioann. Baptistae milites quidam in praesentia*
cleri et populi Parisiis congregati, Papae Bonifacio multa imposuerunt
enormia, puta haeresim, simoniam, homicidia, propter quae per Regem
Franciae appellatum est contra eum, ad illum cuius interest; donec,
convocato consilio, se a criminibus purgaret obiectis. Circa festum
15 *nativitatis beatae Virginis, videlicet in vigilia nativitatis eiusdem, venit*
summo mane magnus exercitus hominum armatorum missus ex parte
Regis Franciae repente ad portas civitatis Anaguinae, in quam Papa
confugerat pro tutela, quia ibidem natus fuerat. Invenientes igitur
portas apertas ingressi sunt civitatem, et mox dederunt insultum
20 *Palatio domini Papae. Communitas vero villae comperto, quod*
Willelmus de Longaretto (legendum est Nogaretto) seneschallus
Regis Franciae advenisset, ut Papam deponeret, vel necaret, statim pul-
sata communi campana, et tractatu habito, elegerunt sibi capitaneum
quendam Adnulphum, qui quidem illis ignorantibus extitit domini
25 *Papae capitalis inimicus.* Hi omnes communibus votis tantum
irruerunt in Papam, et nepotem suum, et tres Cardinales (qui a
tergo per latrinam evaserunt) quod diu (ut putabatur) eis
resistere non valerent. Ob quam caussam Dominus Papa timens
sibi, treugas petiit.[12]

[10] To here, from previous note, from *ibid.*, I, 84–5.   [11] To here, from last
note, from *ibid.*, I, 98.   [12] To here, from last note, from *ibid.*, I, 100–1.

summoned to appear before him at Rome on 1 November, together with the doctors in theology and in canon and civil law. The king of France then published an edict prohibiting anyone from taking from his kingdom any gold or silver or any revenues whatsoever, and he also had all persons leaving or entering the kingdom very carefully watched.[10] The bishops of France sent three of their number to the pope to excuse themselves for not appearing on the day appointed in the summons. When the French bishops did not appear, the pope sent to France John the Monk, who had been made a cardinal, to call the prelates together in Paris and hold a secret meeting with them.[11]

'Later, at about the time of the festival of Saint John the Baptist, a number of knights met together in Paris in the presence of the clergy and the people, and accused Pope Boniface of many frightful crimes including suspicion of heresy, simony and murder, and on these counts a process was begun against him through the king, in whose interest the matter lay, requiring the pope to summon a council and purge himself of the crimes with which he was charged. At the time of the festival of the nativity of the Blessed Virgin, and actually during the vigil for the nativity, a strong force of armed men, sent without warning on behalf of the king of France, arrived at dawn at the gates of the city of Anagni, where the pope had taken refuge, since it was the city of his birth. As they found the gates open, the soldiers entered the city, and soon afterwards they violated the security of the lord pope's palace. The town community soon found out that Guillaume de Longaret (the name should be read as Nogaret), the seneschal of the king of France, had come to depose or murder the pope. The town bells were at once tolled and a meeting was held, where the citizens elected a man named Arnolfi as their captain, not knowing that he was a confirmed enemy of the lord pope. All the people rushed to the pope, his nephew and three cardinals (who escaped through a lavatory at the back of the house) to offer their common prayers and promises of support, but it was thought not to be worth trying to resist the soldiers. For this reason the lord pope, who was in great fear for his safety, sought a truce.[12]

Quibus finitis, exercitus per vim ad Papam est ingressus, quem tunc permulti verbis contumeliosis sunt aggressi. Cum autem ad rationem positus esset, an vellet renuntiare Papatui, constanter respondit, 'Non', imo citius vellet perdere caput suum, dicens in suo vulgari: 'Ecco il 5 collo, Ecco il capo', quod est dicere, 'ecce collum, ecce caput'. Et statim protestatus est corram omnibus, quod Papatui nunquam renuntiaret, quandiu posset habere vitam; exercitus vero postquam irrupit palatium, mox despoliavit Papam, et eius cameram, atque thesauriam suam, et asportavit vestimenta cum ornamentis, et aurum atque argentum, cum 10 omnibus aliis rebus inventis ibidem. Et revera creditur, quod omnes Reges mundi non possent tantum de thesauro reddere, infra unum annum, quantum fuit de Papali palatio asportatum.

Remansit autem Papa sub custodia militum et custodum usque ad diem tertiam; sed populus Anagum, facta convocatione secreta usque ad 15 decem millia hominum concurrunt, et Papam deliberaverunt. Sed ante haec omnia sciendum, quod cum illi primo Papam comprehendissent, in equum posuerunt effrenem, facie ad caudam versa, et sic coegerunt discurrere, fere ad novissimum halitum, et tandem pene fame neca-verunt; donec eum populus Anagum (ut praemittitur) liberasset. Tunc 20 populus fecit Papam deportari in magnam plateam, ubi Papa lacry-mando populo praedicavit, et tandem in fine sermonis dixit: 'Boni homines et mulieres, constat vobis, qualiter inimici mei venerunt, et abstulerunt omnia bona mea, et non tantum mea, sed etiam bona Ecclesiae, et me ita pauperem, sicut Iob fuerat, dimiserunt; propter quod 25 dico vobis veraciter, quod nihil habeo ad comedendum vel bibendum, et ieiunus remansi, usque ad praesens. Et si sit aliqua bona mulier, quae me velit de sua iuvare eleemosyna, in pane vel vino, et, si vinum non habuerit, de aqua permodica, dabo ei benedictionem Dei et meam, et omnes qui quicquam portaverint, quantulumcumque modicum, absolvo 30 eos ab omnibus peccatis suis.' Tunc omnes haec audientes ex ore Papae, clamabant, VIVAS PATER SANCTE. Et mox cerneres mulieres currere certatim ad Palatium, ad offerendum sibi panem, vinum, vel aquam, in tantum, quod statim camera Papae victualibus repleta fuit.

'When this had been effected, the French forced their way into the presence of the pope and many of them insulted him with words of derision. But when it was put to him that he should renounce the papacy, he firmly refused, indicating he would rather lose his head, and saying in Italian: "Ecco il collo, ecco il capo", which means "here is my neck, and here my head". And he immediately protested before all present that he would never resign the papacy while life remained to him. Whereupon the soldiers rushed through the palace, pillaging the pope's chamber and his treasury, and carrying off his ornate vestments, together with gold and silver and anything else they could find there. Indeed it is believed that no king in the world could have paid out from his treasury in a single year as much as was carried off from the papal palace.

'The pope remained in the custody of the soldiers and guards until the third day. However, the people of Anagni secretly met together and mustered as many as ten thousand men, who freed the pope. Before this occurred it should be understood that when the soldiers arrested the pope they placed him on an unbridled horse with his head facing the tail, and forced it to gallop about in all directions until he was almost at his last gasp and nearly dead from hunger. It is reported that this continued up to the point when the people of Anagni delivered him. Then the people had the pope taken to an open square where he preached so effectively that he drew tears from his audience. At the conclusion of his sermon he said: "Good men and women, it is well known to you how my enemies came and took from me all my goods, and those of the church as well, and thus reduced me to a pauper, as Job once was. And I tell you truthfully that as a result I have had nothing to eat or drink, and I have been starving right up to the present time. And if some good woman out of her charity wishes to help me with bread or wine, or, failing wine, a small quantity of water, then I shall bestow upon her God's blessing and my own, and I shall absolve from all their sins all those who bring anything, however small." Then all those who heard the pope called out: "Long live the Holy Father." And the women ran eagerly to the palace to offer him bread, wine and water in such great quantities that the

Et cum non invenirentur vasa ad capiendum allata, fundebant vinum
et aquam in area camerae Papae, in maxima quantitate. Et tunc potuit
quisque ingredi, et cum Papa loqui, sicut cum alio paupere, qui volebat.
Tunc Papa exiens absolvit omnes existentes in civitate ab omnibus
5 *peccatis eorum.*

His itaque gestis, Papa subito et inopinate, recessit de villa Anagum,
progrediens versus Romam, cum maxima multitudine armatorum. Et
cum pervenisset ad sanctum Petrum, ex timore, quem conceperat, quando
fuit captus, et maerore rerum inaestimabilium perditarum, cito defecit,
10 *et sic completa est prophetia praedecessoris sui, quae dixit:* 'Ascendisti
ut vulpes; regnabis ut leo; morieris, ut canis.' [13] Haec Walsinghamius,
totidem verbis, primum in Historia sub Eduardo primo, deinde
in Annalib.; quinetiam sub anno 1307 haec adscribit:[14] *Rex*
Franciae per hoc tempus petiit per suos nuntios a domino Papa Bene-
15 *dicto, ossa praedecessoris sui* Bonifacii, ad comburendum, tanquam*
haeretici.

---

15 c² omits '*sui*'.

[13] To here, from last note, from *ibid.*, I, 102–4.   [14] *Ibid.*, I, 28.

papal chamber was at once crammed full with victuals. When a sufficient number of jars to hold the wine could not be found, they poured a vast quantity of both wine and water in the yard of the pope's dwelling. And any one who wished to do so was able to go in and speak with the pope, as they would with any pauper.

'After these events the pope suddenly and unexpectedly withdrew from the town of Anagni, and made his way towards Rome with a great multitude of armed men. And when he arrived at the city of Saint Peter he died in a brief space from the terror he had conceived at the time of his capture and the sorrow he had for the inestimable things he had lost. Thus was fulfilled the prophecy of his predecessor, who had said: "You will climb to power like a fox; you will reign like a lion; you will die like a dog."'[13] This is the full account of the matter provided by Walsingham in his *History of England* under Edward I and also in his book of annals for the year 1307, where he writes:[14] 'At this time the king of France sought through his ambassadors from the lord pope, Benedict, to have the bones of his predecessor, Boniface, burnt as those of a heretic.'

^aCAPUT XVIII [^bXIX, ^{cc²}XXIII, ^{c¹}XXII]

De memorabili auctoritate concilii in
regem Ludovicum XI

Magna igitur ac plane sacrosancta Concilii et Ordinum co-
actorum vis et potestas ex superioribus testimoniis apparuit. Sed
quoniam in hoc genere versamur,* non praetermittenda videtur
eiusdem Concilii auctoritas, patrum nostrorum memoria interposita contra Regem Ludovicum XI qui superiorum Regum
5 omnium versutissimus et callidissimus est habitus. ^cEx quo intelligi facile poterit, quod iam saepe diximus, maiores nostros non
sibi ferum aliquem tyrannum aut carnificem imposuisse, qui
suos cives in pecudum loco ac numero haberet, sed Regem iuris
ac libertatis suae custodem ascivisse, qui iustitiae praeses esset.*
10 ^aAnno igitur MCCCCLX cum ita Regnum ab illo Ludovico
gereretur, ut multis in rebus boni Principis et patriam amantis
officium desideraretur, coepta est Concilii auctoritas requiri, ut
in eo Boni publici ratio haberetur. Et quoniam ei Rex minime
sese subiecturus putabatur, Proceres Regni, assiduis plebis queri-
15 moniis et expostulationibus incitati, manus cogere, exercitusque
comparare instituerunt, ut Bonum publicum procurare, *et Regi
perditam Reipublicae administrationem* (verba sunt Philippi
Cominii lib. 1, cap. 2¹) *vi demonstrare possent. Instructi enim et parati
cum exercitu esse volebant,* *ut si Rex consulere bono publico, et bonis
20 consiliis parere detrectaret, vi cogere invitum possent, qua de caussa
bellum illud Bono publico susceptum dicebatur, vulgoque Bellum boni*

---

3 *bc* 'Sed quoniam hoc in argumento et quasi campo versamur'.   **9 *c*¹** omits
this sentence, 'Ex quo...praeses esset.'.   **19 *c*¹** inserts here a parenthetical
expression '(quod tamen exemplum periculosum est, eiusque auctor aut suasor
esse nolim)'.

¹ *Mémoires*, I, 2; SHF, I, 14.

The memorable authority of the council against King Louis XI

The foregoing authorities reveal how great and, indeed, how holy was the force and authority of the council and the assembled estates. But, since we are involved with this theme,* we must not overlook an occasion when, within the memory of our fathers, the authority of this same council was exercised against King Louis XI, who is regarded as the most shrewd and crafty of all the kings we have mentioned. ^cFrom this example it is easy to understand, as we have already said on many occasions, that our ancestors did not impose upon themselves some fierce tyrant or butcher who would treat his subjects like cattle, but rather did they accept a king who would be the guardian of their rights and liberties and the protector of justice.†

^aIn the year 1460 the kingdom was being governed by Louis in such a fashion that in many matters the rule of a good prince and lover of his country was wanting. Consequently the authority of the council began to be needed, so that it might provide for the public welfare. Because it was thought that the king would be most unlikely to submit himself to it, the magnates of the kingdom, who were aroused by the continued queries and complaints of the common people, assembled their local forces and began to prepare an army to secure the public welfare and, in the words of Philippe de Commines,¹ 'to be able to show the king ^bby force ^athe corruption of his administration of the commonwealth. They intended to be ready and prepared with an army‡ so that, should the king refuse to take advice on the public welfare or to obey good counsels, they could oblige him by force against his will. Hence the

---

* **bc** theme *becomes* debate *and, so to speak, field of battle.* † **c¹** *omits the preceding sentence.* ‡ **c¹** *adds* (nevertheless, this is a dangerous instance, and I do not wish to be taken either for the author or the supporter of such a sentiment).

publici appellatum est. Procerum nomina idem Cominius,[2] Gillius,[3] Lamarcius[4] haec prodiderunt: Dux Borbonius, Dux Biturigum Regis frater; Comites Dunensis, Nivernensis, Armeniacus, Albretius; et is ad quem summa imperii respiciebat,

5 Dux Carolensis. Quacunque autem iter faciebant, pronuntiari iubebant, se *ᵇ*bellum *ᵃ*illud Bono publico instituere, tributorumque et vectigalium immunitatem indicebant (quae omnia Gillii verba sunt lib. 4, fol. 152[5]) legatosque et literas Lutetiam ad Parlamentum, Ecclesiasticos et Academiae rectorem miserunt

10 (verba haec eiusdem Gillii sunt fol. eodem[6]) ne putarent exercitum illum in Regis perniciem comparatum fuisse, verum ut illum ad boni Regis officium revocarent, sicuti boni publici ratio postulabat.

Verba autem Annalium, qui Chronica Ludovici XI inscripti

15 sunt, Lutetiae a Gallioto impressa, haec fere sunt, fol. 27:[7] Primum et summum postulatorum caput hoc fuit, ut Trium ordinum conventus haberetur, quippe, quod unicum omnibus seculis, malorum omnium remedium fuisset, vimque semper eiusmodi incommodis medendi habuisset. Rursus pag. 28:[8]

20 *Procerum legatis Senatus datus est Lutetiae, die XXIIII in Curia quae Domus civitatis dicitur, in quo affuerunt delecti ex Academia, ex parlamento, et ex Magistratibus. Responsum est, eorum postulatum aequissimum videri, conciliumque trium Ordinum indictum est.* Haec, inquam, Historici verba sunt, fol. 28, ex quibus verissimum istud

25 M. Antonii vetus verbum esse apparet:[9] *Etsi omnes molestae semper seditiones sunt, iustas tamen esse nonnullas, et prope necessarias. Eas vero iustissimas, maximeque necessarias videri,** cum populus Tyranni saevitia oppressus, auxilium a legitimo Civium conventu implorat. *ᵇQuid? deteriorne Civium conditio esse*

30 *debet, quam olim servorum fuerit?** qui saevitia dominorum

---

27 'videri': *c* 'quis non dicet'.   30 *c* 'fuit'.

[2] *Ibid.*; SHF, I, 14–17.   [3] Ed. 1551, II, fol. ci\.   [4] La Marche, *Mémoires,* Introd., c. 24; SHF, I, 124.   [5] Cf. ed. 1551, II, fol. ci\.   [6] *Ibid.*   [7] Roye, *Chron. scandaleuse*; SHF, I, 87–8. Quite distorted: an assembly of the King and those of his blood to hear grievances is called for, but not of the 'three orders'. [8] *Ibid.*, I, 91.   [9] Cicero, *De oratore*, II, 199; Loeb, 342.

war that was undertaken was said to be for the public welfare, and it was commonly called the War of the Common Weal.' Commines,[2] Gilles[3] and La Marche[4] have recorded the names of these magnates. They were the duke of Bourbon, the king's brother, the duke of Berry, the counts of Dunois, Nevers, Armagnac, and Albret, and the duke of Charolais, on whom was conferred the high command. Wherever they marched they ordered it to be proclaimed that they had started *b*the war *a*for the public welfare. They declared immunity from dues and taxes (all these matters are related by Gilles[5]), and they sent envoys and letters to the parlement of Paris, the clergy and the rector of the university (as indicated by Gilles in the same passage[6]), to prevent them from thinking that the army had been raised to destroy the king, whereas they wished to recall him to his duty to rule as a good king, as the public need demanded.

Moreover, a passage from the annals entitled the *Chronicles of Louis XI*, which was printed in Paris by Galliot du Près, reads as follows:[7] 'Their first and principal demand was that an assembly of the three estates should be held because to all men who were not of the priesthood it had been the sole remedy for all ills, and had always possessed the power to adjust difficulties of this sort.' On the next page occur these words:[8] 'On the twenty-fourth day an audience was given at the Hôtel de Ville in Paris for the envoys of the magistrates, at which were present the delegates of the university, the parlement and the magistrates. It was replied that their demand seemed most just, and a council of the three estates was summoned.' These are the very words of the historian, and they appear to confirm that old saying of Marcus Antonius:[9] 'Although in every age all seditions are troublesome, yet there are some that are just and even necessary.' But those that seem* the most just and necessary of all occur when a nation is oppressed by the savagery of a tyrant and implores the help of a lawful assembly of citizens. *b*What! Should the condition of citizens be worse than that of the slaves of former times, who were so oppressed by the savagery of

---

* *c* But those that seem *becomes* But who would not say that.

pressi ad urbis praefectum confugiebant, et de suis dominis verecunde (ut ait Ulpianus[10]) expostulabant.*

^aItaque Guaguinus in vita eiusdem Ludovici, ubi responsum Caroli Burgundiae Ducis ad Regis legatos exponit, his utitur
5 verbis, pag. 265:[11] *Audivit,* inquit, *Carolus legatos, verum ad Pacem nihil commodius esse respondit, quam trium Ordinum conventum, ubi tantas animorum et belli discordias componi oporteret; quod postquam per nuntios legati Ludovico retulerunt, ipse in dilatione spem reponens, Concilium apud Turones ad Kal. April. anni MCCCCLXVII*
10 *indixit. Conventionis definito tempore, affuere ex toto Regno,* etc. Quod idem totidem verbis traditur in iis quae diximus Annalibus, fol. 64,[12] et in Magno Chron., vol. 4, fol. 242,[13] ubi etiam illud additum est, quod memoria dignum ^bet ^asummopere observandum videtur, placuisse in eo Concilio, ut certi pro-
15 batique viri ex singulis ordinibus deligerentur, qui Rempublicam constituerent, et (ut ad verbum interpretemur) iuri ac iusticiae providerent. At N. Gillius, eo quem ostendimus loco:[14] *Post praelium,* inquit, *Montlerinum, delecti sunt complures egregie cordati et prudentes viri, qui boni publici curatores essent, quemadmodum inter*
20 *Regem et supradictos Proceres convenerat; primusque in eo numero fuit Comes Dunensis, qui primus discessionis illius auctor fuerat.*

Erat autem (ut superius dictum est) antiquae consuetudinis, postquam Ecclesiasticorum opes in tantam potentiam excreverant, ut populus in tres ordines describeretur, quorum unum
25 Ecclesiastici obtinerent, cumque Reipublicae curatores constituerentur, duodeni ex unoquoque ordine deligerentur. Itaque in eo Concilio constitutum fuit, ut XXXVI Reipublicae curatores crearentur, qui communi consilio publicis incommodis mederentur. Qua de re Monstrelletus vol. 4, fol. 150 ita scribit:[15]

---

2 *c*[1] suppresses the previous 67 words, 'ex quibus verissimum...expostulabant'.

10 Non invenio.   11 Bk. 10; ed. 1528, fol. cclxv.   12 Roye, *Chron. scand.*; SHF, I, 198ff.   13 *Grandes chroniques*; ed. 1518, IV, fol. 242^v. On Hotman's rendition of this passage, in the following lines, see above, p. 56.   14 Ed. 1551, II, ci^v.   15 Since the events related occurred after Monstrelet's time, the reference here must be to one of the early 16th-century editions of his chronicle which were brought up to date by using a mélange of other authors. The ordonnances regarding the commission of reformers are given in Isambert, X, 515f. & 529.

their masters that, as Ulpian tells us,[10] they fled to the prefect of the town and timidly complained about their lords?*

*a*Thus in his life of this same Louis, Gaguin, who is describing the reply of Duke Charles of Burgundy to the king's envoys, states:[11] 'Charles heard the ambassadors and replied that nothing would better advance the cause of peace than a meeting of the three estates, where it was proper for such discords, whether armed or unarmed, to be composed. When the ambassadors had reported this to Louis through messengers, the king relied upon the hope of delay, and summoned the council to Tours on 1 April 1467. At the time fixed for the assembly, there were present from the entire kingdom...' etc. The same is reported in so many words in the annals we have cited,[12] and in the fourth volume of the *Great Chronicle*,[13] where something is also added that is pre-eminently worth noting and remembering, namely that certain proven men should be chosen from each estate to restore the commonwealth and (we are reporting the writer to the letter) to provide for law and justice. Further, Nicolas Gilles, in the passage already quoted, states:[14] 'After the battle of Montlhéry, a number of exceptionally wise and prudent men were chosen as guardians of the public welfare in the manner agreed between the king and the magnates. The first among them was the count of Dunois, who had been the first author of the uprising.'

As we have said earlier, it was an ancient custom, after the wealth of the clergy had grown to excessive proportions, to rank the people in three orders, one of which had been taken over by the clergy. When the guardians of the commonwealth were established twelve were chosen from each order. Thus it was decided in that council that thirty-six guardians of the commonwealth should be created to remedy the public difficulties through joint consultation. In his fourth volume Monstrelet writes as follows about this matter:[15]

---

* *c*[1] *omits a large section of this paragraph, from* and they appear to confirm *to* complained about their lords.

Principio decretum est, ut ad Rempublicam constituendam, plebemque tributis et detrimentis sublevandam XXXVI viri auctoritate Regia deligerentur, duodeni ex clero, totidem ex equitibus, et totidem iuris et iustitiae periti, quibus potestas
5 permitteretur videndi, quibus vitiis atque incommodis Regnum laboraret, iisque vitiis remedium adhibendi; fidemque Rex regali dicto promissoque dedit (ad verbum, *Et promisit Rex in verbo Regis*) ratum se habiturum, quicquid illi XXXVI viri constituerent.

10 Haec Monstrelletus, cui Oliverius Lamarcius Belga, in historiae suae cap. 35 totidem prope verbis subscribit,[16] eundemque XXXVI Curatorum Reipublicae numerum prodit; simulque ascribit, cum Rex ei dicto promissoque non stetisset, fidemque publicam et publice iuratam violasset, miserrimum in
15 Francogallia bellum exarsisse, quod annos prope XIII duravit. Ita Regis periurium cum ipsius infamia, tum etiam populi pernicie expiatum est.

Utcunque sit, perspicuum est, nondum centesimum annum abiisse, ex quo Francogalliae libertas, solennisque Concilii
20 auctoritas vigebat, et vigebat adversus Regem, neque aetate, neque animo imbecillum, sed et iam annorum XL maiorem, et tanta ingenii magnitudine praeditum, quantam nunquam in ullo Rege nostro fuisse constat. Ut facile intelligatur, Rempublicam nostram libertate fundatam et stabilitam, annos amplius centum
25 et mille statum illum suum liberum et sacrosanctum, etiam vi et armis adversus Tyrannorum potentiam, retinuisse.

Neque vero praeclarum hac de re Philippi Cominii clarissimi viri et ornatissimi historici elogium praetermittendum videtur, qui lib. Hist. 5, cap. 18 in hanc scribit sententiam, quam ad verbum
30 convertemus:[17] *Quare ut in instituto sermone pergamus, ecquis est in orbe terrarum Rex, aut Princeps, cui ius sit tributum unius teruncii subiectis suis sine ipsorum consensu et voluntate imponere? nisi violentia et tyrannide uti velit. At enim (dixerit aliquis) potest tempus incidere,*

---

[16] La Marche, *Mémoires*, I, 35; SHF, III, I. [17] V, 19; SHF, II, 141.

'In the first place it was decreed that thirty-six men should be chosen with royal authority to reform the commonwealth and relieve the common people of the burden of taxes and exactions. Twelve were to be from the clergy, twelve from the nobility and twelve from men experienced in law and justice. To them would be entrusted the power to find out what faults and difficulties the kingdom was enduring and to bring forward a remedy for these defects. The king pledged his faith and promised with his royal word (the actual phrase used is: the king promised by the king's word) that he would accept whatever those thirty-six men decided.'

Such are the words of Monstrelet, and his account is confirmed by Olivier de la Marche the Belgian in almost the same words in his history.[16] He also records the number of guardians of the commonwealth as thirty-six. He adds at the same time that, since the king did not stand by his word and violated the oath he had publicly sworn, a most lamentable war was kindled in Francogallia, which lasted for nearly thirteen years. In this way the king's perjury was expiated both by his own disgrace and the ruin of the people.

However this may be, it is clear that less than a century ago the liberty of Francogallia and the authority of the solemn council flourished, and the council directed its vigour against a king who was neither young in age nor deranged in mind, but who was over forty years of age and endowed with greater talents than was any other of our kings. So it may readily be understood that our commonwealth, which was founded and established upon liberty, retained that free and holy condition for more than eleven centuries, and even resisted the power of tyrants by armed force.

Nor should we fail to mention the celebrated encomium on this matter by that most famous man and excellent historian, Philippe de Commines, who offers the following opinion which we quote verbatim:[17] 'Wherefore let us continue with the argument we began, and ask whether there is a king or a prince in the whole wide world who has the right to levy a farthing's tax upon his subjects without their consent and free will unless he wishes to practise violence and tyranny. But, someone might say, there may

cum ^b*publicum* ^a*populi Concilium expectandum non est, neque tantam moram res patitur. Verum* in bello suscipiendo nihil tanta celeritate est opus; satis ad eam rem temporis suppeditat. Addo etiam illud, cum Reges et Principes bellum civium suorum consensu susci-*
5 *piunt, multo et potentiores sunt, et hostibus suis formidabiliores.*

    Et rursus aliquanto post:[18] *Regem Galliae minime omnium decet his uti verbis: 'Habeo potestatem exigendi a meis civibus, quantum mihi libet.' Nam neque ipse, neque quisquam alius eam potestatem habet. Qui vero his utuntur verbis, nullum ei honorem tribuunt, neque*
10 *illius auctoritatem et existimationem apud exteras nationes augent. Verum ex contrario, terrorem finitimis iniiciunt, qui nulla conditione dominatum illius subire vellent. At si Rex noster, aut ii qui potentiam eius praedicant, ita loquerentur: 'Habeo subiectos ita mansuetos et obsequentes, ut nihil eorum quae impero facere detrectent, neque quis-*
15 *quam Princeps subiectos habet aeque obsequentes, quique calamitatum et incommodorum suorum facilius obliviscantur', haec oratio magnae illi laudi atque ornamento esset. Verum illa Regem non decet: 'Exigo, quantum volo, eiusque rei potestatem habeo, quam mihi conservare* volo.' Rex Carolus quintus hac oratione non utebatur. Neque sane*
20 *Regem ullum nostrum illis utentem verbis audivi, sed quosdam ipsorum comites et ministros, qui sibi bonam Regibus navare operam videbantur. Verum meo iudicio adversus illos peccabant, et tantum assentandi causa ita loquebantur, neque satis quid dicerent, considerabant.*

    Atque ut certius mansueti Gallorum ingenii argumentum pro-
25 *feramus, consideremus Concilium trium Ordinum Turonibus, post Regis nostri Ludovici XI excessum, habitum, anno nimirum 1484. Existimari per id tempus poterat, bonum illum Ordinum conventum periculosum esse; dicebantque nescio qui, non magni pretii homines, saepiusque post id tempus dixerunt, crimen esse laesae Maiestatis,*
30 *siquis de trium Ordinum concilio convocando verba faciat. Id enim ad minuendam Regis auctoritatem pertinere. Verum illi ipsi sunt, qui*

---

2 *bc* 'Sane'.   18 *bc* '*conservatam*'.
[18] *Ibid.*, SHF, II, 142–3.

be a time when one should not wait for a *b*public *a*council of the people, and the matter does not brook such a delay. Yet,* in the undertaking of a war, preparations do not require such haste, and there is time enough to make ready. I might also point out that when kings and princes undertake a war with the consent of their subjects, they are much more powerful and formidable to their enemies.'

In a later passage he writes:[18] 'It becomes the king of France least of all to say: "I have the power to exact as much as I like from my subjects." For neither he nor anyone else has such power. Those who employ such words do their king no honour, nor do they increase his authority and reputation in the eyes of foreign nations. On the contrary, they inspire their neighbours with fear, and they become unwilling to submit to his rule under any circumstances. But if our king, or those who proclaim his power, were to say, "I have such gentle and obedient subjects that nothing will prevent them from doing what I ask of them, nor does any prince have subjects so obedient, or subjects who will more easily forget their disasters and misfortunes", then such a speech would be greatly to the king's praise and glory. It certainly does not become a king to say: "I take what I like. I have the power to do so, and I intend to keep it." King Charles V did not use such words. Nor, indeed, have I heard any other king speak so, but only certain officials and ministers, who considered they were acting in the king's best interest. In my view they did him a disservice, and spoke in this way merely for the sake of flattery, without sufficiently considering what they said.

'To offer a more certain proof of the peaceful disposition of the French, let us consider the council of the three estates that was held at Tours in the year 1484, after the death of our King Louis XI. At that time it could be thought that that wise assembly of the estates was a dangerous thing, and there have been some men of no great account who said then, and often said since, that it was high treason to speak of convening the council of the three estates, since it tended to diminish the authority of the king. But indeed these were

* *bc* Indeed.

crimen illud adversus Deum, et Regem et Rempublicam committunt.
Neque verba eiusmodi aliis prosunt, quam iis, qui nullo suo merito
gradus honorum et dignitatum obtinent, neque ad illos obtinendos sunt
idonei, sed assentari et servire auribus didicerunt, et nugatoriis de rebus
5 *verba facere; magnosque conventus hominum reformidant, ne quales*
sunt, tales agnoscantur, eorumque opera vituperentur.

*b*Haec *c*ad verbum *b*Cominaeus, ex quibus aliisque quae
superius de retenta publici concilii in Ludovicum XI auctoritate
diximus, perspicue intelligitur, etiam usque ad id tempus nobile
10 illud praeceptum, a Turcica tyrannide alienum, viguisse: SALUS
POPULI SUPREMA LEX ESTO. Sed hanc conventus publici
libertatem *c*palpatores aulici, *b*regum assentatores, et qui malis
artibus honores adepti sunt (ut Cominaeus scribit[19]) omni studio
et contentione aversantur. Qua de re Budaeus quoque libro de
15 Asse IIII sic scribit:[20] *Quare, si moribus iam nostris, qui rerum*
summam tenent, tenebuntque in posterum, IN DISQUISITIONEM
CONVENTUUM aliquando vocentur, nonnulli saepe qui sese
nasutos videri volunt, haud dubie (quod aiunt) apprime simi, atque ea
parte deformes ab omnibus cernerentur.

20 *c*Haec Budaeus, circiter illud tempus, quo Rex Franciscus
primus ex Hispania (quo captivus abductus fuerat) reversus, ut
redemptionis suae nomine pecuniam conficeret, tributum Ordinibus sui Regni non pro suo iure imperavit, sed (ut auctores
omnes affirmant) ab iis bona sine gratia, sine venia impetravit;
25 qua de re Nic. Boerius Decis. cxxvi ita scribit:[21] *Anno Domini*
MDXXVII, Princeps noster in mense Decemb. convocavit praelatos,
nec non nobiles de eius sanguine, et alios regni sui, et ex quolibet
Parlamento unum praesidentem, et duos consiliarios, qui omnes ita
REGI ANNUERUNT TALLIAM, USQUE AD SUMMAM DUO-
30 *RUM MILLIONUM, pro redemptione sua, imponere et levare posse.*

---

[19] Cf. *ibid.*; SHF, II, 152.   [20] Ed. 1532, III.   [21] Decis. 126, §11; ed. 1567, 217–18.

the very men who committed that crime against God, the king and the commonwealth. Words of this kind profit no one save those who obtain positions of honour and dignity through no merit of their own. Nor are these men capable of acquiring such places except by learning to flatter and gratify and to talk about trifles. They dread large assemblies of men in case they should be recognized for what they are and have their deeds denounced.'

*b*From Commines' words, *c*cited verbatim, *b*and those of the other authors we have mentioned earlier about the preservation of the authority of the public council against Louis XI, it can clearly be understood that that noble precept, so alien to the Turkish tyranny, 'LET THE WELFARE OF THE PEOPLE BE THE SUPREME LAW', retained its vigour right up to that time. But *c*the courtly sycophants, *b*the flatterers of kings, and those who acquire honours through their evil arts (as Commines writes[19]) shun the liberty of the public assembly with all the effort and exertion they can apply. In the fourth part of his book *De asse* Budé writes on the matter as follows:[20] 'If, according to our customs, those who hold high office today, or are likely to hold it in the future, are on some occasion summoned to an inquest of the estates, there will be some who often want to put on airs, and unquestionably everyone will see these men in particular for what they really are.'

*c*Budé wrote these words at about that time when King Francis I, who had been led away as a captive, returned from Spain. In order to complete the sum stipulated for his ransom, the king demanded a subsidy from the estates of his kingdom. However, he did not order it by his own right, but rather, as all authors affirm, he procured contributions from the estates without courtesy or politeness. On this matter Nicolas Bohier writes in his collection as follows:[21] 'In December of the year 1527 our prince called together the bishops (but only those of noble family) together with others from his kingdom and one president and two counsellors chosen at random from the parlements. These men all agreed that the king could raise and levy a tax of up to two million livres for his ransom.'

Alterum eiusdem publici concilii facinus insigne in papa Benedicto XIII damnando et repudiando

Hactenus quanta publici Francogalliae concilii auctoritas in damnanda Papae Bonifacii VIII insania fuerit, satis explicatum arbitramur. Nunc alterum eiusdem auctoritatis exemplum in Papa Benedicto XIII damnando ac repudiando proponamus.
5 Quo tempore Rex Carolus VI Galliae gubernacula tenebat, circiter illud tempus mirificum quoddam Antipaparum aliquot certamen extitit, quod annos amplius XXX factionibus exitiosis, summa cum omnium rerum perturbatione et piorum animorum cruciatu, moerore ac prope desperatione duravit, neque ullus in
10 orbe Christiano Princeps fuit, neque Rex neque Imperator, qui non omne suum studium in illa funesta et calamitosa Anti-paparum contentione sedanda interposuerit, quam historiam Platina,[1] Krantzius[2] et Guaguinus[3] memoriae prodiderunt, sed omnium copiosissime is, qui assiduus tragoediarum illarum
15 spectator fuit, Theodor. Nyhemius, lib. de schismate 3.[4] Sed quoniam hanc operam Gallis nostris potissimum navamus, com-modius fore arbitramur, unius Enguerrantii Monstreletti, qui Gallorum prope omnium manibus teritur, testimonium sequi, totamque ipsius hac de re narrationem breviter comprehendere.
20 Sic enim fere ad verbum sub cap. XL, et aliquot insequentibus scriptum reliquit:[5] Rex Carolus VI per legatos denuntiavit Petro

---

Cap. c[1] suppressed this entire chapter.

[1] Ed. 1530, ccciiᵛff.   [2] *Metropolis*, XI, 30; ed. 1568, 354.   [3] Cf. Bk. 8; ed. 1528, fol. cxciᵛ.   [4] A general reference to Dietrich von Nieheim's *De schismate*. [5] Everything from here to the end of this chapter is drawn from Monstrelet, I, 41–3 (SHF, I, 255–67), but so highly condensed and paraphrased that only the documents quoted verbatim out of Monstrelet have been italicized.

^{cc2}CHAPTER XXIV*

The other remarkable deed of that same council in condemning and repudiating Pope Benedict XIII

So far we believe we have sufficiently explained the extent of the authority of the public council of Francogallia in condemning the madness of Pope Boniface VIII. Now we may offer another example of this same authority in condemning and repudiating Pope Benedict XIII. At this time King Charles VI controlled the government of France and in this extraordinary period a certain conflict was waged between a number of antipopes. This situation lasted for more than thirty years, with pernicious factions, a general disturbance in all spheres of life, and a state of anxiety, lamentation and near despair for pious souls. Nor was there any prince in Christendom, be he king or emperor, who had not applied all his energy to resolving that fatal and disastrous dispute of the antipopes. This is recorded by Platina,[1] Krantz[2] and Gaguin,[3] but the most complete account of all is provided in the third book of the work on the schism by Dietrich von Nieheim,[4] who was a zealous observer of those tragic events. Since, however, we have preferred to devote this work to our fellow countrymen, we think it more convenient to follow the account of Enguerrand Monstrelet alone, whose work has been used exhaustively by nearly every Frenchman, and briefly to recount his whole description of the affair.

This is what Monstrelet wrote, almost word for word, in his history:[5] 'After the nomination of Boniface (the name should be

---

* c¹ omits this chapter.

de Luna, Bonifacio [*leg.* Benedicto] XIII per papificationem
nominato, nisi intra tempus illud, quod de communi Christianorum Principum sententia praestitutum erat, finem illi
funesto certamini imponeret, ac de papatu cum aemulo suo
5 transigeret, fore, ut ipse, suique omnes Galliae populi sibi consilium caperent, ac neutri Antipaparum obedientiam praestarent.
Hac denuntiatione Papa Benedictus graviter indignatus, animi
tamen offensionem vultu atque oratione tegens, blanda oratione
legatos dimisit, confirmans se propediem responsum per certum
10 hominem ac nuntium Regi missurum. Pauculis post diebus
diploma quam Bullam appellant, Regi per emissarium quemdam
misit, qua et Regem et omnes ipsius imperio subiectos excom-
municabat, sacrisque omnibus tanquam impios ac profanos
arcebat. Ea bulla perlecta, eiusque rei fama per universam
15 Galliam disseminata, Rex Concilium publicum Lutetiam
Parisiorum indicit, quo in conventu de communi ordinum
sententia decreta haec fuerunt:⁶ *primum ut Benedictus Papa deinceps*
pro schismatico, haeretico, et Ecclesiae Christianae perturbatore
haberetur; neve illi obedientia ulla praestaretur; utique acta illius omnia
20 *irrita essent; tum ut bulla Regi missa pronuntiaretur impia, scelerata,*
et in regiam Maiestatem contumeliosa; atque iccirco palam inspectante
populo laceraretur; postremo, ut tam atrox illata Regi et regno iniuria
tum adversus Papam, ipsius auctorem, tum etiam adversus omnes
ipsius factionis socios vindicaretur.
25   His decretis palam in conventu pronuntiatis confestim Rector
Academiae Parisiensis e sella exsurgens bullam cepit, eamque
inspectante Rege in procerum delectorumque omnium conspectu suis manibus discidit. Nuntius autem Papae qui eam
attulerat, atque alter quidam eiusdem Pontificis emissarius
30 talaribus amicti togis, in quibus inversa Papae insignia depicta
erant, mitra capitibus imposita, in qua grandibus literis elogium
hoc scriptum erat: HI SUNT IN ECCLESIAM ET REGEM

---

⁶ *Ibid.*, I, 41; SHF, I, 256–7.

read as Benedict) XIII by the papal electoral machinery King Charles VI informed Piero de Luna [i.e. Benedict] through his ambassadors that, unless he put an end to that fatal contest within the time specified by the common agreement of the Christian princes, and brought the rivalry for the papacy to a conclusion, the king and all the people of France would take counsel together and offer allegiance to neither of the antipopes. Pope Benedict deeply resented this declaration. However, by his expression and the words he spoke he concealed his anger, and sent the ambassadors away with mild words, asserting that he would send an early reply to the king through a reliable nuncio. After a few days he sent the king, by means of a certain emissary, a document known as a bull, by which he excommunicated the king and all those under his rule, and forbad such impious and profane men all religious observances. When that bull had been carefully examined, and a report of the matter circulated throughout the whole of France, the king summoned a public council to Paris. There the following decrees were enacted with the general approval of the estates:[6] "First that thenceforth Pope Benedict would be regarded as a schismatic, a heretic and a disturber of the Christian church; no kind of obedience would be offered him; all his pronouncements would, without exception, be annulled; the bull he had sent the king would be declared impious, criminal and derogatory to kingly majesty, and would publicly be torn to pieces before the eyes of the people; and, last, that so horrible was the insult hurled at the king and the kingdom that it should be avenged against the pope, its author, and against all those who belonged to his party."

'When these decrees had been openly announced in the assembly, the rector of the University of Paris forthwith rose from his seat, took the bull, and, with the king looking on and in the presence of the nobles and delegates, tore it asunder with his own hands. Moreover, the pope's nuncio who had brought the bull, together with another emissary from that same pontiff, were clad in long robes reaching to their ankles, on which the papal insignia had been painted upside down; and turbans were placed upon their heads, on which the following inscription had been written in large letters:

PERFIDI,[7] e carcere usque ad palatii Parisiensis aream advecti
sunt, atque in contabulato ex tempore extructo destituti, summa
cum Papae infamia ac dedecore catamidiati, omnium irrisui ac
ludibrio expositi, ioculare Parisiensibus spectaculum praebu-
5 erunt. Tertio denique post die iterum in plaustrum impositi
ac per urbis vias circunvecti, convitiis, sibilis, clamoribus
omnium vexati, vix e populi insultantibus manibus effugerunt.

---

[7] *Ibid.*, I, 43; SHF, I, 265.

"These men are traitors to both church and king."[7] They were carried from their prison to the open space before the palace in Paris, set down upon a hurriedly constructed wooden platform, and flogged as a mark of the pope's infamy and shame. They were exposed to the mockery and derision of all, and provided a public spectacle for the amusement of the Parisians. Finally after the third day they were again placed upon a cart and carried through the streets of the city, where they were subjected to the insults, hisses and shouts of all, and barely escaped alive from the humiliation inflicted by the people.'

CAPUT XXV [c¹XXIII]

Regem Francogalliae non infinitam in suo regno
dominationem habere, sed certo iure certisque
legibus circumscriptam*

Satis igitur demonstratum esse arbitramur, Regibus Francogalliae non immensam atque infinitam potestatem a suis civibus
permissam fuisse, ut legibus omnibus soluti dici possint, sed eos
certis legibus et pactionibus obligatos esse, quarum primam esse*
5 summam hanc fuisse ostendimus: ut publici Concilii auctoritatem sanctam inviolatamque servarent, eumque conventum,
quoties utilitas Reipublicae postularet, sua praesentia concele-
brarent. Ac leges quidem, quibus Reges astrictos esse constat,
permultae sunt. Verum nos eas solas de quibus nemo nisi
10 amentissimus, nemo nisi patriae, parentum ac liberorum suorum
hostis ambigit, ut quaeque memoratu dignae videbuntur,
exponemus.

Prima igitur haec esto: Ut ne quid quod ad statum Reipublicae in universum pertineat, Regi sine publici Concilii
15 auctoritate statuere liceat, cuius rei cum antea certissima testimonia protulimus, tum etiam expressissimum et evidentissimum
usque ad hanc aetatem nostram vestigium illud manet, quod
senatus Parisiensis, qui veteris illius Parlamenti auctoritatem sibi
magna ex parte ascivit, nullas Regis constitutiones, nulla edicta
20 rata esse patitur, nisi quae apud se pro consilio cognita, et
consiliariorum suorum sententiis comprobata fuerint; ut non
incommode dici possit, similem hoc quidem in genere videri

Cap. c¹ omits words 'non infinitam' and 'sed'.   **4** c¹ 'ac'.

That the king of Francogallia does not have unlimited
authority within his kingdom but is circumscribed
by well-defined right and specified laws*

We believe, therefore, that it has been sufficiently shown that a
boundless and unlimited power was not allowed the kings of
Francogallia by their subjects, and they cannot be described as free
from all laws. Rather were they restrained by defined laws and
compacts, and we have shown the first and foremost of these was
that they should preserve the authority of the public council as
something holy and inviolate, and should honour that assembly
with their presence as often as the need of the commonwealth
might demand. There are, indeed, a great many laws established to
restrict kings. But we shall set forth only those of our own laws
which no one who is not completely mad, or admits himself to
be the enemy of his country, his parents and his children, will
deny to be worth relating.

The first of these particular laws may be defined as follows: That
it is not lawful for the king to determine anything that affects the
condition of the commonwealth as a whole without the authority
of the public council. In this regard we have put forward irrefutable
evidence from earlier times and, equally, there is a very precise and
clear remnant of the practice which has lasted right down to our
own age, namely, that the parlement of Paris, which in great part
has appropriated to itself the authority of the ancient parliament,
allows neither the king's laws nor his edicts to be enacted unless
they have been examined and given the parlement's consideration,
and approved by the opinions of its judges. So it may not be inappropriate to say that the authority of the parlement seems to be

* **c¹** *changes title of chapter to read* That the king of Francogallia has an authority
in his kingdom which is circumscribed by well-defined right and specified laws.

Senatus illius auctoritatem veterum Tribunorum plebis potestati, quos Val. Maximus scribit,[1] in vestibulo Senatus expectare solitos, dum ad se decreta eius ordinis afferrentur, quae* ipsi pro Concilio cognoscerent, ut si plebi utilia viderentur, literam T
5 quasi assensus sui notam atque indicem subscriberent[2]; sin minus, vetarent, atque intercederent.

Quanquam Budaeus, vir doctissimus, aliunde similitudinem sumit:[3] *sicuti populo Romano* (inquit) *sciscente aliquid, Senatum auctorem fieri oportebat, quod nunc verbo Graeco 'Homologare'*
10 *dicimus, ita Principum nostrorum constitutionibus, ut vim sanctionum habeant, huiusmodi actis ad Rempublicam pertinentibus auctorem Curiam fieri hodie necesse est, easque in curia promulgari.* Et paulo post:[4] *In hac curia praefecti provinciarum ac iuridici, quos Ballivos, Seneschallos, et huiusmodi nominibus vocamus, in leges iurare solent.**
15 *In huius acta referri diplomata, regiaque beneficia solent, ut perpetua esse possint, ac nunquam antiquabilia. Huius auctoritate rata irritave Principum acta, ne ipsis quidem recusantibus, fiunt. Una haec curia est, a qua sibi ius dari Principes (legibus soluti) civili animo ferunt, quam auctorem fieri sacrandis promulgandisque sanctionibus suis volunt.*
20 *Cuius concilii censurae constitutiones suas eximi, edictaque sua nolint, imo cuius decretis acta sua consecrari aeternitati velint.* Haec Budaeus.

Ut* igitur hanc sibi potestatem Senatus ille tyrannice usurpavit, ut Regiis edictis atque imperiis intercederet, quod certe credibile non est; aut illud fateamur necesse est, Regibus non liberam et
25 infinitam rerum omnium potestatem permissam antiquitus fuisse quod etiam Auffrerius,[5] Boerius,[6] Montanius,[7] Chassanaeus[8] aliique summae apud Gallias* auctoritatis pragmatici, una voce, sine ulla varietate, attestantur.

---

3 *c*[1] 'qui'. 14 *c* actually reads 'soleat'. 22 *c*[1] 'Aut'. 27 *c*[1] 'Gallos'.

[1] Cf. II, ii, 7; Teubner, 65. [2] Valerius Maximus reads 'C', not 'T'; see the remarks of the editor, *loc. cit.* [3] *Annot.* §Ex l. ult. de Senat.; ed. 1557, 93.
[4] *Ibid.*, 69. [5] Probably a reference to ch. 2 of *Instructiones abbreviatae ad habendum notitiam stili curiae Parlementi*, which is usually part two of 16th-century editions of Du Breuil's *Stilus curiae parlamenti*; cf., *e.g.*, ed. 1551, 132. [6] See above, p. 416, n. 5. [7] Montaigne, *Tract. de auct. parlamentorum.* [8] Undoubtedly *Comm. in consuetud. Burg.*

similar in kind to the power of the ancient tribunes of the people, who, as described by Valerius Maximus,[1] were wont to wait in the vestibule of the senate while its decrees were brought out to them. They examined these decrees on behalf of the council to see if they appeared to be of value to the common people, and signed them with the letter T as a mark and indication of their consent.[2] But, if they did not agree, they signified their prohibition and opposed the measure.

On the other hand, that very learned man, Budé, sees the similarity from a different point of view:[3] 'Just as it was necessary', he writes, 'for the Roman people to find out what was done by the authority of the senate – a process we now describe with the Greek word *homologare* – so it is necessary today to give the laws of our princes the force of ordinances in this way by making the court sanction those which pertain to the commonwealth, and by promulgating them in the court.' A little further on Budé states:[4] 'In this court the governors and judges of the provinces, whom we call bailiffs, seneschals and suchlike names, customarily swear to observe the laws. In this court it is customary for public deeds, documents and royal grants to be registered so that they can be permanent and never grow out of date. With the court's authority the ordinances of princes are either confirmed or rendered invalid, when the princes do not themselves object. This is the one court through which princes (who are free from the laws) act to give law to themselves, as though it were a public mind which they wish to see as authorising, sanctifying and promulgating their ordinances. Instead of desiring their laws and edicts to be exempted from the critical judgment of this council, they wish that through its decrees their enactments may be consecrated for all eternity.' Such are the words of Budé. Thus either the senate tyrannically usurped this power to oppose the royal edicts and commands, which is certainly not credible, or else we must acknowledge that kings were not granted a free and unlimited power over all things in antiquity, which is also what Aufrier,[5] Bohier,[6] Montaigne,[7] Chasseneuz[8] and other practising lawyers of the highest authority in France attest with a single voice and without any variation.

Age, reliquas leges regias videamus, atque hanc in primis: Ut Regi ius non sit neque filium adoptare, neque de suo regno, vel inter vivos, vel per testamentum disponere, sed in regni successione maiorum instituta et antiqua consuetudo servetur. Nam
5 Ioannes de terra rubea tracta. 1, concil. 9, ita scribit:[9] *Reges Franciae non potuerunt unquam, neque posset Rex modernus facere testamentum de regno, nec primogenitum aut alterum haeredem facere in illo. Item, adeo ex vi consuetudinis in regno Franciae succeditur, quod sicut nec ex voluntate dispositiva et testamentaria regis successio*
10 *defertur eius successori, nec deferri potest; sic nec ex tacita voluntate eius ab intestato dispositiva ei succedi potest, sed solum Consuetudo succedenti defert regnum.* Haec Terrirubrius. Cuius sententiam cum omnis comprobat antiquitas, tum vero vel maxime historia haec memorabilis, quam subiungam.

15 Anno MCCCCXX, cum Rex Carolus VI Henrico Angliae Regi suum regnum mortis caussa donasset, eumque sibi successorem designasset, repente populus ad publicum gentis concilium provocavit, in quo summa omnium consensione pronuntiatum est, donationem illam ipso iure nullam, inutilem atque irritam
20 fuisse; neque Regi Galliae fas esse, ullam sui regni partem sine publico gentis suae consensu alienare; cuius rei auctores sunt Enguer. Monstrel. cap. hist. 225, et aliis inseqq.;[10] itemque Guill. Benedict. in cap. Raynut. in verb. nume. 188:[11] *Cum Carolus sextus,* inquit, *ex matrimonio iusto filium haberet, cui regnum*
25 *debebatur, non potuit Regem Angliae adoptare in filium, in praeiudicium filii sui legitimi, et naturalis, nec adoptio valuit, nec tenuit, quinimo regnum dicto Carolo septimo delatum fuit.* Item in verb. In eodem testamento, numer. 151:[12] *Ex quibus,* inquit, *confutatur, et penitus confunditur, ut ipso iure nihil valuerit ille tractatus pacis, quem*
30 *Angli praetendunt passatum fuisse inter Carolum sextum, Francorum*

---

[9] Terre Rouge, *Tractatus,* I, i, x–xi; ed. 1585, 83–4.   [10] SHF, III, 388ff.
[11] Benedicti, *In cap. Ray. de test.,* 'Et uxorem nomine Adelasiam', 188; ed. 1575, I, 109ᵛ.   [12] *Ibid.,* 'In eodem testamento relinquens: 1', §151; *ed. cit.,* I, 195ᵛ.

Very well then, let us consider the other royal laws, and among the first the law that the king has no right to adopt a son or to dispose of his kingdom either by distribution among the living or by making a will. Rather is the established and ancient custom preserved that succession to the kingdom goes to the elder. For Jean de Terre Rouge writes as follows in his first treatise:[9] 'The kings of France were never able to bequeath the kingdom by testament, nor to make their first born or any other their heir, and neither can any modern king do so. Further, since the succession is established by the force of custom in the kingdom of France, it cannot be conferred on a successor by the king's express disposition, whether testamentary or otherwise, and in the same way it cannot be disposed of by a decision which is not formally expressed, as in the case of one who dies intestate. But established custom alone confers the kingdom on the successor.' So writes Terre Rouge. Although all antiquity may serve to prove this opinion, there can be no more memorable instance of it than the history I now provide.

In the year 1420, when King Charles VI had promised his kingdom to King Henry of England at his death, and had designated him as his successor, the people unexpectedly appealed to the public council of the nation. There it was proclaimed with the entire agreement of all present that the donation was legally without value and quite invalid, and that a king of France had no right to alienate any part of his kingdom without the public consent of his people. The authorities for this are Enguerrand Monstrelet in his history[10] and Guillaume Benedicti in his gloss on a certain decretal of Canon Law.[11] 'Since Charles VI', he writes, 'had a son in legal matrimony, who was due to inherit the kingdom, he could not adopt the king of England as his son to the prejudice of his own legitimate and natural son. Hence the adoption was invalid and had no force, and the kingdom was instead passed to Charles VII.' In another of his comments, when referring to that same will, he states:[12] 'Hence that argument may be refuted and shown to be false throughout, since under the law there was no validity in the peace treaty which the English claim was agreed between King

regem, et Henricum quintum, Regem Angliae, per quem dictus
Carolus dominam Catharinam filiam suam nuptui dedit praefato
Henrico, eumque sibi adoptavit in filium, nec non sine proceribus solus
existens declaravit coronam Franciae eidem pertinere, et post sui
5 *decessum totum Franciae regnum ad ipsum perventurum. Sed dictus*
tractatus a proceribus regni reprobatus fuit, qui Carolum eius filium
ungi* et coronari fecerunt. Haec Bened. Secunda igitur Regni
Francogalliae illa lex esto.

Deinceps tertiam videamus, quam esse constat huiusmodi, ut
10 Rege mortuo regni hereditas filio ipsius natu maximo deferatur,
neque regi vel natu minorem maiori anteferre, vel alium sibi
successorem instituere liceat. Cuius haec ratio est certissima,
quoniam parentes ea demum adimere suis liberis possunt, quae
ab ipsis proficiscuntur, quae vero vel natura, vel lege atque
15 institutis maiorum iis addicta sunt, in iis parentes ius nullum
habent: l. si arrogator 22, D. de arrogat.;[13] l. 3, D. de interd. et
releg.[14] Filius autem natu maximus suitatem et spem hereditatis,
non parentis sed legis communis beneficio adeptus est, neque
illam suo patri acceptam ferre debet, sed legibus atque institutis
20 maiorum. Itaque rectissime doctores omnes uno consensu
affirmant, Regem Francorum non posse auferre primogenito ius
primogeniturae, sine spe regni, et dare secundo genito, vel alteri:
Ioan. Andr. in c. licet, de voto;[15] Bald. de prohib. feud. alien.
per Frid. § illud;[16] Panorm. cons. 3, nitar in praesenti, lib. 2;[17]
25 Iason in l. nemo potest, De legat. 1;[18] Bald. in c. 1, De feud.
March. ducat.;[19] sed praecipue Ioan. Terrirubius tract. 1,

---

7 c[1] 'ungere'.

[13] *Dig.* 1, 7, 22; Mommsen, I, 38. (Read *de adopt.* for *de arrogat.* at the end of Hotman's allegation.)   [14] *Dig.* 48, 22, 3; Mommsen, I, 871.   [15] Cf. Joh. Andreae on c. 6 X 3, 34: *Decretalia commentaria,* ed. 1581, III, 170, §12.   [16] Baldus, *In usus feud. comm.;* ed. 1585, 79ᵛ–80. More to the point is 'Quibus modis feudum amittantur', §Praeterea; *ed. cit.,* 17.   [17] Panormitanus, Cons. 3 (of Bk. II), §4; ed. 1547, fol. 58ff.   [18] (*Dig.* 30, 55, 3) Jason de Maino, *Infort. comment.;* ed. 1573, 75ᵛ. But note that after saying that the first-born's right is inviolable, Jason goes on: 'Tu intellige, nisi primogenitus esset sufficiens tunc pater in testamento posset regnum demittere secundo genito.'   [19] Baldus, *In usus feud. comm.;* ed. 1585, 23.

Charles VI of France and King Henry V of England, whereby the said Charles gave his daughter, the lady Catharine, in marriage to the aforesaid Henry, and adopted the latter as his son. On his own authority and without the magnates he declared that the crown of France should belong to Henry, and that upon his own death the whole kingdom of France would go to him. But the said treaty was rejected by the magnates of the kingdom, who had his son, Charles, anointed and crowned.' So writes Benedicti. This, therefore, should be the second law of the kingdom of Francogallia.

Next, let us consider the third law, which consists in this, that at the death of a king the hereditary claim to the kingdom passes to his eldest son by birth, and it is unlawful to substitute a younger son for an elder, or to institute any other person as his successor. There is the best of reasons for this, since while parents can deprive their children of anything that originated from the parents themselves, they have no right over their children in anything awarded them either by nature or by the law and customs of their ancestors. In support of this we may cite the twenty-second book of the *Digest* concerning the rights of sons,[13] and the third book concerning prohibitions and rejections.[14] Moreover, the eldest son by birth acquires his personal claim and hereditary expectation not as a favour granted by a parent but rather as one granted through the common law. Nor should such a son regard this right as a thing received from his father, but as one received by the laws and customs of his ancestors. All the learned doctors of the law most correctly agree, and with unanimity, that the king of the Franks can withdraw neither the right of primogeniture nor the expectation of reigning from his first born son, and that he cannot give it to a second son or to another. We cite Johannes Andreae,[15] Baldus in his commentaries on feudal usage,[16] Panormitanus,[17] Jason de Maino,[18] Baldus on feudal usage in the dukedom of Marche,[19]

concl. 9, ubi sic scribit:²⁰ *Reges Franciae nunquam consueverunt de regno testari, sed solum ex vi consuetudinis defertur successio primogenitis maribus ex linea recta eorum, quibus succeditur, et illa desinente succedunt mares transversales iuxta gradus praerogativam.* Item,

5   concl. 9, 10, 11, & 12, ubi sic loquitur:²¹ In regno Franciae non habetur successio hereditaria sive patrimonialis, sed simplex successio, sive subrogatio primogeniti, vel proximioris agnati, cui regnum debetur ex sola lege vel consuetudine regni, a qua sola ius accipit, et non a patre vel alio praedecessore.

10   Et sic ius primogeniturae, quantum ad tale regnum non habetur a patre, sed a lege regni, unde nec est hereditarium, nec patrimoniale, sed mero iure filiationis, vel sanguinis competit. Ita quod non posset Rex de regno testari, etiam primogenitum vel proximiorem, cui regnum debetur, instituendo, quia nullo

15   modo posset institutus capere regnum vi testamenti, vel alterius dispositionis paternae, quae non valuit, sed solum virtute legis immutabilis regni, a qua vocatur. Et in eandem sententiam Guill. Benedict. in c. Raynutius, in verb. In eodem testamento, num. 148, ita scribit:²² *Natura regni Franciae, inquit, requirit, et*

20   *exigit, ne de eo fiant testamenta, legata, vel aliae dispositiones. Unde Ioan. de terra rub. in quodam libro, quem intitulavit Vinea Ecclesiae, tract. 1, q. 9, concludit, dicens,²³ quia regnum Franciae debetur primogenito ex sola regni consuetudine, nunquam consueverunt Reges de ipso regno testari, quod vi et medio consuetudinis defertur primogenito.*

²⁰ Terre Rouge, *Tractatus,* I, I, ix (up to *successio*) and viii; ed. 1585, 83 & 81. This reversed quotation does no injury to fact, since the 9th conclusion does say that the succession goes to those referred to in the preceding conclusion.   ²¹ *Ibid.,* I, I, ix–xii, ed. 1585, 83–5. The important concept of *ius filiationis* is actually developed in I, I, xvi–xvii (ed. 1585, 89–91), and more importantly, in I, 2, vi (ed. 1585, 105–6); see Giesey, *Dynastic Right,* 14, nn. 42–3.   ²² Benedicti, *In cap. Ray. de test.,* 'In eodem testamento relinquens: I', §§145–50; ed. 1575, I, 195ᵛ. As indicated in the above quotation, Hotman inserted the word *lege* into Benedicti's text in two places, making succession derive from 'law and custom'. ²³ Benedicti refers here to the same passages that Hotman quotes in note 19 above. The curious title *Vinea ecclesiae* which Benedicti gives to Terre Rouge's tract comes, apparently, from a twisted reading of the preface to the tract where an elaborate metaphor concerning the *vinea regni* is employed. This preface can be found printed only in the *editio princeps* of Terre Rouge (Lyons, 1526); Benedicti, writing earlier, possessed the manuscript.

and, especially, Jean de Terre Rouge, in the passage where he writes as follows:[20] 'The kings of France were never accustomed to make wills concerning the disposal of the kingdom, but from force of custom the succession passed only to the eldest males in direct line, and when that line came to an end the males of the most closely related cognate branch had the right of succession.' In four subsequent passages[21] Terre Rouge concludes that in the kingdom of France the succession is neither hereditary nor patrimonial but a straightforward succession, that is, the appointment of the eldest son by birth or the nearest agnate, to whom the kingdom is due solely by the law or custom of the kingdom. His right derives from this alone and not from a father or any predecessor.

Thus the right of primogeniture, in so far as it is held to a kingdom of this sort from the law of the kingdom and not from a father, is neither hereditary nor patrimonial, but rather belongs to the claimant by the mere right of filiation or of blood. Thus the king cannot dispose of the kingdom by testament, even to the eldest born or closest by blood to whom the kingdom is due, because in no way can the person authorized hold the kingdom by the power of a will or of any other paternal provision, since such an arrangement is invalid. He holds it only by virtue of that immutable law of the kingdom by which he is called to office. Guillaume Benedicti is of the same opinion in his gloss on the decretal, where he writes on testamentary law as follows:[22] 'The nature of the kingdom of France demands and exacts that no wills, legacies or other dispositions be made concerning it. Thus Jean de Terre Rouge states in a certain book he entitles *The Vineyard of the Church*[23] that, since the kingdom of France must go to the first-born son solely because of the custom of the kingdom, the kings were never accustomed to make wills concerning the kingdom itself, which passes to the eldest son by force and by means of custom. For

Nam Reges Franciae nunquam potuerunt, neque posset Carolus octavus Rex noster modernus testamentum facere de regno, etiam heredem instituendo dominum Delphinum eius primogenitum, quia regnum Franciae non debetur primogenito, ex successione testamentaria, 5 *vel ab intestato, sed solum ex* lege et *consuetudine regni. Igitur Rex ipsum dare non potest primogenito, neque auferre per alienationes inter vivos, testamenta, neque debita voluntaria, legata exheredationis,* ex caussa, quia primogenitus Franciae non habet regnum a patre, sed ab ipsa regni* lege et *consuetudine. Et sic pater potestatem non habet* 10 *ipsum gravare, et de tali dignitate disponi non potest, vel alius in praeiudicium primogeniti, qui cum ius illud habeat, non patris iudicio, sed legis beneficio, per eum gravari non potest, a quo beneficium non habet, nec commodum sentit.* Haec ad verbum Bened.

Sequitur quarta lex regni, de qua tamen superius cap. 10 dis-15 seruimus. Ne virgo, neve mulier ad regni hereditatem admittatur, sed agnatus defuncto Regi proximus, quavis gradu foemina posterior, ei tamen praeferatur, qua de lege nobilis Pragmaticus Iacob. Petr. in sua Pract. cap. 63 ita scribit:²⁴ *Carolo,* qui rex Franciae et Navarrae fuerat, *mortuo, filia Ludovici, sui quon-*20 *dam fratris successit in regno Navarrae, quia illud regnum venerat per foeminam, sed in regno Franciae non successit, quia non admittitur foemina, quamdiu masculus de genere invenitur; successit ergo Philippus filius Caroli, qui erat ei in quarto gradu,* quamvis dicta fratris filia tantum esset in tertio. Item Guill. Bened. in verb. duas 25 habens, num. 78:²⁵ *unde restat,* inquit, *neque filias, neque masculos ex ipsis descendentes in regno Franciae secundum ipsius leges et con-*

---

7 'vivos...exheredationis': c¹ 'vivos aut testamenta, aut debita voluntaria, aut legata, aut exhereditationem'.

²⁴ Pierre Jacobi Rub. 63, §30; ed. 1575, 281.   ²⁵ Benedicti, *In cap. Ray. de test.,* 'Duas habens filias', §78; ed. 1575, I, 17.

the kings of France could never make a will concerning the kingdom, nor can our present king, Charles VIII, do so, even in respect of appointing his eldest son and heir the Lord Dauphin. This is because the kingdom of France is not due to the eldest son through testamentary succession or through a claim from a king who dies intestate, but only through (the law and) the custom of the kingdom. Therefore, the king cannot give his eldest son the kingdom, nor can he alienate parts of it to the living, nor do so through wills or voluntary undertakings or bequests involving disinheritance. The reason for this is that the first-born son does not hold the kingdom from his father but rather from (the law and) the custom of the kingdom. Hence the father does not possess the power to interfere with the succession, and cannot tamper with an official dignity of this kind, or do anything which would prejudice the right of the first-born. This right is not dependent on the father's judgment but is conferred by the law, and the son cannot be deprived of it by one from whom he does not derive his privilege and advantage.' Such are the very words of Benedicti.

There follows the fourth law of the kingdom, which we have discussed earlier in chapter ten. It is that no girl or woman is admitted to the inheritance of the kingdom, but at the death of a king his nearest male agnate is preferred to a woman, even though she may have the better claim in terms of proximate family relationship. The noble lawyer Pierre Jacobi writes of this law in his *Golden Practice* as follows:[24] 'At the death of Charles (who was the king of France and Navarre) the daughter of his brother, Louis, succeeded to the crown of Navarre, since that kingdom had descended through the female line. But she did not succeed to the crown of France, since a woman was not admitted while any male representative of the family existed. Thus Philip, the son of Charles [of Valois], succeeded, and Philip was related to the late king in the fourth degree (whereas his brother's daughter was related in the third degree).' In this respect we may cite Guillaume Benedicti:[25] 'So it is that neither daughters, nor males who are the offspring of such daughters, may, according to the laws and custom of the kingdom of France, succeed to that kingdom, and,

suetudinem succedere, quinimo liberis masculis non existentibus reliqui parentes et consanguinei in regno succederent, servata gradus prae-rogativa. Haec Bened., quae multo copiosius confirmat num. 119 et 120.²⁶

5   Item Cosm. Guim. in proemio pragmat. sanct., ubi sic scribit:²⁷ *Regnum Franciae est ita nobile, et clarum, quod in eo nun-quam succedit foemina, licet bene in regno Navarrae; et huiusmodi quaestio orta fuit post mortem Philippi Pulchri, Regis Francorum, qui habuit unam filiam, nomine Isabellam, et tres filios; dictam Isabellam* 10 *duxit in uxorem Eduardus Rex Angliae, ex qua habuit unum filium, qui similiter dictus est Eduardus, qui successit in regno Angliae, de-functo dicto Philippo. Tres eius filii fuerunt reges Franciae sigillatim, qui tandem decesserunt sine liberis, quibus successit in regno Franciae Philippus, filius Caroli de Valesio, fratris dicti Philippi, de consensu et* 15 *approbatione XII Parium Franciae, qui noluerunt dare regnum dictae Isabellae, Reginae Angliae, nec filio eius Eduardo; unde ortae sunt magnae guerrae, inter Reges Angliae et Franciae, et iniuste, quia sicut filia Regis non succedit in regno Francorum, ita nec natus ex ea: § hoc autem Qui feud. dar. poss.;*²⁸ *De gradib. success. in feud. c. 1, § ad* 20 *filias.*²⁹ *Excluso enim ascendente, excluduntur descendentes ex persona ascendentis: l. fin. C. de natur. lib.;*³⁰ *l. si viva, C. de bon. matern.*³¹ *Ideo non potuit dictus Eduardus filius dictae Isabellae praetendere ali-quod ius in regno Franciae: dicit Bald. in repet., l. 1, C. de summa trinit.*³² Sed nemo uberius hanc historiam exponit, quam Claudi- 25 us Seyssellus, archiepisc. Taurin., in lib. de lege Salica,³³ ubi utriusque Regis Angliae et Franciae iusta copiose exponit, et ad extremum publici concilii, sive trium statuum iudicium sub-iungit.*

---

28 *c*¹ adds here this sentence: 'Sed nos hac de re paullo copiosius in libello De iure success. regiae disseruimus.' See above, p. 99, for remarks about this work, written in 1588.

²⁶ *Ibid.*, §§119–20; ed. 1575, I, 22ʳ⁻ᵛ.   ²⁷ Proem. §In Qua quidem, *ad verb.* 'consanguineis'; ed. 1555, 20ᵛ.   ²⁸ *Lib. Feud.* I, 1; ed. 1562, 719.   ²⁹ *Ibid.*, II, 11; *ed. cit.*, 756.   ³⁰ *Cod.* 5, 27, 12; Krueger, II, 219.   ³¹ *Cod.* 6, 60, 3; Krueger, II, 288.   ³² Cf. Baldus, *Comm. in cod.*, *ad* I, 1, i; ed. 1585, 12–17ᵛ. ³³ Seyssel is not the author of this: see above, p. 418, n. 11, which is the same place to which this allegation refers.

indeed, if there are no surviving male children other relatives and members of the family succeed to the crown according to the degree of relationship.' Benedicti confirms these views with much greater detail in two later references.[26]

In the foreword to his *Pragmatic Sanction* Cosmas Guimier states:[27] 'The kingdom of France is so noble and famous because a woman never succeeds to it, although this is permissible in the kingdom of Navarre. A question of this kind arose after the death of Philip the Fair, the king of France, who had one daughter, Isabella and three sons. Edward, king of England, took the said Isabella to wife, and had one son by her, also called Edward, who succeeded to the English crown after the death of the said Philip. The latter's three sons were one after another kings of France, but, as they died childless, Philip, the son of Charles of Valois, who was a brother of Philip the Fair, succeeded to the French crown with the consent and approbation of the twelve peers of France, who were unwilling to give the kingdom to the said Isabella, queen of England, or to her son, Edward. From this affair arose great wars between the kings of England and France. This was a great error because, just as the daughter of a king does not succeed to the French crown, so a son by her does not succeed either. See the appropriate section of the feudal law,[28] and the first chapter of the same concerning daughters and succession according to family relationships.[29] For when a claimant is excluded, the descendants of the claimant are excluded also. This is stated in two sections of the *Code*.[30,31] Hence the said Edward, son of the said Isabella, could not claim any right to the French crown, as Baldus says in his commentary on the *Code*.[32] But no one explains this affair more fully than does Claude de Seyssel, the archbishop of Turin, in his book on the Salic law,[33] where he sets forth in great detail the claims of the kings of England and France, and subjects them in the end to the final judgment of the public council or three estates.*

* **c¹** *adds this sentence:* But we have dealt with this small matter at length in our book *On the Right of Royal Succession.*

Quinta lex ad Regis domanium pertinet de qua superius suo loco commemoravimus. Ne videlicet Regi ius sit, ullam domanii sui partem sine publici Concilii auctoritate alienare, quippe, quod ei ad tuendam tantum regiam dignitatem fruen-
5 dum datum est ut parem in eo potestatem habeat, atque marito in uxoris dote conceditur. Itaque anno MCCCXCIX, cum Rex Carolus VI Comiti Sampaulino particulam quandam sui domanii sive donasset, sive alia ex caussa cessisset, Senatus Parisiensis pro vetere veteris Parlamenti iure intercessit, ac pro-
10 nuntiavit alienationem regii dominii nullius esse momenti, nisi cuius author Senatus ille Parisiensis fuisset, quod decretum Paponius inter Aresta sua retulit, lib. 5, tit. 10,[34] ubi alia complura generis eiusdem senatusconsulta commemorat, quibus omnibus definitum hoc ius est, alienationem dominii a Rege,
15 sine causa in illo Senatu cognita et probata, factam, ipso iure nullam esse, qua in cognitione haec potissimum exquiruntur. At non aliunde confici pecunia possit? ecqua necessitas urgeat? an pretium sit idoneum? et auctione constituta summum illud ac postremum oblatum.
20   Sed operaepretium est Claudii Seyssellii testimonium in hanc rem exponere, cuius verba ex lib. de monarch. Franc. 1, cap. 10, sic convertimus:[35] *Tertium frenum quo Reges Franciae coercentur est politia, hoc est instituta et mores regni multas per aetates comprobati, et longinqua consuetudine retenti, quorum abrogationem non susci-*
25 *piunt; et si forte susciperent, frustra id tentarent, quoniam eorum imperio non pareretur, quod vel ex dominio et patrimonio regali cognosci licet, cuius alienandi ius sine caussis magnis et necessariis non habent; quas caussas cognosci et probari oportet in consilio et curia parlamenti et Rationalium, qua in cognitione ita caute et diligenter,*
30 *tantaque cum disquisitione proceditur, ut pauci admodum reperiantur*

---

[34] Art. 2 & 4; ed. 1574, 273ff. & 277ff.   [35] I, 11; ed. 1961, 119.

The fifth law concerns the royal domain, which we have related above in its proper place. It is that no king has the right to alienate any part of his domain without the authority of the public council, since it is given to the king and enjoyed by him in order that the royal dignity may be maintained, and he has authority over it in the same way that a husband is granted power over the dowry of a wife. Thus in the year 1399, when King Charles VI had granted a certain section of his domain to the count of Saint-Pol, and had ceded other things to him without good reason, the senate or parlement of Paris interceded on behalf of the ancient right of the old parliament, and declared an alienation of the royal domain to be invalid unless the parlement of Paris had authorized it. Papon gave this decree among his judgments,[34] where he lists many other pronouncements of this kind, and they all serve to define the law that any alienation of the domain effected by the king, without the reason for it being known and sanctioned by the parlement, is invalid by the law itself. In the process of recognition the following matters are the subject of searching enquiry: Cannot money be provided for other sources? Is there any necessity which is really pressing? Is the amount of money really sufficient? And does it represent the best and final bid at a public auction?

In the operation of financial matters the best explanation is provided by Claude de Seyssel, whose words we may cite from his *Monarchy of France*:[35] 'The third rein by which the kings of France are restrained is the constitution, that is the institutions and practices of the kingdom which have been sanctioned throughout many ages and confirmed by long-standing custom. The kings do not attempt their abrogation, and should, perchance, they try to do so their endeavours would be vain. Since these matters are not at the disposal of the government, and the issues concerning the domain and the royal patrimony may lawfully be examined, kings do not possess the right of alienating the domain without great and necessary reasons. It is proper for these reasons to be examined and approved in the council, the court of the parlement and the chambre des comptes. This examination proceeds so cautiously and carefully and with such intensive investigation that very few

*qui eiusmodi alienationes expetant. Etsi autem Reges ius habent dis-
ponendi de fructibus et reditibus regni pro sui arbitrio, quandiu regni
administrationem obtinent, tamen ratio sumptuum tum ordinariorum
tum extraordinariorum ad Rationalium curiam et notionem revocatur.*
5 *Hi rationales sumptus illos regios, si inconsulte facti videntur, coer-
cent. Quae sane lex Reipublicae perquam utilis est, ad Regii dominii
conservationem, quia tum demum ad tributa et indictiones extra-
ordinarias, quibus plebs oneratur, decurri tanquam ad subsidium solet,
cum illud dominium regium exhaustum est, ut omittam, quod hac*
10 *praeclara Regni lege nimia Principis liberalitas quae ad prodigalitatem
accedit, coercetur.*

Haec Seyssellus, sed lib. ɪɪ, cap. ɪɪ, insuper haec addit:³⁶
*Iterum dico: Regem non posse gratius obsequium Deo praestare, aut
suorum civium utilitati, aut suae dignitati atque existimationi melius*
15 *consulere, quam illas Regni leges observando. Tum enim boni et
Christianissimi Regis et Patris patriae cognomentum acquirit, ceteraque omnia nomina, quae sibi magnus aliquis et gloriosus Princeps potest
acquirere. Ex contrario vero simulatque limites et fines illos sibi prae-
scriptos egreditur, et voluntate pro ratione uti instituit, habetur ac*
20 *numeratur improbus, tyrannus, crudelis, et intolerandus, quibus de
caussis in Dei et civium suorum odium incurrit.* Hactenus Seyssellus
Taurinensis Archiepiscopus et Regis Ludovici XII intimus con-
siliarius. In eandemque sententiam, de Rege Franciae, cui non
licet urbes Regni sui alienare, scribunt Hosti.;³⁷ et Io. Andr. in
25 c. dilecti, De maior. et obed.;³⁸ Martin. Laud. in trac. de confoed.,
q. 13.³⁹

Sexta Regni lex numerari haec potest, ut Regi abolendi
criminis et capitalis poenae, sine parlamenti auctoritate, remit-
tendae ius non sit. *In* hoc regno,* inquit Boerius, *criminosus*

---

29 **c**¹ but not **c** or **c**² begins a new sentence here.

³⁶ Ed. 1961, 143.   ³⁷ Non invenio; but see below, n. 39.   ³⁸ Cf. Joh.
Andreae on c. 13 X 1, 33; *Decretalia commentaria,* ed. 1581, ɪ, 268, 4.   ³⁹ Q. 14
in the edition of 1506. Laudensis quotes Hostiensis and Johannes Andreae in the
same manner that Hotman does; I have found the Andreae citation (see previous
note) but not the Hostiensis (above, n. 37).

reasons are found to justify such alienations. Moreover, even if the kings have the right, while they control the government, of disposing of the fruits and revenues of the kingdom at their own discretion, the basis of both ordinary and extraordinary expenditure may be called into question before the court and investigatory commission of the chambre des comptes. These officials in matters of expenditure may restrain the royal officers if they seem to have acted without consulting them. This very sensible law of the commonwealth is particularly useful in preserving the royal domain because it is just at such a time, when the royal domain is exhausted, that it is customary to have recourse, in the form of a subsidy, to tributes and extraordinary taxes, under which the common people are burdened. I shall say nothing of the fact that this celebrated law of the kingdom restrains the excessive liberality of the prince, which may tend towards extravagance.'

In a latter passage Seyssel makes these additional observations:[36] 'Let me say it again. A king cannot show obedience more pleasing to God, or attend better to the ease of his subjects or his own dignity and reputation than by observing those laws of the kingdom. For thereby he will obtain the name of a good and most Christian king and the father of his country, together with all the other names that a great and glorious prince is able to acquire. But, on the other hand, if he oversteps those prescribed bounds and limits and begins to use arbitrary will in place of reason, he will be labelled as a reprobate, a tyrant, a man of cruelty and intolerance, and for these reasons he will incur both the hatred of God and that of his own subjects.' This is the view of Archbishop Seyssel of Turin, the intimate counsellor of King Louis XII. Others who express the same opinion, namely that it is not lawful for the king of France to alienate the towns of his own kingdom, are Hostiensis,[37] and Johannes Andreae in his commentaries on the Decretals,[38] and Martinus Laudensis in his treatise on confederations.[39]

It can be listed as the sixth law of the kingdom that in France the king does not have the right of cancelling or remitting the punishment for a capital crime without the authority of the parlement,*

* c¹, but not cc², begins a new sentence here.

deferens literas remissionis aut abolitionis, sive pardonii, debet in-
carcerari, et suas literas offerre Parlamento, etc. Haec ille Decis.
Burdegal. 65.[40]

    Septima est, ut Regi non liceat magistratum aliquem Regni,
5 sive Reipublicae Franciae, nisi caussa in Parium consilio cognita
et probata, exauctorare. Quae lex ita passim tota Gallia nota et
decantata est, ut testimonii non egeat.

    Octava Regni lex numerari haec potest:* Ne Regi sine publici
concilii auctoritate monetae mutandae ius sit. Nam Guill.
10 Budaeus lib. de Asse 3 et 5 testatur[41] ex antiquis omnibus quae
viderat monimentis constare rei nummariae ius, hoc est potestatis nummorum vel augendae vel imminuendae semper penes
populum fuisse. Quinetiam Carol. Molin. diligentissimus
monetalium ratiociniorum investigator, extremo commentario
15 de contract. et usur. scribit,[42] se in archivis parlamenti et
monetalium praefectorum quamplurimas leges Francicas reperisse, quibus sancitum erat, ne qua rei nummariae mutatio sine
populi consensu fieret, semperque in eiusmodi mutationibus
populi consensum (quippe cuius plurimi intererat) intervenisse,
20 quemadmodum a Iurisconsultis dici solet: *Quorum quid fieri*
interest, eorum in eo negotio gerendo requiritur assensus, vel hoc
modo, quod aliquos tangit, debet ab iis approbari. Quinetiam
Hostiensis Canonista celebris et magnae inter suos auctoritatis,
in summa de censibus, ita scribit:[43] *Quaeritur, nunquid Rex*
25 *Franciae habeat privilegium concedendi pedagia, vel mutandi novam*
monetam. Respondeo, sicut Papa in simili quaestione, sic videretur
aliquibus: c. per venerabilem, qui fil. sint legit.[44] *Mihi vero non*
videtur, nisi populus ei potestatem illam dederit, quae et Imperatori
data est argu. l. 2, § deinde, D. de orig. iur.[45]

---

8 *b* has the substance of the following paragraph several chapters earlier; see
p. 424, variant note on line 28.

[40] By Bohier, §10; ed. 1567, 117.   [41] Ed. 1532, lx^v & cxlviii.   [42] Du Moulin,
as above, p. 424, n. 30.   [43] 'De censibus, & exactionibus, & procurationibus',
§9; ed. 1573, 927.   [44] *Corp. jur. can.*, c. 13 X 4, 17; Friedberg, II, 714ff.   [45] *Dig.*
I, 2, 2, 6; Mommsen, I, 20.

and, in this kingdom, as Bohier says, a convicted criminal should be imprisoned and his letters of remission, cancellation or pardon ought to be submitted to the parlement. Bohier states this in his *Decrees of Bordeaux*.[40]

The seventh law is that it is not permitted for the king to dismiss a magistrate of the kingdom or commonwealth of France without the reasons being examined and approved in the council of the peers. This law is so well known and is so often quoted throughout the whole of France that no supporting testimony is needed.

It can be listed as the eighth law of the kingdom* that the king has no right to change the coinage without the authority of the public council. For in his work *De asse* Guillaume Budé gives examples[41] from all the ancient authors that the right of establishing numerical systems and measurements, that is to say the power of increasing or diminishing values, always lay with the people. Indeed Charles du Moulin, that most diligent investigator of monetary relationships, writes at the end of his commentary on contracts and usury that he himself found in the records of the parlement and the chambre des comptes a great many Frankish laws, by which it had been established that no change of values could be effected without the consent of the people, and the consent of the people was always involved in changes of this kind (for most of them were directly concerned). As the jurists are accustomed to say, when the interest of certain persons is at stake, their consent is necessary in arranging the matter, or, to put it another way, what touches certain persons ought to be approved by them.[42] Indeed Hostiensis, a canonist of celebrated and great authority among his fellows, writes as follows in his work on censors:[43] 'It has been asked whether the king of France has any right to withdraw standards of measurement or to introduce new coinage. I reply, just as the pope did to a like question, that it would seem to some that matters which acquire respect are of a lawful kind.[44] But it does not seem so to me, unless the people gave him the power which was given to the emperor, as is stated in the *Digest*.'[45]

---

* *b has the substance of what follows in this paragraph at the end of chapter ᵃXVII above.*

An mulieres, non ut ab hereditate regni, sic ab
eius procuratione, Francogallico iure, arceantur

---

*b*Sed *a*quoniam de Regni procuratione et summa Reipublicae administrandae instituta disputatio est, non praetereunda quaestio
videtur, An mulieres non ut ab hereditate Regni, sic etiam ab eius
procuratione arceantur. Primum autem illud aperte testatum
5 volumus, nos neque de Romanorum, neque de aliarum gentium
iure, sed tantum de huius nostrae Francogalliae institutis disserere. Nam, ut notum omnibus est, Romanorum institutis
mulieres propter infirmitatem consilii in perpetua tutorum
potestate fuisse, atque ab omnibus non modo publicis, verum
10 etiam civilibus negotiis arceri,* ita nonnullis aliis in gentibus
mulieres summam imperii vetustis moribus obtinent. *Britanni
sexum in imperiis non discernunt*, inquit Tacitus in Agric. vita.[1]

Hoc igitur constituto, et testificatione nostra plane ac dilucide
proposita, deinceps ad quaestionem accedamus. Nam ei caussam
15 praebuisse superiorum aliquot temporum exempla videntur,
quibus constat, Regnum Francogalliae a Reginis, praesertim
viduis, et Regum *b*vel *a*puerorum *b*vel absentium *a*matribus, administratum fuisse. *b*In quibus haud scio an ullum ad muliebrem
audaciam insignius commemorari possit, quam illud reginae
20 Blancae, Ludovici Transmarini matris, de qua posterius dicemus, quae Rege filio in Africam ad bellum gerendum profecto,
summam sibi potestatem non modo in Reipublicae sed etiam in
Ecclesiarum et Episcopatuum administratione ascivit, quemadmodum ex veteribus quibusdam monimentis nuper in lucem

10 'arceri': *bc* 'exclusas esse'.
[1] Cap. 16; Loeb, 196.

^aCHAPTER XIX [^bXX, ^{cc2}XXVI, ^{c1}XXIV]

Whether under Francogallican law women are not as
much excluded from the government of the
kingdom as they are from inheriting it

---

^bBut ^asince our theme concerns the government of the kingdom
and the most important customs in the administration of the
commonwealth, it seems that we ought not to omit this question,
whether women are not excluded from the control of the kingdom
just as much as they are also from inheriting it. First, we wish
openly to state that we shall not discuss the laws of the Romans or
those of any other people, but only the practices of this our own
Francogallia. For everyone knows that under Roman customs
women were always under the authority of guardians, and were
excluded from both public and private affairs because of the
weakness of their judgment. Yet in some other nations women
acquired supreme authority by ancient customs. Tacitus says in his
Life of Agricola:[1] 'The Britons do not distinguish between the sexes
in government.'

Now that this has been established, and our own position has
been plainly and clearly stated, let us proceed with the question.
For in this regard examples from some early times seem to indicate
that it was the practice for the kingdom of Francogallia to be
administered by queens, especially by those who were widows, or
mothers of kings who were boys ^bor who were absent from the
kingdom. Among them it is scarcely possible to find a womanly
boldness more deserving of remembrance than that of Queen
Blanche, the mother of Saint Louis, who, when her son, the king,
set out for Africa to wage war, took to herself supreme authority in
the government of the commonwealth and also in that of the clergy
and bishops. The manner in which this was achieved can be known

editis cognosci potest:² *Nos charissimae Dominae nostrae et matri*
Reginae concessimus, et voluimus, quod ipsa in hac nostrae peregrina-
tionis absentia plenariam habeat potestatem recipiendi et attrahendi ad
regni nostri negotia, quos sibi placuerit, et amovendi quos viderit amo-
5 *vendos; Baillivos etiam instituere valeat, castellanos, forestarios, et*
alios in servitium nostrum et regni nostri ministros ponere et amovere;
dignitates etiam et beneficia ecclesiastica vacantia conferre, fidelitates
Episcoporum et Abbatum recipere, et eis regalia restituere, et eligendi
licentiam dare capitulis et conventibus vice nostra.

10   ᵃEx contrario tamen pugnat primum ratio disputandi usitata,
ut cui per se Reginam esse ius non est, eidem regendi ius ac
potestas non sit. Per se autem Reginam esse mulierem non posse,
neque Regni hereditatem ei ex eave prognatis deferri, sed si
Reginae appellantur, per accidens, et propter Reges maritos id
15 fieri, superius ex antiquis MCC annorum monimentis demonstratum est. Eo accedit, quod superius docuimus, quemadmodum
omnis et creandorum et abdicandorum* Regum potestas penes
publicum Concilium erat, ita Curatoris Reipublicae sive
Moderatoris deligendi ius summum penes idem Concilium fuisse.
20 Quinetiam creatis Regibus, tamen summam imperii administrandi potestatem ab eodem Concilio retentam fuisse, neque
centesimum adhuc exisse annum cum regnante Ludovico XI
quantumvis astuto* et callido, XXXVI Reipublicae curatores,*
tanquam Ephori, ab eodem Concilio constituti sunt. Quod si
25 maiorum nostrorum auctoritatem quaerimus, extat insignis apud
Aimoin. lib. 4, cap. 1, ubi de Brunechilde, Regina matre Childeberti Regis commemorans ita loquitur:³ *Simul*, inquit, *quia*
Brunechildis summam Regni solicitudinem sibi reservare velle intel-
ligebatur, et primates Franciae tanto tempore foemineo dominatui dedig-

---

17 *c*¹ omits 'abdicandorum' as well as 'et' before it and before 'creandorum'.
23 *c*¹ 'vasto'.   **23** *c*¹ adds 'ut sup. diximus'.

² Choppin, *De dom. Fran.*, 2, 9, 8; ed. 1621, 209. Also in Eusèbe de Laurière,
Ordonnances des rois de France (Paris, 1723), I, 60.   ³ PL, CXXXIX, 765.

from certain ancient records which have recently been published.[2] They state: 'We wish and grant to our dearest lady and mother, the queen, that during our absence on this journey she should have complete authority to receive and conduct such affairs of our kingdom as it may please her to do, and authority to dismiss those who she may think should be dismissed. She may also appoint to our service bailiffs, châtelains, captains of the forests and others, and she may appoint and dismiss the chief officers of our kingdom. She may also confer offices and vacant ecclesiastical benefices; she may receive oaths of loyalty from bishops and abbots and may restore regalian rights to them; and acting on our behalf she may grant chapters and clerical assemblies licence to elect.'

[a]Yet, on the other hand, the kind of reasoning employed in disputation opposes the practice, for, if a woman docs not have the personal right to be queen, neither does she have the right and power to rule. A woman cannot be a queen in her own right, nor can an hereditary claim to the kingdom be derived from her or her descendants. If they are termed queens it is only so accidentally and because they are married to kings, and we have already shown this from the ancient records for twelve hundred years. A point we have explained above may here be added, namely that, just as all power to appoint and depose[*] kings lay with the public council, so also the supreme right to choose a regent or administrator of the commonwealth rested in that same council. Even after kings had been appointed, the supreme authority in government was retained by the council, and[†] a century has not passed since thirty-six guardians were created by that same council to act as though they were ephors, and this even occurred when Louis XI was reigning, cunning[‡] and crafty as he was. If we seek the authority of our ancestors in this matter, there exists the remarkable instance in the chronicle of Aimon, where he writes as follows about Brunhild, the queen mother of King Childebert [Childebert II]:[3] 'At the same time, because it was discovered that Brunhild wished to keep the sovereign administration of the kingdom in her own hands, the nobility of France, who for so long had disdained to be dominated

---

* c^1 *omits* and depose. † c^1 *adds* , as we said above,. ‡ c^1 immensely strong.

nabantur subiici, etc. ^cItaque Fran. Connanus Senator Parisiensis lib. 1, cap. 8:*⁴ *Quod Panormitanus putat* (inquit) *Reginis more nostro ius esse in Gallos, multum fallitur. Nulla enim gens minus passa est foeminarum imperium, cum lex Saliorum, id est Gallorum,*
5 *eas regni successione excludat. Itaque videmus Reginas viro mortuo redigi fere in ordinem, sic ut ne umbram quidem Regiae dignitatis retineant.* Haec Connanus.

^aEt profecto ita est, ut si quando Regni procurationem apud maiores nostros mulieres adeptae sunt, semper ea res miras in
10 Republica nostra tragoedias, ^bsumma denique miseriarum incendia ^aexcitarit. Cuius rei non alienum videtur exempla quaedam proponere. Dominata est quondam Chrotildis, Regina mater Childeberti et Clotarii Regum, quae dum alterius filii nomine Chlodomeris demortui filios insano quodam amore prose-
15 queretur, summam contentionem adhibuit, ut nepotes remotis filiis in regiam dignitatem producerentur.* Itaque capillitium eorum, pro eo instituto, de quo superius diximus, summa cum cura et diligentia nutriebat. Cuius rei Reges fratres certiores facti, confestim Arcadium quendam ad eam miserunt, qui nudum
20 gladium simulque forcipem ei ostentans, optionem illi faceret, utrum illorum nepotum suorum capiti admoveri mallet. *At illa,* inquit Gregorius Turon.⁵ *nimium felle commota, praecipue cum gladium cerneret evaginatum ac forcipem, amaritudine praeventa, respondit: Satius mihi est, si ad regnum non eriguntur, mortuos eos*
25 *videre, quam tonsos.* Ita nepos uterque in ipsius conspectu interfectus est. Auctore eodem Gregor. lib. 3, cap. 18,⁶ ubi tamen subiungit, Reginam hanc liberalitatibus et donationibus in monasteria collatis plebis et vulgi benevolentiam conciliasse.

Date frenos (inquiebat Cato⁷) *impotenti naturae, et indomito*
30 *animali, et sperate ipsas modum licentiae facturas.* Quid? quam effrenatum illud fuit animal, illa, inquam, Theodorici Regis

---

2 *c*¹ 'Lib. 1, Cap. 1, Cap. 8'.   **16** *c* 'perducerentur'.

⁴ *Francisci Connani commentariorum,* 1, 8, §5; ed. 1557, 1, 43.   ⁵ III, 18; *MGH SS Mer.,* 1:1², 118, 17.   ⁶ Cf. *ibid.; ed. cit.,* 120, 1.   ⁷ Quoted in Livy, XXXIV, ii, 13; Loeb, IX, 416.

and ruled by a woman etc.' *c*François Connan, a judge in the parlement, states:[4] 'Panormitanus made a great mistake when he claimed that queens have any right among the French by our custom. For there is no people less exposed to the government of women, since the law of the Salians, that is to say the law of the French, excludes them from succession to the kingdom. Thus we see that on the death of their husbands queens are almost completely degraded in rank so that they do not retain even a shadow of the dignity of queen.' So writes Connan.

*a*Indeed it has so happened that, if ever women acquired control of the administration of the kingdom in the times of our ancestors, they always caused extraordinary calamities *b*and subsequently a vast crop of troubles *a*in our commonwealth. It may be appropriate to provide a number of examples of this. There was a time when Queen Clothild, the mother of the kings Childebert [Childebert I] and Lothar, held sway. She favoured with a love akin to madness the sons of another of her own sons, Chlodomir by name, who had died, and she caused a very great dispute by trying to exclude her surviving sons and promoting their nephews to royal dignity. Hence, because of the practice we have earlier described, she took the greatest care to nourish their long hair. When the two royal brothers were informed of her intention, they at once sent a certain Arcadius to her, who offered her a naked sword and a pair of scissors and made her choose which she preferred to have applied to the heads of her grandsons. 'But she', says Gregory of Tours,[5] 'was choked by excess of gall, especially when she saw the unsheathed sword and the scissors, and in her bitterness replied: "I should rather see them dead than shorn if they are not to be raised to the throne."' Thus each of her grandsons was killed before her eyes. In another place the same author adds[6] that this queen won the favour of the common people with the gifts and donations she bestowed upon the monastic orders.

As Cato used to say,[7] 'If you loose the reins with women, as with an unruly nature and an untamed beast, you must expect uncontrolled actions.' What an unbridled beast was that daughter of King Theuderic, of Italian birth, who fell madly in love with her

filia, natione Itala, quae servi sui amore insana, ubi matris iussu illum interfectum cognovit, per speciem reconciliatae cum matre gratiae sacramentum se dominicae coenae cum illa communicare velle ostendit, venenoque in calicem infuso impietate simul et
5 crudelitate nefaria matrem sustulit. Verba Gregorii Turonensis lib. 3, cap. 33, haec sunt:[8] *Erant sub Ariana secta viventes, et quia consuetudo eorum est, ut ad altarium venientes de alio calice Reges communicent, et de alio populus minor* (notanda consuetudo calicis cum plebe communicati) *venenum in calice illo posuit, de quo mater*
10 *communicatura erat, quo illa hausto protinus mortua est.*

   *b*Age, reliquas videamus. *a*Dominata est quondam Frede-gunda, Regina mater, Chilperici primi vidua. Haec marito superstite cum Landerio quondam adulterii consuetudinem habuerat. Ubi Chilpericum id sensisse animadvertit, interficien-
15 dum eum curavit, confestimque Regni procurationem filii sui Regis Clotharii nomine, tanquam Regina, mater suscepit, eam-que annos XIII sustinuit. Primum Childebertum filii sui patruum, eiusque uxorem veneno sustulit, tum Hunnos adversus ipsius filios concitavit, bellumque civile in Rempublicam immisit, fax
20 denique illorum incendiorum fuit, quibus Francogallia multos annos exarsit, auctore Aimoino lib. 3, cap. 36,[9] et lib. 8, cap. 29,[10] *c*et scriptore Chronici Besnensis.[11]

   *a*Dominata est Regina mater Childeberti, Brunechildis, Sige-berti Regis vidua. Haec Italum quendam nomine Protadium in
25 deliciis habebat, eumque omnibus honoribus amplificabat. Haec eadem* filios suos Theodebertum et Theodoricum adolescentes in eam vitae flagitiosae consuetudinem adduxit, ut tandem capitales inter se inimicitias gererent, belloque diuturno conflic-tati praelium atrocissimum committerent. Meroveum nepotem
30 suum Theodeberti filium sua manu interfecit. Theodoricum

---

6 'Haec eadem': *c* 'eademque' – i.e., a new clause, not a new sentence.

8 III, 31; *MGH SS Mer.*, I:1², 127, 2.   9 Garbled; cf. III, 57 & 85; *PL*, cxxxix, 730 & 754.   10 Meant to be Gregory of Tours, as below, n. 13.   11 Cf. *PL*, clxii, 770.

own servant! When she found out that he had been killed by her
mother's command, she pretended the appearance of reconciliation
with her mother and feigned a wish to take the sacrament of the
Lord's supper with her. She mixed some poison in the chalice, and
offered it to her mother with both sacrilegious impiety and
execrable cruelty. These are the words of Gregory of Tours:[8]
'They lived under the Arian form of worship, and, because it was
their custom that the royal family should, on approaching the
altar, take communion from one cup and people of lesser rank from
another (and here it is worth noting the practice of giving the communion cup to the people), she placed poison in that chalice from
which her mother was to communicate, which killed her as soon
as she tasted it.'

[b]Very well, let us look at the other examples. [a]Fredegund,
queen mother and widow of Chilperic I, obtained power at one
time. While her husband was alive she had adopted the habit of
living in adultery with a man named Lander. When she noticed
that Chilperic had become aware of this she had him murdered,
and as queen mother promptly undertook the administration of the
kingdom in the name of her son, King Lothar, retaining it for
thirteen years. First she poisoned her son's uncle, Childebert, and
his wife. Then she stirred up the Huns against his sons and caused
a civil war in the commonwealth. Finally she was the instigator of
those conflagrations which consumed Francogallia for many years.
This is related by Aimon on two occasions[9, 10] [c]and also by the
writer of the Dijon chronicle.[11]

[a]Queen Brunhild, the mother of Childebert and the widow of
King Sigebert, also ruled. She had a certain Italian, Protadius by
name, as her companion in vice, and she puffed him up with all
possible honours. She* brought up her sons Theudebert and
Theuderic in such a vicious kind of life when they were youths that
they became mortal enemies of one another, and they fought a
fearful conflict in the course of a protracted war. She killed
Merovech, the son of Theudebert and her own grandson, with her
own hands. She poisoned Theuderic. Need we go on? As Cato

* [c] honours. She *becomes* honours, and she.

veneno sustulit. Quid amplius? *Date frenos* (inquibat Cato[12])
*impotenti naturae, et indomito animali et sperate ipsas modum licentiae
facturas.** Decem Principibus Regiis necis caussam attulit.
Cumque ab Episcopo quodam obiurgata esset, rogataque ut se
5 ad frugem converteret, illum in profluentem deturbari* iussit.
Ad extremum Concilio Francorum indicto, in iudicium vocata,
damnata, et ab equo currente distracta membratimque dilaniata
est. Auctoribus Greg. Turon., lib. 5, cap. 39, et lib. 8, cap. 29;[13]
et Adone Aetat. 6;[14] Ottone Frisingens. Chron. 5, cap. 7;[15]
10 Godfrid. Viterb. Chron.* parte 16;[16] et Aimoino lib. 4, cap. 1;[17]
itemque Appendice Gregor. Turon. lib. 11, cuius haec verba
sunt:[18] *Reputans,** *ei quod X* Reges Francorum per eam interfecti
fuissent, id est, Sigebertus, Meroveus, et genitor suus Chilpericus,
Theodebertus* et filius suus Clotharius, item Meroveus filius Clo-*
15 *tharii, Theodoricus, eiusdemque tres qui ad praesens extincti fuerant,
per triduum eam diversis tormentis afflictam iubet prius camelo* ^b(legendum puto, Caballo)* ^a*per omnem exercitum sedentem perducere,
posthaec comam capitis uno pede et brachio ad ferocissimi equi caudam
ligare, a quo calcibus et velocitate cursus membratim disrumpitur*;
20 ^cquam eandem historiam reperio in Chronico Monasterii
Besnensis manuscripto his verbis:[19] Nam camelo superpositam
girari fecit per exercitum; quam cum omnes inclamando hor-
ruissent, velut sub carnis vel animae zabulum iterum iussit reduci,
et inter equos quatuor indomitos ligari, ad quorum primam
25 erumpentium fugam partibus rupta, postea igne combusta cum
satellitio peccatorum ab ipsis inferioribus est immersa. Item alio
loco:[20] *Tanta mala et effusiones sanguinum Brunechildis consilio in
Francia factae sunt, ut Prophetia Sibyllae impleretur, dicentis,*

3 *c*[1] omits the entire sentence, '*Date frenos…facturas.*'.   5 *bc* 'praecipitari'.
10 *bc* inadvertently skip several words, so that Godfrey of Viterbo is not
mentioned, and the passage reads 'Ottone Frisingens. Chron. parte 16'.   12 *bc*
'*Reputantes*'.   12 *bc* '*V*'.   14 *bc* '*Theobertus*'.   17 *b* alone has '(legendum puto, Caballo)'.

[12] As above, n. 7.   [13] *MGH SS Mer.*, 1:1², 245 & 391.   [14] Cf. *PL*, CXXIII,
112.   [15] *MGH SS*, XX, 218f.   [16] Cf. Partic. XXII, 26; *MGH SS*, XXII, 194,
30ff.   [17] *PL*, CXXXIX, 766–7.   [18] XI, 41; ed. 1568, App., 29.   [19] Non
invenio; but cf. Besuensis in *PL*, CLXII, 777.   [20] Besuensis; *PL*, CLXII, 766.

said,[12] 'If you loose the reins with women, as with an unruly nature and an untamed beast, you must expect uncontrolled actions.'* She caused the death of ten royal princes. When she was reproved by a certain bishop and asked to be more temperate, she ordered him to be thrown into a river. In the end a council of the Franks was convoked, and she was summoned to judgment, condemned, and torn limb from limb by wild horses. This is attested by Gregory of Tours,[13] Ado,[14] Otto of Freising,[15] Godfrey of Viterbo,†[16] and Aimon.[17] The following passage is taken from the appendix to Gregory of Tours:[18] 'She was held responsible for the death of ten‡ kings of the Franks, namely Sigebert, Merovech, his father Chilperic, Theudebert§ and his son Lothar, Merovech the son of Lothar, Theuderic and his three children who had been recently put to death. It was ordered that for three days she be tortured in various ways. She was first to be placed upon a camel *b*(I think the word should be read as pack-horse)¶ *a*and paraded before the entire army, and then she was to have her hair, one foot and an arm tied to the tails of ferocious horses, which with kicks and swift plunges would tear her apart.' *c*I find the same event described in the manuscript of the chronicle of the Dijon monastery in these terms:[19] 'She was placed upon a camel and taken on a circuit of the army. All shuddered with horror at her cries, as if she commanded body and soul to be taken down again to the infernal regions. She was tied to four wild horses and torn in pieces as they stampeded apart. Then a fire was lit and her remnants, together with her retinue of criminals, were thrust into it by the common people.' In another passage the same chronicler writes:[20] 'So many evils and effusions of blood occurred in France as a result of the counsels of Brunhild that the prophecy of the Sibyl was

---

* *c*[1] omits this sentence. † *bc* omit reference to Godfrey of Viterbo (by inadvertence)
‡ *bc* five. § *bc* Theobert. ¶ *b* alone has the parenthetic passage.

'*Veniens, Bruna de partibus Hispaniae, ante cuius conspectum gentes peribunt. Haec vero equitum calcibus disrumpetur.*'

ᵃAge, de ceteris videamus. Dominata est Plectrudis non Regis, sed Regii praefecti Pipini vidua, qui tum Regium imperium
5 obtinebat, dum inane Regium nomen Dagobertus secundus sustineret. Haec Plectrudis propter adulterii et flagitiosae vitae turpitudinem a Pipino repudiata, marito mortuo multarum in Gallia seditionum auctor fuit. Carolum Martellum Palatii magistrum, fortissimum virum, abire Magistratu coegit, alium-
10 queTheobaldum impurum et nefarium hominem in ipsius locum suffecit. Tandem funestum civile bellum inter Francos ipsos excitavit, qui variis praeliis, et (ut* ait Aimoinus) *durissimis caedibus sese mutuo prostraverunt*; lib. 4, cap. 50, et cap. seq.²¹ Quinetiam auctor libelli cui titulus est, Status regni Franciae, sub
15 Dagoberto II his utitur verbis:²² Cum Franci Plectrudis furores atque insanias ferre non possent, neque in Dagoberto Rege spem ullam reliquam viderent, Danielem quendam sibi Regem delegerunt, qui antea monachus fuerat, eumque Chilpericum nominarunt; quam historiam superius quodam loco perstrinximus.

20 Sed reliquas videamus. Dominata est Regina mater Caroli Calvi, nomine Iuditha, Ludovici cognomento Pii coniux, qui non modo Francogalliae Rex, verumetiam Italiae et Germaniae Imperator fuit. Haec miserum fataleque bellum inter Ludovicum et ipsius filios privignos suos excitavit, unde nata horum ad-
35 versus parentem tanta coniuratio, ut illum imperio se abdicare, suamque illis dignitatem cedere, magno totius prope Europae incommodo cogerent. Quorum incommodorum culpam Historici omnes magna ex parte in illam Reginam matrem Iuditham conferunt, cuius rei testes* Abbas Ursperg.;²³ Michael
30 Ritius;²⁴ et Otto Frising. Chron. 5, cap. 34:²⁵ *Ludovicus*, inquit, *propter mala opera uxoris suae Iudith regno pulsus est.* Itemque Rhe-

---

12 *bc* 'ut' put outside parentheses.   **29** *bc* omit 'cuius rei testes'.

²¹ Ed. 1567, 388.   ²² Non invenio. The essentials of this are found, however, in *Liber historiae Francorum*, 51–2; *MGH SS Mer.*, II, 325ff.   ²³ Cf. Ekkehard, *Chronicon*, A.D. 833, 840; *MGH SS*, VI, 172, 29 & 35ff.   ²⁴ *De reg. Franc.*; ed. 1534, 28.   ²⁵ *MGH SS*, XX, 228, 3.

fulfilled, namely "Bruna will come from distant Spain and peoples will perish before her gaze. But she will be torn apart by the hooves of horses."'

^aWell then, let us look at some other instances. Power was acquired by Plectrudis, who was the widow not of a king but of the minister Pepin, who had obtained the royal authority while Dagobert II held the empty title of king. This Plectrudis was repudiated by Pepin because of the vileness of her adultery and her vicious life. After her husband's death she was the author of many seditions in France. She forced that bravest of men, Charles Martel, mayor of the palace, to resign his office, and put in his place a certain Theobald, a vile and wicked man. At length she stirred up a civil war of dire consequence among the Franks, who, as Aimon says,[21] 'slaughtered each other savagely' in a series of battles. Moreover, the author of the book entitled the *State of the Kingdom of France under Dagobert II* speaks of the matter in these terms:[22] 'As the Franks could not endure the furies and insane acts of Plectrudis, and saw no hope remaining in King Dagobert, they chose a certain Daniel as their king, who had previously been a monk, and called him Chilperic.' This is an event we have earlier related in its proper place.

Let us look at other examples. Power was seized by the queen mother of Charles the Bald, Judith by name, who was the wife of Louis known as the Pious, the king of Francogallia and also the emperor of Italy and Germany. She stirred up a disastrous and fatal war between Louis and her stepsons, from which sprang so great a conspiracy against the king that they forced him to abdicate and cede them his office, to the great detriment of nearly all Europe. All historians place a large share of the blame for these troubles upon Judith, the queen mother, for instance the abbot of Ursperg,[23] Michael Ritius,[24] and Otto of Freising.[25] 'Louis', writes Otto of Freising, 'was expelled from the kingdom because of the evil works of his wife Judith.' This is also the view of Regino in his chronicle

gino in Chron. anni DCCCXXXVIII, ubi sic scribit:[26] *Ludovicus a suis imperio privatur, et privatus custodiae traditur, Regnique monarchia Lothario filio eius per electionem Francorum datur. Fuit autem haec deiectio pro maxima parte facta propter multimodam forni-*
5 *cationem Iudithae uxoris eius.*

Aliquot post seculis dominata est Blanca Regina, mater Ludovici cognomento Divi, natione Hispana. Ut primum gubernaculum arripuit, concurrere ad arma Galliae proceres coeperunt, Duce Philippo, Comite Bolonico, Regis patruo, qui
10 (ut summus auctor scribit Ioan. Ionvillaeus cap. histor. 4[27]) ferendum non esse clamitabant, tantum Regnum a muliere, eaque peregrina, administrari. Itaque Comitem Philippum proceres illi, repudiata Blanca, Regni procuratorem delegerunt. At Blanca nihilominus in instituto perseverare, et auxilia undique accersere,
15 Ferdinandum denique Hispaniae Regem foedere sibi atque amicitia adiungere instituit. Cum Duci Philippo Dux Britanniae et Comes Eboracensis ipsius frater sese coniunxissent, de improviso oppida aliquot interceperunt, eaque praesidiis firmarunt, quod Ionvillaeus cap. 5 commemorat,[28] atque ita
20 gravissimum in Gallia bellum, propter occupatam a Regina matre Regni procurationem, exarsit. Forte tum accidit, ut Rex Stampas a matre armorum caussa missus, proficisceretur. Eo confestim multis ex partibus Proceres advolarunt, Regemque obsidere coeperunt: non laedendi (inquit Ionvillaeus[29]) aut vio-
25 landi illius consilio, sed (ut idem testatur) ut eum a matris potestate abducerent. Qua re ad illam perlata, quae tum Lutetiae permanserat, celeriter armari Parisienses, et Stampas proficisci iubet. Vix eae copiae Montlerium pervenerant, cum Rex obsidione liberatus, ad eos accedit, Lutetiamque una cum ipsis
30 revertitur. Ubi se Philippus domesticis copiis minus instructum animadvertit, Reginam Cypri, quae in regno controversiam quandam habebat, subsidio accersit. Haec magnis copiis in Campaniam ingressa, late regionem illam populatur. Blanca

---

[26] *MGH SS,* I, 567, 18ff.   [27] Cap. XVI–XXII; SHF, 26ff. See above, p. 56, for comment on Hotman's use of Joinville.   [28] Seems to be a reference to c. 16; SHF, 26–7 (if so, quite distorted).   [29] Cap. 16; SHF, 26–7 [?].

for the year 838, when he says:[26] 'Louis was deprived of his government by his own people, and was placed in solitary confinement, while the crown was bestowed upon his son Lothar by the election of the Franks. Moreover this deposition was due mainly to the many adulterous liaisons of his wife Judith.'

In a later age power was exercised by Queen Blanche, who was Spanish by birth and the mother of Saint Louis. When she first seized the helm of the ship of state, the nobility of France began to take up arms under Duke Philip, count of Bologne and uncle to the king. As that most excellent author Jean de Joinville writes,[27] the nobility protested that it was not to be borne that so great a kingdom should be governed by a woman, and she a foreigner. Thus the nobles repudiated Blanche and chose Count Philip as the regent of the kingdom. But Blanche persevered in her purpose nonetheless, and sought help wherever she could, finally arranging to ally herself in treaty and friendship with Ferdinand, the king of Spain. The duke of Brittany and the count of Evreux, his brother, allied themselves with Duke Philip, and suddenly seized a number of towns, making them secure with garrisons. Joinville describes this,[28] and explains how a most intense conflict flared up in France because the government of the kingdom had been taken over by the queen mother. It so happened that the king set out for Etampes at this time, having been sent there for military reasons by his mother. The nobility at once flocked there from all parts of France, and began to surround the king in the town, not for the sake of harming him or doing him violence, but, as Joinville says,[29] to remove him from his mother's authority. This news was related to her when she was still in Paris, and she swiftly ordered the Parisians to arm themselves and march on Etampes. These forces had scarcely reached Montlhéry when the king, who had been freed from his restriction, joined them and returned with them to Paris. When Philip saw that he was equipped with too few troops of his own, he sought help from the queen of Cyprus, who had been conducting a certain legal suit in the kingdom. The latter invaded Champagne with strong forces and pillaged the province extensively. Nevertheless Blanche

nihilominus in sententia permanet. Itaque Anglorum auxilium
Proceres ad extremum in Regni fines introducunt. Hi magnis
incommodis Aquitaniam, ceterasque maritimas regiones affi-
ciunt, quae incommoda omnia ex Reginae illius matris impo-
5 tentia atque ambitione nata fuisse, Ionvillaeus multis verbis
commemorat, cap. 6, 7, 8, 9, et 10.³⁰

 Et quoniam longe alia de Blancae ingenio et moribus nostrorum hominum opinio est, propter eorum (ut credi par est) qui
per ea tempora scripserunt, assentationes (nam Reginis matribus
10 Scriptores fere vel supplicii metu, vel propter Regum filiorum
existimationem parcunt)* non praetermittendum videtur, quod
idem Ionvillaeus cap. 76 commemorat,³¹ illam usque eo filium
in potestate sua habuisse, usque adeo illum timidum abiectumque
redegisse, ut cum ipsius uxorem, nurum suam, Margaretam odio
15 haberet, raro admodum Regem cum illa versari pateretur. Itaque cum Rex iter faceret, Blanca metatoribus imperabat, ut
hospitium Reginae separatim a Rege assignarent. Quinetiam si
quando Rex noctu furtim ad coniugem accedebat, tum hostiarios
in speculis collocabat, et si forte Blancam adventare intelli-
20 gerent, tum fuste canes ab illis caedi imperabat, quorum clamore
de sese occultando commoneretur. Quid amplius? *Die quodam*
(inquit Ionvillaeus³²) *cum Regina Margareta e puerperio aegrotaret,
Rexque pro amicitia ad illam venisset, repente Blanca intervenit.* Rex
clamore canum admonitus, sese in lectuli angulum abdidit,
25 cortinisque involvit. *Illa nihilominus inventum Regem manu,
inspectantibus omnibus, prehendit, ac simul e cubiculo eduxit: ' Tu hic,
inquiens, nihil agis. Egredere.'* At puerpera cum tantam contumeliam
acerbius tulisset, dolore exanimata est, coactique sunt cubicularii
Regem revocare, cuius adventu puerpera recreata est, animumque
30 recepit. Atque haec quidem Ionvillaeus, cap. hist. 76, totidem
prope verbis commemorat.

 Rursus aliquot intermissis annis dominata est Isabella Caroli VI

---

11 **c¹** omits this parenthetical remark.

30 Presumably cc. 17–22 (SHF, 27–37), but very garbled and distorted.
31 Cap. 119; SHF, 217 (a close paraphrase).   32 *Ibid.* – but see above, p. 57,
for comment.

remained resolute in her purpose. In response the nobility finally called in the help of the English to the outlying provinces of the kingdom. They in turn caused great devastation in Aquitaine and other maritime provinces, and all these troubles arose from the passion and ambition of that queen mother, as Joinville records at length.[30]

Since a very different opinion is held among us concerning Blanche's ability and habits – an opinion, one may believe, caused by the flattery of those who wrote at that time (for writers generally hesitate to criticize queen mothers, either out of fear of punishment or out of respect for the kings their sons)* – it seems we should not omit to mention Joinville's remark[31] that she had her son so much in her power, and had reduced him to such a state of timidity and despair, that she would rarely allow the king to converse with his wife Margaret, her own daughter-in-law, whom she hated. Thus when the king went on a journey, Blanche ordered those who laid out the lodgings to give the queen quarters apart from the king. Indeed, if ever the king secretly went to join his wife at night, he placed servants on watch. If they happened to learn that Blanche was approaching they were under orders to thrash some dogs, whose howls might remind him to hide himself. Need we say more? 'One day', writes Joinville,[32] 'when Queen Margaret was ill through pregnancy, the king came to visit because of his fondness for her, and Blanche unexpectedly appeared. The king was warned by the howling of the dogs, and hid himself behind a corner of the bed, wrapping himself in some curtains. Nevertheless, the queen mother found him and, with everyone looking on, laid hold of him and dragged him out of the room. "You had no business to do here", she said. "Get out." But the pregnant queen reacted so strongly to this great insult that she fainted in her exasperation, and the servants were obliged to call back the king. At his return the queen was brought round and recovered consciousness.' Such is Joinville's literal account.

Another example occurred some years later, when Isabella the

---

* c[1] *omits parenthetic passage.*

dementis vidua. Prius enim quam Concilii auctoritate Regni
procuratio certis ac delectis viris mandari posset, multae ab
hominibus ambitiosis contentiones exortae sunt. Sexies denique
controversiae renovatae, sexies interpositis pactionibus sedatae
5 sunt. Tandem Isabella Parisiis exacta, Carnutum se recepit. Ibi
Philippum Morvillerium veteratorem nacta, Senatum sibi, et
Praetorem, et Cancellarium Morvillerium illum instituit, eiusdemque consilio Typum regium (quod Cancellariae sigillum
vulgo appellant) insculpi iussit, suamque in eo imaginem
10 demissis brachiis imprimi, cum in diplomatibus hac praefatione
uteretur: 'Isabella Dei gratia Regina Franciae, quae propter in-
commodam Regis valetudinem Regni procurationem obtinet.'
Verum ubi Respublica multis affecta incommodis, ac prope iam
ad interitum adducta videretur, publico consilio Turones aman-
15 data est, quatuorque illi tutores attributi, qui belluam illam
indomitam domi continerent, viderentque ne quam rem agere,
ac ne literam quidem ullam sine ipsorum permissu scribere
posset. Cuius rei extat apud Monstrelletum copiosa historia
cap. 161 et 168.³³
20   ᵇMultoque vetustius eiusdem severitatis exemplum extat in
Placidina Childeberti Regis matre, quam propter impietatem et
nimiam in episcopo Quintiano vexando et ecclesiae pace con-
turbanda insaniam, in oppido Cadurco comprehensam, et rebus
omnibus spoliatam ac nudatam Franci exilio damnarunt, ut
25 testatur Gregor. Turon. lib. 3, cap. 12.³⁴

---

³³ The seclusion at Troyes, mentioned at the end, actually predates the other
events, and is found in Monstrelet c. 168; SHF, III, 176. All the rest is from c. 180;
SHF, III, 234–5.   ³⁴ Cf. *MGH SS Mer.*, I: I², 108, 12.

widow of the mad Charles VI held power. Before the government of the kingdom could be vested by the authority of the council in tried and chosen men, many disputes had been instigated by ambitious men. On six occasions these quarrels flared up, and six times they were settled by agreement. Finally Isabella was driven out of Paris and proceeded to Chartres. There she discovered a crafty fellow named Philippe de Morvilliers, and set up a parlement for herself with a president and Morvilliers as chancellor. On his advice she ordered a royal seal (commonly called the chancery seal) to be engraved, and upon it to be depicted an image of herself with arms folded in prayer. She used the following preface on official documents: 'Isabella by the grace of God Queen of France, who by reason of the King's ill-health exercises the government of the kingdom.' However, when the commonwealth was afflicted by a multitude of troubles and it seemed that nearly everything was then reduced to ruin, she was removed to Tours by the public council, and four custodians were appointed to keep that wild beast in her lodgings and to see that she was able to do nothing, not so much as to write a letter without their leave. There is a very full account of this affair in Monstrelet.[33]

*b*There is a much older example of such severity in the case of Placidina, mother of King Childebert, who, because of her extreme blasphemy in persecuting Bishop Quintian and her madness in disturbing the peace of the church, was shut up in the town of Cahors. For all these offences the Franks condemned her to be stripped and deprived of her goods and exiled, as Gregory of Tours relates.[34]

^aCAPUT XX [^bXXI, ^{cc²}XXVII, ^{c¹}XXV]

De parlamentis iuridicialibus

*Sub eadem Capevingiorum familia exortum est in Franco-
gallia Regnum iudiciale,* de quo nobis propter incredibilem
artificum industriam, et inauditam seculis omnibus solertiam
dicendum videtur. Dominatur hoc tempore passim in Gallia
5 genus hominum, qui Iuridici a nonnullis, Pragmatici ab aliis,
^bitemque Rabulae ^aappellantur. Horum tanta trecentis fere ab-
hinc annis fuit solertia, ut non modo publici Concilii auctoritatem (de qua superius diximus) prope iam oppresserint, verum
etiam omnes Regni Principes, atque adeo Maiestatem Regiam
10 amplitudini suae parere coegerint. Itaque quibus in oppidis illius
Regni sedes positae sunt, in iis tertia fere civium, et incolarum
pars tantis excitata praemiis ad illius se artis Rabulariae studium
ac disciplinam applicavit, quod vel Lutetiae, quae ceterarum
civitatum omnium princeps numeratur, cuivis licet animadver-
15 tere. Quis enim vel triduum in illa urbe versatus, non animadvertit, tertiam civium partem, artem istam Pragmaticam* et
litigatoriam factitare?
Itaque summus in ea Pragmaticorum conventus (qui Pur-
puratus Senatus dicitur) tantarum opum, tantaeque dignitatis
20 est, ut quemadmodum Iugurtha de Senatu Romano quondam
dixisse fertur,* non iam Consiliariorum, sed Regum ac Satra-
parum consessus videatur quippe, cum ^bplerique ^ain illum
allecti, quantumvis abiecto loco nati, tamen paucorum annorum
spatio regales prope opes sibi concilient. Itaque aliae civitates
25 complures* omni contentione pugnarunt, ut eiusdemmodi con-

---

1 *c¹* omits the first 300-odd words of this chapter, beginning it instead with
'Nomen autem Parlamenti...', as below, p. 498, l. 27.   **2** 'iudiciale': *bc*
'Rabularium'.   **16** *c* 'rabulariam'.   **21** *bc* change this clause to read 'ut
quemadmodum de Senatu Romano quondam dictum est,'.   **25** *bc* 'Qua de
caussa civitates aliae complures'.

^aCHAPTER XX [^bXXI, ^{cc2}XXVII, ^{c1}XXV]

The parlements as courts of law

---

*Under the Capetian dynasty there arose in Francogallia a judicial kingdom,† on which we must have something to say in the light of the incredible industry of the makers of this structure and their unprecedented shrewdness throughout all ages. In France today a certain kind of man is to be found everywhere in a position of authority. Some call them jurists, others lawyers, ^band others again pettifoggers. ^aSuch was the craft of these men over the last three hundred years or so that not only have they now virtually crushed the authority of the public council (as described above), but also they have obliged all the princes of the kingdom, and even the royal majesty itself, to yield to their might. Thus, in all those towns where branches of this legal kingdom have been established, nearly a third of the citizens and inhabitants have been moved by hopes of financial gain to apply themselves to the study and discipline of that profession of pettifoggery. Anyone may notice this in Paris, which is ranked as the chief among all other towns in this respect. For who could dwell there for three days without noticing that a third part of the citizens are engrossed in the art and practice‡ of litigation?

The supreme assembly of lawyers in Paris (which is called the senate in purple) is so replete with wealth and dignity that, as Jugurtha is reported to have said once of the Roman senate,§ it seems no longer a gathering of councillors but rather one of kings and satraps, since ^bmost of ^athose who are tempted to join it, however humble their birth, acquire wealth of almost royal proportions within the space of a few years. So it is that many other cities struggle desperately to be host to judicial assemblies of this

---

* *c*¹ *omits following three paragraphs.* † *bc* judicial kingdom *becomes* kingdom of pettifoggers. ‡ *c* chicanery. § *bc* as Jugurtha is reported to have said once of the Roman senate *becomes* in the manner in which it was once said of the Roman senate.

sessus iuridiciales apud se haberent, iamque celeberrima haec
Parlamenta numerantur: Parisiense, Tholosanum, Rhoto-
magense, Gratianopolitanum, Burdegalense, Aquense, Divion-
ense, quae omnia stataria et sedentaria sunt. Octavum vero
5 mobile et ambulatorium quod Grande consilium appellatur.
*b*Fuit et nonum Armoricis attributum, edicto Henrici regis anno
MDLIII.¹ *a*In horum Regnorum finibus sunt et aliae, ut sic
dicam, Satrapiae, quae superiorum illorum amplitudinem, quoad
possunt, imitantur, et vulgo Sedes praesidiales nominantur; tan-
10 taque huius morbi vis, atque contagio est, ut quemadmodum
olim Aegyptiorum bona pars, Tyrannorum suorum imperio, in
pyramidibus, et eiusmodi molibus extruendis occupata erat, sic
maximus gentis Gallicae numerus in litibus et calumniis exer-
cendis, et forensibus scriptitationibus operam consumat.
15 *b*Extat Claudii Seyssellii Archiepiscopi Massiliensis libellus
Gallice scriptus, cui titulus est, De Monarchia Franciae, cuius in
cap. 15 verba haec sunt:² *Opinione mea, plures sunt in una Francia
scribae, procuratores, advocati, et similes circumforanei, quam in uni-
verso orbe Christiano, si alii omnes unum in locum conferantur.* Neque
20 dissimilis illa est Philippi Cominaei querimonia lib. 6, cap. 6,
ubi de rege Ludovico XI scribens:³ *Habebat,* inquit, *in animo leges
de publico et privato iure, Gallico sermone scriptas, unum in volumen
conferre, quo facilius captiones et praestigiae advocatorum vitari
possent; quorum numerus tantus est in hoc Franciae regno, ut par in
25 mundo non reperiatur, id Nobilitas Francica iampridem sensit, atque
experta est.* Haec ad verbum Cominaeus.
*a*Nomen autem* Parlamenti antiqua nostrorum hominum
lingua colloquium* significat, multorum variis ex locis certum
aliquem in locum* convenientium, ut de communibus rebus
30 communicent.* Itaque in Chronicis veteribus, siquando principes

27 *c*¹ (which begins the chapter here, as remarked above) omits 'autem'.
28 *c* 'collocutionem'. 29 *c*² inadvertently omits 'certum aliquem in locum'
– a typographer's homoioteleuton. 30 'communicent': *c* 'inter se conferant,
ac sermocinentur'.

¹ *Cat. gén. de la (Bib. Nat.), actes Royaux,* I, 194, No. 1122. ² I, 15; ed. 1961,
123. ³ *Mémoires,* VI, 5; SHF, II, 209–10.

kind, and we may now list the following most celebrated parlements: Paris, Toulouse, Rouen, Grenoble, Bordeaux, Aix and Dijon, all of which are settled and established. The eighth, which is movable and on circuit, is called the grand conseil, *b*and a ninth was granted to Brittany by an edict of King Henry in the year 1553.[1] *a*Within the boundaries of these judicial kingdoms are other courts or, so to speak, satrapies, which ape the grandeur of the higher courts so far as they can, and are commonly called présidiaux. So great is the strength and infection of this disease that, just as a large proportion of the Egyptians were once occupied in building pyramids and other undertakings of this kind on the orders of their tyrants, so the greater part of the French nation uses up all its energy in prosecuting law-suits and legal subterfuges and in writing briefs.

*b*In a book written in French by Claude de Seyssel, archbishop of Marseille, and entitled the *Monarchy of France*, there is a passage which reads as follows:[2] 'In my opinion there are more clerks, procurators, advocates and such-like legal hangers-on in France alone than there are in the whole of Christendom, if all the others could be gathered together in one place.' There is a somewhat similar complaint in the memoirs of Philippe de Commines, where he writes of King Louis XI in these terms:[3] 'He intended to bring together the written laws concerning public and private law and have them set out in French in a single volume so as to avoid more easily the frauds and deceits of the lawyers. So numerous are the latter in this kingdom of France that as many cannot be found in the rest of the world. For a long time the French nobility had known this and suffered from it.' These are the very words of Commines.

*a*In the language of our ancestors the word parliament, moreover,* meant a conference of many men coming to meet in some fixed place† from different localities to discuss matters of common concern.‡ According to our ancient chronicles, whenever princes

* c¹ *omits* moreover. † *c omits* in some fixed place. ‡ *c* to discuss matters of common concern *becomes* to confer in discourse among themselves on matters of common concern.

legative principum de pace aut bellicis pactionibus convenerunt, semper colloquium illud condictum,* Parlamenti nomine appellatur. Eademque ratione publicum ordinum Concilium vetusta lingua *b*nostra *a*Parlamentum dicebatur. *b*Quod nomen
5 adhuc in Anglia retinetur. *c*Thom. Walsimgamius in hist. Angl. sub anno 1287:[4] *Hoc anno Rex Angliae in Gallias transiens, Ambianos pervenit, et fecit homagium Regi Franciae, pro terris quas de eo in regno Franciae tenebat Parisius, et interfuit parlamento, quod Rex Francorum tenuit.*

10   *b*Itaque Philipp. Cominaeus lib. 4, cap. 1:[5] *Rex Angliae,* inquit, *tributa suae genti imperandi ius non habet, sine consensu atque auctoritate sui Parlamenti, quod apud nos Trium statuum Concilium appellatur.* Eodemque, nomine conventus ordinum Britanniae Armoricae, quandiu gens illa Regem proprium habuit, semper
15 appellatus est, quemadmodum ex illius Annalib. cognosci licet, multis quidem locis, sed praesertim lib. 3, ubi Ducis Maliclerici, hoc est indocti indocta cum Franciae Rege pactio profertur, ex anno MCCXXX:[6] *Item Dux in signum submissionis praedictae, voluit quod a suo parlamento de cetero appellaretur ad parlamentum*
20 *Franciae, in duobus tantum casibus.* Et mox:[7] *A falso et pravo iudicio sui parlamenti Britanniae appellabitur de cetero ad Franciae parlamentum.*

   Dicebatur etiam Curia parlamenti trium statuum, ut Stephanus Aufrerius Burdegalensis Praetor, nobilis pragmaticus, testatur in Commentario styli curiae parlamenti.[8]* Quinetiam
25 video Bartolum aliosque Doctores Italos hac eadem voce passim pro publico regionis alicuius concilio sive comitiis, usurpare. Nam Bartolus in l. 2, C. de legation., lib. 10:[9] *Praeses*

---

2 *c* 'colloquium' and 'condictum' change places.   **24** *c*[1] adds this sentence: 'Videoque iam ita usurpatum a Ioa. Feraldo Regis Ludovici consiliario in tract. de iur. reg. Franc. privileg. ult. [*i.e.* no. 20.] *Iudicia sub secuta,* inquit, *quae ex registris curiae parlamenti trium Statuum extraxi.* [Ferrault, in Du Moulin, *Opera* (1681), II, 549.]

[4] An. 1288; ed. 1863, I, 28.   [5] SHF, I, 314.   [6] Bouchart; ed. 1541, 89.   [7] *Ibid.*
[8] I do not find this in Aufrier's commentary to Du Breuil's *Stilus curiae parlamenti* (ed. 1551, 95–131), but Charles Du Moulin's marginal gloss to the *Stilus* itself (*ad verbum* 'Franciae' of the Preface) says: 'Parlamentum Parisiense dicebatur antiquitus curiae Franciae. Ioan. Fab. l. 1. C. de sum. tri.' (ed. 1551, 1).
[9] Bartolus, *In tres cod. lib. comm.,* on *Cod.* 10, 63, 5; ed. 1574, 26.

or their envoys met together to negotiate about peace or war such an agreed conference was always described by the term parliament. And for the same reason the public council of the estates was always called the parliament in *b*our *a*ancient tongue. *b*In England this word is retained even to this day. *c*Under the year 1287 Thomas of Walsingham writes in his history of England:[4] 'In this year the king of England crossed to France, and, arriving at Amboise, did homage to the king of France for the lands he held from him in the kingdom of France and attended the parliament the king of France held.'

*b*Philippe de Commines writes:[5] 'The king of England has not the right to order his people to pay taxes without the consent and authority of his parliament, the institution which among us is called the council of the three estates.' The assembly of the estates of Brittany was always called by the same name while that people had their own king, as may be seen from their annals in many passages, and especially in the third book where the treaty of the year 1230 is set out between the incompetent Duke Mauclerc, and the king of France:[6] 'When signing the aforesaid agreement the duke wished that in other respects it be referred from his parliament to the parliament of France, sitting as two houses only.' A little further on the annals read:[7] 'Appeals may be made against a false and perverse judgment of his Breton parliament to the parliament of France.'

It was also called the court of the parliament of the three estates, as that excellent lawyer Etienne Aufrier, a president of the parlement of Bordeaux, tells us in his commentary on the procedure of the court of the parlement.[8]* Indeed I notice that Bartolus and other Italian doctors of the law make use of the term universally to apply to the public council or assembly in any territory. For in his treatise on embassies Bartolus writes:[9] 'The governor of a province

---

* **c**[1] *adds this sentence:* I now see that this expression has been made use of in this sense by Jean Ferrault, councillor of King Louis, in his treatise on the rights and privileges of the king of France, for he claims that he has copied certain judgments from the registers of the court of the parliament of the three estates.

provinciae, inquit, *convocavit parlamentum in provincia, et in eo pro-*
ponit, quod respicit utilitatem publicam. Et mox:[10] *Nota, quod prae-*
sides provinciarum coadunant universale parlamentum provinciae,
quod intellige non quod omnes de provincia debeant ad illud ire, sed de
5 *omnibus civitatibus deputantur ambasiatores, qui civitatem reprae-*
sentant. Et in eandem lib. Ioan. de Platea:[11] *Ubi super aliquo,*
inquit, *providendum est pro utilitate totius provinciae, debet congre-*
gari generale concilium seu parlamentum, non quod omnes de pro-
vincia vadant, sed de qualibet civitate aliqui ambasiatores vel syndici,
10 *qui totam civitatem repraesentent, in quo concilio seu Parlamento*
petitur proponi sanum et utile consilium. Item Lucas de Penna:[12]
Modus proponendi in consilio generali, seu parlamento est, ut
petatur proponi sanum et utile consilium.

    ^{c}Budaeus autem in Pandect.:[13] *Nihilo secius* (inquit) *curiae*
15 *Parisiensis originem a conventibus iuridicis manasse, haud dubia con-*
iectura crediderim, quibus olim Principes interesse, praeesseque sole-
bant, quoniam indictivi erant, nec loco, nec tempore stati. Vagam enim
Parlamenti rationem fuisse constat, quasique praetorianum Principis
concilium.

20   ^{a}Quod cum maximae auctoritas esset, eamque* auctoritatem
imminuere Capevingii molirentur, et certorum Senatorum
numerum in eius Concilii locum substituere, augustum illud
Parlamenti nomen in illum Senatum* transtulerunt, eique hanc
auctoritatem attribuerunt:* primum ut nulla Regia Lex, nulla
25 constitutio rata esset, nisi cuius illi consiliarii auctores compro-
batoresque fuissent; deinde ut nullus tota Gallia Magistratus, non
modo urbanus, verumetiam militaris esset, quem non ab illo
consessu inaugurari, et apud eundem in leges iurare oporteret;

---

20 bc change this sentence, up to this point, to read: 'Cum autem in Gallia nostra summam illam Publici concilii'.   **23** 'Senatum': **bcc²** 'pragmaticorum et iudicum consessum [but **cc²** 'concessum']'; **c¹** 'iudicum concessum'.   **24 bc** 'tribuerunt'.

[10] *Ibid.*   [11] *Super tribus lib. cod.,* on *Cod.* 10, 63, 4; ed. 1537, 61ᵛ. By diverse elisions, Hotman here exaggerates Parliament's initiative.   [12] *Non invenio.* But Lucas de Penna's commentary on *Cod.* 12, 16 (*Lectura,* ed. 1544, ccxxxiᵛ–ccxxxiiᵛ) is replete with similar statements about good counsel.   [13] *Annot.* §Ex. l. ult. Senat.; ed. 1557, 96.

convenes the parliament of the province, and there proposes any-thing that concerns the public welfare.' Later Bartolus states:[10] 'It should be noted that the governors of provinces call together the entire parliament of a province. This does not mean that everyone from the province has to go there, but that deputies from all the cities are authorised to represent their city.' Johannes de Platea writes as follows on the same book:[11] 'When something more has to be arranged for a whole province, a general council or parlia-ment should be called together. Not everyone from the province goes to it, but deputies or syndics from every city attend, repre-senting the entire city. This council or parliament is intended to present wise and useful advice.' Again, Lucas de Penna writes:[12] 'The method of procedure in a general council or parliament is that one asks for wise and useful advice to be offered.'

*c*However, Budé writes on the *Pandects*:[13] 'Nevertheless I would scarcely give credence to this doubtful speculation that the origin of the Parisian court stemmed from those judicial assemblies at which princes were formerly accustomed to be present and to preside, since they were proclaimed at no particular place or fixed time. For it is certain that the business of the parliament was con-ducted at no precise centre, as if it were the executive council of the prince.'

*a*As the authority of the council was supreme, the Capetians endeavoured to diminish it* and to substitute a number of approved judges for the council. Then they transferred the august name of parliament to the senate† and gave it authority as follows: first, no royal law or ordinance might be established unless these councillors had authorised and approved it; second, no magistrate anywhere in France, be he a municipal officer or even a military one, could take up his office without appearing before the body of the judges and

---

* **bcc²** *the preceding part of this sentence altered to read:* But the Capetians endeavoured to diminish the authority of the public council in its supreme place within our France. † **bcc²** senate *becomes* assembly of lawyers and judges; **c¹** assembly of judges.

tum ut ab eorum iudiciis appellandi ius non esset, sed ut eorum
decreta rata et fixa essent. *b*Is qui Princeps est senatus (inquit
Conannus lib. 1¹⁴) cum ius dicit, nemini, praeterquam regi ipsi
honore sedendi cedit; *c*quo tamen loco Connanus Cancellarii
5 oblitus est, cui Princeps ille senatus loco cedit, *quasi* (ut Budaeus
scribit¹⁵) *magistratuum omnium antistiti.* *a*Postremo quicquid
potestatis, imperii, auctoritatis penes publicum Concilium *b*et
Statuum parlamentum *a*per tot annos fuisse docuimus, id totum
Senatus ille subdititius sibi usurpavit,* in quem Reges cooptandos
10 curabant, quos ad suas rationes accommodatos fore videbant;*
*c*eaque tum Curia Parlamenti vocata est, ut in Anglico libello,
cui titulus est A learned commendatum, cap. 52:¹⁶ *sunt quippe in*
regno Franciae, in curia ibidem suprema, quae Curia Parlamenti voci-
tatur, processus quidam, qui in ea plus quam triginta annis pepend-
15 *erunt. Et novi ego appellationis causam unam quae in curia illa agitata*
fuit iam per decem annos, et adhuc verisimile non est, eam infra annos
decem alios posse decidi. Item cap. 48:¹⁷ *Omnes advocati in Francia*
etiam in curia parlamenti solent placitare caussas suas in lingua
Gallica.

20   *a*Quare quibus initiis ac radicibus in tantam amplitudinem
excreverit, paulisper considerandum est. Primum igitur Basilica
Regia Lutetiae opere magnifico extructa est, imperio, ut plerique
affirmant, Regis Ludovici Hutini, quo nomine prisca lingua
nostra Turbulentus significatur; vel, ut nonnulli disputant, Regis
25 Philippi Pulchri, circiter annum MCCCXIIII studio certe atque
opera Enguerrantii Marignii, Comitis Longuevillii, qui aliquot
interiectis annis in patibulo Parisiensi propter peculatus crimen
reste* suspensus est. Utcunque sit, quod Aegyptii Reges fecisse

---

9 'subdititius sibi usurpavit': *c*¹ 'subdititio tributum est'.   **10** *bc* 'iudicabant'.
28 'reste': *c*¹ 'falsum an verum recte'.

¹⁴ Should be *Fran. Connan. comment.* 1, 14, which speaks of privileges of the
princeps senatus, but I did not find the exact words used by Hotman.   ¹⁵ *Annot.*
§Ex. l. ult. Senat.; ed. 1557, 108.   ¹⁶ Fortescue, *A Learned Commendation,* cap.
53; ed. 1567, fol. 126ᵛ.   ¹⁷ *Ibid.*; ed. 1567, fol. 110ᵛ.

taking an oath to uphold the laws; third, there would be no right of appeal from their judgments, and their decrees would be established and immutable. *b*Connan says in his treatise:[14] 'When the senate speaks the law it is the prince, and yields precedence to no one except the king himself.' *c*However, in this passage Connan forgot the chancellor, to whom that prince-senate yields precedence, 'as if (writes Budé[15]) he were the president of all magistrates'. *a*The final point is that all aspects of the power, dominion and authority which we have shown to have reposed in the public council *b*and parliament of the estates *a*throughout so many long years were entirely arrogated to itself by* that spurious senate, and the kings saw† that those coopted to its ranks could be depended on to be accommodating to their intentions. *c*Then that body was named the court of the parlement, as is set out in an English work entitled *A Learned Commendation*:[16] 'Indeed in the kingdom of France there are certain suits in the supreme court, which is called the court of the parlement, that have been under deliberation there for more than thirty years. I myself know of one such case of an appeal which has now been in progress for ten years, and it is probable that it cannot be settled in less than ten more years.' In an earlier chapter the same author states:[17] 'In France, too, all advocates in the court of the parlement are wont to plead their cases in the French tongue.'

*a*For these reasons we should briefly consider the origins and roots from which the parlement grew to so great a size. First, the royal palace of justice was constructed in Paris on a magnificent scale at the command, as many affirm, of King Louis Hutin, whose name in our early tongue means turbulent. Others say that it was built about 1314 by command of King Philip the Fair, through the zeal and labour of Enguerrand de Marigny, count of Longueville, who some years later was hanged with a rope‡ on the gallows in Paris for embezzlement. Whoever was responsible, the Francogallican kings can be said to have taken as much trouble in handing down to posterity the art of litigation as the Egyptians kings are

---

* *c*[1] entirely arrogated to itself by *becomes* all granted to. † *bc* judged. ‡ *c*[1] hanged with a rope *becomes* , rightly or wrongly, hanged.

narrantur, ut imperio suo subiectos in pyramidibus extruendis
occuparent, in quibus Rex Chemnis praecipue memoratur, qui
hominum 360 millia ad pyramidem extruendam conduxit,
idem tum Francogalliae Reges in arte rabularia tradenda fecisse
5 dici possunt.* Guaguini autem Historici in Hutini Regis vita,
verba haec sunt:[18] *Hic Ludovicus instituit Parlamenti curiam Parisiis
stabilem esse, et loco non moveri, ne litigatores crebris circuitionibus
vexarentur.* Haec ille.

Nam quod nonnulli ad Pipinum vel Carolum Magnum insti-
10 tutum illud referunt, quam absurdum id sit, facile ex iis quae
mox docebimus, constabit. Quinetiam *b*eiusdem *a*Caroli Magni
leges et constitutiones complures extant, quarum in nulla neque
parlamenti, neque maioris illius Senatus mentio interponitur,
sed tantum sancitur, ut certis locis forum a Iuridicis agatur, et
15 conventus habeantur, quae ille usitata consuetudine Placitum, et
Mallum* appellat; veluti legis Francicae lib. 4, cap. 35:[19] *Ut in
anno tria sollummodo generalia placita observare compellat, nisi forte
quilibet aut accusatus fuerit, aut alium occupaverit, aut ad testimonium
perhibendum vocatus fuerit.* Multaeque aliae in eandem sententiam
20 eiusdem Regis leges extant, ex quibus de litium paucitate existimare licet. Ac plane verissimum arbitror, quod video a nonnullis hominibus nostris traditum, tantam litium, calumniarum
et sycophantiarum* sementem factam primum a Papa Cle-
mente V, qui Philippi illius Pulchri tempore Papatus sedem
25 Avenionem transtulit, cumque magna ipsius aulici et pragmatici
consuetudine cum hominibus nostris implicarentur, semina
Romanae artis rabulariae in mores nostros sparsisse.

Sed ne tam longe abeamus.* *b*Nam Eguinarthus in vita Caroli
Magni sic scribit:[20] *Cum calciaretur, aut amiciretur, non tantum
30 amicos admittebat; verumetiam si comes palatii litem esse aliquam
diceret, quae sine eius iussu definiri non posset, statim litigantes intro-*

---

5 *c*[1] omits the sentence 'Utcunque sit...dici possunt.'.   16 *c* 'Mallam'.
23 *c*[1] inserts here 'de quibus Philippus Comin. lib. 6, cap. 6 graviter con-
questus'; cf. ed. SHF, II, 225.   28 *bc* omit this short sentence.

[18] Bk. 7; ed. 1528, fol. cxxxi^v.   [19] Ansegius, IV, 55; *MGH LL*, II: 1, 444.
[20] C. 24; *MGH SS*, II, 456, 21–4.

said to have done in commanding the employment of their subjects upon the construction of the pyramids. Among these kings King Chemnis is especially remembered for using 360,000 men to build one pyramid.* In his history of the life of King Hutin, Gaguin writes in these terms:[18] 'This Louis enacted that the court of the parlement should be fixed in Paris, and should not be moved from that place, to avoid troubling suitors with many journeys.'

Some claim that Pepin or Charlemagne was responsible for the establishment of the court, but this is quite absurd, as we shall presently show with ease from the very rulers concerned. Indeed there exist many laws and edicts of *b*this same *a*Charlemagne, and in none of them is any mention made of either the parlement or that supposedly greater senate. He merely ordains that in specified places assizes should be held by the judges, and an assembly should be arranged, which he calls a *placitum* or *mallum* according to his usual practice. In the Frankish law it is stated:[19] 'He shall oblige no more than three general *placita* to be held in any year, except where somebody is charged with a grave crime, or seizes the property of another, or is called upon to provide judicial evidence.' Many other laws to the same effect have survived which were authorized by that king, and from them we may notice the paucity of litigation at that time. What I see related by some of our people is, I think, very clearly true, namely that the seed of so many law-suits, artifices and tricksters† was first sown by Pope Clement V, who translated the seat of the papacy to Avignon in the time of Philip the Fair. His courtiers and lawyers involved our people with their widespread practice, and the seeds of the Roman art of legal pettifoggery were planted among our customs.

But let us not depart so far afield.‡ *b*Einhard writes as follows in his life of Charlemagne:[20] 'When he was dressed, he admitted others besides his friends. If a court palatine said that anyone had a lawsuit which could not be determined without his order, he commanded that the litigants be led in at once, and, sitting in his

---

* *c*¹ *omits the two preceding sentences.* † *c*¹ *adds* , about whom Philippe de Commines complains so loudly. ‡ *bc* *omit this sentence.*

duci iussit, et velut pro tribunali sederet, lite cognita, sententiam dixit.
Itaque eiusdem Caroli Magni in Capitulari haec lex extat:[21] *Hoc*
missi nostri notum faciant comitibus et populo, quod nos in omni septi-
mana unum diem ad caussas audiendas sedere volumus.

5   Age, ceteros videamus. ^{*a*}Regnavit circiter annum MCCXXX
Ludovicus cognomento Divus, cuius vitam Ioan. Ionvillaeus, de
quo superius aliquoties meminimus, conscripsit. At ex huius
commentario quanta per id tempus litium et calumniarum esset
raritas, vel hinc licet intelligatur, quod Rex ipse Ludovicus vel
10 controversias disceptabat, vel disceptandi negotium nonnullis e
suo Comitatu mandabat. Itaque cap. 94, ita scribit:[22] *Solebat,*
inquit, imperare Domino Nellio, Domino Suessionensi, et mihi, ut
iudiciis quae ad portam appellantur, operam daremus. Tum mittebat
qui nos ad se accerseret, quaerebatque ex nobis, quo statu res esset,
15 *ecquod esset iudicium, quod sine ipso exerceri non posset; ac saepe*
accidit, ut re per nos ad ipsum delata, litigatores ipsos accersiri ad se
imperaret, caussamque ex bono et aequo disceptaret. Saepenumero in
saltum Vicennam animi caussa exibat, viridique in cespite ad quercus
alicuius radicem considens, sibi nos assidere iubebat, et, si qui negotii
20 *quippiam habebant, eos vocari ad se iubeat.** Quinetiam ipse clare*
pronuntiabat, siquis litem et adversarium haberet, ut accederet, et iusta
sua exponeret. Tum siquis accedebat, Rex attente ipsum audiebat, ac re
cognita, sententiam ex bono et aequo pronuntiabat. Interdum negotium
dabat Petro Fontanio, et Godefrido Vilettio, ut litigatoribus operam
25 *darent, et caussas disceptarent. Vidi etiam aliquoties, cum bonus ille Rex*
Lutetiae in hortum suburbanum exiret, tunica mediocri indutus, ibique
mensam tapeto insterni imperabat. Tum silentio facto introduci ad se
litigatores iubebat, caussasque suas agere, iusque ex tempore reddebat.
Haec Ionvillaeus. Ex quibus existimari potest, quanta litium et

---

20 '*sibi nos... ad se iubebat*': **bc** '*sibi nos assidere, et, si quis negotii quid habebat, eum*
ad se vocari iubebat.'.

[21] *Hludowici Pii capit.*, 192; *MGH LL*, II:2, 16. In the first edition this passage
came later in the text; see p. 532, n. 2.   [22] Joinville, Cap. 12, SHF, 21–2 (with
many ellipses; see above, p. 37, for comment upon Hotman's use of Joinville).

place of judgment, he heard the case and gave his verdict.' In the capitulary of the same Charlemagne there exists this law:[21] 'Let our commissioners make it known to the nobles and the people that for one day in every week we desire to hold a sitting to hear legal cases.'

Let us look at other examples. *a*About the year 1230 there reigned the king known as Saint Louis, to whose life by Jean de Joinville we have referred on several occasions. From his commentary it may be seen how rare were lawsuits and legal trickeries at that time, since King Louis either judged them himself, or referred them to some of his retinue to be determined. Thus Joinville writes:[22] 'He was wont to command the Lord of Nesle, the Lord of Soissons, or myself to take in hand the cases that were brought to him. Then he would summon us to him and enquire from us the state of the case and whether it was such as could not be handled except by himself. It often happened, if we transferred the matter to him, that he would summon the disputants before him and give judgment on the issue in justice and equity. Sometimes it pleased him to go to the forest of Vincennes and, seating himself upon the green sward at the root of some oak, to command us to sit by him. If any persons had a certain matter of business, he would have them called to him.*

Indeed he would proclaim it aloud that, if anyone had a dispute with an opponent, he should approach and expound the justice of his cause. Then, if anyone did come, the king would listen attentively, and when the case had been presented he would give judgment in justice and equity. At other times he would give Pierre Fontaine and Geoffroy Vilette the task of listening to the litigants and determining the case. Also, when that good king went to some garden outside of Paris, I have often seen him clad in simple garb, ordering a table there to be covered with a cloth. Then, when silence had been obtained, he would order litigants to be brought before him, and, when their cases had been pleaded, he would promptly give them justice.' These are the words of Joinville, and one can judge from them how few were the number of lawsuits and litigants in

---

* **bc** *the sentence is joined to the previous one as:* , and, if anyone had a certain matter of business, for that person to be called to him.

litigatorum illis temporibus esset paucitas, quantaque Regum
illorum in cavendis* litium molestiis solicitudo.*

  *b*Quin ne illud quidem praetermittendum est, quod scribit
Speculator sub tit. dc Feriis, cum suo tempore, hoc est circiter
5 annum MCCLXX graviores caussae ac lites in Concilio publico
(quod, ut iam ante dictum est, Parlamentum appellabatur) agi
solerent, atque illuc omnibus ex regni partibus in ius adiretur,
moris fuisse, propter eos qui longinquis ex regionibus venerant,
ut etiam festis diebus iudicia exercerentur:[23] *Potest*, inquit,
10 *excusari consuetudo Curiae Regis Franciae, quae tempore Parla-*
mentorum omni die ius reddit, ut venientes de longinquis partibus
citius expediantur. At successu temporis, arte rabularia, sensim,
gangraenae modo, serpente, institutum est, ut et saepius et
pluribus locis iurisdictio exerceretur.

15   *a*Nam ex* Philippi IIII cognomento Pulchri constitutione
caput hoc profertur,* ex anno MCCCII:[24] *Praeterea propter sub-*
iectorum nostrorum commodum, et caussarum expeditionem pro-
ponimus ordinare, quod duo Parlamenta Parisiis, et duo Scacaria
Rhotomagi, Diesque Trecenses bis tenebuntur in anno. Et quod
20 *Parlamentum apud Tholosam tenebitur, sicut teneri solebat temporibus*
retroactis, si gentes terrae consentiant. Item, quia multae caussae
magnae in nostro Parlamento inter magnas et notabiles personas agun-
tur, ordinamus et volumus, quod duo Praelati et duae aliae personae
sufficientes, Laicae, de nostro consilio, vel saltem unus praelatus, et una
25 *persona Laica, caussas praedictas audiendi, deliberandique gratia con-*
tinue in nostris Parlamentis existant. Quibus ex verbis intelligi
potest, primum quam raro per ea tempora iudicia exercerentur,
deinde quam pauci iudices in illo Parlamento sederent. Nam
quantum ad ceteras praefecturas Regnique provinciales,* extat

---

2 *bc* 'avertendis'.   2 *bc* from here to l. 15 replace a suppressed *a* passage
which will be found in Appendix A, p. 532.   15 *bc* 'Itaque'.   16 'constitutione...profertur': *bc* 'constitutio haec extat'.   29 *bc* 'provincias'.

[23] Durandus, *Spec. iuris*, lib. II, Partic. 1 'De Feriis': *quod sunt genera feriarum*, 9;
ed. 1602, II, 506.   [24] *Ordinationes regiae antiquae* (see bibliography under Du
Breuil, *Stilus*), Tit. I, §§1–2; ed. 1551, 157.

those times, and with what care the kings avoided the vexations of legal disputes.*

*b*But let us not omit what that author who writes under the name of Speculator [Durand] says under the heading of *Festivals*. In his time, that is about the year 1270, important causes and disputes were customarily dealt with in the public council (which, as we have already said, was called the parliament), and a matter would be submitted there in law from any part of the kingdom. It was the custom for sittings to be held even on feast days in order to accommodate those who had come great distances.[23] 'It is possible', writes Speculator, 'to excuse the practice of the court of the king of France to render justice every day when the parliaments were in session, since those who came from distant parts would have their business attended to the sooner.' But in the course of time through the profession of pettifoggery, which imperceptibly insinuated itself after the manner of gangrene, it gradually became the practice for jurisdiction to be exercised more frequently and in more places.

*a*We offer† this ordinance taken from an edict of Philip IV, known as the Fair, in the year 1302:[24] 'Furthermore, for the convenience of our subjects and the rapid determination of legal causes, we propose to ordain that two parlements shall be held at Paris and two exchequers at Rouen, and that the duration of the judicial term every year shall be doubled, and that, if the people in that region agree, the parlement of Toulouse shall be held as it used to be in former times. Also, because many great causes between great and notable persons are dealt with in our parlement, we wish and ordain that two prelates and two other sufficient persons from our council who are laymen, or at least one prelate and one layman, shall be constantly present in our parlements in order to hear the aforesaid causes and deliberate upon them.' We can see from this passage, first, how rarely judicial sessions were held in those times, and, second, how few judges sat in that parlement. The extent to which this applied to other provincial governments of the kingdom

* *bc omit the following passage, which will be found in appendix A.*   † *bc We offer* becomes *There exists.*

*^b*eiusdem *^a*Philippi Pulchri constitutio, in eodem libello his verbis edita, anno MCCCII.²⁵ *Praecipimus insuper, quod Seneschalli et Ballivi nostri teneant suas assisias in circuitu Seneschalliarum et Balliviarum summarie, de duobus mensibus in duobus ad minus.*

5 Quinetiam Budaeus eodem quem superius notavimus loco scribit,²⁶ anno MCCXCIII a Rege Philippo Pulchro constitutum fuisse,* ut in Parlamento trifarii generis sederent, Praelati, Barones, et mixti Clerici cum Laicis: *Cum laici,* inquit, *partim ex equitibus, partim ex promiscuo genere hominum deligerentur.* Item, ut
10 Praelati et Barones ex illo tertio genere statuerent, qui ad quanque iurisdictionem exercendam idonei viderentur. Simul ut tres viros deligerent, qui in eas regiones mitterentur, quae iure scripto utebantur, ut in iis ius dicerent, et si qua capitalis quaestio habenda esset, literatissimos quosque adhiberent.

15 Quo loco Budaeus horum temporum consuetudinem, hoc est Regnum iuridiciale deplorans,* *^b*simulque vilissima rabularum capita forensia, togatosque vulturios (ut Apuleius loquitur²⁷) detestans,* *^a*ex Iuvenalis versu sic exclamat:²⁸ *Quondam hoc indigenae vivebant more, simulque ita subscribit: Ita enim nobis ex-*
20 *clamare in mentem venit, antiquioribus illis seculis, florente tamen hoc Regno (quod ex numismatis apparet, auro obryzo percussis) simplicem et facilem ius reddendi rationem, rarasque lites, nec diuturnas, ut nunc, aut etiam seculares fuisse, cum nondum ista turba interpretum Iuris Rempublicam invasisset, necdum scientia iuris latissime, atque etiam in*
25 *infinitum patere crederetur, sed aequum bonumque et iudex prudens integritate atque innocentia praeditus, instar sexcentorum voluminum essent. Nunc vero quo res reciderit, nemo quidem non videt, sed omnes*

---

7 *bc* make this clause read 'anno MCCXCIIII [*sic*] ab eodem Rege Philippo constitutum fuisse'. **16** 'consuetudinem...deplorans': *bcc*² 'corruptelam deplorans'. **18** *c*¹ omits 'simulque vilissima...detestans'.

²⁵ *Ibid.,* Tit. 6, §30; ed. 1551, 170. ²⁶ The following lines, up to the top of the next page beginning 'Hactenus Budaeus...', are paraphrased or quoted from Budé, *Annot.* §Ex lege ult. de Senat.; *Opera,* 1557, III, 98–100 – with the exception of the classical quotation interpolated by Hotman (next note). ²⁷ An allusion to *Metamorphoses,* x, 33 [235]; Loeb, 532. ²⁸ Budé, *Annot.,* as above, n. 29; the words 'simulque ita subscribit: Ita enim nobis exclamare' are Hotman's paraphrase of Budé's quoting verses of Juvenal, XIII, 38; Loeb, 248.

may be judged from this surviving ordinance by *b*the same *a*Philip the Fair, dated 1302, and published in that same book in the following terms:[25] 'We enjoin in addition that our seneschals and bailiffs shall hold their assizes in summary form throughout the *sénéchausées* and bailiwicks at least every two months.'

Furthermore, in the passage already quoted Budé writes[26] that in the year 1293* King Philip the Fair enacted that three kinds of persons should sit in the parlement: prelates, barons and clergy mixed with laymen, 'because', says Budé, 'the laymen are chosen partly from the knights and partly from the ordinary sort of men without distinction'. He ordered also that the prelates and barons should appoint men from the third estate who seemed suitable to exercise any jurisdiction, and that at the same time they should choose three men to be sent to those provinces using the written law and administer justice there, and, if any important legal issue should arise, they should take with them men of great learning in the law.

In this passage Budé deplores the practice of these times, that is, the kingdom of the lawyers,†*b*and at the same time he condemns the detestable legal habits of these pettifoggers and robed vultures (to borrow a phrase from Apuleius[27]).‡ *a*Quoting a line from Juvenal he cries out as follows:[28] '"There was a time when primitive men lived by custom alone", as the poet expressed it. Thus it occurs to me to remark that in those ancient days when this kingdom flourished (which is clear from the fact that coins were minted in standard gold) there was a simple and easy method of giving justice, and lawsuits were rare and of short duration and were not, as now, unending. That rabble of interpreters of the law had not as yet invaded the commonwealth, and skill in the law was not thought to stretch out to some limitless extent. Rather was it considered that equity and honesty, and a judge equipped with integrity and innocence, were worth six hundred legal tomes. Now there is no one who does not see to what a pass things have come, but everyone

---

* *bc* 1293 *becomes* 1294 the same. † *bc* the practice of these times, that is, the kingdom of the lawyers *becomes* the corruption of these times. ‡ *c*¹ *omits* and at the same time...Apuleius).

dicere mussant. Hactenus Budaeus gravissimus ubique et acerrimus artis rabulariae adversarius.

Nunc ut ad nostram historiam redeamus, doceamusque* quibus initiis ac fundamentis Regnum istud litigatorium excitatum
5 fuerit, quemadmodum Cicero scribit:[29] *Pontifices veteres propter sacrificiorum multitudinem, tres viros Epulones instituisse, quamvis essent ipsi a Numa, ut etiam illud ludorum epulare sacrificium facerent, instituti*; eodemmodo ex illo perexiguo Iudicum Parlamentariorum numero, crescente litium multitudine, incredibilis
10 Iudicium et Consiliariorum* soboles propagata est. Ac primum Basilica ingens, sumptuosa, magnifica, Regis, ut superius diximus, Ludovici Hutini, vel Philippi Pulcri imperio aedificata est, tum ex mediocri iudicum numero tres decuriae factae,* Magnae Camerae, Inquisitionum, et Postulatorum. Quam partitionem
15 Budaeus eodem illo loco,[30] sed copiosius Gaguinus in Regis Hutini vita commemorat.[31]

*b*Video tamen, qui ad Stilum curiae parlamenti ubi Stephanus Auffrerius eundem numerum servat, hanc notam ascripserit:[32] *Imo initio duae tantum camerae fuerunt, quia Camera Requestarum est*
20 *tribunal inferius. Postea addita est tertia, quae parva Camera Inquestarum appellatur. Sed anno MDXXII rex Franciscus, ut corraderet sexaginta millia aureorum quartam Cameram e viginti novis consiliariis creavit, a singulis capiens ter mille aureos, unde curia valde deturpata fuit. Postea praesidentium quoque numerus pretio auctus est.*
25 *Rursus idem Rex anno MDXLIII alios XX quaestus caussa creavit.*

*a*Quo loco praetermittendum non videtur, quod uterque illorum memoriae prodidit* atque insigne est ad omnem memoriam documentum, illum iudicum conventum non perpetuum et perennem (ut hoc tempore) sed indictivum fuisse, nec nisi

---

3 *c*¹ omits the following 70-odd words, 'doceamusque...aedificata est, tum'.
10 *c* 'Conciliariorum'.   **13** *c*¹ adds 'sunt'.   **27** *bc* render this sentence to this point as follows: 'Quin ne illud quidem praetermittendum videtur, quod et Gaguinus et Budaeus eodem loco memoriae prodiderunt'.

[29] *De oratore*, III, 19, 73; Loeb, II, 58.   [30] As above, n. 26.   [31] Cf. Bk. 7; ed. 1528, fol. cxxx^vff.   [32] *Instructiones abbreviatae* (see bibliog., Du Breuil, *Stilus*), cap. 1, gloss *ad verb.* 'Tres', by Charles Du Moulin; ed. 1551, 131.

mutters it silently.' Thus far Budé, who was in every aspect a most weighty and bitter opponent of the profession of pettifoggery.

Let us now return to our story and reveal* from what beginnings and foundations that kingdom of unnecessary litigation was called into being. As Cicero writes:[29] 'Because of the vast numbers of sacrifices, the ancient priests instituted three men as assistants or *epulones*, although they were also appointed by Numa to sacrifice at the epularian religious banquets.' In the same way from that very small number of judges in the parlements an incredible progeny of judges and councillors was spawned to meet the growing quantity of litigation. First, as we have said earlier, a huge, sumptuous and magnificent palace was built under either King Louis Hutin or King Philip the Fair. Then, from a moderate number of judges three divisions of the parlement were created, the *grand'chambre*, the *enquêtes* and the *requêtes*. This subdivision is mentioned by Budé in the passage cited,[30] but it is discussed in more detail by Gaguin in his life of King Hutin.[31]

[b]I see, however, that in the treatise on the procedure of the court of parlement where Etienne Aufrier has kept the same number of chambers, he has added this remark:[32] 'At first indeed there were only two chambers, since the chamber of the *requêtes* is an inferior tribunal. Later a third chamber was added, known as the small chamber of the *enquêtes*. But in the year 1522 King Francis raised sixty thousand crowns by creating a fourth chamber of twenty new councillors, from each of whom he took three thousand crowns. The court was greatly discredited by this act. Later the number of presidents was also increased for monetary gain. Again, in the year 1543 the same king created twenty more judges because of the profit he secured thereby.'

[a]We should not here omit something mentioned by both Budé and Gaguin, which is remarkable enough to be recorded for all time, namely that this assembly of judges was not perpetual and

---

* c[1] *omits the remainder of this sentence and the three succeeding sentences, ending with* Philip the Fair.

certo Principis mandatu* exerceri solitum, quod quotannis
ineunte mense Novembri edictum Regis proponi oportet, ut
eum renovari liceat. Atque ut huius, inquit Gaguinus,[33] sacro-
sanctae coitionis* Regem auctorem esse certum sit, regia singulis
5 quibusque annis rescripta eduntur, quibus ad D. Martini diem
festum, id est, II Id. Novem. Parlamentum inchoandi iudicibus
a Rege auctoritas datur. De mirabili autem et celeri huius Regni
incremento etiam illud argumento esse potest, quod circiter
centum post annis, hoc est, anno MCCCCLIII regnante Carolo
10 VII, haec ab illo constitutio promulgata est:[34] *A festo Paschae,
usque ad finem Parlamenti, Praesidentes et Consiliarii hora sexta de
mane debent in suis cameris esse congregati; a festo S. Martini, post
horam praedictam.* Et aliquanto post:[35] *Pernecessarium est, ut Praesidentes et Consiliarii Curiae post prandium veniant ad Parlamentum
15 iudicandi et expediendi caussa.*

Haec Carolus VII. At Caroli Magni tempore, qui Regnum
triplo maius obtinebat, quam dissimilis iudiciorum ratio fuerit,
vel ex hac ipsius lege facile intellectu est, Legis Francicae lib. 4,
cap. 74:[36] *Ut comes placitum non habeat, nisi ieiunus.*

20 Iam de voce Parlamenti ac nominis etiam auctoritate illud
argumentum extat, quod cum in ea parte Allobrogum, quae
Delphinatus dicitur, antiquitus Senatus institutus fuisset, cum
summa auctoritate, quod Concilium Delphinale dicebatur,
tamen* Ludovicus XI,* qui bene de se meritis Delphinatibus
25 benigne facere studebat, nomen Consilii* in Parlamentum
mutavit, quanvis nihil ad ius atque auctoritatem adderet; cuius
rei Guidopapius testis est, quaest. *b*Gratianop. *a*43 et rursus
q. 554.[37] [*a*FINIS.*]

---

1 *c* 'mandato'. **4** *bc* '...inquit eodem loco Gaguinus coitionis'. **24** *c* 'tam'.
24 *bc* 'Ludovicus VI'. **25** *bc* 'Concilii'. **28** *c¹* closes here with these final
words: 'Addita sunt deinceps alia parlamenta, praeter illud quod Magnum consilium vocatur et eiusdem auctoritatis est atque dignitatis, qua de re, quia ab aliis
dictum est, plura hoc loco non adiiciemus. FINIS.'

[33] Non invenio, although supposedly the same as n. 31 above. [34] Ordonnance
of April, 1453, art. 3; Isambert, *Recueil général des anciennes lois françaises* (Paris,
1821 ff), IX, 204. [35] *Ibid.*, art. 4; *loc. cit.* [36] Ansegius, III, 38; *MGH LL*, II: 1, 429.
[37] Guy Pape, *Decisiones Gratianopolitanae*, quaest. 43 & 554; ed. 1609, 27, 345.

everlasting (as at the present time), for it was not originally proclaimed as such, and was not usually held except on the specific
commission of the prince, and it required a royal edict to be issued
every year at the beginning of November for the court to be
renewed. Gaguin states[33] that it is certain that the king is the author
of this holy convocation since the royal writs are issued every year
to give royal authority to the judges to inaugurate the parlement on
the feast of Saint Martin, that is on 10 November. The extraordinary
and rapid expansion of this legal kingdom can also be verified from
the fact that about a century later, that is in 1453 during the reign
of Charles VII, the following ordinance was issued by that king:[34]
'From Easter until the conclusion of the parlement, the presidents
and councillors should meet together in their chambers at six o'clock
in the morning, and after Saint Martin's day they should meet after
that hour.' At a later point the ordinance states:[35] 'It is necessary
that the presidents and councillors of the court should come to the
parlement after dinner to give judgments and expedite business.'

Such was the instruction of Charles VII. But in the time of
Charlemagne, who acquired a kingdom three times the size of
France under Charles VII, a very different method of providing
justice was observed. This is easily understood from his law given
in the Frankish law:[36] 'No count should give judgment unless he
has fasted first.'

Now, as to the word parlement and the authority of that name,
it is our view that when the ancient senate was instituted in that part
of south-eastern France known as Dauphiné it had the highest
authority and was called the council of Dauphiné. However,*
Louis XI,† who took pains to do favours for the people of
Dauphiné (which they well deserved), changed the name of the
council to that of parlement, although he added nothing by way
of privilege or authority. Guy Pape is our source for this fact in
his *Judgments of Grenoble*.[37]‡ (*a*FINIS)

---

* *bc* Thus. † *bc* Louis VI. ‡ *a* ends here; *bcc*² *continue as shown;* *c*¹ *ends here*
with an additional sentence as follows: Thereafter the other parlements were added,
besides that which is called the grand conseil, which is of the same authority and
dignity, and on this issue we shall not say more here since it is described by
other authors.

^bCum autem in his iuridicialibus parlamentis, regnisque rabulariis permulta sint, quae boni et cordati viri graviter et acerbe ferunt, tum vero quatuor haec in primis numerantur, quod publica iurisdictionis nundinatio exerceatur, quod magis-
5 tratus publico periurio ineantur, quod parlamenta litium semi-naria sint, postremo quod tertia prope Galliae pars rabulariam artem exerceat. Nam quod ad primum attinet, quotusquisque hodie numerari potest, qui iudicandi munus non et praesenti pecunia sit mercatus, et praesenti pecunia venditet? ut verissime
10 Alexander Caesar dixisse videatur,³⁸ necesse esse ut qui magis-tratum emit, vendat, nec sine rubore puniri posse, qui quod emit, vendit. *Et nummarium tribunal* (inquit Seneca lib. de benefic. I³⁹) *audita utrinque licitatione alteri addici, non mirum; quando quae emeris, vendere gentium ius est.* Hanc boni viri Gallicae iuris-
15 dictionis nundinationem, hoc commercium, hoc forense latro-cinium appellant, quod res quae humanarum rerum sanctissima esse debuit, promercalis facta sit, pretioque et vendatur, et ematur; neque quicquam aeque Galliae existimationem apud exteras nationes onerat, quam quod, sicuti lanii bovem opimum
20 uno pretio emptum, post in macello per partes venditant, ita magistratus uno pretio comparatur, cuius administratio singulis postea ius postulantibus divendatur.

De quo Deum immortalem, Solemque, et coelum, et genus hominum qui hodie vivunt, quique posthac victuri sunt, con-
25 testor, si non optimo iure ac meritissimo tam foedam patriae labem, infamiam, dedecus, ac turpitudinem deploro, neque me Matharelli, aut Massoni,⁴⁰ aut nescio cuius eiusmodi rabulae scabiosi ac sycophantae meretricia impudentia, aut cuiusquam palpatoris aulici pretio conducta calumnia de hoc iuvandae
30 patriae studio, si Dei voluntas ferat, dimovebit. Quid? an quis-quam est, qui cogitare illud sine lachrymis possit, quod non modo clientes et beneficiarii Romani Pontificis, et clerici iureiurando ei devincti, et opimis sacerdotiis praediti, magnam illorum magis-tratuum partem obtinent, verumetiam ii qui se Laicos appellari

---

³⁸ *Scr. hist. Aug.*, Severus Alexander, XLIX, I; Loeb, II, 276.   ³⁹ I, ix, 5; Loeb, III, 30.   ⁴⁰ See above, pp. 76–80, for a discussion of these works.

*b*Moreover in these courts of the parlements and kingdoms of the pettifoggers there are many things which worthy and prudent men do gravely and sorrowfully. Among the first of these the following four may be enumerated: that a public trafficking of jurisdiction takes place, that magistrates are openly installed under false pretences, that the parlements are the breeding grounds of disputes, and that nearly a third of the population of France is engaged in the profession of pettifoggery. As to the first abuse, how many can be listed today who have not bought and sold judicial office for money? As Alexander Severus very truly said,[38] it follows that he who buys a magistracy sells it, and he who sells what he has bought cannot be punished without embarrassment. Seneca says in the first book of his *Benefices*:[39] 'It is not surprising that any tribunal should be passed from one person to another by a monetary offer, since it is the right of people to sell what they buy.' Worthy men call it traffic in national office, base commerce and public robbery, because office, which ought to be the most sacred of human affairs, has been made a piece of merchandise to be bought and sold for cash. Equally, it damages any kind of esteem in which other nations may hold France when a magistracy is offered at a single price and later its administration is divided up among individual claimants, just as a fine ox is bought from a butcher at a single price and is afterwards sold in pieces at a meat-market.

I call upon Almighty God, the sun and the heavens, together with the men who are alive today and those who will live hereafter, to witness this iniquity, and I ask whether I have not the best and most deserved right to lament this detestable lapse in our country and to decry its infamy, dishonour and vileness. Nor shall I be deterred by the meretricious impudence of Matharel and Masson[40] and I know not what other mangy pettifogger and sycophant of this sort. And, if it be God's will, I shall not be turned aside from helping my country through this work by the chicanery of any paid hireling or flatterer of the court. Can anyone refrain from tears when he reflects that the clients and beneficiaries of the Roman pontiff, those clerics bound to him by oath, and those endowed with fat livings, acquire a large share of these magistracies; and, in addi-

volunt istiusmodi beneficiis in suos liberos conferendis eiusdem
Pontificis tyrannidi se, suamque fidem ac religionem venditant?

Iam vero, de periurio passim tota Gallia usitato, quid dicemus?
Vetus Imp. Theodosii lex est, gentium, ut opinor, omnium usu
5 ac moribus comprobata, ut qui magistratum ineunt; publice
iusiurandum dent, se nihil eo nomine neque per se, neque per
alium dedisse, aut promisisse: l. ult. C. de repetund.[41] Hoc
quidem iusiurandum, in Gallia quoque, omnibus magistratuum
mercatoribus in Parisiensi aliove Parlamento defertur; at quid
10 dixi defertur? Imo vero confidenter accipitur, conceptisque
verbis praestatur, ^ccum tamen admodum pauci ac prope dicam
nulli, tota Gallia numerari possint, qui non praesenti numerata
ad manum quaestoris pecunia suum Officium, ac iurisdictionem
sit mercatus. ^bAtque is primus sacris istis initiantibus aditus in
15 Gallia patet.

Age, reliqua videamus. Nam complures istiusmodi iudicum
conventus qui ad dirimendas lites, ad cives iudicialibus molestiis
liberandos instituti sunt, meras esse litium officinas et ergastula,
quis ignorat? aut cui tandem notum in Gallia non est, litem semel
20 institutam hominum istorum artificiis non modo immortalem
reddi, sed etiam in alias complures propagari? Quod vero postremo loco positum est, cui non miserum atque indignum videatur, gentem Gallicam, omnium quas sol videt ad bonas quasque
artes, ac praesertim ad literarum, addo etiam ad pietatis studium
25 aptissimam, tamen in calumniis litium, in sycophantiis exer-
cendis, in sordibus denique rabulariis, quasi in ^ccloacis ac
^blatrinis exhauriendis aetatem consumere? Quae natio trecentis
abhinc annis litium prope expers, Reipublicae et (ut tum loquebantur) boni publici curam in annuis comitiis gerebat, eam in
30 istis lutulentis sordibus occupatam, totam Reipublicae curam
paucis aliquot asseclis atque assentatoribus regiis permittere?

---

[41] *Cod.* 9, 27, 6; Krueger, II, 385.

tion, that those who wish to be known as laymen, and want
benefices of this sort to be conferred upon their children through the
tyranny of this same pontiff, sell their faith and religion?

What shall we say of the falsehood that is everywhere employed
throughout the whole of France? There is an ancient law of the
Emperor Theodosius, which, I believe, has been approved by usage
and custom among all peoples, that those who undertake an office
should publicly swear not to give or promise anything in the
name of that office, either themselves or through the agency of
another. See the last book of the *Code* on extortion.[41] In France, too,
this oath is required of all those who traffic in offices in the Parisian
or any other parlement. But is what I have said carried out? In
actual fact it is scandalous that office is accepted and assumed with
this form of words. *c*For in all France there are very few, and
I would say virtually none, who do not put the requisite price for
their office in the hand of the treasurer and buy their jurisdiction.
*b*And the first access to this in France is provided by accepting
holy orders.

Let us look at the remaining issues. For who does not know that
many assemblies of judges, established to dispose of lawsuits and to
free citizens from legal vexations, become nothing but factories and
workhouses of litigation? And who in France is not aware of the
fact that once a lawsuit is begun it not only becomes unending
through the artifices of these men but is also extended into many
other lawsuits? And finally, let me ask who does not see the misery
and shame of the fact that the French people (among all of whom
the sun shines and the fine arts, and especially literature, flourish,
and who are also so well suited to apply themselves to religion)
should waste their energies in the chicaneries of litigation, in the
practice of deceit, in squalid affairs – in short, in pettifoggery – as
if they were draining their strength in *c*sewers and *b*latrines? Can
this nation which until three hundred years ago was almost devoid
of litigation, this commonwealth (as it was then called) which saw
to the public welfare through its annual assemblies, allow itself to
be occupied by these vile and squalid affairs and resign the entire
care of the state to a few sycophants and flatterers of royalty?

Atque huius ego morbi Rabularii, quam verissime scabiem Gallicam appellare possumus, quo magis magisque originem investigo, eo magis in illa quam superius protuli, opinione confirmor, ut superstitionum lues, ut alia complura, ex Romanorum
5 Pontificum officina profluxerunt, sic rabulariae artis disciplinam ex eorundem curia et iurisdictione ad nos defluxisse, quod peradmodum paucis post Decretalici iuris promulgationem annis contigisse constat. Nam in Gratiani Decretum (c. vides, 10 dist.⁴²) relata est Epistola Leonis Papae (quem illi in Deorum
10 suorum numerum retulerunt) ad Ludovicum II utriusque Franciae Regem et Imperatorem scripta, qua testatur, se Imperatorum legibus, et constitutionibus, et iuri ab illis constituto parere; et in c. ult.⁴³ ab eodem Imp. pro sua clementia petit, ut iuris Romani leges ubique observari velit; quinetiam
15 extat Papae Honorii III, Decretalis in c. 1, Ext. de Iuram. cal.,⁴⁴ ubi dilucide ostendit, Papales clericos usque ad illud tempus Romani iuris legibus et Christianorum Imperatorum constitutionibus, quae in Codice Iustiniani extant, paruisse, iisque etiam in iurisiurandi controversiis usos esse.
20 Ecquodnam igitur (dicet aliquis) tantis malis remedium afferemus? Caussam quidem illorum omnium constat esse partim impietatem, partim incredibilem gentis nostrae superstitionem, quae per eadem illa tempora ex eodem illo fonte ad nos fluxit, quibus immensa caligo universum orbem Christianum obtex-
25 erat, et unico Christianae religionis lumine extincto, sacris scilicet Bibliis obrutis ac sepultis, omnia densissimis superstitionum tenebris oppressa tenebantur. Quare si per nostros Alastoras, si per furias civilium bellorum incentrices licebit, vel (ut verius loquamur) per singularem Dei benignitatem dabitur,
30 ut sacrorum Bibliorum auctoritas in Gallia valeat, et iuventus in iis se studiis exerceat, non dubium est, quin, ut exorto sole tenebrae fugantur, sic artes rabulariae una cum superstitionibus ex eodem fonte deductis, depellantur. Quod ut Deus optimus

---

⁴² *Corp. jur. can.* D. x, c. 10; Friedberg, I, 22.   ⁴³ *Ibid.*, c. 13; *loc. cit.*   ⁴⁴ *Ibid.*, c. 1 X 2, 7; Friedberg, II, 265.

The more I track down the origin of this disease of pettifoggery, which we can very truly call the French pox, the more I am certain of the view I earlier advanced, namely that, just as the plague of superstition, and many other plagues beside, flowed out from the workshop of the Roman pontiffs, so too did the practice of the art of legal chicanery reach us from the court of Rome, because it is known to have expanded to its full extent a few years after the promulgation of the decretals. For in the decretals of Gratian[42] there is reference to a letter from Pope Leo (whom they list in the calendar of their saints) to Louis II, who was both king of France and emperor. There it is stated that the pope submits to the edicts and ordinances of the emperors and the law established by them. The letter goes on to say[43] that the pope begs that same emperor for his clemency and wishes the constitutions of Roman Law everywhere to be observed. Indeed, there exists a decretal of Pope Honorius III[44] where it is clearly shown that right up to that time the popes had obeyed the provisions of Roman Law and the constitutions of the Christian emperors contained in Justinian's *Code*, and that these were used in disputes on oath.

Someone may ask whether we have any remedy to suggest for such ills. It is clear that the cause of all these troubles is in part impiety, and in part the incredible superstition of our people, which flowed in to us throughout those times from that same font. This shrouded the whole Christian world like a huge fog, and, when the single light of the Christian religion was extinguished as the holy scriptures were obscured and buried, all things continued to be weighed down by the thick darkness of superstition. Wherefore, if it is permitted by those among us who fancy themselves for the rôle of Alastor and in the midst of the crazed instigators of civil wars – or, as we may more properly say, if it be granted us through the singular charity of God – let the authority of the holy scriptures prevail in France, and the youth of our country devote their energy to studying them. Then without doubt the darkness would be put to flight by the risen sun, and the arts of legal chicanery, together with the superstitions drawn from the same font,

maximus propter Christi filii sui, et Emmanuelis nostri gloriam, nostrae huic aetati concedat, assiduis ab eo precibus petendum erit.*

FINIS

3 'assiduis...erit': *cc²* 'toto pectore ab eo precor, quaesoque.'.

would be driven out. Since God, the all-good and almighty, may grant this to our generation for the glory of Christ His son and our saviour, it should be asked of Him in earnest prayer.*

FINIS

---

* cc² *change final phrase to read* I pray and entreat this of Him with all my heart.

APPENDICES

Appendix A – major passages
suppressed in later editions

1. *Property at the disposition of the king*
(p. 246, line 13, after 'est')

*a*Earum rerum quae in Regis ditione sunt, quatuor a Iurisconsultis genera numerari: nimirum res (ut illi loquuntur) Caesaris; res fisci; res publicas; et res privatas. Ac res quidem Caesaris eae dicuntur, quae in privato cuiusque principis patrimonio sunt;
5 non quatenus est Princeps, sed quatenus est Ludovicus, aut Lotharius, aut Dagobertus. Institutis autem Gallicis, patrimonium hoc Regis dominium nominatur, quod sine publico Gentis concilio alienari non potest; quemadmodum aliquanto post (ubi de Concilii auctoritate differemus) intelligetur. Res
10 vero fisci dicuntur, quae populi voluntate Regi partim ad tuendam dignitatem suam, partim ad usus Reipublicae repentinos attributae sunt. Publicas autem res Iurisconsulti appellant, quae in ipsius regni ac Reipublicae dominio positae sunt; privatas vero, quae in patrisfamilias cuiusque fortunis ac facultatibus numerantur.
15 Ergo Rege patre demortuo, si ad extraneum regni hereditas deferatur, res quae propriae Regis, et (ut Iurisconsulti loquuntur) ipsius patrimoniales fuerunt, et quas alienari ab ipso non licere diximus, hereditatis iure liberis ipsius relinquuntur. Quae vero regni et Reipublicae ipsius sunt, quoniam regni pars sunt, ad
20 quem regnum defertur, ad eum quoque necessario deferendae sunt;* quanquam tuendae liberorum dignitatis caussa, ratio postulat, ut Ducatus, et Comitatus illis in populi Comitiis assignentur.

21 'necessario deferendae sunt': *b* 'illa deferri'.

1. *Property at the disposition of the king*
(see above, p. 247)

The jurisconsults enumerate four kinds of property which are at the disposition of the king: indisputably there are what they call the things that belong to Caesar; there is the property of the fisc; there is public property; and there is private property. Those things which are said to be Caesar's are such as belong to the private patrimony of every prince, not inasmuch as he is a prince, but inasmuch as he is is Louis or Lothar or Dagobert. Under French law this patrimony is called the king's domain, which cannot be alienated save through the public council of the nation. This will be understood later, when we discuss the authority of the council. The property described as belonging to the fisc is that which is given to the king by the will of the people, partly to preserve his dignity and partly for the unexpected needs of the commonwealth. Public property, in the definition of the jurisconsults, is that which is placed at the disposal of the kingdom and commonwealth itself. Private property consists of those things which are listed as the wealth and possessions of every head of a household. Hence if the inheritance of the kingdom be passed to a foreigner upon the death of a king, the goods belonging to the king, his patrimonial estate (as the jurisconsults say), and the property we have described as that which he cannot lawfully alienate, remain with his children by right of inheritance. But that which belongs to the kingdom and commonwealth, seeing that it is part of the kingdom, must necessarily pass* to him on whom the kingdom has been bestowed. Nevertheless reason demands that in order to maintain the status of the sons, dukedoms and counties may be assigned to them by the assembly of the people.

---

* *b* must necessarily pass *becomes* passes.

2. The origin of the peers
(p. 376, l. 23, after 'afferatur')

Gervasio Tilesberio assentior, quem Guaguinus testatur in libro
quem ad Imp. Ottonem IIII de ctiis imperialibus scripsit,[1]
memoriae prodidisse, institutum illud Arturi Anglorum Regis
fuisse, qui annos aliquot in Galliae parte dominatus fuerat. Nam
5 illius instituti rationem hanc esse arbitror, ut quemadmodum
feudali iure Pares Curiae appellantur beneficiarii, sive clientes
ὁμότιμοι, et convassali, qui ab eodem Seniore ac patrono beneficia et feuda sua acceperunt, eoque nomine fide et obsequio illi
devincti sunt; sic in novo Regno occupato, Arturus Principes XII
10 delegerit, quibus Regni sui partes, ac tanquam satrapias attri-
bueret, quorumque ope et consilio imperium administraret.
Magnumque eorum iudicium requirere cogimur, qui propterea
Pares Franciae appellatos scribunt, quod Regi pares essent, cum
paritas non ad Regiam, sed ad communem ipsorum dignitatem
15 atque auctoritatem referretur. Nomina autem haec fuerunt:
Duces Burgundiae, Nortmanniae, et Aquitaniae; Comites
Flandriae, Tholosae, et Campaniae; item Archiepiscopi Re-
mensis, Laudunensis, et Lingonensis; Episcopi Bellovacus,
Noviodunensis, et Catalaunensis. Et quemadmodum Pares
20 Curtis sive Curiae feudali iure neque creari nisi pro collegio,
neque abdicari, nisi caussa in collegarum consilio cognita, neque
ad aliud ullum, nisi collegarum iudicium vocari possunt, ita hi
nullo nisi Parlamenti, hoc est, imaginarii concilii iudicio tenerentur, et non nisi pro collegio vel cooptari, vel exauctorari possent.
25 Etsi autem a Rege peregrino et advena Magistratus illi primum
instituti fuerint; tamen cum illo exacto, restitutis Regibus institutum illud ad suas rationes accommodatum videretur, consentaneum est illud ab iis retentum atque usurpatum fuisse. Primam
quidem Parium mentionem video notari in Philippo Pulchro
30 inaugurando, a quo ipso multi affirmant sex Pares ecclesiasticos
creatos fuisse.

---

[1] De otiis imperialibus; ed. Rolls Series, 437. All the information that follows,
about King Arthur, is found in this source. Further, see above, p. 90.

2. The origin of the peers
(see above, p. 377)

I would agree with Gervase of Tilbury, who, as Gaguin declares in the book he wrote to Otto IV on the emperor's leisure,[1] recorded that the dignity was instituted by Arthur, king of the English, who for a few years controlled a part of France. For I take the explanation of that institution to be what in feudal law are called equal [*pares*] beneficiaries of a particular jurisdiction, or clients ὁμότιμοι [with an equal share of honour], or joint vassals, who hold their benefices and fiefs from the same overlord or patron, and in his name are bound in fealty and obedience. Thus, when King Arthur had taken possession of the new kingdom, he selected twelve leading men, to whom he distributed the various parts or, in manner of speaking, satrapies of his kingdom. And while he administered the sovereignty he looked to them for support and counsel. And we are obliged to question the sweeping opinion of those who write that they were called peers of France because they were the equals of the king, since their parity has nothing to do with kingship but rather with their common rank and authority. Their titles were as follows: dukes of Normandy, Burgundy and Aquitaine; counts of Flanders, Toulouse and Champagne; archibishops of Reims, Laon and Langres; bishops of Beauvais, Noyon and Châlons. And insofar as they were equals in jurisdiction by feudal law they could not be created unless it were done through their collegiate body, nor could their status be degraded unless the reasons were recognized within their collegiate council. Nor could they be indicted before any tribunal other than that of their colleagues. Thus the peers were not bound by any judgment other than that of the so-called parlement, that is, of the fictitious council, and they could not be admitted into that collegiate body, nor expelled out of it, save only by the college itself. Although these magistrates had first been instituted by a strange and foreign prince, when he had been driven out and the kings restored it seems that the kings found the institution to suit their own ends, and it is generally agreed that they retained and made use of it. I see that the first mention of the peers is in the inauguration of Philip the Fair, who, many declare, created the six ecclesiastical peers.

3. Budé on judicial assemblies
(p. 510, l. 2 after 'solicitudo')

Nam Caroli quoque Magni haec lex in Capitulari extat:[1] *Hoc missi nostri notum faciant Comitibus et populo, quod nos in omni hebdomada unum diem ad caussas audiendas sedere volumus.* Eiusdemmodi testimonium extat apud Guilliel. Budaeum, virum claris-
5 simum, et Galliae nostrae ornamentum insigne. Nam in Annot. in Pandectas, ubi hoc idem argumentum tractat,[2] et Regnum Rabularium insectatur, commemorat se in Regiis venerandae vetustatis commentariis (quorum copiam pro sua dignitate summam habere potuit) reperisse, dominante illo eodem Rege
10 Ludovico, anno 1230, orta inter Regem et Comitem Britanniae controversia castrense iudicium Enceniaci coactum fuisse (utriusque ut credi par est, consensu), in eoque Iudices sedisse, non Iustinianici iuris peritos ac doctores, sed tantum Episcopos, Comites, et Barones; damnatumque Britannicum, et decretum
15 ut incolae iureiurando et fide illis data solverentur. Rursus eodem imperante, anno 1259 cum orta controversia esset de Comitatu Claromontano inter Regem et Comites Pictaviensem, et Andegavensem, constitutum ex eodem hominum genere iudicium fuisse, sedisseque Episcopos, Abbates, Maximum fratrum prae-
20 dicatorum Magistrum, Constabularium, Barones, et aliquot Laicos. Simulque ita subiungit. *Duo tamen quotannis Parlamenta cogebantur, ad natalem, Purificationemque divae Dei genitricis, quomodo et duo quae vocantur Scacaria apud Northmannos, ad Pascha et ad Divi Michaelis.* Haec Budaeus, cui consentaneum est, quod
25 extat in veteri libello de institutione Parlamentorum.[3]

---

[1] *Hludowici Pii capit.*, 192; *MGH LL*, II: 2, 16. Starting with the edition of 1576, this passage was cited earlier in the text (see above, p. 508, n. 21).   [2] *Annot.*, Ex. l. ult de Senat.; *Opera*, 1557, III, 99. This is a paraphrase until the sentence quoted at the end, '*Duo tamen*...etc.'   [3] Probably a reference to Du Breuil, *Stilus curiae parlamenti*, or the *Ordinationes* usually published with it.

3. Budé on judicial assemblies
(see above, p. 511)

Moreover, the following law has survivived in the capitulary of Charlemagne:[1] 'Let our commissioners make it known to the nobles and the people that for one day in every week we desire to hold a sitting to hear legal cases.'* There is testimony to the same effect in the work of that most famous man and outstanding ornament of France, Guillaume Budé. In his *Annotations on the Pandects*, where he deals with this same theme,[2] and inveighs against the kingdom of pettifoggers, he records that he has found in royal commentaries of venerable antiquity (to which he was able to have complete access because of his status) that in the year 1230, during the reign of the same King Louis, disputes arose between the king and the count of Brittany. With the consent, it seems, of both parties, a court was assembled at the camp of Enceny, in which there sat as judges not those learned in Roman Law but simply bishops, counts and barons. The count of Brittany was condemned, and it was decreed that the inhabitants should be absolved from the oath and loyalty they had given. During the same reign Budé found another instance when, in the year 1259, a dispute had arisen concerning the countship of Clermont between the king and the counts of Poitou and Anjou. It was decided that a court would be composed of men of this kind, and upon it sat bishops, abbots, the provincial of the Dominicans, the constable, barons and some laymen. At the same time he adds the following statement: 'This was despite the fact that two parliaments were convened every year, one at Christmas and the other at the feast of the purification of the Holy Mother of God, just as there were two known as *Scacaria* [exchequers] among the Normans, summoned at Easter and at Michaelmas.' These words of Budé are consistent with a passage in an ancient book concerning the institution of parliaments.[3]

---

* **bc** relocate this quotation earlier in the text; see above, p. 508, note 21.

Appendix B – correlation of editions

This list shows on what page of an earlier edition will be found the first usage of a word from that edition on a given page in this edition. For example, on p. 158 of this edition the first word from **a**, 'sed', will be found at some point on p. 10 of the 1573 edition.

1972	Latin¹ a 1573	a¹ 1574	b 1576	c 1586	c¹ 1600	c² 1665	French² 1574	1577	1578	1578	German³ 1968	English⁴ 1711	1721, 1738	1972
136	2^r	¶2^r	3	*2^r	36	*2^r	(:) 2^r	577	271	375^v	203	i	i	137
138	3^r	¶2^v	4	*3^r	37	*3^r	(:) 3^r	578	271^v	376^v	204	ii	ii	139
140	4^r	¶3^r	6	*4^r	37	*4^r	(:) 4^r	579	272	377	205	iii	iii	141
142	5^v	¶4^r	8	*5^v	37	*5^v	(:) 5^v	581	273	378^v	206	v	v	143
144	6^v	¶4^v	10	*6^v	38	*6^v	(:) 6^v	582	273^v	379^v	207	vi	vi	145
146	1	1	13	1	1	1	1	583	274	379^v	210	1	1	147
148	2	2	14	2	1	2	2	584	274^v	380	210	2	2	149
150	4	3	16	3	2	4	5	585	275	381	211	3	3	151
152	5	5	17	4	3	6	7	586	276	382	212	5	5	153
154	7	6	19	6	3	8	10	588	276^v	383	213	6	6	155
156	9	8	21	7	4	10	12	589	277	384	214	8	8	157

¹ See above, p. 129, for details of Latin editions. The anomaly of c¹, that the preface bears a later page number than the text, is due to the fact that the prefaces of all Hotman's works were assembled as a separate section at the end of volume III of the *Opera*, in 1600, while the text of the *Francogallia* comes at the beginning of that volume.

² See p. 82, nn. 2 and 3, for details of the French editions.

³ Jürgen Dennert (ed.), *Beza, Brutus, Hotman: Calvinistische Monarchomachen* (Cologne & Opladen, 1968), pp. 203–327. On p. 203, n. 1, we learn that this is truly a hybrid translation, consisting of all the 1573 Latin, additions [?] found in the 1574 French, and selected additions from the 1586 Latin as found in the 1665 reprint.

⁴ See above, pp. 124–5, for details of the English editions.

1972	Latin a 1573	a¹ 1574	b 1576	c 1586	c¹ 1600	c² 1665	French 1574	1577	1578	1578	German 1968	English 1711	1721, 1738	1972
158	10	9	22	8	4	12	14	590	277v	384v	214	8	8	159
160	11	10	23	9	5	14	15	590	278	385	215	9	9	161
162	12	11	25	11	6	16	17	592	278v	386	215	10	10	163
164	14	12	26	12	6	18	19	593	279	386v	216	11	11	165
166	15	13	27	13	7	20	20	594	279v	387	217	12	12	167
168	16	14	29	14	7	21	22	595	280	388	217	13	13	169
170	16	14	30	16	8	23	22	595	280v	388v	217	13	13	171
172	17	15	32	17	8	25	23	596	281	389	218	14	14	173
174	18	16	33	18	8	27	25	597	281v	390	218	15	15	175
176	20	17	35	19	9	29	27	599	282	391	219	16	16	177
178	21	18	36	21	9	31	28	600	282v	391v	220	17	17	179
180	22	20	38	22	10	33	30	601	283	392	220	18	18	181
182	24	21	40	24	11	36	33	602	284	393	221	20	20	183
184	25	23	41	25	11	37	34	603	284	393v	222	21	21	185
186	26	23	42	26	12	39	35	603	284v	394	222	21	21	187
188	27	24	43	27	12	41	36	604	285	394v	222	22	22	189
190	29	25	45	29	13	43	38	605	285v	395v	223	23	23	191
192	30	27	47	30	13	45	40	606	286	396	224	25	25	193
194	32	28	48	31	14	47	42	608	286v	397	225	26	26	195
196	33	30	50	32	14	49	43	608	287	397v	225	27	27	197
198	35	31	51	34	15	51	45	609	287v	398	226	28	28	199
200	35	31	52	34	15	52	46	610	287v	398	226	29	29	201
202	36	32	53	35	16	53	47	610	288	398v	227	29	29	203
204	37	33	53	36	16	55	49	611	288	399	227	30	30	205
206	—	—	55	38	17	57	—	612	288v	400	228	—	—	207

Appendix B (cont.)

1972	Latin						French				German	English		
	a 1573	a^1 1574	b 1576	c 1586	c^1 1600	c^2 1665	1574	1577	1578	1578	1968	1711	1721, 1738	1972
208	38	34	56	39	17	59	50	613	289	400^v	228	31	31	209
210	40	35	58	40	18	60	52	614	289^v	401	229	32	32	211
212	41	37	60	41	18	62	53	615	290	401^v	229	33	33	213
214	43	38	61	43	19	64	55	616	290^v	402^v	230	35	35	215
216	44	40	63	44	19	67	57	617	291	403^v	231	36	36	217
218	46	41	65	45	20	69	58	618	291^v	404	231	37	37	219
220	46	41	66	46	20	70	59	619	292	404^v	232	38	38	221
222	48	42	68	47	21	72	61	620	292^v	405	232	39	39	223
224	48	43	69	49	21	74	61	620	293	405^v	233	39	39	225
226	50	44	70	50	22	75	62	621	293	406	233	41	41	227
228	50	45	71	51	22	77	63	622	293^v	406^v	233	41	41	229
230	51	45	73	52	23	79	63	622	294	407	234	41	41	231
232	52	46	75	54	23	81	65	623	294^v	407^v	234	42	42	233
234	53	48	76	55	24	83	66	624	295	408	235	44	44	235
236	55	49	78	56	24	84	67	625	295	408^v	236	44	44	237
238	56	50	79	57	25	86	69	626	295^v	409^v	236	46	46	239
240	57	51	81	59	26	88	70	627	296	410	237	46	46	241
242	—	—	83	60	26	90	—	628	296^v	411	—	—	—	243
244	58	52	84	62	27	92	72	629	297	411^v	—	48	48	245
246	—	—	85	63	27	94	—	630	297^v	412	238	—	—	247
248	—	—	—	63	28	95	—	—	—	—	238	—	—	249
250	—	—	—	65	28	97	—	—	—	—	239	—	—	251
252	—	—	—	66	29	99	—	—	—	—	240	—	—	253
254	—	—	—	66	29	99	—	—	—	—	240	—	—	255
256	—	—	—	67	29	101	—	—	—	—	241	—	—	257

1972	Latin a 1573	Latin a¹ 1574	Latin b 1576	Latin c 1586	Latin c¹ 1600	Latin c² 1665	French 1574	French 1577	French 1578	French 1578	German 1968	English 1711	English 1721, 1738	English 1972
258	60	54	87	68	30	103	74	631	298	413	242	49	49	259
260	61	54	88	70	31	105	75	632	298[v]	413[v]	243	50	50	261
262	61	55	90	71	31	107	76	632	299	414	243	50	50	263
264	62	56	91	72	32	109	77	633	299[v]	414[v]	244	51	51	265
266	64	57	93	74	33	111	78	634	300	415	245	52	52	267
268	65	58	95	75	33	113	80	635	300[v]	416	246	54	54	269
270	67	59	96	76	34	114	82	636	301	416[v]	246	55	55	271
272	69	61	98	77	34	116	84	637	301[v]	417[v]	247	56	56	273
274	70	62	99	79	35	118	86	639	302	418	248	57	57	275
276	71	63	100	79	35	120	87	639	302[v]	418[v]	248	58	58	277
278	72	64	102	80	36	121	89	640	303	419	249	59	59	279
280	73	65	104	82	36	123	90	642	303[v]	420	250	61	61	281
282	75	66	105	83	37	125	92	643	304	421	250	62	62	283
284	—	—	107	84	37	127	—	644	304[v]	421[v]	—	—	—	285
286	76	67	108	85	38	128	94	644	304[v]	421[v]	251	63	63	287
288	77	68	109	86	38	130	95	645	305	422[v]	252	64	64	289
290	78	69	111	87	39	132	96	646	305[v]	423	252	64	64	291
292	78	69	113	89	39	134	97	647	306	424	252	65	65	293
294	79	70	114	90	40	136	97	648	306[v]	424[v]	253	65	65	295
296	80	71	115	91	41	138	99	649	307	425	254	66	66	297
298	81	72	116	92	41	139	100	650	307[v]	425[v]	254	67	67	299
300	82	73	118	94	42	141	102	651	308	426[v]	255	68	68	301
302	82	73	120	95	42	143	102	652	308[v]	427	256	68	68	303
304	83	74	122	96	43	145	103	653	309	427[v]	257	69	69	305
306	84	74	122	97	43	146	104	654	309	428	257	70	70	307

Appendix B (*cont.*)

1972	Latin						French				German	English		
	a 1573	*a*^{1} 1574	*b* 1576	*c* 1586	*c*^{1} 1600	*c*^{2} 1665	1574	1577	1578	1578	1968	1711	1721, 1738	1972
308	85	76	124	98	44	148	106	654	309^{v}	428^{v}	258	71	71	309
310	—	—	—	100	44	150	—	—	—	—	—	—	—	311
312	—	—	—	101	45	152	—	—	—	—	—	—	—	313
314	86	76	124	102	46	154	106	655	309^{v}	428^{v}	258	71	71	315
316	—	—	125	104	46	156	—	656	310	429	—	—	—	317
318	—	—	127	105	47	158	—	656	310^{v}	430	—	—	—	319
320	86	76	128	106	47	160	107	657	311	430	259	72	72	321
322	87	77	130	107	48	162	108	658	311^{v}	431	259	73	73	323
324	89	79	131	108	48	163	110	659	312	431^{v}	260	74	74	325
326	90	80	133	109	49	165	112	660	312^{v}	432	261	75	75	327
328	92	81	134	111	50	167	113	660	312^{v}	432^{v}	261	76	76	329
330	92	82	136	112	50	169	113	661	313	433	262	77	77	331
332	93	83	137	114	51	171	115	662	313^{v}	434	—	78	78	333
334	93	83	138	115	51	173	115	663	314	434^{v}	262	78	78	335
336	95	84	140	116	52	175	116	664	314^{v}	435	263	80	80	337
338	96	85	142	117	53	177	118	665	315	435^{v}	264	80	80	339
340	98	87	144	119	53	178	120	666	315^{v}	436^{v}	264	82	82	341
342	99	88	145	120	54	180	121	667	316	437	265	83	83	343
344	100	88	147	121	54	182	122	667	316^{v}	437^{v}	266	83	83	345
346	101	89	148	122	55	184	123	668	316^{v}	437^{v}	266	84	84	347
348	101	90	148	124	55	186	124	668	316^{v}	438	267	85	85	349
350	103	91	149	124	56	187	125	669	317	438^{v}	268	86	86	351
352	104	92	151	125	56	188	127	670	317^{v}	439^{v}	268	87	87	353
354	106	94	153	126	57	190	130	672	318^{v}	440^{v}	269	88	88	355
356				128	57	192								357

1972	Latin a 1573	a¹ 1574	b 1576	c 1586	c¹ 1600	c² 1665	French 1574	1577	1578	1578	German 1968	English 1711	1721, 1738	1972
358	107	95	155	129	58	194	131	673	318[v]	441	270	90	90	359
360	108	95	156	130	58	195	132	673	319	441[v]	270	90	90	361
362	109	97	157	131	59	197	133	674	319[v]	442	271	91	91	363
364	111	98	159	132	59	199	135	675	320	442[v]	271	93	93	365
366	112	99	160	134	60	201	136	676	320[v]	443	272	94	94	367
368	113	100	162	135	—	203	137	677	320[v]	443[v]	273	95	95	369
370	115	102	163	136	—	205	139	678	321	444[v]	274	97	97	371
372	116	102	165	138	61	207	140	678	321[v]	445	274	97	97	373
374	117	104	167	139	61	209	142	680	322[v]	446	275	98	98	375
376	119	105	168	140	62	211	144	681	323	446[v]	276	100	100	377
378	122	108	170	142	62	212	148	682	323[v]	447[v]	277	102	102	379
380	123	109	172	143	63	214	149	683	324	448	278	102	102	381
382	—	—	174	144	64	216	—	684	324[v]	448[v]	279	—	—	383
384	—	—	176	146	64	219	—	685	325	449[v]	280	—	—	385
386	—	—	178	147	65	221	—	686	325[v]	450	281	—	—	387
388	124	109	179	149	66	223	150	687	326	450[v]	282	103	103	389
390	124	109	181	150	66	225	151	687	326	451	282	104	104	391
392	125	110	182	151	67	226	152	688	326[v]	452	283	105	105	393
394	126	111	184	152	67	228	153	689	327	452[v]	283	105	105	395
396	127	112	185	153	68	230	154	690	327[v]	453	283	106	106	397
398	128	113	187	155	68	232	155	691	328	453[v]	284	107	107	399
400	128	114	188	156	69	233	157	692	328[v]	454[v]	285	108	108	401
402	130	115	189	157	69	235	159	693	329	455	286	109	109	403
404	131	116	191	158	70	237	161	694	329[v]	456	286	110	110	405
406	131	116	193	160	71	239	161	695	330	456[v]	287	110	110	407

Appendix B (*cont.*)

1972	Latin a 1573	a¹ 1574	b 1576	c 1586	c¹ 1600	c² 1665	French 1574	1577	1578	1578	German 1968	English 1711	1721, 1738	1972
408	133	117	194	161	71	241	163	696	330^v	457	288	111	111	409
410	134	119	196	162	72	243	165	697	331	458	288	113	113	411
412	135	119	198	163	72	245	165	698	331^v	458^v	289	113	113	413
414	135	120	198	164	72	245	166	699	332	459	289	114	114	415
416	—	—	199	165	73	247	—	699	332	459^v	290	—	—	417
418	135	120	199	166	74	249	166	700	332	459^v	290	114	114	419
420	136	121	200	167	74	251	168	700	332^v	460	291	115	115	421
422	138	122	202	168	75	252	170	701	333	460^v	292	116	116	423
424	139	123	204	170	75	254	171	702	333^v	461	292	117	117	425
426	—	—	—	—	76	—	—	—	—	—	—	—	—	427
428	—	—	205	170	—	255	—	703	334	462	293	—	—	429
430	—	—	207	171	—	257	—	704	334^v	462^v	293	—	—	431
432	—	—	—	173	—	259	—	—	—	—	294	—	—	433
434	—	—	—	174	—	261	—	—	—	—	295	—	—	435
436	—	—	—	175	—	263	—	—	—	—	296	—	—	437
438	—	—	—	177	—	265	—	—	—	—	297	—	—	439
440	140	124	208	178	76	267	171	704	334^v	463	297	118	118	441
442	141	125	209	179	76	268	173	705	335	463^v	298	119	119	443
444	142	126	211	180	77	270	175	706	335^v	464	299	120	120	445
446	144	128	212	181	77	272	177	707	336	465	299	121	121	447
448	146	129	214	183	78	274	178	708	336^v	465^v	300	123	123	449
450	148	131	216	184	78	276	180	709	337	466^v	301	124	124	451
452	—	—	—	185	79	278	—	—	—	—	302	—	—	453
454	—	—	—	186	—	280	—	—	—	—	302	—	—	455
456	—	—	—	188	—	282	—	—	—	—	303	—	—	457

1972	Latin						French				German	English		
	a 1573	a^1 1574	b 1576	c 1586	c^1 1600	c^2 1665	1574	1577	1578	1578	1968	1711	1721, 1738	1972
458	—	—	—	188	79	283	—	—	—	—	303	—	—	459
460	—	—	—	189	79	284	—	—	—	—	304	—	—	461
462	—	—	—	190	80	286	—	—	—	—	305	—	—	463
464	—	—	—	192	81	288	—	—	—	—	306	—	—	465
466	—	—	—	193	81	289	—	—	—	—	306	—	—	467
468	—	—	—	194	82	291	—	—	—	—	307	—	—	469
470	—	—	—	195	82	293	—	—	—	—	308	—	—	471
472	—	—	—	196	83	295	—	—	—	—	309	—	—	473
474	—	—	—	198	83	297	—	—	—	—	310	—	—	475
476	—	—	—	199	84	299	—	—	—	—	311	—	—	477
478	148	131	217	200	85	301	181	710	337^v	467	312	125	128	479
480	149	132	219	201	85	302	182	711	338	467^v	312	126	129	481
482	150	133	220	202	86	304	183	712	338^v	468	313	126	129	483
484	152	134	222	204	86	306	185	713	339	469	313	128	131	485
486	153	136	223	205	87	308	187	714	339^v	469^v	314	129	132	487
488	154	137	225	206	87	310	188	715	340	470	315	130	133	489
490	156	138	226	208	88	312	190	716	340^v	471	316	131	134	491
492	158	140	228	209	89	314	193	717	341	472	316	132	135	493
494	160	141	230	210	89	316	195	719	342	473	317	134	137	495
496	161	142	232	212	—	318	197	720	342^v	473^v	318	135	138	497
498	162	144	233	213	90	319	199	721	343	474	318	136	139	499
500	163	144	235	214	90	321	200	722	343^v	475	319	136	140	501
502	164	145	236	215	91	323	200	723	343^v	475^v	319	137	140	503
504	164	145	237	216	91	325	201	723	344	476	319	137	140	505
506	165	146	238	218	92	327	202	724	344^v	476^v	320	138	141	507

Appendix B (cont.)

1972	Latin						French				German	English		
	a 1573	*a*¹ 1574	*b* 1576	*c* 1586	*c*¹ 1600	*c*² 1665	1574	1577	1578	1578	1968	1711	1721, 1738	1972
508	166	147	240	219	92	329	204	725	345	477	321	139	142	509
510	168	148	240	220	93	331	205	726	345ᵛ	478	321	140	143	511
512	170	151	244	221	94	333	207	727	346	478ᵛ	323	141	145	513
514	172	152	245	223	94	335	209	728	346ᵛ	479	323	143	146	515
516	173	153	247	224	94	336	211	729	347	480	324	143	147	517
518	—	—	249	225	—	338	—	730	347ᵛ	480ᵛ	325	—	—	519
520	—	—	250	227	—	340	—	731	348	481ᵛ	326	—	—	521
522	—	—	252	228	—	342	—	732	348ᵛ	482	327	—	—	523
524	—	—	254	229	—	345	—	733	349	482ᵛ	327	—	—	525

BIBLIOGRAPHIES

Ado of Vienne. Archbishop of Vienne; *c.* 800–73.
  Chronicon. In Migne, *Patrologia latina*, vol. CXXIII.
Aemilius, Paulus. Italian historian in France; *fl.* 1500.
  De rebus gestis Francorum libri IV.
Agathias. Byzantine historian; *fl. c.* 500.
  Gothic Wars. In Migne, *Patrologia graeca*, vol. LXXXVIII.
Aimon of Fleury. Abbot of Fleury-sur-Loire; *c.* 950–1008.
  Historia Francorum (lib. I–IV). In Migne, *Patrologia latina*, vol. CXXXIX.
  *Aimoni monachi qui antea annonii nomine editus est, Historiae Francorum
  lib. V.* Paris, 1567.
Ambrose, Saint. Bishop of Milan; d. 397.
  Epistolae. In Migne, *Patrologia latina*, vol. XVI.
Ammianus Marcellinus. Roman historian; 4th century.
  Ammianus, ed. J. C. Rolfe (Loeb Classical Library). London,
  1935–9.
Andreas of Isernia. Italian jurist; *c.* 1220–1316.
  In usus feudorum commentaria. Frankfort, 1598.
Ansegius. Abbot of Fontenelle; d. 833.
  Capitularia regum Francorum, ed. A. Boret. *Monumenta Germaniae
  historica, Libelli de lite,* vol. II.
Antoninus Pius. Roman emperor; 86–161.
  Itinerarium, ed. A. Manutius. Venice, 1518. (Also attributed to Marcus
  Aurelius, 121–80, and Caracalla, 188–217.)
Appian. Greek historian; 2nd century.
  The Civil Wars, ed. Horace White (Loeb Classical Library). New York,
  1913.
Apuleius, Lucius. Roman author; *c.* 128–90.
  The Golden Ass, ed. S. Gaselee (Loeb Classical Library). New York,
  1915.
Aristotle. 384–322 B.C.
  The Politics, ed. H. Rackham (Loeb Classical Library). New York,
  1932.
  Nicomachean Ethics, ed. H. Rackham (Loeb Classical Library). New
  York, 1926.

Aufrier, Etienne. French jurist; 16th century. See Du Breuil.

Augustine, Saint. Bishop of Hippo; 354–430.
  De civitate Dei, ed. E. Hoffman (Corpus scriptorum ecclesiasticorum latinorum, vol. 40). 2 vols., Vienna, 1898.

Ausonius. Roman poet; 309–*c*. 400.
  Ausonius, ed. H. G. Evelyn White (Loeb Classical Libary). London, 1919–21.

Aventinus, Johannes. German historian; 1477–1534.
  Annalium Boiorum libri VII. Leipzig, 1710.

Baldus de Ubaldus. Italian jurist; 1327–1400.
  Commentarium in primum (–tertium) codicis. Lyon, 1585.
  Consiliorum volumen primum (–quintum). Venice, 1575.
  In usus feudorum commentaria. Lyon, 1585.

Bartolus of Sassoferato. Italian jurist; 1314–57.
  In tres codicis libros commentaria. Turin, 1574.

Beatus Rhenanus. German scholar; 1485–1547.
  Rerum Germanicarum libri tres. Basel, 1551.

Benedicti, Guillaume. French jurist; *fl*. 1500.
  Repetitio . . . in cap. Raynutius de testamentis. Lyon, 1575.

Besuensis. Anon. writer of St Bénigne, Dijon; 11th century.
  Anonymi chronicon S. Benigni Divionensis. In Migne, *Patrologia latina*, vol. CLXII.

Biblia sacra.

Bohier, Nicolas. French jurist; 1470–1539.
  Decisiones Burdegalenses. Lyon, 1567.

Bouchart, Alain. French historian; 16th century.
  Les grandes annales ou croniques parlans tant de Angleterre que de Bretaigne. N.p., 1541.

Bouchet, Jean. French historian; 1476–1550.
  Les annales d'Aquitaine. Poitiers, 1557.

Budé, Guillaume. French humanist; 1467–1540.
  Annotationes in quattuor et viginti pandectarum libros. Basel, 1557.
  De asse et partibus eius libri quinque. Paris, 1532.

Caesar, Julius. 100–44 B.C.
  Bellum Gallicum, ed. H. J. Edwards (Loeb Classical Library). London, 1917.

Cassiodorus. Roman statesman; *c*. 480–575.
  Variarum, ed. T. Mommsen. *Monumenta Germaniae historica, Auctores antiquissimi*, vol. XII.

Cato the Censor. Roman statesman; 234–149 B.C.
M. Porcii Catonis Origines. In *Veterum historicorum Romanorum reliquiae.* Leipzig, 1870.

Cedrenus, Georgius. Greek monk; 11th century.
Historiarum compendium. In Migne, *Patrologia graeca,* vol. CXXI.

Chasseneuz, Barthélemy de. French jurist; 1477–1541.
Commentaria in consuetudines ducatus Burgundiae. Lyon, 1517.

Choppin, René. French jurist; 1537–1606.
De domanio Franciae. Paris, 1621.

Chronicum majoris monasterii. Composed at abbey of Marmoutier, Tours; 13th century.
Chronicum abbatum majoris monasteriensis, ed. A. Salmon. *Recueil de chroniques de Touraine.* Tours, 1854. Pp. 318–38.

Cicero, Marcus Tullius. 106–43 B.C.
Epistolae ad Brutum II, ed. L. C. Purser. In *M. Tulli Ciceronis Epistolae.* 3 vols., Oxford, 1902.
De inventione, ed. H. M. Hubbell (Loeb Classical Library). Cambridge, Mass., 1949.
De legibus, ed. C. W. Keyes (Loeb Classical Library). London, 1928.
Oratio quam pro domo suo habuit, ed. N. H. Watts (Loeb Classical Library). London, 1923.
Orationes in Verrem, ed. L. H. G. Greenwood (Loeb Classical Library). 2 vols., London, 1935.
De oratore, ed. H. Rackham (Loeb Classical Library). 2 vols., London, 1942.
Philippics, ed. W. C. A. Ker (Loeb Classical Library). London, 1926.
Pro C. Rabirio Postumo oratio, ed. N. H. Watts (Loeb Classical Library). London, 1931.
Pro M. Fonteio oratio, ed. N. H. Watts (Loeb Classical Library). London, 1931.
Pro rege Deiotaro oratio, ed. N. H. Watts (Loeb Classical Library). London, 1931.
De re publica, ed. G. W. Keyes (Loeb Classical Library). London, 1928.
Tusculanarum disputationum, ed. J. E. King (Loeb Classical Library). London, 1927.

Claudian. Roman poet; 4th century.
De bello gothico, praefatio, ed. M. Platnauer (Loeb Classical Library). London, 1922.
De consulatu Stilichonis, ibid.

Panegyricus de quarto consulatu Honorii Augusti, ibid.

In Rufinum, ibid.

Commines, Philippe de. Burgundian chronicler; 1445–1511.
  Mémoires, ed. E. Dupont (Société de l'histoire de France). Paris, 1840.

Connan, François. French jurist; d. 1551.
  Commentariorum iuris civilis, ed. B. Faye. Basel, 1557.

Corpus iuris canonici. Compiled in 12th century.
  Corpus iuris canonici, ed. E. Friedberg. Leipzig, 1879–81.

Corpus iuris civilis. Compiled in 6th century.
  Corpus iuris civilis, ed. Krueger, Mommsen, Schoell and Kroll. Berlin, 1954.

Dante Alighieri. 1265–1321.
  Divina commedia.

Dietrich von Nieheim. German cleric; d. 1418.
  De schismate. Basel, 1566. Book IV also known as *Nemus unionis*, in 6 chapters.

Dionysius of Halicarnassus. Graeco-Roman author; *fl.* 25 B.C.
  Roman Antiquities, ed. E. Cary (Loeb Classical Library). London, 1937.

Du Bellay, Guillaume. French general; 1491–1543.
  Epitome de l'antiquité des Gaules et de France. Paris, 1556.

Du Breuil, Guillaume. French jurist; 14th century.
  Stilus supremae curiae Parlamenti Parisiensis cum novis annotationibus Caroli Molinaei & antiquis additionibus Do. Stephani Auffrerii. Paris, 1551.

Du Moulin, Charles. French jurist; 1500–66.
  Tractatus contractum et usuarum. Ed. *Opera omnia*, vol. II. Paris, 1681.

Durandus, Gulielmus ('Speculator'). French jurist; 1237–96.
  Speculum iuris Gulielmi Durandi. Venice, 1602.

Du Tillet, Jean. French scholar; d. 1570.
  Les mémoires et recherches de Jean du Tillet. Rouen, 1578.

Einhard (or Eginhard). French statesman; c. 770–840.
  Vita Karoli, ed. G. Pertz. *Monumenta Germaniae historica, Scriptores*, vol. I.

Eumenius. Gallic rhetorician; *fl.* 300.
  Eumenii oratio de scholis, ed. Fr. Baudouin. Paris, 1570.

Eutropius. Roman historian; 4th century.
  Breviarium ab urbe condita, ed. H. Droysen. *Monumenta Germaniae historica, Auctores antiquissimi*, vol. II.

Faber, Johannes (Jean de Faure de Roussines). French jurist; d. 1340.
In cod. Justiniani Imp. priores libros IX annotationes codicis breviarium nuncupatae. Lyon, 1594.

Fortescue, John. English jurist; c. 1394–1476.
A Learned Commendation of the Politique Lawes of England. London, 1567.

Francis I. King of France; reigned 1515–47.
Ordonnance royaulx sur le faict de la justice [1530], ed. Fr.-A. Isambert. *Recueil général des anciennes lois françaises,* vol. XII. Paris, 1828.

Frederick II. Holy Roman Emperor; reigned 1215–50.
Placita principum seu constitutiones regni Neapolitani cum glossis ('Neapolitan Constitutions'). Lyon, 1534.

Frodoard. Presbyter of Reims; d. 966.
Chronicon Frodoardi. In Bouquet *et al., Recueil des historiens des Gaules et de la France,* vol. VIII.

Froissart, Jean. French chronicler; 1333–c. 1400.
Chroniques, ed. S. Luce *et al.* (Société de l'histoire de France). Paris, 1869–1957.
Chroniques. Lyon, 1559.

Gaguin, Robert. French historian; 1433–1501.
De Francorum regum gestis. Paris, 1528.
Rerum Gallicarum annales. Frankfort, 1577.

Gellius, Aulus. Roman grammarian; A.D. 125–75.
Noctium Atticarum, ed. J. C. Rolfe (Loeb Classical Library). London, 1928.

Gervase of Tilbury. English jurist; *fl.* 1211.
De otiis imperialibus, ed. J. Stevenson. (Rerum Britannicarum medii aevi scriptores – 'Rolls Series'). London, 1875.

Gilles, Nicolas. French historian; d. 1503.
Chroniques et annales de France. Paris, 1551.

Glareanus (Heinrich Loriti of Glarus). Swiss humanist; 1488–1563.
Commentariolus in Taciti Germaniam. Augsburg, 1579.

Godfrey of Viterbo. German chronicler; d. *c.* 1198.
Pantheon, ed. G. Waitz. *Monumenta Germaniae historica, Scriptores,* vol. XXII.

Grandes chroniques. Compiled from 13th to 16th century.
Le premier (–troisième) volume des grans croniques de France. Paris, 1514.
Le quatriesme livre de la mer des hystoires et croniques de France. Paris, 1518.

Gregory of Tours. French bishop; *c.* 535–94.
  Gregorii episcopi Turonensis libri historiarum X, ed. B. Krusch and
    W. Levison. *Monumenta Germaniae historica, Scriptores rerum Mero-*
    vingicarum, I: I. 2nd ed., 1951.
  Gregorii Turonici historiae Francorum libri decem...appendix item sive
    liber XI. Basel, 1568.
Guimier, Cosmas. French jurist; 15th century.
  Pragmatica sanctio, cum glossis Cosmae Guimier. Paris, 1555.
Henri II. King of France; reigned 1547–59.
  Edict...qui établit dans cette province [Bretagne] un parlement [1553], ed.
    Fr.-A. Isambert, *Recueil général des anciennes lois françaises*, vol. XIII.
    Paris, 1828.
Herodotus. Greek historian; 484–*c.* 406 B.C.
  Herodotus, ed. A. D. Godley (Loeb Classical Library). London, 1921–4.
Homer.
  Odyssey, ed. A. T. Murray (Loeb Classical Library). London, 1924.
Honorius, Flavius. Roman emperor; reigned 395–423.
  Corpus legum ab imperatoribus Romanis ante Justinianiam latarum, ed.
    G. Hänel. Leipzig, 1857.
Hostiensis (Cardinal Henricus de Segusio). Italian jurist; d. 1271.
  In primum decretalium librum commentaria. Venice, 1587.
  Summa aurea. Basel, 1573.
Hotman, François.
  De feudis commentatio tripertita. Lyon, 1573.
  De jure successionis regiae in regno Francorum. n.p., 1588.
Hunibaldus. Supposed 5th-century chronicler.
  De origine gentis Francorum compendium Ioannis Trittenhemii abbatis, ex
    duodecim ultimis Hunibaldi libris. In S. Schard (ed.), *Historicum opus in*
    quatuor tomos divisum. Basel, 1574.
Isocrates. Greek orator; d. 338 B.C.
  Oration on the Peace, ed. G. Norlin (Loeb Classical Library). London,
    1929.
Ivo of Chartres. Bishop of Chartres; d. 1117.
  Epistola. In Migne, *Patrologia latina*, vol. CLXII.
Jacobi, Pierre. French jurist; 14th century.
  Aurea practica libellorum. Cologne, 1575.
St Jerome. 340–420.
  Epistolae. In Migne, *Patrologia latina*, vol. XXIII.
  Vita S. Hilarionis eremitae. In *ibid.*

Johannes Andreae. Italian jurist; *c.* 1270–1348.

In primum (–tertium) decretalia librum novella commentaria. Venice, 1581.

Joinville, Jean. French historian; 1224–1318.

Histoire de Saint Louis, ed. Natalie de Wailly (Société de l'histoire de France). Paris, 1868.

Josephus. Jewish historian; 37–*c.* 100.

Josephus, ed. H. St J. Thackeray *et al.* (Loeb Classical Library). London, 1926–43.

Justinian. See Corpus iuris civilis.

Justinus. Roman historian; 2nd century.

Trogi Pompei historiarum philippicarum epitoma, ed. J. Jeep. Leipzig, 1862.

Krantz, Albert. German theologian; d. 1517.

Chronica regnorum Aquilonarium, Daniae, Suetiae, Norvagiae. Frankfort, 1546.

Ecclesiastica historia, sive metropolis. Basel, 1568.

La Marche, Olivier de. French chronicler; 1426–1501.

Mémoires, ed. H. Beaune and J. d'Arbaumont (Société de l'histoire de France). Paris, 1883.

Lambert of Hersfeld. German monk; d. after 1077.

Historiae Germanorum. In S. Schard (ed.), *Germanicarum rerum quatuor chronographi.* Frankfort, 1566.

Landulphus Sagax. Italian chronicler; *fl.* 1000.

Historiae miscellae a Paulo Aquilegiensi diacono primum collectae, post etiam a Landulpho Sagaci. Basel, 1569.

Laudensis, Martinus. Italian jurist; 15th century.

Tractatus de confederatione, pace et conventionibus. In *Tractatus d. Martini Laudensis.* Pavia, 1506.

Leges Alamannorum. Germanic law; 7th and 8th centuries.

Monumenta Germaniae historica, Leges: Legum sectio I; Leges nationum Germanicarum, tom. V. Leges Alamannorum, ed. K. Lehmann.

Lex Angliorum. Germanic law; 8th century.

Originum ac Germanicarum antiquitatum libri, leges videlicet Salicae, Alemannorum, Saxonum, Angliorum, etc., ed. B. J. Herold. Basel, 1557.

Lex Ripuaria. Frankish; 7th century.

Monumenta Germaniae historica, Leges: Legum sectio I; Leges nationum Germicarum, tom. III. Lex Ribuaria, ed. F. Beyerle and R. Buchner.

Lex Salica. Frankish; 6th century.

As above, *Lex Angliorum.*

Lex Saxonum. Germanic, 8th century.

   As above, *Lex Angliorum.*

Libri feudorum. Compiled in 12th century.

   Volumen locupletus posteriores tres libros Codicis, Novellas & Feuda, Lyon, 1562. Bound (as then usually) with *Institutionum Iustiniani libri IV,* in a complete set of the Roman Law.

Liutprand of Cremona. Italian churchman; d. 762.

   Antapodoseos, ed. G. Pertz. *Monumenta Germaniae historica, Scriptores,* vol. III.

Livy, Titus. Roman historian; 59 B.C.–A.D. 17.

   Livy, ed. B. Foster, E. Sage, F. G. Moore and A. Schlesinger (Loeb Classical Library). London, 1919–59.

Loi Salique. Anonymous treatise, 15th century.

   La loy Salique, premiere loy des François, appended to Seyssel, *La grand' Monarchie de France.* Paris, 1557.

Lucan. Roman poet; A.D. 39–65.

   The Civil War ('Pharsalia'), ed J. D. Duff (Loeb Classical Libary). London, 1928.

Maino, Jason de. Italian jurist; 1435–1519.

   In secundam infortiati partem commentaria. Venice, 1573.

Marinaeus, Lucius. Italian historian; d. c. 1533.

   De rebus Hispaniae memorabilibus opus. In R. Bel, *Rerum Hispanicarum scriptores,* vol. I. Frankfurt, 1579.

Marsiglio of Padua. Italian scholar; d. 1342.

   De translatione imperii. In M. Flacius and W. Weissenberg (eds.), *Antilogia Papiae.* Basel, 1554.

Masson, Papire. French humanist; 1544–1611.

   Iudicium de libello Hotomani. Preface to A. Matharel, *Ad Franc. Hotomani Francogalliam...responsio.* Paris, 1575.

Matharel, Antoine. French jurist; 16th century.

   Ad Franc. Hotomani Francogalliam...responsio. Paris, 1575.

Monstrelet, Enguerrand de. French chronicler; c. 1390–1453.

   La chronique d'Enguerran de Monstrelet, ed. L. Douët d'Arcq (Société de l'histoire de France). Paris, 1857–62.

Montaigne, Jean. French jurist; 16th century.

   Tractatus de auctoritate sacri magni concilii et parlamentorum regni Franciae. Paris, 1512.

Mutius, Henricus. German humanist; 16th century.

   De Germanorum prima origine, moribus, institutis. Basel, 1539.

Nauclerus, Johannes. German chronicler; d. 1510.

Chronica res memorabiles saeculorum omnium et gentium. Cologne, 1579.

Newburgh. See William of Newburgh.

Nieheim. See Dietrich von Nieheim.

Oldradus de Ponte. Italian jurist; d. 1335.

Consilia. Lyon, 1583.

Ordonnances des roys de France, vol. 1, ed. Eusèbe de Laurière. Paris, 1723.

Orosius. Roman historian; 5th century.

Historiarum libri septem. In Migne, *Patrologia latina,* vol. XXXI.

Otto of Freising. German chronicler; d. 1158.

Gesta Frederici imperatoris, ed. R. Wilmans. *Monumenta Germaniae historica, Scriptores,* vol XX.

Chronicon, ibid.

Ovid. Roman poet; 43 B.C.–A.D. 17.

Epistolae ex Ponto, ed. A. L. Wheeler (Loeb Classical Library). London, 1924.

Panegyrist. Anonymous Roman rhetorician; 4th century.

Panégyriques latins, ed. E. Galletier. Paris, 1949–55. 3 vols.

No. IV: *Incerti Panygericus Constantino Caesari dictus.* Vol. I, pp. 81 ff.

No. VI: *Incerti Panegyricus Maximiano et Constantino dictus.* II, 16 ff.

No. VII: *Incerti Panegyricus Constantino Augusto dictus.* II, 53 ff

No. X: *Nazarii Panegyricus Constantino Augusto dictus.* II, 166 ff.

Panormitanus (Nicolaus de Tudeschis). Italian jurist; 1386–1445.

Consilia. Lyon, 1547.

Pape, Guy. French jurist; 15th century.

Decisiones Gratianopolitanae. Frankfort, 1609.

Papon, Jean. French jurist; 1505–90.

Recueil d'arrests notables des cours souveraines de France. Paris, 1574

Paradin, Guillaume. French historian; *c.* 1510–90.

Annales de Bourgogne. Lyon, 1566.

Paris de Puteo (Paride del Pozzo). Italian jurist; 1413–93.

De syndicatu. In *Tractatus de formatione libelli in syndicatu.* Venice, 1578.

Paul the Deacon. Italian historian; 8th century.

Historia Langobardorum, ed. G. Waitz. *Monumenta Germaniae historica, Scriptores rerum Langobardicarum.*

Paulus, Julius. Roman jurist; *fl.* A.D. 200.

Sententiarum receptarum ad filium libri, ed. J. Cujas. Lyon, 1556.

Petrus de Vinea. Italian statesman; *c.* 1190–1246.

Petri de Vineis epistolarum libri VI. Basel, 1740.

Platea, Johannes de. Italian jurist; 15th century.
Super tribus ultimis libris codicis. Lyon, 1537.
Platina, Battista (Bartolommeo de'Sachi). Italian historian; 1421–81.
De vita et moribus summorum pontificum historia. Paris, 1530.
Plato. 427–348 B.C.
Laws, ed. R. G. Bury (Loeb Classical Library). London, 1926–51.
Phaedrus, ed. H. N. Fowler (Loeb Classical Library). London, 1953.
Pliny the Elder. Roman statesman; 23–79.
Natural History, ed. H. Rackham (Loeb Classical Library). London, 1952.
Plutarch. Greek author; *c.* 50–140.
Plutarch's Lives, ed. B. Perrin (Loeb Classical Library). London, 1917 ff.
Polybius. Greek historian; *c.* 204–124 B.C.
The Histories, ed. W. R. Paton (Loeb Classical Library). London, 1923.
Pomponius Leta. Italian humanist; 1425–97.
De Romanis magistratibus, sacerdotiis, iurisperitis & legibus. Paris, 1552.
Postel, Guillaume. French savant; 1505–81.
La loy Salique; les origines & auctoritez de la loy Gallique nommée communement Salique. Paris, 1552.
Procopius. Byzantine historian; *c.* 500–65.
Gothic War, ed. H. B. Dewing (Loeb Classical Library). London, 1919.
Ptolemy. Greek geographer; 2nd century.
Geographia, ed. C. F. A. Nobbe. Leipzig, 1898.
Quintilian. Roman rhetorician; *c.* 42–95.
The Institutio Oratoria of Quintilian, ed. H. E. Butler (Loeb Classical Library). London, 1922.
Regino. Abbot of Prüm; d. 915.
Chronicon, ed. G. Pertz. *Monumenta Germaniae historica, Scriptores,* vol. I.
Ritius (Michael du Rit). Italian historian; *fl.* 1500.
De regibus Francorum. Basel, 1534.
Rolevinck, Werner. German historian; d. 1502.
Fasciculus temporum. Venice, 1480.
Roye, Jean de. French historian; 15th century.
Journal de Jean de Roye connu sous le nom de Chronique Scandaleuse, ed. B. de Mandrot (Société de l'histoire de France). Paris, 1894–6.
Sabellico, Marc Antonio. Italian historian; 1436–1506.
Rapsodie historiarum Enneadii. Paris, 1517.

Sallust. Roman historian; 1st century B.C.

The War with Catiline, ed. J. C. Rolfe (Loeb Classical Library). New York, 1921.

The War with Jugurtha, ibid.

Salvian. Priest of Marseille; c.390–484.

De gubernatione Dei libri VIII, ed. C. Halm. *Monumenta Germaniae historica, Auctores antiquissimi*, vol. I.

Scriptores historiae Augustae. Roman historian collection; 4th century.

Scriptores historiae Augustae, ed. T. E. Page, E. Capps, and W. H. D. Rouse (Loeb Classical Library). London, 1932.

Seneca. Roman philosopher; c. 4 B.C.–A.D. 65.

De beneficiis, in *Moral Essays*, ed. J. W. Basore (Loeb Classical Library). London, 1935.

Epistolae morales, ed. R. M. Gummere (Loeb Classical Library). London, 1925.

Seyssel, Claude de. French statesman; 1450–1520.

La monarchie de France, ed. J. Poujol. Paris, 1961.

Sextus Rufus. Roman historian; 4th century.

The Breviarium of Festus, ed. J. W. Eadie. London, 1967.

Sidonius Apollinaris. Roman poet; c. 430–89.

Epistolae et carmina, ed. C. Luetjohann. *Monumenta Germaniae historica, Auctores antiquissimi*, vol. VIII.

Sigebert of Gembloux. Benedictine monk; 1030–1112.

Chronicon, ed. L. C. Bethmann. *Monumenta Germaniae historica, Scriptores*, vol. VI.

Strabo. Greek geographer; c. 50 B.C.–A.D. 30.

Geographica, ed. G. Müller and F. Dübner. Paris, 1853.

Suetonius. Roman historian; c. 70–160.

Lives of the Twelve Caesars, ed. J. C. Rolfe (Loeb Classical Library). London, 1914–20.

Suidas. Greek lexicographer; 10th or 11th century.

Suidae lexicon, ed. Bernhard. Halle, 1843–53.

Tacitus. Roman historian; c. 55–120.

Agricola, ed. W. Peterson (Loeb Classical Library). London, 1914.

Annals, ed. J. Jackson (Loeb Classical Library). London, 1937.

Germania, ed. W. Peterson (Loeb Classical Library). London, 1937.

Histories, ed. C. H. Moore (Loeb Classical Library). London, 1925–31.

Terre Rouge, Jean de. French jurist; 15th century.

Tractatus, ed. F. Hotman. Bound with Hotman's *Disputatio de contro-versia successionis regiae*. Basel, 1585.

Theodosian Code. 5th century.
Theodosiani libri XVI, ed. T. Mommsen and P. M. Meyer. 2nd edition. Berlin, 1954.

Thomas of Walsingham. English monk; d. *c.* 1440.
Historia Anglicana, ed. H. T. Riley. (Rerum Britannicarum medii aevi scriptores – 'Rolls Series'.) London, 1863.

Tiraqueau, André. French jurist; *c.* 1480–1558.
Opera omnia. Frankfort, 1597.

Trithemius, Johannes. German theologian; 1462–1516.
Compendium de origine regum et gentis Francorum. Paris, 1539.

Turnebus, Adrianus. French savant; 1512–65.
Adversariorum tomus primus (–secundus). Paris, 1564–5.

Turpin. Archbishop of Reims; d. *c.* 800.
In S. Schard (ed.), *Germanicarum rerum quatuor chronographi*. Frankfort, 1566.

Urspergensis, Abbas. Compiled by several abbots of Ursperg: covers 1125–1226.
Chronicon universale, ed. G. Waitz. *Monumenta Germaniae historica*, *Scriptores*, vol. VI.

Valerian Maximus. Roman author; 1st century.
Factorum et directorum memorabilium, ed. C. Kempf. Leipzig, 1888.

Vasaeus, Ioannis. Flemish historian; 16th century.
Hispanicarum chronicon. In R. Bel (ed.), *Rerum Hispanicarum scrip-tores*. Frankfort, 1579.

Venericus. See Walramus.

Virgil, Polydore. Italian historian in England; 1470–1555.
Historiae Anglicae libri XXVII. Leyden, 1651.

Walramus. Bishop of Naumburg; d. 1111.
De unitate ecclesiae conservanda, ed. E. Dümmler. *Monumenta Germaniae historica*, *Libelli de lite*, vol. II.

Walsingham. See Thomas of Walsingham.

Widukindus. German historian; 12th century.
Res gestae Saxonicae, ed. G. Waitz. *Monumenta Germaniae historica*, *Scriptores*, vol. III.

William of Newburgh. English monk; d. 1208.
Historia rerum Anglicarum, ed. H. C. Hamilton. (Rerum Britannicarum medii aevi scriptores – 'Rolls Series'.) London, 1856.

Xenophon. Greek philosopher; *c.* 430–355 B.C.
Memorabilia, ed E. C. Marchant (Loeb Classical Library). London, 1923.
Zonaras. Byzantine historian; 12th century.
Annales, ed. M. Pinder (Corpus scriptorum historiae Byzantinae). Bonn, 1891–4.
Epitomae historiarum libri XVIII, ed. Th. Buttner-Wobst (*ibid.*). Bonn, 1897.
Zosimus. Greek historian; 5th century.
Zosimus, ed. J. Bekker (*ibid.*). Bonn, 1837.
Zurita, Géronimo. Aragonese historian; 1512–80.
Indices rerum ab Aragoniae regibus libri tres. In Andr. Schottus (ed.), *Hispaniae illustratae*, vol. III. Frankfort, 1606.

Allen, J. W. *A History of Political Thought in the Sixteenth Century.* London, 1941.

Armstrong, E. 'Political Theory of the Huguenots', *English Historical Review*, IV (1889), 13–40.

Baird, H. M. 'Hotman and the Franco-Gallia', *American Historical Review*, I (1895/6), 13–40.

Baron, J. *Franz Hotmanns Antitribonian, ein Beitrag zu den Codifications-bestrebungen vom 16. bis zum 18. Jahrhundert.* Bern, 1888.

Bayle, Pierre. 'Hotman', in *The Dictionary Historical and Critical.* 2nd Eng. ed.; III, 518–24. London, 1736.

Blocaille, E. *Etude sur François Hotman, la Franco-Gallia.* Dijon, 1902.

Blok, P. J., ed. *Correspondance inédite de Robert Dudley, comte de Leycester, et de François et Jean Hotman.* Haarlem, 1911.

Caprariis, Vittorio de. *Propaganda e pensiero politico in Francia durante le guerre di religione (1559–1572).* Naples, 1959.

Cardauns, Paul Ludwig. *Die Lehre vom Widerstandsrecht des Volks gegen die rechtmässige Obrigkeit im Luthertum und im Calvinismus des 16. Jahrhunderts.* Bonn, 1903.

Church, William Farr. *Constitutional Thought in Sixteenth-Century France.* Harvard, 1941.

Cougny, Ed. 'Etudes sur le XVIe siècle; théories politiques; François Hotman, La "France-Gaule"', *Mémoires de la Société des sciences morales, lettres et arts de Seine-et-Oise*, X (1875), 241–322.

Dareste, Rodolphe. 'Dix ans de la vie de François Hotman (1563–1573)', *Bulletin de la Société de l'Histoire du Protestantisme français*, XXV (1876), 529–44.

'Documents inédits relatifs à d'anciens jurisconsultes français: Pierre de Fontaines, Antoine Leconte, François Hotman', *Revue historique de droit français et étranger*, I (1855), 487–99.

Essai sur François Hotman. Paris, 1850.

'François Hotman et la conjuration d'Amboise – deux lettres inédites de Jean Sturm', *Bibliothèque de l'Ecole des Chartes*, XV (1854), 360–75.

'François Hotman. Extraits de la correspondance inédite', *Séances et travaux de l'Académie des Sciences Morales et Politiques*, CIV (1875), 644–68.

'François Hotman, sa vie et sa correspondance', *Revue historique*, II (1876), 1–59, 367–435.

Dareste, Rudolphe. 'Hotman d'après de nouvelles lettres des années 1561–1563', *Revue historique*, XCVII (1908), 297–315.

Dennert, Jurgen, ed. *Beza, Brutus, Hotman: calvinistische Monarcho-machen*. Cologne, 1968.

Ehinger, Ludwig. *Franz Hotmann; ein französischer Gelehrter, Staatsmann und Publizist des XVI. Jahrhunderts*. Basel, 1896.

Elkan, Albert. *Die Publizistik der Bartholomäusnacht und Mornays 'Vindiciae contra Tyrannos'*. Heidelberg, 1905.

Fournol, E. 'Sur quelques traités de droit public au XVIe siècle', *Nouvelle revue historique de droit français et étranger*, XXI (1897), 298–325.

Franklin, Julian H. *Jean Bodin and the Sixteenth-Century Revolution in the Methodology of Law and History*. New York, 1963.

Constitutionalism and Resistance in the Sixteenth Century: Three Treatises by Hotman, Beza, and Mornay. New York, 1969.

Giesey, Ralph E. *If Not, Not: The Oath of the Aragonese and the Legendary Laws of Sobrarbe*. Princeton, 1968.

The Juristic Basis of Dynastic Right to the French Throne. Transactions of the American Philosophical Society, LI: 5. Philadelphia, 1961.

'The Monarchomach Triumvirs: Hotman, Beza, and Mornay', *Bibliothèque d'Humanisme et Renaissance*, XXXII (1970), 41–76.

'When and Why Hotman Wrote the *Francogallia*', *Bibliothèque d'Humanisme et Renaissance*, XXIX (1967), 581–611.

Haag, Eugene and Emile. *La France protestante*. 10 vols. Paris, 1846–55. Article on Hotman: V, 525–40.

Harsin, Paul. 'Le parrain d'une école germaniste: Fr. Hotman et sa Francogallia', *Revue des sciences politiques*, XLIX (1926), 607–22.

Hauser, Henri. 'Antoine de Bourbon et l'Allemagne', *Revue historique*, XLV (1891), 54–61.

Hölzle, Erwin. *Die Idee einer altgermanischen Freiheit vor Montesquieu*. Berlin, 1925.

(Hotman) F. et J. *Hotomanorum et clarorum virorum ad eos epistolae*. Amsterdam, 1700.

Huppert, George. *The Idea of Perfect History: Historical Erudition and Historical Philosophy in Renaissance France*. Urbana, 1970.

Kan, Joseph van. 'François Hotman en de Codificatiepolitiek van zijn tijd', *Tijdschrift voor Rechtsgeschiedenis*, III (1921), 1–11.

Kelley, Donald R. *The Foundations of Modern Historical Scholarship: Language, Law and History in the French Renaissance*. New York, 1970.

Kingdon, Robert M. *Geneva and the Coming of the Wars of Religion in France, 1555–1563.* Geneva, 1956.

Kleyser, Friedrich, 'Calvin und Franz Hotman', *Geschichtliche Kräfte und Entscheidungen; Festschrift für Otto Becker*, 47–64. Wiesbaden, 1954.

Lagarde, Georges de. *Recherches sur l'esprit politique de la réforme.* Paris, 1926.

Lemaire, André. *Les lois fondamentales de la monarchie française d'après les théoriciens de l'ancient régime.* Paris, 1907.

Lureau, Henri. *Les Doctrines démocratiques chez les écrivains protestants français de la seconde moitié du XVIe siècle (Junius Brutus, François Hotman).* Bordeaux, 1900.

Maffei, Domenico. *Gli inizi dell'umanesimo giuridico.* Milan, 1956.

Méaly, Paul-F.-M. *Origines des idées politiques libérales en France: les publicistes de la Réforme sous François II et Charles IX.* Paris, 1903.

Mercier, C. 'Les théories politiques des Calvinistes en France au cours des guerres de religion', *Bulletin de la Société de l'Histoire du Protestantisme français*, LXXXIII (1934), 225–60.

Mesnard, Pierre. *L'essor de la philosophie politique au XVIe siècle.* Paris, 1951.

'François Hotman (1524–1590) et le complexe de Tribonien', *Bulletin de la Société de l'Histoire du Protestantisme français*, CI (1955), 117–37.

Moussiegt, Paul. *Hotman et Du Plessy-Mornay, théories politiques des réformés au XVIe siècle.* Cahors, 1899.

Murray, A. H. 'The Franco-Gallia of François Hotman: a Study in Political Pluralism', *Butterworth's South African Law Review*, 1956, 100–18.

Murray, R. H. *The Political Consequences of the Reformation.* London, 1926.

Naef, Henri. *La Conjuration d'Amboise et Genève.* Geneva, 1922. Also in *Mémoires de documents de la Société d'histoire et d'archéologie de Genève*, t. XXXII.

Nevelet, Pierre (Doschius). *Elogium Franc. Hotomanni jurisconsulti.* [1592.] Frankfort, 1595.

Pocock, J. G. A. *The Ancient Constitution and the Feudal Law.* Cambridge, 1957.

Polenz, Gottlob von. *Geschichte des französischen Calvinismus.* 5 vols. Gotha, 1857–69.

Reynolds, Beatrice. *Proponents of Limited Monarchy in Sixteenth-Century France: Francis Hotman and Jean Bodin*. New York, 1931.

Salmon, J. H. M. *The French Religious Wars in English Political Thought*. Oxford, 1959.

'Bodin and the Monarchomachs', in *Jean Bodin: Verhandlungen der internationalen Bodin Tagung in München*, ed. Horst Denzer. München, 1972.

Sayous, Pierre. *Etudes littéraires sur les écrivains français de la réformation*. Paris, 1854.

Schickler, Fernand. 'Hotman de Villiers et son temps', *Bulletin de la Société de l'Histoire du Protestantisme français*, XVII (1868), 97–111, 145–61, 401–13, 464–76, 513–33.

Schnur, Ramon. *Die französischen Juristen im konfessionellen Bürgerkrieg des 16. Jahrhunderts*. Berlin, 1962.

Smith, David Baird. 'François Hotman', *Scottish Historical Review*, XIII (1915/16), 328–65.

Strohl, H. 'Le droit à la résistance d'après les conceptions protestantes', *Revue d'histoire et philosophie religieuses*, X (1930), 126–44.

Treumann, R. *Die Monarchomachen*. Leipzig, 1895.

Viguié, Ariste. *Les théories politiques libérales au XVIe siècle: études sur la 'Francogallia'*. Paris, 1873.

Vogel, Werner. *Franz Hotman und die Privatrechtswissenschaft seiner Zeit*. Freiburg-im-Bresgau, 1960. Thesis.

Vuilleumier, H. 'Le séjour de Fr. Hotman à Lausanne (1549–1555)', *Bulletin du bibliophile et du bibliothécaire* (1901), 125–9.

Weill, Georges. *Les théories sur le pouvoir royal en France pendant les guerres de religion*. Paris, 1891.

INDEX

Page references between 1 and 134 relate to the editors' introduction. Subsequent references relate to Hotman's Latin text, those in bold type signifying that the corresponding entry and/or subentry appeared in Hotman's index to the 1586 edition of *Francogallia*. The only book titles shown here are anonymous or pseudonymous works where authorship is uncertain. Place names occurring in the text have been indexed, but not those in the introduction.

Reynolds, William (Rossaeus), 109, 115, 117
Rhemi, 148, 174
Rhine, river, 176, 180, 188, 190, 192, 196, 210, 212, 214, 216, 280, 328
Rhône, river, 176, 280, 318
Richard I, 90, 288–90
Richard of Normandy, 396
Richemer (son of Chlogio), 262
Rigunthis, queen, 356
Ripuarian Franks, 55, 272
Ritius, Michael, 488
Robert II, 358
Robert (first duke of the Franks), 228, 242, 394, 408, 410
Robert the Strong of Anjou, 228, 408, 410
Rodibert, 336
Roissy, 384
Roman Law, 4, 9–10, 11, 13, 14, 16, 27–9, 33–6, 42, 44, 52, 55, 70, 97, 98, 102, 113, 246–52, 334, 414, 465, 478
    Code cited, 105, 194, 246, 248, 250, 256, 260, 344, 374, 376, 470, 520, 522
    Digest cited, 105, 158, 162, 248, 250, 260, 344, 346, 476
    Institutes cited, 398
Romans, 138, 140, 172–80, 204, 298–300, 460
    their art of seducing other nations, 150
    their language, 186
    their tyranny over Gaul, 63, 176–8
Ronsard, 74
Rossaeus, see Reynolds
Rossant, André de, 109
Rouen, 384, 498, 510
Roye, Jean de, 54, 442
Rudolph of Burgundy (elected king at death of Charles the Simple), 228, 230, 240, 242, 394
Rufinus, 280
Rymer, Thomas, 122–3

Sabellico, Marc Antonio, 202

Saint Bartholomew, massacre of, 8, 15, 30, 31, 48, 50–1, 59, 62, 63, 74, 75, 93
Saint-Brieu, 384
Saint-Maclou, 384
Saint-Maur, treaty of, 39
Saint-Paul, 382, 384
Saint-Pol, count of, 472
Sala, river (Saar), 184, 212, 270, 348
Salian Franks, 21, 55, 68, **212**, **270**, 482
Salic law, 21, 36, 56, 59, 60, 68, 78, 97, 108, **268–74**, 470, 482; see also Succession
Sallust (Gaius Sallustius Crispus), 172, 204
Salogast, 270
Salvianus (bishop of Marseille), 168, 180
Sancerre, 384
Saône, river, 280
Saumaise, Claude de, 117
Saxons, 46, 55, 120–1, 122, 123, 166, 182, 194, 212, 214, 218, 280, 328, 334, 352, 398
Saxony, 186, 326
Scandinavia, 196
Scipio Aemilianus, 162
Sciron, 138
Scots, 214
Scottish constitution, 6–8
Seditions, sometimes just though troublesome, **444**
Seine, river, 184, 186, 336
Selden, John, 115
Semiramis, 402
Senate, Roman, 460, 496
Seneca, 43, 83n., 140, 252, 300, 518
Seneschal, office of, 90, 358
Senlis, 382
Senones, 148, 152
Sens, 384
Sequani, 150, 152, 154, 214
Servin, Louis, 113
Severus, Alexander, 86, 518
Sextus Rufus, 178
Seydlitz, Caspar, 29, 30, 45

CAMBRIDGE STUDIES IN THE HISTORY AND THEORY OF POLITICS

TEXTS

LIBERTY, EQUALITY, FRATERNITY, *by James Fitzjames Stephen.* Edited, with an introduction and notes, by *R. J. White*

VLADIMIR AKIMOV ON THE DILEMMAS OF RUSSIAN MARXISM 1895–1903. An English edition of 'A Short History of the Social Democratic Movement in Russia' and 'The Second Congress of the Russian Social Democratic Labour Party', with an introduction and notes by *Jonathan Frankel*

TWO ENGLISH REPUBLICAN TRACTS, PLATO REDIVIVUS or, A DIALOGUE CONCERNING GOVERNMENT (*c.* 1681), *by Henry Neville* and AN ESSAY UPON THE CONSTITUTION OF THE ROMAN GOVERNMENT (*c.* 1699), *by Walter Moyle.* Edited by *Caroline Robbins*

J. G. HERDER ON SOCIAL AND POLITICAL CULTURE, translated, edited and with an introduction by *F. M. Barnard*

THE LIMITS OF STATE ACTION, *by Wilhelm von Humboldt.* Edited, with an introduction and notes, by *J. W. Burrow*

KANT'S POLITICAL WRITINGS, edited with an introduction and notes by *Hans Reiss*; translated by *H. B. Nisbet*

MARX'S CRITIQUE OF HEGEL'S 'PHILOSOPHY OF RIGHT', edited with an introduction and notes by *Joseph O'Malley*; translated by *Annette Jolin* and *Joseph O'Malley*

STUDIES

1867: DISRAELI, GLADSTONE AND REVOLUTION. THE PASSING OF THE SECOND REFORM BILL, *by Maurice Cowling*

THE CONSCIENCE OF THE STATE IN NORTH AMERICA, *by E. R. Norman*

THE SOCIAL AND POLITICAL THOUGHT OF KARL MARX, *by Shlomo Avineri*

MEN AND CITIZENS: A STUDY OF ROUSSEAU'S SOCIAL THEORY, *by Judith Shklar*

IDEALISM, POLITICS AND HISTORY: SOURCES OF HEGELIAN THOUGHT, *by George Armstrong Kelly*

THE IMPACT OF LABOUR 1920-1924. THE BEGINNING OF MODERN BRITISH POLITICS, *by Maurice Cowling*

CAMBRIDGE STUDIES IN THE HISTORY AND THEORY OF POLITICS

TEXTS

LIBERTY, EQUALITY, FRATERNITY, by *James Fitzjames Stephen.* Edited, with an introduction and notes, by *R. J. White*

VLADIMIR AKIMOV ON THE DILEMMAS OF RUSSIAN MARXISM 1895–1903. An English edition of 'A Short History of the Social Democratic Movement in Russia' and 'The Second Congress of the Russian Social Democratic Labour Party', with an introduction and notes by *Jonathan Frankel*

TWO ENGLISH REPUBLICAN TRACTS, PLATO REDIVIVUS or, A DIALOGUE CONCERNING GOVERNMENT (*c.* 1681), by *Henry Neville* and AN ESSAY UPON THE CONSTITUTION OF THE ROMAN GOVERNMENT (*c.* 1699), by *Walter Moyle.* Edited by *Caroline Robbins*

J. G. HERDER ON SOCIAL AND POLITICAL CULTURE, translated, edited and with an introduction by *F. M. Barnard*

THE LIMITS OF STATE ACTION, by *Wilhelm von Humboldt.* Edited, with an introduction and notes, by *J. W. Burrow*

KANT'S POLITICAL WRITINGS, edited with an introduction and notes by *Hans Reiss*; translated by *H. B. Nisbet*

MARX'S CRITIQUE OF HEGEL'S 'PHILOSOPHY OF RIGHT', edited with an introduction and notes by *Joseph O'Malley*; translated by *Annette Jolin* and *Joseph O'Malley*

STUDIES

1867: DISRAELI, GLADSTONE AND REVOLUTION. THE PASSING OF THE SECOND REFORM BILL, by *Maurice Cowling*

THE CONSCIENCE OF THE STATE IN NORTH AMERICA, by *E. R. Norman*

THE SOCIAL AND POLITICAL THOUGHT OF KARL MARX, by *Shlomo Avineri*

MEN AND CITIZENS: A STUDY OF ROUSSEAU'S SOCIAL THEORY, by *Judith Shklar*

IDEALISM, POLITICS AND HISTORY: SOURCES OF HEGELIAN THOUGHT, by *George Armstrong Kelly*

THE IMPACT OF LABOUR 1920–1924. THE BEGINNING OF MODERN BRITISH POLITICS, by *Maurice Cowling*